*

GEORGIA

A Guide to Its Towns and Countryside

*

GEORGIA

A GUIDE TO ITS TOWNS AND COUNTRYSIDE

COMPILED AND WRITTEN BY WORKERS OF THE WRITERS'
PROGRAM OF THE WORK PROJECTS
ADMINISTRATION

IN THE STATE OF GEORGIA

Illustrated

Sponsored by the Georgia Board of Education

THE UNIVERSITY OF GEORGIA PRESS

ATHENS

1 9 4 0

Republished 1973
SOMERSET PUBLISHERS – a Division of Scholarly Press, Inc.
22929 Industrial Drive East, St. Clair Shores, Michigan 48080

FIRST PUBLISHED IN APRIL 1940

FEDERAL WORKS AGENCY

JOHN M. CARMODY, *Administrator*

WORK PROJECTS ADMINISTRATION

F. C. HARRINGTON, *Commissioner*

FLORENCE KERR, *Assistant Commissioner*

R. L. MACDOUGALL, *State Administrator*

LC-7284467

ISBN 0-403-02162-6

PRINTED IN U.S.A. BY THE UNIVERSITY OF GEORGIA PRESS

Executive Department
Atlanta

All progressive Georgians are awaiting, with more than usual interest, the appearance of this story of our State's advantages and accomplishments. Those who knew the Georgia of relatively a few years ago will see in it a story of progress, showing conclusively that Georgia is taking its place among other States of the Nation in the matter of developing its natural resources and promoting the active interest of its citizens in such a program.

Georgia, over the past decade, has grown beyond the fondest hopes of most of its ambitious people--industrially, educationally and commercially. And our growth has not been of the mushroom variety. It has been a steady, progressive climb, the trend always upward. Of course, the line of progress has sagged momentarily at times under the pressure of various influences. But it has seemed always to come back to a higher level. We can ascribe this to the fact that through the programs of the State and Federal Governments our people have come to be more familiar with the objectives of these programs and are cooperating in these several activities. In other words, our people have become alert to the importance of conserving and developing our natural re- sources, promoting erosion control and reforestation and attracting new industries.

We have been awakened to what Georgia has and have set ourselves to the task of teaching the rest of the country. This book, I believe, is destined to prove of tremendous worth to us in our efforts toward advancing the interest of Georgia.

Few states in the Union have a greater forest area than ours. No State can boast a finer year-round climate than Georgia's. No State can rival our natural resort advantages--5,000-foot altitudes in the mountains of North Georgia for summer tourists and the tidewaters of our coast line for vacationists in winter and summer.

E. D. RIVERS
GOVERNOR

People who have viewed the grandeur of our mountains, in spring, summer and autumn, will tell you that nowhere will you find more natural beauty. Shimmering lakes and racing streams are set like jewels in the hills. And now the State and Federal Governments have lent a hand to Nature in adding to the natural wonders of the section by providing resort facilities, human comforts and a fine system of roads, so that the average citizen can visit our mountains, spend some time there and enjoy real recreation without great expense.

We are providing recreation spots also in Middle Georgia and down in the Piney Woods region, as well as on the Coast.

Historic sites are being marked; ancient landmarks, linked with Georgia's early history, are being restored, so that we of today can look back on the days of our forefathers and, looking, give our minds to building a greater Georgia for other generations to come.

We are proud of our work in public health in the past few years.

We are proud of our advances in education, the progress made in our common school system and in higher education.

We are proud of Georgia's preeminence in the way of a vacation place for our friends of the North and other parts of the country--a place to golf, play polo and tennis, a place to hunt and fish to the heart's content.

All of these things are emphasized in this great book.

I commend this work to Georgians who are interested in their State and I commend it to the people of other States who are interested in finding a hospitable place to visit and a grand place to live.

Governor of Georgia

Preface

WHEN THE Federal Writers' Project of Georgia began work on a
guidebook of the state, no one knew exactly where to start. We
knew that various points of interest should be located and described,
but we had little conception of how patiently facts must be examined
to show Georgia as it really is. Thus, many of us who had been
Georgia residents for years began for the first time to be acquainted
with our own state.

Soon it became evident that we must be a little of everything—
farmer, map maker, historian, architect. We traveled broken roads,
struggled out of ditches, shivered in frigid old houses, climbed mountains, and forded streams. We shouted questions at deaf caretakers
and puzzled over the peals of mirth our questions sometimes evoked.
Our research was made more difficult by the constantly changing conditions in Georgia; for, while we worked, historic houses were destroyed by fire, rocks that had formed the faces of famous statesmen
crumbled again into mere rocks, Federal and state governments acquired more lands, and new state parks came into being. We went to
many sources and sometimes discovered that hitherto unquestioned
"facts" were fables.

Although we have assiduously sought to be accurate, we have not
desired to strip Georgia history of its authentic romance. If we have
dealt somewhat shortly with legends of cliff-leaping Indian maidens
and their scarcely less suicidal lovers, we have given as much attention
as space permitted to such vitally arresting Georgians as Nancy Hart
and Elijah Clarke. The question of space was, of course, always with
us. This must be our explanation to consultants in many fields who
rendered us invaluable assistance, and who sometimes felt that we
were giving their subjects insufficient treatment. We had to be selec-
tive. With the vast quantity of information that was placed at our
disposal, it would have been far too easy to lose perspective and write
of the state in a one-sided way, to show it as a vast factory or farm or
Indian mound. It is the task of the specialist to know his field thor-

oughly; it has been our task to learn something about many fields—
and to make every sentence count.

Georgia's size and its great diversity demanded a variety of talents
in order to study it well and set it forth truly. We have called on
these talents in ourselves and in others, and now we present the
finished work.

We wish to acknowledge gratefully the assistance given us by Federal,
state, and local organizations, libraries, newspapers, historical societies,
and colleges. Although space is lacking to thank individually all who
have helped us, we take this opportunity to mention a few: Miss Alma
Hill Jamison, head of the reference department of the Carnegie Library
in Atlanta, gave us almost daily assistance. Mr. Richard C. Job, Director of the State Planning Board, and Mrs. Louise Hays, Georgia State
Historian, read the entire manuscript and offered many valuable suggestions. Mrs. Carolyn P. Dillard, now State Supervisor of the
Workers Service Program of the W.P.A., did much of the early
work on the guide as state director of the Federal Writers' Project,
1935-37, and frequently gave her services as consultant after she re-
signed. Among the many who assisted us in special fields the follow-
ing consultants made essential contributions: Harold Bush-Brown;
E. Merton Coulter; General Walter H. Harris; Dr. C. C. Harrold;
Reverend W. F. Hollingsworth; A. R. Kelly; Bishop H. J. Mikell;
George S. Mindling; Eugene Mitchell; Mrs. Wayne Patterson;
Haywood Pearce, Jr.; Reverend Alfred M. Pierce; Arthur Raper;
Louis Skidmore; Richard W. Smith; Linton H. Solomon; Helen Knox
Spain; Melvin Thompson; and Raiford S. Wood.

SAMUEL Y. TUPPER, JR., *State Supervisor*
KATHRYN A. HOOK, *Assistant State Supervisor*

Contents

Part Four: Appendices

Illustrations

Maps

General Information

(*State map, in pocket inside back cover, shows highways, waterways, principal towns, recreational areas, and points of interest*)

Railroads: Thirteen Class 1 railroads, with 5,825 miles of main line track, and more than a score of smaller railroads, with 889 miles of track, making a total of 6,714 miles, constitute the railroad facilities of Georgia. The foregoing figures exclude side tracks and switching yards. The Class 1 lines are: Alabama Great Southern R.R.; Atlanta & West Point R.R.; Atlanta, Birmingham & Coast R.R. (A. B. & C.); Atlantic Coast Line R.R.; Central of Georgia Ry.; Charleston & Western Carolina Ry.; Georgia R.R.; Georgia & Florida R.R.; Georgia Southern & Florida Ry.; Louisville & Nashville R.R. (L. & N.); Nashville, Chattanooga & St. Louis Ry. (N. C. & St. L.); Seaboard Air Line Ry.; and Southern Ry.

Highways: Twenty Federal highways, of which three traverse the United States. Highways patrolled by state police; a few counties provide their own. Filling stations are well distributed, but many close at dark. State gasoline tax 6¢. Since there are no stock laws in many counties of south Georgia, motorists are warned to watch for cattle and pigs. North Georgia counties have stock laws.

Bus Lines: Interstate: Alaga Coach Lines, Inc., Atlantic Greyhound Lines, Carolina Scenic Coach Lines, Crescent Stages, Inc., Georgia Stages, Inc., Service Stages, Inc., Smoky Mountain Stages, Inc., Southeastern Greyhound Lines, Southeastern Motor Lines, Inc., Southeastern Stages, Inc., Teche-Greyhound Lines, and Tennessee Coach Co. Many smaller lines connect principal cities and towns.

Waterways: Two principal seaports, Savannah and Brunswick, of which Savannah is by far the more important. Several steamship lines, both passenger and freight, ply between Savannah and other ports,

American and foreign. The Ocean Steamship Co. (Savannah Line) maintains passenger service between Savannah, New York, and Boston; the Merchants & Miners Transportation Co., between Savannah, Jacksonville, and Miami, and between Savannah, Norfolk, Baltimore, Philadelphia, and Boston. Brunswick is a port of call for tramp steamers. Freight carriers make use of the inland waterway, while both freight carriers and pleasure craft ply the principal rivers.

Air Lines: Two companies, the Eastern and Delta, operate seven main routes through the state. Regular transport service is offered at Atlanta, Augusta, Savannah, and Macon. Atlanta has twenty-eight arrivals and departures daily at Candler Field.

Motor Vehicle Laws (digest): Maximum speed 55 m.p.h., 10 m.p.h. at slow signs; non-resident drivers of vehicles properly registered under the laws of another state are exempt from registration for 30 days. Hand signals must be used for stops and turns. Turns on traffic lights vary with cities. Full stop must be made at grade crossings. Driver's license required. Minimum age for driver, sixteen. Two front lights and one rear must be in good order; spare bulb required.

Prohibited: Passing streetcars on left; passing vehicle on left without sounding horn; passing school bus or streetcar while passengers are getting on or off; driving into a boulevard without stopping. Bright lights are prohibited in some cities.

Liquor Laws: State law permits the sale of light wines and beer; county option on sale of whisky.

Accommodations: First-class commercial hotels in large cities of uniformly good quality; although accommodations in small towns vary widely in quality, a good number have new, comfortable hotels. Many private homes advertise for tourists, and regular tourist camps are found at frequent intervals; variations in quality of these make inquiry at AAA desirable. The winter resorts of south Georgia generally have more luxurious accommodations than the summer resorts of the north Georgia mountains. Most hotels have no seasonal fluctuations in rates.

Climate and Equipment: The climate is generally mild. Topcoats needed for spring and autumn evenings in the mountains. Sudden rain may be expected, but this varies considerably from season to season. Throughout the state quick changes make weather predictions difficult, and travelers should be well provided with wraps from November to April.

Recreational Areas: Nine state parks, widely scattered from mountain top to seacoast: Indian Springs, 5 m. S. of Jackson on US 341; Vogel, between Cleveland and Blairsville on US 19; Santo Domingo, 5 m. S. of Darien off US 17; Alexander H. Stephens, near Crawfordville on State 12; Pine Mountain, 2 m. SW. of Warm Springs off State 41; Chehaw, 2 m. N. of Albany just off US 19; Little Ocmulgee, 2.4 m. N. of McRae on State 31; Fort Mountain, between Chatsworth and Ellijay on US 76; and Jefferson Davis, 1 m. N. of Irwinville off State 32. Accommodations maintained all year at Pine Mountain and Vogel.

Three recreational demonstration areas: Alexander H. Stephens Memorial Recreational Demonstration Area, near Crawfordville on State 12; Pine Mountain Recreational Demonstration Area, 2 m. SW. of Warm Springs off State 41; and Hard Labor Creek Recreational Demonstration Area, 2 m. N. of Rutledge off State 12.

In the mountains of north Georgia are many small summer resorts, including Cloudland, Lakemont, Clayton, and Tate. Recreation is afforded by several large lakes formed in the course of hydroelectric power development and several smaller lakes made by private resort owners. The larger lakes include Burton, with a water surface of 2,775 acres; Rabun, 834 acres; Tugalo, 557 acres; Yonah, 325 acres; and Tallulah, 63 acres. The Georgia Power Co. owns these lakes in fee simple and uses a permit system in exercising control over fishing, swimming, and boating. There is no charge, but permits are issued only to residents of Georgia. Comparable in size to Lake Burton is Lake Blue Ridge (Lake Toccoa), formed when the Tennessee Electric Power Co. impounded the waters of the Toccoa River.

Augusta, Savannah, and Thomasville have long been known to northern people as winter resorts. The coastal section of Georgia is noted for its islands, which are year round resorts; all are privately owned except Tybee and St. Simon. Several rivers and numerous inlets and bays afford fresh- or salt-water fishing, swimming, and boating. The luxurious Sea Island, adjoining St. Simon, is a new resort appealing to northern people in winter and Georgia people in summer.

Fishing: No fishing permitted in any fresh water from Apr. 15 to June 1 except in the trout streams of Catoosa, Chattooga, Dade, Dawson, Fannin, Gilmer, Gordon, Habersham, Lumpkin, Murray, Pickens, Rabun, Stephens, Towns, Union, Walker, White, and Whitfield counties, in which the closed season is Nov. 15 to Mar. 31. In the lakes and streams (generally stocked) of north Georgia are rainbow trout, speckled or brook trout, small-mouthed black bass, and goggle-eyed perch; in middle and south Georgia are blue, channel, and mud cat, perch, jackfish, mullet, and pike; common to all sections are bream, large-mouthed black bass, and suckers. Shellfish and salt-water varieties, such as mullet and sea trout, are found along the coast.

Licenses: Residents, $1.25; non-residents, $5.25. Licenses issued by the commissioner of game and fish and sold throughout the state by authorized agents, such as deputies, ordinaries, and hardware dealers.

Limits: Rainbow trout, 20; brook or speckled trout, 25.

Prohibited: Taking fresh-water fish in any manner except with hook and line (this does not apply to shad, which may be taken with net from Feb. 1 to Apr. 20, except in the St. Marys River, or to mullet, carp, and gar, which may be taken with 3-in. mesh net during December, January, and February); to peddle fresh-water fish without license; to obstruct passage of fish in streams by means of dams or other obstacles.

Hunting: Open season for deer (antlered only may be killed) is Nov. 15 to Jan. 5; quail and wild turkeys, Nov. 20 to Mar. 1; marsh hens, Sept. 1 to Nov. 30; squirrels, Oct. 1 to Jan. 15; raccoons and bears, Nov. 20 to Feb. 28; opossum, Oct. 1 to Feb. 28; doves (in Troup, Meriwether, Pike, Lamar, Monroe, Jones, Baldwin, Washington, Jefferson, Burke, and all counties north thereof), Sept. 15 to Oct. 15 and Dec. 20 to Jan. 31; doves (all other counties) Nov. 20 to Jan. 31. No closed season on rabbits or foxes, but license is required. For Federal regulations on migratory game, inquire of local postmasters for seasons and bag limit.

Licenses: Residents: state, $3.25; county, $1. Non-residents: state, $12.50; county, $5. License must be carried on person while hunting.

Limits: Wild turkeys and deer (bucks only), 2 a season; doves and squirrels, 15 daily; marsh hens, 25 daily; quail, 15 daily, 30 weekly; raccoons, bears, and opossums, no limit.

Prohibited: To hunt at night; to hunt without permission of landowner; to buy, sell, or offer for sale any game; to possess game outside open season; to hunt doves on, over, or near a baited field; to hunt grouse; to trap any game bird or game animal except raccoon, fox, and opossum; to kill or trap female deer (bucks must be reported within 5 days); to hunt deer at any time in the following counties: Catoosa, Chattooga, Dade, Dawson, Fannin, Gilmer, Gordon, Habersham, Lumpkin, Murray, Pickens, Rabun, Stephens, Towns, Union,

Walker, White, Whitfield, Bartow, Floyd, Marion, Schley, Webster, Chattahoochee, Muscogee, and Stewart.

Trapping: The following fur-bearing animals may be trapped from Nov. 20 to Mar. 1: mink, otter, muskrat, raccoon, opossum, and fox. Bobcats and skunks may be killed at any time.

Licenses: Resident, $3; non-resident, $25.

Prohibited: To trap, kill, or molest beavers at any time.

Poisonous Snakes and Plants: Rattlesnake, water moccasin (cottonmouth), and highland moccasin (copperhead) found in rural and wooded areas of entire state; coral snake, in extreme south Georgia. Poison ivy grows to some extent in woods.

Information Service: Georgia State Planning Board, Atlanta.

Calendar of Annual Events

(Information on local holidays and other state observances not listed here is mentioned in connection with the places where they occur. "nfd" means no fixed date)

JAN.	*nfd*	**Augusta**	Woman's Titleholders Open Golf Championship
	nfd	**Coastal Plain**	Opening winter tourist season
	nfd	**Waynesboro**	Georgia Field Trials
	nfd	**Albany**	Southeastern Field Trials
FEB.	*12*	**State-wide**	Georgia Day. (Pageant at Savannah commemorating Oglethorpe's landing.)
	nfd	**Atlanta**	Southeastern Golden Gloves Boxing Tournament
	nfd	**State-wide**	MacDowell Festival
MAR.	*nfd*	**Augusta**	South Atlantic States Tennis Tournament
	nfd	**Augusta**	Augusta Woman's Invitation Golf Tournament
(BIENNIAL)	*nfd*	**Atlanta**	Young Artists' and Student Musicians' Contest
	nfd	**State-wide**	Peach trees in bloom
APRIL	*I*	**Augusta**	Augusta National Golf Tournament
	24	**Thomasville**	Rose Show
	26	**State-wide**	Confederate Memorial Exercises
	nfd	**Atlanta**	Opening Southern Baseball Assn. Season
	nfd	**Savannah**	Dog Show
	nfd	**Atlanta**	Georgia Federation of Music Clubs Contest
	nfd	**Atlanta**	Dogwood in bloom

xxvii

MAY	6-11	State-wide	Flower Week (Garden Club Flower Show in Atlanta)
	8-10	Atlanta	Horse Show
	14-16	Columbus	Chattahoochee Valley Cotton Carnival
	nfd	Athens	Little International Livestock Show
	nfd	Atlanta	Uncle Remus May Festival
JUNE	nfd	Mountains and Coast	Opening of summer tourist season
JULY	4	Atlanta	Automobile races on dirt track
	2nd Thurs.	Savannah	Interstate Sailboat Regatta
AUG.	2nd Fri.	Atlanta	Sacred Harp Singers' Southeastern Convention
SEPT.	Labor Day	Atlanta	Automobile races on dirt track
	nfd	Atlanta	Georgia Old Time Fiddlers' Assn. Convention
OCT.	11	Savannah	Pulaski Day
	nfd	Atlanta	Southeastern Fair
	nfd	Columbus	Chattahoochee Valley Fair
	nfd	Macon	Georgia State Exposition
NOV.	3	State-wide	Forget-Me-Not Day
	9	Waycross	Slash Pine Festival
	11	State-wide	Poppy Day
DEC.	nfd	Augusta	Augusta Open Golf Tournament

*

PART ONE

GEORGIA:

General Background

*

Georgians at Home

THE AVERAGE Georgian votes the Democratic ticket, attends the Baptist or Methodist church, goes home to midday dinner, relies greatly on high cotton prices, and is so good a family man that he flings wide his doors to even the most distant of his wife's cousins' cousins. But these facts, significant as they are, should not be taken as all-revealing. In this, the largest of the southeastern states, there is no one characteristic type, even though the racial texture is relatively simple. The lethargic Georgia cracker of popular legend, with his drawl, his tattered overalls, and his corncob pipe, is no more typical than several other figures. The term "cracker," which originated in connection with the cracking whips of the early tobacco rollers, has evolved into a term of double meaning. Since it may designate any Georgia citizen or the most slovenly of the poor-white class, the visitor would be wiser not to thank his hostess for her delightful cracker hospitality.

Even in politics it is unsafe to make predictions. The average Georgian, close to the land and to family life, is inclined to be the protector of things as they are and the enemy of violent change. Often he is far more ready to acknowledge the presence of bad conditions than he is to suggest remedies, for he has the conservative feeling that the cure may be worse than the disease. Nevertheless, his political traditions sometimes compel his tacit support of a disturbingly liberal program merely because he cannot bring himself to change his party. In ante bellum and Reconstruction times the Georgian was hot with conviction as he hurried to the ballot box; in the twentieth century a crucial issue is needed to bring out a large poll. Although many citizens of the more populous centers, particularly businessmen, have broken wholly away from the political tradition of the Solid South, many a farmer and small-town merchant preserves a rather bewildered allegiance to his party merely because he finds any other course unthinkable.

This respect for ancestral usage, however, does not impel the Georgian to conceal himself from the modern world. Often he is boldly and genuinely liberal; almost always he responds to innovations that make his life more comfortable and efficient. Perhaps his attitude toward old ways is less one of respect than of an indulgent but unblinking affection. Old houses in Georgia have not been well preserved unless they were also agreeable to live in, and it is only in recent years that organizations in the state have begun to commemorate its historic spots. In most ways the Georgian does not linger long in the shadow of his forbears.

Nor is this condition entirely of modern times. With certain mutations, it is a normal evolution from Colonial days, when the settlers, despite the financial aid extended to them by the trustees, had to rely largely upon their own energy for economic survival. The Georgia colony, created partly as a protective rampart between South Carolina and the hostile Spaniards of Florida, was regarded as a stepsister of South Carolina, peopled by adventurers. Various visiting chroniclers of the early nineteenth century made allusion both favorable and unfavorable to the Georgian's shrewdness, his readiness to bargain keenly, and his energy in the pursuit of prosperity. Similar comments came from within. The state's own commentators seemed content to see their ideal embodied in the canny but honest country gentleman of Augustus Baldwin Longstreet's *Georgia Scenes*.

The modern prototype of that gentleman, equally robust, is found less frequently on the farm than in the small town. Other types may be more numerous, but none is more important or more characteristic of sectional culture. In this state the big man in a small town is so powerful that in certain communities he has the prerogatives of a patriarch and a dictator. Usually his despotism is benevolent, but it is seldom questioned. In a remote hamlet of south Georgia a stranger who wished to go hunting was informed that he must secure not only a hunting license but also the permission of the town's leading citizen. This gentleman not only granted that permission but offered free bed and board, and enthusiastically joined the visitor in the hunt. But without this royal consent the reception would not have been so pleasant. Far from resenting his highhanded ways, the autocrat's friends usually chuckle, "Well, you know how Mr. Ed is."

Although this Main Street monarch no longer lives on a farm, he usually owns one and is never very far away from it in spirit. If any generalization could be patterned to fit Georgians, it would be that even the most urbane ones have seldom traveled far from plowed fields and country lanes. About two thirds of the state population is actually engaged in agriculture, and the remaining third—although some do not realize it—is powerfully affected by the cotton crop. Rare indeed

AMICALOLA FALLS

LAKE NACOOCHEE, CHATTAHOOCHEE NATIONAL FOREST

BRASSTOWN BALD, FROM TRAY MOUNTAIN

PROVIDENCE CAVERNS, NEAR LUMPKIN

COUNTRY ROAD, NEAR IRWINVILLE

CONTOUR PLOWING ON GEORGIA'S ROLLING UPLANDS

WORM FENCE, BLUE RIDGE MOUNTAINS

WILD DUCKS, SAVANNAH WILDLIFE REFUGE

MINNIE LAKE, OKEFENOKEE SWAMP

LAKE TRAHLYTA, VOGEL STATE PARK

PALMETTOS NEAR BRUNSWICK

DOGWOOD BLOSSOMS

STONE MOUNTAIN

is the citizen with more than two generations of city life behind him. Even the most hard-driven city banker holds fast to his father's farm; · even the most fashionable urban society takes pleasure in the rural amusements of barbecues, fish fries, and possum hunts. For all its industrial wealth, its factories, and its capital city of bright eastern smartness, Georgia is still an agricultural state.

The wagon-rutted red-clay roads of Georgia are not only farm-to-market but farm-to-courthouse highways; for the rural voter, stoutly fortified by the county-unit electoral system, is a powerful force in state politics. The norm is found neither in the lackadaisical poor-white sharecropper nor in the keen young graduate of a modern agricultural college, but somewhere between these two—in a rangy, slow-speaking man, red with sunburn and a little stiff from outdoor work in all sorts of weather. He gathers with his own kind at the crossroads store, which is often the real seat of legislative decisions. To a stranger asking a direction he is as polite as he is loquacious, very ready to answer with "ma'am" or "sir," but in argument he is no easier to overcome than his own mule. Riding to town in his rumbling wagon or well-worn Ford, he is quietly aware that his place in the community is an important one. Although many of his kindred and friends have left the farm in poverty, he still keeps it the center of power.

Although the family has felt shattering forces here as elsewhere, there still persists the fierce and tenacious clan loyalty that was so mighty a cohesive force in Colonial society. This quality explains many common phenomena: the interminable "little visits" among brothers and sisters, the tolerance for crabbed uncles and crotchety aunts, the care for old family servants, the vigilance for favors from cousins in high places, the long and intricate tribal conferences whenever a daughter marries or a son changes his job.

Even in Atlanta, least typically southern of southern cities, a host will heartily urge his guests to stay even though he whisper to his wife that night in the bedroom, "How long do you reckon Cousin Annie Mae means to visit us?" Accepting all "kinfolks" as inevitable, he invites them to his daughter's wedding, which is likely to be a lavish affair with lovely bridesmaids in pastel dresses, and several rooms set aside for the sparkling display of wedding gifts. In their turn, the guests feel bound to send gifts, no matter how slight the actual intimacy. Georgia's tradition of social obligation seems unlikely to be lost, for it has survived almost intact through the War between the States and the bitter years of poverty that went on even into the new century.

Although Georgians are not "still fighting the Civil War," they mean that conflict and nothing later when they refer to "the war." Margaret Mitchell's *Gone with the Wind* did not arouse, but merely confirmed, the sectional feeling of the old people who remember General Sherman's march to the sea, and even readers who did not like Scarlett O'Hara or Rhett Butler acclaimed the book for its picture of Georgia plantation life. The fire of sectional resentment no longer flames fiercely, but the invaders are not wholly forgotten. Although Georgia is only beginning to be well adorned with historic markers, the Union invasion has left towering monuments in the minds of its oldest citizens and of their children reared in the years of famine. With each generation the fire burns lower, but it still smoulders enough to make the War between the States a rather dubious topic to be introduced by the northern visitor. Only the most modern young Georgians can discuss impersonally the reasons for the destructive march to the sea.

Georgia's young people, more widely traveled than their parents, have lost much of their sectional individuality as they have acquired closer resemblance to young people throughout the nation. They have learned to accept many conditions formerly rejected in their state. Their attitude toward the educated Negro, for instance, may be different from that of their elders who still prefer the old-fashioned unlettered kind. The college-bred Negro is likely to be lonely except in Atlanta, the world's largest center of Negro education, where he finds many of his own kind. The older Georgian generally meets this type with civility but with aloofness, feeling a half-conscious distrust because he has not grown accustomed to the educated Negro's new and precise enunciation. The rich slurring tones of his old nurse are to him more natural.

But, however cool he may be toward the cause of Negro education, the Georgian is usually kind to his own servants and not a little apprehensive of hurting their feelings. Although many Georgia women do their own housework, many others still employ a general servant who is usually referred to as "the cook." Likewise, the gardener is called "the yard man." If these servants have been long with the families which they serve, they are loquacious, assured, and quite capable of showing strong preferences among their masters' friends. Only very old servants will go so far as to invite their favorites to dinner without first consulting higher authority, but few southern women would be heedless of the warning tone in which a cook mutters, "It's time you wuz havin' Miss Grace to supper."

In Georgia the past and the present sometimes are blended harmoniously, sometimes are separated sharply. Although many parts of the state move slowly, they almost never have that museum stillness which some visitors apparently expect. Change may come very gradually, but it does come, even in decorous Savannah, the most aristocratic of Georgia's larger cities; and often the younger generation appears more jaunty than it is because of the contrasting quiet background. Even in the villages of the north Georgia mountains is seen the sleek, tightly waved hair of native daughters who have visited the traveling "beautician." In many ways Georgia has become very much like other states.

Where, then, can a tourist expect to catch the characteristic flavor and experience the real "feel" of Georgia? He will not always find it in Atlanta, sprawling and rich; or in sedate and beautiful Savannah; or in Augusta, where the past is thrown into sharper relief by the smartness of wealthy tourists. Perhaps he will come nearest to finding it in rolling hills of red clay, brown cornfields, white patches of cotton, and green fields of watermelons. He will find it on many a quiet farm, where the plow has left long undulating furrows over the hills, and where, each Saturday, the children sweep the yard very clean and bare. He will find it after church on Sunday, when the young married couples join their parents about a table loaded with fried chicken, ham, hot biscuits, jelly, preserves, and all the vegetables from the garden. Afterward the men smoke and sit on the worm fence, talking crops and politics, and the women gossip on the porch while they watch the children at play.

This characteristic atmosphere may also be caught in the typical Georgia town, where the wide streets are bordered by magnificent trees and a rather sparse planting of grass. Downtown, amid brick shops of the 1880's and 1890's, a Confederate soldier of granite or marble leans on his musket as he watches over the quiet courthouse square. Sometimes the passing automobiles are packed tightly with boys and girls in slacks, polo shirts, and sun-back dresses, looking like young people everywhere. Their faces may seem very young to a visitor, for a Georgia girl begins "going out" a year or two earlier than northern girls, so that her debut is less an introduction than a triumphant affirmation of popularity.

In these towns the center of sociability has shifted from the livery stable to the corner drug store, the garage, and the filling station. Spanish mission bungalows and scrollwork cottages have sprung up amid the columned ante bellum houses, and even some of these latter have been modified by additions of bandsaw banisters or screened porches. The porch is a real Georgia institution. Here throughout the summer evenings sit thousands of Georgians, neither rushing into the future nor running away from it, but waiting to accept it as it comes.

Natural Setting and Resources

GEORGIA, THE largest state east of the Mississippi River, has an area of 59,265 square miles. Its extreme length is approximately 320 miles and its extreme width about 260 miles. The northern boundary, which is near the thirty-fifth parallel of latitude, separates the state from Tennessee and North Carolina. On the east Georgia is bounded by South Carolina and the Atlantic Ocean, on the south by Florida, and on the west by Alabama. It has approximately a hundred miles of direct coast line, with many deep indentations, and 540 square miles of inland water surface.

Throughout most of Georgia, the rolling character of the land makes for undulations in the roadways, the fields, and the pine forests that border them. The clay hills are deeply gullied by erosion, and their red color against the dark pines of the wooded regions creates a perpetually vivid landscape.

The state is divided among five of the major physiographic provinces of the United States: the Appalachian Plateau, the Valley and Ridge Province, the Blue Ridge Province, the Piedmont Plateau, and the Coastal Plain. Local custom, however, recognizes only three main divisions: the mountains of north Georgia, the plateaus of middle Georgia, and the Coastal Plain of south Georgia.

That part of the state which lies within the Appalachian Plateau—the extreme northwestern corner—has an altitude ranging from one thousand eight hundred to two thousand feet. Separated by mountain ridges from the rest of Georgia, this small section until recently could be entered directly only from Alabama or Tennessee over US 11, which threads the narrow valley between Lookout and Sand mountains. Scattered along the upper reaches of Lookout Mountain are several peaks or rounded domes rising from two hundred to four hundred feet above the general level, and near the Alabama boundary is a projecting spur known as Pigeon Mountain.

That part of the Appalachian Valley which extends through northwestern Georgia, called the Valley and Ridge Province, is from twenty-eight to fifty-three miles wide, with a general elevation of six hundred to eight hundred feet. Although its "floor" is broken by sharply serrated ridges rising from two hundred to seven hundred feet, this section is described topographically as a valley because of the contrasting height of the mountains on each side. The Oostanaula and Etowah rivers, which join at Rome to form the Coosa River, drain most of the valley.

The Appalachian Mountains in North Georgia, known as the Blue Ridge Province, are made up of the Blue Ridge Mountains on the east and the Cohuttas (a continuation of the Smoky Mountains) on the west. Between them are cross ridges separated by intermountain valleys such as the Nottely River Valley and the Hiawassee River Valley. In the ridge dividing these two valleys is Georgia's highest peak, Brasstown Bald or Mount Enotah (4,784 alt.), approximately eight miles from the northern boundary of the state. Apart from the connected mass and outlying in the Piedmont section are many separate ridges, such as Pinelog, and many separate peaks, such as Yonah and Walker mountains. The Blue Ridge is the major watershed in Georgia, and many rivers have their sources here. Some, like the Savannah, flow southeastward directly to the Atlantic Ocean; others, like the Chattahoochee, flow southwestward to the Gulf of Mexico; and several small rivers, like the Toccoa, flow northwestward into the Tennessee River and thence to the Mississippi. The headwaters of these rivers are impressive because of the volume of clear, swift-flowing water descending in numerous falls. Power development has destroyed the beauty of Tallulah Falls, but it has created several large reservoirs such as Lake Burton and Lake Rabun.

The Blue Ridge section, because of its general inaccessibility and scarcity of tillable land, has a small and scattered population. Good highways lead through Ellijay Valley, Neel Gap, and Rabun Gap, the only three places where the mountains can be crossed without a formidable climb. The Louisville & Nashville Railroad passes through Ellijay Valley, and a branch of the Southern Railway crosses Rabun Gap.

Most of the state's larger cities are in the Piedmont region of middle Georgia. This region, comprising 31 per cent of the state's area, is predominantly rolling upland broken occasionally by fairly deep river valleys and a few bold hills and ridges that rise from a hundred to a thousand feet above the general level. These hills or small mountains are formed of rock more resistant to erosion than the surrounding plain. Conspicuous among them are Stone Mountain near Atlanta and Kennesaw Mountain near Marietta. The general elevation ranges from approximately four hundred feet along the fall line to fifteen hundred feet along the northern edge. This section is well drained by the principal rivers of the state, the Savannah, Chattahoochee, Oconee, Ocmulgee, and Flint, all red or reddish-yellow in color.

The entire southern half of Georgia is a part of the Coastal Plain. It is separated from the Piedmont area by the fall line, which extends across the state from Augusta through Macon to Columbus and marks the coast line of an earlier geologic era. The rivers descend in numerous small rapids from the fall line hills, some of which have an elevation of seven hundred feet. Great stretches near the coast are very low and almost flat.

The southeastern portion of this region is covered by five coastal terraces that have gradually emerged above sea level. The highest of these is the Hazlehurst (Brandywine) Terrace, with an altitude of from 215 to 260 feet. The Okefenokee Terrace, ranging from 100 to 160 feet in altitude, is 50 miles wide in some places; it contains the famous Okefenokee Swamp, which is the second largest fresh-water swamp in the United States. The lowest is the Satilla Terrace, ranging from sea level to an altitude of 60 feet. This terrace, the last of the five to emerge, comprises the mainland shore, the salt marshes, and the sea islands. The shore land, which is partially submerged at flood tide, is broken by tidal rivers and by marshes covered with dense grasses and sedges. Of the fringe of sandy islands off the coast of Georgia, the most important are Tybee, Wassaw, Ossabaw, St. Catherines, Sapelo, St. Simon, Jekyll, and Cumberland.

CLIMATE

The climate of Georgia is mild. Long summers and short winters are usual, although prevailing westerly winds sometimes bring sudden cold waves. Minor windstorms are not uncommon, but it is very seldom that Georgia suffers a tornado such as the one that ravaged Gainesville in 1936.

An error regarding Georgia's climate has long been perpetuated in encyclopedias and reference works, many of which give mean annual temperatures ranging from less than 40° on some mountain tops to more than 70° in the southern interior. According to weather bureau records covering a long series of years, the January average is 40° or slightly higher in such towns as Blue Ridge, Clayton, and Dahlonega. The annual average is not less than 57° in these mountain towns and not less than 50° on the highest mountain tops. In the warmest parts of Georgia the annual average is between 68° and 69°.

In the mountain area, where the first killing frost usually occurs during the latter part of October and the last near the middle of April, the mean annual temperature (disregarding the uninhabited mountain summits) ranges from about 55° to 61°. The hilly region, between the mountain area and a line running through Columbus, Macon, and Augusta, has mean annual temperatures ranging from about 61° to 64°. In this region the first and last killing frosts usually occur in early November and late March. Farther south the mean annual temperature increases to a little under 69° with subtropical conditions along the coast and near the Florida line. In this section of the state the first and last injurious frosts usually come in late November and early March.

The number of days a year on which the mercury falls below the freezing point averages only eight on the coast, twenty-two at Waycross and Albany, forty at Atlanta and Athens, fifty at Rome and Gainesville, and eighty at Clayton in the extreme northeastern mountains. Even on these days the mercury rarely fails to rise above the freezing point. Periods of out-of-season warmth often occur in the winter months, temperatures of 80° having been recorded as far north as Rome even in January. The summers are usually warm, but the thermometer rarely reaches extremely high temperatures; heat prostrations are almost unknown.

Rainfall in Georgia averages almost fifty inches a year, but varies from about seventy inches in the extreme northeast to forty-five or forty-six inches between Macon and Augusta. Where long records have been made, the wettest year usually shows about twice as much rain as the driest year. Snowfall averages seven to ten inches a year in the mountain area, about three inches in Atlanta, and diminishes to negligible amounts near the coast.

GEOLOGY AND PALEONTOLOGY

The entire range of geologic time, beginning with the Archeozoic era of unicellular life, is represented in Georgia rocks. The records of these rocks indicate that the land was subjected to a long series of upheavals and erosions before it assumed its present form.

The northern portion of the state is by far the older. The sedimentary deposits of this section were formed in layers during the Pre-Cambrian period, when much of the North American continent was under water. At the close of this period a vast mountain range was thrust upward. At one time this range towered as high, perhaps, as the Rocky Mountains but it has been worn down by erosion to form the gently rolling plain of the Piedmont Plateau. By the same pressure that built up this range, the earlier layers, now metamorphosed into sedimentary rocks, were pushed upward and forced into gigantic folds. Tightened, condensed, and intruded by granites, these folds hardened into the crystalline formations that now make up the underlying rocks of north Georgia.

Later, when the mountains had been worn down and the debris deposited in the inland sea that covered what is now northwestern Georgia, thousands of feet of sedimentary rock were piled up in successive layers. Then the land was lifted above sea level, and the formation of the present Appalachian Mountains began. The same subterranean activity that pushed up these mountains exerted a tremendous lateral pressure, forcing the sedimentary rocks into great folds and thrusting entire beds of rock over one another. Again the older crystalline rocks of the mountain and Piedmont sections were intruded by more granites, such as Stone Mountain and those found at Elberton.

The Appalachian Valley, which now separates the Lookout and Blue Ridge ranges in northern Georgia, was formed by erosion after the entire area of this section of the state was above water. Not all the rocks of this region were as hard as the crystallines of the Piedmont and mountain lands, and the lesser resistance to erosion of certain shales and limestones is cited to explain the forming of this valley.

The belt of ancient crystalline rocks from northeastern New York to eastern Alabama extends throughout the Appalachian Mountains and Piedmont Plateau and underlies almost one-fourth of Georgia. These formations, belonging to the remotest geologic age, are classed as Carolina gneiss, Roan gneiss, and granite. In the northwestern corner of the state, the predominant formations are the much younger sandstones, shales, and limestones, the youngest of all being the coal deposits found on the tops of Lookout and Sand mountains.

The geologic formations in the southern half of the state are much simpler than those of the northern half, for the Coastal Plain section did not begin to appear until many millions of years after the formation of the mountains. At the time when the Appalachian Mountains were forming, the land now embraced by Georgia was tilted, so that its lower section was covered by the ocean and the erosion of the upper section was increased. During a long period of erosion vast quantities of debris were carried southward to the ocean, forming the layers of sands, clays, and marls of the present Coastal Plain.

Beginning with the fall line hills, this southern section presents a slope gradually descending toward the seacoast with formations laid down in successive layers, of which the oldest is at the fall line and the youngest is at the coast. The deposits near the fall line hills are largely gravel, clays, and coarse light-colored sands, derived from the granites of the adjoining Piedmont Plateau. Red sands make up most of the southern part of these hills, although white limestone forms part of the surfaces of the Flint and Chattahoochee river valleys. The lands farther southeast contain varying amounts of sand, gravel, loam, and flint. The flat lands of the coast line in the southeastern part of the state are coastal terraces, where thin beds of marls and sands overlie the older sedimentary beds.

Evidences of prehistoric life in Georgia have been exposed both by accident and by geological research. Discoveries have been made in various sections, but especially in the northern mountains and the coastal marshes.

The mountains of northwest Georgia have yielded many fossilized examples of ancient life, ranging from the earliest forms of trilobites and corals to fishes, tree ferns, and primitive insects, and dating from the Proterozoic through the Paleozoic era. These remains came from the bed of a broad shallow sea, which covered an immense area west of the Appalachian Mountains; this region was elevated during the era following the Carboniferous or coal period, when these mountains underwent their most recent upheaval.

Other discoveries above the fall line include fossilized larch twigs and leaves found at Dahlonega in the mountainous region of northeast Georgia. At Lithia Springs, in upper western Georgia, a few teeth of the mastodon—a large prehistoric elephant—have been taken from stream deposits of the Pleistocene or Glacial epoch overlying crystalline rock.

Below the fall line the rich alluvial land is valuable for a preservative quality that has kept many fossils intact. Fossil discoveries in Georgia began in 1823, when Samuel L. Mitchill, in his natural history researches, came upon partially decomposed bones on Skidaway Island, twelve miles southwest of Savannah. These bones belonged to the giant ground sloth (*megatherium cuvierri*), an animal more massive than the largest existing elephant and an ancestor of the present sloth found in South American forests.

Among the first fossils in Georgia to be preserved and recorded were those discovered in 1838 by James Hamilton Couper, a southern planter who became well known for his agricultural experiments. These fossils, taken from Skidaway Island and from the Brunswick and Altamaha Canal, included remains of several large prehistoric animals such as the megatherium, mammoth, and mastodon, as well as extinct species of the hippopotamus, horse, ox, and hog. Most of these are kept in the natural history museum of the state capitol. Mr. Couper collected all his fossils from the coastal district, where they were found buried at the bottom of alluvium and resting on white sand.

· In the same fertile Savannah region Sir Charles Lyell, the eminent English geologist, discovered mastodon remains in 1854, and findings have continued down to recent years. In 1935 the fossilized bones of a mammoth were turned up by F.E.R.A. drainage workers at Sackville, five miles south of Savannah.

Giant oyster fossils, four inches wide and ranging from twelve to twenty-two inches in length, have been taken from Shell Bluff, forty miles south of Augusta on the Savannah River. They were dug from a formation twenty-four feet thick, and are regarded as belonging to the Cenozoic era, or Age of Mammals. Other large oyster fossils have been found in a limestone sink near Sandersville in middle Georgia and at Stormy Branch and Cox Springs in southeastern Georgia. One of the most important discoveries in the middle Georgia section was the remains of a toothed whale, a species of the extinct genus Zeuglodon.

Petrified wood has been found in several parts of south Georgia. One specimen, a petrified tree of the pine family, belonging to the Cretaceous or chalk period, was without annular rings, indicating a climate of little or no seasonal variation.

Shark teeth are probably the most abundant fossils of south Georgia. Almost every large dredging project uncovers many of these teeth, which are black, with a grayish-brown outer coating of enamel, and are from one to six inches long. These fossils have been turned up frequently, not only along the coast, but as far north as the fall line.

PLANT LIFE

Georgia possesses a native flora of exceptional variety and interest. Many trees and flowers are common to the entire state and flourish almost everywhere. The pine, cedar, oak, elm, sycamore, and poplar are the most prevalent trees. In all sections the red maple shows its rust-red buds and scarlet leaves, and streams are bordered by feathery-leaved willows. The hickory, the persimmon, the symmetrical black gum, the sweet gum with its green burs, and the tall tulip tree with its pale saffron-streaked flowers fill the wooded areas.

The most famous of Georgia's flowering trees is the magnolia, with glossy ovate leaves and creamy, heavy-scented blossoms—a tree that has won a place in the romantic literature of the South. Almost as well known is the spreading mimosa, with its fragrant "powder-puff" blooms and ferny foliage. The chinaberry, once extensively cultivated to counteract miasma, has lost popularity because of the cloying sweetness of its lavender flowers.

The flowering dogwood has a slender crooked trunk and boughs arranged in flat, irregular layers. Green in summer and covered with crimson leaves and clusters of red berries in fall, it bursts into fullest beauty in spring with a glory of snow-white bloom. Pink dogwood, native to the state but less common than white, appears occasionally in the woods and is frequently planted on lawns.

The streets of many Georgia towns are lined with crape myrtles, thick in late summer with clusters of fluted cerise flowers. Less common varieties have white, lavender, or pink blooms. One of the earliest-blooming spring shrubs is the yellow January jasmine, and this is closely followed by the vivid flowering quince. Early-blossoming trees are the Japanese magnolia, the weeping dwarf cherry, and the redbud tree with its lavender-pink blossoms.

Georgia's state flower is the hardy Cherokee rose, a flat white blossom with a yellow center. Its name is derived from an Indian legend concerning the romance of a young Seminole warrior and the daughter of an enemy Cherokee chieftain. As the lovers were fleeing, the girl broke off a sprig of the rose as a souvenir of her native hills, and when she went to live among the Seminoles she planted the sprig and nourished it. Afterward the flower was regarded as a symbol of the land that later became Georgia.

Roses thrive throughout the state in all but the high mountain regions, and the yellow of daffodil, crocus, forsythia, and marigold is seen almost everywhere. In their seasons, goldenrod, wild asters, morning-glories, red sumac, and crimson-flowering trumpet vine are gay along the roadsides; and graceful white spirea, blue larkspur, multicolored zinnias, and ragged chrysanthemums bloom successively in the gardens. Red clay banks are hidden by fragrant climbing honeysuckle, and blue iris, yellow jasmine, and pink and yellow primroses grow wild throughout the countryside.

Many trees and plants grow only in certain sections of the state. On the higher peaks of north Georgia are numerous species of plant life usually found only in New England and eastern Canada. Among these adventurers from northern forests are wild columbine, Dutchman's-breeches, lily of the valley, coreopsis, trillium, corydalis, and striped maple or moosewood.

In the mountainous areas the hemlock reaches a great size, and massive red oaks grow to a height of eighty feet. The white pine, so common in the North Carolina mountains, occurs only in scattered areas, but the slow-growing scrub pine is found throughout the region. Chestnut trees, often seventy-five feet high, were plentiful until decimated by a blight that spread southward from the northern Appalachian regions in the present century; the new growth, which springs from the roots of the old trees, reaches a height of only twenty or thirty feet before it dies. The chinquapin or bush chestnut still flourishes; and here also is found the buckeye, whose smooth brown nut is cherished as a good-luck talisman. At the foot of the large trees grow the spicy wild ginger or heart-leaf, the glossy-leaved galax prized by florists, the delicate maidenhair fern, the thin silver stems of the Indian pipe, and the starry white blossoms and red fruit of the partridgeberry. A delicious wild strawberry grows here, as well as the more common blackberry and blueberry. Cleared fields and pastures are covered with daisies and Queen Anne's lace, while streams are bordered with rhododendron, mountain laurel, and flame azalea, ranging in color from pale flesh tints to light scarlet. The apple orchards of the foothills are filled in spring with pale pink blossoms.

Farther south, where the mountains merge into the Piedmont Plateau, hardwood trees are scarcer and such conifers as the loblolly, shortleaf, and pitch pines are more plentiful. Here, too, grows the small sassafras tree, with aromatic roots from which a fragrant tea is made. In many parts of this area, as well as in central Georgia, peach orchards in spring form a cloud of pink.

Some of the flowers native to the more northerly region have gained a foothold in the upper Piedmont region. The trailing arbutus lies hidden under pine needles, but the large bird's-foot violet comes out boldly, carpeting the slopes in spring. The purple blossoms of the low maypop vine are known as passion-flowers because they have a crosslike marking in the center, nail-shaped pistils, and a group of stamens resembling a crown of thorns. The small green fruit of the maypop is often used by countrywomen for making jelly.

Street plantings in the towns of middle Georgia are likely to include crape myrtle, the water oak, and the ginkgo or maidenhair tree with its large, fan-shaped leaves. The sweet, musk-flavored scuppernong grape, as well as several varieties of fig trees, commonly grow in the back yards. Also popular are the pomegranate, prized for its flame-colored blossoms and rosy fruit, and the sweet-scented Cape jasmine, a variety of gardenia.

Below the fall line hills, near the central part of the state, the topography changes abruptly into the flat lands of south Georgia, where longleaf pines tower above an undergrowth of wire grass, wild leguminous plants, or gallberry bushes. Also plentiful in this region is the slash pine of great potential value for paper making. The trunks of many of these pines are gashed for turpentine, and the air is sharp with its clean and pungent odor. Throughout south Georgia and on the coastal islands grows the mighty live oak, its gnarled trunk supporting thickly foliaged branches hung with waving streamers of gray Spanish moss. The trunkless saw palmetto, commonly called the scrub palmetto, sends out long, tough roots into the sandy soil of the extreme southern portion of the state. On the coastal islands it grows a short trunk and, with its large fan-shaped leaves, frequently attains a height of twelve feet. The more decorative cabbage palmetto, sometimes called cabbage palm, is a native of the coastal region and is widely used in that section for avenue planting. The young terminal bud of this species is edible.

Vivid red poinsettias, growing under cultivation in this southermost region, often reach the eaves of houses. Several varieties of hibiscus abound; the Confederate rose, belonging to this genus, grows to the size of a small tree and bears large double roselike blooms that are white in the morning and deep rose at nightfall. Throughout town and countryside in south Georgia grows the camellia, a shrub with glossy evergreen leaves and white, pink, or red blossoms with waxy petals.

The trees most abundant in the southern swamps are the tupelo gum and the stately bald cypress, with dark frondlike foliage and projecting "knees" that supply a beautiful burl wood used in furniture making. These swamp lands are almost impenetrable because of their subtropical growth of cane, greenbriar, holly, and thorny vines. Here, too, are white clematis, white marsh lilies, wild orchids, and greenish-yellow insectivorous pitcher plants. Streams are choked by blossoming reeds, aquatic grasses, and water hyacinths; and water lilies float on the still ponds and lakes. The Ogeechee lime tree, a rare species belonging to the same genus as the tupelo, grows abundantly in the swamps along the Ogeechee River and produces a small fruit often used for flavoring. In the swampy bottom lands of the Coastal Plain grow the water oak, willow oak, and laurel oak; the first two varieties have been widely planted as shade trees along the streets and in the parks of Georgia towns.

The various garden clubs of Georgia have performed inestimable service to the state, not only by planting gardens in the cities but also by promoting the cultivation of shrubs and flowers along the highways. Even some of the drabbest villages have been improved with plots of grass and hardy shrubs. Every spring a garden pilgrimage is conducted through the larger towns in the state, and various camellia shows held in February in south Georgia have stimulated much interest in this flower. An annual rose show at Thomasville in south Georgia has become widely known, and a tour of the Augusta gardens is conducted each spring. The most notable feature of the spring blooming in Augusta and Savannah is the azalea, which in hedges and massed plantings forms sheets of color ranging from white and palest pink to coral, flame, and rose red.

The general aspect of Georgia gardens has changed greatly since ante bellum days. Then a popular form of planting included a row of magnolia trees across the front of the grounds and a grove of cedars hiding the slave quarters. Between these the gardens were laid out in small beds, which were circled by sandy walks bordered with box hedges. The beds were planted with roses, lilies, larkspur, poppies, and violets. Near the house were planted oleanders, camellias, and fragrant Cape jasmine bushes; and over trellises climbed white star jasmine, white and purple wistaria, and old-fashioned roses. While the same flowers and shrubs are being planted in modern Georgia gardens, the arrangement has been greatly altered. Emphasis is placed now, not on trees and precise beds, but on shrubbery banked against the house and sweeping expanses of unbroken lawn.

ANIMAL LIFE

Concerning the "animal productions" of the Georgia territory, as he observed them during his travels in the early 1770's, the famous naturalist William Bartram wrote: "They are the same which originally inhabited this part of North America, except such as have been affrighted away since the invasion of the Europeans. The buffalo, once so very numerous, is not at this day to be seen in this part of the country; there are but few elks, and those only in the Appalachian Mountains. The dreaded and formidable rattlesnake is yet too common, and a variety of other serpents abound. . . . The alligator, a species of crocodile, abounds in the rivers and swamps, near the sea coast, but it is not to be seen above Augusta. Bears, tygers [panthers], wolves, and wild cats are numerous enough."

These animals became less numerous, however, because pioneers cleared new land and hunters saw no reason to stint themselves amid such plenty. Despite excellent breeding grounds provided by the well-watered mountain slopes, river valleys, semidry flatlands, and swamps, the wild life of Georgia continued to dwindle until the first quarter of the twentieth century. In 1911, however, the state legislature organized a department, which, now functioning as the division of wild life, is doing much to preserve the native animal life. Nine state parks provide protection to small animals and birds, and one game farm releases quail for distribution throughout the state. In 1938 the division of state parks announced the acquisition of twelve additional tracts of land for conversion into state parks and natural resource reservations.

By co-operative agreement, the state and Federal governments have established in the Chattahoochee National Forest of north Georgia four game management areas, including the 23,000-acre Chattahoochee Game Refuge, a region well stocked with large game. The United

States Bureau of Biological Survey has charge of eight similar Georgia areas, comprising more than 330,000 acres: the Okefenokee Swamp Wildlife Refuge (*see* TOUR *4A*), the Blackbeard Island Migratory Bird Refuge, the Wolf Island Wildlife Refuge, 3,000 acres of the Savannah River Wildlife Refuge, the Wilson Wildlife Refuge near Springfield, the Piedmont Wildlife Refuge near Gray, the South Sapelo Island Refuge, and the Tybee Wildlife Refuge on Oysterbed Island. Rearing pools for bass and bream are maintained by the Federal fish hatcheries at Warm Springs and at Lake Park near Valdosta; Georgia lakes and streams are restocked each year from these and from the state hatcheries at Summerville, Millen, Fitzgerald, Macon, and Ways.

Most of the animals now found in Georgia are small, for only in the sparsely inhabited regions is any natural protection afforded the larger species. Although bear and deer formerly abounded over the entire state, unrestricted hunting resulted in their virtual disappearance from north Georgia; but they continued to thrive in the natural shelter afforded by the forests and marshes of the Coastal Plain. They were reintroduced into the protected portions of the Chattahoochee National Forest in 1926, and there are now about a thousand deer in that region. The U. S. Biological Survey has estimated that there are (1939) about seventeen thousand deer and about four hundred bear in Georgia as a whole. The wildcat, as always, still roams the thinly settled areas throughout the state. Both the gray fox and the more common red fox are indigenous to the mountains of north Georgia and the forests of south Georgia. Among the larger marine mammals are dolphins, which inhabit the coastal sounds. The porpoise or bottlenosed dolphin often grows to be nine and a half feet long.

Small fur-bearing animals are plentiful. The muskrat and raccoon are common in swampy areas, and the gray squirrel, hunted in the forests for food and pelts, scampers unmolested over city parks and lawns. The flying squirrel is also found in urban areas, and the small, quick ground squirrel, or chipmunk, with its prettily striped back. Across Georgia's rural highways dart many rabbits; the swamp rabbit can be distinguished from the more familiar gray cottontail by its dark-brown color and its lack of a powder-puff tail. One of the most numerous of mammals is the marsupial opossum, with coarse light-gray hair, a sharp muzzle, and a face that appears comically human because of its wide grin. Mink are not uncommon along many Georgia streams.

Among the less abundant mammals are the otter, now increasing along the Savannah River and in the Okefenokee Swamp; the woodchuck, occasionally to be seen in the north Georgia highlands; the pocket gopher, a native of the pine barrens in south Georgia; the arboreal fox squirrel; and the red squirrel, found but rarely in north Georgia's highest mountains. Beavers are indigenous in several river swamps of central Georgia; in other areas they have been introduced and protected. There is an abundance, however, of such small rodents as the field and meadow mouse, and fields and gardens are broken by the burrows of the mole as it goes its blind, destructive way underground.

No fewer than 350 species of birds have been recorded by observers in Georgia at different seasons. Among those most common to the entire state are the mockingbird, brown thrasher, towhee, cardinal, bluejay, catbird, robin, crow, ruby-throated hummingbird, and several species of woodpecker, wren, thrush, and warbler. One of the most familiar sounds in spring and summer is the song of the mockingbird in endless repetition. The brown thrasher, chosen by school children as the state bird, sings much like the mockingbird, but its song has a wilder quality and can be identified because each phrase is repeated only once. Vacationists in the Blue Ridge Mountains of Georgia remember the rising inflection of "tze–tze–tze," song of the black-throated green warbler, the booming voice of the barred owl, and the ecstatic flight song of the plain-colored ovenbird, which confines itself to a sober "teacher–teacher–teacher" song when in treetops.

Georgia is a transition area in the distribution of many northern and southern birds. A camper in the foothills region can frequently hear the whippoorwill from the North as well as the chuck-will's-widow, native of the South, both belonging to the goatsucker family. Many migratory species, such as the robin and bluebird, are common all the year round, and visitors, accustomed to associating the robin and bluebird with spring, are surprised to find these birds even in north Georgia during winter. Some species, like the red-headed woodpecker, remain only when the winters are mild.

Georgia's scavengers are the turkey and black buzzards. Its common predatory birds are the barred owl, screech owl, and various species of hawk; less common are the entirely white-headed bald eagle and the white-breasted osprey or fish-hawk. Only among the highest and most isolated peaks of north Georgia do ravens live. They have been photographed during their nesting season on Mount Enotah, a peak that has long been known alternatively as Ravens' Cliffs.

Georgia's chief game birds, quail and doves, are common in all sections. Quail are especially abundant in south Georgia, where private preserves are constantly restocked and carefully managed for maximum bird productivity; doves are as plentiful in the Piedmont and mountainous sections as in the lower part of the state. Wild turkeys are particularly prevalent in the southwestern part of the state, where they have multiplied in the Coastal Plain forests. Ducks are plentiful in the vicinity of lakes and streams along the coast, and rails or marsh hens abound in the eight coastal counties. Jacksnipe (Wilson's snipe) are common in marshy lands during winter months and woodcock during spring and fall migration. Wild geese are found in late fall and winter near Elberton. The wide variety of Georgia game bird life is indicated by the presence in north Georgia of the ruffed grouse, now so rare that it is under legal protection.

Because of its bountiful supply of plant food the Okefenokee Swamp affords a rich natural refuge for many kinds of birds, especially waterfowl. Eighty-five species of birds have been recorded within its boundaries during the summer and ninety during the winter. One of the most unusual birds within the swamp is the anhinga or water turkey, which belongs to a rather primitive species and uses its wings to swim under water, catching fish for food. At various seasons eleven species of duck have been seen; the wood or summer duck is the only year-round inhabitant, but this region has been adopted as a winter home by the ring-necked, the pintail, and the black duck, as well as by the mallard, the hooded merganser, and the green-winged teal. The Okefenokee is also a refuge for the smoky gray sandhill (Florida) crane, the snowy egret, and the white ibis, birds that were almost extinct during the early part of the present century.

Representatives of America's four common species of poisonous snakes are found in Georgia: the rattlesnake, the highland moccasin, the water moccasin, and the coral snake. The rattlesnake is the most dangerous, especially the diamondback that inhabits south Georgia. The north Georgia varieties, such as the timber rattler, are less irritable and secrete less venom. The highland moccasin, scarcely less venomous than the rattlesnake, is not so numerous in the open fields as among the rocks and in wooded lands. Native to north Georgia, and commonly known as the copperhead, it can be distinguished by its reddish bands, alternately bright and dull. The water moccasin, also called the cottonmouth because its mouth is white inside, is not commonly found north of Atlanta. It is a dull-colored and flat-headed snake that lives near bodies of water and particularly around stagnant swamp pools where it feeds on fish, lizards, frogs, and other snakes. In central and southern Georgia lives the rare coral snake, small but conspicuous because of its vivid alternate bands of red, yellow, and black. Unlike the other venomous species, it has grooved instead of hollow fangs, and its poison affects the nervous system rather than the lymphatic glands.

Among the nonpoisonous snakes are the water snake, green arbor snake, spreading adder, black snake, common garter or grass snake, king snake, and rainbow snake. The king snake is often protected by the farmers because it destroys rodents that harm their crops. The rainbow snake—brightly colored with blotches of yellow, red, and black—is a burrowing species with a blunt head and a strong body; it occurs principally in Georgia and South Carolina.

Turtles found in the state range from the musk turtle, with a small shell three inches long, to giant sea turtles often weighing 300 pounds or more. These large creatures nest from May to August on the ocean beaches of the coastal islands. Alligator terrapins sometimes weigh as much as seventy-five pounds. The gopher terrapin thrives in the dry pine barrens, and the Florida terrapin and soft-shelled turtle, along the boggy edges of swamps and rivers. The coastal estuaries are a habitat and breeding ground for diamondback terrapin, which are also raised commercially on the Isle of Hope near Savannah and shipped to clubs and restaurants throughout the United States and in Europe.

The largest of Georgia's reptiles are the alligators, some of which grow to a length of fourteen feet. Formerly inhabiting many south Georgia swamps, alligators have gradually retreated from the populated regions and are now abundant only on the coastal islands where they have been given a measure of protection and in the Savannah River, Blackbeard Island, and Okefenokee Swamp Wildlife Refuges. Among the many species of lizards are the common striped lizard, the blue-tailed skink, and the chameleon, which conceals itself by rapidly changing color against foliage or rocks. The legless lizard, commonly called the glass snake, is interesting because it is able to escape by disjointing its tail when caught by that part of its body. Since the tail grows again, there is a Negro superstition that the two parts unite before nightfall. In the dense low forest there is a ceaseless rustle of small scaleless amphibians—toads, frogs, newts, and salamanders.

Lakes and streams of the Appalachian Highland region of north Georgia are breeding waters for many fresh-water fish such as bream, pike, sunfish, and large-mouthed and small-mouthed black bass. There are a few Georgia streams with rainbow trout, and brook trout are known to occur in Georgia but are even less plentiful. In the muddy rivers of middle Georgia are numerous mud catfish, yellow catfish, and eels; and these streams have been restocked with bream, sunfish, and German carp, which had been diminished greatly by intensive seining. Redfish, bass, mullet, drum, shad, and mackerel are plentiful in the rivers of the Coastal Plain.

An abundance of edible shrimp, blue swimming-crabs, and tide-water oysters along the seacoast has led to the establishment of shellfish industries in Brunswick and Savannah. The rivers of Georgia are well known among naturalists as the habitat of many varieties of mussels. Several species occur only in Georgia waters, and some are limited to a particular river system. There are about fifteen species of fresh-water crayfish that grow to a maximum length of six inches and are a favorite food for bass. Among the common but little-known forms of animal life are many kinds of micro-crustaceans that occur in rivers, lakes, and temporary pools throughout the state and are eaten by minnows.

Because of Georgia's mild winters and long hot summers, its bogs and woods contain almost every form of insect life native to the southeastern United States. Portions of the state once were infested with mosquitoes, but extensive malaria control has greatly decreased their number. The most destructive of Georgia insects is the boll weevil, which farmers have learned to control in some measure since its first serious attack on the cottonfields in 1921. Among the many species of spiders is the black widow, which lives in damp places, particularly in crevices of old logs. The black widow is a poisonous species, and its bite is sometimes fatal. Moths and butterflies range from the small white and yellow varieties to the gorgeous broad-winged specimens typical of semitropical climates.

Of considerable interest to students of wild life are the specimens in the zoological garden of Grant Park in Atlanta, the mounted specimens in the State Capitol museum, and the Emory University collection of beetles, moths, butterflies, and unmounted birds.

NATURAL RESOURCES AND THEIR CONSERVATION

Forests: From northern mountains to coastal lowlands the lands are heavily wooded, principally in pine. Despite extensive destruction by fire and commercial exploitation for turpentine, Georgia's forests still cover 23,750,000 acres, or roughly two-thirds the total area of the state.

The principal species of Georgia pine are the loblolly, Virginia scrub, shortleaf, longleaf, pond, pitch, and slash. Of these the longleaf and slash pines of the Coastal Plain predominate. They are used for building construction, poles, piling, railroad ties, and flooring; and both contribute greatly to the production of naval stores, especially rosin and turpentine, in which Georgia leads all the states. Recent experiments have shown that the rapidly growing pine is also particularly suited to the manufacture of pulp paper. The timber of the loblolly, Virginia scrub, shortleaf, pitch, and pond pines is inferior, although adequate for use in cheap construction. White pine, a less prevalent but more valuable species found in the mountainous regions, is a soft wood used chiefly for furniture, wallboarding, and matches.

While the pines predominate, being more adaptable to varying soil conditions, hardwood trees are plentifully scattered throughout the state. The white oak is by far the most important and is particularly preferred for general construction purposes requiring massive beams, such as bridge building and housing. The live oak, common throughout the Coastal Plain, supplies a hard, well-wearing timber that is especially adapted to use as veneering. In both the northern and southern sections numerous hardwood varieties are used in furniture manufacture. The cypress of the swamp regions, although depleted by lumbering, is still found in sufficient quantity to be important to the industry; the durability of this wood under exposure to the weather makes it desirable also for exterior trim of buildings and for boat and ship building.

Georgia has three state forests—a 100-acre tract near Augusta, a 1000-acre tract near Baxley, and a 3,800-acre tract near Waycross—all planted in pine to be used for experimental purposes in determining the best types of pine for seedlings. Reforestation is aided by the maintenance of several state nurseries; especially important among these are the one at Flowery Branch in the national forest district and the one at Albany in the southwestern part of the state. During the planting season of 1938-39 about fifteen million pine seedlings from these nurseries were set out on waste lands throughout the state. Nine state parks and three recreational demonstration areas, totaling more than fifteen thousand acres, are further aids in the conservation of forest resources.

On July 1, 1936, the Georgia districts of the Cherokee and Nantahala national forests were consolidated with additional lands purchased by the Federal Government to form the Chattahoochee National Forest, with more than 500,000 acres. The purchase area of the forest includes 1,165,000 acres and extends from the Tennessee and North Carolina boundaries southward for forty-five miles at some points and from the South Carolina border westward almost across the state.

A reforestation program is aided by several Federal and state agencies, including the school of forestry established at the University of Georgia in 1906, now the oldest and largest school of its kind in the South. The state division of forestry functions to protect and develop Georgia's timber resources by aiding in the conservation of trees and encouraging their adaptation to new commercial uses. In its development program the division has initiated or aided three outstanding activities:

Groups of persons owning 10,000 or more acres of forest have been organized into timber protective associations for mutual cooperation in providing fire service, purchasing fire-fighting equipment, and constructing fire-breaks and telephone lines. These organizations now have under their protection more than five million acres of land and are making every effort to reduce forest fire losses, which have some- times amounted to five million dollars annually. This cooperative plan, originated by the division of forestry, has been adopted by many other states.

In 1929 the division, with the aid of the state department of voca- tional education, established forestry projects in 192 rural high schools. These projects are designed to teach farm boys how to get the greatest returns from woodlands. Each school is required to have ten or more forested acres, and each boy must have a small wooded tract of his own. The course of instruction covers every phase of tree conservation and development, and a special training camp is conducted each summer at one of the state colleges.

In 1931 the Chemical Foundation, Inc., offered Charles H. Herty $50,000 to carry out his experiments on the paper-making possibilities of Georgia pine, provided he could secure $20,000 a year for the main- tenance and operation of a laboratory. The state legislature appropri- ated this amount and on January 1, 1932, authorized that the work proceed as the Pulp and Paper Division of the State Department of Forestry and Geological Development.

Herty's activities were also aided by donations from the city of Savannah and from private sources.

Minerals: Clays, granite, and marble are Georgia's most important minerals. Although many others occur in varying quantities, develop- ment has been slow because of lack of funds, distance from markets, and the state's preoccupation with agriculture. Some of the north Georgia deposits are rich and diverse; but, contrary to general belief, south Georgia minerals produce a larger income, principally because of the sedimentary clays of the Coastal Plain.

Kaolin, the most valuable of the various clays, was found near Augusta and Macon in early Colonial days and was mined for ship- ment to the famous Wedgwood Pottery in England. When English kaolin became available, the mining of the Georgia product was aban- doned for more than a century, but at present approximately 65 per cent of that produced in the United States is from the deposits of mid- dle Georgia. It is used extensively as a paper filler and in the manu- facture of white ware, firebrick, and terra cotta.

The alluvial and residual clays of middle Georgia are used for com- mon building brick and structural tile, and the shale of the north- western region is important in making face brick, building and roof- ing tile, and sewer pipe. Jugs, churns, and art pieces are made by a few small potteries in middle and north Georgia. The state stands first in the Union in the production of fuller's earth, a claylike material of various colors, which differs from common clay in being porous, carrying a high percentage of water, and having little or no plasticity.

Granite occurs in large quantities throughout the Piedmont Plateau, and Georgia ranks seventh among the states in its production. At Elberton, in northeast Georgia, the granite industry has been developed most extensively. At Stone Mountain, sixteen miles northeast of Atlanta, an important quarry was operated for three-quarters of a century. Also of commercial importance is the Lithonia mass, extending over a considerable area near Atlanta. The light-colored stone from these quarries is of great strength and uniformity, is remarkably free from chemical and physical defects, and is used extensively for road material as well as for buildings and monuments.

In the value of the marble quarried, Georgia ranks higher than any other state except Vermont. A single large vein in the north Georgia mountains is three-eighths of a mile wide, four miles long, and from two hundred feet to half a mile deep. Although the marble usually has a coarse texture, it takes a high polish and is admirably suited both for building purposes and for monuments. Tests made by the state geological survey prove that its durability equals that of any other marble on the market. The color of the stone varies from white and pink to almost black.

Less than 3 per cent of the mineral production of Georgia is derived from the metallic minerals. Manganese ores are confined principally to northwestern Georgia, large and productive deposits near Cartersville having been worked for many years. Formerly these ores were shipped to England, but in recent years they have found a ready market in this country. Georgia produces approximately half of the manganese of the United States.

The state ranks second in the production of barite, which is mined in the rich mineral belt near Cartersville. It is used as a substitute for white lead and in the manufacture of paper, rubber, and oilcloth, as well as for refining sugar, glazing pottery, and enameling iron. Bauxite, in the production of which Georgia is third among the states, is mined in both northwestern and middle Georgia. It is important in the manufacture of firebrick, aluminum, alum, and artificial abrasives. The first bauxite discovered in the United States was found near Rome in northwestern Georgia in 1887.

Gold deposits occur in a number of parallel belts in the Appalachian region. Before 1849 these fields produced most of the gold mined in the United States, but with the discovery of richer fields in the West all but a few mines were abandoned. Coal and iron are found in small quantities in the extreme northwestern corner of the state, but the general isolation of the section and the difficulties of transportation have made development unwarrantable. Although some deposits of copper, feldspar, and asbestos occur also in the northern half of Georgia, low prices make mining unprofitable.

A large variety of minerals suitable for gems and ornamental cabinet specimens has been found in the mountainous northeastern section of the state. Mining for gems, however, has never been systematic, and the discoveries have been either accidental or incidental to other mining.

Water Power: With its swift streams descending from sharply sloping mountains and the rolling central plateau, Georgia has potential hydroelectric resources estimated at nearly two and a half million horsepower daily. Only half of this power has yet been utilized, for need did not arise until recent years, when the state's rapid industrial growth created a demand for increased hydroelectric service.

Most of the principal rivers of Georgia rise in the mountainous northern section and flow southward, dropping in numerous waterfalls and rapids to the broad and flat Coastal Plain below the fall line. Power facilities are greatest in the northeastern section, where some of the rivers have precipitous falls. The Tallulah River drops more than six hundred feet within less than two miles; the Broad River drops sixty-five feet in approximately the same distance; and the Towaliga River, ninety-eight feet in a quarter of a mile. In the hilly middle Georgia region the river fall is gradual, but even as low as the fall line it is sufficient for development. On the almost flat Coastal Plain there are few natural facilities for power projects.

The earliest use of water power in Georgia was made along the fall line by water-driven cotton and woolen mills. During the latter part of the nineteenth century, the Augusta Canal was the most important water power achievement in the southern states, but since then it has been greatly surpassed by hydroelectric advances in north Georgia.

Forty-three hydroelectric plants with a capacity of 586,301 horsepower have been established on the major rivers in Georgia and some of their tributaries. In the Savannah River basin, including the Tugalo and Tallulah rivers, are ten plants with a capacity of 321,007 horsepower. The adjoining basin on the west, the Ogeechee River basin, is smaller and has one plant with a capacity of 100 horsepower. Ten plants with an aggregate capacity of 52,936 horsepower are in the basin of the Altamaha River, formed by the junction of the Oconee and Ocmulgee rivers. The basins of the Chattahoochee and Flint rivers, part of the greater Apalachicola River basin, have nineteen hydro-electric plants with a capacity of 180,708 horsepower. In the extreme northern part of the state is a small portion of the Tennessee River basin, having one plant with a capacity of 30,000 horsepower, and the two plants of the Coosa River basin in the Appalachian Valley of northwest Georgia have a combined capacity of 1,550 horsepower.

Archeology

ALTHOUGH THE State of Georgia is one of the richest in the country in archeological remains, systematic exploration has been confined to limited areas and the picture of aboriginal cultures in this region is far from complete. Georgia is of special significance because of the great variety in the types of its archeological remains and the vast span of time indicated between the findings of the earliest and the latest periods—from the ancient flint-using people who dwelt on the site of the Old Ocmulgee Fields near Macon at a very early period to the Indians of historic times whose buried artifacts are mingled with trinkets and tools of European manufacture.

In recent years archeological research in Georgia has been conducted principally at Macon, but there are indications that the prehistoric Indians occupied every part of the state where lands could be easily cultivated. Important evidence of early man in America has been disclosed in pottery fragments and flints along the coast, where there are extensive shell heaps and mounds; rock shelters have been found close to Macon; caves have been explored near Cartersville in northwest Georgia; and petroglyphs have been reported, not only in the mountains of northern Georgia, but along streams in the central portion of the state.

According to M. W. Stirling, Chief of the Bureau of American Ethnology of the Smithsonian Institution, Georgia possesses, in the Eagle Mound near Eatonton, the most perfect effigy mound in America. Stirling also states that Georgia has three of the four most interesting archeological sites east of the Rocky Mountains—Etowah near Cartersville in northwest Georgia, Old Ocmulgee Fields near Macon in central Georgia, and Kolomoki near Blakely in southwest Georgia. Archeologists consider the site of Etowah one of the most important in North America.

· Of all the traces of ancient peoples, those of the mound builders are undoubtedly of greatest general interest. Scattered profusely throughout the Mississippi Valley, and in some places approaching the eastern seaboard, are uncounted thousands of ancient earthworks that served a variety of purposes—defensive, ceremonial, mortuary, and domiciliary. Archeologists believe that these earthworks were built, occupied, and reoccupied over a period of hundreds of years and then abandoned by the ancestors of historic tribes or possibly, in some instances, by tribes that were later absorbed or became extinct.

Their existence, coupled with the character of tools and implements found on the sites, indicates that during the period of mound building the American Indians in general were more settled and sedentary in their habits than in historic times. Many theories have been advanced to account for the gradual cessation of this stupendous labor by primitive man in America, but the most cogent theory assumes an invasion or series of invasions by warlike nomadic tribes from the northward who upset the agricultural economy of the mound builders. Whatever the actual circumstances, the first Europeans who landed on the Atlantic seaboard found only a few of the mounds still occupied, and it is by no means certain that these late mound dwellers were also mound builders.

After four years of intensive exploration of mounds and village sites in the vicinity of Macon (*see* TOURS *9A and 9B*), A. R. Kelly, for the Smithsonian Institution, tentatively identified six successive levels of occupation that afford a cross section of cultures extending from 1821, the year in which the land was ceded to the state, back to an ancient period, the exact date of which cannot be determined. Collections from more than fifty archeological sites throughout the state have been brought to Macon for study, and the culture revealed at many of these sites has been identified with one of the cultures disclosed at Old Ocmulgee Fields.

The oldest evidence of human occupation is represented by many primitive flint implements found in the weathered plateau soils. These implements include cutting and scraping tools of various types, primarily designed for use in skin dressing, and bear a certain resemblance to those of undisputed antiquity found in the Great Plains. The absence of pottery or any indication of agriculture supports the belief that these are the remains of hunting peoples who lived on the Ocmulgee terraces before the advent of the mound-building peoples.

In the most recent cultural levels the materials represent the historic phase of occupation, tentatively identified as that of the Creek Indians, or at least of members of the Muskhogean linguistic stock. From this assumption, the time of the historic and proto-historic occupation at Macon is referred to as the Late Muskhogean Period. In addition to Indian artifacts of late workmanship, excavations have uncovered the foundations of a trading post in which were found glass trade beads, pipe stems, brass hawks' bells, flintlock guns and pistols, swords, knives, axes, leaden bullets, and harness. Although this trading post unquestionably was constructed and occupied by Europeans, it is debatable whether they were Spanish or English. The most generally accepted opinion, however, is that they were traders from Charleston, South Carolina, who established the post at some time between 1690 and 1715.

According to Kelly, the Late Muskhogean was the last of six major cultural developments tentatively identified, the earliest being that of the flint-using people. Not all of these cultural periods, however, were those of mound builders.

The origin myths of the Creek recount that when their ancestors arrived in this region they found it already occupied by strange Indians. Some of these tribes they drove out; others they absorbed. Exploration near Macon has uncovered the remains of many swamp villages that may be considered as the habitations of these strange tribes.

Ethnological sources imply that these people spoke languages belonging to the same linguistic stock as that of the invaders. Evidence from both ethnological and archeological sources indicates that they had different customs and that the conquering tribe had no particular sense of kinship. Archeological evidence supports the theory that the aboriginal Muskhogeans had been settled in the region for a long time. It is probable that one of the most numerous and most powerful tribes resident in the area was the Hitchiti, and it is virtually assured that Lamar, Mossy Oak, and Horseshoe Bend are representative village sites of this tribe. There is evidence that the Hitchiti were living on the Ocmulgee River at the time of De Soto's journey in 1540, and that they had been living in the same area for hundreds of years before that date. This second period in the cultural development of the Ocmulgee basin people may confidently be designated as the Middle Muskhogean.

It is evident that the Indians of the swamps and lowlands belonged to the Middle Muskhogean Period and had developed their natural culture to a rather high level. The excellence and distinctiveness of their arts and industries show that their civilization was at a point of efflorescence. This does not mean that these people had reached a very high cultural phase but that they had developed their peculiar arts of pottery decoration, house building, and town planning and had achieved a stable equilibrium with assured economic subsistence in their natural environment. Evidence of the full-blown culture of the Middle Muskhogean era is exemplified specifically in the pottery. The profusion of designs, the boldness of execution, and the elaboration of detail are all traits of an advanced evolutionary stage. The archeologist immediately discerns that these people had been living in the area long enough to become adapted to their particular environment and that there must have been an earlier phase of development.

No definite line has yet been isolated as the ancestral stem from which the main cultural development came. It is highly probable that, in their turn, the Hitchiti and the other strange tribes present in the Piedmont region and along the fall line when the legendary Creek first came in had also come into the area as immigrants. Exploration of Old Ocmulgee Fields has revealed refuse pits beneath the council chamber and an occupation level below Mound A that was inhabited before the mound was built. Early types of stamped pottery, found in such deep archeological levels as these, show a more primitive treatment of the same designs found at Lamar. The origin of the Middle Muskhogean phase may not be found by archeological exploration in the Ocmulgee region, but the presence of the more primitive type of pottery indicates that an earlier development is represented in some degree. A safe conclusion, therefore, is that the third period is partly represented at Macon and that it may be called the Early Muskhogean Period.

The indexes of the pottery collection at Macon show a difference between the culture represented at Lamar and that of the prehistoric peoples of the Macon Plateau. Indications that more than one cultural phase is represented on the Macon Plateau are evident in the number of different kinds of pottery, the varieties of flint artifacts, and a marked difference in house types. In general, the pottery of the Macon Plateau Indians is almost completely lacking in the highly ornate paddle-marked designs found at Lamar. Most of the plateau pottery is plain, but some pieces show impressions of baskets and nets that were used to support the soft clay before firing. The baskets evidently were used as cores around which the paste was built, and the nets were pressed around the clay until it had hardened.

On the Macon Plateau, at least two kinds of ordinary residences have been distinguished: large square houses with round corners and small round or oval sod-covered houses with semi-subterranean floors and post walls. Around the plateau there are extensive trench systems broken by occasional post holes. There are also two types of public buildings: one is represented by the so-called Macon Council Chamber or ceremonial earth lodge; the other, which W. S. Webb of Kentucky has called the "small-post town house," was a square structure with small verandas or galleries, used also for conferences. On the basis of these classifications the cultural sequence may then include a fourth and a fifth period. The extensive prehistoric trench system near Mound A shows a deliberate filling of the pits by the mound builders. This fact implies that the mound-building phase is the later and belongs to the fourth or Macon Plateau II Period, whereas the pits belong to the older occupation or Macon Plateau I Period.

In the Etowah Group (*see* TOUR 2), on the Etowah River near Cartersville, are three large mounds and three almost indistinguishable burial mounds enclosed by a ditch. The central mound, sixty-five feet high and covering almost three acres at the base, is larger than any other in the United States except the Cahokia Mound in Illinois. A terraced ramp formerly led up the east side. From excavation of the smaller mounds in this group and in the village site, objects of remarkable workmanship and a high degree of artistic merit have been recovered. Among them are a stone sculptured image of a small boy, copper plates depicting eagles and dancing human figures, carefully chipped flint blades twenty-two inches long, and pottery with designs in color. Even more remarkable are incised shell gorgets, showing a spotted serpent, the world symbol with the four directions and the sun, and other designs of artistic merit. These designs have a striking resemblance to those of the prehistoric civilization of Middle America and Mexico. Determination of the time and the nature of the contacts between these two civilizations is one of the large problems awaiting future research.

The Eagle Mound (*see* TOUR 16), seven miles north of Eatonton in central Georgia, is a remarkable example of another type of mound. This typical effigy mound is owned by the Federal government. It was built by ingeniously arranging rocks and soil in the shape of a gigantic eagle, measuring 102 feet from head to tail and 120 feet across the outspread wings. The body is built up ten to twelve feet above the level of the ground and is sixty feet long and thirty-five feet wide. Head, beak, neck, and tail are all carefully constructed, but it is not possible to get the effect of the figure in its entirety except from a height. Near the west bank of the Oconee River seven or eight miles east of this mound is another rock eagle effigy. Although it is not in as good condition as the other, it can easily be restored from measurements made by the Smithsonian Institution. The Georgia Power Company, which owns this mound, has offered to co-operate with the Society for Georgia Archeology in its restoration.

Among a number of mounds in the swamps of Richmond County in eastern Georgia, the most notable are the Rhodes Group—two immense piles, one oval in shape and the other resembling a giant horseshoe. A few miles north of this pair is the Hollywood Mound, covering about four acres and elevated about fifteen or twenty feet above the swamp. Excavation here has disclosed two distinct periods of occupation, the later one apparently within the period of European contact. An extensive shell heap lies a short distance north of the Hollywood Mound. Other shell heaps and kitchen middens, which in some instances give the appearance of deliberate arrangement, abound along the Georgia coast and on the sea islands. A mound on Creighton Island yielded 220 skeletons and a number of interesting artifacts including a chisel of slate, one of copper, shell gorgets, bone objects, pipes, and earthenware vessels.

Explorations of widely separated sites in Georgia river valleys have revealed pottery and other relics suggesting the rather advanced cultural phase exemplified at Lamar. Among these are the Irene Mound on the Savannah River (*see* TOUR *1*), Bull Creek village site on the Chattahoochee near Columbus, the Nacoochee Mound near the headwaters of the Chattahoochee, and the Neisler Mound on the Flint River near Roberta. At Bull Creek village, revealed by an old railroad cut, were found whole pottery vessels, three resembling a dog. The significance of these effigies is not known, but they are highly regarded by archeologists. Since they were found in burial heaps, a mortuary significance is attached to them. The Nacoochee Mound, 20 feet high, 190 feet long, and 150 feet wide, was explored in 1915 by the Heye Foundation. A published report of the excavation states that a "dog pot" was also found here. Another vessel of this type, along with good examples of stamped pottery, was found at the Neisler Mound, which was partly uncovered by the overflow of the river but has never been scientifically studied.

It must be remembered that only the most general and tentative ideas can now be advanced concerning the sequence of history brought to light by these various excavations. The ultimate schematic arrangement of the results of archeological study must come from detailed analysis of the great mass of materials taken from the many sites explored or reconnoitered.

Some of the material recovered is in the U. S. National Museum at Washington, the Phillips Academy Museum at Andover, Massachusetts, and the American Museum of Natural History and Museum of the American Indian at New York City, but these specimen collections are incomplete. A number of private collectors, as well as the University of Georgia and other schools, have assembled artifacts. The collection resulting from the Works Progress Administration excavations at Macon has not yet been arranged for exhibition, but will eventually be housed in a museum at Macon.

History and Government

WHEN THE Creek and Cherokee Indians came into the territory that is now Georgia, they found mysterious ceremonial mounds of former civilizations. The Creek, who pushed on to the south, and the Cherokee, who settled in the highlands, established their villages on these ancient sites. Hernando de Soto, believed to be the first white man to traverse the territory, explored it in 1540 searching for gold and found these Indians and other tribes near the coast living in well-developed communities and carrying on a highly organized trade with tribes of the upper eastern country.

After De Soto had continued on to the Mississippi River, the region was left open for the French navigators, who were beginning to explore the islands of the southeastern coast. The small and scattered settlements were little more than temporary headquarters for the trappers and explorers, but their mere existence so angered Spain that in 1565 Philip II sent a force under Pedro Menendez de Aviles to assert Spain's claim to the entire southeastern region. Constructing forts on several of the islands, Menendez pressed on into the mainland, followed by priests who established missions in his wake. His progress was marked by strong opposition from the Indians, and within two years both soldiers and priests were driven back to the coastal islands, where they entrenched themselves against attack from French and English pirates on the sea front and from the Indians of the interior.

Although the territory remained ostensibly under Spanish rule, it was deeded by English kings several times to individuals who, failing to undertake expeditions against the Spanish, permitted it to revert to the Crown. For more than a century bands of English and French freebooters harried the coast, but not until the coming of Oglethorpe in 1733 did English influence become so formidable as to challenge the power of Spain.

The earliest organized colonization was motivated at the outset by a philanthropic purpose. Under the first two Hanoverian monarchs,

35

widespread extravagance, speculation, and unemployment in England had resulted in the imprisonment of many persons for debt. These unfortunates excited the sympathy of James Edward Oglethorpe, a member of Parliament. At once a philanthropist and a shrewd promoter, Oglethorpe conceived the idea of transporting a large number of the debtors to America as settlers in the development of a new Crown colony. He enlisted the aid of John, Viscount Perceval, noted for his work among the poor, and the project was so enthusiastically received that plans were broadened to make the proposed colony a refuge for persecuted Protestants of continental Europe. These two groups were later augmented by a gentry class of adventurers who came to the colony at their own expense and in many cases received large land grants.

Geographical knowledge of America was vague at this time, and the territory granted to Oglethorpe and his associates was "the land lying between the Savannah and Altamaha rivers and westward from the sources to the South Sea." On June 9, 1732, the charter was signed by King George II, for whom the new colony was named. The twenty petitioners for the grant formed a board of trustees, which was given legislative and executive powers for a period of twenty-one years, as well as the prerogative of distributing land to the settlers.

The trustees' determination to keep the colony strictly communal and nonspeculative made this experiment one of the most interesting relief projects of English record. It must not be forgotten, however, that the underlying philanthropic motive was far from being the only consideration that prompted the new venture. The trustees' purposes might have been idealistic; the calculations of the Crown were wholly practical. In petitioning King George II for a grant of land "on the southwest of Carolina for settling poor persons of London," Oglethorpe was wise in stressing the economic advantages of the project. He pointed out that many raw materials would become available for England, that a new market for home manufactures would be opened, and that by providing another outlet for excess population the colony would help to improve the economic conditions in the home country.

Political considerations also were powerful. South Carolina had been calling for royal aid against the possible encroachments of Spaniards who, though living principally on the coastal islands, laid claim also to the inland country. George II saw in the settling of Georgia the establishment of a buffer colony between the English settlements along the upper seaboard and the Spanish forces in Florida. South Carolina itself welcomed these new defenders; at first there was no intimation of the rivalries and jealousies that were soon to spring up between the two colonies.

Because of the philanthropic aims of the trustees, great care was taken in the selection of the first colonists, who were to be drawn principally from the impoverished classes. Nevertheless, persons of high estate, provided they were not speculators, were eligible. In the period 1732-40, 2,500 emigrants, about two-thirds of whom were foreign Protestants, were sent to Georgia by the funds of the trustees. Provisions were made (1733-35) for groups of Salzburgers and Moravians, German Protestant people who sought escape from the ruling Catholic order in their own countries. For effective military defense a considerable company of Scottish Highlanders was recruited in 1735.

In the autumn of 1732 the first Georgia colonists, a group of about 125 persons, under the leadership of Oglethorpe, set sail from England on the *Anne*. On February 12, 1733, they landed eighteen miles up the Savannah River on a bluff secured by agreement from Tomochichi, chief of the Yamacraw Indians, an outlawed tribe of the Creek. The colonists laid out a town, which they named Savannah, and began immediate construction of houses.

Upon completion of the little settlement, Oglethorpe negotiated a treaty of peace with the eight principal Creek tribes and then turned to a consideration of defenses against the Spanish. After fortifying several strategic points along the coast and among the islands, he went back to England in 1734 to obtain more money and additional settlers, especially those who were skilled in military affairs. Returning in February, 1736, he continued his military preparations. Three years later England was at war with Spain, and open warfare soon began in Georgia. For three years the opposing forces fought, with shifting advantages, until the struggle culminated in a decisive English victory at the Battle of Bloody Marsh on St. Simon Island, July 7, 1742.

Oglethorpe returned to England in 1743 and never revisited Georgia. His victory had made conditions in the colony safer, and in the year of his departure the military rule was changed to that of a civil body directed by a president and five councilors. This group, however, was still under the supreme authority of the trustees, and the colonists were not permitted to direct the course of their political or economic destiny. With the threat of Spanish dominion removed, the trustees hoped that the colonists would immediately focus their energies on making Georgia the Utopia it was originally designed to be. But their suggestions met with rude rebuffs. The victory over the Spanish had given the colonists a sense of independence that led them to make new demands on the trustees.

· Knowing that some of the colonists were indolent, the trustees had limited each settler who came at public expense to fifty acres and withheld complete possession of even that small grant. This precautionary limitation was to prevent the less industrious settlers from selling their lands and becoming mere hired laborers. Moreover, a thickly settled population was desirable as a protection from invasion by the Spaniards in Florida.

There was constant agitation concerning slavery. The trustees felt that the introduction of slaves would defeat the primary purpose of the experiment, which was the development of a colony sustained by its own labor. Since many of the colonists owed their release from debtors' prisons to the trustees, their unwillingness to carry on the trustees' communal plan was denounced as ingratitude. The Scottish Highlanders, who had fought so valiantly, supported the trustees in most respects, especially in regard to slavery which they considered degrading both to masters and to slaves. But the majority of the colonists held very different views and expressed them hotly. They felt that the service they had rendered in helping to protect South Carolina entitled them to privileges similar to those granted to that colony. By smuggling in slaves of their own they sought to emulate the ease afforded by slave labor in South Carolina.

The manufacture and sale of whisky in the colony had also been forbidden, but nonobservance of this law was so general that juries frequently refused to convict persons arrested for violating it.

Thus the restrictions on land, slaves, and whisky generated an attitude of opposition and lawlessness that persisted for several generations. In time complaints became bitter denunciations which, although the English government upheld the trustees, eventually won for the colonists most of the legislation they had demanded. The trustees sought to keep at least the appearance of authority and hastened to legalize practices that had become general. The liquor law was repealed in 1742, the ban on slaveholding was removed in 1749, and by 1750 complete possession of the land was permitted.

Although philanthropic hopes were fading, cultural interests were being advanced. Later settlers in the growing colony were fascinated by the strange country, less resentful of the trustees' supervision and regulations, and more given to pride in their communities. Schools were built at Savannah, Frederica, Irene, and Ebenezer. In 1740 the Reverend George Whitefield and James Habersham established near Savannah the Bethesda Orphan House, a combined school and orphanage that proved to be the most successful charitable and educational endeavor of this early Colonial period. Religion was not neglected by the trustees, who appropriated about £7,500 for the construction of churches and the purchase of Bibles, but the only material achievements were one structure in Savannah and the formal organization of a church or two among the Salzburgers. John and Charles

Wesley, who later became known as the founders of Methodism, came to Georgia in 1736 as young Anglican clergymen, but they found life in the colony uncongenial and soon returned to England.

So intent were the trustees on the sociological aspect of their experiment that they gave little attention to local government. A general court had been established with three judges called bailiffs, a recorder, and a few constables—an arrangement that lent itself to petty tyranny. The colonists had but small part in regulating their own affairs and this led to much open flouting of the laws. Although an assembly of delegates from each town was called and first met in January, 1751, it had no authority to pass laws. It could only hear reports from the various towns, discuss measures for betterment, and make suggestions that the trustees were free to accept or disregard as they chose.

In 1752, adequate financial aid for the colony having been refused by both Parliament and the Crown, the trustees yielded to the King's suggestion that they give up the charter at once. It was surrendered on June 23, but not until the trustees had secured a promise that the separate colonial status of Georgia would be maintained.

Two years later the colony became a royal province, with a governor and a royal council or upper house of fourteen members appointed by the King and a house of commons elected by the people. The first assembly convened at Savannah, the capital of the province, in 1755. This change in government ended all hopes for success of the original philanthropic purpose. Georgia was now a military and commercial enterprise; and although its citizens were endowed with some of the privileges of Englishmen at home, England still levied taxes and meted out punishment. The colonists were subject to strict duties and substantial payments. The first royal governor was John Reynolds, who served from 1754 to 1757. His two successors in office were Henry Ellis (1757-60) and James Wright (1760-76, 1779-81).

In 1758 the assembly declared official adherence to the Church of England, and the province was divided into eight parishes. Anglican churches were already functioning at this time in the parishes of Savannah and Augusta, but it was planned to erect a church in each of the others. Although there was no compulsion to belong to the Church of England there was no exemption from taxes for its support. The Roman Catholic church was banned in the colony, but otherwise Georgians were permitted to belong to any of the numerous sects that had been established here.

Progress was continually interrupted by troubles with the Indians within the colony and with the Spanish on the southern border. Even more serious were the colonists' disputes with their own countrymen, which were never settled as long as boundaries were not precisely determined. South Carolina claimed the lands lying south of the Altamaha River, where public and private interests were promoting vast speculative enterprises.

By the Treaty of Paris in 1763, Georgia's western boundary was defined as the Mississippi River, and its southern boundary was fixed as extending from the head of St. Marys River westward to the confluence of the Chattahoochee and Flint rivers, up the Chattahoochee River to the thirty-first parallel, and thence westward to the Mississippi. Treaties with the Indians providing for their further removal westward gave the colony room for growth. By this time the character of Georgia's population had completely changed, and all signs of the intended Utopia had vanished. Not only did the people own land and slaves, but the original charity class had disappeared, and Georgia now had its own debtor laws and debtor prisons. New and varied elements in the population were becoming evident, among them a group of Massachusetts Puritans who settled at Midway in 1752, and who not only aided in the colony's material development but reinforced its moral and intellectual standards. Since land could be bought on very easy terms, many wealthy South Carolinians moved in, bringing their slaves. According to the estimate of Governor James Wright, Georgia in 1766 contained nearly 10,000 white persons and at least 7,800 Negroes.

Life in this growing country was simple. Agriculture, cattle and horse raising, lumbering, and the fur trade brought a measure of wealth, but Georgia still depended upon England for its sale of raw materials and its purchase of finished products. There was no established currency, although England permitted the colony to issue paper money in limited amounts as needed. In 1763, with the establishment of a printing press at Savannah, the colony's first newspaper, the *Georgia Gazette,* made its appearance.

During the French and Indian War, England incurred heavy indebtedness for the protection of the colonies, and now felt that the latter should share this indebtedness as well as provide soldiers or pay part of the cost of maintaining British troops in future wars. To this end the Crown imposed certain taxes and trade regulations designed to bring in additional revenue. In the discontent aroused by this and other actions of the British government, Georgia at first had little interest. It was the youngest of all the colonies, the weakest and least protected, and its energies had been spent in seeking to establish and maintain itself. At length, however, internal agitation, resulting in the organization of the Liberty Boys, aroused a state of such excitement that when the British warship *Speedwell* unloaded stamps at Savannah on December 5, 1765, it was necessary to keep the storehouse under heavy guard. By February the citizens had become so riotous that the stamps were removed from the colony.

When the Townshend Act (1767), levying heavier taxes, was passed, the situation became tense indeed. The act of Parliament (1774) which revoked the Massachusetts Bay Charter agitated Georgia, in common with other American colonies. Georgia's reaction is expressed in the records of a general meeting held at Savannah on August 27, 1774. Eight resolutions were adopted, including one declaring "That we will concur with our sister colonies in every Constitutional measure to obtain redress of American grievances, and will . . . maintain these inestimable blessings for which we are indebted to God and the Constitution of our country—a Constitution founded upon reason and justice and the indelible rights of mankind."

A general committee of correspondence, representative of Georgia, was appointed to correspond with the other colonies, and only the persuasiveness of the royal governor, James Wright, prevented Georgia from sending a delegate to the First Continental Congress (1774). This postponement of action, misunderstood by the other colonies, was considered cowardly, and when the Second Continental Congress convened on May 10, 1775, without delegates from Georgia, the province was excoriated. Three days later a lone Georgian, Lyman Hall, presented his credentials. But these showed him to be the representative, not of Georgia, but only of his own parish, St. Johns. After some discussion, however, he was admitted to Congress, with power to take part in debates but not to vote; and when, on May 17, Congress put Georgia under a ban of colonial nonintercourse, Lyman Hall's parish was excepted.

However, Georgia was fast drawing into line with the rest of the colonies. In June a group of aroused citizens met in Savannah and appointed a council of safety to establish good will with the other colonies and to stimulate Georgians to a sense of their obligations in the movement for independence. This council called a provincial congress, which convened in Savannah on July 4, 1775, and appointed a permanent council of safety to act with full authority when the congress was not in session. On July 10 Archibald Bulloch, John Houstoun, Lyman Hall, Noble Wymberley Jones, and the Reverend John Joachim Zubly were elected delegates to the Continental Congress then in session at Philadelphia. Word of Georgia's decisive action reached Philadelphia on July 20, and the Continental Congress immediately withdrew its ban of colonial nonintercourse. Georgia was received enthusiastically into the Union of Colonies, and on September 13 three of its delegates —Bulloch, Houstoun, and Zubly—were seated in Congress. Jones and Hall were unable to attend.

The provincial congress that met in Savannah in January, 1776, chose five delegates for the next meeting of the Continental Congress. They were given no specific instructions, but were directed to act as they thought best for the common good. When the vote for independence was cast, the three Georgians present to approve and eventually to sign the Declaration were Button Gwinnett, Lyman Hall, and George Walton. The reading of the Declaration of Independence in Georgia produced great enthusiasm. Ominous preparations were made: food and munitions were sent to the army, and the home militia was strengthened.

No actual fighting took place on Georgia territory until 1778, when British forces attacked along the coast and from Florida. Savannah was captured on December 29, and General Robert Howe, who commanded the colony's forces, retreated into South Carolina. Sunbury and Augusta were taken in January, 1779, and by the end of the year every important town had fallen into the hands of the British. Only the sparsely settled northern region known as Wilkes County was left unoccupied.

The Revolutionary period in Georgia was not one of planned strategic warfare, but of incessant guerrilla strife. With their means of communication cut off, the people had little knowledge of what the patriot forces were doing. A man would fight for a few weeks, hurry home to plant his crop, and then rush back to military duty. Confiscation, plunder, torture, and outright murder for revenge were common occurrences. Tories who had been thrashed or tarred by hotheaded Liberty Boys did not fail to take revenge when Whig settlements fell into their hands. Because the Church of England had been predominantly Loyalist in sentiment, taxes for its support were revoked and its churches closed, and parishes that had been named after the saints were renamed for eminent public men in Great Britain who had shown friendship for the colonies. A scarcity of food and the prevalence of smallpox caused suffering everywhere.

Georgia's greatest weakness lay within. Unable to co-operate effectively in either civil or military affairs, its people were demoralized by the lack of powerful leadership, the presence of strong Tory sentiment, and angry division within the Whig party. There were sometimes three separate governments, one Tory and two Whig, in a state that could not effectively support one. Although there was much heroism on both sides, it was the heroism of individuals rather than that of organized forces.

After the close of the war those who had supported the Revolutionary cause were rewarded with gifts of confiscated property, and many soldiers and sailors received land grants. Although unjust exactions and penalties were later rectified in part, hundreds of worthy citizens left Georgia because of extreme confiscatory laws and hostile sentiment. With half its private property destroyed and the institution of slavery disorganized, the state's poverty was appalling. Taxes could not be collected, repeated new issues of paper money were rendering valueless the currency already in circulation, and slaves, land, livestock, and personal belongings were all accepted as mediums of exchange. Nevertheless, there were many who considered that Georgia's new status as a sovereign state was well worth the price paid in this fearful confusion, and they immediately set about restoring orderly processes.

Taking an active part in affairs as far west as the Mississippi, Georgia in 1783 expanded its legislative jurisdiction to include the Natchez district along that river. Bourbon County was established there in 1785, although Georgia's title to this region was not recognized by Spain until ten years later. Meanwhile, two additional Georgia boundaries had been fixed. In 1783 the northern boundary was established along the 35th parallel, extending from Nickajack Creek 140 miles eastward to the Chattooga River. In 1787 the eastern boundary was established as extending from the Atlantic Ocean northward along the Savannah, Tugalo, and Chattooga rivers to the 35th parallel.

The Articles of Confederation had been signed on behalf of Georgia on July 24, 1778, by Edward Telfair and Edward Langworthy. To the convention that met at Philadelphia in May, 1787, to revise the Articles of Confederation, Georgia elected six delegates, of whom only four attended—William Few, Abraham Baldwin, William Pierce, and William Houstoun. Two of these men, Few and Baldwin, signed the Constitution of the United States, as drafted and adopted by that convention. On January 2, 1788, Georgia became the fourth state to ratify the Constitution. In order that state procedure might conform to national principles, a convention was called to make necessary changes in the state constitution of 1777. The revised constitution, adopted in May, 1789, provided for the election of a governor and formulated his prerogatives, established a senate and house of representatives, and extended the vote to all male citizens of twenty-one years or older. Several later constitutional conventions were held from time to time; an entirely new document was adopted at the convention of 1798, while the others were for amendment or revision.

It was in Georgia that Eli Whitney, in 1793, invented a practicable cotton gin. Other inventors had worked for years to devise a machine that would separate cotton lint from the seed, but their efforts had been unsuccessful. Eventually, young Whitney's invention tremendously affected the economic trend of the entire United States. Slavery, which had become a dying institution, was now revived as more cotton was planted and more Negroes were needed to cultivate it. Cotton gins were not quickly available, but the potential value of Whitney's gin probably contributed to the sudden growth of the state in the decade of 1790-1800, when the population increased from 82,548 to 162,686. Meanwhile, Savannah had proved unsatisfactory as a seat of government because the center of population had moved westward and bad roads made travel difficult. Augusta became the temporary capital in 1786, while Louisville was being laid out as a permanent capital. A statehouse was completed at Louisville in 1795, and the Georgia records were moved there. Nine years later Milledgeville became the state capital.

The cession of more Indian territory was followed by wildcat land speculations, the most flagrant example of which was the so-called Yazoo fraud. Thirty-five million acres in the present states of Alabama and Mississippi were bought from Georgia in 1795 by land companies for less than a cent and a half an acre. These companies became so notorious for their unscrupulous dealings that in 1796 the entire state was aroused to wrath, the legislative transfer of the land was rescinded, and the documents of sale were burned in front of the statehouse at Louisville.

As pre-Revolutionary conditions had bred conflict with England, so now the seeds of a new conflict were being sown. This time the issue was that of states' rights. When the United States Supreme Court ruled that individuals had the right to sue a state and in 1793 handed down a decision against Georgia in the Chisholm *vs.* Georgia case, the state legislature promptly proposed an act to the effect that anyone seeking to enforce judgments based on this decision should be hanged. This act was never passed, however, for other states, formerly submissive, rallied to the support of Georgia. As a result, the Eleventh Amendment, denying individuals the right to sue a state, was added to the United States Constitution in 1798.

The same fundamental issue was also involved in Georgia's sharp disagreement with the national government concerning treaties with the Indians. The troubles resulting from such treaties were caused not only by the greed of the white settlers and their Indian intermediaries but by a lack of unity and organization in the Indian population. A Creek or Cherokee leader might be authorized by one group of his people to sell lands to the white man and then be denounced and punished by another group which refused to relinquish its claims. The buyers, considering themselves defrauded, turned angrily to the national government, which tried in vain to keep peace.

With the deeding of its western territory to individuals in settlement of debts, as rewards to deserving citizens, or by sale to speculators, the state's relations with the Indians became more tense. In 1802, Georgia ceded to the United States Government all its remaining lands north of 31° and west of the Chattahoochee River and a given line running north from near the mouth of Uchee Creek to Nickajack Creek. This cession was made in order that the state might extricate itself from complications arising out of the many fraudulent land operations, and in return it was to receive a cash consideration and certain lands then in possession of the Indians. In the same year, by the treaty of Fort Wilkinson, the Creek ceded to Georgia tracts of land south of the Altamaha River and west of the Oconee. The legislature divided this land into lots of various sizes and in 1803 began to dispose of it by a lottery system, devised to encourage rapid settlement of the new land. Various other treaties ceding land followed.

Soon after taking office in 1824, Georgia's militant Governor, George M. Troup, insisted that the United States government should comply with an agreement of 1802, whereby it had assumed the obligation of removing all Indians from Georgia to the western territory. President Monroe therefore called the leading Creek chieftains to a conference at Indian Springs, in February, 1825, to negotiate further land concessions. By a treaty drawn up at this conference, the lower Creek, led by William McIntosh, mixed-breed Indian chief and cousin of Governor Troup, ceded to the United States "all the lands within the boundaries of the present state of Georgia as defined by the compact of 1802," in exchange for an equal amount of western land and the sum of $400,000. Governor Troup obtained permission to survey the new lands, and the friendly Indians prepared to depart. But the Creek who were hostile to the treaty held a general council, appealed to the Federal government, and sentenced McIntosh to death. On the night of April 30, 1825, a group of 170 Indians carried out this sentence. Nevertheless, the legislature ordered the tract to be surveyed, preparatory to opening it for white settlement.

In the litigation that followed, President Adams favored the hostile Creek. Governor Troup declared that if the Creek were not removed immediately a state of war would exist between Georgia and the United States. The President then called thirteen Creek chiefs to a conference in Washington, where in January, 1826, a treaty was signed ceding to the Federal government all the Creek lands east of the Chattahoochee River except a tract of 300,000 acres that was retained by the Indians. After further difficulties all the remaining Creek land was ceded to the United States for $28,000, and soon afterward the Creek left Georgia and moved west of the Mississippi.

The state now turned its attention to evicting the Cherokee. A nation within a nation, having their own capital city at New Echota, their own constitution (adopted in 1827 and patterned after the Federal Constitution), and a newspaper printed in their own language, the Cherokee sent delegates to Washington where they were received on the same footing as the diplomats of foreign countries. Georgia passed a law late in 1828 extending its jurisdiction over the Cherokee country and refusing recognition of Indian self-government within the state. When Andrew Jackson, a noted Indian fighter, was elected to the Presidency in 1828, the Indians received no further sympathy from the Federal government.

Gold was discovered in north Georgia in 1828-29. Rough and lawless prospectors immediately flocked to the mining area and, protected by a hurriedly enacted law that prohibited an Indian from bringing suit or testifying against a white man, seized the Cherokee lands. Indians who resisted were forcibly removed or even killed. In 1832 the state arbitrarily divided the territory into ten counties and subdivided these into land lots of 140 acres and gold lots of 40 acres each. The lots were then raffled off to the homesteaders. In the same year a law was passed forbidding the Cherokee to hold public meetings, thereby forestalling any organized move toward the defense of their property. Not satisfied until the last Indian claim was permanently revoked, Georgia again called upon the Federal government to carry out its part of the agreement of 1802 by evicting the remaining Indians. In 1835 the Cherokee were offered five million dollars and new lands in the West in exchange for their Georgia holdings. Realizing the futility of further opposition, they accepted this offer, and the last Indians were removed from the state three years later.

From 1800 to 1840, Georgia's population grew from 162,686 to 691,392, and 68 new counties were formed. With the growth in population, the need for better transportation became increasingly acute. A system of wagon roads and turnpikes was evolved to supplement the already well-traveled waterways. Beginning in 1833, when companies were chartered for constructing the Georgia Railroad and the Central of Georgia, railroad transportation developed rapidly. The first satisfactory educational program was established in 1858, when the sum of $100,000 a year derived from the rental of the state-owned Western & Atlantic Railroad was appropriated to maintain a free school system. The decade or two immediately preceding the war constituted the most prosperous period of Georgia's history. But its prosperity rested upon large cotton plantations and slavery. Intimately interwoven with the economic texture of the state, slavery had long been a subject of internal dispute. Georgia was divided by the controversies concerning the admission of Texas as a slave-holding state, the agitation over slavery in the new territory acquired from Mexico in 1848, and the Compromise of 1850. Its attitude was certain to be very influential, if not decisive, in determining the attitude of the entire South; for its population of about a million and its large area and economic importance had given it national political prominence. Talk of secession was current throughout Georgia and the South, but to save the Union the state accepted the compromise with the definite statement that it would yield no further.

Within the state, northern and southern Whigs drew apart in opinion until the greater portion of southern Whigs went over to the Democrats. When the new Republican party arose, its leaders declaring that they would not yield in their stand against the extension of slave territory, the southern states recognized a common enemy. In the election of 1860, Democrats were divided among themselves, but Georgians were united against Lincoln. From their viewpoint his election left no alternative to secession.

In the governor's chair was Joseph E. Brown, one of the boldest and most turbulent leaders in Georgia's political history. A fiery proponent of states' rights, he urged the legislature to withdraw immediately from the Union without waiting for the other states to act, to appropriate $1,000,000 for defense, and to proceed toward preparations for war. Even before Georgia voted for secession, Governor Brown, on January 3, 1861, ordered Fort Pulaski near Savannah to be occupied, and five days after Georgia seceded he secured the surrender of the Federal arsenal at Augusta. When the state declared for secession on January 19, 1861, Governor Brown at once set about procuring arms. Agents were sent to Europe, the penitentiary at Milledgeville was converted into an armory, and munitions plants were established at Augusta, Macon, Columbus, and Athens. The people offered church bells and household metals to be melted down and molded into cannon.

President Davis and Governor Brown differed sharply concerning military administration. President Davis, believing that each state should stand or fall with the common fortune, commanded that soldiers enlist in the Confederate Army, not in the army of any particular state, and upheld the right of the Confederacy to draft soldiers directly and to appoint all the commanders of highest rank. Governor Brown acted upon the assumption that each state should enlist its own fighting force, control it subject to a quota call from the Confederacy, and appoint its own commanders. Time after time he collected an army, only to have it drafted into the larger service. To form a state militia he ignored the age limits fixed for the draft, only to have the Confederacy widen its age limits and take in his militia. As the Union forces drew nearer to Atlanta in June, 1864, he made a last desperate call for recruits "from the cradle to the grave," and succeeded in gathering about 10,000 men and boys known as "Joe Brown's Malish."

Within the state also there was dissension. Alexander H. Stephens, Vice President of the Confederacy, supported Governor Brown's views on the subject of states' rights, as did Linton Stephens and Robert Toombs; but Howell Cobb and Benjamin Hill were equally outspoken on the other side. Governor Brown hotly charged President Davis with being as great an enemy to Georgia as Lincoln, and Davis himself came to Georgia to checkmate Brown's activities.

Georgia was near the center of the Confederacy, and for the first three years of the war there was little fighting within its territory except along the coast. Fort Pulaski was retaken by Union forces on April 10, 1862, and an attack was directed toward Savannah but was not pushed. Darien was burned, and Fort McAllister was attacked without success. But after the fall of Vicksburg on July 4, 1863, the invaders concentrated their forces for a drive against Chattanooga and subsequently Atlanta. During the following months Federal operations resulted in the occupation of Chattanooga on September 9, followed by the Battle of Chickamauga on September 19 and 20—frequently called "the two bloodiest days of the war." The following spring Federal troops under General Sherman began their campaign in north Georgia. The greatly outnumbered Confederate Army under General Joseph E. Johnston adopted the strategy of defensive fighting, but by a series of flanking movements Sherman turned Johnston's position again and again and forced him to retreat. The Confederates were defeated in engagements at Dalton, Resaca, and New Hope Church, but the Federal Army suffered a heavy loss at Kennesaw Mountain on June 27, 1864. Disapproving of Johnston's evasive tactics, President Davis replaced him with General John B. Hood, who flung his forces against the Federal Army on the outskirts of Atlanta. After about six weeks of fighting, the city was occupied by Sherman on September 2, 1864.

Six weeks later, on November 14, Sherman set fire to Atlanta and with an army of about 60,000 men set out on his famous march to the sea, ruthlessly laying waste the villages, towns, and countryside through which he passed. His own estimate of the value of the property destroyed in this march was $100,000,000. By December 22 he had occupied Savannah, which he held until early in February of the following year.

Even before Sherman marched into Georgia there was a strong sentiment in favor of peace negotiations, and the suspicion was growing in some quarters that Davis was postponing peace because a treaty could not be consummated according to his own cherished theories.

Now that Georgia lay ruined and the Confederacy was crumbling on all fronts, this sentiment increased in strength. When a new invasion was begun from the west through Columbus, the legislature was called into session and Georgia surrendered its armies to General James H. Wilson.

During the four years of war, Georgia had sent into battle nearly 125,000 men and boys and had lost three-fourths of its material wealth. The economic structure of the state had been shattered, its plantation system destroyed, its industry demoralized, its banks ruined. Nevertheless, with the establishment of peace, public morale proved equal to the tremendous task of rebuilding and readjustment. Many freed slaves remained on the plantations and were hired by their former masters. Farmed by white and Negro tenants, the land began once again to yield profitable harvests. The existing railroads began to restore their physical equipment, and new roads were chartered within a year after the close of the struggle. Although few Georgians had salvaged substantial funds that could be invested, outside capital was attracted, and twenty banks and loan associations were chartered by 1867. With the appointment of a state superintendent of education in 1866 and the reopening of schools that had been closed during the war, public education gained new impetus.

The more thoughtful Georgians were appalled at the possible consequences of President Lincoln's assassination. On October 26, 1865, the state accepted with bitter submission all the requirements of the new President, Andrew Johnson, for readmission into the Union—repeal of secession ordinances, repudiation of Confederate war debts, and emancipation of slaves. Soon, however, the racial question aroused angry conflicts, and when the state refused to ratify the Fourteenth Amendment, giving the Negro full citizenship, Congress in 1867 placed Georgia under military rule.

Thus for the first time the state had its officials forced upon it by outside military appointment. In the election of 1868 a new constitution was adopted, Rufus Bullock was chosen governor, and Atlanta was made the state capital. When the legislature assembled, it had among its members thirty-two Negroes—twenty-nine in the house and three in the senate. The Fourteenth Amendment was ratified by this body on July 21, 1868, Bullock was inaugurated, and the troops departed.

The Loyal or Union League first appeared in the state in 1867 and organized the Negroes to cast their first ballot. Formed in the North as a secret Republican organization, the league had actively supported the Union cause; but with the coming of peace, it had declined and survived only in a few places as a club or local social unit. In the South during Reconstruction years, it was revived under northern leadership in changed form. Negroes were admitted to membership and taught the doctrine of equality. The league frequently formed militias, ostensibly in defense of the civil rights of the Negroes, but actually in many cases to safeguard the privileges and support the corrupt policies of the carpetbaggers and other unscrupulous politicians. The southern white people organized the Ku Klux Klan to combat the league, the carpetbaggers, and the scalawags and to oppose Congressional Reconstruction measures. Like the Union League, the Klan, which first began to operate in the state in the spring of 1868, gained effectiveness by costume and ceremony, and its white-robed night riders brought terror by their acts of violence. Its membership, which was kept strictly secret, included many men prominent in the state, and its leader was General John B. Gordon. The frightened Negroes soon withdrew from the polls.

In September the state legislature decided that enfranchisement did not necessarily confer the right to hold office, and expelled all Negroes from the legislature except four members of the house. When white members supplanted the expelled Negroes, Governor Bullock began to fear that his control over the legislature might fail and he inaugurated a movement to have the Federal government restore the military regime. By this time the activities of the Ku Klux Klan in Georgia provided Governor Bullock with another argument for the reestablishment of military rule. When Georgia rejected the Fifteenth Amendment in 1869, he succeeded in securing the return of Federal troops, and once more Georgia was out of the Union.

Bullock now called the legislature into session, and, as it reassembled, the military authorities enforced the reinstatement of the Negro members and prevented the seating of those white members who were hostile to the Governor. With power thus supported by the sword, the Bullock administration entered upon a brief period of financial debauch. On February 2, 1870, the legislature ratified the Fifteenth Amendment, and Georgia was readmitted to the Union in the following July. A committee from the United States Congress investigated the procedure of this legislature, found it "improper, illegal, and arbitrary," and ordered a new election. In this legislative election the Democrats obtained control of both houses, and Bullock, knowing that impeachment awaited him, resigned and fled from the state. In a special election the Democrats chose James M. Smith as Governor and set out to redeem the government from the misdeeds of the previous administration.

After the departure of the carpetbaggers and the flight of Governor

Bullock, a group of Georgians, including Robert Toombs, Charles J. Jenkins, and Thomas J. Simmons, began reorganizing the government of the state and forming a new constitution. This constitution, adopted in 1877, is still in force with numerous amendments to fit changing conditions. The Democrats had by this time divided into opposing factions, the dominant element being the conservatives or Bourbons. The outstanding leaders of this faction were John B. Gordon, Joseph E. Brown, and Alfred Colquitt, who focused their attention on the state's industrial future. Henry W. Grady's speeches and writings also called for a new South of broader and more modern opportunities. Perceiving something of Georgia's great industrial potentialities, these men endeavored to establish the state as a powerful manufacturing area rather than permit it to slip back into the plantation tradition of ante bellum days.

At length the dominance of this group was threatened by W. H. Felton and Emory Speer in the Forty-sixth Congress (1879-81). The spoils system, together with a growing belief that the leaders of the Colquitt administration were in league with "big business" and that the administration was corrupt, brought about an upheaval in the party.

Investigations followed, with impeachments and exonerations, but although a special committee pronounced the charges made by political enemies against Governor Colquitt (1876-82) to be "vile and malignant slanders," the discontent of the insurgent Democrats continued. The Republicans, seizing upon the opportunity thus afforded, rallied their forces in a convention that endorsed the nominee of the insurgents. The result was the election in 1882 of Alexander H. Stephens as Governor.

For years discontent had been spreading because of the unprofitableness of agriculture and the increase of sharecropper tenancy with its accompanying evils of poverty and ignorance. Bankruptcy came to owner and tenant alike when overproduction of cotton resulted in falling prices and increased taxation. When the Farmers' Alliance, originating in the West in 1876, reached Georgia in 1887, it found an enthusiastic response to its program of restoration of property and the establishment of social and economic justice. Although its adherents were called "wild men" by the conservatives, their strength was so great that Democratic office seekers hastily pledged their support to the Alliance's advanced platform, and the farmer became the dominant factor in Georgia politics. Out of the Farmers' Alliance and similar people's bodies sprang the Party of the People, or the Populist party, led by Thomas E. Watson. The farmers' group elected him to Congress on the Populist ticket in 1888; Watson became widely known and was the party's candidate for Vice President in 1896 and for President in 1904. But after the turn of the century the party weakened and soon ceased to be a factor of importance in national politics.

Georgia's growing importance as an industrial state had by this time definitely established it in co-operative relationship with the industrial North and East. Scars of the civil struggle were being eradicated gradually, and divergent social and political views were tacitly subordinated to the requirements of commerce and trade.

In 1898 the Spanish-American War, to which Georgia contributed more than three thousand soldiers, brought the state into still closer affiliation with the country as a whole. Training camps were set up at Atlanta, Augusta, Chickamauga, Savannah, Macon, and Griffin. Forty thousand soldiers were concentrated at Chickamauga alone. When President McKinley attended a national peace jubilee in Atlanta immediately after the close of the war, he further strengthened friendship between North and South by his gracious words about the Confederate dead.

At the turn of the century, Georgia, now a state of more than 2,200,-000 people, still faced many problems, political, economic, and social. The principal issue of the times was state prohibition. Sponsored by numerous religious and other organizations, the prohibition movement became so powerful that office seekers were compelled to identify themselves with it in order to secure election. Employers of labor endorsed it; merchants were pressed to lend it their support. A series of campaigns culminated in 1907 in the passage of a state prohibition law, which remained in force until March, 1938.

In the World War Georgia contributed 93,321 men and 238 nurses to the American forces. Its casualties totaled 525 killed and 2,321 wounded.

The important national trends and events of recent years, particularly the sudden prosperity of the 1920's, the financial crash of 1929, and the depression of the 1930's, have affected Georgia as they have affected other states. Under Federal grants for unemployment relief, administered by the Works Progress Administration and its predecessors, hundreds of projects have been completed, including the construction of highways, public buildings, airports, and sewer and drainage systems. Recreational and conservation areas have been developed, and professional service activities in education and public health have augmented the work of state agencies in these fields.

"Deaths from all the principal diseases considered amenable to public health measures" showed an appreciable decline in 1937, according to the annual report of the state's department of health for that year. The control of malaria, one of the state's most pressing public health problems, has been aided by the drainage projects and work of other Federal agencies. Statistics published in 1939 show that there has been a marked decrease in the death rate from malaria during the past ten years.

In education, an important step was taken in 1931 when the state's institutions of higher learning were reorganized to promote efficiency and economy. Seventeen units were brought together into a university system under the direction of a board of regents, and the numerous agricultural and mechanical schools were abolished or converted into junior colleges. This was part of a general reorganization bill that grouped more than a hundred state agencies under twenty principal divisions. Old age insurance and other social security legislation was enacted in 1937, in line with the provisions of the Federal social security law. In the same year a state planning board and a state department of natural resources were created.

A state board of penal corrections, composed of three members appointed by the governor with the approval of the senate, was created by legislative act in March, 1939. The board has complete jurisdiction over all misdemeanor and felony convicts in the penal institutions of the state. The granting of parole or probation and the supervision of parolees and probationers are vested in a state prison and parole commission, composed of three members elected by the qualified voters of the state for a term of six years. Several steps have been made in recent years to improve the Georgia penal system, long the subject of adverse criticism. The practice of leasing convicts to private individuals was abolished in 1908, and the use of the lash was legally prohibited in 1923. Convicts are still used for road work, and some counties still retain the striped uniforms. The act establishing the board of penal corrections also prohibits industrial output by convict labor "of such nature as to compete with products of private industries in the state."

U. S. Supreme Court decisions were handed down on Georgia cases in 1937 and 1938. Angelo Herndon, a Negro Communist organizer, was arrested in Atlanta on July 11, 1932, following a mass demonstration of the unemployed, and sentenced to twenty years under an insurrection statute of 1866. The case attracted wide attention. The trial judge granted Herndon his freedom and declared the statute unconstitutional. But the state supreme court reversed this decision, and the case was carried to the U. S. Supreme Court which ruled in 1935 that it was not within its jurisdiction. Finally, on April 26, 1937, the U. S. Supreme Court set aside the verdict of the state supreme court and upheld the trial judge's decision on the ground that the statute under which Herndon had been convicted "was so vague and indeterminate that the law necessarily violates the guarantees of liberty embodied in the Fourteenth Amendment." In December, 1937, the U. S. Supreme Court in *Breedlove vs. Suttels* upheld the constitutionality of the Georgia poll tax laws. The third case involved the constitutionality of an ordinance in Griffin, prohibiting the distribution of literature without a permit. The U. S. Supreme Court decision, March 29, 1938, voided the ordinance.

Georgia, with its three million people, is still predominantly rural and agricultural, and this fact determines in large measure the character of the state's social, educational, and religious life. Yet there are many signs that tradition is being modified. Increasing industrialization, the growing tendency toward diversified farm production, the building of farm-to-market roads, the raising of general educational standards (particularly in the field of Negro education), are linking the state more closely with the rest of the nation.

GOVERNMENT

Georgia adopted its first state constitution on February 5, 1777. One hundred years later, on December 5, 1877, the state ratified its seventh constitution, which has remained in effect ever since. Framed at the close of the turbulent Reconstruction period, when the wild extravagances of that era were uppermost in the minds of the drafters, this document imposed limitations upon taxation that have made Georgia one of the most conservative of the southern states. Its many curbs on the legislative body have occasioned the addition of 144 amendments to the 13 original articles, approximately half of these amendments having been adopted since the World War. Counties and municipalities are prohibited by the constitution from incurring debts amounting to more than 7 per cent of the assessed value of their taxable property. The state itself may not issue bonds or otherwise incur debts except by popular vote.

The constitution arbitrarily apportions the legislative representation of Georgia's 159 counties, the largest number in any state except Texas. The 8 largest counties in population have three representatives each, the 30 next largest, two each, and the remaining 121, one each. The county unit electoral system, long in use as a Democratic party rule, was established by law in 1917. It is designed to enable the rural areas to offset the voting strength of the more heavily populated urban counties, but actually the system gives control to the rural areas.

Since Georgia is overwhelmingly Democratic, nomination in the Democratic primary is tantamount to election, the nominees of the dominant party rarely being opposed in a general election. A candidate carrying a given county receives the full electoral vote of that county—two unit votes for every representative in the lower house of the legislature. Following the primary, the chosen delegates gather in the party convention, ratify the results of the primary, adopt a party platform, and choose state and national party officers and representatives. United States Senators and all state-wide elective officers are chosen under this primary system. Although Negroes represent more than 35 per cent of the population, they have little or no influence on the state government since they are virtually barred from the white primaries by party rules.

The executive branch of the government is similar to that of other states. The governor is elected for a period of two years and may serve a second term, but he is not eligible for a third term without an intermission of four years. He may call an extraordinary session of the legislature to consider a specific question but cannot adjourn the body. He has the right of veto, which may be exercised against any item of an appropriation bill, but a two-thirds vote of each house overrides his veto. Though advised by a pardon board, the governor has unlimited pardoning power. As there is no lieutenant governor, the president of the state senate is next in line to the governor, and second to him is the speaker of the house of representatives.

The legislature, which convenes every two years for a period of sixty days, is bicameral and operates similarly to that of other southern states. It may convene in extra session by its own volition. Deliberations are protracted because of the large number of members in both houses, there being 52 state senators and 205 representatives. With the exception of Fulton County, which is the only single county that elects a senator, from two to five counties are combined to make a senatorial district; the counties within a senatorial district rotate in electing a senator.

Georgia has a decentralized system of courts; there are approximately two thousand judicial tribunals in the state. The supreme court is a bench of six, consisting of a chief justice and five associate justices, all elected by the people for a term of six years. Constitutional provision was made for this court in 1835 but it was not established until 1845. A court of appeals, composed of a bench of six, was established in 1906 by constitutional amendment to relieve the supreme court. Each of the thirty-three judicial districts has one superior court judge elected for four years, except the Atlanta circuit which has seven judges and the Macon circuit which has two. The people elect an attorney general for the state and a solicitor general for each superior court.

A jury commission, appointed by the superior court judges for six-year terms, draws the names from which all juries must be selected.

Women have never served on juries in Georgia, for according to the state code, "Females are not liable to discharge military, jury, police, patrol, or road duty."

The most important sources of revenue for the state are the motor fuel, income, and general property taxes. Motor fuel and motor vehicle license taxes produce more than half the total revenue collected; one-sixth of the motor fuel tax is allotted to the counties on the basis of their highway mileage, one-sixth to the common school fund, and two-thirds to the state highway department. The ad valorem tax, limited by the constitution to a levy of five mills on each dollar's valuation of property assessed, is unusually low, but the combined city and county rates average about thirty mills to the dollar. According to two constitutional amendments ratified on June 8, 1937, homesteads up to $2,000 in value were exempted from state and county taxes, and household personal property up to $300 in value was exempted from municipal as well as state and county taxes. The income tax, introduced in Georgia in 1929, is modeled upon the Federal system. A poll tax of one dollar exacted of every registered voter goes to the common school fund.

The state constitution sets forth the general form of county government, naming certain officers such as tax collector, sheriff, and ordinary, all of whom must be elected by the people. The office of ordinary, a ranking county official, is peculiar to this state, although his duties are similar to those of a probate judge elsewhere. In counties having no board of commissioners the ordinary is the executive officer. Most counties at present are administered by county commissioners, varying in number from one to six for each county, the exact number being specified by the state legislature. In most of the smaller counties the officers are paid according to the fee system rather than by a fixed salary.

There are 593 incorporated cities and towns, each created by a special act of the legislature. There is much duplication in city and county government in the larger cities, but no consolidation between the two has yet been effected. The expense of local government is so great that only a few of the 159 counties pay as much into the state treasury as they receive from the state for school funds and other purposes.

Georgia is in the fifth United States judicial circuit, which also includes Florida, Alabama, Mississippi, Louisiana, and Texas; and the state contains three Federal judicial districts—northern, middle, and southern. There are ten congressional districts, and United States Senators and Congressmen are elected as in other states, after being nominated at the Democratic primary.

Agriculture

SINCE EARLY in the nineteenth century, farm life in Georgia has centered around the production of cotton, a commodity that dominates the state's industry as well as its agriculture. This prevailing one-crop system, however, is rooted in historical rather than in natural causes, for Georgia's clay and loam soils and mild climate are well adapted to a wide diversity of farm products. Because almost half of the state's population is engaged in agriculture, the self-sustaining farm is vitally essential, and recent trends point toward a more balanced farm economy and more varied foodstuff production.

Before the establishment of the English colony in Georgia, Indian women cultivated corn, beans, and pumpkins, and Spanish missionaries set out fig, orange, peach, and pomegranate orchards and planted mulberry trees for silkworm culture. The reasons given by the trustees in 1732 for supporting Oglethorpe's colony were to some extent based on the extravagant reports of the varied plant life and the favorable climate of this land. In addition to the military and philanthropic motives, imperialists declared that Georgia could provide all the wine needed for British consumption, could release England from dependence on Russia for flax and potash, and could produce enough silk to supply all England and still have a surplus for foreign export. The high expectations of the benefactors of the province are evident from their donations of varied plants, roots, and seeds, for which Oglethorpe established a public nursery in Savannah called the Trustees' Garden.

The garden was a ten-acre plot laid out with crosswalks bordered with orange trees; in the squares between the walks were planted not only fruits and vegetables common in England but Egyptian kale, madder, bamboo, chestnuts, olives, grapes, peaches, figs, strange medicinal herbs, and "vast quantities" of white mulberry trees. In the squares protected from the north wind the gardeners grew coffee, cotton, "cocoa-nuts," and other tropical plants. The colonists obtained growing shrubs and trees from the garden for their own plots.

Especially important were the mulberry plants, for the trustees were determined that the new colony should succeed in silk culture, which had been supplanted in Virginia by tobacco growing and in South Carolina by the cultivation of rice and indigo. Therefore, every Georgia colonist was required to plant mulberry trees, and for a time silk culture flourished. In 1764, the year of highest production, more than 15,000 pounds of silk were delivered to the filature at Savannah. After this date, however, interest began to wane because of a climate unfavorable to silk culture, the high cost of skilled labor, the removal of the bounty on silk shipped to England, and the colonists' increasing preoccupation with the growing of foodstuffs. Since manufactured articles were imported and mining operations had not yet been undertaken, an interest developed in raising varied farm products, and many plantations became self-sustaining.

Attempts to cultivate olives, grapes, and indigo were unsuccessful, but cattle raising soon proved remunerative because of the mild climate and good pasturage. Late in the Colonial period rice plantations began to spread over the marshy lands along the coast and the Savannah River, giving a new direction to the development of southeastern Georgia. Since rice could be grown only in the lowlands, corn, potatoes, peas, and wheat were planted in the higher sections.

Although the trustees did not encourage the growing of cotton, it was planted at Frederica, and the energetic Salzburgers near the coast experimented with the cultivation of a few plants in 1738. It was not until 1793, when Eli Whitney invented the cotton gin, that large-scale cotton growing became profitable. Slave labor then became a tremendous factor in maintaining the low cost necessary for successful cotton production. From the latter part of the eighteenth century until the War between the States there was an enormous increase in the cotton output of Georgia. In 1791 the state production was only 1,000 bales; in 1800 it was 20,000 bales; it doubled in the following decade, reached 150,000 bales in 1826, and continued to rise until 1860, when 701,000 bales were produced. During this period slavery spread throughout the southeastern and central sections of the state, and the owners of great plantations established their dominion.

As early as 1810 the legislature chartered the Agricultural Society of Georgia, an organization that had little lasting influence. It was revived in 1847 as the Southern Central Agricultural Society and became the Georgia State Agricultural Society in 1860. As a result of the efforts of this and other agricultural organizations, a few planters experimented with crop rotation and diversification. In 1860 the state produced more than thirty million bushels of corn, more than two million bushels of wheat, and sweet potatoes, oats, rice, tobacco, syrup, and honey in marketable quantities. There were also numerous cattle, sheep, hogs, and work animals.

Even at the height of the plantation system the importance of large plantations was out of all proportion to their number. In 1860, when the population of the state was 1,057,286, there were 31,000 farms of 100 acres or less, 3,564 of more than 500 acres, and only 902 of 1,000 acres or more. The ratio of nonslaveholders to slaveholders was about two to one. The greatest number of those engaged in cotton cultivation were members of a class intermediate between the wealthy landowners and the thriftless "poor whites." These small farmers, who lived in plain abundance, sometimes owned a few slaves but more often sustained themselves entirely by their own labor. The large slaveholders exercised a predominant influence on the state's development in the heyday of the great cotton plantations. The leisure and superior education enjoyed by these men gave them so strong a position in political and social life that their downfall after the War between the States meant a drastic revision of the entire system.

Their slaves freed and their currency worthless, the large landowners could not afford to maintain their holdings and were compelled to break them up into small units. Most of these were leased to white and Negro tenants, who could seldom meet a cash rental and usually paid in shares of the cotton crop. Often the renters had no cash with which to finance the initial cultivation or to provide for their own maintenance during the growing season, and their landlords had to advance supplies and money against the expected yield. Some landlords established stores of their own, but to cover credit and risk they charged from 20 to 50 per cent more for their goods than did stores of normal commercial character.

Tenants still raise cotton, partly because it is the crop with which they are familiar, and partly because the landlords want a crop that can be readily marketed. Since fluctuations in price make cotton a highly speculative commodity, it is produced with the lowest possible cash outlay. Fertilizer—a necessity in raising cotton—farm equipment, and whatever the tenant needs for bare living must all be bought on credit with the crop as collateral. Banks, landowners, merchants, and tenants are all involved in a precarious credit system, since the crop is mortgaged before it is planted and tenants and landlords alike are perennially in debt. Thus tenant farming perpetuates itself to the disadvantage of both tenants and landowners and results in the impoverishment of the soil.

· Tenants may be divided into three classes: renters, who lease farms for a fixed price to be paid in cash or its value in crops; share tenants, who supply much of the farm equipment and pay a third or fourth of their crops for rent; and sharecroppers, who have nothing to contribute but their labor. The landlord provides the sharecropper with land, a house, farm implements, work animals, seed, fertilizer, stovewood, and sometimes food; and when the crops have been harvested and sold the proceeds are divided equally between the two after all debts have been paid. Since the landowner keeps the books and the sharecropper generally has no records, this system is subject to abuse through dishonest bookkeeping. On the other hand, generous landlords have gone bankrupt in their efforts to carry their tenants through hard times. The sharecropper is the burden of the conscientious landlord and the prey of the unscrupulous one.

Because the improvements that a tenant makes to property merely enhance its value for the landowner without giving the tenant any additional claim, he has little incentive to exert himself beyond routine demands. After years of work he has no more share in the land he tills than at the beginning; and poverty, ignorance, and disease tend to make him improvident and lackadaisical. He frequently lives at a subsistence level in a dilapidated shack, far too small for his usually large family. Because he plants cotton up to his door and raises few food crops, his family lives on a diet consisting principally of salt pork, corn meal, and sorghum or sugar-cane syrup, and frequently suffers from pellagra.

As long as land was abundant in Georgia, farmers preferred to move westward to new acres rather than to conserve soil fertility by crop rotation. Even when new lands were no longer available, Georgia farmers were reluctant to plant crops other than the cotton which they could easily sell. By this one-crop policy, many thousands of acres have been worn out and the soil has been robbed of its vital nitrogen content.

Equal to the loss of soil fertility in its destructive consequences has been the rapid advance of soil erosion. The Soil Conservation Service of the U. S. Department of Agriculture reports that approximately 22,000,000 of the 37,584,000 acres in Georgia have lost all or part of their topsoil, that 20,000,000 are affected by gullying, and that more than 2,000,000 acres have been ruined for further tillage. The situation is grave enough in north Georgia, where the soils vary from sandy loam to clay loam with red clay subsoils, but the most appalling picture of erosion is near Lumpkin in southwestern Georgia, where the clay and marl soil is brittle. Half the farms in Stewart County have at least one gully not less than fifty feet deep which has ruined for cultivation at least fifteen acres of land; one such gully, three hundred feet wide and two hundred feet deep, affects more than three thousand acres.

The Federal Soil Conservation Service conducts five demonstration projects in Georgia to aid farmers in the reclamation of wasted land. With headquarters in Athens, La Grange, Gainesville, Rome, and Americus, these projects deal with areas varying in size from 25,000 to 100,000 acres and covering a total of approximately 250,000 acres in portions of 12 counties. Expert technicians co-operating with the farmers within these areas are showing that erosion can be controlled by rotating cash crops and cover crops, by strip cropping, by building proper terraces and ditches, and by planting trees, bushes, and vines in gullies. At Athens and Americus nurseries have been established to supply farmers with the necessary plants, and at Athens a soil conservation experiment station has been set up to work out new methods and improve former practices. The conservation service directs the soil conservation activities of nine of the Civilian Conservation Corps camps which have been assigned to the state.

In 1937 the state general assembly passed an act authorizing the establishment of soil conservation districts. Landowners within any proposed area may petition the state soil conservation committee for the organization of a soil conservation district. In December, 1938, ten districts located in forty-five counties had been established, and farmers from many other counties had asked for organization. Supervisors have secured the co-operation of various state and Federal agencies in conserving soil resources, but the greatest contribution comes from the Federal Soil Conservation Service, which furnishes technicians and some equipment for detail work. Experiments in diversified crop production are conducted by the Georgia Agricultural Experiment Station near Griffin, the Mountain Experiment Station near Blairsville, and the Coastal Plain Experiment Station near Tifton.

Because of soil erosion and other factors, farm depression in Georgia began long before the general depression of the 1930's. Probably widespread pauperization began in 1921, when the boll weevil first wrought serious damage within the state. This pest, together with low cotton prices, so impoverished the farmers that they were unable to re-establish stability during the ensuing years of general prosperity, and the nation-wide depression that began late in 1929 drove many below the subsistence level. In 1934 more than 30,000 families, approximately 12 per cent of the farm families in Georgia, were on county relief rolls, and still more were being helped by various agencies. Most of those on county rolls were tenant farmers and wage hands; about one out of six was a landowner.

In the summer of 1934 the Georgia Rural Rehabilitation Corporation initiated a program to relieve destitute farmers and to direct them toward a sounder farm policy. In 1934 and 1935 the organization selected from the relief rolls 12,981 farm families, to whom it made loans of $4,349,605, or an average of $335 a family. Each of these loans was secured by a bill of sale covering capital, equipment, household goods, livestock, and crops. The program gave promise of permanent success, for during 1935 repayments amounted to more than 45 per cent of the total amount lent. On July 1 of that year the Georgia Rural Rehabilitation Corporation was transferred to the National Resettlement Administration, now the Farm Security Administration. During the following year loans were reduced still further, for most of the families raised a large portion of their food supplies and livestock feed. In 1934 and 1935 the average assets of the families receiving loans were less than $50; in 1936 this average had increased to $245. Although about 10 per cent of the original borrowers were dropped because of unfitness or lack of co-operation, loans to other low-income families brought in 1936 the total to 11,511; of these 1,500 paid their loans in full, bringing the total repayment in that year to $1,590,000, and some made down-payments on farms.

In 1937, almost two hundred white families had received assistance from the following resettlement projects of the Farm Security Administration: Briar Patch Farms near Eatonton, Piedmont Homesteads near Monticello, Irwinville Farms near Irwinville, and Wolf Creek Farms near Cairo. Flint River Farms, near Montezuma, provide 107 farm units for Negro families. The most striking example of farm rehabilitation work in the state is that of the Pine Mountain Valley Rural Community Corporation, which has rehabilitated about 160 families on 12,000 acres of western Georgia land.

The state board of health, with the co-operation of Federal agencies, has recently undertaken a program to improve the health conditions of the farm population. An expanded program has reduced such common health hazards as malaria and hookworm, and efforts are being made to control pellagra and other dietary diseases.

Of Georgia's 37,584,000 acres, 25,300,000 acres were included in farms and more than 11,000,000 acres were cultivated in 1935. There were 250,544 farms, of which 164,000 were worked by tenants, a percentage of 65.6 for farm tenancy in Georgia as compared with 42.1 for the the entire country. A further analysis shows 177,259 white farm operators of whom 101,649 were tenants, and 73,285 Negro farm operators of whom 62,682 were tenants. The evils of the system are intensified by the short tenure of tenant farms. In 1935, according to the report of the President's committee on farm tenancy, 48.4 per cent of tenants in the state had occupied their farms for less than a year, while only 5.2 per cent had 15 years or more of occupancy.

Crops: Although cotton is still by all odds the leading Georgia product, farmers are deriving profits not only from crops relatively new to the state but from others that have flourished in the past. Georgia leads all other states in the production of sweet potatoes, peanuts, watermelons, and improved varieties of pecans; its pimiento production is twice that of California, the only state competing in this commodity. In 1938 the value of its cotton and cottonseed was $46,096,000; corn $29,772,000; tobacco $19,045,000; peanuts $16,837,000; sweet potatoes $7,841,000; and peaches $5,320,000.

Corn, second only to cotton in value of the annual crop, is now cultivated on almost every Georgia farm. Meal, starch, and syrup are made from the grain, and the blades are used for fodder.

Tobacco, now one of the state's most important cash crops, was introduced into Georgia by settlers from Virginia after the War of the Revolution. Much land about Augusta and in north Georgia was cleared for tobacco and its culture became extensive, but after the invention of the cotton gin this crop was displaced by cotton. Since about 1911, however, tobacco has brought so large a measure of prosperity to planters of middle and south Georgia that it is generally known as Georgia's "miracle crop." The introduction of tobacco in this area was sponsored by southeast Georgia bankers, who through foreclosure had acquired many thousand acres of unprofitable land. During the depression of the 1930's the tobacco planter suffered less severely than most other farmers because of the greatly increased consumption of cigarettes.

Potatoes, requiring neither a rich soil nor expensive fertilizer, can be grown at low cost and are planted in almost every Georgia county. The Georgia yam, a sweet potato widely known for its delicious flavor, is marketed throughout the United States. Agricultural chemists reported in 1937 that the sweet potato can be used to make adhesive products, laundry starch, and sizing. The soil of the Coastal Plain is particularly well suited to Irish potatoes but, because other crops have proved more profitable, they have not been raised in such quantities as the soil and climate of Georgia permit. Irish potatoes are intensively cultivated, however, in the small but fertile Appalachian Valley section.

Peanuts were first grown commercially when the boll weevil forced many farmers to substitute other cash crops for cotton. Their cultivation is most extensive in southwest Georgia, where the Spanish and runner varieties are best adapted to the soil and climate. Their vines are valued as fodder, and their nuts are utilized for peanut butter, candy, and oil. After the crops are harvested, farmers allow their hogs to root for the remaining nuts. Because peanut-fed hogs are prized for the flavor of their hams, farmers often turn their swine loose on unharvested crops grown especially for hog feed.

Although Georgia is surpassed by California in peach production, it ranks first in volume of fresh peaches marketed. The best-known varieties, the Georgia Belle, Hiley Belle, Elberta, and Hale, were originated in Georgia. The fruit was not a major commercial crop until after 1890, when refrigeration and rapid transportation made it possible for Georgia growers to market their fruit in northern cities. Storms and late freezes sometimes bring disaster to the crop, but peaches are cultivated successfully without extraordinary care in both the central and northern sections of the state. The region of the heaviest production is near the fall line and formerly centered about Fort Valley; but because the "phony" peach disease has attacked the trees of central Georgia, peach culture has moved northward about Thomaston. Even the mountainous regions have been planted successfully, and the land about Cornelia, widely known as an apple section, is now also a flourishing peach-growing area.

Paper-shell pecans were introduced about 1905, and Georgia soon took the lead among the states in their cultivation. Pecan production, which centers about Albany, fluctuates greatly in quantity, and because of a short crop and low prices, its value was only $886,000 in 1938. Watermelons are grown in most sections of the state; the value of the crop was $830,000 in 1938. The vicinity of Cairo in southwestern Georgia is so rich in the production of sugar cane that Cairo ranks second to New Orleans as a syrup market. This region also produces an abundance of vegetables and supplies 98 per cent of all the collard seed marketed. Here and in most other parts of the state every farm has its patch of collards (a variety of kale), for this hardy vegetable provides green food late into the fall.

The production of tung oil also centers about Cairo, where the soil and climatic conditions are similar to those of the section of China which is the native home of the tung nut. The first trees in the state were planted in 1908, but large-scale development was only recently begun, and reliable statistics concerning the value of the commodity are not available. The fact that the nut is poisonous and consequently pest proof greatly aids in maintaining a low production cost. Because tung oil has more than a hundred commercial uses, it is one of the most promising orchard products of the state. The chief use of the oil is in the manufacture of lacquers, paints, and varnishes.

Other cash crops promising well for the future are various vegetables and fruits grown for canneries that are being developed on a small scale throughout Georgia. Pimientos are extensively planted near Griffin, where a pimiento cannery has been established. Since 1935, when the former state prohibition law was modified to permit the sale of light wines, thick-skinned scuppernong grapes have been cultivated more extensively on Georgia farms.

Control of the boll weevil has permitted again the cultivation of sea-island cotton, a variety preferred by makers of fine cloth because it has an unusually long staple. The first sea-island cotton in America was introduced into Georgia from the Bahama Islands in 1786. It was found to be suited to the climate of the coastal islands and the extreme southern part of the state, where it was grown successfully until the boll weevil ended its cultivation. Because sea-island cotton matures late in the growing season, it is especially subject to the attack of this pest.

Despite almost year-around pasturage available in some sections, the possibilities of livestock raising have not been fully developed. Only within the last twenty-five years have stock raising, dairying, and meat packing become important industries in Georgia. Scrub cattle and razor-back hogs have been replaced to a great extent by finer breeds of stock. Dairies and creameries, usually near cities where good markets are assured, now supply much of the milk and butter locally consumed. Georgia produces more cattle and has more meat-packing plants than any other southeastern state.

It is possible that livestock and foodstuffs will displace cotton and become the major cash crops of the future. The obstacles to the development of a balanced farm economy in place of one-crop production are formidable, but various agencies in the field of farm education are seeking to overcome them. The Georgia Department of Agriculture, established in 1874 as the first state department of agriculture in the Union, aids farmers in marketing their produce and sends out market bulletins. Its general educational work is augmented by that of the extension service of The University of Georgia, the agricultural experiment stations, and Federal and county agencies.

Industry

As COTTON is the leading farm product of Georgia, so cotton textile manufacturing leads the state's industries. Extensive industrial development did not begin until after the War between the States, but its foundations were laid much earlier. It was in Georgia that Eli Whitney invented and perfected the cotton gin, which made possible the removal of lint from seed by machinery instead of by hand. This machine immediately stimulated cotton production. From 487,-000 pounds in 1793, the year the gin was invented, the national export of cotton soared to 1,601,700 pounds in 1794 and 6,276,300 pounds in 1795. By 1800 the country was exporting 17,789,800 pounds of cotton. This machine radically reduced the number of laborers employed in processing but, by expanding cotton culture, greatly increased the demand for field hands. Since Negro slaves were paid no wages and could be sustained cheaply, Georgia's cotton profits rested on a slave economy.

Several Georgia mills were erected early in the nineteenth century, but they were short-lived. The most successful mill of the period, built near Augusta by John Shly in 1828, spun between 200 and 300 pounds of yarn and produced 300 to 400 yards of cotton bagging daily on four looms. Later the plant manufactured osnaburg, a coarse cloth used extensively for slaves' clothing. Shly provided houses, fuel, and garden plots for his fifty employees. In 1834, when the factory was moved nearer Augusta, it began the manufacture of "Georgia Plains," a woolen cloth which sold at half the price of the imported "British Plains." It also installed a dye house and made the first striped or checked cotton goods produced in the state, as well as blue and brown denims for overalls. The mill was probably the first in Georgia to manufacture duck, a cloth used for tents and caisson coverings during the War between the States.

A seven-mile power canal, constructed at Augusta in 1845 at a cost of $1,500,000, made the waters of the Savannah River available for industrial power and established Augusta as a leader in cotton manufacturing. After Shly had demonstrated the practicability of the cotton textile industry, several mills were built in Georgia, and in the 1840's progress in cotton manufacturing was exceeded only by that in Massachusetts and New Hampshire. At the outbreak of the War between the States Georgia had more than fifty textile mills.

The war temporarily stunned industrial activity, but within little more than a year after its close the state had granted more than seventy charters for railroads, streetcar lines, petroleum companies, and various manufacturing concerns. From 1870 to 1890 the capital invested in manufacture quadrupled, railroad mileage trebled, and property values increased from $215,000,000 to $280,000,000.

Southern men often pooled their resources, borrowed additional capital from the North, and established mills. Northern capitalists also began to establish various enterprises in Georgia, where they found rich natural resources and little industrial development. There was an abundance of unorganized labor and a warm climate that permitted cheap living. Moreover, there was virtually no outlay for transporting raw material to the factory, since textile mills could be established in the midst of the cotton-growing region.

By 1881, when the International Cotton Exposition was held in Atlanta, the urbanization of industries was well under way. The introduction of steam power removed the necessity for building factories near waterways; instead, manufacturers began to look for sites where transportation facilities made abundant coal supplies available. Thus cities gained in importance. Later, with the long-distance transmission of hydroelectric power, the trend was reversed, and industrial concerns now prefer to establish their plants in smaller communities where production costs are lower.

According to the U. S. Census of Manufactures for 1937, the manufacture of cotton woven goods was valued at $164,173,282. Georgia's peak year in cotton production was 1911, when 2,768,627 bales were compressed. But with the coming of the boll weevil in 1921, cotton crops were so blighted that two years later only 588,236 bales were produced. The annual average production from 1923 through 1937 was 1,156,548 bales, with the largest crop (1,592,439 bales) in 1930. Although cotton production and cotton consumption in Georgia have been almost equal, local textile manufacturers have bought most of their raw material outside of the state because the Georgia product failed to meet spinning requirements. In recent years, however, through the efforts of the State College of Agriculture, the United States Bureau of Plant Industry, and the Cotton Manufacturers' Association, the quality and staple of Georgia cotton has been so improved that an increasingly larger portion is consumed by local mills.

Cotton is also important as a basis for the cordage and cottonseed industries. With the assistance of northern capital, Georgia has become the leading state in the production of tire cord. In 1937 the value of cottonseed products was $27,268,138. Cottonseed oil is used in the production of cooking compounds and soaps, meal in making fertilizer and cattle feed, and linters in the manufacture of rayon.

Georgia's second largest industrial income is derived from forest products. Its vast pine forests give the state a high position in the production of naval stores, a well-established industry, and in paper manufacturing, a new one. These forests were neglected until the Reconstruction era, when cotton plantations were destroyed, Confederate currency was worthless, and it became necessary to find natural resources for immediate industrial development. In this critical period the people exploited south Georgia's pine trees and developed two great industries, naval stores and lumber. By 1882 a naval stores exchange had been founded at Savannah, and that city is now the world's foremost market for these products. Georgia leads all the states in this industry, producing more than half the gum turpentine in the United States; its turpentine and rosin produced in 1937 were valued at $16,557,756.

Paper making is still in a speculative stage, although investments of millions of dollars have followed the experiments of Charles H. Herty. From the results obtained in his paper-pulp laboratory in Savannah, Herty offered proof that newsprint produced at $47.48 a ton in the North can be made from southern pine at $27.50 a ton. The investment of more than $12,000,000 in paper mills at Savannah and Brunswick indicates confidence in the future of this industry.

Georgia timber is largely utilized by woodworking enterprises; the value of finished products in 1937 was $37,663,894. Plants include coffin factories, planing mills, furniture factories, broom and box factories, and cooperage works.

Although fertilizer sales declined sharply in 1931, when retailers put the business on a cash basis, Georgia usually ranks second or third in the annual output of this product. In 1937 there were 143 fertilizer factories and mixing plants in the state, and the output was valued at $21,711,717.

The peanut products industry has been growing since 1921 when farmers planted more peanuts as a substitute crop for cotton, which was ravaged by the boll weevil for the first time in that year. In the late 1930's limitation of cotton acreage through the Federal control program also resulted in an increase of peanut acreage. Many cottonseed refineries now include peanut crushing in their process plan, producing pulp for peanut butter and oil for salad dressing.

Forty-three hydroelectric plants in the state have a total capacity of 586,301 horsepower. According to the reports of the drainage basin committee (published by the National Resources Committee, December, 1937), the state has many potential sites for water power development. Some of these undeveloped sites have already been investigated by the U. S. Corps of Engineers.

Although total mineral production was valued at $12,640,232 in 1936, the state is not making full use of its mineral resources. In 1937, the value of stone products (including marble, granite, and slate) was $4,139,349; clay products, other than pottery, ranked next at $3,641,-371; and minerals and earths (ground or otherwise treated) were valued at $2,127,708. The value of foundry products was $2,835,522, but the raw material used was largely imported from other states, as Georgia's supply of iron ore is negligible.

Each of Georgia's principal cities has a strategic place in the general industrial pattern. Atlanta, a center for transportation, distribution, and banking, is also Georgia's leading industrial city; Savannah, with its tar products, naval stores, and sugar, is the principal port; Columbus has textile mills and iron foundries; and Augusta and Macon have textile mills and clay works. Brunswick is a port and naval-stores market, and Rome, Griffin, La Grange, Gainesville, Dalton, Canton, Silvertown, and West Point are busy textile centers.

Despite industrial advance, Georgia still presents a striking disparity between the potential wealth of its natural resources and the value of industries utilizing these resources. Moreover, industrial growth has not been marked by diversification of production. This is to some extent a result of the prevailing low wages paid to technicians in the state. Chemists, mining engineers, and other trained industrial workers educated in Georgia usually seek employment in other sections of the country, where wages are higher, and remain to aid in the development of the resources of those areas. Perhaps a more direct cause of Georgia's failure to develop diversified industries is that its people are accustomed to think in terms of agriculture and are slow to realize the potential industrial value of the abundant natural resources. The easier marketing of the cotton crop, made possible through the invention of the cotton gin, served to perpetuate the agricultural pattern.

Almost all parts of the state are linked by rail to the market areas of the Mississippi Valley, Chicago, and New York, and indirectly, by way of the Gulf and the Atlantic Coast, to world markets. But despite this apparent advantage and the greatest railroad mileage of all southern states except Oklahoma and Texas, the division of the nation's railway system on a regional basis, with concomitant freight-rate disparities, has done much to bar Georgia from a greater share in the country's industry and commerce. Freight charges on pottery, for example, shipped from Gordon, Georgia, to Cincinnati, Ohio, a distance of 584 miles, are 68 cents per hundred pounds, while the rate on the same product shipped from East Liverpool, Ohio, to St. Louis, Missouri, a distance of 588 miles, is only 42 cents. As a result, most of Georgia's clays are shipped North to be made into finished products.

J. R. Bachman of the Atlanta Freight Bureau states, "Freight rate parity is imperative not only because the present situation is indefensible and monstrously unfair to the South, but for the more compelling reason that the entire nation is suffering from the subnormal per capita income of the South and the industrial congestion of the North." In 1937 Georgia's per capita income was only $288, whereas that of Massachusetts was $668 and that of New York, $859. Industrial leaders of all southern states are now urging a reduction in rates on the interstate shipments of a dozen major commodities and expect that the establishment of these lower rates will result in a general rate slash.

Labor

THE FOUNDERS of Georgia intended to keep the colony communal, but failure seemed inevitable from the beginning. Many settlers, envying the prosperity of slave-holding South Carolina, clamored for the right to possess slaves, and when slavery became legal in 1749 the pattern of Georgia's labor was set for more than a century. There were many white and some free Negro laborers during slavery days, but they were without organization and had to work in competition with slaves.

Immediately after the War between the States the newly emancipated Negroes, believing that land was to be confiscated by Congress and allotted to them, refused to enter into contracts to work for wages. At first this situation caused an acute labor shortage, but during Reconstruction the Negroes were absorbed as paid laborers by industry.

With the expansion of industry desire for organization arose among the workers. When unions appeared they worked zealously to effect the political and social improvement of the laboring classes, but most of these early organizations were short-lived. In the late 1880's the Knights of Labor, which dominated the American labor movement at this time, led a few strikes in Georgia mill villages. In 1888 nineteen machinists of Atlanta organized the United Machinists and Mechanical Engineers of America, the first machinists' union in the United States. A convention, held in Atlanta in the following year, formed the association which became the International Association of Machinists. In 1889, also, the International Brotherhood of Blacksmiths, Drop Forgers, and Helpers was organized in Atlanta.

A central labor body was formed in Augusta in 1890 and one in Atlanta in the following year. The Georgia Federation of Labor, a state body of the American Federation of Labor, was founded in 1899. Within the next ten years central labor bodies developed in Columbus, Macon, Savannah, Rome, and Waycross. Short-lived organizations were formed in Athens, Valdosta, Douglas, Fitzgerald, and Brunswick in 1913 and 1918.

The railway employees in Georgia were fairly well organized by 1890, and their unions continued to develop during the first two decades of the twentieth century. But the open shop drives of 1920-22, part of a nation-wide movement, largely disrupted the unions in the maintenance divisions. The railway transportation unions, known as the railway brotherhoods—engineers, firemen, trainmen, and conductors—were, and still are, independent; but other unions in the skilled trades, organized soon after the turn of the century, were affiliated with the Georgia Federation of Labor.

Some newspaper publishers conceded union recognition as early as the 1880's, and the important book and job printing plants in Atlanta were completely organized by 1903. Within the next fifteen years the chief printing plants of the state were organized. The International Paving Cutters' Union of the United States of America and Canada was formed at Lithonia in 1901, and stone-working unions now exist in other parts of the state. The longshoremen of Savannah were unionized in 1900, but the fact that there were strikes as early as 1881 indicates that formal unionization was preceded by some sort of organization. Unions in the building trades, strongest in Atlanta, have operated widely but their strength has varied with construction booms and depressions. In other branches of industry also unions flourished during the boom period of the 1920's, weakened during the depression years, and revived to some extent under the National Recovery Act (1933-35).

Georgia musicians and stage employees have organizations in most of the important cities. Public employees of Atlanta and Fulton County, including teachers and fire-fighters, are unionized. Street transportation employees have been organized in Augusta since 1912, in Atlanta and Macon since 1918, and in Rome since 1926. In Columbus and Savannah they were organized for a short while in 1918 and 1919; in Columbus they were again organized in 1933.

The Committee for Industrial Organization (now the Congress of Industrial Organizations) became active in Georgia in 1935, soon after it was formed. In August of that year the United Automobile Workers of America, who had a union in Atlanta, became affiliated with the C.I.O. Since that time C.I.O. unions have been organized in the meat-packing, steel, and textile industries in the state.

With the rise of the C.I.O. a split occurred in the Georgia Federation of Labor. During the annual state convention in April, 1937, William Green, president of the American Federation of Labor, ruled that A. Steve Nance, president of the Georgia Federation of Labor, was ineligible to preside because he had become southeastern director of the Textile Workers Organizing Committee, a C.I.O. body. Some unions, however, continued to support Nance, and until after his death on April 3, 1938, there were two groups that called themselves the Georgia Federation of Labor. The united organization is now making a continued drive to organize textile workers within the framework of the A.F. of L. The Textile Workers Organizing Committee and part of the older United Textile Workers merged in May, 1939, to form the Textile Workers Union of America, affiliated with the C.I.O., while some of the local textile unions remained with the A.F. of L.

The formation of the C.I.O. gave great impetus to labor organization. Both the C.I.O. and the A.F. of L. wished to increase their membership, and organizing campaigns brought many new members into existing unions and led to the formation of new unions. Some A.F. of L. unions do not admit Negroes and, in those that do, the Negro members are organized in separate locals. Negroes are not excluded from C.I.O. unions, but when they belong to a local with white membership they meet separately.

Many of Georgia's labor disturbances can be traced to the industrial boom of the 1920's, during which many workers left the farms for the factories and failed to be absorbed into industry. This situation became more acute during the depression of the 1930's. In August and September of 1930 the American Fascisti Association and Order of Black Shirts was organized in Atlanta in an attempt to drive Negro workers out of jobs and replace them with white laborers. Some employers yielded to its demands, others stood firm against them. The movement swept the state in a few weeks and there were some strikes, but the organization was short-lived.

Though the number of strikes in the state for the twenty-year period of 1916-36 was less than one per cent of the national total, some have been spectacular. In general, strikes have been called because of grievances over working conditions, long hours, low wages, discharges, and anti-union discrimination. Sometimes they have been called to secure the closed shop, union recognition, and collective bargaining. Georgia's most serious strikes, part of the nation-wide textile strike of 1934, lasted from September 14 to October 8 of that year and affected thousands of workers in almost every textile mill in the state. The Governor declared martial law and called out the state militia.

Troops were also used in the stove foundry strike in Rome, October 15-29, 1934, and in hosiery and textile strikes in 1935. In November, 1936, the United Automobile Workers of America organized one of the first sit-down strikes in America in the Fisher Body Company, Atlanta. This method spread northward to Flint and Detroit and was used in the General Motors strikes during the winter of 1936-37.

The longest labor struggle in the history of the state was settled on December 14, 1938, when employees of an Atlanta department store ended seventy-two weeks of picketing for a wage increase and returned to work on the basis of a compromise agreement.

In general, employers have opposed unionization and maintained a paternalistic attitude toward their employees. This is due to some extent to the historic development of industry and labor in the state and is fostered by the conditions under which the majority of industrial workers live. As textile mills and other industrial plants were established in Georgia during the latter half of the nineteenth century, mill villages appeared. They followed the pattern of New England textile towns and were generally found wherever mills were established in isolated communities. These communities, with their company-owned houses and in some cases company-owned stores, provide a way of life that has long been a subject of controversy. Sociologists hold that mill-owned villages give the employer-landlords the power to control the political and social as well as the economic life of the workers. On the other hand, spokesmen for industry stress the advantages of mill villages in providing low-cost housing and social and recreational opportunites. They point to the attractive and well-kept villages that have been built in recent years by several companies, while those who criticise the system point to the squalid conditions in other mill villages.

Of Georgia's total population of 2,908,506, almost half (1,162,174) ten years of age and over were gainfully employed in 1930. This group is almost entirely native and, with the exception of agricultural workers and domestic servants, predominately white. Except in the building trades Negroes usually hold only unskilled positions in industry. Between 1910 and 1930 the number of workers engaged in manufacturing rose from 12.2 to 20.1 per cent and the number engaged in agriculture fell from 63.3 to 43.2 per cent. Despite the rise of manufacturing all those unable to find a livelihood in agriculture have not been absorbed, and this has resulted in a surplus of labor competing for jobs and a consequent decline in the bargaining position of workers. Industrial wages are lower in Georgia than in other sections of the country. In 1937 the average annual wage in manufacturing was $692 for Georgia, $843 for the South Atlantic states, and $1,180 for the United States as a whole.

Labor is attempting to interest the public in its aims through an extensive educational program. Many unions, particularly those of the C.I.O., conduct weekly classes for their members, and the Georgia Federation of Labor publishes a weekly newspaper with an open circulation available to the public. The unions also are taking steps to check the establishment of "runaway industries" from states where wages and living standards of the laborer are higher. Georgia workers declare that the lower wages paid by these concerns tend to depress all wages still further. Small independent merchants conduct a similar but separate fight based on the argument that these industries, largely financed by eastern capital, are draining money out of the state. Both organized labor and small local businesses also oppose the overtures and aid sometimes extended to these industries by civic bodies—including new buildings and equipment, payment for training machine operators, long-period tax exemptions, free water power, and a guarantee of protection against interference of organized labor. Because of the rights granted to the worker under the National Labor Relations Act of 1935 and the Fair Labor Standards Act of 1938, migration to Georgia of industries paying substandard wages and imposing long working hours has been checked to some extent.

Efforts to pass a child-labor law in Georgia began in 1887, and in 1906 the legislature enacted a law prohibiting the employment in manufacturing establishments of children under ten years of age. Children ten to twelve years old could be employed if they could read and write simple sentences or if they were offspring of indigent parents. In 1914 the minimum age limit was raised to fourteen years. Although the general assembly rejected the Federal child-labor amendment in 1924, in the following year it adopted further child-labor legislation modeled after the Federal laws of 1916 and 1919. Children under sixteen may not be employed in any manufacturing establishment between the hours of 7 P.M. and 6 A.M., the employment of children in certain hazardous occupations is prohibited, and boys under sixteen may not be employed as messengers between the hours of 9 P.M. and 6 A.M. Despite legislation on child labor, 14.7 per cent of Georgia's workers, according to the 1930 census, were children ten to fifteen years of age. In 1938, however, the annual report of the Georgia Commissioner of Labor stated that no child under sixteen years of age is employed in Georgia's industries. No laws have been enacted regulating child labor in mercantile or street trades.

Operatives in cotton and woolen mills may not be required to work more than ten hours a day or sixty hours a week, railroad trainmen may work only thirteen hours in any twenty-four and are guaranteed ten-hour rest periods, and under an act of 1865 only works of necessity and charity may be performed on Sunday. In 1930 the leading textile mills voluntarily banned night work for women and children. The effects of the Fair Labor Standards Act in Georgia cannot yet be determined.

A workmen's compensation act has been in effect since 1921. In

1937 provision for medical care was raised from $100 maximum with a thirty-day limit to $500 with a ten-week limit, and maximum benefit was raised from $15 to $20 a week. Under the laws passed in 1899 employers are required to provide seats for women laborers during inactive hours and to equip the buildings with fire-safety devices. An act of 1933 requires the provision of safeguards for workmen on building construction jobs.

Other protective laws relate to garnishment of laborers' wages and to special liens on the property of employers and on the product of a laborer's work for wages due him. Laws have been passed to regulate many occupational qualifications, and practitioners of virtually every trade or profession are required to meet minimum standards set up by the state or its designated agent. Although progressive labor laws have been passed in recent years, Georgia has not yet made sufficient provision for raising funds to enforce them. The commissioner of labor, an elected official, is entrusted with the supervision and administration of all the state's labor laws and regulations.

Transportation

THE FIRST English settlers, who came to Georgia more than two centuries ago, found only a few primitive trails. These and the navigable streams served well enough for inland travel while the settlements were huddled near the coast. Military need brought about the construction of the first roads in the colony, one of which was the road cut by Oglethorpe's regiments through St. Simon Island from Fort Frederica to Fort St. Simon.

As agriculture developed, the need for better transportation became more acute, but waterways long continued to serve as the main arteries of trade. Market towns were conveniently located along the rivers. Augusta shipped its cotton directly to Savannah on river boats; Milledgeville and Macon sent their cotton down the Oconee, Ocmulgee, and Altamaha rivers to Darien and then up the coast to Savannah. The return trips upstream were long and arduous; the boats were poled by gangs of slaves, and the average distance covered by a crew of twenty men was only about ten miles a day. Canoes and bateaux (flat-bottomed rowboats), small sloops, and piraguas (flat-bottomed boats with both sails and oars) traveled between the coastal islands and on the rivers. Great one-way "cottonboxes," which were actually shallow wooden barges, were floated down the rivers of the coastal plain to the market towns, where they were broken up and sold for lumber.

Need for better means of land travel grew more pressing as settlements moved farther inland. Trails, made by years of steady travel on foot and on horseback, gradually became roads. Wagons carried crops to market and returned laden with supplies. Large groups traveled and camped together on hard and perilous journeys made in canvas-covered wagons like the prairie-schooners used later in the West. Tobacco was drawn to market in hogsheads fitted with axial poles to which mules were harnessed. To avoid streams men rolled the hogsheads over highland ridge trails such as the present Tobacco Road, celebrated in Erskine Caldwell's novel of that name and its dramatization. At the end of the road the hogsheads were put on flatboats and taken down the river to Savannah.

Before the end of the eighteenth century a network of roads connected Savannah, Augusta, Sunbury, Darien, Washington, and Louisville. By 1799 a stagecoach line was running twice a week between Savannah and Augusta, and a few years later stages were carrying passengers on regular schedule in other parts of Georgia. A coach ran six days a week between Augusta and Milledgeville, then the state capital, and stages traveling between Columbus and Milledgeville and between Athens and Augusta made connections with lines to other growing towns. By 1840 the New Southern Line was operating a regular service between New York and New Orleans by way of Charleston and Savannah. The state encouraged road building by granting charters to private companies to build turnpikes and operate stage-coach systems. Georgia's early transportation development was aided further by the Federal government's military and post roads, one of which was constructed in 1811 from Milledgeville westward across the Chattahoochee River and another in 1815 from Athens northward into Tennessee.

Early in the nineteenth century, Georgia staked its hope of a better transportation system on the building of canals and the improvement of waterways. Of three canals chartered in 1818, however, only that connecting the Ogeechee River with the Savannah was actually begun. Despite public interest, construction lagged and this thirteen-mile waterway was not completed until 1831, after the state had appropriated $44,000 for the purchase of stock. Many other canals were planned. In 1826 the Brunswick Canal Company was organized and began work on a canal to carry cargoes of rice and lumber from the Altamaha River to Brunswick harbor. Beset by many difficulties, the company ten years later completed a ditch twelve miles long, fifty-four feet wide, and six feet deep, with locks at each end and a towpath along its eastern bank. But the canal was never opened to traffic.

River travel developed more rapidly as the streams were improved. At first the inhabitants along the rivers were responsible for keeping them navigable. The work done under this arrangement was negligible, and about 1810 the state adopted the plan of chartering private companies to improve the river beds and charge tolls on river traffic. Because of the expense involved, this plan in turn proved unsuccessful; and it became apparent that if the rivers were to be made and kept navigable the state would have to appropriate funds for water development. By 1828 the legislature had spent $321,500 of a $500,000 fund appropriated in 1821, and yet little improvement had been made. This, however, did not hinder the development of watercraft.

About the time of the launching of Robert Fulton's *Clermont* in 1807 William Longstreet, of Augusta, built a steamboat that attained a speed of five miles an hour on the Savannah River. The state encouraged steamboat development, but not wisely, for in 1814 it granted to Samuel Howard a monopoly for steam navigation on all Georgia streams. Howard built the *Enterprise* and sent it up the Savannah River to Augusta in 1817; and in the following year he organized the Steamboat Company of Georgia, for which he secured another monopoly. In an effort to combat the high rates and other public disadvantages resulting from this monopoly, the state later chartered the Savannah River Navigation Company, but the terms of Howard's charter prevented this new company from using steamboats. An ineffectual expedient was the *Genius of Georgia,* which plied the Savannah in 1820, its paddle wheels driven by nineteen horses treading an endless belt. Howard's charter was nullified in 1824 by a decision of the United States Supreme Court, which ruled in a New Jersey case that no state could grant a monopoly on the use of its waterways. Thus freed, steamboat transportation expanded rapidly, and vessels appeared on one river after another, connecting the interior with the coast. The *Georgia,* one of Howard's boats, had navigated the Altamaha and Oconee rivers as far as Milledgeville in 1819, and by the late 1820's between ten and fifteen steamboats were running regularly between Savannah and Augusta. Their chief cargo was cotton, some carrying loads of twelve hundred bales.

The Savannah Steamship Company was incorporated in 1818, and the first trans-Atlantic "steamer," the *Savannah,* was built for this company in New York and launched in the spring of 1819. For practical reasons its steam power was auxiliary, supplementing sails with which it was fully equipped. After a trial trip to its home port, where it was inspected by President James Monroe, the *Savannah* left on May 22, 1819, for Liverpool, England, where it docked on June 20 after a hazardous voyage. From Liverpool it went to St. Petersburg, Russia, returning to Savannah in November of the same year. Because this pioneer voyage was a financial failure, the *Savannah* abandoned the use of engines but continued to ply the Atlantic Coast as a sailing vessel until it was lost off Long Island in 1822. National Maritime Day, May 22, was proclaimed by President Franklin D. Roosevelt in 1935 to commemorate the epochal voyage of the *Savannah.*

Steamboats and stagecoaches could not meet the increasing transportation demands of the state as population and production continued to expand. Yet Georgia for a time was indifferent to the idea of railroads. Not until construction was begun on the Charleston & Hamburg Railroad in South Carolina did the state take notice; and only when the line from Charleston to the Savannah River opposite Augusta was completed in 1833 was it roused to action. Savannah, especially, feared the loss of its shipping commerce, knowing that Charleston with its railroad could capture the trade of the South and Middle West. The first railroad in the state was the Georgia, sponsored by merchants of Athens to connect that city with Augusta and the South Carolina lines. It was chartered in 1833, and four years later trains were carrying passengers and freight between Augusta and Berzelia, a distance of twenty miles. Although construction had begun in Augusta, the citizens of that city did not at first approve of the venture, fearing that Augusta would become only a way-station between Athens and the port of Charleston. The line did not reach Athens until 1841.

The Central of Georgia also was chartered in 1833, to run from Savannah to Macon, the center of a rich cotton belt. Despite the obtuseness of some inland towns, which refused to aid or even to accept the railroad and later suffered severely for their shortsightedness, the Central of Georgia finally reached Macon in 1843 and assured Savannah's commercial security.

Meanwhile, the ambition of both Georgia and South Carolina was to reach the trade of the Middle West by rail through Tennessee. Georgia had the advantage over its rival state in its geographical position nearer the goal and in a natural route that could be followed northward through the mountains. In the absence of private initiative the state itself decided to initiate this project, and in 1837 it started the construction of a line between the Chattahoochee River, at a point near Bolton, and Chattanooga, Tennessee. To connect this line with Savannah, Augusta, and Macon, plans were made for extending the Georgia Railroad from Union Point westward and for building a new line—the Macon & Western, now a part of the Central of Georgia—from Macon northward to a point where these two lines would meet the southern terminus of the state railroad, the Western & Atlantic. That meeting place, first known as Terminus and then (1843-47) as Marthasville, was the site of the present city of Atlanta. It was reached by the Georgia Railroad in 1845 and by the Macon & Western in the following year. The three railroads converging here were chiefly responsible for the phenomenal development of Atlanta, which soon became the most important inland transportation center of the state.

The Western & Atlantic was completed to Chattanooga in 1851. Within a few years thereafter, connecting rails from other roads enabled the Western & Atlantic to move its freight as far west as Nashville and Louisville and eastward into Virginia. State operation of the road was a failure until Governor Joseph E. Brown began in 1857 to reorganize it. Three years later it was earning half a million dollars annually for the state. Since 1870 the road has been privately operated under lease

from the state, first by ex-Governor Brown, and since 1890 by the
Nashville, Chattanooga & St. Louis Railroad at an annual rental, since
1919, of $540,000.

Railroad development was seriously retarded during the War between the States, when tracks, stations, and equipment were destroyed
on a large scale in military operations. The post-war recovery was
rapid, however, even in the difficult times of Reconstruction. Demolished tracks were relaid, and new lines were constructed throughout the state. In 1938, thirty-nine railroad companies, including ten
trunk lines, were operating in Georgia on 6,700 miles of track, exclusive of sidings and yard trackage.

Highway construction and improvement, however, failed to keep
pace with railway development. Indeed, for many years the standard
of Georgia's highways was very low. Until 1908 convicts were leased
to private individuals or companies for work on railroads and other
enterprises. After the abolishment of the system in that year, the state
for a time used convict labor in road construction, but now uses it
only for the maintenance of highways. In 1916 the state prison board
began to serve also as a highway board. This arrangement was discontinued in 1919, when an independent highway board was created.

The first concrete highway in Georgia, an experimental five-mile
strip north of Griffin, was constructed in 1919. The through traffic to
Miami during the Florida boom did much to stimulate interest in improved highways, and soon roads were being paved throughout the
state. The gasoline tax was greatly increased, and in 1931 the highway board was spending more than half of the state's annual income.

Recent road development by the Civilian Conservation Corps and
the farm-to-market road program under the Works Progress Administration have done much to expand and improve intra-state highway transportation and consequently to raise the standard of living in
rural districts. At the end of 1936 nearly four thousand miles of rural
roads were either completed or under construction. Of more than
10,740 miles of highways in Georgia (including 20 U. S. highways),
44 per cent are paved. The principal bus and motor transport systems
follow virtually the same routes as the principal railways, and touch all
sections of the state.

For air, as well as for motor and railroad transportation, Atlanta is
the foremost traffic center of the Southeast. When two large air lines
simultaneously established routes through Georgia in 1927, they
selected Candler Field near Atlanta as the center of their operations.
Of Georgia's fifty-three airports, more than twenty are equipped with
beacons and field lights. Ten emergency landing fields are now maintained by the U. S. Civil Aeronautics Authority, and forty-five other
emergency landing fields have been developed by the W.P.A.

The Negro

THE GEORGIA colony, conceived primarily for the purpose of giving English debtors an opportunity to improve their economic condition by their own labor, did not at first permit slavery. By 1749, however, public sentiment had forced the authorities to remove the ban on slaveholding, and from that time the Negro population increased at a rapid rate.

In Georgia as a state, the number of Negroes reached its peak in 1880, when it represented 47 per cent of the total population. Because of the migration to northern and eastern cities, where opportunities for industrial employment were greater, the percentage has declined steadily since then; but Negroes still comprise almost 37 per cent of the population. The 1930 United States census showed 1,071,125 Negroes in Georgia, a larger number than in any other state.

The 50-per-cent increase in Atlanta's Negro population during the past decade is indicative of rapid urbanization, but more than 70 per cent of the total Negro population of the state is still rural. Most of it is concentrated in the old plantation section of middle Georgia and the coast, where Negroes outnumber the whites in some counties. Southwest Georgia, the last portion of the state to be settled, contains relatively few Negroes. Still fewer live in the mountainous region of north Georgia; there are none in Towns County and only a small number in the other counties of this area. In this mountainous land the people were never large slaveholders; and their strong prejudice against the Negro race, perhaps economic in origin, persists to the present.

Though the Negroes are a distinct and segregated group, they are not homogeneous ethnically. The original African slaves came from diverse tribes which varied in their degree of social development. The mingling of people from these tribes and widespread miscegenation has produced what may be considered a new race—Afro-American— which bears little or no relation to its African origin.

Christianity, with its biblical imagery and promise of a happier life in another world, provided an acceptable religion to the slaves, who adapted its concepts to their own needs with peculiar twists and modifications. The emotional fervor of the Baptists and Methodists, as well as their willingness to permit individual interpretation of the Bible, endeared them to the Negro, and consequently most of the Negro churches in Georgia are of the Baptist or Methodist denomination. According to the church census of 1926, there were 5,201 Negro churches in the state, of which 618 were urban with 236,145 members and 4,583 were rural with 401,948 members.

Negro labor has played an important part in the economic development of the state. The slaves, whose labor was chiefly utilized in the cultivation of cotton and rice, were closely supervised and controlled according to strict codes. Those who showed mechanical skill in iron-working, wagon-making, carpentry, or masonry commonly practiced these trades, and some even bought their freedom through such work. Indeed, skilled Negro labor reached such proportions that the white mechanics of Georgia protested, saying that the practice of trades made the blacks restless and unhappy. As a result, the state in 1845 passed an act forbidding all Negro mechanics, slave or free, to make contracts under penalty of a $200 fine.

After the War between the States, most of the freed slaves were at first employed as day laborers or tenants by their former masters. Later, when the plantations were broken into smaller units, the Negro worked with little or no direct supervision and paid a fixed share of his crop for the use of the land and a home. This change marked the beginning of opportunities for Negroes to buy land, although actual ownership has been severely limited by the state's economic and social pattern.

The records of the comptroller of Georgia from 1899 to 1926 give some indication of the general trend of Negro land ownership. The total of 1,062,223 acres owned by Negroes in 1899 had increased by 1920 to 1,839,129 acres, the largest amount of land ever under the control of Negroes in Georgia. Beginning in 1920 there was a steady decline, with a total loss of 351,141 acres in the succeeding six-year period; and the trend is still downward, though at a somewhat diminishing rate. In 1935 fewer than two per cent of the rural Negroes owned the farms they worked (see AGRICULTURE).

Most urban Negroes are either day laborers or house servants, although a considerable number find regular employment as waiters, bellboys, janitors, and in other more or less menial capacities. Low wages and restrictive practices of one sort or another force almost all of them to segregate in the least desirable sections of cities and towns. Some of the house servants still live under the sort of benevolent paternalism that not uncommonly marked the relations between master and slave in ante bellum days, and their lot is upon the whole better than that of many of their fellows.

The position of Negroes in industry has always been a submarginal one, white workers being given preference both in jobs and wages. In recent years group competition along racial lines has been intensified by the collapse of market farming, which has forced both white and black agricultural workers to seek industrial employment at a time of low production. In this situation the Negroes have suffered greatly, and in many cases they have been replaced by white workers even in the most menial tasks. In the summer of 1930 the Black Shirts, a Georgia organization of white laborers, threatened serious trouble by their demands against the employment of Negroes.

Because of economic discrimination and lack of capital, only a few Negroes have been successful in organizing business enterprises or in accumulating wealth. There are four Negro insurance companies in Georgia, and one bank is controlled and operated wholly by Negroes. In the field of smaller business enterprises, 2,099 retail establishments were being operated by Negroes in the highly prosperous year of 1929. These were principally restaurants and lunchrooms, filling stations, and cigar, drug, and grocery stores.

There were 4,986 Negroes engaged in professional services (including trained nursing) in 1930, according to the U. S. Census. The group included 2,056 clergymen, 86 college presidents and professors, 190 physicians, 59 dentists, 573 trained nurses, and 6 engineers. Many of these workers were educated in Georgia institutions founded to train Negroes for professional careers.

Negroes have no direct influence and virtually no part in Georgia politics. Most of them are virtually disfranchised by the white primary system and discriminatory party rules. In 1935 there were only 65,972 Negro poll-tax payers on the lists, as against 337,992 white poll-tax payers. Literacy is judged by the registrar, who may disqualify voters by means of tests left to his discretion. For all practical purposes, the primary system serves to disfranchise the Negro completely. Consequently Negroes hold no office in Georgia, although they are sometimes called for jury service.

Despite an earlier law prohibiting education for the Negro, clandestine classes were conducted by and for Negroes early in the nineteenth century. The most noted of the early schools for free Negro children was started in Savannah by a French Negro, Julien Froumontaine, about 1818. This school functioned openly until December, 1829, when the law making it a penal offense to teach a slave or free person of color to read and write was enforced. Froumontaine's school continued secretly for many years.

The first conference of white and Negro men in Georgia to make plans for educating Negroes met in Savannah in 1864. The convention decided to open schools for all who should apply, but it was difficult to find buildings. By December, 1865, however, Savannah Negroes had contributed $1,000 for the support of teachers and had opened a number of schools. The Negroes of the state organized an educational association in January, 1866, to foster the establishment and support of schools, and in the following year 191 day schools and 45 night schools were reported as functioning.

The constitution of 1868 made provision for state-supported elementary schools for Negroes. The practice of maintaining separate schools was embodied in the constitution of 1877, which stated that "separate schools shall be provided for the white and colored races." The Negro schools were generally of low grade, poorly equipped, and poorly staffed, and until recent years no effort was made to establish high schools. Although the illiteracy rate among Negroes in Georgia decreased from 92.1 per cent in 1870 to 19.9 per cent in 1930, discrimination against Negroes in respect to educational opportunities still exists. In 1930 Georgia spent an average of $35.42 a year for the schooling of each white child, while for the Negro the yearly expenditure was only $6.32 per child. In addition to common schools, the state maintains three colleges for Negroes.

Soon after the War between the States, Atlanta was selected by several missionary societies as an advantageous place in which to establish advanced schools for Negroes. Seven such institutions, providing excellent training in various fields, now make Atlanta the country's foremost center for the higher education of Negroes. Other Negro colleges are in Augusta, Macon, Savannah, and Albany.

The first Negro newspaper in Georgia, the *Colored American,* was begun in Augusta in 1865 with "no political battles to wage and nothing to promote but the intellectual and moral advancement of its constituents." This paper lasted only six months. The *Savannah Tribune,* established in 1875, is still in existence and is the oldest Negro paper in Georgia in point of continuous publication. The *Columbus Messenger* began as a weekly in 1887, changed to a semiweekly and finally to a daily, and was perhaps the first Negro daily in the South. The *Atlanta Independent,* founded in 1903, reached a circulation of 22,500 in the period from 1918 to 1927, and continued publication until 1932. At present, the *Atlanta World,* established in 1928, is the only daily newspaper entirely owned and operated by Negroes. Most of the white papers publish matter of special interest to Negroes, including releases by several regional and national Negro news agencies; and the *Macon Telegraph* publishes a special daily edition for Negroes.

The Negro frequently appears in Georgia police courts for petty violations of the law but seldom figures in serious crimes, most of his offenses being directly traceable to ignorance and poverty. Realizing this fact, governmental agencies are seeking to improve housing and sanitation in Negro sections of the larger cities, and to construct more schools, playgrounds, and libraries in such sections. Negro welfare organizations and institutions are now generally included in community chest budgets, and the aid of the more advanced Negroes is solicited in support of the indigent and otherwise unfortunate members of their race. Negro social workers are increasingly in demand, and play an important part in the state program for social work.

Health among Negroes has received attention in the past few years through the work of the state board of health, county health units, municipal health officers, and public nurses. The death rate is declining, although it is still higher than that of the white population. Hospital facilities are provided only in the larger cities and are inadequate not only for the care of patients but also for the training of doctors, since Negro physicians are not allowed to practice in white hospitals even where there are wards for Negro patients. Grady Hospital in Atlanta, however, gives medical attention to approximately one-third of the Negro population of the city each year, at a cost of more than $200,000, and offers training as nurses to Negro women.

The Commission on Interracial Cooperation, organized in Atlanta in 1919, has rendered effective service in advancing the welfare of Negroes in the state and throughout the South. The Association of Southern Women for the Prevention of Lynching, which was sponsored by this commission, has done much to arouse public sentiment against mob violence.

Religion

AFTER PEDRO MENENDEZ DE AVILES had established a garrison on St. Catherines Island in 1566, Spanish missions were set up along the coast of what is now Georgia, and for more than a century first the Jesuit and then the Franciscan priests of these missions made zealous efforts to convert the Indians to Christianity. It was not until 1686 that the Carolina English forced the Spanish to retreat south of St. Marys River, leaving the missions to crumble into ruins.

The royal charter granted to the "Trustees for establishing the Colony of Georgia in America" accorded to all except Roman Catholics the free exercise of religion within the colony, provided no ministrations were offensive to the government. Roman Catholics were excluded because it was feared that they would act as spies for the French in Louisiana and the Spanish in Florida. The persecuted Protestants of Europe were welcomed, and within six years after its founding the colony contained Swiss, German, Italian, Scottish Highlander, Salzburger, and Moravian settlers. The trustees, constantly solicitous for promoting religious thought and observance among the colonists, kept them supplied with catechisms, devotional exercises, Christian guides, and spiritual advisers.

Aboard the *Anne* in Oglethorpe's party of first settlers was the Reverend Henry Herbert, an Anglican clergyman, who served as the first minister and baptized the first child born in the colony. Temporary church quarters were found immediately, and on July 7, 1733, the colonists met before Oglethorpe's tent to select a site for their first religious edifice, Christ Church. In the following year, forty-two families of Salzburger Lutherans with their spiritual leader, John Martin Bolzius, settled at Ebenezer, where they established Jerusalem Church. A small party of Moravians landed at Savannah in 1735 and waited for twenty-five others, who in February, 1736, came over with Oglethorpe on his second voyage to America. Instead of proceeding to the land allotted them on the Ogeechee River, the Moravians remained in Savannah and set up a mission school for Indians at Irene.

Their pacifist principles debarred them from fighting against the Spanish and soon caused them to migrate to Pennsylvania and elsewhere. In the nineteenth century, Moravians from North Carolina established missions at Spring Place and New Echota for the Cherokee Indians of north Georgia.

On board ship with Oglethorpe and the Moravians in 1736 were the gifted brothers Charles and John Wesley, who were then ordained clergymen in the Church of England and later were identified with the founding of Methodism. After a month in Savannah, Charles went to Frederica on St. Simon Island, where he preached at Christ Church and acted as Oglethorpe's secretary. John remained in Savannah where he served as rector of the established church, translated German hymns, founded the first Sunday School on the banks of the Savannah River. and aided the Moravians in their mission work among the Indians. But Oglethorpe and the more worldly of the colonists were not sympathetic toward these two zealous clergymen. The hardships of life in the colony were great, and the Indians were unresponsive. Charles resigned within less than six months and returned to England, but the sterner John remained until the latter part of 1737. While in Georgia, John Wesley was closely associated with the Moravians, whose simple devotion modified his High Church views and notably influenced the direction of his later career.

The eloquent George Whitefield, another Church of England clergyman, arrived in Savannah on May 7, 1738. Having heard from Charles Wesley of the need in the colony for homes for orphan children, he visited the orphanage conducted by the Salzburgers at Ebenezer and after four months returned to England to raise funds for another such institution. While there he received an appointment as Anglican minister at Savannah, obtained a grant of 500 acres from the trustees, and collected £1,000 for his charitable enterprise. Upon his return to Savannah in January 1740 he rented temporary quarters for use as an orphanage and began the construction of a permanent home, which he called Bethesda. The maintenance of this institution required him to make five later voyages to England and to spend much time in itinerant preaching, which aroused fervent religious excitement along the Atlantic seaboard from New England to Georgia.

The Church of England's influence grew steadily in the colony until the Revolutionary period, when the American patriots closed the doors of its houses of worship and banished its preachers because of their British affiliation. Afterward, however, Georgia members united with those of other states to form the Protestant Episcopal church. So vigorous was the organization's growth in Georgia that in 1840, at a convention held in Grace Church, Clarkesville, the Episcopalians were of sufficient number to elect their own bishop, the Reverend Stephen Elliott. The church prospered until the War between the States, when it suffered from the fall of the landed gentry who constituted the greatest part of its membership. In 1907 the Episcopal organization in the state was divided into the Diocese of Georgia under Bishop Frederick F. Reese at Savannah and the Diocese of Atlanta under Bishop Cleland Kenloch Nelson. According to the latest U. S. census (*Religious Bodies: 1926*), the organization as a whole comprised 107 congregations with 19,888 members.

The first Presbyterian colonists in Georgia were Scottish Highlanders who came in 1735 with their minister, John McLeod, and settled at Darien, which they called New Inverness. Twenty years later some of their number petitioned for permission to build the Independent Presbyterian Church in Savannah. In 1752 a group of Massachusetts Puritans founded the church at Midway, and this organization, Congregational in polity but served by Presbyterian ministers, later counted among its members many prominent religious and political leaders of the state.

Presbyterian communities developed more rapidly toward the end of the eighteenth century. In 1785 the Reverend John Newton, the first Presbyterian evangelist to enter Georgia, established Beth-Salem near Lexington, and in 1790 the first ordination on Georgia soil took place when the Reverend John Springer was consecrated as a Presbyterian minister under a poplar tree in Washington, Georgia. Pioneer missionaries were sent by the Synods of New York and Philadelphia, and in 1825 the Domestic Missionary Society was organized to fill the needs of a sparsely settled land. Soon four men were preaching throughout the state and setting up camp-meeting sites, of which only Smyrna Campground near Conyers now remains. In 1845 the Synod of Georgia was formed and held its first meeting at Macon.

Throughout the first half of the nineteenth century the Presbyterian denomination retained the severe and rigorous attitude of the first Scottish settlers. One congregation protested against the installation of an organ because the Scripture did not authorize the "worship of God with machinery." Many Presbyterian churches distributed tokens a week in advance and collected them before the communion service in order to debar the unworthy from receiving the sacrament. Refusing to "make slaveholding a sin or nonslaveholding a term of communion," forty-seven southern presbyteries renounced their general assembly and appointed commissioners who met in Augusta on December 4, 1861, and formed the Presbyterian Church in the Confederate States of America. This group united in 1864 with another seceding body, the United Synod of the Presbyterian Church, and in the following year became the Presbyterian Church in the United States. In Georgia in 1926 this branch of the Presbyterian church had 250 churches with 29,675 members and the Presbyterian Church in the United States of America had 32 churches with 2,158 members.

Since the Presbyterian ministry has always had to meet high educational requirements, this denomination has strongly influenced the general culture of the state. As early as 1836 the Presbyterian Church established Oglethorpe College near Milledgeville. This school was closed in 1862, and efforts to refound it in Atlanta were not successful until 1913. Other schools founded by Presbyterians are Agnes Scott College and Columbia Theological Seminary in Decatur and Rabun Gap-Nacoochee School in the north Georgia mountains.

The Baptist denomination is now the largest in Georgia. Although a few Anabaptists landed with Oglethorpe, the greatest power of the Baptist church came later with emigration from other states. There was a small Baptist mission on the Savannah River in 1765, but it was not until 1772 that the first church, the Anabaptist Church of Kiokee, was organized by the Reverend Daniel Marshall near Appling. In this church five Baptist congregations organized in 1785 the Georgia Baptist Association, which nine years later included sixty churches with a membership of forty-five hundred—a number greater than that of any other denomination in the state at this time. To fill the places of leaders who had died, the Reverend Jesse Mercer and William Rabun called a meeting at Powelton on May 1, 1801,—the first of many conferences that brought together the ablest Baptist preachers in Georgia and carried the church forward in a steady growth.

Because the Foreign Mission Society would not accept slaveholders as missionaries the various southern state conventions met at Augusta in May, 1845, seceded from the American Baptist Union, and organized the Southern Baptist Convention. This schism on the issue of slavery, however, served only to vitalize the Baptist denomination, for fifteen years later the number of Baptists in the state had more than doubled.

Georgia's 814,148 Baptists in 1926 included 6,317 Free Will Baptists, 15,317 Primitive Baptists, and 400,560 Southern Baptists. The Primitive Baptist Church, formed in 1835 by the believers in extreme Calvinistic doctrine, flourishes chiefly in rural districts. Retaining many early religious practices, this "hard-shell" sect periodically observes the ceremony of foot-washing. The Baptist denomination as a whole is strongly rooted in urban as well as rural areas. In Atlanta, for example, there were more than 46,000 Baptist church members in 1926.

The best known Baptist institutions in Georgia are Mercer University at Macon, Shorter College at Rome, Bessie Tift College at Forsyth, the Baptist Orphans Home at Hapeville, and the Georgia

Baptist Hospital in Atlanta. The oldest continuously published church periodical in the South is the *Christian Index,* edited by the Georgia Baptist Convention in Atlanta.

The Methodist Episcopal Church has the second largest membership in the state. According to John Wesley, the second Methodist society in the world was organized in Savannah in the early Colonial period, but it was not until 1785 that the first seventy members were converted by an unknown preacher. So well suited to pioneer conditions was the Methodist itinerant system that Georgia soon became a church district, and Bishop Francis Asbury held the first Methodist Conference near Elberton in 1788. Because of "their revival services, class meetings, love feasts with closed doors, and stern rebukes of all sin," the Methodists aroused such an enthusiastic response that by 1806 there were 130 congregations with 5,000 members.

The early itinerant ministers—clean-shaven, short-haired, and wearing straight-cut coats and broad-brimmed hats—had to be men of fervid faith and powerful physique. Preaching every day but Monday, they traveled through rough and undeveloped country in order to serve the congregations of their large circuits. Their flocks were lavish with food and lodging but penurious in paying the minister, who rarely gave instruction in stewardship lest he be charged with preaching for money. At first a minister received 25 cents quarterly for each member of his congregation; this was later increased to an annual salary of $64 and still later to $84 for himself and a like amount for his wife. In his absence the pulpit was filled by one of the numerous local preachers, who supplemented their scant stipends with other work. The pastor, himself under severe discipline, was held responsible for enforcing attendance and throwing such fear into his flocks that all frivolity would be shunned. Conversion was scarcely orthodox unless accompanied by shouting; frequent public prayer was expected of all, and women were forbidden to wear frills or ribbons.

Because their ministers found it impracticable to hold evangelistic services at each of their numerous churches, Georgia Methodists adopted from Kentucky the custom of holding annual camp meetings. Gathering at a suitable location for the "camp," the people of a district would erect a stand for the preachers, with near-by log shacks for living quarters, and remain for a few days of sermons and psalm-singing. In time almost every county had one or more campgrounds where thousands attended annual revival meetings with services three or four times daily. The temporary stands were often replaced by permanent tabernacles, wooden shelters with open sides.

Although early Methodism appealed principally to humble folk, membership by 1830 included many leaders of the state, and among the ministers were such learned men as George F. Pierce and Ignatius Few. In 1831 the Georgia Conference of the Methodist Episcopal Church held its first annual session. The national General Conference in 1844 adopted a resolution, asking Bishop James O. Andrew, eminent Georgia preacher, to refrain from exercising his official duties as long as he owned slaves whom he had obtained by "inheritance and marriage." The issue thus raised with respect to slavery caused the Georgia Conference to secede from the national organization and join other southern conferences in forming the Methodist Episcopal Church, South. In 1886 the Georgia Conference of this body was divided into the North Georgia and South Georgia Conferences, which in 1926 comprised 1,620 churches with 249,722 members. In 1938 delegates to the General Conference of the Methodist Episcopal Church, South, voted for the unification of the three Methodist church organizations—the Methodist Episcopal Church, South, the Methodist Episcopal Church, and the Methodist Protestant Church. This unification was ratified at a convention held by the delegates of the three organizations at Kansas City, Missouri, in May, 1939, and the three branches of Methodism are now united under the name of the Methodist Church.

Georgia Methodists have long been interested in educational and social development. They maintain two colleges for women, Wesleyan and La Grange, five junior colleges, and (in co-operation with the general conference) Emory University in Atlanta and the Vashti School in Thomasville. A theological school is maintained by Emory University, and two hospitals and two orphanages in the state are under Methodist control.

The first Roman Catholics to be admitted into Georgia were Irish Redemptionists, who had pledged their services for a number of years to plantation owners and traders in return for passage to the new country. It is not known when the first Roman Catholic church was built, but as early as 1792 a small chapel stood in Liberty Ward, Savannah. Two years later a few Catholic refugees fled to Savannah from the massacres of Santo Domingo, and in 1796 settlers from Maryland established a church at a place called Locust Grove near Washington. By 1802 the number of Roman Catholics in Savannah had increased so greatly that the Church of St. John the Baptist was erected near Liberty Square. Georgia was made a separate diocese in 1850 with the Right Reverend Francis X. Gartland as bishop.

The Roman Catholic church in Georgia now functions principally in urban centers, Savannah having the largest number of members and Atlanta the next largest. Recently the Church of Christ the King in Atlanta has been elevated to equal rank with the Cathedral of St.

John the Baptist in Savannah as official seat of the Savannah-Atlanta Diocese. The religious census of 1926 showed 17,871 members for the state as a whole, with forty-nine urban and twenty-four rural churches. The Roman Catholics established their first academy in Savannah in 1845, and they now own five preparatory schools and two hospitals.

Although the trustees were wary of permitting any non-Christian sect to enter the colony, a group of Jewish people came to Savannah in 1733, and Oglethorpe on the advice of his lawyers allowed them to remain. Among the forty members of this group were Spanish and Portuguese Jews who had sought refuge in Holland. Bringing with them the Scroll of Laws and Ark of the Covenant, they soon set up in Market Square a house of worship called Mickve Israel. Later this congregation was augmented by German Jews sent to the colony as charity wards of Oglethorpe, and gradually the prevailing opposition diminished as the Jews quietly adapted themselves to the city's mercantile life. In 1820 they were sufficiently numerous to build a new synagogue in Savannah. As early as 1847, a group of twenty-five Jewish families was supporting a religious school in Atlanta; and during the War between the States the Hebrew Benevolent Society was formed in that city. On May 14, 1875, the members of this society laid the cornerstone of the first Jewish house of worship in Atlanta. The congregation, now occupying its third synagogue, the Temple, has been served since 1895 by Rabbi David Marx, whose scholarly and liberal mind has made him a power in civic and social betterment.

Although in 1826 Georgia had only 400 members of the Jewish faith, a century later there were 18,366 members organized into 22 congregations with 13 synagogues. Charitable and educational work is carried on through the Independent Order of B'nai B'rith, and hospitalization work in Palestine is promoted through Hadassah. Aid to the blind, regardless of religion, is offered by the Kriegshaber Memorial Lighthouse in Atlanta.

Many other religious denominations and sects are represented in Georgia, though their members are relatively few. The Congregational church, less prominent than in northern states, had only 3,469 members in Georgia in 1926, but has grown constantly more active. Piedmont College at Demorest, often cited as an example of intelligent economy in college organization, is supported by northern members of this church. Georgia members of the Lutheran faith numbered 5,759 in 1926. Throughout the rural sections are Holy Rollers, who express their religious impulses with emotional and physical freedom, and members of the more restrained Holiness sect, who congregate annually at Indian Springs for a two-weeks' service.

After the introduction of slavery into the state in 1749, northern churches sent white missionaries into Georgia to convert the Negroes to Christianity. But when local religious denominations became stronger, they admitted Negroes as members of their churches. The slaves, occupying galleries set apart, attended the services of their masters, for independent Negro congregations were suspected of breeding rebellion against white authority.

Soon after the Revolution a few independent Negro churches were established in the North, but Georgia has two that antedate any of these. The Springfield Baptist Church of Augusta was organized by members of the Silver Bluff Baptist Church, near Augusta in South Carolina. When the white members of that church moved into a new building in 1773, they allowed their Negro slaves to use the old edifice for worship. Dispersed by the Revolution, the Negro congregation was reorganized at Augusta in 1793. Andrew Bryan, a slave, instituted in 1775 a prayer meeting in the barn of his master's Brampton Plantation near Savannah. With the aid of Jesse Peters, a Negro preacher, and the Reverend Abraham Marshall, a white Baptist minister, Bryan was able in 1788 to organize at Savannah the First African Baptist Church.

Most of the Negroes continued to worship with their masters, and by 1830 about six thousand slaves were listed on the rolls of the Methodist Episcopal Church alone. Their number increased until after emancipation, when they joined other Methodist bodies that had already established separate churches for them. In 1870 they combined with the Negro Methodists from other states in forming the Colored Methodist Episcopal Church.

With improved educational facilities for Negroes, many of their churches have developed a more restrained form of worship and a deeper sense of social responsibility. Negroes in Georgia are affiliated with about twenty-five religious bodies, but the majority are either Baptists or Methodists; in 1926 there were 391,954 Negro Baptists and 135,650 Negro Methodists. Widespread denominational interest in Negro education is indicated by four schools maintained for Negroes by the Methodists, three by the Baptists, and one by the Presbyterians.

In recent years certain religious cults have attained some popularity among Georgia Negroes. In Augusta and in Savannah Bishop Grace's House of Prayer has a devout though not extensive following, and Father Divine, who was born in Savannah, numbers some Georgia Negroes among the members of his Peace Mission. One of the many lesser known religious organizations in the state is a Moslem sect in Augusta, of more than 150 Negroes. This sect is attempting to convert all local Negroes to Mohammedanism, in the belief that all American

Negroes were originally Asiatics and that Mohammedanism is their rightful religion.

That fully half the people of Georgia belong to religious denominations is the result of two centuries of strenuous labor. So difficult was the task of founding churches in this wild land that in 1831, almost a century after the arrival of the first little band of settlers, only a tenth of the state's inhabitants had become affiliated with any church. In 1926, more than fifty denominations in Georgia listed 10,898 churches with 1,350,184 members and 567,449 Sunday school pupils.

Education

WITH THE presentation of a thousand spelling books to James Edward Oglethorpe by James Leake in January, 1732, the first step was taken toward public education in Georgia. This gift, antedating the departure from England of the first colonists, was followed by other donations; and before Oglethorpe sailed in November of the same year, the trustees of the new colony possessed more than two thousand volumes as the nucleus of a public library.

The trustees, who had received contributions for educational purposes from missionary bodies such as the Society for the Propagation of the Gospel in Foreign Parts, arranged with the Reverend Benjamin Ingham to accompany the original settlers as the colony's first teacher. Later, at the request of the practical-minded Oglethorpe, who realized the inadequacy of Ingham's catechistic instruction, the trustees sent Charles Delamotte to the colony as the first in a succession of secular schoolmasters.

In 1734 Lutheran emigrants from Salzburg settled at Ebenezer and immediately established the first two schools in which German was the principal language to be used for more than fifty years. Members of the Moravian religious sect arrived in 1735 and 1736 and built a three-room schoolhouse at Irene. But the most successful of Georgia's early educational institutions was at the "orphan house" Bethesda, founded near Savannah in 1740 by George Whitefield, noted preacher, and James Habersham, acting Colonial Governor. During the winter of 1746-47 a "Latin school" was established at Bethesda, and in 1764 Whitefield petitioned Governor James Wright for a charter to elevate the institution to college rank. Approved by the Colonial assembly, the petition was sent to the English authorities, who wanted the head of the proposed institution to be an Anglican clergyman. Whitefield, who believed that such a stipulation would not be pleasing to the colonists, let the petition drop. The institution was bequeathed to the Countess of Huntingdon upon Whitefield's death in 1770. Two years later the Countess sent students from her seminary in Wales to serve as teachers at Bethesda, which she tried unsuccessfully to convert into a mission school for the training of evangelists. Under the auspices of the state, an academy was established at Bethesda in 1788.

In 1743 the common council of Savannah passed a resolution to establish a free school, with a salary of £20 a year for a teacher; and a similar school was opened in Augusta. But since the Colonial assembly made no provision for education, these institutions were left to exist as best they could on local support. When Georgia became a royal province in 1752, there was enough wealth in the colony to establish and maintain private schools, and throughout the rest of the Colonial period education was chiefly a luxury limited to those who could afford it.

Recognizing the need for systematized public education, the authors of the original state constitution (1777) inserted a clause providing that "schools shall be erected in each county and supported at the general expense of the state, as the legislature shall hereafter point [out] and direct." Each of the state-supported schools thus authorized was given land for a campus and was endowed with 1,000 acres of land. The academies of Richmond, Wilkes, and Burke counties, chartered in 1783, were the first of many county academies to be established. In 1792 the land endowment was changed to £1,000 secured from the sale of confiscated Tory property.

Offering instruction to both boys and girls in elementary and high school courses, the academies stressed Latin, Greek, English, and mathematics, and classes in these subjects were taught by learned men. Georgia, although founded as a colony to give employment to poor Englishmen, thus adopted the traditional system of classical education. After 1821 these academies received in the aggregate an annual sum of $20,000, the income from $250,000 set aside as an "academic fund." Although this sum was greater than any similar appropriation made by other states, it was not sufficient; the schools were forced to operate as private institutions and to rely on tuition fees, usually $10 a quarter. In 1837 all state aid was discontinued, but the academies continued to function. In 1838 there were 166 county academies with 10,145 pupils.

Considering an institution of higher learning "as necessary to the public prosperity and even existence of a free people," the legislature, on February 25, 1784, set aside 40,000 acres of public land to endow a college and appointed a board of trustees. As a result the University of Georgia was granted a charter on January 27, 1785, but it was not until 1801 that the institution was opened in Athens. Although one other (the University of North Carolina) was in operation earlier, this was the first state university to be chartered in America. According to its charter, all state-aided schools in Georgia were considered members of the university, and the supervision of all public educational activities within the state was vested in a board of visitors and a board of trustees, which together formed the "Senatus Academicus." Because of public indifference this system never functioned effectively and was finally removed from the statute books in 1859.

The rural sections of the state endeavored to meet their educational needs with small elementary institutions called Old Field schools, established jointly by patrons and teachers and conducted without state or county control. The buildings were log cabins, and the poorly qualified teachers frequently moved from one school to another. From sunrise to sundown the children, often studying aloud, were taught "reading, writing, and the usual rules of arithmetic." Textbooks were scarce, and instruction was principally a matter of memory and drill work directed toward the pupils' making a good showing at the annual "exhibitions." In 1850 there were 3,000 Old Field schools in Georgia.

In 1817 the legislature appropriated $250,000 for aiding elementary education and in 1821 increased this amount to $500,000. The income from this fund was to be used in paying the tuition of children whose parents were unable to bear the expense of educating them. Schools receiving this aid were known as "poor schools." No child whose parents paid a tax exceeding fifty cents, in addition to the poll tax, could participate in the fund's benefits. Children from eight to eighteen years of age were permitted to go to any convenient school that would receive them for the small tuition fee allowed and were taught only elementary subjects. The school period was limited to three years and the school day to three hours. Children attended school for only four months of the year, and teachers received as compensation seven cents a day for each pupil.

Since many of the children who took advantage of this plan attended the Old Field schools, these institutions mark the beginning of Georgia's public educational system. A few cities, such as Savannah in 1818 and Augusta in 1821, and a few counties, such as Glynn in 1823 and Emanuel in 1824, established separate schools for needy children, but the state made no effort to found such institutions.

In 1837 a more ambitious scheme of free education, sponsored by Alexander H. Stephens, was adopted. A "common school" fund, composed of the "academic fund," the "poor school fund," and about $350,000 of the "surplus revenue" obtained from the Federal government in 1836, was allocated to provide schools for all white children in the state and books for the needy. But the expense involved in this plan alarmed the legislators, who repealed the act in 1840. Unspent appropriations reverted to the "poor school" fund, and the stigma of charity was still attached to tax-paid education.

Through the influence of Governor Joseph E. Brown, $100,000 of annual income from the state-owned Western & Atlantic Railroad was added in 1858 to the school fund for instruction in elementary branches. With this legislation the word "poor" disappeared from the statute books, and local school systems were authorized. It was not until 1860, however, that the first free county schools for all classes were established; these were in Gordon and Gilmer counties. So, along with the state system, there grew up a series of special schools regulated and controlled by local laws. Chatham County in 1866 was followed by the cities of Columbus, in 1866, and Atlanta, in 1870; and soon all the larger towns and many counties had local systems.

In the decade following 1830 "manual labor schools" were sponsored by various churches and private groups. These were not trade schools but academies where young men could pay in part for their tuition by working, usually three hours a day and five days a week, on the school farm. Of ten such schools established in Georgia, three developed into colleges that are prominent today. Mercer Institute, opened at Penfield in 1833, later became Mercer University; the Georgia Conference Manual Labor School, begun at Covington in 1835, was later incorporated as Emory College, now Emory University; and Midway Seminary, opened near Milledgeville in 1835, developed into Oglethorpe University.

The first academies to admit students of both sexes offered a classical education, but as a rule the girls studied "moral and intellectual philosophy," geography, and the history of music. In the 1830's so many girls were in attendance that educators felt the need of separate female academies, and wealthy planters demanded better institutions for the education of their daughters. Many of the women's academies that sprang up throughout the state were short-lived, for a strenuous pioneer society could not give continuous support to such genteel enterprises. One that has lasted for more than a century is La Grange College, established in 1831 as La Grange Female Academy. The Georgia Female College, under Methodist auspices, was established at Macon in 1836; this institution, which later became Wesleyan College, was the first college in the world chartered to grant degrees exclusively to women. Bessie Tift College was founded in 1847 as the Monroe Female College.

Many of Georgia's private and semiprivate educational institutions were permanently closed as a result of the War between the States. After the war a general movement for state-supported schools resulted in a legislative act in December, 1866, providing for a "complete system of Georgia schools." A state superintendent of schools was to be appointed by the governor, and teachers were to be examined and certified. This act never came into effect, however, for during reconstruction the state government was taken from the hands of native citizens.

The carpetbagger Constitution of 1868 provided that Georgia should have "a thorough system of general education to be forever free to all children of the State." The State Teachers Association, organized in 1867, was instrumental in persuading the legislature to pass an adequate educational law; and J. R. Lewis was appointed state commissioner to supervise a system of free schools in which white and Negro children should be taught separately. Lewis was soon replaced by Gustavus Orr, who was so successful in this work that he is often referred to as "the father of the Georgia free school system." When control of the state government reverted to native white citizens in 1877, a new constitution once more declared for a thorough system of common schools.

It was fortunate that numerous local systems had been established, because the makers of the Constitution of 1877 (the seventh and last to be adopted) were not sure that the state owed its children a well-rounded education. They provided for county taxation and state aid for instruction in the "elementary branches of an English education only"; the only concession to higher education was for donations to the University of Georgia. Thus, outside the larger towns and cities, there was no connecting link in the state educational system between the elementary schools and the colleges. In the ensuing quarter-century the need for such a link became so pressing that, in 1903, the state university appointed Joseph S. Stewart as a special agent to encourage the establishment of high schools by municipal initiative and support. Through his efforts, Georgia was one of the first states in the Union to adopt an accrediting system for its university. The state constitution was amended in 1910 to permit county taxation for the support of high schools, but it was not until 1912 that these schools became a part of the state's public educational system.

Georgia was equally slow to finance its institutions of higher education other than the state university. The North Georgia Agricultural College, now North Georgia College, was opened at Dahlonega in 1873 as a land-grant school under a Congressional act of 1862, which donated land to the states to provide colleges for training in the agricultural and mechanical arts. As the need arose for specialized colleges in other sections of the state, some of the post-war politicians who were cautiously attentive to the demands of their local constituents

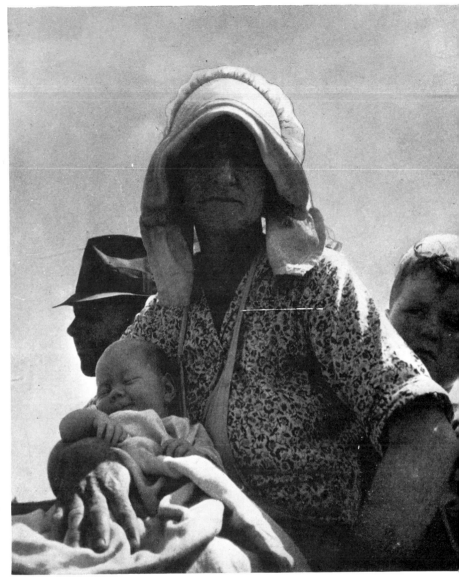

SHARECROPPER FAMILY

COTTON—GEORGIA'S FIRST CROP

WEIGHING COTTON AT THE GIN

CHOPPING COTTON

PICKING COTTON

TOBACCO IN THE FIELD

TOBACCO AT THE BARN

SATURDAY AFTERNOON

SHARECROPPER CABIN

MODERN FARMHOUSE, IRWINVILLE FARMS RESETTLEMENT PROJECT

CORN—GEORGIA'S SECOND CROP

PEACH PICKING, NEAR MACON

devised a plan for establishing such colleges as branches of the state university, thus securing state sponsorship and support. Each institution, with its own board of trustees and president, was to be connected loosely with the others by a parent board. Under this plan the Georgia School of Technology was opened at Atlanta in 1888; the Georgia Normal and Industrial College, now the Georgia State College for Women, at Milledgeville in 1891; and the State Normal School, now Co-ordinate College, at Athens in 1895. Dissatisfaction with the agricultural and mechanical department at the university led to the establishment of the Georgia State College of Agriculture as a separate institution in 1906. The new institution was located in Athens on a site adjacent to the university but was given a separate administrative organization. For preliminary work in agriculture and mechanic arts the legislature created a system of agricultural and mechanical schools, establishing one in each congressional district of the state.

Reverting in part to the original centralized plan for the control of its colleges, Georgia adopted in 1931 a reorganization bill that abolished the local boards of trustees and organized the University System of Georgia, vesting control in a board of regents—a new "Senatus Academicus." The seventeen distinct units of this system include the University of Georgia at Athens, in which are combined the Co-ordinate College and the State College of Agriculture; the Georgia School of Technology at Atlanta; the Georgia State College for Women at Milledgeville; and three Negro institutions—The Georgia Normal and Agricultural College at Albany, the State Teachers and Agricultural College at Forsyth, and the Georgia State College near Savannah. The agricultural and mechanical schools that had been established in each congressional district were either abolished or converted into junior colleges. In 1937, eight junior colleges were being supported by the state, five by churches, two by cities, and one by private enterprise.

Public education for Negroes presented no problem to pre-war Georgia, inasmuch as a law was passed in 1770 forbidding their being taught to read and write. Despite this law, however, some slaves surreptitiously received a rudimentary education. After the abolition of slavery, the Freedmen's Bureau and various missionary and betterment societies established private schools for Negroes, but not until after the Constitution of 1868 had been adopted was public education permitted for them. The Constitution of 1877 requires separate schools to be maintained for white and Negro children, and there are now 3,425 elementary and secondary schools for Negroes in Georgia, most of them one-teacher schools. These are supervised by the state division of Negro education, which also serves as a medium through which philanthropic agencies may render aid.

Soon after the War between the States, a movement was initiated for the creation of higher educational institutions for Negroes. The American Missionary Association took the initiative in this movement by founding Atlanta University in 1865; the Baptists organized Augusta Institute, now Morehouse College, in 1867; and the Freedmen's Aid Society of the Methodist Episcopal Church founded Clark University in 1870. Miss Sophia B. Packard and Miss Harriett E. Giles opened Spelman College in 1881. Morris Brown University was begun in 1885 by Negro Methodists; Paine College was established by southern Methodists in 1883; and the Fort Valley Normal and Industrial College was founded in 1896 by the American Church Institute, affiliated with the Episcopal Church. Georgia's present institutions for the higher education of Negroes comprise nine colleges, a graduate school, and a social service training institute. Atlanta University, Morehouse College, and Spelman College were affiliated in 1929 to provide an inclusive program of university activities for Negro men and women. Atlanta is now the world's largest center for Negro education.

Most of the early denominational colleges for white students were continued after the war, and a number of new institutions were chartered. The Baptists established at Rome in 1873 the Cherokee Female College, which became Shorter College in 1877, and at Gainesville in 1878 the Georgia Baptist Seminary, now Brenau College. The congregation of the Decatur Presbyterian Church in 1889 founded the Decatur Female Seminary, which later became Agnes Scott College, one of the state's outstanding colleges for women.

Of special interest are several schools established in north Georgia during the present century to provide educational facilities for the boys and girls of this sparsely settled mountain region. Comparable to the nineteenth-century "manual labor schools," these institutions enable students to pay for their tuition by farming and by domestic work. Miss Martha Berry opened the first of these schools in a log cabin near Rome in 1902. The famous Berry Schools now comprise four units on an extensive campus and receive students not only from rural Georgia but from many other states. The Tallulah Falls Industrial School, established by the Georgia Federation of Women's Clubs in 1909 to stimulate interest in mountain arts and crafts, is still supported by that organization. The Rabun Gap-Nacoochee School, including a junior college department, was founded under Presbyterian auspices in 1920 and is supported by state and Federal funds as well as by private donations. At Ways, in south Georgia, Henry Ford has established an experimental crafts and trades school similar to the one at Dearborn, Michigan.

The National Vocational Education Act of 1917 was sponsored by two Georgians, Senator Hoke Smith and Representative Dudley Hughes. Since the adoption of this act, vocational courses have become increasingly prominent in the state's secondary schools. With the aid of Federal funds, the division of vocational education has become responsible for the introduction of courses in agriculture and home economics, trade and industrial education, and vocational rehabilitation in schools throughout the state.

In recent years the Works Progress Administration has assisted in providing Georgia with many new or rehabilitated school buildings. It has also organized and maintained numerous courses for young and old in general and vocational education, as well as in such special subjects as public affairs, homemaking, safety, and first aid, and has offered instruction for the deaf and blind. The broad vocational work includes training in business, agriculture, domestic service, sewing, cooking, millinery, and the native arts and crafts. Negroes are given special attention in general and vocational instruction. Forty-seven per cent of the W.P.A. teachers are Negroes, and 78 per cent of these give instruction in reading and writing.

Because of its inadequate public education laws, Georgia has always had a large percentage of illiteracy; but the compulsory school law of 1916 and various programs of adult education have done much to improve the situation during the past two decades. Among white inhabitants the illiteracy rate has been reduced from 27 per cent in 1870 to 3.3 per cent in 1930, and among Negroes from 56.4 per cent in 1900 to 19.9 per cent in 1930. The percentage for the state population as a whole was 9.4 in 1930 as compared with 15.3 in 1920. Through adult education classes of the W.P.A., from its beginning in July, 1935, up to March, 1937, 14,785 white and 28,632 Negro pupils were taught to read and write.

The Georgia school system, long fettered by inadequate and conflicting laws and lack of revenue, lagged behind that of many other states. Promises of educational advancement, however, are evident in recent progressive enactments. The state now allots 30 per cent of its total revenue to educational purposes, and this fund is disbursed to the counties on an equalization basis, but in no county does the state contribution provide for more than 50 per cent of the total school expenses. The law of 1910 permits any county to vote a tax not exceeding five mills on the dollar as an additional means of maintenance, yet in 1930 Georgia spent an average of only $35.42 for each white and $6.38 for each Negro pupil in the state. It is hoped that increased appropriations will improve the quality of education in Georgia's 6,149 elementary and secondary schools, where more than 700,000 children are taught by 20,781 teachers. Although the number of small and inefficient schools has been reduced by consolidation, there are still many unaccredited schools.

In 1937 the state legislature passed a law fixing a minimum term of seven months for all schools and providing for free text books for pupils in all grades and for reorganization of the state board of education to administer the enlarged program. This law helps to equalize conditions that have given some children the advantage of good schools with a term of nine months and restricted others to inferior schools with a term as short as three months.

Sports and Recreation

THE AVERAGE American reader of the sports section in his daily newspaper is likely to think of Georgia chiefly as the home state of Bobby Jones, Charlie Yates, Ty Cobb, and Bryan Grant. But the exploits of a few "native sons" who have won fame as amateur or professional performers make up but a very small part of the complete story of sports and recreational activities in Georgia. From the days when the Indians played a game that was a mixture of American football, soccer, and lacrosse and the white pioneers depended for their amusement chiefly upon wrestling, boxing, and cock-fighting, there has been an ever increasing interest in sports as something to be participated in not merely by a few experts but by the great mass of the people. This interest has gained immense impetus in recent years, when Federal aid has enabled many urban and rural communities to set up adequate public facilities for sports and recreation, including athletic fields, playgrounds, swimming pools, and the like.

From mid-March until well into October, the climate of Georgia is ideal for such outdoor sports as baseball, swimming, and tennis, while golfing and riding are popular throughout the year in most sections. Georgia's greatly varied topographical features, ranging from highlands to seashore, from swift mountain streams to sluggish lowland rivers, from pine forests to swamps and marshlands, provide an equal variety of recreational activities.

All sections of the state provide excellent hunting. In south Georgia, especially near Thomasville, many large estates with private preserves have been established. Bird hunting attracts the largest number of sportsmen. Many Georgians own trained pointers and setters that are entered each spring in the Southeastern Field Trials at Albany, a competition attended by some of the best dog handlers with the finest bird dogs in the country. Quail abound throughout the state, particularly in the southern and central regions. This is Georgia's principal game bird, but there are also wild turkeys in the southern area, geese in the Savannah River basin, woodcock and jacksnipe near any boggy lands, and marsh hens in the coastal swamps. Thirty species of duck have been identified near the small lakes of Georgia, and in the northern section there are ruffed grouse, now so rare that they are under legal protection.

The chief game mammals are the rabbit, opossum, raccoon, bobcat, gray squirrel, fox squirrel, and gray fox. Deer, although most plentiful on private preserves of the coastal islands, are hunted in the southern pine belt. They had become extinct in the north Georgia highlands, where they were once abundant, but the Chattahoochee National Forest has been restocked recently, and here the deer are under legal protection until 1940.

Hunting is so popular in Georgia that even the poorest farmer usually keeps a few coon and possum hounds. Fox hunting is common in the north Georgia mountains; unlike the English hunt of pink coats, hounds, and horns, it is here a hillbilly sport, in which the dogs are loosed at dawn and the fox is trailed up mountainsides, across streams, and over fences. The mountaineers enjoy the chase, rather than the catch, and usually let the fox get away so that they may hunt it again. The possum hunt, popular in autumn, is a night sport, the hunting being done with torches and flashlights. When the dogs have treed the possum the hunters flash their lights in its eyes, and the frightened animal clings to its perch until the hunters shake it down or climb up and bag it.

The angler has a wide choice of opportunities in Georgia, ranging from fresh-water fishing in the northern lakes to deep-sea fishing off the Atlantic coast. Small-mouthed black bass, goggle-eyed perch, and rainbow, speckled, and brook trout are plentiful in the Toccoa, Tallulah, and upper Chattahoochee rivers, in Lake Blue Ridge, and in the six lakes constructed by the Georgia Power Company for electric power production. The waters of middle and south Georgia contain jackfish, perch, pike, and speckled, channel, and mud catfish. Bream and large-mouthed black bass are found in streams and lakes all over the state. In spring the shad run the lower courses of the Satilla, Altamaha, Ogeechee, and St. Marys rivers. Fishermen along the coast make good catches of such salt-water fish as red snapper, drum, sheepshead, flounder, mullet, redfish, and sea bass. Shrimp, oysters, and especially crabs are also abundant in coastal waters. Wire baskets baited with raw meat can be rented at beach resorts for crabbing; and at Savannah, St. Simon, Darien, and Brunswick, yachts can be chartered for deep-sea fishing. State and Federal hatcheries supply the trout, bass, and bream with which lakes and streams are constantly restocked.

Golf has been played in Georgia since 1736, when Scottish settlers introduced the game at Darien. As far back as the late eighteenth century there was at least one golf club in the state, as evidenced by a notice in the *Georgia Gazette* of September 22, 1796, announcing the annual meeting of the Savannah Golf Club, an organization that is still in existence. Throughout Georgia many courses are open to the public at small greens fees, and there are about 150 private clubs. The widespread popularity of the game throughout the state in recent years is due in no small degree to the influence of Bobby Jones, of Atlanta, internationally famed as the "greatest golfer of all time" and "grand slam" winner of the American Amateur, American Open, British Amateur, and British Open tournaments in a single year. Georgia has produced other noted players: Charlie Yates, a member of the Walker Cup Team in 1936 and 1938 and winner of the British Amateur Tournament in 1938; Alexa Stirling, women's national champion in 1916, 1919, and 1920; and Howard Wheeler, winner of the Negro national golf championship in 1938.

Private and municipal tennis courts are common throughout the state and tennis squads of colleges and high schools compete in regional and state tournaments. In March of every year the South Atlantic States Tournament is held at Augusta, and exhibition matches featuring the country's leading players are held regularly in Atlanta. Georgia's best known tennis player is Bryan ("Bitsy") Grant, who won the national clay courts championship in 1930, 1934, and 1935, achieved third place in the national ratings in 1936, and in 1937 was a member of the Davis Cup Team.

In addition to the sand-lot variety of baseball and softball, played nearly everywhere in Georgia, few towns of any size lack baseball fields where teams representing social, civic, religious, or business organizations vie in amateur competition. The outstanding professionals are the Atlanta Crackers of the Southern Baseball Association, a Class A league composed of teams from the larger southern cities. Macon and Savannah teams play in the Class B Southeastern League, and several of the smaller towns are represented in the Georgia-Florida and Georgia-Alabama leagues. Tyrus Raymond ("Ty") Cobb, of Augusta, known to millions as "the Georgia Peach," was an outstanding figure in major-league baseball for twenty-one years. In 1905 he joined the Detroit Tigers, led the American League in batting for twelve years, and served as manager of the club during the last five years of his professional career.

As a spectator sport, football is only slightly less popular than baseball. College, high school, and preparatory school games draw large crowds. The two best known teams are the Georgia School of Technology Yellow Jackets and their traditional rivals, the University of Georgia Bulldogs; both of these play most of their schedules in the state, with a few important games in other parts of the country. In 1929 the Yellow Jackets won national renown by defeating the University of California in the Rose Bowl game at Pasadena.

Swimming, basketball, track sports, and boxing also hold a more or less prominent place among athletic activities; and in some of these, individual Georgia athletes have achieved national or even international fame. Forrest ("Spec") Towns, of the University of Georgia, won the hurdles championship at the 1936 Olympics. An Atlanta Negro, Ralph Harold Metcalf, considered one of the fastest runners in the world, equaled or bettered world track and field records in the Olympics of 1932, 1933, and 1936. Louisa Robert was national junior back-stroke swimming champion in 1932. The names of W. L. ("Young") Stribling, one-time contender for the world's heavyweight boxing championship, and "Tiger" Flowers, famous Negro pugilist, are prominent in the annals of prize-fighting.

For the horseman and horsewoman, there are riding clubs in various communities and many bridle trails in and near the larger towns. Along these trails the rider can enjoy a wide variety of scenic interest and beauty—the rolling wooded country around Atlanta and Augusta, the salt-water marshes and semitropical woodland near Savannah, the magnificent winter estates and large hunting preserves at Thomasville, the moss-hung live oaks and cypresses along the Flint River at Albany, the luxuriant growths of palmettos and oleanders at Sea Island. The Atlanta Horse Show Association sponsors an annual exhibition and competition in May.

The average Georgian is not very enthusiastic about hiking, but many hikers and campers tramp the foot trails of the highlands. The Appalachian Trail, which begins at Mount Katahdin in Maine and ends at the foot of Mount Oglethorpe in Georgia, is known to all hikers. At intervals along this well-marked route are log shelter-huts for overnight camping and vantage points for panoramic views of the mountain country.

In recent years the development of state parks has been undertaken with the aid of Federal funds and private donations, and there are now nine such parks. Indian Springs, Santo Domingo, Alexander H. Stephens, and Jefferson Davis parks are established on sites of historical interest; Chehaw, Fort Mountain, Little Ocmulgee, Pine Mountain, and Vogel parks were created because of the natural beauty and recreational possibilities of their areas. With the exception of Jefferson Davis Park, which is solely a historical memorial, all have foot trails, winding drives, and picnic grounds equipped with shelters, outdoor stoves and tables. Several have lakes for boating and swimming and furnished cabins with convenient equipment. Stone inns have been built as recreational headquarters in most of the parks.

The Federal government has established three recreational demonstration areas in Georgia: Alexander H. Stephens Memorial Recreational Demonstration Area, Pine Mountain Recreational Demonstration Area, and Hard Labor Creek Recreational Demonstration Area. These areas provide lakes for swimming and boating and cabins available for use by organized camping groups. In the Chattahoochee National Forest, containing more than 500,000 acres, picnic areas and camp sites are maintained and provided with sanitary facilities, protected water, and firewood. Hunting and fishing are permitted in some sections of the forest.

In June 1938 the Georgia Department of Natural Resources announced a program for adding several new parks. Two of these, Fort King George and Kolomoki Mound, will occupy sites of historical interest; the remaining, including Sitton's Gulch, Black Mountain, Little Tybee Island, Lakeside, Old Mill, and Winona Wayside, will be developed in areas of exceptional scenic beauty. The department also plans to develop a natural resource reservation of 1,000 acres or more in each county, to be used for forestry demonstration, a wild life preserve, and a recreation area.

Press and Radio

"Moscow: Nov. 15. The Empress keeps her apartments, not through illness but precaution." Thus reads the first news item in the first issue of Georgia's first newspaper. This irrelevant item referred to Catherine the Great and the newspaper was the *Georgia Gazette*, which made its appearance in Savannah on April 7, 1763.

During the preceding thirty years of its existence the colony had depended for its news on the South Carolina papers, supplemented by the accounts of sailors and adventurers who, since they usually spread their tidings at the village tavern, were frequently more entertaining than accurate. Thus a genuine need was filled by the *Gazette*, a small folded sheet of four pages, with two closely printed columns to the page. The editor, James Johnston, suspended publication in 1765 because of difficulties about the Stamp Act tax, but he revived it after seven months. This newspaper followed the tendency of early periodicals in becoming a political organ, and in 1774 it issued a call for "lovers of liberty" to convene for the consideration of Parliamentary acts depriving American subjects of their political rights.

Discontinued because of the Revolution, the paper reappeared in new guise during the British occupation of Savannah in 1779, when John Hammerer issued it as the *Royal Georgia Gazette,* counter-Revolutionary in policy. Within a few months it was taken over by its original editor, the ambitious Johnston, who retained its pro-British sympathies. It failed in the following year; but Johnston, whose political convictions seemed adaptable to all circumstances, revived it in 1783 as the *Gazette of the State of Georgia,* in recognition of Georgia's newly acquired statehood. After five years it again became known as the *Georgia Gazette* and, except for an interruption during the great fire of 1796, it continued publication until November, 1802.

Other journals sprang up in the late eighteenth century, but all were short-lived with the exception of one. The *Augusta Chronicle,* oldest active newspaper in the South, first appeared in 1785 and has had continuous publication since that year. The masthead of early issues carried the following: "Georgia. The Augusta Chronicle and Gazette of the State. Freedom of the press and trial by jury shall remain inviolate. Printed by John E. Smith, printer to the State. Essays, articles of intelligence and advertisements will be gratefully received and every kind of printing performed." In the columns of the *Chronicle,* Georgia's progress can be traced from almost the beginning of statehood to the present day.

During the prosperous first half of the nineteenth century, Georgia newspapers reshaped political policies, caused new towns to grow, and powerfully influenced rural economy. Some of the editors, who often were local politicians, later became distinguished in other fields. In Milledgeville the *Southern Recorder* was established in 1819, and the *Federal Union,* in 1825; these were combined in 1872 to form the *Union Recorder,* Georgia's oldest existing weekly. Myrom Bartlett, a fearless editorial writer, inaugurated the *Macon Telegraph* three years after the founding of the city. The first attempt to establish a daily newspaper in the state was made by Bartlett in 1831, when he issued his paper as a daily for two months. Mirabeau Buonaparte Lamar, later president of the Republic of Texas, instituted the *Columbus Enquirer* in 1828. The *Athens Banner-Herald* can be traced to the *Athenian,* begun in 1828 and renamed the *Banner* six years later. In 1850, William Tappan Thompson, author of the humorous *Major Jones's Courtship* (1840), launched the *Savannah Morning News,* which became financially successful and politically powerful. At the middle of the century, Georgia had fifty-one newspapers, including five dailies.

The few early periodicals that appeared in the state were of a religious or otherwise specialized character. Two in the denominational field have been familiar in Baptist or Methodist homes for more than a century. In 1833 the noted pioneer preacher, Jesse Mercer, bought the *Christian Index,* which for twelve years previously had been published in Philadelphia, and transferred it to Washington, Georgia, where he served as its editor for seven years before turning it over to the Georgia Baptist Convention. The *Wesleyan Christian Advocate,* the official organ of the Methodist Church in Georgia, was founded in Charleston, South Carolina, in 1836 as the *Southern Christian Advocate;* its present name was adopted when the publication offices were moved to Macon in 1865. *The Southern Cultivator,* established in Augusta in 1842, maintained uninterrupted publication throughout the War between the States and remained in existence until 1935. Another pioneer journal in its field, although one that had a shorter life, was the *Southern Medical and Surgical Journal,* established in Augusta in 1845 by Dr. Paul F. Eve and Dr. Ignatius P. Garvin.

Unique among Georgia publications was the *Cherokee Phoenix,* published at New Echota, the capital of the Cherokee Indian Nation. The completion in 1821 of an 86-character Cherokee syllabary by the half-breed Indian Sequoyah aroused much interest, and in 1824 the national council of the Cherokee voted to establish a weekly paper. Elias Boudinot, an Indian who had been educated at a mission school in Cornwall, Connecticut, was engaged as editor for $300 a year. It was not until February 21, 1828, however, that Boudinot, assisted by the Reverend Samuel A. Worcester, a medical missionary, produced the first official issue. The paper, with at least a fourth of its contents printed in the syllabary, was favorably received by the Indians and was effective in teaching many of them to read both English and Cherokee. The last issue appeared in October, 1835, when the paper was suppressed by Georgia authorities because of its unfavorable comments on the attitude of the state toward the Cherokee Nation.

In the decade of 1850-60, as relations between North and South grew more strained and interest in national affairs more intense, the number of newspapers in Georgia more than doubled, increasing from 51 to 105, with the number of dailies increasing from 5 to 12. Along with advertisements, poetry columns, weather reports, and the record of local events, lengthy discussions of the slavery issue became increasingly prominent. Editorials were powerful factors in winning allegiance to the newly organized Democratic party and in formulating Georgia sentiment with respect to secession from the Union.

On Monday morning, April 15, 1861, the *Macon Telegraph* appeared with the screaming headline: "War! War!! War!!! 75,000 Barbarians Coming Down on the South!" Four years later, on April 16, 1865, the *Savannah News,* which had been confiscated by Federal soldiers and renamed the *Daily Herald,* printed a boldface headline representative of anything but southern sentiment: "Most Glorious News of the War. Lee Has Surrendered to Grant."

Throughout the conflict, Georgia newspapers constantly encouraged men to enlist in the army, helped to sustain the morale of the people at home with optimistic editorials, and worked to enhance an already strong feeling of nationalism within the Confederacy. At first the papers were chiefly dependent on official dispatches for their war news, but it was not long before special correspondents in the battle areas and letters from soldiers at the front were adding colorful human details to the bare announcements of troop movements and engagements.

Under the difficulties and hardships imposed by four years of war, many newspapers suspended publication or appeared only at irregular intervals. In addition to writing and assembling their material, editors were often obliged to serve as typesetters, proofreaders, pressmen, and delivery men as well. Paper became scarce throughout the South, and some journals were printed on wallpaper, wrapping paper, or even cardboard. With the depreciation of Confederate currency and the ever-rising cost of materials, subscription rates rose rapidly; in 1865 the price of a year's subscription to the *Macon Telegraph* was $120. Many presses had to be hidden in out-of-the-way places to escape destruction, or (as in the case of the *Atlanta Intelligencer's* equipment) shifted about the state in freight cars, the newspapers being issued wherever and whenever circumstances permitted. By the close of the war, fifty-nine Georgia newspapers had ceased publication; and, of those remaining, thirty-three failed during the subsequent hard years of Reconstruction.

When General Sherman occupied Savannah in December, 1864, he seized the offices of the *Republican,* a journal which had upheld the traditions of the state since 1802. An editor with the Federal army took charge of the paper, and on December 29 issued a salutatory announcing that it was his purpose "to avoid the shoals of intolerance and endeavor to show . . . in the darkest hours the light of magnanimity and justice." Because of its new adherence, however, many southerners dropped their subscriptions to the journal, and it was forced to abandon publication in 1875. Augustus P. Burr of the *Macon Journal and Messenger* took the required oath of allegiance to the Union in 1865, and soon thereafter stated editorially that he had had to fortify himself for the occasion with "Dutch courage." This statement resulted in his arrest and the suppression of his paper by Federal authorities.

The disastrous effects of the war on Georgia journalism were but temporary, however, and new publications were soon taking the place of those that had vanished; so by 1870 the number of papers had increased to 110. The *Atlanta New Era* was founded soon after the war by Dr. Samuel Baird, previously a fiery Democrat but now a supporter of the Republican party. As his allegiance to the North became stronger, his subscription list dwindled, and the paper failed in 1872. The most successful journal to appear during the Reconstruction era was the *Constitution,* Atlanta's oldest existing newspaper, founded in 1868 by Colonel Carey W. Styles, who advocated the abolishment of military government, white supremacy over newly emancipated Negroes, and the ejection of northern political scalawags. Thus the paper plunged immediately into politics, and to it is attributed the Democratic victory in the election of 1871.

· The rapid growth of Georgia in the last quarter of the nineteenth century brought forth several of the state's leading daily papers. The *Atlanta Journal* was founded in 1883 by Colonel E. F. Hogue; the

Macon News, in 1884 by J. B. Pound; the *Columbus Ledger,* in 1886; the *Savannah Press,* in 1891 by Pleasant A. Stovall; and the *Augusta Herald,* in 1897.

When Evan P. Howell gained control of the *Atlanta Constitution* in 1876, he engaged two brilliant writers, Henry W. Grady and Joel Chandler Harris, both exponents of "the New South," a phrase coined by Grady to symbolize the energy and courage with which the southern states were fighting their way back to· prosperity. Through his editorials and speeches, Grady not only encouraged the reestablishment of friendship between North and South but urged the South to rebuild itself as a powerful industrial region and to avoid slipping back into the retarding romanticism of ante bellum days. In this program he was effectively aided by Harris, who later became known as the author of the Uncle Remus stories. Frank L. Stanton, a well-known Georgia poet, was a colleague of these two men on the *Constitution* staff.

From the staff of the *Atlanta Journal* have risen many noted journalists and authors, among them Don Marquis, Laurence Stallings, Erskine Caldwell, Ward Morehouse, Grantland Rice, Ward Greene, and Margaret Mitchell. Also associated with this paper have been Hoke Smith, Secretary of the Interior under President Cleveland, and Major John S. Cohen, former United States Senator. The *Journal* won the 1937 Pulitzer award for its campaign to end corruption and inefficiency in the city police department.

An outstanding representative of Georgia journalism was John Temple Graves. Born in South Carolina in 1856, he attended the University of Georgia and began his career as a newspaper man on the *Rome Daily Tribune.* After serving at various times in Atlanta as editor of the *Journal, News,* and *Georgian,* he became editor of the *New York American* in 1907 and held a prominent place in the journalistic world until his death in 1925. His oratorical brilliance equalled that of Grady, and as an editorial writer he did much to elevate the standards of national journalism.

Julian La Rose Harris, son of Joel Chandler Harris, has twice won distinguished recognition in the field of journalism. In 1926, while he was editor of the *Columbus Enquirer-Sun,* and again in 1931, while he was managing editor of the *Atlanta Constitution,* his paper received the Pulitzer prize "for the most disinterested and meritorious service of any American newspaper." W. T. Anderson, editor of the *Macon Telegraph* since 1914, is also well known for his vigorous editorials in denunciation of intolerance and political graft.

The most colorful of all Georgia newspapermen was W. B. Townsend (1855-1934), for many years owner, business manager, editor, reporter, typesetter, and printer of the *Dahlonega Nugget*. His country newspaper, established in 1892, was printed on an old-fashioned hand-press in a little town twenty miles from the nearest railroad station. His homespun wit and salty philosophy were often quoted in the nation's leading newspapers. Lacking even a grammar school education, Townsend made his faulty spelling a part of his stock in trade. He did not take time to write out his copy but composed his news stories and editorials while setting them up in type. As the popularity of his paper increased, he became unable to supply the demand; so in characteristic fashion he solved the problem, not by installing a more modern press, but by limiting his subscription list to 1,000. Busy as he was with his paper, Townsend found time to serve as county ordinary, banker, justice of the peace, constable, mayor, alderman, and herb seller. Since his death in 1934 the *Nugget* has been edited by his son, Phil Townsend.

The weekly newspapers in the many small towns and county seats have exercised an important influence on the people of an essentially rural state. In 1887 the editors of these papers met at Milledgeville and formed the Georgia Weekly Press Association. Daily newspapers were admitted to membership in 1918, and the word "Weekly" was dropped from the title of the association. Ten years later its members organized the Georgia Press Institute, which holds an annual session at the Henry W. Grady School of Journalism at the University of Georgia, for the consideration and discussion of journalistic matters. (*For the Negro press see* THE NEGRO.)

In present-day Georgia (1939), only 5 of its 159 counties are without any kind of newspaper. Although the circulation of the state's 29 city dailies is much more widespread than formerly, there is no essential conflict between these and the 218 weeklies and 4 semiweeklies. People in the small towns and rural areas read the dailies for current news of state and national events, the weeklies for local and personal items. The dailies in some of the smaller cities combine in issuing enlarged Sunday editions, with special magazine and comic sections. Most of the state's 73 miscellaneous periodicals are specialized in character, ranging from trade journals to poetry magazines.

RADIO

The first two radio stations in the South were established in Atlanta. WSB's initial broadcast was made on March 15, 1922, and that of WGST (then WGM) just two days later.

WSB has established many precedents. It was the third licensed station in the nation, the first sponsored by a newspaper (the *Atlanta*

Journal), the first to feature regular nightly programs, and the first to employ a broadcasting slogan, "The Voice of the South." The custom of sounding musical notes with station identification also originated with WSB and was later adopted by the National Broadcasting Company, with which the station became affiliated in 1927. WSB also broadcasts the "Atlanta Journal School of the Air," designed to promote public school interest in the arts. Approximately three hundred thousand high school and grammar school students compete each year in the music and oratory contests on these programs, and winners are awarded scholarships in Georgia colleges of their choice. This station also carries a program from the extension service of the State College of Agriculture, giving instruction in all phases of animal husbandry and agronomy and interviews on the marketing of farm products.

Station WSB has confined its NBC broadcasts to the programs of the Red Network since 1937, when the *Journal* established WAGA as Atlanta's Blue Network station. WATL, established by Oglethorpe University in 1931 and sold to a group of business men in 1935, broadcasts local programs and recorded music.

The history of Radio Station WGST dates back to March 17, 1922, when the station first went on the air with the call letters WGM. At this time the station was owned by the *Atlanta Constitution*. It was later transferred to the Georgia School of Technology, and was operated as Radio Station WBBF by Georgia Tech. On January 8, 1925, the call letters were changed to WGST, the present call letters of the station. WGST is now licensed to the Georgia School of Technology, a division of the University System of Georgia, and operates on a frequency of 890 K.C. with a power of 5,000 watts day and 1000 watts night, as assigned by the Federal Communication Commission, with studios on the top floor of the Forsyth Building in Atlanta, Georgia. WGST is on the air 18 hours each day, and studio visitors are always welcome.

Georgia also has stations in Albany, Athens, Augusta, Columbus, Griffin, Macon, Rome, Savannah, Thomasville, and Waycross. There are about a thousand amateur, two emergency, two aeronautical, one coastal, and seven police stations, all licensed by the Federal Communications Commission. Near Marietta the commission maintains a monitor station which checks the time and subject matter on all broadcasts in the Southeast and enforces the power and wave length specifications for the various stations of the region.

Georgia has contributed several performers to the ranks of nationally known radio entertainers. These include the Pickens Sisters, Pat Padgett of "Molasses 'n' January," James Melton, Bert Parks, and "Smilin' Ed" McConnell.

Literature

Iт is natural that the earliest writings in the Georgia colony should be valuable to a newer generation for content rather than literary merit. Such records as the businesslike reports of James E. Oglethorpe, founder of the colony, have survived two centuries principally because they present the practical problems of settling a new land. Only in relation to the practical is the broader social aspect present; only by inference do these reports show the more subtle difficulties of making men from debtors' prisons feel and behave as free men.

The colonists have left some record of their own inner life in the stories, poems, and sermons that have been preserved. These documents reveal the wonder and dismay of prisoners who have been set free to master a land of unimaginable richness and terror. Most of these writings show little concern for literary effect, and thereby gain in significance as the expression of genuine, sometimes passionate, feeling. Probably without realizing it, these men were writing the first circumstantial and social history of Georgia.

Some of the most vital colonial records are the diaries and journals. William Stephens' journal of pioneer life between 1737 and 1741 is now a valuable source book preserved in the DeRenne Collection at the University of Georgia. Other early writers introduced a powerful religious overtone, as did the famous Anglican minister John Wesley. Too impassioned to be objective, Wesley has left not so much a factual account as a monument to his own character—earnest, intolerant, tragic in its capacity for suffering for a cause. This religious intensity is shown also by his brother Charles in such famous hymns as "Jesus, Lover of My Soul." Since the way pointed by the Wesleys was either one of darkness or of blinding splendor, it was fortunate that there were steadier lights held by such men as the genial and popular Anglican rector George Whitefield.

Written more for practical purposes than as a release of creative energy, these compositions remained simple; but, as communication spread, Georgia writers began to adorn their works with the current conceits. Later literary development here was similar to that of all the South, with leisured slaveholders forming a limited reading public that regarded writing not as a profession but as an elegant diversion. At a time when New England was fostering its most renowned groups, Georgia had only a few isolated individuals whose voices were scarcely heard. Neither then nor later did literary groups and salons flourish. Beginning without large cities where it might have become focalized, Georgia literature has remained varied and difficult to classify.

During the leisured first half of the nineteenth century the popular literary forms were the love story, the historical romance, and the sentimental poem. Characteristic of the period is the graceful melancholy verse of Richard Henry Wilde, preserved most enduringly in the brief lyric "My Life Is Like the Summer Rose." Caroline Lee Hentz, although born in the North, sentimentalized the days of slavery in her flowery romances.

It is noteworthy, however, that even at that time some writers flung off the ornateness which fashion had bred. A pioneer historian, Major Hugh McCall, set down with admirable directness a history of the era between the first settling and the end of the American Revolution. Still less conforming were the Georgia humorists, who imparted to their work a stout native quality that reached its best known expression in the Uncle Remus stories, but which had its robust prophets at a much earlier date. The first widely known humorist was Augustus Baldwin Longstreet, founder of the *Augusta Sentinel,* whose famous *Georgia Scenes* appeared serially as early as 1833. These sketches made him known as a social commentator, since his accounts of horse trading, fights, and fox hunts clearly depicted the vigorous, crudely abundant life of the 1830's. Though never ribald, Longstreet was unmoved by the genteel affectations that had begun to flower; he merely noted them with scornful amusement. His regionalism, which is often the most pugnacious provincialism, probably influenced later humorists. At any rate the prose of William Tappan Thompson, Bill Arp, Richard Malcolm Johnston, Harry Stillwell Edwards, and the famous Joel Chandler Harris has a native character as tenacious as the red clay of middle Georgia.

Although Thomas Holley Chivers, author of *The Lost Pleiad and Other Poems* (1842), may be justly charged with overornamentation, he cannot be charged with conventionality. His tortuous idioms are his own, and since he was solitary and lacking in critical sense these expressions range from genuine majesty to absurdity. The technical innovations that made his verse at once arresting and obscure were later used advantageously by poets of clearer utterance. According to S. Foster Damon, Chivers' work influenced the metrics of Swinburne, Rosetti, and Poe. In his biography *Thomas Holley Chivers, Friend of Poe* (1930) Damon writes: "Chivers is kin to Coleridge and Poe; but he so far surpassed them in audacity that he anticipated for himself the fundamental theory of Symbolist poetry . . . Chivers also tried to build poems out of pure sound, with results that are surprisingly modern." Remembered principally for his correspondence with Poe, whom he accused of plagiarism, Chivers is more interesting for his technical accomplishments and for the enigmatic personality that shines darkly through his verses.

In the years immediately preceding the War between the States, Georgia writers found a contemporary subject vital enough to challenge their creative faculties. Audiences went wild when they heard speeches against abolition, secession crackled in the air, and soon everyone was hearing the words of Benjamin H. Hill, Alexander H. Stephens, and the fiery, sardonic Robert Toombs. In the newspapers, vitriolic opinions appeared thinly disguised as fiction and poetry. By offering rousing themes the war gave Georgia literature its greatest impetus, and if the writings of these days lack reflectiveness they at least live with a fierce sincerity.

Some of the verse became famous without making its authors famous. Probably few now recall that "Maryland, My Maryland" was written by James Ryder Randall, who served for many years on the staff of the *Augusta Chronicle,* or that Francis O. Ticknor, who practiced medicine near Columbus, was the author of "Little Giffen of Tennessee." Hundreds of boys have thundered forth "The Conquered Banner" and "The Sword of Lee" but have forgotten the name of Father Abram J. Ryan, Confederate poet and Roman Catholic priest who served in Augusta and Macon. The more firmly fashioned, less sentimental verses of Paul Hamilton Hayne, who lived in Augusta for many years following the war, were once frequently declaimed from grammar-school platforms, but now only mature readers know his *Legends and Lyrics* (1872) and *Mountains and Lovers* (1875).

Georgia's most celebrated poet, Sidney Lanier, lived out his brief life through war and reconstruction. With him music was almost an obsession, and he wrote his philosophical prose work *The Science of English Verse* (1880) to prove that the laws of music and verse are inseparable. He became well known as the author of "Corn" and "The Symphony," but it is for the sensuous magic and singing cadences of his less pretentious poems that he is best loved. Readers of his famous "Song of the Chattahoochee," "Ballad of Trees and the Master," and "The Marshes of Glynn" cannot but admire the adroit craftsmanship of his musical rhythm.

Lanier, writing to a friend in 1866, characteristically deplored, not the material hardships of the Reconstruction era, but its intellectual stagnation. These years produced little writing worthy of preservation, for the embittered people had little heart for creative expression. It was not until later, when time had brought a measure of calm, that Reconstruction history, memoirs, and stories were published. Before the war Georgia's best writers had been writers only secondarily, but soon afterward a number of Georgians began to gain their livelihood by their pens. This trend was shown by the widely read romances of Eliza Frances Andrews and William Henry Peck. Still more popular was Augusta Evans Wilson's *St. Elmo* (1866), whose Byronic hero and overwhelming vocabulary are still remembered. Inclining toward a more realistic view was Will N. Harben, who wrote with some penetration of the Georgia mountaineer, formerly almost unknown in fiction.

Oratory, always a popular art, continued to flourish. Especially notable are the speeches of Henry W. Grady, who used all his tremendous magnetism to urge amity between North and South. Although his phrases are too fluent, too rounded, for twentieth-century taste, they embody the noblest idealism of his time.

Histories of the Colonial, Revolutionary, and Confederate periods continued to be written. Alexander H. Stephens, Vice President of the Confederacy, turned his fine scholarship and incisive mind to recording his times; Bill Arp (Major Charles H. Smith), best known for his humorous sketches, also wrote Georgia history; and Myrta Lockett Avary became known for several memoirs such as the recently reissued *Dixie after the War* (1937). W. B. Stephens and Charles Colcock Jones also wrote of their own land and people. The vigorous Thomas E. Watson, well known in state and national politics, stands apart from his contemporaries in selection of foreign subjects for his two most popular works, *The Story of France* (1898) and *Napoleon* (1902).

If the closing decades of the century produced nothing else, they would still be worthy of record because of Joel Chandler Harris, the first writer to use Negro dialect prominently in his work. A gentle, shy man who shunned celebrity, he never was known by the general public, but his personality has been set forth in two biographies by his daughter-in-law, Julia Collier Harris (Mrs. Julian La Rose Harris). In the Uncle Remus tales, beloved for their adroitly personified animals and rich Negro humor, the material is compiled from African folklore but is stamped with Harris' unique treatment. Mingling gayety with reflection, the tales of Br'er Rabbit, Br'er Fox, Sis' Cow, and the fabulous Tar Baby are American classics. A discerning critic has pointed out that one of the most engaging traits of the stories is the triumphant trickery of the rabbit, actually the least shrewd of animals but a picaresque hero in the hands of Harris.

Harry Stillwell Edwards, of Macon, also won praise for his stories of the southern Negro. During his long lifetime he was a popular columnist on the *Atlanta Journal,* and his mystery novel *Sons and Fathers* was awarded the *Chicago Record* Prize in 1896. He is most widely remembered, however, for *Eneas Africanus* (1919), a tragicomic story of an old Negro slave in search of his master.

The poetry written in the late 1890's and early 1900's, though neither profuse nor striking, is not without variety. The work of Frank L. Stanton, Georgia's poet laureate and most popular poet of the period, was chiefly notable for its dialect. He is best known for the lyrics "Mighty Lak a Rose" and "Just a-Wearyin' for You," but during his connection with the *Atlanta Constitution* he wrote hundreds of similar pieces. (Ernest Neal, present poet laureate, also writes the type of verse commonly known as homespun.) Other poets of the time expressed themselves in the more conventional lyrical form. Robert Loveman is best remembered for his delicate and rhythmic "Rain Song," while Roselle Mercier Montgomery left behind her a number of classical verses, such as "Ulysses Returns."

For many years Georgia's only novelist of national reputation was Corra Harris, whose first book, *A Circuit Rider's Wife* (1910), called forth both praise and indignation for its outspoken portrayal of a Methodist minister's life. Most of her books can scarcely be called fiction, for they are weak in plot and usually slight in characterization, but they are pithy with humorous comment and serious reflection.

Although in her time Corra Harris was censured for her candor, her work is reticent beside that of newer writers. *Tobacco Road* (1932), Erskine Caldwell's startling novel, outraged some readers by its insistence on the ignorance, poverty, and disease that handicap the sharecropper class. But present-day awareness of social problems and the success of the drama which was made from Caldwell's novel have aroused national interest. Presented with laconic, amused naturalism, Jeeter Lester has become a living type of the thriftless sharecropper.

Equally downright but more sympathetic is Caroline Miller, who won the 1934 Pulitzer Prize for her novel of the wiregrass section, *Lamb In His Bosom.* Bitter and violent as are some of the incidents, they are softened by the religious perceptions of the characters and the poetic style of the author. John Fort also clothes drabness in dignity in such mountaineer novels as *Stone Daugherty* (1929) and *God in the Straw Pen* (1931), and Fisewood Tarleton's *Some Trust in Chariots* (1930) and Evelyn Hanna's *Blackberry Winter* (1938) lay the mantle of sympathy over people almost savagely near to the earth.

Other Georgia writers have turned to urban scenes. Isa Glenn and especially Frances Newman are known as book critics as well as novelists, and a critical, frequently satirical note sounds through their fiction. Although many of their characters are southern, local color is not an outstanding characteristic of their work. In the last years of her life Miss Newman published two sharply ironic novels, *The Hardboiled Virgin* (1926) and *Dead Lovers are Faithful Lovers* (1928). Miss Glenn's more numerous books frequently have a foreign setting, as *Transport* (1929) and *Mr. Darlington's Dangerous Age* (1933), but *A Short History of Julia* (1930) is laid in Georgia.

But even when Georgia writers have selected foreign lands as background they have remained acutely aware of their own region. Berry Fleming has written of many places, but his best known work, *Siesta* (1935), has a southern setting; Harry Hervey, who takes his restless heroes into exotic ports, still shows them as haunted by their childhood environment, as in *Ethan Quest* (1925). Samuel Tupper, Jr., who does not indicate any local problems, has laid both of his rapid, lightly written novels, *Some Go Up* (1931) and *Old Lady's Shoes* (1934), in his native Atlanta. The scene of Willie Snow Ethridge's gay and amusing memoirs, *As I Live and Breathe* (1937), is Macon, and her novel, *Mingled Yarn* (1938), deals with the problem of a young couple in a southern mill town. Ward Greene, once a star reporter on the *Atlanta Constitution,* brings a reporter's remorseless objectivity to his southern pieces, *Cora Potts* (1929) and *Death in the Deep South* (1936). Mildred Seydell also had wide newspaper experience before she published her problem novel, *Secret Fathers* (1930). Minnie Hite Moody has sometimes used a midwestern setting, but in *Death is a Little Man* (1936) she employs her exquisite prose to depict an urban community of southern Negroes. Harry Lee's vividly subjective novel *The Fox in the Cloak* (1938) tells of the adjustment of a young artist to a commercial community.

The novels of Gertrude Capen Whitney, Mary Granger, and Parker Hord treat both the historical and spiritual aspects of religion. Performers on lighter themes are both numerous and capable, and readers throughout the nation are familiar with the adventure stories of Edison Marshall, the animal tales of Elmer Ransom, the collegiate gayeties of Nunnally Johnson, the bright sophisticated novels of Marian Sims, the mystery novels of Medora Field, Dorothy Ogburn and Linton C. Hopkins, and the pleasing romances of Marie Conway Oemler, whose *Slippy McGee* (1917) and *Two Shall Be Born* (1922) are still popular.

Historical fiction has been somewhat neglected by contemporary Georgia writers, but in 1936 a Georgian's novel was acclaimed as an outstanding historical novel and was awarded the Pulitzer Prize in 1937. *Gone with the Wind,* by Margaret Mitchell, is a long but rapidly paced story of the War between the States, with the scene laid in the section of middle Georgia ravaged by the invading Federal forces of General Sherman. Striking an adroit balance between the romantic and realistic methods of story telling, Miss Mitchell recounts the incidents from the southern point of view.

Some of the best-known Georgia playwrights, including Anne Nichols, Laurence Stallings, and Ward Morehouse, have gone far from home in selection of subjects. Only two dramatists have reached large audiences through folk or sectional plays. Nan Bagby Stephens' play *Roseanne* (first presented in 1924) introduced a new note of seriousness in the depiction of the Negro race, and Lula Vollmer's *Sun Up* (1924) is a vivid dramatization of the life of the southern mountaineer.

The number of modern Georgia poets is very large, as is shown by the statement of Richard Moult that Atlanta alone has contributed more poetry to his anthologies of British and American verse than any other municipality except New York. A well-selected anthology has been compiled by Ruth Elgin Suddeth under the title of *An Atlanta Argosy* (1938). On the whole, Georgia's poets have been most successful in the traditional forms; only Lola Pergament has established a reputation in the more experimental patterns. The other leading Georgia poets, though conventional in technique, are often fresh and acute in theme and idiom. There is real poetic quality in Daniel Whitehead Hicky's imagery, Anderson Scruggs' somber wisdom, Agnes Kendrick Gray's adroit fancies, Mary Brent Whiteside's spirituality, Arthur Crew Inman's dynamic movement, Carrie Fall Benson's warm emotion, James Warren's sensitive perceptions, and in the music of Gilbert Maxwell's sonnets. Conrad Aiken was born in Savannah and spent his boyhood there, but his well-known poems have no bearing on Georgia themes. Rae S. Neely is known for a compact and restrained narrative poem on Queen Marguerite of Navarre. Ernest Hartsock, who was only twenty-seven years old when he died in 1930, showed promise of becoming Georgia's most distinguished poet. The title poem of his third volume, *Strange Splendor* (1930), won him the annual award of the Poetry Society of America, and much of his work is notable for its intellectual power and dazzling phrases.

The critical, questioning spirit which swept the country in the 1920's has been embodied not only in the fiction of Georgia but in the newer history books. Perhaps the most iconoclastic of the biographers is W. E. Woodward, whose reputation rests partly on his satiric novels, chiefly on his trenchant biographies and histories. John D. Wade's biographies are kindlier, although a suave irony is often present in his comments on Augustus Baldwin Longstreet and John Wesley. Haywood Pearce, Jr., has shrewdly presented one of the most complex individualities in Confederate annals in his biography of Benjamin H. Hill (1928). A penetrating biography (1938) of the radical and brilliant Thomas E. Watson has been written by Vann Woodward. Merton Coulter's *A Short History of Georgia* (1933) questions some of the more fabulous traditions, but does not divest Georgia history of its authentic romance.

The newer authors also have written with distinction on economic and social themes. Ulrich B. Phillips' *Life and Labor in the Old South* (1929) is one of the most complete and enlightened works of its kind. Howard Odum has not only written memorably of southern life in several well documented volumes, such as *Southern Regions* (1936), but has also caught the plaintive quality of a race in his compilations of words to Negro songs. Arthur Raper, nationally known for his work in interracial relations, has written two books that are outstanding for their frankness and vigor: *The Tragedy of Lynching* (1933) sharply analyzes mob frenzy, and *Preface to Peasantry* (1936) studies two Georgia counties in relation to the farm tenancy situation. In *Road to War* (1935), Walter Millis has coolly analyzed the folly of war as revealed in the propaganda which in the years 1914-17 aroused America to chauvinistic hysteria. Such works as these contrast with the readable but less critical earlier histories of Lucian Lamar Knight and Clark Howell. Robert W. Burns' *I Am A Fugitive from a Georgia Chain Gang* (1932) and John L. Spivak's *Georgia Nigger* (1932), although not written by natives of the state, indicate a new approach to social problems in Georgia.

The textbook histories of R. Preston Brooks and Lawton B. Evans have been used in the Georgia schools for a generation, and juvenile psychology has been kept well in mind by Eva Knox Evans and Madge Alford Bigham, who have written successful books for children. With the exception of Joel Chandler Harris, however, Georgia's best-known writer of juvenile books is F. R. Goulding, whose *Young Marooners* (1852) and *Marooner's Island* (1869) are known to boys in all parts of the United States.

Only in recent years has the Negro in Georgia contributed to the literature of the state. The most widely known of the Negro writers is Walter White, author of two novels—*Fire in the Flint* (1924) and *Flight* (1926)—and one nonfictional work on racial injustice, *Rope and Faggot—a Biography of Judge Lynch* (1929). W. E. Burghardt Du Bois, distinguished Negro sociologist of Atlanta University, has interpreted his race in *The Souls of Black Folk* (1903) and *Black Recon-struction* (1935). The Negro poets also used this theme in their work, but it is significant that there is also a growing interest in the broader aspects of life. Thomas Jefferson Flannagan, Victor Wellborn Jenkins, Frank Marshall Davis, and Georgia Douglas Johnson are the Negro poets in Georgia who have received most recognition.

A survey of Georgia writers indicates that in general they have been most effective when they have been most strongly regional. If their best scenes are native, however, their view of life is frequently far broader; they have extended this more profound recognition into the past. A more critical view of history is a salient characteristic of the newer Georgia writers, and the more popular ones are not blind worshipers of familiar customs and institutions. Neither are they predominantly destructive or satiric. The most eminent are making notable efforts to show their state in relation to the rest of the world.

Music

ALTHOUGH JOHN and Charles Wesley wrote some hymns during their brief visit to the colony in 1736 (*a Collection of Psalms and Hymns* by John Wesley was published at Charleston in 1737), there is little record of music in Georgia before the nineteenth century. In the early decades of that century, people played naive mazurkas, polkas, and waltzes and sang plaintive songs of hearts bowed down or Scottish and English ballads about lovelorn maidens. In the churches, hymns were "lined out" and the tunes "raised" by some member of the congregation who was considered skilful in "hitting the right key."

The songs of the Scotch-Irish who settled in north Georgia have had a lasting influence on the folk music of the Georgia mountains. A blend of Irish mysticism and Scottish realism, these songs have been handed down by word of mouth through several generations. Although ballads were denounced as "devil ditties" by the preachers, mothers would sing their children to sleep with adventures of lords and fair ladies or would compose verses and tunes that were recorded only in memory. A traveling "ballad maker" was always welcome at mountain homes for his ability not only to sing old ballads but also to make new ones out of a local romance, an accident, or a feud. As the songs were handed down orally, they were often expanded until some of them comprised a hundred stanzas or more.

At rural social gatherings, games with songs were played to the accompaniment of the fiddle, and often songs were improvised about local events. "That's What Made Denmead Build his Chimney up so High" concerned a high chimney built for the Kennesaw Mill in Marietta in 1856-57. "The Death of Mary Fagan" had its origin in a widely publicized murder case.

Throughout the state, especially in northern and western Georgia, it has long been common for country people to hold singing schools, Sunday afternoon song services, and "all day singings with dinner on the ground." An interesting development of this rural music is the

Sacred Harp singing, in which the performers read from shaped-note song books with triangle, circle, square, and diamond standing respectively for *fa, sol, la*, and *mi*. Because they begin by vocalizing the notes, the participants are called "fasola" singers. No instrumental accompaniment is used, the vocal cords being considered the "sacred harp." Since the women sing only the alto parts and the men carry the melody, the music has its own peculiar tone. In addition to old ballads and well-known hymns, they sing religious verses set to popular tunes—as for example, the piece called "Be Joyful in God," in which the tune is that of "Nellie Gray."

The first song book used by these groups, *The Sacred Harp,* was published in 1844 by B. F. White and E. J. King. Realizing that rural singers needed a musical organization, White founded in 1847 the Southern Musical Convention, of which he was president until 1862. Other early "fasola" collections were William Hauser's *Hesperian Harp* and John G. McCurry's *Social Harp,* both of which contain simple folk melodies as well as original songs named for prominent Georgians and Georgia towns. The United Sacred Harp Musical Association was founded in 1904, with headquarters in Atlanta, where a Sacred Harp convention is held each spring.

To the accompaniment of fiddle, banjo, or guitar, the Georgia cracker sings old ballads, songs of the War between the States, and local ditties, or "calls the turns" for spirited breakdowns at country dances. Since 1885 a fiddlers' convention has been held annually in Atlanta; among the hundreds who have played at these conventions are Fiddling John Carson, Gid Tanner, and Riley Puckett, well known through national radio broadcasts. Throughout north Georgia many hillbilly bands have been organized and provide the music for country dances and other entertainments.

The Negroes, introduced into Georgia in the early years of the colony, brought with them their own peculiar music, characterized by a vigorous rhythm. Although none of their tunes can be definitely traced to an African origin, the early background of the race had a definite influence upon the Negro music. Through the adaptation of the white man's religious songs to their own manner of expression and through many creations of their own, the Negroes evolved the spirituals, songs of supplication, and jubilees. Since they sang at both play and work, their music came to include breakdowns, sorrow songs with occasional Biblical references, and work songs such as corn-shucking and cotton-picking tunes. Many Negroes had a gift for "matchin' de words" and "snatchin' a tune out er de haid," and as the songs were passed from one singer to another the tunes were changed and new words added. When Negroes are at work, one laborer is sometimes chosen to lead the group in singing, so that all may work in rhythmic unison with the music. The line, "Done bus' dat rock, boys, f'om hyeh to Macon," seems to indicate a Georgia chain-gang origin for "Water Boy."

Lowell Mason (1792-1872), the composer of "Nearer My God to Thee," "My Faith Looks Up to Thee," and other hymns, began his musical career as a choir leader and organist in Savannah at the age of twenty. Remaining in that city for about fifteen years, he published a collection of psalm tunes and wrote the music for Bishop Heber's hymn "From Greenland's Icy Mountains," a composition first sung in the old Independent Presbyterian Church of Savannah.

From 1825 until the War between the States, music gradually acquired a sounder technical basis and a more native character. The popular French and German songs which had enlivened so many musical programs were replaced by the indigenous melodies of Stephen Foster. Sopranos, warbling florid opera arias and heroic songs meant for male voices, were succeeded by performers of greater artistic merit. The New Orleans Opera Company was heard in Augusta in 1854, and during the ensuing decade many musical societies came into being. Throughout the war, a blending of sentimental and martial music held first place in popularity, and singers became known for their rendition of such songs as "Rock Me to Sleep, Mother" and "You are Going to the Wars, Willie Boy." A group of musicians called the Atlanta Amateurs gave concerts in Savannah, Augusta, Macon, and other cities for the benefit of Confederate soldiers.

With the revival of musical interest after the Reconstruction era, the appreciation of good music became more widespread. In Atlanta during the 1870's a succession of musical organizations, such as the Beethoven and Mendelssohn societies, made their appearance. In Augusta in 1875, the German pianist and composer Scharwenka played on the last piano made by Peter Brenner, noted piano maker; later Gustave Satter, French pianist, used the same instrument. After about 1890, oratorios were occasionally sung in the larger churches, and opera companies and symphony orchestras gave performances in the principal cities. The Damrosch and New Orleans Opera companies came with their German and French repertoires. In 1898 the Atlanta Concert Association brought such artists as De Pachmann, Paderewski, Nordica, and Melba for a season of music, and with the Grau Opera Company came Eames and Schumann-Heink.

All this imported talent stimulated greater local activity. The Savannah Music Club was formed in 1897. The Atlanta Music Festival Association was organized in 1909 to celebrate the official opening of the municipal auditorium-armory and inaugurate an annual music festival. At the first season of the festival, concerts were given by the Dresden Philharmonic Orchestra, Geraldine Farrar, and Albert Spalding. In the following year, through the efforts of Colonel William Lawson Peel and others, the Metropolitan Opera Company presented a week of opera. Thereafter until 1931, except for a period during the World War, the Metropolitan Opera season in Atlanta was a yearly event that attracted music-lovers from all the southeastern states.

Percy Starnes was chosen municipal organist of Atlanta in 1910 and gave many Sunday afternoon recitals on the large organ of the auditorium-armory. He was succeeded in this position by Edwin Arthur Kraft and later by Charles Sheldon, Jr. Such famous organists as Clarence Eddy, Joseph Bonnet, and Edwin H. Lemare have played at the auditorium-armory. A Georgia chapter of the American Guild of Organists was organized by Edwin Arthur Kraft in 1914.

Through the efforts of George Folsom Granberry, director of summer school music at the University of Georgia, an annual opera season became an interesting feature of that institution for several years preceding and including 1932. The various departments of the school cooperated in creating the scenery, costumes, and lighting arrangements; and with the exception of the principal roles, which were assigned to visiting artists, the casts consisted of students and local singers.

In 1927 the Atlanta Music Club, organized in 1915 as the Woman's Choral Club, instituted a series of civic concerts, with orchestral and solo numbers, and continued to sponsor performances for several years. At present an annual series of such concerts is jointly sponsored by the Atlanta Music Club and the Atlanta Philharmonic Society.

The activities of musical organizations throughout the state are coordinated and promoted by the Georgia Federation of Music Clubs, which had its inception in 1919. With a membership of about 140 clubs and 3,800 individuals, this organization sponsors study programs and concerts and fosters the formation of junior music clubs. In 1930 Miss Evelyn Jackson, then president of the federation, organized the MacDowell Festival as a nation-wide tribute to the American composer Edward MacDowell and as a means of raising funds for the Peterborough colony which he founded.

As there is neither state nor county provision for musical education in the public schools, many communities have developed activities of their own in this field. School choruses, glee clubs, and orchestras are numerous, and special music contests are sponsored each year by the State Federation of Women's Clubs, the Georgia Education Association, and the Atlanta Journal School of the Air. The radio programs, for which a different school is responsible each week, arouse keen competition between towns.

The University of Georgia and several women's colleges, especially Brenau and Wesleyan, have excellent music departments, and there is musical activity in other higher educational institutions. The Emory University Glee Club, under the direction of Malcolm H. Dewey, was one of the first college musical organizations to eliminate jazz bands and mandolin clubs from their programs and to present only choral music. It has sung before President and Mrs. Coolidge in Washington, and before President Roosevelt in Georgia Hall at Warm Springs. During two concert tours in England, the club appeared at the Lord Mayor's reception in Old Guildhall, London and filled engagements at the London Coliseum. This group is especially well known for its presentation of Negro spirituals. The Emory Little Symphony Orchestra, now in its seventeenth year, has presented fifty-four Sunday afternoon concerts of classical music.

A contemporary group of musicians has won more than local reputation through their compositions and their efforts to raise the standard of musical appreciation. Elizabeth Hopson, Jane Mattingly, and William O. Munn have achieved wide recognition for their children's pieces: outstanding in their fields are William Arnaud's church music, W. C. Dieckmann's organ pieces, and Eldin Burton's compositions for piano and for voice. Hugh Hodgson, head of the music department at the University of Georgia since 1928, has a broad influence as pianist and teacher. Georg Lindner directed the Atlanta Conservatory of Music for twenty-seven years and has been conductor of the Atlanta Philharmonic Orchestra since 1933.

During recent years the popular interest in Negro music has resulted in the formation of many Negro choruses and choirs and the recording of many of the older Negro songs. Few of the singers have had formal training, but their natural aptitude for harmonic singing imparts richness to the music. Although musical notation often fails to convey the vigor of the original songs, much elemental feeling remains. Big Bethel Choir in Atlanta is known for its folk play called *Heaven Bound,* which includes a number of gospel songs.

Prominent among those who have worked to preserve and popularize Negro melodies are Mrs. Maxfield Parrish, wife of the noted painter, and Howard W. Odum, of the University of North Carolina. At her Sea Island home, Mrs. Parrish has recorded coastal Negro music; and the Spiritual Singers Society of Coastal Georgia, which sponsors concerts and choral singing among the coastal Negroes, was organized through her efforts. Dr. Odum has collected many Negro songs in his books *The Negro and His Songs, Rainbow Round My Shoulder,* and *Negro Workaday Songs.*

Several Georgia Negroes have made notable contributions in the field of music. Roland Hayes, born of former slave parents in Curryville, has attained international fame for his work as a concert singer and for his rendition of Negro spirituals in particular. Hall Johnson, of Athens, is known for his arrangements of Negro spirituals and his Negro choir, which sang in *Green Pastures.* He is the author of the folk opera *Run, Little Chillun* and other compositions. Frederick Douglas Hall, born and educated in Atlanta, is director of music at Dillard University in New Orleans and a composer of national reputation. Kemper Harreld, since 1911 director of music at Morehouse College, Atlanta, is widely known for his activities in organizing glee clubs and orchestras in Negro schools and for his work in the field of Negro folk music.

Among Negro musicians of an earlier day was Robert Cole (1868-1911) of Athens, gifted comedian who wrote popular songs and musical comedies. *A Trip to Coontown,* written in collaboration with William Johnson, was the first musical comedy worked out by a Negro for Negro talent. Thomas Green Bethune, known as "Blind Tom," occupied a unique place on the concert and vaudeville stage for more than forty years before his death in 1908. He was born a slave on the Bethune plantation near Columbus in 1849. Although mentally deficient as well as blind, he displayed from childhood a remarkable musical instinct and a phenomenal musical memory, and without professional training he achieved international fame as pianist and composer.

In 1922 the legislature adopted Lollie Belle Wylie's musical setting of Robert Loveman's "Georgia" as the official state song, but this choice was not generally approved, and various state organizations subsequently sponsored the adoption of other songs. When the Atlanta Chamber of Commerce received a letter from Oklahoma in 1935 requesting a copy of the state song, "Marching Through Georgia," the reaction was one of consternation and amusement, since this song commemorates the destructive invasion of Federal troops in the state. Frank L. Stanton's "Georgia Land" sung to the tune of "Maryland, My Maryland" is the favorite among school children.

Art

AMONG GEORGIA's first colonists were a number of officials and soldiers of fortune accustomed to fine living and eager to provide themselves with attractive and well-made things. Under their influence Savannah, for several decades the most important settlement, soon developed a certain degree of urbanity. Brick making, iron mongering, wood carving, and pottery were carried on locally; and these crafts might have attained a high level of excellence but for the competition of superior commodities imported from England. In the first days of the colony the pottery ware of Andrew Duché reached a standard far exceeding that of provincial craftsmanship. The Earl of Egmont considered Duché's "porcelane" of such excellence that he ordered "China Cups" to be made for display in England.

By 1741, only eight years after the building of the first pioneer cabins in Savannah, English travelers spoke of the fine houses that had been erected in that town. In the 1750's, when the trustees' government was replaced by Royal Governor and Council and the slave and land prohibitions were abrogated, there was an influx of prosperous planters from the West Indies and from South Carolina. These new arrivals, who settled in and about Savannah and down the Georgia coast as far as the St. Marys River, augmented the cultural resources of the older Georgia families.

Towards the latter part of the century Augusta, established in 1735 as an Indian trading post and slowly expanding into an interior river town, was beginning to serve as a market for fine goods for near-by planters who were entering the region from Virginia and South Carolina. On the interior as well as the coastal plantations, slaves were trained in the practice of the useful arts, and slave craftsmen produced implements and household furniture of sturdy native wood or of mahogany imported from the West Indies. These examples of early plantation skill are much admired today for their excellent simple designs.

The prosperous families maintained relatively close contacts with

Europe and the urban centers of the New World and, especially in Savannah and the coastal islands, were able to preserve a fairly cosmopolitan atmosphere. Sons were often educated in London, Edinburgh, or Philadelphia, and visitors were lavishly entertained. Merchants and planters furnished their homes in the most elegant manner of the times: inventories of the latter half of the eighteenth century indicate that mahogany furniture, books, silver plate, and fine china were common in households of well-to-do citizens. To this period belong many costly laces, embroidered linens, waistcoats, and ballroom dresses which are now in museum collections.

The leisure and luxury of the pre-Revolutionary period also fostered an interest in the fine arts, particularly portraiture. Itinerant painters known as "rider artists" traveled from town to town with collections of stock canvases on which sumptuous clothing and settings had been painted, leaving the faces to be filled in from life. Other wandering artists, working out of Philadelphia or Charleston, portrayed the gentry in silhouettes, miniatures, and portraits, many of which are scattered throughout the state among descendants of their subjects. The work of Jeremiah Theus, the Swiss portrait painter, who made his home in Charleston about 1739 and died there in 1774, was much in demand in coastal Georgia, particularly Savannah, where eleven of his portraits are still in existence.

The well-balanced life of affluent Georgians was shaken by the Revolution. Many Tory families lost their property through confiscation and banishment, though some returned to the state and reestablished themselves after the war. Goods from abroad continued to be imported, however, by both royalists and patriots.

By the close of the eighteenth century a high living standard had been reached by the wealthy. In this period portraiture gained in popularity. On April 7, 1792, a notice appeared in the *Augusta Chronicle* that "William Anson, from London, Portrait, Miniature, Sign, and House Painter" was serving the public "with elegance and expedition." In 1804 Rembrandt and Raphael Peale, the distinguished sons of Charles Willson Peale, established a shop in Savannah where they cut silhouettes and painted portraits. Rembrandt Peale did a number of large oil studies, and Raphael painted both miniatures and portraits, as shown by a contemporary newspaper advertisement: "Portraits in miniature 30, and in oil, 50 dollars . . . RAPHAELLE PEALE." Samuel F. B. Morse, the New England artist and inventor, stayed for a time with a clergyman friend in Darien and painted many portraits of Georgians. These artists no doubt obtained commissions in the newer agricultural districts, as well as in Augusta, Savannah, and Darien.

Perhaps the most notable artist associated with the history of art in Georgia is Edward Greene Malbone, the miniature painter, who died in his cousin's house in Savannah in 1807 and was buried in the Colonial Cemetery of that city. His miniatures are to be found throughout the state, and several especially fine ones are in Augusta, Rome, Brunswick, and Savannah—in the Savannah group is a portrait of Rachel Gratz, sister of Rebecca Gratz whom Sir Walter Scott used as his model for the tragic heroine of *Ivanhoe*. Other miniature artists found a demand for their work in Georgia, and the signatures of Isabey, de Saint-Memin, Charles Fraser, T. S. Dubourjal, Arthur Haycock, Charlotte Cheves, and Louisa Catherine Strobel are on miniatures in the possession of old Georgia families.

In addition to the work of the painters and artists who came to the state, portraits were brought home by citizens traveling to Philadelphia, New York, London, or Paris. Thus, Sir Joshua Reynolds, Gilbert Stuart, John Durand, Charles Willson Peale, John Wesley Jarvis, Thomas Sully, John Singleton Copley, Chester Harding, and other late eighteenth- and early nineteenth-century artists contributed portraits to local collections. Sully in particular was popular and is represented today by five portraits in Savannah, two in Rome, and others in Augusta, Macon, Columbus, Milledgeville, Washington, Brunswick, and the rural coastal section. One of the Savannah portraits is a likeness of General Nathanael Greene, possibly copied from a Gilbert Stuart.

Masters in other arts also found their products welcomed in the larger centers and on the plantations. Georgia cities still possess furniture by Chippendale, Sheraton, Hepplewhite, Duncan Phyfe and the Adam brothers. The work of the silversmiths of England and Boston was highly prized. Numerous examples of hallmarked silver and fine china remain, among them silver spoons of Thomas Jefferson, eight Sevres plates brought from France by John Adam Treutlen, Georgia's first governor under the constitution, a pair of Dresden jardinieres, and a priceless set of Davenport lusterware.

Through the establishment of Athens, Milledgeville, Rome, Macon, and other towns, the culture of the coastal region penetrated the interior of the state. The wealth and leisure of the first half of the nineteenth century gave little impetus, however, to local creative activity, for the upper classes considered art as a drawing room accomplishment rather than a serious vocation. Young men were trained to be barristers, planters, or merchants; young ladies could avail themselves of courses in art like those advertised by Thomas Addison Richards, the portraitist, in 1839: "He gives instructions in Landscape, Fruit, and Marine painting in oil colors: Landscape and Flower

Drawing in water colors; Sepia and India tinting; Pencil Drawing and Perspective."

In the ante bellum period when Atlanta was developing into a thriving town, treasures of the coastal country were brought into the interior. Examples of early craftsmanship and of the heavy, dignified Colonial and Empire pieces, which so well complemented the tall-columned southern mansions, are to be found also in Athens, Milledgeville, Washington, Madison, Macon, and Columbus.

The burning of Atlanta during the War between the States destroyed many fine objects, and Georgians lost countless household treasures during Sherman's seaward march. Portraits, silver, and fine cabinet work were seized or destroyed. After the war economic and political chaos discouraged the arts. The founding of Telfair Academy of Arts and Sciences in Savannah in 1875 indicated, however, the reawakening of a desire for artistic advancement.

Portraiture remained for many decades the chief genre of Georgia painters. At length, however, landscapes and scenes from everyday life became popular subjects. Towards the end of the nineteenth century, a number of native Georgians worked and studied in Paris and New York, where they acquired thorough artistic training. This tendency towards improvement of technique through work and study in the metropolitan centers was a distinguishing characteristic of American art during this period and was to have important consequences for the later development of local art. Edward Kemeys, sculptor, was born in Savannah in 1843 and studied in New York and Paris. His work, represented by fifty bronzes at the National Gallery in Washington, depicted the wild animals of America. William Posey Silva (b. 1859), widely known landscapist, Kate Flournoy Edwards (b. 1877), portraitist, and Annie Laura Blackshear (b. 1875), painter, writer, and lecturer, are Georgia-born artists who received instruction in Europe and New York. Among their contemporaries are: Alexander John Drysdale, born in Marietta in 1870; Wyncie King, illustrator, born in Covington in 1884; and Lucy May Stanton, miniaturist, born in Atlanta in 1875.

Fine arts departments have been established at the University of Georgia and other colleges. The most important center, however, is the High Museum of Art in Atlanta, founded in 1926, which exhibits the work of old and modern masters and conducts the High Museum Art School. The Association of Georgia Artists, organized in 1929, gathers an annual exhibit of the work of members and circulates it, with accompanying lectures, in many Georgia towns. Art organizations in Athens, Augusta, Macon, and Savannah sponsor art education and exhibitions. In Atlanta and Savannah camera clubs of recent organization have attained recognition in national exhibits and competitions.

Several outstanding American artists have lately lived and worked in Georgia cities. Carl Brandt, muralist, was director at Telfair Academy; Gari Melchers, who married into a Savannah family, assisted with the selection of paintings for the Academy during visits to that city. Joe Cranston Jones, noted as a silhouette cutter, spent most of his short life in Augusta. Hale Woodruff, celebrated Negro modernist painter, is now art instructor at Atlanta University. The gigantic heads of Stonewall Jackson and Robert E. Lee carved by Augustus Lukeman on Stone Mountain have received much attention.

In the decades following the World War, Georgia has seen a marked increase in creative activity, and several of its younger artists have begun to emerge into national prominence. If art in the state has lost much of its aristocratic orientation, it is compensating itself by a new interest in technical problems and an attentive observation of the local scene. Familiar Georgia places and types are today making their appearance on the walls of the nation's galleries. The following titles, of works accepted for exhibition at the New York World's Fair in 1939, will give some notion of the type of subject-matter that has replaced official and upper-class family portraiture as the main theme of Georgia painting: *Blues Singer Over XYZ* by Marjorie C. Bush-Brown, *Copper Hill* by Lamar Dodd, *Negro Head* by Julian H. Harris, *Old Brewery* by George Ramey, *Between Courses* by Edward S. Shorter, and *Little Boy* by Hale Woodruff.

Architecture

WHEN HERNANDO DE SOTO in 1540 explored the region that later became Georgia, he found Indians living in huts constructed of poles and canes plastered with clay. These circular or rectangular huts, with curved cane and bark roofs rising flush from the walls, were carefully constructed dwellings rather than mere rude shelters. The missions and presidios erected by the Spanish in the southeastern part of the region and on the coastal islands were the first structures built by white men. These buildings were constructed of wood, adobe bricks, and sometimes of tabby, a cement made of oyster shells, lime, and sand in equal proportions. Tabby, also employed by the English who settled Georgia under Oglethorpe in 1733, was used in the fortifications of Frederica on St. Simon Island.

Log cabins predominated in the early settlements. The typical pioneer cabin consisted of a single room with a large end chimney of brick, mud, or field stone. The walls were of logs dovetailed together, the cracks were chinked with mud, and the roofs were covered with hand-split shingles. The floors often were of puncheons, split logs roughly smoothed by strokes of the axe, for it was not until later that hand-hewn boards were used for floors, ceilings, and sometimes walls. Openings were few and the small windows were closed by wooden shutters. The log cabin house was sometimes enlarged by adding rooms or a second story. An old tavern (Eagle Hotel) at Watkinsville is an example of this larger type, but the original logs later were covered with clapboards. Another type of log building that was common on the frontier as late as the first half of the nineteenth century is the blockhouse, a two-story square structure with a stone foundation. On the site of Fort Hawkins at Macon, such a structure has been restored on the foundations of the original blockhouse.

An interesting variation of the log cabin is the breezeway, or dog-trot house, still fairly common in southwest Georgia. Since the early log cabin did not lend itself readily to additions, the settlers found that the simplest method of enlargement was to erect another unit opposite

137

the first and to cover the connecting passage, thus making a windy combination of porch, washhouse, kennel, woodshed, and general catch-all. Even in comparatively recent years south Georgia farmers have constructed such houses of vertical boards with the joinings battened, or of logs with the passages between the units floored as well as covered. Many breezeway houses are still standing in the vicinity of Albany and Thomasville, contrasting sharply with the handsome winter homes of northern millionaires.

In Savannah the settlers' log huts were replaced by houses of clapboard, for which timbers were hewed from the dense forests bordering the Savannah River. Because of the careful planning and able craftsmanship of the early builders, and because the settlers modeled their houses after those of English cities, the town had less of a frontier appearance than had later outposts to the west. In general, architecture in Georgia evolved from frontier simplicity to the more pretentious building styles of the nineteenth century with few intermediate stages. Because economic expansion was not well under way until after 1800, there were not many fine Georgian Colonial houses and these were built for the most part only in the older communities. Since the recent razing of the old Mackay-Hunter and Houstoun-Johnston houses in Savannah, probably the most distinguished Georgian Colonial buildings in the state are Lowther Hall in Clinton, the Old White House in Augusta, and the Davenport and Pink houses in Savannah.

During the late Georgian Colonial period, when frontier cabins were still being built along the edge of the Cherokee country, a simple but pleasing transitional type of domestic architecture developed along the coast, especially in Savannah and Augusta. A small frame house was constructed on a high basement, which really constituted a first story and necessitated the building of a long, straight flight of steps to reach the main entrance on the second floor. It had a roof projecting over a porch in a long sweep, slender wooden columns, gable ends with outside chimneys, and dormer windows, usually three. The high basement is believed to have been evolved in order to raise the principal rooms above the level of the miasma, popularly considered a cause of malaria. Most cottages of this type have disappeared from the coastal countryside, but variations, with a small stoop in the center or at one side, are still frequently found in the older areas of Savannah. In the country versions, the porch was carried all the way across the front, as at Wild Hern on the Ogeechee River and at Refuge Plantation near Woodbine.

In Augusta this style was developed with such individuality of design that the Augusta Sand Hill Cottage is often designated as a definite type. The characteristic high basement is commonly explained here as having been adopted as a safeguard against floods, but probably it is only a derivative of the Georgian precedent. Many of the pleasing examples found in the city and in the surrounding country have been retrimmed with cast iron, Victorian latticework, or the jigsaw decorations of the 1880's. The interiors, usually designed with restraint, harmonize well with "peasant furniture" and simple antiques. Of the Augusta examples the best known are Meadow Garden, the Mell Cottage, the Chafee House, the Verdery Cottage, and the Dickey Cottage.

Because taste in architectural styles did not change rapidly, late Georgian elements and Adam details were carried over into the houses of the subsequent Federal era, when the effect of English Regency influence was felt. Consequently, the buildings of the period had the characteristics of both Georgian and Federal architecture. Some of the best houses of Milledgeville, Augusta, and Savannah have details showing the effects of this transition, as do the Blount House near Macon and the Mitchell-McComb House (Mount Nebo) near Milledgeville.

In the early decades of the nineteenth century a number of beautiful Federal houses, designed by the well-known English architect William Jay, were erected in Savannah and its vicinity. Although Jay remained only a few years in Georgia, the taste and beauty of his work is still an influence, reflecting as it does the elegance of his native Bath and suggesting the English dwellings in the West Indies from which he migrated to Savannah. Perhaps Jay's best known building was the Habersham House in Savannah, razed in 1916. Other Savannah buildings attributed to him are the Richardson-Owens House, the Scarborough House, and Telfair Academy, all of which are well preserved.

In 1805 Thomas Spalding reintroduced the use of tabby when he built a house on Sapelo Island. The structure was later destroyed by fire, and Howard E. Coffin erected a magnificent modern house on the old foundations. For coastal defense during the War of 1812, Isaiah Davenport built for the Government the round tabby Martello Tower near the lighthouse on Tybee Island, where it stood until well into the twentieth century. During the prosperous period following the war, Jay and other builders favored tabby as a structural material for the larger buildings. It is said that in Darien the exterior walls of the Dent House, traditionally credited to Jay, were made of tabby, as were those of Ashantilly, Spalding's old mainland house, which was burned in 1937. Rice mills and other plantation structures were also built of this material.

Expanded land holdings followed the increase of cotton production in the second quarter of the century, and larger, more sturdily built houses began to appear in the agricultural regions. During this era of prosperity Georgia, like other sections, evinced interest in the balanced architectural forms and classic details of ancient Greece. The characteristic feature of the Greek Revival house was the two-story colonnade of four or six columns across the entire front, but often there was a central portico with two or four columns supporting a front pediment. The interior followed the plan set by the first formal houses of the Georgian era. Two large rooms opened from each side of a wide central hall that usually had a stairway on one side. The broad verandas and high ceilings were particularly suited to the long hot summers of Georgia. Soon this style also reached the cities, and the entire state was dotted with the spacious columned houses that gave so lustrous a tradition to the ante bellum era.

The many Greek Revival buildings still remaining make Georgia outstanding for those who wish to study this architectural style. Examples of public buildings range from the handsome Old Medical College Building in Augusta and the University of Georgia Chapel in Athens to the simple Harrison Hotel on the square at Jefferson. Dwellings range from the elaborately detailed Orange Hall at St. Marys, the beautiful Ralph Small house in Macon, and the exquisitely proportioned Greenwood house near Thomasville to Mimosa Hall in Roswell, which follows the design of a classical temple without modification. The type includes not only skilfully detailed buildings such as the old Executive Mansion in Milledgeville but dwellings designed, often with engaging crudities, by plantation owners. Despite the ravages of war and time, innumerable Greek Revival houses stand along the route from Atlanta to Savannah by way of Covington, Madison, Eatonton, Milledgeville, and Louisville; and from Atlanta to Augusta by way of Athens and Washington. They are also found in Sparta, where the Middlebrooks and the Wynn-Clinch houses are notable examples.

Some Greek Revival houses, like those of the Carolina lowlands, have porticoes with two galleries and superimposed columns, sometimes of a different order. Examples are the Brown-Stetson-Sanford house and the Williams-Ferguson house in Milledgeville and the Sayre-Turner-Shivers house in Sparta. In general, however, they have two-story columns and are more closely akin to the upper Carolina and Virginia residences built by the Scotch-Irish pioneers who followed more closely the Classical Revival tradition.

The Gothic Revival, which spread throughout the state during the latter part of the Greek Revival period, is represented in the cities by such excellent examples as the Old Richmond Academy in Augusta, the Old Capitol in Milledgeville, and the Green-Meldrim mansion in

Savannah, where Sherman established headquarters after capturing the town. Since the classical influence continued strong until the War between the States, Gothic details were often combined with Greek and Roman themes. One of the most popular forms was the combination of small, square, one-story columns with elaborate latticework of wood or cast iron, as exemplified frequently in Augusta cottages. Occasionally this hybrid variety with two-story columns added an odd note to the classical plan, as in the Evans house in Sandersville. The Victorian Gothic style brought to the state many elaborate dormered dwellings with steep roofs, the forerunner of the jigsaw extravagances of the prosperous 1880's. Frequently, beautiful cast ironwork on porches and stair rails is combined with Greek columns and door trim, as in the T. R. R. Cobb and Howell Cobb houses in Athens. The Jones house at Birdsville, near Millen, is a good example of the combination of classical and Victorian details, often used in older houses.

During the War between the States there was naturally a complete cessation of building in Georgia. By the 1880's, however, the more progressive centers had recovered sufficiently to fall into line with the development of the French Renaissance style, which had been popular for a decade in other sections of the country. The Wesleyan Conservatory, the Marshall-Johnston house in Macon, and some of the older houses on Peachtree Street in Atlanta are conservative examples of buildings with the Mansard roofs of the Richard Morris Hunt vogue.

After the 1880 era, building reflected the current modes of the nation and resulted in both good and bad examples of Romanesque courthouses, neo-Gothic churches, and Italian Renaissance post offices. Because of the strong classical tendency, however, a restraining influence was more evident than in other states. In many towns twentieth-century neo-classic houses, called "Colonial," were built with hipped roofs, ornate banisters, and intricate entablatures, showing Victorian influence. With the softening effect of time, however, and the planting of shrubbery, these neo-classic houses harmonize with those of 1850 that antedate them by more than half a century. There are numerous examples on West Peachtree Street and Ponce de Leon Avenue in Atlanta, on Vineville Avenue in Macon, and along the highway in Montezuma.

No single style predominates in the architecture of Georgia today. Atlanta, with a serrated and sharpcut skyline, has the most noteworthy flat-surfaced, modern buildings in its downtown section. In its residential sections, especially the Paces Ferry and Druid Hills areas, Gothic, Greek Revival, Georgian Colonial, Spanish, half-timbered Elizabethan, French Chateau, and Italian Renaissance types provide interest and variety. This commingling of period designs is also evident in Augusta, known for its beautiful residential section, The Hill. Augusta lost many of its fine buildings in 1916, when the older portion of the city burned. The fad for Spanish Colonial architecture that spread from Florida in the 1920's resulted in the building of many schools, hospitals, and houses of this type in south Georgia. The Archbold Memorial Hospital at Thomasville and the Cloister Hotel at Sea Island are good examples.

Gothic, Georgian Colonial, and Greek Revival designs have long been popular for churches throughout the state. Gothic influence is seen in the crenellated parapets of the First Presbyterian Church, built in Augusta during the first quarter of the nineteenth century, while the design of the new Church of Christ the King in Atlanta reverts to the older Gothic style of the thirteenth century. The old Independent Presbyterian Church in Savannah and the new Glenn Memorial Church in Atlanta have the single tall spire and other characteristics of the Georgian Colonial religious edifices. Churches such as the Vineville Methodist Church in Macon and Christ Church in Savannah are of Greek Revival design. Examples of the simple type of church with a central overhead steeple are the frame Midway Church on the coast and the brick Jerusalem Church at Ebenezer.

During the nineteenth century the red-brick buildings of educational institutions were built with little regard for architectural styles. Many of those still standing, however, have the overornamentation of the Victorian period. The newer college buildings, such as those of Agnes Scott in Decatur and the Georgia School of Technology in Atlanta, are red-brick structures characterized by the pointed arches and limestone trim of the Collegiate Gothic style. Those of Oglethorpe University near Atlanta and of the girls' college at the Berry Schools near Rome are of stone in the traditional Gothic manner. The Wesleyan College buildings and those of the men's college at the Berry Schools show Greek Revival influence, and the pink marble buildings of Emory University are of Italian Renaissance design.

The three-story red-brick apartment buildings of the Techwood and University (Negro) housing projects in Atlanta are severely plain structures, showing the influence of modern utilitarian design. They are characteristic of the type of design used by the Federal Housing Authority in the slum areas of Savannah, Augusta, Macon, Columbus, Rome, and other Georgia cities. Four additional projects, each with 650 units, have been announced for Atlanta. Simple rectangular white frame cottages with front porches have been built for the families on the five resettlement projects of the Farm Security Administration. Another experiment in low-cost housing has been made by this organization near Athens where prefabricated dwellings constructed of steel sheeting have been built on individual farm units.

It is worthy of note that marble is used comparatively little, although the value of Georgia's production ranks second only to Vermont's. Its use in domestic work is negligible except around Tate, the great marble center, but it is employed to some extent in public buildings. Brick is used more frequently, and a ready supply is always assured by the abundance of red clay. Wood, however, is the material in most general use. Georgia's bountiful yellow pine, though less adaptable than white pine to the execution of intricate detail, has proved a strong and durable building material.

The architecture of Georgia in recent years has lost much of its indigenous quality by conforming to more universal patterns, but it has gained immeasurably in variety and in fineness of execution. With the predominant classical influence still strong, Georgia is becoming aware of other styles equally suited to its climate and topography. Examples of this trend are appearing with increasing frequency, not only in the larger cities, but throughout the entire state.

*

PART TWO

CITIES

*

Athens

Railroad Stations: Thomas and Mitchell Sts. for Central of Georgia Ry.; foot of Broad St. for Georgia R.R.; College Ave. and Ware St. for Seaboard Air Line Ry. and Gainesville Midland R.R.; Hoyt and Hull Sts. for Southern Ry.

Bus Station: Union Bus Depot, 220 W. Broad St., for Atlantic Greyhound, Bass Bus Lines, Neel Gap Lines, Smoky Mountain Stages, and Southeastern Stages.

Taxis: 10¢ a passenger within city limits; 10¢ additional for each suitcase or large parcel.

Local Busses: Fare 5¢.

Traffic Regulations: Right, left, and U turns at all intersections except where traffic lights direct otherwise. Right turns on red light, provided full stop is made. Speed limit in business district, 15 m.p.h.; in residential section, 30 m.p.h.

Accommodations: Six hotels, five tourist homes, one tourist camp.

Information Service: Athens Chamber of Commerce, Civic Hall, Washington St.

Football: Sanford Field Stadium, University of Georgia Campus.

Baseball: Old Sanford Field, Lumpkin St., for University of Georgia games.

Swimming: American Legion Pool, Lumpkin St.; children 10¢, adults 25¢.

Golf: Athens Country Club, 2 m. NW. on US 129 (Jefferson Rd.), 18 holes, 75¢ for non-residents.

Radio Station: WGAU (1310 kc.).

Motion Picture Houses: Four, including one for Negroes.

Annual Events: Little International Livestock Show, Hardman Hall, State Agricultural College, May. American Legion Fair and Carnival, on Legion grounds, 500 block Lumpkin St., October.

ATHENS (771 alt., 18,192 pop.), on a hill in a curve of the Oconee River, is known both as the home of the University of Georgia and as a city of fine ante bellum houses. Greek porticoes with pediments and large Doric columns are the dominant architectural feature. Old-fashioned boxwood gardens, towering oaks and elms, and white-blossomed magnolias with their sweet, heavy perfume, all embody the romantic traditions of the Deep South.

The small downtown section ends abruptly at the university campus. During the school season the collegiate atmosphere is dominant, and college performances are attended by enthusiastic citizens who, despite their deep

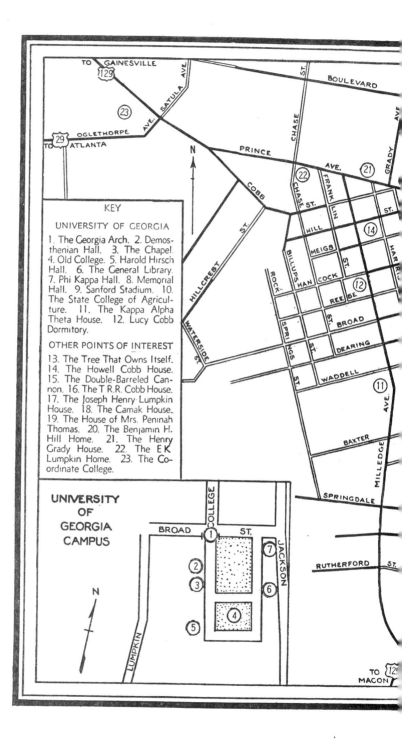

KEY

UNIVERSITY OF GEORGIA

1. The Georgia Arch. 2. Demosthenian Hall. 3. The Chapel. 4. Old College. 5. Harold Hirsch Hall. 6. The General Library. 7. Phi Kappa Hall. 8. Memorial Hall. 9. Sanford Stadium. 10. The State College of Agriculture. 11. The Kappa Alpha Theta House. 12. Lucy Cobb Dormitory.

OTHER POINTS OF INTEREST

13. The Tree That Owns Itself. 14. The Howell Cobb House. 15. The Double-Barreled Cannon. 16. The T.R.R. Cobb House. 17. The Joseph Henry Lumpkin House. 18. The Camak House. 19. The House of Mrs. Peninah Thomas. 20. The Benjamin H. Hill Home. 21. The Henry Grady House. 22. The E.K. Lumpkin Home. 23. The Coordinate College.

UNIVERSITY OF GEORGIA CAMPUS

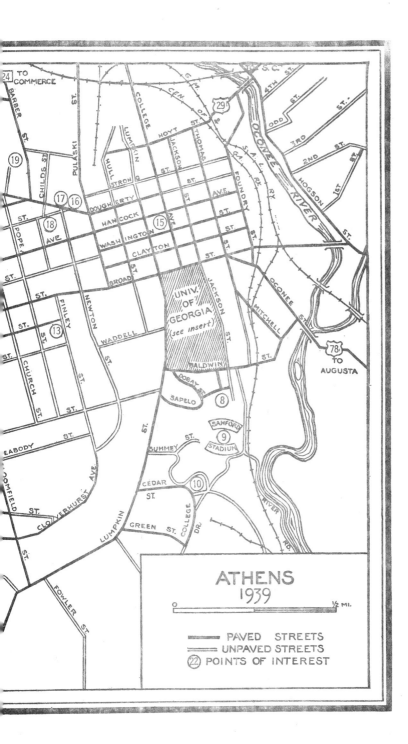

ATHENS
1939

0 ————————————— ½ MI.

═══════ PAVED STREETS
══════ UNPAVED STREETS
Ⓐ POINTS OF INTEREST

conservatism, are indulgent toward student pranks. The student body, coming principally from the small towns and farm areas of the state, is in general not wealthy, and the usual vehicles are superannuated Fords, gaily painted and piled with an amazing number of passengers.

The larger industrial plants of Athens lie along the banks of the Oconee River, but the smaller establishments are scattered throughout the city. Among widely diversified products manufactured by approximately forty plants are commercial fertilizers, tire cord, piece goods, hosiery, overalls, and cottonseed oil. Negroes, who constitute approximately 35 per cent of the population, have congregated principally in east Athens near the industrial plants, but many also live along the alleys throughout the city. Their social life centers about the churches and burial societies.

In 1784 the legislature allocated 40,000 acres of land for sale to provide an endowment for a university. Appointed on a board of trustees were Governor Lyman Hall, a signer of the Declaration of Independence, and Abraham Baldwin, alumnus of Yale, educator, and lawyer. Baldwin, as a member of the legislature, drew up a charter that was legally passed the following year. He was elected president of the proposed institution and held the entirely nominal office for fifteen years before he resigned to become a member of the United States Senate. His former pupil at Yale, Josiah Meigs, was elected to fill the position in 1801, and a committee was appointed to select a site for the college. The committee members were delighted with a tract of land in the bend of the Oconee because of the majestic oaks, clear spring, and delicious river shad that they ate for lunch. Consequently John Milledge, later Governor of Georgia, donated 633 acres here as the site for a town, which the committee named Athens.

In the fall of 1801 Meigs hastily erected a few log and frame buildings, sold town lots to raise money for the university, and soon began to impart his precise culture to a handful of young men in a wild and lonely land. The peaceable Cherokee did not interfere, and in 1805 construction was finished on the first permanent building, which was named Franklin College, a term applied for years afterward to the entire institution. At this time there were not a dozen houses in the settlement, that had been named hopefully for the ancient Greek city. In 1807 a newspaper was printed, but this journal and others immediately following it were short-lived. In 1824 a Methodist church was erected, and in 1841 the Georgia Railroad was laid from Carr's Hill, across the river from Athens, to Union Point. The Southern Mutual Insurance Company and a branch of the state bank were also established during this period.

The genteel church and college groups sometimes clashed with the rough pioneers in the new settlement. The Franklin House was prohibited from serving intoxicants under penalty of losing some of its rented land, but a bar, ingeniously connected by a bridge with a house in the rear, was well known to initiates. Another early hostelry, the Newton House, is remembered for its churchlike belfry and the enormous bell that clanged forth the noon dinner hour. Town Hall, built in 1845, contained a bell that was equally practical. The basement of this distinguished edifice served as a meat market, and it was customary to ring the bell whenever an animal was slaughtered so that housewives could purchase their meat while it was fresh.

The mid-nineteenth century was marked by a rising interest in girls' schools, of which Lucy Cobb Institute, opened in 1859, survived the longest. The university commencement had a state-wide significance, for not only did graduates meet old friends but business men and politicians gathered to solicit favors. The most illustrious statesmen of the period kept the students' minds upon vital issues, until all others were blotted out by secession.

Aroused by the wrathful eloquence of Thomas R. R. Cobb's secessionist speeches, so many students enlisted in the Confederate Army that the small attendance forced the university to close in 1863. The Athens Guards, which had been chartered in 1855, drilled in gay uniforms trimmed with gold braid and later marched to battle while their wives sewed for the Soldiers' Aid Society. At first Athens felt no impact of actual warfare, but in 1864 the buildings of the university were converted into hospitals and barracks to accommodate the refugees and wounded soldiers who crowded into the city.

The increase in population, caused by the many refugees who remained after the war, led to the incorporation of Athens as a city in 1872. About the same time it became the seat of Clarke County. A city school system was established in 1885, and the State Normal school, now Co-ordinate College, was opened ten years later. Also in the 1890's Georgia included in its annual appropriation bill funds for the State College of Agriculture and the Mechanic Arts, which had been established in 1872 as a department of the university and supported partly by federal funds. In 1906 the general assembly made the department a separate institution under the name of the State College of Agriculture. In 1932, when all state institutions of higher learning were incorporated into the university system, the college again became a department of the state university. The emphasis placed by the college on modern farming methods and diversification of crops has profoundly affected the farm life of Georgia.

Although many sports-loving Georgians regard the university as a mere adjunct to its football team, a high scholastic standard is maintained. The faculty of nearly two hundred and the student body of thirty-five hundred leave their imprint on the civic and social fabric of Athens; otherwise, it is an aristocratic, old-fashioned southern city, leisured in its tempo, gracious in its manner of living.

THE UNIVERSITY OF GEORGIA

The University has twenty-three principal buildings on the Old Campus, which has a weathered iron fence across the front. The oldest structures, set about the long grassy quadrangle, are uniform neither in style nor material but have a dignified harmony in their setting of trees and shrubbery. The newer buildings, generally of red brick, show the influence of Georgian Colonial architecture.

(Unless otherwise stated, all buildings are open during school hours.)

1. The GEORGIA ARCH, at the main entrance to the campus, College Ave. and Broad St., is a simplified version of the one depicted on the state seal. The cast-iron arch, erected in 1856, is adorned with conventionalized bough patterns and supported by three slender fluted columns. Freshmen are forbidden to pass beneath its portals except on Freshman Night early in the school year, when the entire city falls under their noisy dominion.

2. DEMOSTHENIAN HALL, a small, square, two-story structure of cement-covered brick with a plain elliptical-arch doorway and central Palladian window, was completed in 1824. The ceiling of the upper floor is designed in the Christopher Wren manner, with a beautiful central medallion and molded plaster frieze. The hall houses the university's first literary society, founded in 1803. The Demosthenian Society evolved a custom of making famous men honorary members, and its membership included Andrew Johnson, Henry Clay, and William Cullen Bryant.

During the first half of the nineteenth century literary societies had an importance somewhat comparable to that of modern football teams. Rigid rules governed the meetings, and fines ranging from twenty-five cents to two dollars were imposed upon debaters for eating, standing before the fire, or pulling a fellow member's coattail. Crawford Long, the first physician to use ether in an operation, Robert Toombs, the fiery Confederate orator, and Henry Timrod, the poet, all were punished for infractions during their student days.

3. The CHAPEL is a cement-covered brick building with massive Doric columns. Dominating its auditorium is a large painting of the interior of St. Peter's in Rome by George Cook, a Virginia artist (1783-1857); it was presented to the school by Daniel Pratt, of Prattville, Alabama.

The chapel, completed in 1832, was the first permanent assembly hall of the college. Commencement exercises were held in this old building for almost a century, until a larger enrollment made the custom impracticable. During the War between the States federal troops quartered on the campus used the front columns as rifle targets. The bell in a tower at the rear of the chapel rings for class assembly and to celebrate athletic victories.

4. OLD COLLEGE, a three-story, red brick structure of post-Colonial design completed in 1805, was modeled after Connecticut Hall at Yale, for Josiah Meigs brought the plans with him when he came to Georgia in 1801. The building was named Franklin College to honor Benjamin Franklin, who had acted as London agent for the Georgia colony, and this name is still applied to the College of Arts and Sciences. A plaque on the exterior wall of the second story marks the room once occupied by Crawford W. Long and Alexander H. Stephens. These two men, roommates in college, are Georgia's representatives in Statuary Hall of the National Capitol.

5. HAROLD HIRSCH HALL, occupied by the Lumpkin Law School, was constructed in 1932 largely through alumni contributions and named for Harold Hirsch, a prominent lawyer and alumnus. This handsome, three-story, red brick building, designed in the Greek Revival style, has a small entrance portico adorned with four fluted Doric columns and a central tower and cupola topped with balanced scales symbolic of justice. The Alexander C. King Law Library contains more than fourteen thousand volumes. On the library walls hang seven engravings which William Starr Basinger, an 1846 alumnus, bought from the Arundel Society of England. These engravings are from Raphael's original designs for the Sistine Chapel tapestries.

The Lumpkin Law School was founded in 1859, when the question of secession and states' rights had kindled Georgia to excitement over legislative affairs. The founders, William Hope Hull, Thomas R. R. Cobb, and Joseph Henry Lumpkin, were well-known attorneys, and Lumpkin, for whom the school was named, was the first chief justice of Georgia's supreme court.

6. The GENERAL LIBRARY, a brick and stone building completed in 1905, was the gift of the philanthropist, George Foster Peabody. The library, founded a year before the school opened, contains more than 80,000 volumes, about 150,000 pamphlets, and many maps and manuscripts. Its Georgia collection was greatly increased in 1938 by the acquisition of the noted DeRenne Library from Wormsloe (*see* SAVANNAH). Among the prized documents of this collection are letters of Harman Verelst, Oglethorpe's private agent, James Wright, last Colonial Governor, and General Nathanael Greene, Colonial patriot. William Stephens' *Journal of the Proceedings in Georgia* (1742), a copy of the *Cherokee Phoenix,* and photostat files of the *Royal Georgia Gazette* are other rare items.

7. PHI KAPPA HALL (*lower floor open*), Broad and Jackson Sts., is a two-story, red brick structure with four smooth Doric columns across its portico. The building was constructed in 1836 for the Phi Kappa Literary Society, which was organized in 1820 largely through the efforts of Joseph

Henry Lumpkin. Taking themselves very seriously, the Phi Kappa boys showed their patriotism by adorning their walls with portraits of Presidents of the United States. In selecting their honorary members, they were even more ambitious than their Demosthenian rivals, for they extended invitations to Andrew Jackson, James K. Polk, James Buchanan, Jefferson Davis, John Tyler, and Napoleon III. When the hall was used as a storehouse during the War between the States, its valuable library was damaged irreparably.

8. MEMORIAL HALL, visible from Dobay St., is situated on a high hill overlooking the campus. The imposing cream brick building with its Ionic portico was erected in 1923 by friends and alumni to honor university students who died in the World War.

A plaque in the interior marble and limestone rotunda honors Vonalbade Gammon, a student killed in one of the first football games (1897). Realizing what his wishes would have been, his mother controlled her grief and intervened in behalf of football when excited public opinion resulted in legal steps to ban the game in the state. The library, left of the rotunda, is used by foreign and graduate students, and the lounge serves as a hall for intimate lectures and musicales. The athletic association maintains headquarters in the basement.

9. SANFORD STADIUM, S. end of Dobay St., is the athletic field of the university. The large, oval, concrete structure, with a seating capacity of 33,000, is in a natural ravine. The stadium, named in honor of S. V. Sanford, Chancellor of the University System, was dedicated on October 12, 1929, when the Yale football squad broke a precedent by coming south to play against the Georgia Bulldogs. The dedication occurred amid elaborate ceremonies before many visiting dignitaries, present to pay tribute to Abraham Baldwin.

10. The STATE COLLEGE OF AGRICULTURE, Cedar St. and College Dr., a department of the university, has a campus of 140 acres and an adjoining farm of 1,250 acres. There are nine main buildings, a dairy and livestock barn, greenhouses, and many special buildings, bringing the total number to 110.

LUMPKIN HALL, a two-story, granite building used by the college, was erected by Irish masons in 1842 as the home of Wilson Lumpkin, celebrated jurist and Governor of Georgia. According to tradition, the Governor was seeking to embody in the house his own rock-ribbed personality.

11. The KAPPA ALPHA THETA HOUSE (*private*), 338 Milledge Ave., originally the A. P. Dearing home, is a beautiful red brick Greek Revival building

completed in 1856. Construction is of brick throughout, even to the massive Doric columns covered with cement. The interior woodwork is of curly maple and the flooring is of wide board pine.

12. LUCY COBB DORMITORY, Milledge Ave. between Reese St. and Hancock Ave., a three-story stone building with long piazzas decorated in lacy ironwork, housed Lucy Cobb Institute from the 1860's well into the twentieth century. This school for girls was praised throughout the South for its emphasis on gentle manners and old-fashioned accomplishments. Its founding followed an article in the *Southern Watchman* in which Mrs. Williams Rutherford, writing under an assumed name from feelings of ladylike modesty, deplored the poor facilities for southern female education. Her brother, General T. R. R. Cobb, appealed to Athens people, canvassed for subscriptions, and contributed liberally himself. Lucy Cobb Institute was opened in 1859 and named for General Cobb's little daughter, who had recently died.

From 1880 the institution was directed for many years by Miss Mildred Lewis Rutherford. "Miss Millie," always a champion of southern traditions, was a woman of powerful personality, commanding presence, and fearlessly outspoken opinions; she was known widely for the speeches she delivered in hoop skirts. For all her decorum, she seemed to enjoy her protracted battles over the plaster goats that stood at each end of the dormitory's long veranda. The college boys periodically painted these animals in their school colors, red and black. At last they were broken when the boys attempted to hide them; some of the former belles of Lucy Cobb still cherish pieces of the goats as souvenirs. After Miss Rutherford's death in 1928, interest in the old-fashioned institution declined, and two years later the university annexed the building as a dormitory for women students.

OTHER POINTS OF INTEREST

13. The TREE THAT OWNS ITSELF, SW. corner Dearing and Finley Sts., was on the land of Colonel William H. Jackson, who, according to tradition, in 1820 bequeathed to this white oak in fee simple all land within eight feet of its trunk. It is encircled by chains linked to granite posts and is marked by an inscribed granite block.

14. The HOWELL COBB HOUSE (*private*), 425 Hill St., is a two-story, white frame structure of Greek Revival design. The classic portico is adorned with Doric columns, a small overhanging balcony, and a wide piazza enclosed by an iron balustrade. General Howell Cobb, brother of General T. R. R. Cobb and Governor of Georgia, built this house about 1850.

Howell Cobb, one of Georgia's most eminent statesmen, unwaveringly supported the Union in 1850 during the bitter controversy over the trying problems of the times. In 1861, however, he spoke strongly for secession and later attended the convention to draft the Confederate constitution. When Joe Brown, Georgia's pugnacious wartime Governor, quarreled with President Jefferson Davis over the right of individual states to raise their own armies, Cobb was among Brown's most bitter opponents.

15. The DOUBLE-BARRELED CANNON, SW. corner Hancock and College Aves., made at the Athens Foundry during the War between the States, is believed to be the only gun of its type in the world. The inventors devised a plan for chaining the balls together and mowing down the enemy in great numbers but unfortunately failed to synchronize the firing of the two barrels. An eyewitness of the trial shot states that the chain broke, one ball demolishing a Negro cabin, the other plowing up an acre of ground and killing a yearling calf in a distant field.

16. The T. R. R. COBB HOUSE (*private*), 194 Prince Ave., is a white frame dwelling with a Doric portico, a small balcony, and octagonal wings. The clapboarded exterior walls are accented with Doric pilasters at the corners. This house, built between 1830 and 1840, was bought and remodeled by General T. R. R. Cobb about 1843. General Cobb, an ardent secessionist, was influential in causing Georgia to withdraw from the Union and in drafting the new Confederate constitution.

17. The JOSEPH HENRY LUMPKIN HOUSE (*private*), 248 Prince Ave., was built about 1845 by Lumpkin, a co-founder of the Lumpkin Law School and Georgia's first chief justice. The house is an excellent example of Greek Revival architecture, with a large Doric portico and a hanging balcony above the entrance. For a period following 1869 the dwelling was occupied by the Home School, established by Mme Sophie Sosnowski, a political refugee from Poland, who came to Athens in 1862 to teach at Lucy Cobb.

18. The CAMAK HOUSE (*private*), 279 Meigs St., was erected in 1817 and occupied by James Camak, first president of a branch of the Georgia State Bank established in Athens in 1834. This dwelling is one of the few old Athens homes still owned by descendants of the original owners. The house, constructed of brick painted white, is predominantly Georgian Colonial in style, having a raised basement and a small piazza of wrought iron.

19. The HOUSE OF MRS. PENINAH THOMAS (*private*), 698 N. Pope St., built about 1840 by General Howell Cobb, is a three-story Greek Revival struc-

ture of cement-covered brick painted white. Six Doric columns rest upon concrete pillars between which are low arches that provide for light on the basement terrace.

20. The BENJAMIN H. HILL HOME (*private*), 570 Prince Ave., is a white clapboard house of Greek Revival design with a massive Corinthian portico extending along the front and sides of the structure and a characteristic balcony above the entrance. The front garden, with its oaks, cedars, magnolias, crape myrtles, and formal plantings of boxwood, follows the old-fashioned southern plan. In the rear a Doric colonnade overlooks a modern, landscaped garden.

Built by John Thomas Grant in 1855, this house did not come into Hill's possession until 1869. Benjamin Hill (*see* TOUR 3) was a prominent Georgia statesman despite a temporary unpopularity caused by his freely avowed change of conviction on the secession question.

21. The HENRY GRADY HOUSE (*private*), 634 Prince Ave., was built about 1845 and later was occupied by Henry W. Grady (*see* ATLANTA), whose magnetic personality and equable, progressive attitude did much to reconcile the South with its northern conquerors. Thirteen monumental Doric columns, representing the original colonies, enclose its Greek Revival portico on three sides of the house. Heavily linteled windows extending to the floor are flanked by paneled pilasters.

22. The E. K. LUMPKIN HOME (*private*), 973 Prince Ave., a two-story brownstone house with corner quoins and a wrought-iron piazza, was built about 1850. Here in 1891 Mrs. E. K. Lumpkin formed the Ladies' Garden Club, first organization of its kind in the United States. The gardens, planted by Mrs. Lumpkin, have received national recognition for their boxwood and iris.

23. The CO-ORDINATE COLLEGE, Prince and Oglethorpe Aves., was originally the State Normal School, opened in 1895. When the control of the state colleges was vested in the Board of Regents in 1932, this institution was reorganized as an integral part of the university. The ten buildings are set on a sixty-acre campus.

GILMER HALL (*private*), Prince and Oglethorpe Aves., a brownstone dormitory with iron-railed piazzas and a large bracketed gable, was erected 1859-60 and was called Rock College because it was built of native stone. It was occupied first as a college preparatory school for the university. During the War between the States it was used as a hospital and afterwards as a rehabilitation training school for Confederate soldiers. In 1895 the building was given to the new State Normal School and its name was changed to Gilmer Hall in honor of Governor George R. Gilmer, who bequeathed an endowment fund for the training of Georgia teachers.

WINNIE DAVIS HALL (*first floor open 9-6 daily*), facing main entrance, one of the seven dormitories, was erected in 1902 by various branches of the United Daughters of the Confederacy and named for Jefferson Davis' daughter. The fluted Doric columns of this three-story brick building are thickly covered with ivy. The roof of the portico is bordered by a balustraded parapet. In the reception rooms are two collections of war relics. The Confederate souvenirs were donated by the U. D. C., and the World War relics were assembled by Miss Moina Michael of Athens, who is known as the originator of "Poppy Day," an occasion for raising funds to aid disabled World War veterans.

Atlanta

Railroad Stations: Terminal Station, Mitchell and Spring Sts., for Central of Georgia Ry., Atlanta & West Point R.R., Seaboard Air Line Ry., and Southern Ry.; Union Station, 2 Forsyth St., for Atlanta, Birmingham & Coast R.R., Louisville & Nashville R.R., Nashville, Chattanooga & St. Louis Ry., and Georgia R.R.; Peachtree Station, 1688 Peachtree St., for Southern Ry.

Bus Station: Union Terminal, 169 Carnegie Way, for Southeastern Greyhound of Alabama, Southeastern Management Co., Atlantic Greyhound, Teche Greyhound, Southeastern Stages, Southern Stages, Georgia Stages, Service Stages, Smoky Mountain Stages, Peach Belt Stages, Southeastern Motor, Dahlonega Bus, Neel Gap Bus, Tennessee Coach Co., and Suburban Coach Lines.

Airport: Candler Field Municipal Airport at Hapeville, 9.2 m. S. of city on US 41, for Eastern and Delta Air Lines; special bus, fare 75¢, stops at hotels, Terminal Station, and downtown ticket offices of air lines.

Taxis: 15¢ in business district for one to five passengers; 30¢ for 4 miles; 10¢ each additional half-mile; hand baggage free.

Streetcars and Local Busses: 10¢; four tickets for 30¢; shoppers' busses limited to central business section, 5¢.

Traffic Regulations: Speed limit 25 m.p.h. One-way streets indicated by signs. Right turn permitted on red light after full stop; left turn on green light only. All vehicles must stop six feet behind streetcars or busses except at safety islands. Limited parking in downtown area; no parking at yellow curbs; parking on R. of street enforced even in residential sections.

Accommodations: 70 hotels including 2 for Negroes; many tourist homes.

Tourist Information Service: Atlanta Chamber of Commerce, Chamber of Commerce Bldg., Pryor St. at Auburn Ave.; AAA, Biltmore Hotel, 817 W. Peachtree St.; Dixie Motor Club, 302 Peachtree St.; Atlanta Convention and Tourist Bureau, Rhodes-Haverty Bldg., 134 Peachtree St.

Theaters and Motion Picture Houses: Erlanger Theater, Peachtree St. between Linden St. and North Ave.; Atlanta Theater, 25 Exchange Pl., SE.; Auditorium-Armory, corner Courtland St. and Gilmer St., for occasional concerts and operas; 33 motion picture houses including 8 for Negroes.

Radio Stations: WSB (740 kc.); WGST (890 kc.); WAGA (1450 kc.); WATL (1370 kc.).

Swimming: Municipal pools in Piedmont Park, Piedmont Ave. at 14th St.; Mozley Park, Mozley Dr. at Laurel Ave.; Grant Park, Cherokee Ave. at Georgia Ave.; Maddox Park, Bankhead Ave. at Law St.; Cochran (Oakland City) Park, Holderness St. at Harman St.; small fee.

Golf: Municipal courses: Bobby Jones Course, North Side Dr. (Clubhouse on Woodward Way), 18 holes, $1; Piedmont Park, Boulevard at 10th St., 9 holes, 25¢; James L. Key Course, Glenwood Ave. at Chester Ave., 9 holes, 25¢; John A. White Course, Huff Rd. at Cascade Ave., 9 holes, 25¢; Candler Park, McLendon Ave. at Mayson Ave., 9 holes, 25¢.

Riding: Roxboro Riding Academy, Roxboro Rd., NE.; Biltmore Riding School, Roxboro Rd., NE.; Canter Riding Club, Lindbergh Dr., NE.; Pine Hill Riding Stables, off Roswell Rd.; Tuxedo Hunt Club, Tuxedo Park.

Tennis: 71 courts in municipal parks (*see* SWIMMING); 6 courts for Negroes in Washington Park, Lena and Ollie Sts.

Baseball: Ponce de Leon Park, Ponce de Leon Ave., Southern League (Atlanta Crackers).

Football: Grant Field, Georgia Tech, North Ave. and Techwood Dr.; Rose Bowl Field, Georgia Tech, Fifth St.; Hermance Stadium, Oglethorpe University, Peachtree Rd.; Ponce de Leon Park, 650 Ponce de Leon Ave., NE., for high school games.

Annual Events: Flowering of dogwood trees in residential sections, April; Flower Week (Garden Club Flower Show), May 6-11; Horse Show, May 8-10; "Uncle Remus" May Festival for children at Wren's Nest, home of Joel Chandler Harris, 1050 Gordon St. (date varies annually); automobile races on dirt track, July 4 and Labor Day, Lakewood Park; polo tournament each summer between officers at Fort McPherson and members of Governor's Horse Guard; Southeastern Fair and Educational Exposition, first week in October at Lakewood Park; Joel Chandler Harris Memorial Service, Wren's Nest, December 9.

ATLANTA (1,050 alt.; 270,366 pop.), capital of Georgia, is a lusty off-spring of railroads—restless, assertive, sprawling in all directions and taking in smaller towns in its incessant push toward greater growth. Downtown there is a ceaseless humming beneath the sharper surface noises; even in quiet residential hills sound the distant chug and clatter of trains. Founded little more than a century ago and burned by General Sherman on his march to the sea, Atlanta has grown haphazardly out of the Reconstruction era to be a wealthy industrial metropolis and the southern distributing point for many national products. Unlike most southern cities it has no old houses and few old families, but it has handsome estates and a smart society. It has not many cultural traditions, but it is a flourishing center for education, music, and painting. It has few classic columns but many smokestacks. Gay, modern, colorful, and energetic, it is a city of the New South.

The principal business area extends roughly from North Avenue south-ward to Mitchell Street, and from Courtland Street westward to Spring Street. Within this section, gashed by parking lots and intricately threaded by narrow streets, are the hotels and tall office buildings that make Atlanta's jagged skyline. Here flimsy wooden fronts go up overnight, scaffolding rises high, and riveters keep up their staccato drumming as the city is built, torn down, and built again. Beneath the five parallel viaducts lie gleaming stretches of railroad track lined by sheds and the stores of the former street level. In the sunless gloom of this underground Atlanta is a man's world

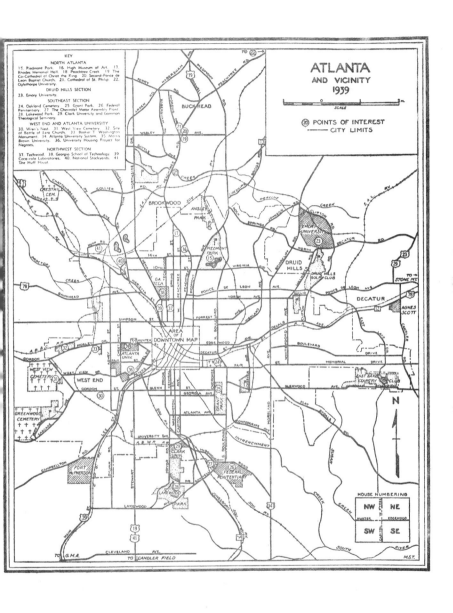

KEY
NORTH ATLANTA
15. Piedmont Park. 16. High Museum of Art. 17.
Rhodes Memorial Hall. 18. Peachtree Creek. 19. The
Co-Cathedral of Christ the King. 20. Second-Ponce de
Leon Baptist Church. 21. Cathedral of St. Philip. 22.
Oglethorpe University.

DRUID HILLS SECTION
23. Emory University.

SOUTHEAST SECTION
24. Oakland Cemetery. 25. Grant Park. 26. Federal
Penitentiary. 27. The Chevrolet Motor Assembly Plant.
28. Lakewood Park. 29. Clark University and Gammon
Theological Seminary.

WEST END AND ATLANTA UNIVERSITY
30. Wren's Nest. 31. West View Cemetery. 32. Site
of Battle of Ezra Church. 33. Booker T. Washington
Monument. 34. Atlanta University System. 35. Morris
Brown University. 36. University Housing Project for
Negroes.

NORTHWEST SECTION
37. Techwood. 38. Georgia School of Technology. 39.
Coca-cola Laboratories. 40. National Stockyards. 41.
The Huff House.

ATLANTA
AND VICINITY
1939

SCALE

⑳ POINTS OF INTEREST
———— CITY LIMITS

of grimy flagmen and overalled Negroes who push baggage carts or drive mail trucks bumping over the cobblestones.

Southeast of Five Points, Atlanta's present hub, is its old center where the state capitol dome, the spires of older churches, and the smokestacks and water towers of many factories are silhouetted against the sky. Once fashionable houses, with ironwork, cupolas, and bay windows, still stand amid the old trees, but they have become dingy. Along the shady streets move shawled Jewish housewives on their way to kosher markets, and occasionally there is a bearded rabbi, venerable in his skull-cap. This is the section of the pushcart man—the scissors grinder, the fruit peddler, the peanut vendor. There is a rich, fruity smell from markets where farmers unload their trucks and arrange their fruit and vegetables in gayly colored rows.

Northward, zoning laws are yielding to the advance of business, and small shopping centers are springing up at street intersections. Old homes are used for boarding houses or are being torn down to make way for apartments, filling stations, chain stores, and open-air eating places. To the northeast are the colorful tile roofs of Druid Hills, famous for its dogwood, and other beautifully landscaped residential subdivisions. To the north extends the Peachtree Road section, and far beyond the city limits are the imposing estates of West Paces Ferry Road. These sections are notable for green lawns and luxuriant shrubbery, and in April there is still greater beauty when the white dogwood blossoms appear like a spring snowfall.

Atlanta's Negroes, one-third of the total population, are segregated, but not always in clearly defined districts. Many of the more prosperous live in well-kept houses along Ashby Street, near the trim campus of Atlanta University, or slightly east of this vicinity in comfortable lodgings newly erected by a Negro slum clearance project. The poorer Negroes live over garages or in frame shacks along the alleys behind the homes of white people and in dilapidated old residences near the business district. These neighborhoods are loud and gay as the rich voices call from porch to porch. Down the streets in winter rumble horse-drawn wagons filled with coal that is sold by the sack for 25¢ and 50¢; Negroes in the backs of the wagons squat about charcoal fires built in old buckets and warm their hands over the flames.

Atlanta's history, characteristic of its adolescence, is a chronology of energetic personalities and rapid changes. The first mention of the region is found in Revolutionary War records dated August 1, 1782, which state that a secret emissary had been delegated to report on rumors of friction between the Cherokee and Creek Indians at The Standing Peachtree. Named, according to legend, for a fruit-bearing tree that grew on a near-by Indian mound, The Standing Peachtree was a Creek settlement on the southern bank of the Chattahoochee River, approximately seven miles from the present site of Atlanta. The Creek are said to have acquired the region south of the river from the Cherokee in a series of decisive ball games, with the land rights at stake.

Because of the disturbances between the Creek and Cherokee, Lieutenant George R. Gilmer, later Governor of Georgia, was commissioned in 1813 to erect a fort at The Standing Peachtree; he and twenty-two recruits constituted the first white settlement in the Atlanta area. After his departure, The Standing Peachtree grew into an important trading post and gateway to northern Cherokee lands.

The founding of Atlanta was due to the enterprise of pioneer railroad men. In 1836 representatives of the existing railroads in Georgia devised a plan whereby the state should build a railroad through the mountains of north Georgia to connect the proposed termini of their lines at the Chattahoochee River with the Tennessee River. The charter of the Monroe Railroad was amended on December 10, 1836, to provide for the extension of that line from Forsyth to the Chattahoochee River, and eleven days later the Western & Atlantic Railroad was chartered to be built at state expense. A year later a legislative act provided for the extension of the Western & Atlantic to a point not exceeding eight miles from the southeastern bank of the Chattahoochee River. The promoters of the Georgia Railroad were permitted by the same assembly to extend their line from Madison to the terminus of the Western & Atlantic.

The proposed junction of the railroads, referred to as Terminus, soon became a trading center for the surrounding country, with two stores, a sawmill, and a railroad office. In 1843 the settlement was incorporated as the town of Marthasville in honor of Martha Lumpkin, daughter of the Governor. When the Georgia Railroad was completed in 1845, Marthasville was considered an inappropriate name for so progressive a community, and the town was given the name Atlanta as a feminine version of Atlantic, taken from the Western & Atlantic Railroad. The following year, when the Macon & Western, formerly the Monroe Railroad, reached Atlanta, the town's commercial importance increased so rapidly that on December 29, 1847, Atlanta was reincorporated as a city. The corporate limits of the new city were within a circle, the center of which was the Western & Atlantic zero milepost near the southwestern corner of Wall Street and Central Avenue.

In 1851 the Southern Agricultural Fair, held on the site now occupied by the Fair Street School, introduced Atlanta as a marketing center for agricultural products and livestock. During the same year two political parties sprang up, the "Orderly" and the "Rowdy." A riot instigated by the "Rowdies" caused Mayor Jonathan Norcross to issue a call for volunteer police, and the response of more than a hundred armed men constituted the beginning of a regular police force.

The new county of Fulton was created from DeKalb County on December 20, 1853, and Atlanta was made its seat. In the same year the Holland Free School, the city's first publicly sponsored educational institution, was opened in the old Angier Academy on the southwest corner of Forsyth and Garnett Streets. In 1854, when the population was approximately 6,000, the Athenaeum Theater was opened and the first city hall was constructed. The Atlanta Medical College was founded in 1855 by the physicians of the city. During the same year a charter was granted to the Atlanta Gas Company, and the city was lighted by gas on Christmas Day. A city directory, published in 1859, gave Atlanta's population as 11,500.

In the late 1850's growing agitation between the North and the South prompted Atlanta merchants to restrict business transactions to southern firms. Several political clubs were organized. Grim gatherings were held by the Gate City Guards and the Atlanta Grays, military organizations engendered by the unrest of the times. The secession of Georgia from the Union on January 19, 1861, aroused the citizens to feverish activity, for it was logical that Atlanta should become an important military and hospitalization center and supply depot for Confederate forces. The city was put under martial law by Confederate forces in April, 1862. During the course of the war many large factories and warehouses were established for the manufacture and storage of supplies. It has been estimated that 80,000 wounded soldiers were quartered in the city.

On May 22, 1863, instructions were given Colonel Lemuel P. Grant to plan fortifications for the defense of Atlanta; by April of the next year breastworks and batteries were in readiness to withstand the expected attack. When General John B. Hood superseded General Joseph E. Johnston in command of the Confederate army on July 17, 1864, General Sherman was already moving his men into position around the outer line of defense. On July 22, two days after General Hood's desperate attempt to break the advancing Union line at the Battle of Peachtree Creek, the fierce encounter known as the Battle of Atlanta occurred in the southeastern part of the city, principally along what is now Moreland and DeKalb Avenues. Losses were heavy on both sides, but the battle was not decisive. A few days later a short conflict at Ezra Church in southwest Atlanta convinced Sherman that it was too costly to take the city by assault. Several of the largest siege guns used in the war were brought down from Chattanooga, and the bombardment of Atlanta was continued throughout the remainder of July and all of August.

By the end of August General Sherman had destroyed all means of Confederate communication with Atlanta except the Central Railroad (formerly the Macon & Western). Finding it impossible to compel the city's surrender by bombardment, he swung a large part of his army to Jonesboro, twenty miles south, in an effort to cut this last line of communication.

STEEL WORKS, ATLANTA

MAKING CANDLEWICK BEDSPREADS, RESACA

TEXTILE MILL—WARPING

TEXTILE MILL—SLASHING MACHINE

POWER DAM, TUGALO

GOLD MINING, DAHLONEGA

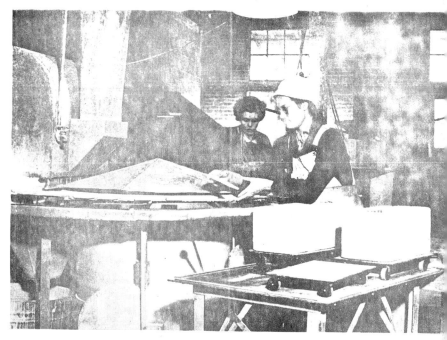

TILE MANUFACTURE, MACON

MARBLE QUARRY, TATE

ROSIN YARDS, SAVANNAH

PAPER MILL, SAVANNAH

LOGS FOR CRATE MANUFACTURE, MACON

LOADING COTTON, SAVANNAH

MULE AUCTION, ATLANTA

General Hood sent General W. J. Hardee with a small force to meet him, but the result was a Confederate defeat at the Battle of Jonesboro, September 1, and the seizure of the railroad. Hood evacuated Atlanta that night by way of the McDonough wagon road, and on September 2 the mayor formally surrendered Atlanta to Colonel John Coburn.

Within the next few days General Sherman ordered the removal of all citizens from the city, an unexpected command, since the terms of surrender specified that the lives and property of all citizens were to be protected. Sherman, however, supplied teams of horses for transporting citizens to Rough and Ready, a settlement one mile south of the present Hapeville, and Hood furnished additional teams from Rough and Ready to Lovejoy Station, ten miles farther south. After the evacuation had been completed, Sherman reorganized his army and gave orders for the destruction of Atlanta by fire and explosives. On November 15, the day after the conflagration, Sherman and his army resumed their march toward the sea, having dispersed the population and razed all but 400 of Atlanta's 4,500 houses and commercial buildings.

The war was a heavy blow to Atlanta's progress and development. Much of the real estate, which had been assessed in 1860 at almost three million dollars, and much personal property had been destroyed by fire. Rehabilitation, however, followed quickly. By January, 1865, many citizens had returned to rebuild the city from salvaged materials and, after the Confederate surrender, there was an influx of people from the North and other parts of the South. On June 24, 1865, at the first public meeting after the surrender of Atlanta, citizens discussed plans for reconstruction and resolved to co-operate with the Union politically and commercially. Although at first financial difficulties made it necessary to appeal for food supplies, immediate steps were taken to reorganize business and repair the wrecked railroad facilities. In 1866, after Atlanta became Federal headquarters for reconstruction in this section, the population was estimated at 20,228, the greatest number in the history of the city up to that time.

The Young Men's Library Association was established in 1867, and in the next year the *Atlanta Constitution,* oldest existing newspaper in the city, was founded. In 1870 the first board of education was elected, and within three years several public schools were opened to 4,000 children. The year 1870 also saw the opening of the DeGive Opera House, one of the finest theaters in the South. The first street railway began operation in 1871, the cars being drawn by mules. Atlanta's importance as a railroad center was further increased in 1873 by the construction of the Atlanta & Charlotte Air Line Railroad and the beginning of the Georgia Western. Atlanta was now the second largest city in the state, surpassed only by Savannah.

A constitutional convention met in Atlanta on December 9, 1867, upon the order of Major General John Pope, officer in charge of the Reconstruction military government. Atlanta offered the state free office space for ten years, and a capitol site, if that body would adopt a resolution to make the city the state seat of government. The proposal was accepted on February 27, 1868, and upon ratification of the constitution the same year, Atlanta became the state capital. There was dissatisfaction in certain parts of the state, however, because the removal of the capital from Milledgeville was made by the Republican administration. Another constitutional convention, held in 1877, submitted the issue to the people who again confirmed the selection of Atlanta, by then a leading center of industry and commerce.

The International Cotton Exposition, held in 1881, focused the attention of the nation on the potentialities of this region as a manufacturing center and attracted investments from eastern capitalists. The fair buildings afterward were taken over by the Exposition Cotton Mills. A second and more ambitious undertaking was the Cotton States and International Exposition, which was held in 1895 in the area that is now Piedmont Park. This exposition, featuring the progress made by the Negro since emancipation, did much to cement the friendship between the New South and other sections of the United States.

Atlanta continued to develop commercially, and its population increased from 89,872 in 1900 to 200,616 in 1920. The meeting of the National Association of Manufacturers in 1905 was among the first of numerous conventions that have brought many visitors to Atlanta during the twentieth century.

In September, 1906, a race riot, precipitated by newspaper accounts of several attacks on white women, reached such proportions that the state militia was called out by Governor Joseph M. Terrell. Seven Negroes and one white man were reported killed, though the actual number of fatalities was probably higher; many hundreds were wounded. As a result of the riot, a racial tolerance group was formed and committees for bettering civic conditions were organized. Neighboring Georgia cities also took steps toward improving racial understanding.

The Federal Reserve Bank, established in 1914, increased the city's prestige as a financial center, and the Southeastern Fair, inaugurated during the same year, stimulated agriculture and livestock raising throughout the surrounding countryside. The greatest catastrophe to the city since the Battle of Atlanta was the conflagration that started on May 21, 1917, near Decatur Street and rapidly burned the section about Boulevard from Decatur Street to Ponce de Leon Avenue. About 2,000 dwellings and business houses were destroyed and the property damage was estimated to be more than five million dollars.

From September, 1917, through November, 1918, more than 230,000 soldiers and officers were mobilized at Camp Gordon, a World War cantonment established near Atlanta. The average monthly population of the camp was about 32,000 men. For several years after the war many houses were built by new citizens, as well as by older inhabitants who moved into newly developed residential sections. Tall buildings were erected to provide additional floor space for industrial corporations that opened distribution offices in Atlanta. Candler Field, established in 1925, was later selected by leading air lines as an airport. The new three-million-dollar post office was completed in 1934.

Atlanta ranks first among cities of the Southeast as a railroad and communications center. It has no dominating industry but manufactures more than 1,500 products, including textiles, beverages, confectionery, paper products, fertilizers, chemicals, agricultural implements, and refrigerators. In 1937 the value of these diverse products made in 442 industrial plants was $152,704,389. The value added by manufacture was $57,420,403. Organized labor in Atlanta, since the forming of the first union in 1891, has had a history comparatively free from serious disturbances. In June, 1932, when the state closed down all its relief stations, Angelo Herndon, a Negro Communist organizer, led a demonstration of white and Negro unemployed at the city hall. His arrest and conviction under an 1833 slave insurrection statute finally ended with a reversal of judgment by the U. S. Supreme Court in April, 1937 (*see* HISTORY). There are approximately a hundred local unions, largely representing railroad and street railway workers, electricians, printers, bakers, garment workers, and those in the building trades.

Throughout the Southeast Atlanta is recognized for its religious, medical, and educational facilities. The church census of 1926 listed 254 churches with 122,855 members. Eighteen registered medical institutions include a cancer clinic and an endocrine clinic, one of the first established in the United States. Among the institutions of higher learning within the metropolitan area are Emory University, Georgia School of Technology, Agnes Scott College, Oglethorpe University, and Atlanta University for Negroes. Atlanta University, together with its affiliated institutions, is the largest Negro educational center in the world. The public school system has fifty-four elementary, nine junior high, and five senior high schools, as well as five special and six night schools.

POINTS OF INTEREST

(*DOWNTOWN*)

FIVE POINTS, at the intersection of Peachtree, Decatur, and Marietta Streets and Edgewood Avenue, is Atlanta's hub from which its principal thoroughfares radiate to all parts of the metropolitan area. Here, in recent years, steel and concrete office buildings have shot up above the low brick structures of

ATLANTA
DOWNTOWN AREA
1939

0   ¼ M.

SCALE

★ FIVE POINTS
① POINTS OF INTEREST

KEY

1. The Old Lamppost 2. Henry Grady Monument 3. Carnegie Library. 4. Candler Building. 5. Municipal Auditorium-Armory 6. State Farmers Market 7. Grady Hospital 8. Big Bethel A.M.E. Church 9. The Atlanta Daily World Building 10. Decatur Street 11. The State Capitol 12. The City Hall. 13. Church of the Immaculate Conception 14. The Kimball House.

the 1880's and 1890's. About the foot of the tall flagpole there is always noise and restless movement as lights change, police whistles blow, and crowds hurry in all directions. Here on gala days the reviewing stand is set up for officials. Important occasions, from Clean-Up Week to the President's visit, are publicized from Five Points.

Soon after the city was incorporated in 1847, this section became its natural center. Here in 1884 the city drilled an artesian well 2,044 feet deep, and a tank and pump were installed to supply water to downtown establishments. In 1893, however, the seepage of surface water caused the condemnation and abandonment of the well.

1. The OLD LAMPPOST, NE. corner Whitehall and Alabama Sts., preserved as a relic of the War between the States, was one of the first lampposts erected in Atlanta. At its base is a hole torn by a shell during the Battle of Atlanta, July 22, 1864.

2. HENRY GRADY MONUMENT, Marietta and Forsyth Sts., was unveiled on October 21, 1891, as a memorial to Henry Woodfin Grady, one of the South's greatest orators and journalists. Draped female figures, representing *Memory* and *History,* are set on two sides of a large granite pedestal, which is surmounted by a bronze figure of Grady delivering an address. Alexander Doyle was the sculptor.

Henry Woodfin Grady, born in Athens on May 24, 1850, devoted his life to furthering the peace and prosperity of his native state. His orations, *The New South,* delivered before the New England Club of New York City in 1886, and *The South and Her Problems,* delivered at the State Fair at Dallas, Texas, in 1887, gave him a national reputation. His most eloquent address, *The Race Problem,* was delivered in Boston ten days before his death on December 23, 1889.

3. CARNEGIE LIBRARY (*open 9-6 weekdays; Sun., reading room only, 2-6*), 126 Carnegie Way, occupies a two-story building constructed of Georgia white marble in conventionalized Ionic design. On the facade above the arched windows of the second story are carved the names of famous writers. Akerman and Ross of New York were the architects.

The library is an outgrowth of the Young Men's Library Association organized on June 30, 1867. The present building was opened to the public in 1902. The library owns approximately 190,000 volumes, including Georgiana and books on genealogy and southern history. It maintains nine branches, two of them for Negroes.

4. CANDLER BUILDING, SE. corner Peachtree and Houston Sts., built 1904-06, rises to a height of seventeen stories and was for so many years Atlanta's only skyscraper that "as tall as the Candler Building" became a popular

local simile. Exterior and interior are of Georgia white marble, elaborately carved by French, Italian, English, and Scottish sculptors who were imported for the work. A series of panels carved on the facades represents the liberal arts and sciences. At the Houston Street entrance are two 26-foot engaged columns cut from single blocks of marble. In two niches above the grand staircase are busts of Asa G. Candler's parents, and carved in high relief in an ornate frieze are the heads of Alexander H. Stephens, Charles J. Jenkins, General John B. Gordon, General Joseph E. Wheeler, Sidney Lanier, Joel Chandler Harris, and Eli Whitney.

5. MUNICIPAL AUDITORIUM-ARMORY, NE. corner Gilmer and Courtland Sts., was erected 1908-09 at a cost of more than $200,000; in 1938, through Works Progress Administration assistance, the entire building was renovated. Besides its main auditorium with a seating capacity of approximately 5,000, the five-story red brick building contains several assembly halls and an armory for the state military forces. The first performance of the Metropolitan Opera Company in the South was presented here in 1910. Except for an intermission during the World War, a week of opera was an annual event from that year until 1931. Among the varied entertainments that have been offered in the auditorium-armory are sports matches, horse shows, automobile shows, annual concert series, food shows, and conventions.

6. STATE FARMERS' MARKET (*open day and night*), occupying a six-acre plot on Gilmer St. between Courtland St. and Piedmont Ave., is one of eight markets financed and operated by the state department of agriculture. Opened February 3, 1936, primarily as an outlet for Georgia farm products, the market is also a distribution center for the farmers of other states.

The selling is done in two large corrugated iron sheds with paved center thoroughfares for the passage of trucks and automobiles. The piles of cabbages, the crates of tomatoes, and the net bags of oranges make masses of vivid color, and there is always a strong, mingled odor of vegetables and fruits. In the morning there is brisk movement, but during the slower buying of the afternoon the farmers visit from stall to stall, making themselves comfortable in rockers, in split-bottomed chairs, or on upturned crates.

7. GRADY HOSPITAL, occupying several buildings along Butler St. between Gilmer and Armstrong Sts., is a municipal charity hospital, built 1891-92 as a memorial to Henry Woodfin Grady. The institution provides 350 beds for white patients and 250 for Negroes. Fifty full-time physicians and surgeons are retained, and 300 others give their services. The medical staff of the Negro division is composed of faculty members of the Emory Uni-

versity School of Medicine. Training schools are operated for white and Negro nurses.

8. BIG BETHEL A. M. E. CHURCH, NW. corner Butler St. and Auburn Ave., is the largest Negro church in Atlanta. The building, marked by large electric signs, is constructed of granite blocks with a circular tower and a large spire. It was erected in 1922 after a fire had demolished an older structure.

Big Bethel Choir, composed of 55 male and 130 female voices, has received national attention for its rendition of Negro spirituals and especially for its many presentations of *Heaven Bound,* a modern form of the medieval miracle play. Saints and sinners, singing hymns, walk down the center aisle toward the golden gates of heaven represented on the rostrum. A chorus of angels behind the gates offers encouragement, but the temptations of the Devil entice many sinners from the true path. Those who succeed in reaching the gates are joyfully ushered into heaven and presented with white robes, golden crowns, and palm leaves; the others are led off by the triumphant Devil.

9. The ATLANTA DAILY WORLD BUILDING, 210 Auburn Ave., houses the only daily and Sunday newspaper in the world published by Negroes. The *World,* founded in 1928 by W. A. Scott, was published first as a weekly. Circulation increased so rapidly that in 1931 the publishers organized a syndicate which now owns or controls papers in more than thirty cities.

10. DECATUR STREET, for about five blocks southeast of Five Points, was once the center of a fashionable residential section, but is now the "East Side" of Atlanta, the principal trading and amusement center of the Negro population. Shabby buildings house pawn shops, poolrooms, beer parlors, shooting galleries, and cheap merchandising establishments. Herb doctors and fishmongers hawk their wares along the street, while Syrians, Jews, and Greeks sit in the doorways, alert for prospective buyers. Passers-by must pick their way carefully to avoid the odds and ends of second-hand furniture cluttering the store fronts and the garments rope-strung along the sidewalks. The powerful, acrid smell of frying fish rises even to the Courtland Street viaduct, which crosses Decatur Street at second-story level.

On Saturday evenings, especially during the summer months, Decatur Street takes on a carnival atmosphere. Groups of Negroes congregate on every corner, leaning against posts or sprawling along the curbs. More active pleasure seekers romp along the pavement, occasionally breaking into dance movements in response to the raucous raspings of phonographs in drug stores or the mechanical thumping of nickel-in-the-slot pianos in second-floor dance halls. Always distinct among the confused sounds breaks the infectious laughter of the Negro.

11. The STATE CAPITOL (*open 8-4 Mon.-Fri.; 8-12 Sat.*), Washington St. between Hunter and Mitchell Sts., was completed in 1889 at an approximate cost of a million dollars. Built of Indiana limestone and patterned after the national capitol, it is one of the few buildings of such scope to be raised within the sum appropriated. Edbrooke and Burnham were the architects. The capitol grounds, beautified by native trees and shrubs, form the setting for monuments and tablets commemorating Georgia personalities and events. The equestrian statue of General John B. Gordon, the first Governor to occupy the capitol, is among the best works of Solon Borglum; a fine natural patina adds to the beauty of the bronze. Joseph E. Brown, Governor of Georgia during the War between the States, and his wife, Elizabeth Grisham Brown, are commemorated by bronze figures posed in the manner of a daguerreotype. A rather crudely executed statue of Thomas E. Watson, United States Senator and leader of the Populist party, depicts the fiery statesman in a characteristic attitude of forensic vehemence.

Within the hallways and rotunda, finished in Georgia marble, are numerous life-sized oil paintings of prominent state leaders, as well as several miscellaneous collections of historical and literary interest. A marble bust of Benjamin Harvey Hill is the work of Alexander Doyle. Through the efforts of the United Daughters of the Confederacy, many historic flags, some torn by shot and shell, have been preserved and are on display. An exhibit of Georgia's natural resources is placed throughout the corridors of the upper floors.

The capitol dome, rising 237 feet above ground, is reached by a staircase from the top floor of the building. Surmounting the dome is a bronze female figure holding a sword in one hand and a torch in the other. The history of the statue and the date of its casting are unknown, since a description of the statue was not included in the building specifications and no stories regarding it have been substantiated.

The STATE LIBRARY (*open 9-4 Mon.-Fri.; 9-12 Sat.; books must be used in library*), on the third floor, contains 79,000 volumes, including many rare books and the largest collection of Georgia material in the state. The names of the owners and the holdings of proprietary lands are shown on a group of old Georgia maps. The nucleus of the literature and historical collection was bequeathed to the state during the 1880's by Everard De Renne, son of the founder of the noted De Renne library of Georgiana.

The STATE OFFICE BUILDING (*open 8-4 Mon.-Fri.; 8-12 Sat.*), Capitol Square SW. of Capitol, houses the state departments of public welfare, health, labor, and education. The six-story building, constructed of marble and granite in 1939, has six bronze relief figures by Julian Harris embossed on the black marble spandrels. Augustus Constantine was the architect.

12. The CITY HALL (*open 8-4:30 Mon.-Fri.; 8-12 Sat.; observation tower same hours*), Mitchell St. between Central Ave. and Washington St., was erected in 1929 at a cost of more than a million dollars. The dignified 14-story structure, Gothic in detail and modern in mass, is of the set-back type of architecture. Its outside walls are of terra cotta, and its main entrance and lobby walls are finished in Georgia travertine. The bronze doors of the four elevators are inscribed with the seal of Atlanta, bearing a phoenix and the words "Resurgens 1847-1864, Atlanta, Georgia." The building, designed by G. Lloyd Preacher, is on the site of headquarters occupied by General Sherman in 1864. The observation tower affords an excellent panoramic view of the city.

13. CHURCH OF THE IMMACULATE CONCEPTION (Roman Catholic), SE. corner Central Ave. and Hunter St., erected in 1869 to replace an earlier frame building damaged by bombardment during the Battle of Atlanta, is the oldest church building in the city. Gothic in design, the church is of red brick with granite embellishments and is partly encircled by an iron picket fence. The interior is softly lighted by tall stained-glass windows. The central altar is carved from white marble. The land on which this building stands was deeded to the Roman Catholics in 1848, and soon afterward a church was erected on the site.

14. The KIMBALL HOUSE, 33 Pryor St., a hotel erected in 1870, burned in 1883, and rebuilt shortly afterwards, is a landmark of eventful years in Atlanta. With its turrets, arched windows, and flat Saracenic ornamentation, the massive brick edifice shows the influence of the romantic revival characteristic of the period. In the marble lobby are an old silver water cooler and a table recovered from the ruins of the original structure after the fire. With its solid mahogany woodwork, stained glass windows, elaborate candelabra, and hand-carved furniture, the Kimball House for many years was the most modern and progressive hotel in the South. When hydraulic elevators were installed in 1883, people came from all parts of the state to ride in them. A long hallway leads from the lobby to a Peachtree Street entrance. For many years this hotel was a popular rendezvous for political leaders from the near-by capitol.

(NORTH ATLANTA)

15. PIEDMONT PARK, Piedmont Ave. between 10th St. and the Southern Ry. belt line, covers approximately 185 acres of rolling tree-dotted land. Curving asphalt drives lead through landscaped grounds past a lake, a golf course, and recreational fields. In 1887 this tract, then the property of the Gentlemen's Driving Club, was used for the Piedmont Exposition which was planned in honor of President Cleveland's visit to Atlanta. Two years later the land was purchased by the Exposition Company, and the grounds were further improved in 1895 for the Cotton States and International Exposition. Atlanta purchased the land for a municipal park in 1904.

The PEACE MONUMENT, near the 14th Street entrance, is a bronze figure of the Goddess of Peace holding an olive branch and commanding a kneeling Confederate soldier to lower his gun. The sculptor was Allen Newman, of New York. The monument, unveiled on October 10, 1911, was presented to the city by the old Gate City Guard. Founded in 1857 for the protection of Atlanta citizens, the Old Guard still survives as a social organization.

At the Orme Circle entrance to the park are three lampposts used by the city in its first street lighting system in 1855.

16. HIGH MUSEUM OF ART (*open 9-5 weekdays: 7-9 P.M. Mon., Wed., Fri.; 2-5 P.M. Sun.*), 1262 Peachtree St., is the only museum of fine arts in Atlanta. The brick and stucco building, of Tudor domestic architecture, was the home of Mrs. James Madison High, who presented it to the citizens of Atlanta in 1926. The building houses the Atlanta Art Association, organized in 1905 and later affiliated with the American Federation of Arts, and the High Museum School of Art, which has an enrollment of 160 pupils and offers courses in commercial and fine arts.

In the museum the Atlanta Friends of Art have assembled permanent collections for exhibition, and loan collections are shown periodically. Early paintings of importance are the *Madonna and Child* of Christoforo Caselli (1455-1521), the *Offering of the Matronali* of Giovanni Battista Tiepolo (1692-1769), both gifts of S. H. Kress, of New York, and a landscape of Salvatore Rosa (1615-73). Among the portrait painters represented are Sir Joshua Reynolds, Thomas Sully, and Sir Henry Raeburn, each by one painting. Except for the French post-impressionistic *Chateau Gaillard* of Maxine E. L. Maufra, most of the other paintings of note are by American artists. Among these are *Isles of Shoals* by Childe Hassam, a student of French impressionism; *Moon Magic,* a good example of the moonlight pictures of Ralph A. Blakelock; the imaginative *Fingals Cave* and the realistic *Pueblo of Acoma, New Mexico,* both by Thomas Moran; and the *Portrait of an Artist* by Frank Duveneck. The French influence of Degas is evident in the ballet dancer of *In the Dressing Room* by Louis Kronberg, and modern treatment and color-conception are evident in the *Girl in Blue Arranging Flowers* by Frederick Carl Frieseke, *Harlem River at Highbridge* by Ernest Lawson, and *The Bathers* by Robert Brackman. *Woman Mounting a Horse* by John McCrady is an example of modernist departure from the realistic method. In addition to the paintings, the museum contains two water colors by Rabindranath Tagore, sketches by James McNeill Whistler and Rembrandt, sculptures, and antique furniture.

17. RHODES MEMORIAL HALL or THE GEORGIA STATE DEPARTMENT OF ARCHIVES
AND HISTORY (*open 8:30-4 Mon.-Fri.; 8-12 Sat.*), 1516 Peachtree St.,
constructed of Stone Mountain granite and modeled after a Bavarian castle,
houses Georgia's documents and historical records, as well as county and
private papers concerning Georgia and Georgians. Its pictorial collection
includes daguerreotypes, photographs, and portrait miniatures. Its HIS-
TORICAL MUSEUM contains a million unbound original documents and 30,-
000 manuscript books and pamphlets. A group of Tiffany painted glass
windows depicts *The Rise and Fall of the Confederacy*. The Rose Room,
to the right of the entrance hall, contains a collection of Colonial china,
lithographs, and steel engravings. A great mahogany staircase winds upward from the reception rooms to the second and third floors, which are
given over to collections owned by patriotic organizations.

Rhodes Memorial Hall was originally the residence of A. G. Rhodes,
whose heir presented it to the state in 1929. The Department of Archives
and History, created by legislative act in 1919, was placed under the supervision of Lucian Lamar Knight, author of various books on Georgia history
and the state's first official historian.

18. PEACHTREE CREEK is the site of the first of the series of engagements
around Atlanta during the summer of 1864. On July 19 the battle lines of
the Confederate forces under General Hood were drawn up south of
Peachtree Creek in preparation for an attack on the Federal troops before
they could cross the creek and get into position. The charge was scheduled
for noon on the 20th, but the Confederate movements were not well coordinated and it was mid-afternoon before hostilities began. The desperate
fighting in the brief hours before dark resulted in failure for the Confederates and heavy losses on both sides.

19. The CO-CATHEDRAL OF CHRIST THE KING, NE. corner Peachtree Rd. and
Peachtree Way, has equal rank with the Cathedral of St. John the Baptist in
Savannah as the official seat of the Bishop of the Savannah-Atlanta Diocese
of the Roman Catholic Church. The building, recalling the thirteenth century Gothic cathedrals in design, towers above a beautifully landscaped
plot of four acres. The plan maintains the traditional cruciform shape,
but departs from the early Gothic norm by the absence of a continuous line
of flying buttresses and lengthy transepts. Above the main portal is a
carved limestone figure of Christ the King beneath a lacy stonework canopy.
On each side of the figure is a stained glass lancet window and above is a
rose window, the group set within a large Gothic frame between twin
pinnacle-like towers.

Adjoining the church is a parochial school, designed in harmony with
the major structure and built of the same materials. The architects of

the co-cathedral and school were Henry D. Dagit & Sons, of Philadelphia; the windows are from the studio of Henry Lee Willet, also of Philadelphia.

20. SECOND-PONCE DE LEON BAPTIST CHURCH, NE. corner Peachtree Rd. and Wesley Ave., is constructed of whitewashed brick in American Georgian design, with a Georgian Colonial doorway and a tall spire of the type originated by Sir Christopher Wren. The white interior of the building, which was completed in 1937, is designed as simply as the exterior. The church was organized in 1930 by the combination of the Second Baptist Church, founded in 1854, and the Ponce de Leon Baptist Church, established in 1904.

21. CATHEDRAL OF ST. PHILIP, 2744 Peachtree Rd., a simple, gray shingled building, stands upon a commanding site in the triangle formed by Andrews Drive and Peachtree Road. The first building of St. Philip's Church, a modest frame structure, was erected between 1847 and 1849 at the northeast corner of Washington and Hunter Streets. In 1864 General Sherman's invading Union army used it as a stable and bowling alley. During the Reconstruction era the members contributed coins, tableware, and jewelry to be fashioned into a communion service. In later years the Federal government reimbursed the church for war damages, and a $5,000 fund was raised by a northern communicant, General George Meade, who had been military commander of the Atlanta district during reconstruction. The second church, a brick structure of Gothic design, was built 1880-82 on a lot adjoining the old frame church. In 1918 the wooden structure was given to the Negroes of St. Philip's Parish, who removed it to Irwin and Fort Streets. When the brick church was torn down in 1935, the old pews, chancel rail, stained glass windows, and silver communion service were removed to the cathedral.

22. OGLETHORPE UNIVERSITY, Peachtree Rd., has an extensive campus embracing 600 acres of woodland and an 80-acre lake. The three Gothic buildings are constructed of Georgia blue granite. A coeducational school, Oglethorpe offers courses leading to the B.A., B.S., and M.A. degrees. The system includes schools of banking and commerce, science, secretarial preparation, liberal arts, journalism, and physical education. The present faculty numbers 28 and the student enrollment is approximately 250.

Oglethorpe University is an outgrowth of Oglethorpe College, which was founded near Milledgeville in 1835 (see TOUR 14). The college was destroyed during the War between the States when its buildings were burned and its endowment lost through the failure of Confederate bonds. The institution was opened in Atlanta during the fall of 1870, but after three years it was forced to close because of financial difficulties. The movement for the present institution was begun in 1912 by Thornwell Jacobs, and four years later the university reopened with Jacobs as president. Since then large donations have been received, and Lupton Hall, Lowry Hall, and Hermance Stadium commemorate the generosity of donors. William Randolph Hearst's donation of $125,000 made possible the purchase of 400 acres of land.

Oglethorpe University owns and operates its own press, all the work being done by student labor. The press issues the quarterly journal *Bozart-Westminster.*

A vault, called the Crypt of Civilization, has been built under the administration building to preserve material illustrative of present civilization. This vault, containing canned food, cameras, phonographs with records, and encyclopedias transferred to microfilms, is not to be opened until the year 8113.

(DRUID HILLS SECTION)

23. EMORY UNIVERSITY occupies a 235-acre campus, roughly bounded by North Decatur, Clifton, and Briarcliff Rds. The natural wooded beauty of the grounds is preserved and enhanced by additional plantings of flowering trees and shrubs. Most of the fifteen buildings, of simplified Italian Renaissance architecture, are finished in Georgia marble and have red tile roofs.

Desiring to establish a university east of the Mississippi River, the General Conference of the Methodist Episcopal Church, South, decided to make Emory College at Oxford (*see* TOUR *17*) the nucleus of a new institution. The university was established in 1914 with a pledge of $500,000 from the city of Atlanta and a gift of $1,000,000 from Asa G. Candler, Sr., whose family has since contributed a large part of the $6,000,000 endowment. The system, which includes the seven schools of the university on the Atlanta campus and two junior colleges at Oxford and Valdosta, has a student enrollment of 1,500 and a faculty of 211.

Although Emory University is primarily for men, women are admitted into the graduate and professional schools, with the exception of the school of medicine, and into the junior and senior classes of the undergraduate college upon special approval. Emory is one of the few universities in the United States that have stressed the development of intramural sports, participating in few intercollegiate contests.

GLENN MEMORIAL CHURCH, on a commanding elevation at the entrance to the campus, is a white stucco building of Georgian design with a tall tower rising from an Ionic portico. The interior, finished in white and lighted by clear glass windows, emphasizes the colonial motif. The auditorium combines the plan of a church with that of a theater, its stage concealed by red velvet draperies suspended from columns forming a Palladian design. The columns can be swung back on large hinges, revealing a stage twenty-nine feet deep and forty-four feet wide, and the pulpit platform can be rolled upon a steel track beneath the stage, leaving an orchestra pit. The building was erected at a cost of $197,650 and presented to the college and to the congregation by Thomas K. Glenn and Mrs. Howard Candler in memory of their father, Wilbur Fisk Glenn. The firm of Hentz, Adler, and Shutze of Atlanta designed the church, which was dedicated in 1931.

The LAMAR SCHOOL OF LAW, E. side of quadrangle, occupies a pink marble building partly covered by ivy. In the interior lobby is a bronze bust of Judge John S. Candler. A gracefully curved marble stairway with a grilled balustrade winds past a two-story arched window. Chartered in 1915, the law school was named for L. Q. C. Lamar, Jr., distinguished alumnus.

The CANDLER SCHOOL OF THEOLOGY, across the quadrangle from the law school, is housed in a building of similar design. In the marble lobby is a bust of Bishop Warren A. Candler, for whom the school was named when it was organized in 1914. In the rear is Emory Chapel, popular among the alumni for small weddings. The lights on the pink marble walls are shaded by marble brackets bearing bronze reproductions of early Christian symbols. The high wooden ceiling gives an atmosphere of spaciousness to the small room. To the right of the lobby is the WESLEYAN MUSEUM, a fine collection of rare books and other possessions of John and Charles Wesley, reputed to be the most extensive Wesley collection in this country and possibly in the world. Also on display in the museum are a pulpit made for John Wesley and a chair used by Bishop Francis Asbury, who was influential in the spread of Methodism in America.

The ASA G. CANDLER LIBRARY (*open 8 A.M.-9 P.M. Mon.-Fri.; 8-12 Sat.*), N. end of quadrangle, is finished in white marble. On the main floor are the administration offices and a museum. Among the twelve varied collections are Egyptian-Babylonian documents and artifacts and three adult mummies, one being that of an aged man buried 5800 B.C. The natural history exhibit includes 252 species of Georgia birds, 210 varieties of eggs, 20,000 specimens of insects, and an extensive display of moths and butterflies. A coin collection, with ancient and modern pieces from 40 countries, contains a Maccabean Hebrew shekel of the Sanctuary.

On the shelves of the reference room on the second floor are 10,000 volumes, and in the stacks below are 90,000 bound books and 60,000 unbound books and pamphlets. On the third floor is the Library School, founded as the Southern Library School in 1905 and affiliated with Emory in 1925.

EMORY UNIVERSITY HOSPITAL, Clifton Rd., occupies a large pink stucco building set on shaded grounds. Established in 1903 as the Wesley Memorial Hospital, the institution was expanded and moved to its present site in 1922. The name was changed in 1925, when the hospital became affiliated with the School of Medicine of Emory University. This institution, established in 1915, is an outgrowth of the Atlanta Medical College, founded in 1854 and later consolidated with several other medical schools. On the second floor is the ABNER W. CALHOUN MEDICAL LIBRARY (*open 9-5 weekdays*) of sixteen thousand volumes and a historical museum displaying old pictures, manuscripts, and surgical instruments.

(SOUTHEAST SECTION)

24. OAKLAND CEMETERY, Fair St. between S. Boulevard and Oakland Ave., is enclosed by an old brick wall. The cemetery, originally a six-acre tract deeded to the city in 1850, was later extended to cover eighty-five acres. The LION OF ATLANTA, on the cemetery grounds, is a copy of the celebrated Lion of Lucerne. Carved from a single block of Georgia marble, it was dedicated to the unknown Confederate dead in Oakland Cemetery on April 26, 1894. The grave of Martha Lumpkin Compton, for whom Marthasville was named, is marked by a large native granite block.

25. GRANT PARK, S. Boulevard and Atlanta Ave., was named for Colonel Lemuel P. Grant, who in 1882 donated a hundred acres of wooded land as the site for a municipal park; forty-four acres have since been added. A large lake is equipped for swimming and boating, and near the center of the park are picnic booths, a bandstand, and a sunken garden designed as an amphitheater. Shrubbery and flowers are cultivated in the greenhouses for use in all the parks of the city. The zoo (*open 7-6 daily*) contains the largest and most varied collection of animals and birds in the Southeast. The extensive Candler collection, added to the zoological gardens in 1935, is housed in quarters made available by funds donated by school children of the state and by the Emergency Relief Administration.

The SITE OF FORT WALKER, at the crown of the hill near the Atlanta Ave. and Boulevard entrance to the park, is a commanding position held by a Confederate battery during the Siege and Battle of Atlanta in 1864. The park is honeycombed with breastworks. The hill was named in memory of William H. T. Walker, Confederate general who was killed in the Battle of Atlanta.

The CYCLORAMA BUILDING (*open 8 A.M.-10 P.M. daily, children 25¢, adults 50¢; lectures according to attendance; no cameras allowed*), facing the Augusta Ave. entrance to the park, houses the colossal *Cyclorama of the Battle of Atlanta*. This battle was fought July 22, 1864, in the territory around Moreland Avenue for control of the Georgia Railroad.

The building, situated on a high terrace, is approached by double stairways leading up to a broad esplanade. The front half of the building is constructed of white stone-flecked terra cotta, while the circular rear section, especially erected to house the great canvas, is of stucco. The facade is dominated by a loggia, two stories high, featuring Ionic columns and pilasters.

From the entrance hallway a short flight of stairs leads downward into a tunnel; at the opposite end a double stairway leads upward into the center of the rotunda where the huge circular picture is displayed. Visitors may view the canvas from two levels, circling to follow the lecturer who speaks from a catwalk on the lower level.

The time of the scene depicted is the crucial moment at 4:30 P.M., when General Cheatham's troops made a counterattack in an effort to restore their line. Beyond the charging soldiers, the exploding shells, and the rising smoke of the fields lies the small city of Atlanta, which at that time had a population of approximately 15,000. Stone Mountain and Kennesaw Mountain are seen in the distance. Above the confusion of the battle, "Abe," the eagle mascot of Union Company C, flies high to avoid the shells. This eagle has since been memorialized on the silver dollar.

The painting is approximately 400 feet in circumference and 50 feet in height, and weighs 18,000 pounds. Suspended from a circular rail, the canvas creates an illusion of a continuous landscape. A striking three-dimensional effect is achieved by continuing the action of the picture into the space (about forty feet) between the canvas and the central platform. The irregular terrain of the battlefield is reproduced with 1,500 tons of Georgia clay, ranging in color from white to red. Tree trunks, dynamited and treated to appear shell-torn, green-tinted excelsior simulating grass, and bushes made of wire and plaster add to the realistic effect. Scores of plaster soldiers—fighting, wounded, and dead—are spread over the battle-field. The figures vary in size from twenty-two inches to slightly under four feet, but they are placed with such precision that in perspective they appear lifesize. Canvas and foreground are so well merged that only the keenest scrutiny can determine where one leaves off and the other begins. The ambulance is partly painted and partly executed in plaster; the railroad tracks start as painting on the hanging canvas and extend with actual rails across the field to the opposite side of the picture.

The Cyclorama was painted about 1886 in Milwaukee, Wisconsin, by a staff of German artists, who executed similar cycloramas of the battles of Gettysburg and Missionary Ridge, both of which were accidentally destroyed. In the early 1890's the *Battle of Atlanta* was brought to this city and lodged in an Edgewood Avenue building, where it remained until 1898, when it was purchased for $1,000 by G. V. Gress, an Atlanta lumber merchant, and presented to the city.

The work of projecting the picture into the third dimension was carried out by a staff of professional painters and sculptors in 1937 with the assistance of Federal funds under the Emergency Relief Program.

On the upper floor is a room in which are displayed enlargements of eight pictures of Atlanta and the trenches and breastworks surrounding the city at the time of the Federal siege. The original photographs were taken by General Sherman's official photographer.

The TEXAS, the engine which participated in one of the most dramatic episodes in the War between the States, is in the basement of the Cyclorama Building. At Marietta, Georgia, on April 11, 1862, James J. Andrews and twenty-one Union men, disguised as Confederates, boarded the train drawn by the locomotive *General*. When the crew and passengers detrained at Big Shanty (now Kennesaw) for breakfast, Andrews and his raiders seized the *General* and directed it toward Chattanooga, Tennessee. The conductor and crew ran after it on foot until they found a handcar at Moon's Station. At the bridge across the Etowah River they took the *Yonah*, an engine used on the spur track to the Cooper Iron Works, and continued the chase. Blocked at Kingston by freight cars that had delayed the *General*, they changed to the *William R. Smith*. A few miles north of Kingston a broken track forced them to abandon this last engine and again proceed on foot. Near Adairsville they commandeered the *Texas*, reputedly the finest and swiftest engine on the road. Andrews and his men attempted to block the path of the *Texas* by hurling obstructions across the railroad tracks, but the pursuing engine, running backward, continued to shorten the distance between them. Within five miles of Chattanooga the *General*, out of fuel and water, was overtaken, and Andrews and most of his men were captured. A trial was held in Chattanooga, after which Andrews and seven of his raiders were brought to Atlanta and executed by hanging, June, 1862.

The *Texas*, a Danforth and Cook engine, was put on the road in 1856, running in freight service before and after Andrews' Raid. Prior to 1895 it was equipped for burning coal. In 1907 it was sent to the Atlanta railroad yards for scrapping, but the pressure of public opinion caused it to be preserved as a historic relic, and in 1911 the city of Atlanta formally accepted the *Texas*. In 1927 the locomotive was removed to the Cyclorama Building and later was completely renovated by employees of the Emergency Relief Administration. The *General* is on display in the Union Station in Chattanooga (*see* TENNESSEE GUIDE).

26. FEDERAL PENITENTIARY (*open only to immediate relatives of prisoners and to those having business to transact*), McDonough Rd. and S. Boulevard, opened in 1902, is one of twenty-eight such institutions in the well-integrated United States prison system. The east half of the massive granite main building on the front of the Federal reservation was erected in 1915 and the west half in 1919. The granite, which came from Stone Mountain, was cut by prison labor. In the rear of this structure twenty-eight acres of

land are enclosed by a wall 4,178 feet long, between 28 and 37 feet high, and from 2 to 4 feet thick. Officials live in houses on the reservation.

The penitentiary has an average population of three thousand inmates, who occupy four cell houses, each five tiers high. Two farms, covering approximately fifteen hundred acres and cultivated by about two hundred and fifty men, supply garden and dairy products for the prison. Within the prison walls are a textile mill and related industrial plants, in which more than a thousand inmates are employed. The mill is the only factory in the nation that manufactures canvas for government mail sacks. Several hundred prisoners are employed in maintenance activities and shops. A hundred patients can be accommodated at a well-equipped hospital, and prisoners who have not completed the third grade are required to attend school. A library contains about twenty thousand books.

27. The CHEVROLET MOTOR ASSEMBLY PLANT (*open, guides 10 A.M. and 2 P.M. Mon.-Fri.*), Sawtell Ave. and McDonough Rd., is housed in two large buildings on a thirty-acre tract of land. The three-story office building, of reinforced concrete, has outer walls of yellow tapestry brick with cement trim. The one-story plant building has a floor area of approximately nine acres and houses various units, including a branch of the Fisher Body Works. The assembly line has a daily capacity of 400 finished cars, which are shipped to points throughout the Southeast.

28. LAKEWOOD PARK, Lakewood Ave., the largest municipal amusement park in the city, covers an area of 366 wooded acres. The original tract of fifty acres was purchased by the city of Atlanta in 1874, and the headwaters of the South River were impounded to form a reservoir for the city water works department. The Lakewood Park Company, organized in 1895, leased the property from the city and converted it into an amusement park. Since 1915 the Southeastern Fair, sponsored by the Atlanta Chamber of Commerce, has been held annually at Lakewood in several large stucco buildings constructed especially for this purpose.

29. CLARK UNIVERSITY and GAMMON THEOLOGICAL SEMINARY (Negro) occupy a joint 100-acre campus on McDonough Rd. S. of the Atlanta & West Point R.R. tracks. Shaded by oaks and pines, the brick buildings stand on a high elevation. Clark University, founded in 1870 by the Freedmen's Aid Society of the Methodist Episcopal Church, offers a four-year high school course and college work leading to a normal certificate and the A. B. degree, and has an average enrollment of 355. Gammon Theological Seminary, established in 1883 as a biblical department of the university, has a student body of about eighty-five. Through a co-operative arrangement, Atlanta University allows students of Clark University to use its library and attend its summer school.

(*WEST END AND ATLANTA UNIVERSITY*)

30. WREN'S NEST (*open 9-5 weekdays; 25¢, children 10¢*), 1050 Gordon St., the former home of Joel Chandler Harris, is a memorial to the creator of the Uncle Remus stories. In 1913 the property was acquired by the Uncle Remus Memorial Association, which sponsors a memorial service in the house on December 9, the author's birthday.

The Wren's Nest is an irregularly shaped frame house with drooping eaves, numerous gables, and elaborate scrollwork. It received its name when a wren built her nest in the mail box and Harris built another box to avoid disturbing her. The two-story house has eleven rooms, six of which were added at intervals after the house was built. The sloping lawn is shaded by tall trees with tangled vines in their branches. A walk leading to the side of the house is made of Georgia pink marble, and each section is inscribed with the name of an Atlanta writer. On display at the Wren's Nest is a collection of autographed pictures, letters, personal possessions, and original editions of Harris' works, more than twenty-five of which were written here.

Joel Chandler Harris (1848-1908), born in Eatonton, was connected with several newspapers, including the *Macon Telegraph* and the *Savannah Daily News,* before he joined the staff of the *Atlanta Constitution* in 1878. In that year, upon the suggestion of Evan P. Howell, editor of the *Constitution,* Harris agreed to write a daily column containing humorous sketches and observations. The Uncle Remus stories, songs, and sayings resulted. Harris' fame spread almost immediately, and in 1880 his first book, *Uncle Remus: His Songs and Sayings,* was published. This was followed by *Nights with Uncle Remus* (1883) and several other volumes of Uncle Remus stories. Harris' use of Negro dialect and Negro characters in his work was a unique contribution to American writing.

31. WEST VIEW CEMETERY (*open 7-6 daily*), Gordon Rd. and Mozley Dr., was granted a charter in 1884. The grounds, with individual lots merging into one another unseparated by walls or copings, form a continuous landscape of green lawns and magnificent trees. Fifty of the 577 acres in the cemetery grounds are used for parks, and an extensive nursery is maintained. The tulip, rhododendron, and azalea seasons in the spring attract many visitors.

On the plot contributed for the Confederate dead is a tall monument erected by the Confederate Veterans' Association of Fulton County.

Burial sections five, seven, and ten are owned by the Irish Horse Traders, descendants of eight Irish families of horse traders. The most unusual memorial, that of John Sherlock, bears photographs of himself and his wife made on porcelain plaques and inserted in the stone. Because the various families are separated most of the year and seldom communicate with one another, many members attend an annual reunion in Atlanta on April 28, have marriage ceremonies performed, and bury their dead. The bodies are shipped to the city and kept in vaults until the date of the reunion. Funeral services are held at the Church of the Immaculate Conception. The horse traders began the custom of burying their dead in Atlanta, where Roman Catholic priests were available, in 1881 when John McNamara died while in Atlanta and was buried at Oakland Cemetery. When no more interments could be made at Oakland Cemetery they purchased lots in West View.

The history of the Irish Horse Traders in this country dates back more than a century, when the first family landed in America and opened a livery stable in Washington, D. C. Other families came, from the clans of Rileys, McNamaras, Carrolls, Sherlocks, Garmans, Costellos, Dartys, and O'Haras. When trade slackened, the clans organized themselves as traveling horse traders, going about in covered wagons with their animals on leads. In Atlanta the clans bought large tracts and settled for a short time, but they soon started out again, retaining their land titles in the Atlanta territory. Several are now in business at the Atlanta stockyards.

These Irish Horse Traders have preserved their entity. Marriage is confined to the limits of the eight original families, and only rarely has this tradition been violated. The families in America now total approximately 10,000 members, some of whom are very wealthy. The traders travel in high-powered motor cars, carrying tents and household goods in trailers and their animals in trucks.

32. On the SITE OF THE BATTLE OF EZRA CHURCH, Mozley Dr. at E. end of Mozley Park, is a public playground. At this place General Hood made a third desperate attempt, July 28, 1864, to drive General Sherman's forces from Atlanta.

33. BOOKER T. WASHINGTON MONUMENT, before the main entrance to the Booker T. Washington High School, SW. corner Hunter and C Sts., is a memorial to the famous Negro educator. The group of bronze figures, executed by Charles Keck, of New York, represents Washington lifting the veil of ignorance from his race. An inscription on the marble base records the educator's words: "We shall prosper in proportion as we learn dignity and glorify labor and put brains and skill into the common occupations of life." The monument was erected from funds donated by the teachers and students of the Booker T. Washington High School and by white and Negro citizens of Atlanta.

34. ATLANTA UNIVERSITY SYSTEM (Negro) comprises Atlanta University, a coeducational graduate school conferring the M. A. and M. S. degrees;

Morehouse College, an undergraduate college for men; and Spelman College, an undergraduate college for women. The three institutions have an enrollment of 850 and an endowment of about $3,500,000. Laboratory schools for training prospective teachers provide instruction for Negro children ranging from kindergarten through high school age. In 1929 the three colleges, on neighboring campuses, adopted a plan of affiliation whereby they would be so co-ordinated that their combined resources would be available to every student. Co-operation is being extended to effect further affiliation and bring Clark and Morris Brown Universities into the system.

The department of fine arts presents music, drama, painting, sculpture, and the dance in a manner to cultivate the taste of the community as well as that of the students. The Spelman-Morehouse Glee Club has toured the eastern states, the University Players offer several dramatic performances a year, and debating teams engage in intersectional and international debates.

Atlanta University was established in 1865, when representatives of the American Missionary Association opened a school in a boxcar. In 1876 the first college class was graduated. With grants from the Federal Freedmen's Bureau, the American Missionary Association, and philanthropic individuals, the school grew rapidly. Morehouse and Spelman are under the direction of the American Baptist Home Mission Board of New York.

Most of the red brick buildings trimmed with white limestone follow the Georgian Colonial design. Atlanta University DORMITORIES and DINING HALL, 50 Chestnut St., three buildings opened in 1933, are the million-dollar gift of an anonymous donor. The dining hall connects the two dormitories.

ATLANTA UNIVERSITY ADMINISTRATION BUILDING, 223 Chestnut St., has a columned portico and a cupola surmounted by a gilded dome. The main facade faces the campus. Completed in 1932, this building houses the administrative offices of the university, seminar rooms, and a conference chamber.

ATLANTA SCHOOL OF SOCIAL WORK, Chestnut St. between the library and the administration building, is the only professional school in the city for training Negro social workers. Organized in 1925, it holds the only Negro membership in the American Association of Schools of Social Work, to which it was admitted in 1928.

The UNIVERSITY LIBRARY (*open 9:30-9:30 weekdays*), 273 Chestnut St., opened in 1932 through donations of the General Education Board of the Rockefeller Foundation, has served as a model for the construction of similar institutions. The library contains 60,000 volumes and accommodations for 115,000 more. In the basement is a hall for lectures and art exhibitions.

The seven buildings of MOREHOUSE COLLEGE occupy a thirteen-acre rectangular campus. Organized in 1867 in Augusta as the Augusta Institute, the school was moved in 1879 to Atlanta and incorporated as Atlanta Baptist Seminary. In 1897 college work was undertaken under the administration of John Hope, who was later the first president of the Atlanta University System. In 1912 the name of the school was changed in honor of Henry L. Morehouse, former secretary of the American Home Mission Society.

SPELMAN COLLEGE, the women's undergraduate school, is built around an oval grassy plot planted with oaks, elms, and magnolias. The campus covers twenty-five acres. In 1881 Miss Sophia B. Packard and Miss Harriet E. Giles, of Boston, opened the school with eleven pupils in the basement of Friendship Baptist Church. Two years later the school acquired the grounds and buildings of old Fort McPherson, formerly a Confederate drill ground.

ROCKEFELLER HALL, facing the campus drive, the administration building, was erected in 1886 as the first permanent building of the college. The old chapel on the second floor has been transformed into a theater for the school of dramatics. This building represents the first major gift of Rockefeller to education.

SISTERS CHAPEL, also facing the campus drive, dedicated in 1935, is a Greek Revival red brick building with six white columns. The building, designed by Hentz, Adler, and Shutze, of Atlanta, has a seating capacity of 1,500 and is used for concerts, commencement exercises, and daily chapel services. It was named in honor of the mother and aunt of John D. Rockefeller.

SPELMAN COLLEGE NURSERY SCHOOL, 365 Leonard St., occupies a house of English Tudor design. Provision is made for the care and training of 100 children between the ages of eighteen months and five years.

35. MORRIS BROWN UNIVERSITY (Negro), 643 Hunter St., a coeducational institution controlled by the African Methodist Episcopal Church, was opened in the fall of 1885 as Morris Brown College. In 1932 it was moved from its original location on Boulevard at Houston Street to the old campus of Atlanta University. The school, which has an enrollment of almost 600, offers a four-year college course and maintains a theological seminary.

36. UNIVERSITY HOUSING PROJECT FOR NEGROES, Greensferry Ave. between Dora and Lawshe Sts., is a 17½-acre tract developed by the Federal government under the Public Works Administration. The severely simple fireproof brick buildings contain 675 apartments ranging in size from two to five rooms. Space is provided in the administration building for a management office, eight stores, offices for doctors and dentists, and a clinic. One central plant manufactures steam for heating all the buildings, and convenient laundries, a kindergarten, and a day nursery are maintained.

Approximately 25 per cent of the area is covered by buildings, and the remainder is being improved for parks, playgrounds, and community activities. The Federal government allocated $2,500,000 to cover the entire cost of the project that replaced 218 squalid shacks.

(NORTHWEST SECTION)

37. TECHWOOD, Techwood Dr. between North Ave. and Mills St., built at a cost of $2,875,000 and opened in 1936, was the first all-Federal slum clearance and low-rent housing project completed by PWA in the United States. Covering eleven blocks, a total of twenty-two acres, it consists of twenty-two fireproof apartment buildings of brick and concrete construction. The Techwood housing development, replacing a slum area, provides modern, sanitary, and conveniently located homes for families with annual incomes not exceeding $1,800. No family whose living conditions have not heretofore been substandard is allowed to rent an apartment in Techwood, and families with children are given preference.

The apartment buildings, severely plain in their rectangular simplicity and economy of detail, are surrounded by landscaped lawns and young trees. All buildings are constructed of steel, hollow tile, and brick and are insulated with cork; the floors and roof are made of five-inch reinforced concrete slabs. The apartments range in size from three rooms to duplex units of six rooms, and all are equipped with modern bathrooms, electric refrigerators, electric stoves, and incinerators. Walls and floors may be washed with soap and water.

At the southern end of the development is a community playground with wading pools for children; at the northern end are three clay tennis courts. The project provides five free laundries completely equipped, a large library room with a book repair shop and a librarian's office, a little theater, and a kindergarten. A motion picture theater and a block of stores serve the community. A large brick building houses the administrative offices and the health center, which includes a clinic, an operating room, a dentist's office, and offices for resident physicians.

A dormitory, accommodating 309 Georgia Tech students, was opened in September, 1935. The dormitory is of the same construction as the apartment buildings.

38. GEORGIA SCHOOL OF TECHNOLOGY, the engineering unit of the University System of Georgia, offers four-year courses leading to the B. S. degree in civil, mechanical, chemical, textile, electrical, and general engineering; architecture; aeronautics; ceramics; and industrial management. Approximately 2,500 students are enrolled, and the faculty numbers 150. Since 1912, in addition to the regular course, Tech has offered a co-operative plan of engineering education designed to co-ordinate theory with practical experience in several engineering fields.

In 1882 the general assembly adopted a resolution to consider the establishment of a state technical school, and in 1885 a law was passed appropriating $65,000 for the institution. The school was established in Atlanta because the city, in competition with four other Georgia towns, made a better offer of money and land. Installation services were held at DeGive's Opera House early in October, 1888. In half a century Georgia Tech has grown from a five-acre tract with two structures to a campus of forty-four acres with thirty buildings.

The State Engineering Experiment Station, an applied science research agency, was placed in operation at the Georgia School of Technology in 1934. The purpose of the station is to serve industry by developing the natural and human resources of Georgia through the utilization of the laboratory equipment and faculty talent of the various departments.

The older buildings have no definite architectural design but were planned solely for utility and are crowded close together on a high central campus. Dominating this group is the ACADEMIC BUILDING, erected in 1888, of Richardsonian Romanesque style with a square tower and pointed steeple, the name TECH in electric lights on each side of the tower. The buildings erected since 1920 conform to the Collegiate Gothic design and are placed according to a definite campus plan, drawn by F. P. Smith and Paul Phillipe Cret.

At GRANT FIELD, North Ave. between Techwood Dr. and Fowler St., is Tech's arched concrete football stadium, with a seating capacity of approximately 40,000. The "Golden Tornado," which has a national reputation, is always a strong contender in the Southern Conference football games.

Three DORMITORIES and the DINING HALL, Techwood Dr. between North Ave. and 3rd St., are all of Collegiate Gothic design. Within the dining hall there is a large stained glass Tudor window with ornate tracery in the pointed, four-centered arch. Fourteen panels contain figures symbolic of activities in the various departments of the school.

The NAVAL ARMORY (*open 9-4 daily during school term*), SW. corner Techwood Dr. and 3rd St., a long, two-story stuccoed building completed in 1934, houses the Tech naval unit of the R.O.T.C. The bell mounted at the right of the entrance and the eagle above the doorway are from the U.S.S. *Georgia,* which was scrapped in 1922. The grilled gates, designed by Julian Harris, were fashioned of iron taken from the same battleship. A submarine torpedo mounted on a pedestal and a modern naval gun are at the side of the building.

The AUDITORIUM-GYMNASIUM, 3rd St. between Techwood Dr. and Fowler St., constructed of reinforced concrete, was erected in 1938 with the aid of W.P.A. and P.W.A. funds. The facade rises above a platform forming the entrance, and the only ornamental detail is a free-cast concrete grille set above each of the four doorways. The building is used both as an auditorium and gymnasium; as an auditorium the seating capacity is 3,000.

The CERAMICS BUILDING, 3rd St. between Fowler and Cherry Sts., a simple red brick structure erected in 1924, contains the classrooms, laboratories, and library of the department of ceramic engineering.

The CIVIL ENGINEERING BUILDING, 3rd St. between Fowler and Cherry Sts., erected in 1938 with the assistance of the P.W.A. is of reinforced concrete faced with brick and trimmed with limestone. Marking the entrance is a wide terrace of brick, with a landing and graduated steps at each end, a pierced wall of brick forming the balustrade. This building contains classrooms of the department of civil engineering and freehand architecture and the laboratories of the highway engineering department.

The MECHANICAL DRAWING BUILDING, erected in 1938, is similar to the other newer buildings in design and structural material. The large windows, which form a major portion of the exterior walls, afford a maximum of natural lighting.

The DANIEL GUGGENHEIM SCHOOL OF AERONAUTICS, NW. corner Cherry St. and North Ave., was established in 1930 through a gift of $300,000 from the Daniel Guggenheim Fund for the Promotion of Aeronautics. The red brick building was designed especially for the laboratory equipment, which includes a nine-foot and a two-and-a-half-foot wind tunnel.

39. The COCA-COLA COMPANY (*open to visitors*), 318 North Ave., maintains here a plant that manufactures syrup for the well-known drink, which received its name from two of its ingredients, coca leaves and cola nuts. This is one of eight similar plants operated in the United States; it supplies syrup to soda fountains and bottling plants throughout the Southeast. Adjoining is an office building, from which many of the company's promotional and sales activities are directed.

Coca-Cola was first made in Atlanta in 1886 by J. S. Pemberton, a wholesale druggist and manufacturing chemist, who had been experimenting to perfect a new beverage. In 1887 Pemberton disposed of two-thirds interest in his commodity for $283.29 and in the following year sold the remaining third to Asa G. Candler's drug firm. Candler (1851-1929) gradually acquired ownership of Coca-Cola, simplified its formula, and in 1892 organized the Coca-Cola Company. He retained controlling interest in the corporation, served as its president, and amassed a fortune. In 1919 the company was sold to a syndicate that has greatly increased the sale of the beverage.

40. NATIONAL STOCKYARDS, Marietta St. and Brady Ave., the largest mule market in the world, is not a corporation but a name used to designate that district off Marietta Street given over to ten independent dealers and two large commission firms. The barns and pens of the National Stockyards

have a capacity of more than 20,000 animals. Two commission merchants hold auctions on Monday and Tuesday of each week. Mules are shipped to Atlanta from ten states.

When the sale starts, all buyers are requested to be in their seats, which are elevated before a well-lighted ring into which the mules are admitted through a gate. As many as 600 mules have been sold in one day. Transactions in the mule market, amounting to more than four million dollars annually, bring more buyers to Atlanta than the activities of any other local business. Cattle, sheep, and hogs are also sold at the stockyards.

41. The HUFF HOUSE (*private*), 70 Huff Rd., an unpretentious frame house on a knoll, was built in 1855 upon the foundations of a former house dating from 1830. During the Siege of Atlanta the neighborhood was occupied by Confederate camps. Later the house became the headquarters of General George H. Thomas, commander of the Army of the Cumberland, and the Confederate flag was replaced by the United States flag. The Huff family fled when Sherman ordered Atlanta to be burned, but a Scottish neighbor saved the house from destruction by raising the British flag above it. Afterward, the Huff house was known as the House of Three Flags.

POINTS OF INTEREST IN ENVIRONS

Candler Field Municipal Airport, **7.6 m.**, Kennesaw Mountain National Battlefield Park, **21.8 m.** (*see* TOUR 2); Fort McPherson, **4.2 m.**, Agnes Scott College, **6.8 m.**, Georgia Military Academy, **7.8 m.** (*see* TOUR 3); Stone Mountain, **16.3 m.** (*see* TOUR 8).

Augusta

Railroad Station: Union Station, 800 block Walker St., for Southern Ry., Atlantic Coast Line R.R., Georgia R.R., Charleston & Western Carolina Ry., Georgia & Florida R.R., and Central of Georgia Ry.

Bus Station: Southern Finance Bldg., 700 block Broad St., for Atlantic Greyhound Lines, Carolina Scenic Stages, Southeastern Stages, Southern Stages, and Bass Bus Lines.

Airport: Daniel Field Municipal Airport, Wrightsboro and Wheeless Rds., 4.5 m., for Delta Air Lines; taxi fare 50¢, bus fare 5¢.

Local Busses: 10-, 15-, and 20-min. schedules; fare 5¢.

Taxis: 25¢ and up according to number of passengers and distance.

Traffic Regulations: Right or left turns at all intersections except where traffic lights or officers direct otherwise. Street signs indicate parking limitations; no all-night parking on paved streets.

Accommodations: Ten hotels (three open during winter only); tourist houses.

Information Service: East Georgia Motor Club, Richmond Hotel, 744 Broad St.; Chamber of Commerce, Southern Finance Bldg., 700 block Broad St.

Tennis: May Park, 3rd and Watkins Sts., 4 courts; Allen Park, 15th St. and Walton Way, 6 courts; Hickman Park, 900 block Hickman Rd., 1 court; Julian Smith Park, west end of Broad St., 10 courts.

Swimming: Lake Olmstead, municipal beach, at Julian Smith Park, west end of Broad St.

Golf: Municipal Golf Course, Wrightsboro and Wheeless Rds., 50¢. Augusta Country Club, Milledge Rd. between Gardner and Broad Sts., $2. Forest Hills Course, in Forest Hills, Comfort Rd. and Magnolia Dr., $2.

Baseball: Municipal Baseball Stadium, Allen Park, 15th St. and Walton Way.

Football: Richmond Academy Stadium, Walton Way and Russell St., October and November.

Motion Picture Houses: Five, including one for Negroes.

Radio Station: WRDW (1500 kc.).

Annual Events: Woman's Titleholders Golf Championship (*open*), late January; Augusta Woman's Invitation Tournament, mid-March; Augusta National Golf Tournament, late March; South Atlantic States Tennis Tournament, late March; Augusta Open Golf Tournament, December.

For further information regarding the city see *Augusta*, another book of the American Guide Series, published in 1938 by the Tidwell Printing Supply Co., Augusta, Ga., and sponsored by the City Council.

AUGUSTA (109-483 alt.; 60,342 pop.), overlooking the Savannah River, is a city of old houses, vivid-flowered parkways, and groves of tall pines. Although the city is in the fall line hills, its climate is that of the Coastal Plain, and its short, mild winters attract tourists from the North and East. Augusta has become nationally known as a smart, lively winter resort. Here the tourists are not hurrying trailer guests but solid permanent citizens who have bought homes, joined clubs, modified local traditions, and made lasting friendships. Yet this element, for all its importance and animation, has not altered the essential texture of the serene and gracious old city. When the winter colony breaks up before the summer heat, the real Augusta emerges, its wide streets empty in the hot noonday stillness— a city where history is not so much exhibited as taken for granted in daily life.

This old-fashioned aspect persists even in the downtown section of Broad Street with its modern office buildings. Along Greene Street and others of the older residential areas there is a stately decorum in the weathered, sometimes shabby dwellings, which range from Colonial cottages and columned Greek Revival mansions to the turreted, jigsaw castles that were popular at the turn of the century. Old houses predominate also in North Augusta, a separately governed city of about 2,000 inhabitants that has grown up across the Savannah River in South Carolina. But in "The Hill" section there are fashionable winter hotels and imposing modern houses set amid smooth lawns and landscaped gardens.

The industry and commerce of Augusta are based principally upon cotton. Merchants and brokers gather around the exchange, and bales are stored in warehouses to be compressed for shipment to distant markets. Four textile mills, with 121,936 spindles and 2,044 looms, manufacture unbleached yard goods and heavy colored cloth, and a fifth mill manufactures coarse yarn. Five companies extract oil from cottonseed; the by-products are cottonseed hulls and meal, both used for cow feed. Four of the various fertilizer plants use hulls in addition to phosphates in the manufacture of their products.

Augusta, in the Savannah River kaolin belt, is one of the largest clay product centers in the Southeast. About 200,000 tons of kaolin a year are produced by five companies, one of which manufactures a kaolin brick that competes successfully with the English product. Red clay is also mined extensively; four companies have an annual capacity of 175,000,000 brick and 50,000 tons of hollow tile.

Augusta has a large candy factory, a barbecue and hash cannery producing 10,000 pounds of food daily, and a company that utilizes human hair imported from China to make oil press cloth, used to extract oils from cotton and other oil-bearing seeds. An ironworks makes boilers, tanks, sawmill machinery, brass, and aluminum castings. Incorporated in 1869,

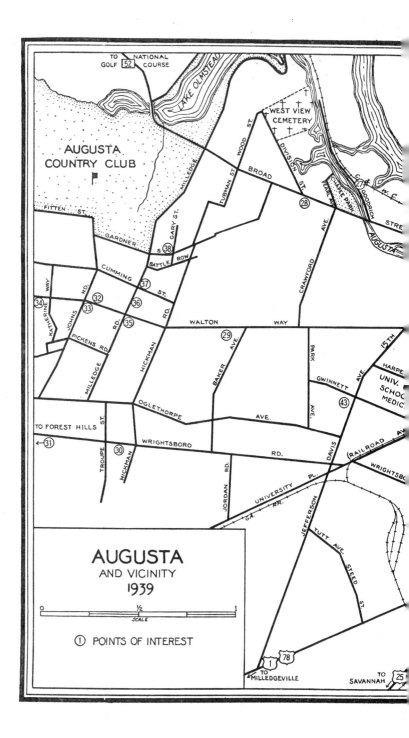

TO NATIONAL
GOLF 52 COURSE

LAKE OLMSTEAD

WEST VIEW
CEMETERY

AUGUSTA
COUNTRY CLUB

WOOD ST.

DIVISION ST.

BROAD

FITTEN ST.

MILLEDGE

TUBMAN ST.

GARDNER

GARY ST.

S 38

CUMMING

BATTLE ROW

37

ST.

WAY

KATHERINE

JOHNS RD.

32

33

36

34

PICKENS RD.

35

HICKMAN RD.

WALTON

28

CRAWFORD AVE.

GOODRICH

27

PARK

AUGUSTA

STRE

WAY

MILLEDGE

OGLETHORPE

BAKER AVE.

29

PARK AVE.

GWINNETT

15TH

HARPE

UNIV.
SCHOO
MEDIC

43

TO FOREST HILLS

31

TROUPE ST.

HICKMAN

30

WRIGHTSBORO

AVE.

RD.

DAVIS

(RAILROAD AV

WRIGHTSB

JORDAN RD.

UNIVERSITY PL.

GA. RR.

JEFFERSON

TUTT AVE.

STEED ST.

AUGUSTA
AND VICINITY
1939

0   ½   1
SCALE

① POINTS OF INTEREST

78

1
TO
MILLEDGEVILLE

TO
SAVANNAH 25

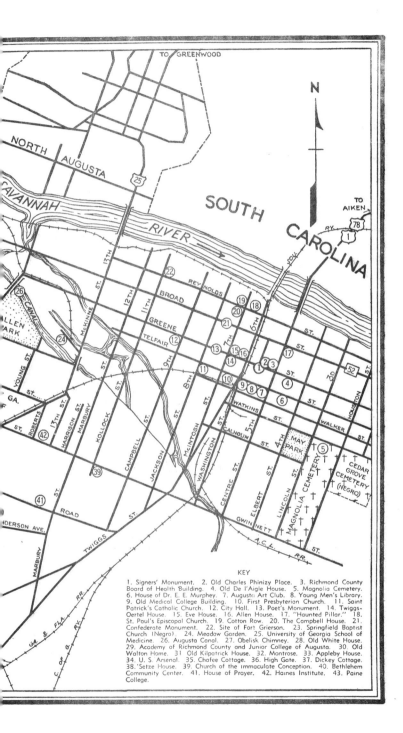

KEY

1. Signers' Monument. 2. Old Charles Phinizy Place. 3. Richmond County Board of Health Building. 4. Old De l'Aigle House. 5. Magnolia Cemetery. 6. House of Dr. E. E. Murphey. 7. Augusta Art Club. 8. Young Men's Library. 9. Old Medical College Building. 10. First Presbyterian Church. 11. Saint Patrick's Catholic Church. 12. City Hall. 13. Poet's Monument. 14. Twiggs-Oertel House. 15. Eve House. 16. Allen House. 17. "Haunted Pillar." 18. St. Paul's Episcopal Church. 19. Cotton Row. 20. The Campbell House. 21. Confederate Monument. 22. Site of Fort Grierson. 23. Springfield Baptist Church (Negro). 24. Meadow Garden. 25. University of Georgia School of Medicine. 26. Augusta Canal. 27. Obelisk Chimney. 28. Old White House. 29. Academy of Richmond County and Junior College of Augusta. 30. Old Walton Home. 31 Old Kilpatrick House. 32. Montrose. 33. Appleby House. 34. U. S. Arsenal. 35. Chafee Cottage. 36. High Gate. 37. Dickey Cottage. 38. 'Setze House. 39. Church of the Immaculate Conception. 40. Bethlehem Community Center. 41. House of Prayer. 42. Haines Institute. 43. Paine College.

this firm has manufactured grills, fences, banisters, and stairs that adorn many of the older houses.

Early in the eighteenth century English fur traders from the South Carolina colony were attracted to this section, and established a trading post, Savannah Town, on the Savannah River opposite the site of the present city of Augusta. It was this lucrative trade with the Indians that later influenced James Edward Oglethorpe to establish a town here.

He marked off the town in 1735, only two years after he had founded the Georgia colony at Savannah, and named it Augusta for the mother of George III. Kennedy O'Brien, an Irish trader, built the first storehouse and began trading with the Indians. Although relations between the two races were friendly on the whole, the watchful Oglethorpe in 1736 instructed that a garrison be built for protection. Trade developed, not only by means of the river, but also along the highway that was built in 1740 to connect Augusta with Savannah and the Indian nations. Each round-up of the fur traders was a spirited occasion, when the pack horses returned to town laden with pelts and followed by Indians. Oglethorpe contrived, despite some dishonest practices among the traders, to preserve peace between the colonists and the Indians. The shrewd George Galphin and others of his kind continued to exchange trinkets and gay clothing for valuable lands, and the trading post grew. In 1745 there were five warehouses but no schools, churches, or doctors. St. Paul's Church was established in 1750, and the following year the Reverend Jonathan Copp came to preach to its congregation of more than a hundred. During the following two decades the village developed as a military outpost.

In the course of trading, regulations were continually evaded, with the result that the Indians fell heavily into debt. In order to settle the claims of their white creditors, the Governor called a conference at Augusta in 1773. At this meeting the Indians ceded an area of 2,100,000 acres as far north as the Broad River.

Growing revolutionary sentiment severed many family ties in Augusta, which like other Georgia towns had its liberty pole and its hot-headed patriots. In 1776 George Walton, an Augusta citizen, signed the Declaration of Independence. St. Paul's Parish became Richmond County. Near the close of 1778, when Savannah fell to the British, Governor John Houstoun and his council fled to Augusta, which, however, was soon captured and held for a brief time. During 1780, a chaotic year with control of the city shifting from one army to the other, the seat of government was officially brought to Augusta. But soon afterward the town was taken by Grierson and Browne, Tory colonels. Browne, who had been tarred and feathered by a patriot mob five years before, took revenge by banishing Whigs and seizing their property.

Fort Augusta, renamed Fort Cornwallis by its British captors, stoutly resisted siege. Colonel Elijah Clarke made an assault in September, 1780, but was driven back. But in 1781 the daring "Lighthorse Harry" Lee contrived to erect a log tower from which his men were able to sweep the interior of the fort with musket fire. This attack was successful and on June 5, 1781, the British surrendered. Thus Augusta again was in patriot hands, but the town was so destitute that planters had to pole cargoes of game and rice up the river to the starving people.

After the Revolution, tobacco culture was introduced into Georgia by settlers from Virginia. Lands about the city were cleared for the crop, casks with axles and shafts were drawn by horses into town, and for the rest of the century Augusta was the principal tobacco market of the state. The town soon began to lay aside its cruder frontier attributes and to make cultural progress. In 1783 the Academy of Richmond County was chartered; two years later it was opened in a Bay Street residence. The *Augusta Chronicle and Gazette,* now the South's oldest newspaper in continuous publication, was issued in the same year.

In 1785 the legislature in Savannah adjourned to meet in Augusta the following year, when it appointed commissioners to choose a suitable site nearer the center of population and name it Louisville. The new site was not ready until 1796; consequently Augusta remained the state capital for ten years and it was during this time, on January 2, 1788, that Georgia ratified the Federal Constitution. In 1798 Augusta, which had been incorporated as a town nine years earlier, was granted a city charter with provision for a council composed of members elected from each district and an intendant elected by this body. It was also in 1798 that Augusta saw its first professional play, *Three Weeks After Marriage.*

During this progressive period William Longstreet worked for fifteen years to perfect the steam engine that he had invented with the financial aid of Isaac Briggs. After having applied for exclusive rights to the use of the engine, he launched an odd-looking craft with heavy oak boilers banded with iron. A fleet of skiffs rowed by jeering onlookers followed the boat downstream; to their astonishment the boat reversed and came back to its dock. Just as Longstreet was about to apply for a patent, news of Fulton's success reached Augusta.

The year 1808 marked a step toward cultural activity in the formation of the Thespian Society and the Library Company of Augusta. In 1810 the Bank of Augusta was chartered, and in 1819 the first arsenal was completed. The War of 1812, which brought a brief financial panic because Augusta merchants had overstocked in certain goods, did not long delay the town's progress. The Augusta Free School Society was organized in 1821 to educate the poor children who could not afford to pay tuition at the academy. The Medical Society of Augusta, the outgrowth of an association organized in 1808, was incorporated in 1822. Dr. Milton Antony, collaborating with his pupil Dr. Joseph A. Eve, opened a school of medicine in connection with the city hospital, a small frame building equipped to accommodate ten persons under ordinary conditions and twenty-one in emergencies. The Augusta Library Society was organized in 1827. The Medical Academy of Georgia, chartered the following year and opened a few years later, was the first in the state.

As the century advanced and cotton supplanted tobacco, Augusta took the lead as a market for the newer product, partly because of its favorable location and partly because all sales here were transacted for cash. Drivers of cotton caravans announced their arrival by sharply cracking their long whips, and Broad Street became jammed with wagons carrying 250-pound bags of cotton. About fifteen steamboats and many poled rafts, plying the Savannah River, carried from eight hundred to a thousand bags from Augusta to Savannah. Eli Whitney set up one of his first experimental gins on Rocky Creek, four miles from the city.

In 1837 the Georgia Railroad, begun in Augusta, started operation over its first twenty miles of track to Berzelia. The largest of the engines, which were called by such descriptive names as *Fairy, Dart,* and *Swallow,* was an eight-wheel passenger engine. In 1845 work was begun on the canal that later became so important in the development of the textile industry. When a plank road was built up Walton Way in 1850, the Sand Hills became a year-round place of residence. In 1851 John W. Houghton, a leather merchant, bequeathed funds to erect a brick school free to Augusta children; the city council provided teachers. The Augusta and Savannah Railroad, now the Central of Georgia, reached Augusta in 1854. The Young Men's Library Association, which had been organized in 1848, sponsored lecture courses and brought the famous William Makepeace Thackeray to Augusta, during his American tour (1855-56), to read *The Four Georges.*

Progress during this era was interrupted by epidemics of yellow fever in 1840 and 1854. The latter epidemic brought such fearful loss of life that there was a shortage of vehicles to take away the dead, and wheelbarrows were used to carry them to the cemeteries.

On January 24, 1861, the United States flag of the arsenal was replaced by a white flag bearing a red star, emblematic of the Confederacy. Because of its central position, water power, and transportation facilities Augusta was selected as the site of the Confederate Powder Works. All sorts of metal articles were offered to make bullets, and Augusta women helped to produce 75,000 cartridges a day. Among more than two thousand soldiers sent to war there were 292 casualties. St. Patrick's, like the other Augusta churches, was dedicated as a hospital. When Sherman left Atlanta for the sea in November, 1864, Augusta citizens feared that he would attack their city. Military leaders caused cotton to be piled five or six bales high on Broad Street so they could burn it rather than let it fall into the hands of the enemy. The mayor, however, prevailed on them to rescind the military order which probably would have destroyed the city. Earth mounds were thrown up around the arsenal. A wing of the Federal army swung by neighboring plantations, but Augusta escaped destruction because Sherman at that time could not afford to lay siege. It was not until after General Lee's surrender in April, 1865, that the army of occupation took the city with little disorder.

Under the military regime Negroes overran the city. The Freedmen's Bureau patiently explained to them the necessity of working for themselves, doled out supplies, instituted schools for them, and quartered them in barns, where, however, many died of disease. Tension between the Negroes and white people steadily increased, and on July 4, 1876, a riot occurred across the river in Hamburg. Negroes hurried to Augusta with their worldly possessions in pillowslips.

During the 1870's and the following two decades, industries developed rapidly, bringing about an increase in population. There was steady growth in the cultural as well as the industrial life of the city, despite an earthquake, a freshet, and a fire which damaged Augusta during this period. In 1908 a flood crippled the city for several days and destroyed several million dollars' worth of property. This flood, and a lesser one in 1912, led to the construction of a fourteen-mile levee, financed by a municipal bond issue and completed in 1916. A street railway strike in 1912 lasted for twelve days, and several men were killed in the rioting. The culminating disaster was the fire of 1916, which destroyed property estimated at $2,500,000 and wiped out many historic houses. When the city was rebuilt, many residents established their new homes in the higher and more spacious Sand Hills section.

Camp Hancock, Augusta's cantonment during the World War, accommodated forty thousand soldiers, and for a time the city took on a war-time atmosphere. The boom years of the 1920's affected Augusta chiefly through increasing its winter colony.

In October, 1929, the river rose to an unusual height and put the levee to a test. Although sandbags were piled on top and there was one ominous rift, the levee held. Further flood control work is now (1939) being undertaken, partly with Works Progress Administration labor.

In 1935 Augusta celebrated its bicentennial. Five thousand white-robed people, each bearing a lighted candle, marched into the arena of Richmond Academy stadium to the accompaniment of anthems of praise. This pageant presented the city's slow yet steady progress in commerce, industry, culture, and education.

POINTS OF INTEREST
(DOWNTOWN)

1. SIGNERS' MONUMENT, Greene St., between 5th and 6th Sts., is an imposing fifty-foot granite shaft rising from the center of the green. At night indirect lighting turns the stone to a warm, pale amber color against the dark sky. Begun with the laying of the cornerstone on July 4, 1848, it was erected by the State of Georgia in honor of its three signers of the Declaration of Independence. The bodies of Lyman Hall and George Walton are buried beneath the monument. Plans were made to reinter here the body of Button Gwinnett, killed in a duel with Lachlan McIntosh, but his burial place was never found.

2. The CHARLES PHINIZY PLACE *(private)*, 519 Greene St., now occupied by an undertaking establishment, is a handsome Georgian house built in 1841. It was originally conceived as a two-story structure over a high basement, but a third story has been added. Hand-made red brick was used in its construction, and the stucco covering the outside walls is painted to resemble brick. A graceful, iron-railed horseshoe stairway leads to a small entrance balcony at the second floor level. Pink marble is used in the floors and the waist-high dadoes of the basement.

3. The RICHMOND COUNTY BOARD OF HEALTH BUILDING *(open 9-5 weekdays)*, 503 Greene St., formerly the Clanton home, was built in 1848-51 and became county health headquarters in 1934. Greek Revival details are the high basement, the four fluted Doric columns supporting a classic pediment, and the small balcony over the entrance. The delicate iron grillwork used lavishly on the facade is hand wrought, and all the brick used in its construction was brought from Philadelphia by ship. Silver-plated doorknobs and hand-carved woodwork are notable features of the interior.

4. The DE L'AIGLE HOUSE *(private)*, 426 Greene St., a three-story, red brick structure, was built in 1818 by Nicholas de l'Aigle, a French *émigré*. The main portion of the house is of Tudor design, but the side wings, added at a later date, have small Corinthian columns in the Greek Revival manner. The front door is elaborately hand-carved, as are the wood trim and brass work throughout the interior. The sidelights and transom of one of the back doors are of red Bohemian glass etched in grape design. A graceful, mahogany-railed staircase winds up to the ballroom on the third floor. On this floor is a small, dark room where, it is said, the gentlemen of the old days stored their arms before entering the ballroom. There are two large wine cellars with iron-barred windows and ledges for kegs and demijohns.

In the back yard is the old kitchen, with a ten-foot fireplace and a large Dutch oven.

5. MAGNOLIA CEMETERY (*open 9-5 daily*), 3rd St. between Watkins and Gwinnett Sts., was named for the rows of magnolia trees that shade its walks and grounds. Although an older cemetery occupied part of this plot, the earliest interment recorded since it was taken over by the city bears the date August 5, 1818. Three Augusta poets, Paul Hamilton Hayne, Richard Henry Wilde, and James Ryder Randall, are buried here.

An UPRIGHT CANNON, its mouth buried in the ground, marks the grave of John Martin, a Revolutionary soldier. It is said that the cannon figured in a riot, when a mob packed it with anything that might be used for ammunition, including nails and bits of glass. The cannon would not fire, however, and rather than risk the danger of unloading it they buried it near this grave.

A large, STONE MAUSOLEUM contains the body of Wylly Barron, a gambler who conducted an establishment in the old Adkins Hotel on Ellis Street. Though a genial and tolerant host, he enforced a rigid rule that no man should play who could not afford it. It is told that this rule was established after a young man who had suffered heavy losses committed suicide, and dying, predicted that Barron himself would die penniless and without a place in which to be buried. Barron, in alarm, erected the handsome vault in Magnolia Cemetery twenty-four years before his death and provided that his body should be placed there in a metal casket, that the door should be locked, the keyhole sealed, and the key thrown off the bridge into the Savannah River. There is no known key either to the vault or to the ornate iron fence that surrounds it.

6. The HOUSE OF DR. E. E. MURPHEY (*private*), 432 Telfair St., was designed by a French architect, probably Gabriel Manigault, of South Carolina, and built as the "Government House" in 1790, when Augusta was the state capital. In 1791, during his visit to the city, George Washington was honored at a state banquet in this home. The stucco-covered brick house is of simple, square design with wings at each end that were added at a later date. There are beautiful white Carrara marble mantels and wide floor boards throughout the interior. A row of old-fashioned service bells hangs across the top of the back porch.

7. AUGUSTA ART CLUB (*open by permission*), 506 Telfair St., formerly a residence, has been remodeled for use as an art school and exhibition hall. This two-story frame building, with ornamentation of Adam style, is considered one of the few almost perfect examples of Georgian architecture in Augusta. The horseshoe entrance steps have balusters with delicate

mahogany railings, and on the interior a handsome mahogany stairway winds to the attic. The house was built by Nicholas Ware in 1818, and because it cost the large sum of $40,000 Augusta citizens called it Ware's Folly. Gabriel Manigault, the well-known architect, is thought to have designed it. When La Fayette visited Augusta in 1825 he was given a ball in this house.

8. YOUNG MEN'S LIBRARY (*open 9:30-6 weekdays*), 540 Telfair St., contains many rare volumes, old music, old newspapers, and bound copies of discontinued publications in addition to current books. It was founded by the Young Men's Library Association in 1848 but was not opened to the public until 1937. In the same building is the AUGUSTA MUSEUM (*open 2-6 weekdays*). Although it was not established until 1933, the museum contains good collections of Indian artifacts, Confederate relics, rifles, and ceramic art. The treasures of the pottery collection are pieces of Wedgwood ware made from Georgia clay and a Greek or Roman flagon bearing illustrations of a pagan festival to harvest gods.

The building is constructed of hand-made, stucco-covered brick in simple Tudor design. Gothic influence is seen in the battlemented parapets of the roof, and Renaissance detail in the columns of the entrance portico. The structure was erected in 1802 for the Academy of Richmond County and during the War between the States was used as a Confederate hospital. After the removal of the academy to its new quarters on Baker Avenue in 1926, the building stood vacant for two years before it was occupied by the library.

9. OLD MEDICAL COLLEGE BUILDING (*open when announced in newspapers*), Telfair St. between 5th and 6th Sts., is a simple Greek Revival structure of stuccoed brick. Six massive Doric columns of the portico support a plain entablature, above which rises an unadorned pediment. The building, designed by C. C. Clusky, was erected in 1835 for the Medical Academy of Georgia, the first school of medicine in the state. When the college was moved to University Place in 1911, the building became the manual training shop and science laboratory of the Academy of Richmond County. Abandoned in 1926, when the academy moved to Baker Avenue, it was made into a garden center by the Sand Hills Garden Club. Marked by a slab to the left of the entrance is the grave of Dr. Milton Antony, founder of the college.

10. FIRST PRESBYTERIAN CHURCH, 642 Telfair St., is a gray, stuccoed brick building of simplified Tudor architecture, showing Gothic influence in its crenelated parapets, rounded Norman arches with mullioned windows, the rose window above the recessed central doorway, and the Chester arch

ceiling. Renaissance influence is evident in the three-tiered Georgian tower surmounted by a spire. The church is set on a large tree-shaded lot surrounded by a hand-turned picket fence. It was built in 1812 from the plans of Robert Mills, designer of the Washington Monument. The Austin organ, installed in 1927, is one of the finest instruments in the South.

The MANSE (*private*), NW. corner Telfair and 7th (McIntosh) Sts., a two-story red brick house, was the boyhood home of Woodrow Wilson when his father, the Reverend Joseph R. Wilson, was pastor of the church.

11. SAINT PATRICK'S ROMAN CATHOLIC CHURCH, SE. corner Telfair and 8th (Jackson) Sts., serves a parish that was created in 1810. The church, designed by J. R. Nierrusse, of Columbia, South Carolina, and completed in 1862, is a Norman style, stuccoed building with a bell tower from which the angelus is daily heard. The members of the parish, unable to raise sufficient funds for construction, joined the hired workmen each day after their own work was done.

12. The CITY HALL (*open 9-5 weekdays*), SW. corner 9th and Greene Sts., is a Victorian Gothic building showing Romanesque influence; Italian influence is suggested in the red brick and terra cotta ornamentation. It was built between 1888 and 1890 as the Augusta post office at a cost of about $85,000, and it was not acquired by the city until 1916, when the new Federal building was erected.

In the foyer is the *Georgia,* the first steam fire engine purchased by a volunteer fire company, the Georgia Independent, in 1869. Among several old portraits in the building are two of George Washington by unknown artists, one showing the general in uniform, the other, in civilian clothes with stock, lace ruffles, and sword.

13. POETS' MONUMENT, Greene St., between 7th and 8th Sts., is a granite shaft standing in the green that runs down the center of the street. The city accepted the gift from Anna Russell Cole to honor four Georgia poets: Sidney Lanier, James R. Randall, Paul Hamilton Hayne, and Father Abram Ryan. The last three at one time lived in Augusta.

14. The TWIGGS-OERTEL HOUSE (*private*), 638 Greene St., is a massive red brick house of Regency style with Greek Revival detail. The iron railings of the steps have the same beautiful design as that of the fence enclosing the front yard. The house was built by Major George Lowe Twiggs about 1810 and later became the home of Johannes A. S. Oertel, who painted *Rock of Ages* and the Biblical series, *Dispensations,* which hang in the assembly hall of the University of the South, Sewanee, Tennessee.

15. The EVE HOUSE (*private*), 619 Greene St., erected in 1814, is a two-story frame building distinguished by a high brick basement. This was the home of Dr. Paul Fitzsimmons Eve, who served as a surgeon in the Polish army during the Polish War of 1830. On the green in front of the house a MONUMENT commemorating his services has been erected jointly by the Polish Government and the Medical Department of the University of Georgia.

16. The ALLEN HOUSE (*private*), 613 Greene St., built in 1859, is a two-story brick structure with a high basement and delicate, vine-covered ironwork of Federal style on the steps, porch, and balcony. The interior plan is unusual because the hallway runs the length of the house on the west side. Three successive generations of Allen men have served as mayors of Augusta.

17. "THE HAUNTED PILLAR," SE. corner 5th and Broad Sts., a Roman Doric stone column about ten feet high, bears a curse that has gained respect because of the peculiar circumstances surrounding it. On the side of the ash-colored column, about three feet above the sidewalk, is a black imprint that is said to have been made by the bloody hand of a slave put up for sale. It has been there since "the memory of man runneth not to the contrary," and the rains of more than half a century have not effaced it.

This pillar is the sole remnant of the old commercial center known as the Lower Market, which stood in the middle of Broad at Center Street until the building was leveled by a cyclone in February, 1878. An itinerant preacher had predicted this catastrophe as a warning to the townspeople for their worldliness, and he had further prophesied sudden death to anyone who attempted to remove the remaining pillar. When construction was begun on a new market a year later, Theodore Eye, a near-by grocer, bought the pillar for $50, according to legend, and engaged a Negro man to remove it to his corner. As the pillar stirred from the tug of ropes, a small boy joker set off a firecracker behind the workman's back; the frightened Negro, shouting of inflicted judgment, leaped down Broad Street and disappeared. Another story recounts that in later years when the street was widened, two men attempting to disturb the column were struck by lightning.

18. ST. PAUL'S EPISCOPAL CHURCH, 605 Reynolds St., with its Doric-columned portico and bell tower surmounted by a small dome, is set behind a brick wall and graceful iron gate. This building, erected in 1918, is a reproduction of the church built almost a century before and destroyed by fire in 1916. It is the fourth on the same site, the first having been established for the men of Fort Augusta in 1750, less than twenty years after Oglethorpe

founded the city. This church was then the farthest outpost of the Church of England on the new continent. A baptismal font, brought from England by the first rector, the Reverend Jonathan Copp, is the only possession saved from the building that burned in 1781. In the crypt beneath the altar is the tomb of Bishop Leonidas Polk, "fighting bishop of the Confederacy," killed at the Battle of Pine Mountain.

The tombs of noted persons in the churchyard include that of General George Brandes Matthews, twice Governor of Georgia; Commodore Oliver Bowen, who captured a British powder ship off Tybee Island in 1775; and William Longstreet, inventor of an early steamboat. It is believed that an Indian chief is buried upright in the tall brick monument in the southwest corner.

The Celtic cross in the churchyard was placed there by the Colonial Dames to mark the SITE OF FORT AUGUSTA, about which the city developed. At its base is a cannon brought from England by Oglethorpe.

19. COTTON ROW, Reynolds Street between 7th and 8th Sts., is composed of the cotton exchange, which has direct communication with the New York and New Orleans exchanges, and of warehouses and compress companies that compress and store the bales for shipment. In the fall the street is congested with trucks and sidewalks are lined with bales. Sometimes marketing more than half a million bales a season, Augusta was for many years rated the second largest inland cotton market in the world.

20. The CAMPBELL HOUSE (*private*), 123 7th St., is unusual in having no windows facing the river on the north side of the house except in the attic. It was believed that miasma rising from the water would cause fever. The residence, built in 1792, was remodeled when it was recently converted into a funeral home.

21. CONFEDERATE MONUMENT, in the center of Broad. St. between 7th and 8th Sts., is Augusta's most impressive memorial. The central shaft, carved in Italy of Carrara marble, is seventy-six feet high. The life-size figures, one at each corner of the column, are of Generals Robert E. Lee and Stonewall Jackson, representatives of the Confederacy; General Thomas R. R. Cobb, of Georgia; and General W. H. T. Walker, of Richmond County. At the top of the shaft is a statue of a Confederate private. Designed by Von Gunden and Young, of Philadelphia, the monument was erected by the Ladies Memorial Association at a cost of approximately $17,000 and was dedicated on October 31, 1878.

22. The SITE OF FORT GRIERSON, near intersection of 11th and Reynolds Sts., is indicated by a granite marker bearing a bronze plate. During British

occupation of the city eighty men were stationed at the fort under Colonel Grierson. In May, 1781, an American force under General Andrew Pickens, aided by Colonel "Lighthorse Harry" Lee and Colonel Elijah Clarke, attacked and captured the fort.

23. SPRINGFIELD BAPTIST CHURCH (Negro), SE. corner Reynolds and 12th (Marbury) Sts., a red brick structure with a gambrel roof, was built in 1910 to house a congregation organized in 1773 as the Silver Bluff or Dead River Church in South Carolina. The congregation of this, the first Negro Baptist church in the United States, was dispersed during the Revolution when many of the Negroes came to Augusta with their masters. Here they were reorganized as the Springfield Baptist Church. Among the six pastors buried in the churchyard is the Reverend Kelly Lowe, who organized the first Negro Sunday school in the nation on January 11, 1869. The wooden school and community house to the rear of the church was originally the St. John Methodist Church (white), moved to this site in 1844.

24. MEADOW GARDEN (*open 3-6 Wed. during winter, also some holidays; 25¢*), Nelson St., between 13th and 15th Sts., was named long before business encroached upon the surrounding fields. The story-and-a-half white frame house with three dormer windows in the sharply sloping roof is surrounded by a white paling fence and privet hedge. In 1794 Thomas Watkins gave the property to his godson, George Walton, Jr., son of the George Walton who signed the Declaration of Independence. The old residence, preserved as a museum by the D. A. R., contains early American relics, including old furniture, portraits, prints, clothes, and a cannon used during the Revolution in the defense of Augusta and in the Battle of Ninety-Six, South Carolina.

25. UNIVERSITY OF GEORGIA SCHOOL OF MEDICINE, Harper St. between Railroad Ave. and 15th St., was chartered in 1828 as the Medical Academy of Georgia, and 45 years later it was made a branch of the University of Georgia. Controlled by the Board of Regents of the University System of Georgia, the school has an enrollment of more than a hundred and fifty and a faculty of ninety. The large, red brick building with a mansard roof and ironwork porches was begun in 1870 for the Tuttle-Newton Orphanage and was not converted into the college building until 1911. It contains a MEDICAL MUSEUM (*open upon application to the dean*) that provides opportunity for research and study in its display of normal and pathological models, charts, and specimens.

Since senior medical students treat city patients free of charge, close contact is maintained with the UNIVERSITY HOSPITAL, situated on the same tract of land. Its main building, with three connected wings of semi-classical architecture, was erected by the city in 1914 at an approximate cost of $500,000. The hospital, which has an A rating from the American College of Surgeons, accommodates 325 patients. The bronchoscopic clinic, established in 1929, is one of the oldest in this section.

The Lamar Wing for Negroes supplants the Lamar Negro Hospital, established upon the bequest of Gazaway B. Lamar, Augusta financier, who willed $50,000 each to Augusta and Savannah for the building of Negro hospitals. These funds were in the form of claims against the U. S. Government for cotton destroyed during the War between the States. The first Federal payment of $7,000 was increased by a city appropriation of $8,000, and the cornerstone was laid on March 11, 1895.

26. AUGUSTA CANAL, spanned by the Butt Memorial Bridge, extends nine miles through the city, running from west to east. In 1844, four progressive citizens, realizing the need of Augusta for additional water power, financed a survey for a canal to be filled with water from the Savannah River. Work was begun the following year on a seven-mile project that was completed on November 23, 1846. Six hundred horsepower was developed, but before many years had passed new factories necessitated additional power. Between 1871 and 1875 the widening, deepening, and lengthening of the canal to nine miles resulted in increasing the horsepower to 14,000. Four cotton mills derive part of their power from the canal system.

27. The OBELISK-SHAPED CHIMNEY, Goodrich St. one block N. of Broad St., 176 feet high, stands as a monument to the Confederate Powder Works, of which it is the only remaining part. From 1862 until 1865 this plant, occupying several acres of land, manufactured 2,270,000 pounds of gunpowder under the direction of Colonel George Washington Rains. Since it was the only powder plant in the South, the area about it was carefully guarded for several miles. The plant was dismantled in 1871.

28. The OLD WHITE HOUSE (*private*), 1822 Broad St., erected about 1750, is the oldest house in Augusta. Situated on an eminence above a brick retaining wall, this two-story frame house has a gambrel roof, substantial end chimneys, and a recessed front porch. It is said that if one standing on the beautiful circular stairway counts to thirteen, he will hear a groan. This tradition dates from the American Revolution when the house was known as McKay's Trading Post. On September 14, 1780, Colonel Elijah Clarke with 500 men attempted to take Augusta from the British, who were under the command of Colonel Grierson and Colonel Thomas Browne, a local Tory. The British, desperately pressed, took refuge in the trading post, protected by earthworks and barred windows. They were on the point of

starvation after a four days' siege when the arrival of reinforcements forced the Americans to retreat, leaving Captain Ashby and twenty-eight patriot soldiers. The wounded Browne caused thirteen of the abandoned soldiers to be hanged from an immense hook in the attic and moved his bed near the door to watch their bodies dangle in the stair well. In the front yard the Indian allies formed a circle about the other prisoners and put them to death by slow torture.

(THE HILL)

On THE HILL, Augusta's most beautiful residential section, handsome houses are designed to blend with oak and pine groves and the natural contours of the Sand Hills. Here are green parkways and landscaped gardens, open each spring during the Sand Hills Garden Club tour, when they are ablaze with red flowering quince, purple wistaria and iris, pink crabapple, and pink and white dogwood. The beauty of the formal houses of winter colonists and the more elaborate residences of Augusta citizens is accented by the simplicity of the Sand Hills cottages, variations of the American Farmhouse type, built about 1800. At that time citizens of low-lying Augusta sought to escape the heat of the long, humid summers and the miasma of surrounding swamplands by building summer residences on the Sand Hills. Carriages first plowed through the sand of an old tobacco road, called Battle Row because boisterous tobacco rollers often engaged in brawls at the tavern on its course. Later they were able to traverse a plank road along what is now Walton Way upon payment of a toll collected at the 15th Street gate. In 1861 people were living on The Hill throughout the year, and the village was incorporated as Summerville. When a streetcar line was laid to the arsenal in 1866, an extra team of mules was necessary to pull the car up the grade. Summerville was not incorporated in the city until 1912.

29. ACADEMY OF RICHMOND COUNTY and JUNIOR COLLEGE OF AUGUSTA, Walton Way and Baker Ave., occupy a $375,000 building erected in 1926 of brick and stucco in the modern Collegiate Gothic style. Both the high school and the college are a part of the city school system and have an enrollment of 1,428 students with 56 teachers.

The high school is the outgrowth of old Richmond Academy, which was one of the first three public schools in the state. Chartered in 1783, the academy moved two years later into its first building, on Bay Street. When President Washington was in Augusta in May, 1791, Governor and Mrs. Edward Telfair gave a ball in his honor in the building. He was present also during an examination of the academy pupils and was so impressed by their progress that he later sent the honor students appropriately inscribed copies of Roman classics. In 1802 the academy moved into the building now occupied by the library, and in 1926, when the junior college was added, transferred to the present structure.

A Spanish convent bell of unknown age, which hung on the porch of the original building and summoned the pupils to school, is a cherished possession of the present school.

30. The OLD WALTON HOME (*private*), 2216 Wrightsboro Rd., is a two-and-a-half-story, white clapboard house now owned by the Harper family, descendants of George Walton. Walton, Georgia signer of the Declaration of Independence, built the house before 1795 for his summer home. The hand-carved exterior and interior trim and the delicate spider web design of the banisters on the first- and second-story porches show good Colonial detail. Massive end chimneys and numerous windows are other features of the house.

31. The OLD KILPATRICK HOUSE (*private*), Comfort Rd. between Buena Vista Rd. and Magnolia Dr., is a large, square Colonial building that was moved here from the southwest corner of Greene and 7th Streets. Its most notable feature is the entrance, with graceful horseshoe stairs. The house, built in 1761, was a fashionable inn on what was then the Old Post Road that led from Savannah. In 1825 when General La Fayette visited Augusta he addressed a large crowd from the porch.

32. MONTROSE (*private*), 2249 Walton Way, a story-and-a-half clapboarded structure, was built in 1849 by Robert Reid. Large Roman columns reach from the level of the brick basement to the roof. On the lawn in front of the house is one of the eight old cannon from the dead town of Sunbury (*see* TOUR 1). During the American Revolution, when the British sent word demanding that the Scottish Highlanders at Sunbury surrender Fort Morris, the dauntless Highlanders are said to have replied, "Come and take it." Years later this cannon was presented to Colonel Charles Colcock Jones, Jr., a Georgia historian. Colonel Jones wrote his vast historical works in the northwest basement room of this house, which is now occupied by his descendants.

33. The APPLEBY HOUSE (*private*), 2260 Walton Way, known as the Montgomery Place, is a two-story white frame building erected about 1830. The large, square structure, recently renovated, is built in Greek Revival style and has massive Doric columns rising to the porch roof. An ornamental iron balcony is suspended over the entrance doorway.

34. U. S. ARSENAL (*grounds open daily*), Walton Way and Katherine St., is the only one in the Southeast and one of the oldest in the country. The six

original buildings, in use since 1829, are built on the sides of a brick quadrangle that encircles a rose garden centered by a stone sundial. The garden was formerly the old parade ground.

The first United States arsenal at Augusta, built in 1819, was on the Savannah River near the site of the King and Sibley Mills. When an epidemic of "black fever" swept the garrison, higher ground was sought and seventy acres on the Sand Hills were purchased for $6,000. Buildings were erected and the arsenal garrisoned in 1829.

In 1861, five days after Georgia's secession from the Union, the arsenal was surrendered with no more struggle than the formality of an exchange of stiffly diplomatic notes between Captain Arnold Elzey, representing the United States, and Colonel W. H. T. Walker, representing Governor Brown. The long building near the main entrance was built soon afterward for a machine shop where harness, gun-carriages, and the like were made. In the front part of the building Augusta women and children picked lint and made surgical dressings.

35. The CHAFEE COTTAGE (*private*), 914 Milledge Rd., is a two-story clap-board house built on a brick basement with an outside kitchen that is still in use. The structure is of the Sand Hills Cottage type with dormers in its gabled roof. Built before 1784, the house remains in the possession of the family that originally owned it. In the house are many objects of art, one of them being a Gilbert Stuart portrait of Mrs. Hanna Few Howard, a direct ancestor of Mrs. Harry L. Chafee, present owner of the cottage.

36. HIGH GATE (*private*), 820 Milledge Rd., was erected about 1800 by slave labor with hand-hewn timber that was felled on the grounds. In 1838 a house that was virtually a duplicate of the original was built in front of the old structure. The two parts are now connected by one-story rooms. The name of the place is derived from the tall wrought-iron gates of the fence. In the gardens, old millstones are used as stepping stones.

37. The DICKEY COTTAGE (*private*), 728 Milledge Rd., is of the Sand Hills Cottage type. The front part of the house was built in 1857, but the kitchen and pantries were part of the house of Colonel John Forsyth (1780-1841), Governor of Georgia and Secretary of State under Andrew Jackson. Colonel Forsyth, as Minister to Spain, secured ratification by Ferdinand VII of the treaty of 1819 ceding Florida to the United States.

38. The SETZE HOUSE (*private*), 635 Gary St., is a white frame house show-ing classical influence in the fluted columns of its two-story portico. John Milledge, elected Governor of Georgia in 1802, built the house soon after the Revolution. For a site he chose a hill on his 5,000-acre tract so that he

could look out over his own broad acres and see Augusta from his front porch. The trees were topped for a better view and still show effects of the topping. Because of the view of the town, he named the place Overton.

(THE TERRY)

Negroes, constituting 40 per cent of the city's population, live principally in THE TERRY (a corruption of The Territory), a section in southeast Augusta. Here are rough, unpaved streets bordered with unpainted, three-room shacks, some with crude wooden shutters, a few with screens. The narrow porches, set flush with streets and alleys, are filled in summer with blooming plants, no less luxuriant for the battered lard cans and worn-out kitchen vessels that hold them. Low fires burn under black washpots and clothes hang on crisscrossed lines in the yards. In the business section the Negroes have their own grocery stores, insurance companies, doctors, dentists, churches, and motion picture theaters. Curious signs, often with misspelled words, advertise that a merchant is "ugly but honest" or that "miners" (minnows) are for sale as fish bait. To many of the alleys the Negroes have applied such descriptive names as Thank God, Tin Cup, Electric Light, or Garbage Can.

39. CHURCH OF THE IMMACULATE CONCEPTION, SE. corner Gwinnett and 11th (Kollock) Sts., is a Roman Catholic church for Negroes. This institution was founded in 1909. In connection with the church is a school where 400 children are taught by two priests and by Franciscan Sisters.

40. BETHLEHEM COMMUNITY CENTER (open 9 A.M.-10 P.M. weekdays), NE. corner Anderson Ave. and Clay St., is maintained by the women of the Methodist Episcopal Church, South. Group co-operation is emphasized by the house staff, by representatives of various churches who participate in leadership classes, and by students of Paine College who gain valuable training by helping with various activities. The building has a modern kitchen for cooking classes, a sewing room for domestic science groups, a library for Bible classes and night school, a gymnasium for Negroes of the section, and club rooms for boys and girls. Community welfare is promoted by family visiting, and interracial understanding is improved by the annual good-will Christmas party and other activities.

41. The HOUSE OF PRAYER, 1269 Wrightsboro Rd., is an unpainted, rough-board tabernacle in which Bishop Grace preaches a highly emotional religion to the accompaniment of much shouting, increased by the four brass bands that provide music for the services. At one end of the auditorium, decorated with streamers of crepe paper, is the "throne" of Daddy Grace, as the preacher is affectionately known. Worshipers sit on wooden benches arranged on the sawdust-covered dirt floor.

42. HAINES INSTITUTE, 1339 Gwinnett St., is a Negro school housed in brick buildings on a four-acre campus and supported in part by the Presbyterian Board of National Missions. From the institution, offering four years of high school and one of college work, more than 2,000 Negroes have been graduated since its establishment in 1886. The enrollment is 370, and the faculty, entirely of Negroes, numbers 12.

To the right of the entrance is a monument marking the grave of Lucy Laney, founder of the school. "Miss Lucy," as she was affectionately called by her students, developed the institution in the face of many obstacles.

43. PAINE COLLEGE, 15th St. (Jefferson Davis Ave.) between Gwinnett St. and Oglethorpe Ave., is an accredited Negro college situated in the midst of a white residential section. A curving driveway leads through the twenty-acre campus to the red brick, Georgian-style main building, one of the six principal college structures. There are also three science laboratories and a library containing 15,000 volumes. The college is attended by between 325 and 400 young men and women from nine states who pay less than one-fifth of the actual cost of their training. It was incorporated on June 19, 1883, by the Methodist Episcopal Church, South, and later the Colored Methodist Church was admitted to joint ownership and control. The faculty is composed of both white and Negro teachers, and it has always been customary to have a white president and a Negro dean.

The MUSEUM (*open on application at office*), in Haygood Hall, contains an assemblage of African relics, including carved ivory pieces, grass cloths, woven baskets, two-faced fetishes, native drums, musical instruments, and farming implements, all brought from Africa by the Reverend W. E. Tabb, a missionary.

POINTS OF INTEREST IN ENVIRONS

AUGUSTA NATIONAL GOLF COURSE (*open to members and guests only*), 1.5 m. NW. on State 52, is an 18-hole links with velvety green fairways that are particularly vivid during winter. Designed by Dr. Alistair McKenzie, noted golf course architect, in collaboration with Georgia's Bobby Jones, it was opened in 1934. Several national tournaments are played here each year.

An avenue of stately magnolias leads to the clubhouse, a broad-verandaed, stucco structure built in 1854 by Prosper J. A. Berckmans on his estate, Fruitlands, now the golf links. Berckmans was a Belgian horticulturist who designed many Georgia gardens and supplied them with shrubs from his nursery here. Consequently, the natural beauty of the grounds is greatly augmented by plantings of unusual trees and shrubs, carefully preserved by the designers. The rare specimens include a Spanish cork tree received from the United States Patent Office about 1880; camellias imported about

1861 from Japan and several European countries; 40 varieties of foreign azaleas more than 60 years old; a Chinese pine about 75 years old; a holly-like tea olive brought from Japan in 1880; and a hardy lemon hedge propagated from a Japanese plant obtained in 1870.

Bath (old Presbyterian Church and cemetery), **15 m.** (*see* TOUR *4*). Cottage Cemetery, **6.1 m.**; Tobacco Road, **8.5 m.**; New Savannah (Savannah River Lock and Dam and New Savannah Cemetery), **10.2 m.** (*see* TOUR *15*).

Columbus

Railroad Stations: Union Station, 12th St. and 6th Ave., for Southern Ry. and Central of Georgia Ry.; Central of Georgia branch stations, Railroad St. and 2nd Ave., and 9th St. and Broadway, open 15 minutes before arrival of trains (no baggage checked).

Bus Station: Union Bus Terminal, 1300 Broadway, for Greyhound, Ader, and Alaga Lines and Southern, Crescent, and Georgia Stages.

Airport: Municipal Field, 2 m. S. of business section on new Fort Benning highway; no scheduled service.

Taxis: 10¢ between any two points in city; 20¢ a mile outside city limits; 10¢ extra for each suitcase or large package.

Local Busses: Fare 5¢.

Inter-urban Busses: Broadway and 10th St. for hourly service to Fort Benning; fare 20¢ at station, 25¢ if boarded en route.

Accommodations: Eight hotels including one for Negroes; boarding houses and tourist camps.

Information Service: Chamber of Commerce, Civic Building, 12th St. and 1st Ave.; Chattahoochee Valley Motor Club, 10th St. and Broadway.

Athletic Field: Memorial Stadium, 4th St. and 1st Ave.

Baseball Park: 4th St. and 1st Ave.

Golf: Municipal Golf Course, 4th St. and 10th Ave., 25¢ for 9 holes; Country Club, Cherokee Ave., 18 holes, grass greens, $1.50.

Riding: Boardman Riding Stables, River Rd., $1 an hour.

Motion Picture Houses: Six, including two for Negroes.

Annual Events: Cotton Festival, May; Georgia-Auburn football game, Oct.; Chattahoochee Valley Fair, Oct.

COLUMBUS (250 alt., 43,131 pop.) is situated on the east bank of the Chattahoochee River at the head of navigation. The city extends into both the Piedmont Plateau and the Coastal Plain at the foot of a series of powerful falls, and its proximity to great hydroelectric power developments has attracted many manufacturing establishments. Machine shops, foundries, clay works, fertilizer plants, confectionery factories, packing houses, cotton gins, and textile mills operating more than half a million spindles, all have contributed to the growth of this municipality.

The original city plan of 1828 has been retained, with streets varying in width from 99 to 164 feet, laid out in orderly pattern with central parkways. Bordering the streets are magnificent trees set in broad grass plots. In spring when the white dogwood and purple wistaria bloom together, the streets are glorious with color.

The important stores and offices are crowded into a few blocks on Broadway, which runs north and south about two blocks from the river front. Shops of twentieth-century smartness are accentuated by the many red brick buildings of the type constructed near the turn of the century. The residential district begins close to the business section and extends over a thickly populated suburban area. The older sections, spread through the downtown area and often intermingled with the business section, lie in the valley and are very flat. Here houses of brick or clapboard are built on small lots fronting the sidewalk, the classic note often appearing with variations in the smaller as well as the larger houses. In the newer residential developments of Green Island Hills and Wynnton, to the north and east, are estates with terraced gardens and landscaped lawns.

Despite the stir of industry, something of a rural atmosphere persists. In the early morning Negro women peddle fresh vegetables from full baskets carried on their heads, and in the spring wildflower vendors gather at the site of the old city market on First Avenue. Front Avenue, an important thoroughfare in the days of river traffic, is crowded with farmers gathered for trading, and here parking spaces have been reserved for buggies, wagons, and carts.

Fort Benning (*see* TOUR *10A*), an infantry training school with a personnel of 6,500, is nine miles from the city. This army post is virtually a self-sufficient unit, but uniforms are frequently seen downtown and many citizens attend the fort maneuvers, polo games, dances, and Sunday morning fox hunts. The officers' club has a large civilian membership.

Though not a college town, Columbus has been a leader in various important educational developments. With the establishment (1905) of an academic trade school under the municipal education system, it became the first city in the United States to provide industrial training in the public schools. The "Columbus Plan" for school architecture originated in this city. By this plan all units are placed on one floor with convenient communication, thus insuring greater efficiency and reducing fire hazard.

Columbus has a number of choral clubs and musical organizations. The non-sectarian Georgia-Alabama Sacred Harp Singing Society, a group that sings without instrumental accompaniment, is one of the oldest organizations of its kind in the South. Its name is derived from the fact that such singers consider the vocal cords sacred harps (*see* MUSIC).

In the early 1800's the site of Columbus was occupied by a Creek village. After the Indian lands in this territory were ceded to the state in 1826, Governor Forsyth saw the desirability of strengthening the border of

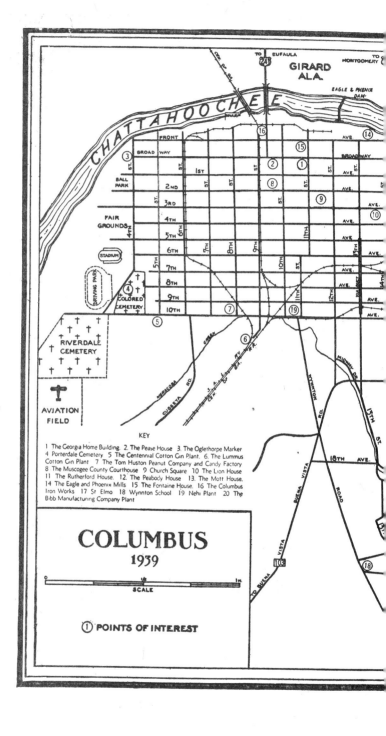

TO EUFAULA

GIRARD ALA.

TO MONTGOMERY

EAGLE & PHENIX DAM

CHATTAHOOCHEE

FRONT AVE.

BROAD WAY

1st ST.

2ND

3RD

BALL PARK

FAIR GROUNDS

4TH

5TH 6TH

6TH

STADIUM

5TH

7TH

8TH

DRIVING PARK

9TH

COLORED CEMETERY

10TH

RIVERDALE CEMETERY

AVIATION FIELD

BROADWAY

AVE.

AVE.

AVE.

AVE.

AVE.

AVE.

AVE.

AVE.

AVE.

AVE.

AVE.

VERACORA RD.

CUSSETA RD.

BUENA VISTA

BUENA VISTA

WYNNTON RD.

WYNNTON

108

18

16TH AVE.

ROAD

KEY

1 The Georgia Home Building. 2. The Pease House 3. The Oglethorpe Marker
4 Porterdale Cemetery 5 The Centennial Cotton Gin Plant. 6. The Lummus
Cotton Gin Plant 7 The Tom Huston Peanut Company and Candy Factory
8 The Muscogee County Courthouse 9 Church Square 10 The Lion House
11 The Rutherford House. 12. The Peabody House 13. The Mott House.
14 The Eagle and Phoenix Mills 15 The Fontaine House. 16 The Columbus
Iron Works 17 St Elmo 18 Wynnton School 19 Nehi Plant 20 The
Bibb Manufacturing Company Plant

COLUMBUS
1939

SCALE

① POINTS OF INTEREST

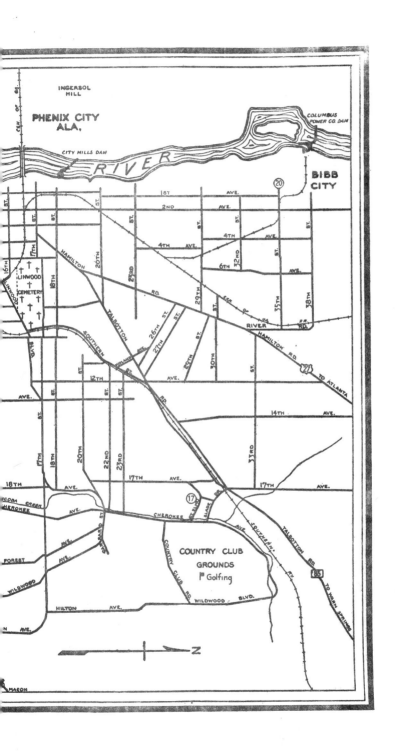

Georgia by the establishment of a trading post. He therefore appointed commissioners to lay out a town, which was to be called Columbus, and to dispose of the lots. Columbus was thus established in 1828 as the last frontier town of the Thirteen Colonies. The first steamboat visited the little town in 1828, beginning a river trade that increased until the coming of the railroads in the 1850's. At the height of river commerce as many as sixteen boats, loaded with cotton and naval stores, plied the Chatta-hoochee. Stagecoaches were already bringing daily mail from the north, and in the early 1830's construction was begun on the first bridge connecting Columbus with Alabama.

During the Indian War of 1836 the town became the center of military operations because of the proximity of the tribes on the opposite side of the Chattahoochee River. Settlers from near-by wilderness cabins fled to Columbus, and many, upon the restoration of peace, remained as residents.

At the outbreak of hostilities with Mexico in 1846, the martial spirit of Columbus was aroused, and the town was the point of debarkation for troops to the Mexican territory. Because of the influence of Mirabeau B. Lamar, renowned soldier in the struggle for Texas independence, three companies were mustered from among the Columbus citizenry and equipped for service.

Textile development began in 1838 when the Columbus Cotton Factory began spinning cotton yarn and carding wool. Between 1840 and 1850 water rights were leased and the cotton mill industry was given added impetus. Gas and telegraph connections were established by 1855. Although the Mobile & Girard Railroad was chartered in 1846, it was not until 1853 that the first track connecting Columbus with Alabama was put into operation. Prior to this time an interstate railway joined the town with points north as far as Fayetteville.

During the first years of the War between the States there was a marked increase in business activity, and plants manufacturing shoes, caps, swords, pistols, cannon, and gunboats ran at full capacity to supply Confederate needs. It was not until April 16, 1865, a week after General Lee's surrender, that Union forces attacked Columbus. General Howell Cobb made a brave attempt to defend the bridge over the Chattahoochee River but was overwhelmed by General James Wilson's Federal troops who entered the city. Mills and public buildings were destroyed, and twelve hundred prisoners and fifty field guns were captured.

The period of reconstruction was one of havoc and distress, but rebuilding was accomplished with such rapidity that by 1874 the city's industries were more numerous and varied than before the war. Concurrent with the decline of shipping at the turn of the century was the impetus given manufacturing through the construction of hydroelectric plants. Since that time Columbus has grown rapidly, the decade from 1920 to 1930 showing an increase in population of almost 28 per cent. The city today ranks second in cotton manufacturing in the South and is one of the great iron-working centers. It is also an important shipping point for products from the surrounding area, including pecans, dairy products, livestock, and diversified crops.

POINTS OF INTEREST

1. The GEORGIA HOME BUILDING, SE. corner Broadway and 11th St., is a three-story bank building erected by William H. Young between 1860 and 1867. Of Italian Renaissance design, it is notable for its narrow, arched windows and for its cast-iron exterior walls that were molded in sections in Pittsburgh, Pennsylvania.

2. The PEASE HOUSE (*private*), 908 Broadway, was built in 1854, the first story being of stuccoed brick and the second of native heart pine. Of the New Orleans or Creole type, it is painted a vivid canary yellow that contrasts strikingly with the iron grillwork on the upper and lower porches and on the horseshoe stairs curving upward from a lower front court.

3. The OGLETHORPE MARKER, Broadway and 4th St., is a boulder erected by the D. A. R. to commemorate General James Edward Oglethorpe's visit to Coweta Town (in what is now Russell County, Alabama) in 1739 to treat with the upper Creek Indians. As a result of this visit Oglethorpe concluded, on August 21, 1739, one of the most important treaties in all his bloodless dealings with the American Indians. Not only did this treaty confirm the colony's first title to the eastern territory lying between the Savannah and Altamaha rivers, but it provided for the considerable enlargement of the colony's territory and forestalled a possible alliance of the western Creek with the Spanish of Florida and the French of Mobile Bay.

4. PORTERDALE CEMETERY, 4th St. near 7th Ave., is a Negro burial ground, where the primitive custom of placing medicine bottles, crockery, snuffboxes, toothbrushes, and other humble decorations on the graves is retained.

The BRAGG SMITH MONUMENT was erected here by the city of Columbus to a Negro who lost his life September 30, 1933, in a vain attempt to save the superintendent of public works from being crushed in a collapsing trench. This is believed to be the only monument ever erected to a Negro by a municipality.

5. The CENTENNIAL COTTON GIN PLANT (*open weekdays during work hours*), 10th Ave. and 5th St., was organized at Fort Valley in 1876 for the manufacture of cotton gins and ginning machinery. In 1921 the business was moved to Columbus, where continued growth necessitated the building of

the present large, modern plant four years later. The output is about forty gins a week.

6. The LUMMUS COTTON GIN PLANT (*open Mon.-Thurs. during working hours*), E. end of 9th St., one of the largest cotton gin manufacturing plants in the South, was established here in 1871 upon its removal from Juniper, Georgia. Lummus gins were the first to be equipped with the air blast feed system, universally recognized as the most important and revolutionary improvement in the cotton gin since its invention by Eli Whitney.

7. The TOM HUSTON PEANUT COMPANY AND CANDY FACTORY (*open 8:30-4:30 weekdays; guide service*), SW. corner 10th Ave. and 8th St., represents the development of an idea conceived by a Columbus business man. The first bag of Tom's Toasted Peanuts, marketed in April, 1925, was packed in a small, one-story building at 4th Avenue and 30th Street. At that time the company's working force numbered only four men; today there are four hundred employees.

8. The MUSCOGEE COUNTY COURTHOUSE, 2nd Ave. between 9th and 10th Sts., a red brick building with massive Doric columns and simple porticoes at front and rear, occupies a well-landscaped city block. The structure was erected in 1928. At the northern entrance of the lawn is a CANNON captured by Federal troops at the Battle of Shiloh. This cannon, cast at the naval iron works in Columbus during the War between the States, was made from household brasses contributed by the ladies of the town—hence the name *Ladies Defender,* crudely engraved near the breech.

A small BRASS SALUTE GUN, at the northern entrance, is the property of the Columbus Guards. This gun fired salutes in 1861 upon the secession of each state from the Union and also upon the occasion of Jefferson Davis' inauguration in Montgomery, Alabama, to the Presidency of the Confederate States. Thrown into the Chattahoochee River to save it from Federal capture, it was later accidentally taken up on an anchor. It was recovered in New York, where it had been shipped to be sold as junk, and was returned to Columbus in 1884 by L. H. Chappell, then captain of the Columbus Guards.

9. CHURCH SQUARE, 2nd Ave. between 11th and 12th Sts., is an entire block occupied by the FIRST BAPTIST CHURCH and ST. LUKE METHODIST CHURCH. The plot was laid out and reserved as a church square when the town was founded. With smooth lawns and interlacing trees, it affords a pleasing contrast to the compact squares of the downtown section. The Methodist Church is of Romanesque style; the Baptist Church is a brick structure of Greek Revival design with massive Doric columns. The Methodist Church was organized in 1828 and the Baptist in 1829.

10. The LION HOUSE (*private*), 1316-3rd Ave., also known as the Ralston Cargill House, is of Greek Revival design, its porch columns copied from those of the Tower of the Winds near Athens, Greece. Several interior decorative features are also Grecian, but an Italian note is displayed in the two massive black Nubian lions guarding the front portals. The house, designed by Stephens Button, of Philadelphia, was built by Dr. Thomas Hoxey about 1840 but was not completed. Before 1864 it was bought by Augustus Marcelin Allen and his mother, who completed the interior according to the original drawings.

It is believed that there is a sub-basement from which an underground tunnel once led to a lake on the present site of the Racine Hotel. According to this story, a drove of mules was hidden in this secret chamber during the Union occupation in 1865. An appreciable hoard of gold coins was found in a window casing of the house in the 1870's.

11. The RUTHERFORD HOUSE (*private*), 321 14th St., a small structure of dark reddish clapboards, was the home of Lizzie Rutherford Ellis, who is credited with having originated the custom of annual decoration for the graves of Confederate soldiers. Here the Ladies' Memorial Association was organized in March, 1866, for this purpose. At this meeting, commemorated by a MARKER on the sidewalk before the house, April 26 was selected as Southern Memorial Day.

12. The PEABODY HOUSE (*private*), SW. corner 15th St. and 2nd Ave., former home of the philanthropist George Foster Peabody, was built in 1853 of red brick from the old First Presbyterian Church. This ivy-covered dwelling is a notable example of ante bellum architecture. Its green shutters, well-proportioned doorway, and trim portico with Doric columns make it one of the most attractive small houses in the city. On the eastern and northern sides of the house are posted signs reading Jackson Street and Bridge Street respectively, the original names of the streets before they were changed in 1885.

13. The MOTT HOUSE (*open 8-12 and 1-4:30 weekdays*), SE. corner Mott St. and Front Ave., a handsome structure of Georgian Colonial design, is used for general offices by the Muscogee Manufacturing Company. Both the house and the wall partly encircling it are of brick, and much wrought iron is used in gates, steps, and the small balcony above the stoop. The most striking interior feature is the winding stair copied from one in a Milanese palace. Since its erection in 1851, the house has changed hands only twice. During the War between the States it was for two nights the headquarters of General J. H. Wilson, the Union leader, and for this reason was not burned. Colonel R. L. Mott, who was owner at that time, was a fearless

Union supporter, who said of his house, "This is a residence that has never been out of the Union." Colonel Mott, however, contributed generously to relieve the suffering of the destitute Confederates.

14. The EAGLE AND PHOENIX MILLS (*not open to public*), Front Ave. between 13th and 14th Sts., is a large textile plant that is a landmark in Columbus history. The company was organized in 1851 as the Eagle Manufacturing Company; its building was burned by Union forces in 1865 and rebuilt by the firm, renamed the Eagle and Phoenix Manufacturing Company. In 1909 this mill began to use hydroelectric power for lighting. It was the first mill in the world to take this important step, which made practicable the employment of night shifts.

15. The FONTAINE HOUSE (*open by permission*), 1044 Front Ave., was built by John Fontaine, first mayor of Columbus, and is now used by the Elks Club. Of brick and frame construction and painted white, the old mansion is noted for its fine wrought iron, large columns, and fanlighted doorway set between small Ionic pilasters. The interior is equally elaborate, with frescoed ceilings, solid mahogany doors, and fireplaces of black Italian marble. The spiral staircase winding upward from the central hall is unusual in its combination of massiveness and grace.

The broad grounds surrounding the house once extended to the river, but when industries moved into this section the street was cut across the front lawn. A small courtyard in the rear is surrounded by a brick wall from which gates open on the street. In its early days the house was supplied with water from a large cistern lined with charcoal, which was sealed when recent additions were made.

16. The COLUMBUS IRON WORKS (*open weekdays during work hours*), SW. corner Front Ave. and Dillingham St., housed in a square, three-story structure of red brick, manufactures general agricultural implements. At the rear is the old steamboat landing where Chattahoochee River packets began to dock in 1828. What is believed to have been the first mechanical ice machine in the world was manufactured here in 1872. It was invented by Dr. John Gorrie of Apalachicola, Florida, in 1851, and has been placed in the Smithsonian Institution. In 1863 the Columbus Iron Works produced a breech-loading cannon, also believed to have been the first of its kind. This cannon, made from the wheel shaft of the sunken river steamer *John C. Calhoun,* now stands mounted in the iron works building.

17. ST. ELMO (*open daily; adm. 50¢*), 2810 St. Elmo Dr., was built 1831-32 by Seaborn Jones, prominent lawyer and congressman. It is a stately two-story Greek Revival house, constructed of handmade brick molded on the

premises by slaves. Its twelve Doric columns rise to a height of forty feet, lending grace and dignity to its massiveness. Blue-green shutters and the black iron grillwork of the swinging balcony afford a contrasting note to the mellow orange bricks of the lower terrace, and an adjacent smokehouse and circular fountain recall plantation days.

Originally called El Dorado, its name was changed to St. Elmo by James Jeremiah Slade, who acquired the property about 1875. Augusta Evans Wilson, born in Columbus, often visited this estate, and her popular romance *St. Elmo* (1860) contains descriptive references to it. Distinguished visitors have included President James K. Polk, President Millard Fillmore, Henry Clay, and William Makepeace Thackeray.

18. WYNNTON SCHOOL, Wynnton Rd. between Wildwood and Forest Aves., is a low building of white stuccoed brick constructed on the plan of one-story-and-court, known as the "Columbus Plan" of school architecture. The original Wynnton School, erected about 1840, is a small brick structure at the rear of the present building.

19. NEHI PLANT (*open weekdays during working hours*), 1000 9th Ave., a Columbus institution, produces bottled soft drinks. Nehi, dating from 1925, evolved from the Chero-Cola Company, which was established by Claude A. Hatcher in 1905. The plant covers almost a city block and has a floor area of six acres.

20. The BIBB MANUFACTURING COMPANY PLANT (*not open to public*), W. end of 35th St., manufactures print goods, shirting, knitting yarns, and tire cords and fabrics. In addition to the six-story main plant, covering thirty-five acres of floor space, other buildings are maintained for the storage of looms and equipment.

The surrounding mill village, laid out along a bluff above the Chattahoochee River, is an independent municipality with its own mayor, council, and police department. The grounds are carefully landscaped, and constant attention is given to shrubbery and greenhouses.

POINTS OF INTEREST IN ENVIRONS

Fort Benning, 9.5 m. (*see* TOUR *10A*).

Macon

Railroad Station: Terminal Station, 5th and Cherry Sts., for Georgia R.R., Central of Georgia Ry., Southern Ry., Georgia Southern R.R., and Macon, Dublin & Savannah R.R.

Bus Station: Greyhound Terminal, 320 Broadway, for Southeastern Greyhound, Bass, and Union Bus Lines, Southern Stages, Inc., and Georgia Central Coaches.

Airport: Herbert Smart Municipal Airport, 6.5 m. E. on State 87, for Eastern Airlines. Taxi to airport $1.

Taxis: Meter service, 10¢ first 1½ miles; 10¢ each additional half mile. Jitney service, 10¢ a passenger to any point within city limits; 15¢ a mile outside city limits.

Local Busses: Fare 5¢; transfers 1¢ additional.

Traffic Regulations: Right turns may be made on red light; no U turns on Cherry St. at traffic lights.

Accommodations: 18 hotels, including 2 for Negroes; numerous boarding houses, tourist homes, and camps.

Information Service: Chamber of Commerce, Municipal Auditorium, 1st and Cherry Sts.

Golf: Cherokee Golf Club (municipal), 6 m. W. on US 80, 9 holes, sand greens, 50¢. Idle Hour Country Club, 5.5 m. N. on US 341, 18 holes, $1.

Tennis: Baconsfield Park, North Ave. and Nottingham Dr.

Swimming: Lakeside Park, 4 m. S. on US 80; Recreation Park, 2 m. SE. on US 80; Y. W. C. A., 453 Cherry St., open to public at night.

Athletics: Municipal Stadium, Morgan Ave.

Riding: Rivoli Riding Club, 7 m. N. on US 41, $1 an hour.

Theaters and Motion Picture Houses: Municipal Auditorium, Cherry and 1st Sts.; Macon Little Theater, Ocmulgee St.; 7 motion picture theaters in downtown area, including 2 for Negroes.

Radio Station: WMAZ (1180 kc.).

Annual Events: Bibb Flower Show and Bibb County Camellia Show, spring; Georgia State Exposition, October.

For further information regarding the city see *Macon,* another book of the American Guide Series, published in 1939 by the J. W. Burke Company, Macon, and sponsored by the Macon Junior Chamber of Commerce.

MACON (334 alt., 53,829 pop.), on the fall line in the center of the state, is the natural clearance point for middle Georgia produce and manufactured products. The city is comfortable and unhurried, with a warm, natural beauty rather than a fashionable smartness. The characteristics of the small town and the industrial center are blended, and even in the crowded downtown district the broad parkways planted in roses, crape myrtles, and palmettoes give an appearance of space and leisure. The old brick stores and the more modern shops glittering with vitrolite and chromium are overshadowed by dignified municipal buildings with columns and massive porticoes.

The plan of the original city area was well conceived, with wide thorough-fares running northwest and southeast and cross streets intersecting at exact right angles, but the newer streets loop about in irregular patterns. The business district has spread to the banks of the muddy Ocmulgee River, which separates East Macon from the city proper, and has pushed the residential sections to the hills north and east of the town. One of these districts, Vineville, is particularly attractive with its juxtaposition of ante bellum and modern houses in an old-fashioned setting of tall trees, boxwood hedges, iron fences, and ivy-covered stone walls. The newer houses are in the suburbs of Stanislaus, Ingleside, and Shirley Hills, where the rolling landscape lends itself naturally to building sites.

Wesleyan College and Mercer University, Methodist and Baptist insti-tutions, have established Macon as an educational center. Wesleyan, the oldest chartered woman's college in the world to grant degrees, has been prominent in the cultural life of the city for three generations. Mercer's students and faculty are also an integral part of Macon.

Negroes, who constitute 44 per cent of Macon's population, live in settle-ments scattered throughout the city. Some have houses crowded into alley-ways behind the homes of white people; the more prosperous live in the subdivisions of Unionville and Pleasant Hill. The few Negro business dis-tricts appear with startling abruptness adjacent to the white sections. Many Negro citizens have taken advantage of the educational opportunities pro-vided by Beda Etta College, Ballard Normal School, Georgia Baptist Col-lege, and a progressive public school system. Two Negro hospitals are maintained. The most eminent Macon Negro is Professor W. S. Scar-borough, born a slave, who was president of Wilberforce University in Ohio and is the author of Greek textbooks adopted by Yale.

The development of the Macon area began when the Indians, by treaties of 1802, 1804, and 1805, ceded to the state all their lands between the Oconee and Ocmulgee rivers with the exception of 100 acres reserved for the estab-lishment of a military and trading post on the eastern bank of the Ocmul-gee. Fort Hawkins, constructed here in 1806 to protect the state against Indian insurrection, served as a meeting place for Federal agents with the

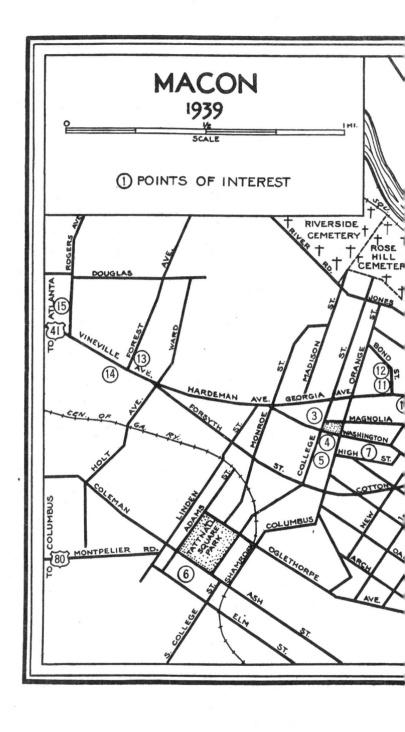

KEY

1. The Citizens and Southern National Bank. 2. The Municipal Auditorium. 3. Wesleyan Conservatory. 4. Washington Memorial Library. 5. The M.G. Ross House. 6. Mercer University. 7. The Home of Sidney Lanier. 8. The City Hall. 9. First Presbyterian Church. 10. The P.L. Hay House. 11. The Marshall Johnston House. 12. The Cowles-Bond-O'Neal House. 13. Vineville Methodist Church. 14. The Coleman-Speer-Birdsey House. 15. The Ralph Small House. 16. The Cowles-Walker House. 17. Christ Church. 18. Clinic Hospital. 19. The Site of Fort Hawkins. 20. Central City Park.

Creek. During the War of 1812 it was an assembling point for troops who were equipped and sent to the aid of General Andrew Jackson.

Settlers from North Carolina came to the reservation in 1818-19 and soon established business houses, a hotel, and a newspaper. When the remaining 100 acres and the land between the Ocmulgee and Flint rivers were ceded to the state in 1821, the village adopted the name Newtown. New immigrants complained that the earlier settlers had the choicest land. Accordingly, when Bibb County was established in 1822, the legislature appointed commissioners to lay out another town on the western bank of the Ocmulgee and name it for Nathaniel Macon, a highly esteemed statesman of North Carolina. The following year the new site was surveyed, lots were sold at auction, and many Newtown inhabitants moved across the river.

The Macon Hotel was built and the Macon Academy was established in 1824. In 1825 Simri Rose moved his newspaper, the *Georgia Messenger,* from Newtown to Macon, and a branch of the Bank of Darien was opened in the first brick building. When General La Fayette visited the town on March 30 he found seven hundred inhabitants. The Fort Hawkins property was sold in 1828, and the following year Newtown became a part of Macon, which thus had its population increased to almost two thousand.

Several factors contributed to the rapid growth of Macon. Its location in a rich agricultural section caused it to become a cotton market and trading center for sixteen counties. Its situation on the Ocmulgee permitted trade with the seaport Darien. At first, flat-bottomed boats, propelled by oars, transported cotton down the river, but these were soon superseded by steamboats. The *Pioneer,* the first built in Macon, was poled down the river to Darien, where machinery was installed, and on January 30, 1833, citizens were delighted to see the loaded ship come steaming up the river, towing two barges. Instead of remaining a river port, however, Macon soon became a railroad center. In 1838 the Monroe Railroad was completed from Macon to Forsyth, and five years later the first passenger train came from Savannah to Macon over the Central Railroad. In 1848 the Southwestern Railroad was chartered to bring trade from the fertile lands of southwest Georgia. All these are now controlled by the Central of Georgia Railway.

In 1836 the Georgia Methodist Conference voted to accept the city's offer of a five-acre site and substantial sums of money from its citizens for the establishment of the Georgia Female College, now Wesleyan. Ex-President Millard Fillmore was given a ball at the Hotel Lanier in 1854, and the following year Alexander H. Stephens and Stephen A. Douglas addressed large crowds from the balcony of the Union Depot. During this decade new stores and handsome residences were constructed, many of brick. In 1860 the Belgian Fair and Cotton Planters' Exposition drew crowds of

CO-CATHEDRAL OF CHRIST THE KING, ATLANTA

GREENWOOD, THOMASVILLE

SIDNEY LANIER HOUSE, MACON

STAIRWAY IN LAMAR SCHOOL OF LAW, EMORY UNIVERSITY

WETTER HOUSE, SAVANNAH

HANGING STAIRWAY IN LOWTHER HALL, CLINTON

"REHABILITATION"—FRIEZE ON STATE PENITENTIARY, REIDSVILLE

SPIRE OF INDEPENDENT PRESBYTERIAN CHURCH, SAVANNAH

OLD MEDICAL COLLEGE, AUGUSTA

visitors including representatives from Belgium. Inspired by the presence of foreigners, the planters determined to establish direct trade with Europe.

During the War between the States the Confederate Treasury Department established at Macon a depository in which $1,500,000 in gold were stored at one time. Fifteen million dollars of the first issue of Confederate notes-were brought to the depository in February, 1864. When the city was made a distribution center for supplies, quartermaster and commissary departments were established and the arsenal moved to Macon from Savannah. Saddles, harness, shot, cannon, and small weapons were manufactured. The city became crowded with refugees from the devastated towns of north Georgia and with sick and wounded soldiers from the Confederate army. The Ladies' Soldiers Relief Society cared for the wounded and made clothing and bandages.

On July 30, 1864, General George Stoneman marched against the city, which was garrisoned by the Georgia Reserves under General Howell Cobb. After destroying the railroads during a day of fighting in the suburbs, the Federal forces retreated toward Clinton, near which they were defeated the following day. Stoneman and five hundred soldiers were brought to Macon as prisoners. On November 20 the city was saved from capture a second time when General Judson Kilpatrick was repulsed. On April 20, 1865, General James H. Wilson advanced on Macon from Columbus. Within thirteen miles of the city his advance guard was met by Confederate officers bearing under a flag of truce a message from General Cobb announcing an armistice between General Johnston and General Sherman. Before the message could be delivered to Wilson, the advance guard hastened into the city and received its surrender over the protest of General Cobb, thus ending the march through Georgia known as Wilson's Raid.

On May 13 Jefferson Davis was brought to Macon after his capture at Irwinville and lodged in a second-floor room of the Lanier Hotel. A rope had been placed in his room and a coach waited in the alley below the window, but Davis would not agree to plans for his rescue and was later imprisoned in Fortress Monroe.

Macon struggled through the subsequent economic paralysis, rebuilt its railroads, resumed its cultural and industrial progress. In 1871 Mount de Sales Academy was established by the Roman Catholics and Mercer University was moved by the Baptists from Penfield. Three years later the public library was founded. Following the establishment of the Bibb Manufacturing Company in 1876, industrial activity expanded.

The new century was marked by the extension of the city limits, by the construction of public buildings, and by large expenditures on business and residential houses. During the first decade the population increased from 23,272 to 40,665. The river levee, begun in 1906, rendered the lowlands safe from floods and available to manufacturing plants. During the same year the Central of Georgia Railway purchased from the city a site on which it later erected shops costing $1,500,000. In 1908 the new post office building was opened.

During the World War period, Camps Harris and Wheeler were located in Macon. Camp Harris was designated as the state mobilization camp for the entire Georgia National Guard, which was sent to the Mexican border in 1916. Camp Wheeler was the mobilization camp for the famed Dixie Division (31st) of the U. S. Army.

Although the city suffered from the depression of the 1930's, its industries have become more diversified and its trade has consistently grown. The annual production of Macon's 165 manufacturing plants has been estimated at $25,000,000. Chief among the products are articles from the twelve textile mills, which use more than 70,000 bales of cotton yearly. The food and farm produce of the surrounding agricultural country have given rise to grain mills and canneries, and the more recent interest in livestock raising, to slaughter houses and tanneries. Twelve lumber companies, three furniture factories, and a crate and basket plant utilize the rich supply of pine timber. A sawmill equipment shop makes boilers and saws that are sold throughout the United States. Other plants use the clay and kaolin deposits in the manufacture of brick, tile, sewer pipe, pottery, and paint.

POINTS OF INTEREST

1. The CITIZENS AND SOUTHERN NATIONAL BANK, NE. corner Cherry and 3rd Sts., of hand-made red brick trimmed with Georgia marble and terra cotta, was completed in 1933. The Georgian detail shows the influence of Sir Christopher Wren's Hampton Court Palace. On the northern wall of the main banking room five murals by Athos Menaboni, an Atlanta artist, depict the original Wesleyan building, old Fort Hawkins, the meeting of James Oglethorpe and Tomochichi, the sailing of the steamship *Savannah,* and the original building of Mercer University.

2. The MUNICIPAL AUDITORIUM, SW. corner Cherry and 1st Sts., with a seating capacity of 4,000, was completed in 1925. It was designed in the neo-Classic style by Egerton Swartwout, of New York, and constructed of Indiana limestone at a cost of $500,000. Broad terraces lead to the arched doorways of the main floor, and the gallery level is adorned with massive Doric columns. The copper-covered dome is 156 feet, 6 inches in diameter. The murals above the proscenium, depicting historical incidents relating to the state as well as to Macon, are the work of Don Carlos du Bois and Wilbur G. Kurtz, of Atlanta.

The ART ROOM (*open 9:30-4 Mon.-Fri.; 8:30-12 Sat.*), in the basement of the auditorium, contains many of the Indian artifacts excavated at the Ocmulgee National Monument (*see* TOUR 9B).

3. WESLEYAN CONSERVATORY, College St. between Georgia and Washington Aves., is the school of music and fine arts of Wesleyan College (*see* TOUR *12*), which was moved from this site to suburban Rivoli in 1928. The original building in which the college opened on January 7, 1839, was remodeled into the present structure about 1881, when George I. Seney, New York philanthropist, made a gift of $125,000 to the institution. The structure is ornamented with gables, towers, and wide porches in the Victorian manner; in pleasing contrast is the simple Greek Revival chapel built in 1860.

4. WASHINGTON MEMORIAL LIBRARY (*open 12-9 weekdays*), SE. corner College St. and Washington Ave., was endowed and presented to the city in 1919 by Mrs. Ellen Washington Bellamy in honor of her brother, Hugh Vernon Washington. The glazed terra cotta building, designed in simple neo-Classic style, contains more than 18,000 volumes, and files of Macon's first newspapers. In the northern wall is a niche containing a white marble bust of Sidney Lanier. The statue and niche were designed by Gutzon Borglum, and the background murals, illustrating Lanier's poems, were painted by Athos Menaboni. On display are a manuscript and first edition of Lanier's poems, a flute that once belonged to the poet, and an invitation to the wedding of Lanier and Mary Day. In the Washington home, which originally stood on this site, William Makepeace Thackeray was entertained when he came to Macon in 1856.

5. The M. G. ROSS HOUSE (*private*), 534 College St., a white frame structure with green shutters, was built about 1913 and designed by Neel Reid, Atlanta architect. It is notable for the chaste simplicity of its Georgian Colonial design and for its handsome doorway, embellished with four fluted Ionic columns and pilasters. Among the antiques within the house are a small Pembroke table, at which it is believed La Fayette drank tea, and a highboy awarded first honor at the World's Columbian Exposition in Chicago.

6. MERCER UNIVERSITY, Ash St. between S. College St. and Linden Ave., housed in 16 red brick buildings of modified Georgian design, is situated on a 63-acre landscaped campus. The institution was originally opened at Penfield (*see* TOUR *17*) on January 14, 1833, as Mercer Institute, a manual labor school with 39 students. In 1837 the school was chartered as Mercer University and included three educational units: the academy, the college, and the theological seminary. Mercer was moved to Macon in 1871, after the city had contributed $125,000 and several acres of land for a campus. The law school, established in 1873, was admitted to membership in the Association of American Law Schools in 1922. The university, with an

enrollment of about 550 and a faculty of 35, is under the control of the Southern Baptist Association.

7. The HOME OF SIDNEY LANIER (*private*), 213 High St., is a gray, story-and-a-half, white-shuttered dwelling marked by a marble tablet set in an ivy-covered terrace. Sidney Lanier (1842-81), Georgia's best-known poet (*see* LITERATURE), was born in Macon. His musical talent, developed at an early age under his mother's tutelage, soon enabled him to play almost every musical instrument. At school he spent much time writing poetry, and he was an inveterate reader, especially of Scott, Bulwer, and Froissart, whose influence later showed in his tendency to use archaic phrases.

At the head of his class Lanier was graduated from Oglethorpe College in 1860, and the following year he accepted a position as tutor there. His hopes for further study in Germany were shattered by the outbreak of the War between the States. Serving with the Macon Volunteers in Virginia, he was captured on a blockade runner and imprisoned at Point Lookout, Maryland, where he cheered his fellow prisoners with the flute that he always carried with him. After the war he returned to Macon, ill from lung trouble contracted in prison, and for a short time practiced law in his father's office. In 1873 he moved to Baltimore, where he played in the Peabody Orchestra and lectured on English literature at Johns Hopkins University. Failing health forced him to retire in 1881 to the North Carolina mountains, and there he completed two of his best known poems, "The Marshes of Glynn" and "Sunrise."

8. The CITY HALL, Poplar St. at intersection with Cotton Ave. and 1st St., built in 1836 as the Monroe Railroad Bank and remodeled in 1933-35, combines the Classical Revival style of the original structure with the utilitarian design of modern architecture. The severely modern side entrances are in pleasing contrast with the columns of the principal facade. On both sides of the main entrance are black vitrolite panels inscribed with the history of the Macon vicinity. This building was the state capitol from November 18, 1864, until March 11, 1865, the date of the last session of the General Assembly of Georgia under the Confederate States of America.

On the third floor is a MUSEUM (*open only for special exhibitions*) containing prehistoric and historic relics and an art collection. The room is used for the meetings of the Macon Historical Society and the Macon Art Association.

9. FIRST PRESBYTERIAN CHURCH, SE. corner Mulberry and 1st Sts., was dedicated in 1858 to house a congregation organized in 1826. Negroes worshiped with the white congregation until 1886, when they withdrew to form their own church. The brick building, of early Christian basilican

type, is covered with cement scored to simulate stone blocks. Above the tall, arched doorway with its carved double doors is a central tower, 183 feet in height.

10. The P. L. HAY HOUSE (*private*), SW. corner Georgia Ave. and Spring St., built about 1855, is a 24-room brick structure on a knoll surrounded by lawns and trees. Almost all the materials were imported from Italy. It is of modified Italian Renaissance design; the interior, with its frescoed ceilings and crystal chandeliers, is finished in solid mahogany and rosewood. During the War between the States the dwelling was used as Confederate headquarters and was a target for the bullets of the besieging Union army.

11. The MARSHALL JOHNSTON HOUSE (*private*), NW. corner Georgia Ave. and Bond St., built in 1883, is of red brick with a number of turrets, gables, and bay windows. The house, surrounded by broad lawns planted with shrubbery and encircled by an iron fence, is impressive because of its situation on a high hill overlooking the older part of the city. Jefferson Davis visited this house during a Confederate reunion in 1887, and from the veranda reviewed the assembled veterans.

12. The COWLES-BOND-O'NEAL HOUSE (*private*), 138 Bond St., built about 1836, is a two-story structure of pale brown stucco with green shutters and a small, circular iron balcony. The architecture shows a blending of Greek and Roman motifs, typical of the Classical Revival style, in the eighteen Doric columns which adorn the front and side of the portico. The entrance door, of heavily carved black walnut, is framed by a fanlight and deeply recessed sidelights.

13. VINEVILLE METHODIST CHURCH, NE. corner Vineville and Forest Aves., erected in 1926, is an unusually well-proportioned limestone structure of Greek Revival design. Six Doric columns on the entrance portico support an entablature and a simple pediment.

14. The COLEMAN-SPEER-BIRDSEY HOUSE (*private*), 304 Vineville Ave., built in 1840, is a notable example of Greek Revival architecture. This two-story frame house, with its "H" plan, is similar to Stratford Hall in Virginia. Four fluted Doric columns adorn the portico, which is set between projecting wings.

15. The RALPH SMALL HOUSE, 115 Rogers Ave., built in 1846, is also an outstanding example of Greek Revival architecture. This green-shuttered, white frame house has a spacious veranda with a small balcony above .the

entrance door. Six Doric columns are topped with an entablature bearing a frieze of laurel wreaths. The first floor is used as an art and gift shop.

16. The COWLES-WALKER HOUSE (*private*), 519 Walnut St., of Greek Revival design, is one story in height, with white stucco-covered brick walls. It was built in 1830. The small entrance portico is adorned with four Ionic columns, and a doorway is framed by sidelights and a fanlight. It is now the property of the Scottish Rite Masons.

17. CHRIST CHURCH, 520 Walnut St., the oldest church in the Atlanta Episcopal Diocese, was organized in 1826, and the cornerstone of the present building was laid in 1851. Of pale, grayish stucco, with a square central tower, pointed arches, and small buttresses, this simple church of Gothic Revival architecture is built in the shape of a cross. Its bell was given to the Confederate government to be melted and made into ammunition.

18. CLINIC HOSPITAL, NE. corner Walnut and 2nd Sts., was designed by Dr. Ambrose Baber as a residence and built in the decade following 1830. The entire structure was put together with hand-made pins. In 1841 the house was bought by Colonel John Basil Lamar, a signer of Georgia's Secession Ordinance, and at his death was inherited by his sister, Mrs. Howell Cobb. In 1920 the building was enlarged and remodeled for use as a hospital, but the fine proportions of the original lines were retained. The construction is of brick and frame covered with stucco, patterned in blocks. A small stoop, a fanlighted doorway, and cast iron railings are distinguishing features of its Classical Revival design.

19. The SITE OF FORT HAWKINS, SW. corner Maynard and Woolfolk Sts., is marked by a blockhouse constructed in 1938 by the Nathaniel Macon Chapter of the D. A. R. Plans have been made to reproduce the frontier fort erected in 1806 and named for Benjamin Hawkins, Federal Indian agent. A stockade enclosing 14 acres was made of hewn posts 14 inches thick and 14 feet high, sunk 4 feet into the ground; every other post had a round hole for muskets. Inside the area two log blockhouses, 28 feet square, consisted of two stories on a stone basement, the upper floors projecting over the lower. Smaller log houses were used as living quarters and trading rooms.

20. CENTRAL CITY PARK, E. end of Walnut St., was first developed in the decade following 1870. During the Spanish-American War it was the site of Camp Price, where the Third Immunes under Colonel Ray encamped for three months. The soldiers called themselves Immunes because they believed that living in the South had given them a natural immunity to

malaria, prevalent in Cuba. Horse and automobile races were held for many years on the mile and the half-mile tracks in the park, and many circuses have pitched their tents within the enclosure of the mile track. The park includes the quarters of the Georgia State Exposition, which is held each October for one week, and the Luther Williams Baseball Park, the home of the Macon Peaches. Most of the buildings are used as the WINTER QUARTERS OF DOWNIE BROTHERS CIRCUS (*open 10-4 daily in winter*).

POINTS OF INTEREST IN ENVIRONS

Lamar Mounds and Village Site, **6.8 m.** (*see* TOUR *9A*). Ocmulgee National Monument, **1.1 m.** (*see* TOUR *9B*). Georgia Academy for the Blind, **2.3 m.**; Wesleyan College for Women, **6.9 m.**; Porterfield, **7.7 m.** (*see* TOUR *12*). Georgia Baptist College, **5.5 m.** (*see* TOUR *16*).

Savannah

Railroad Stations: 301 W. Broad St. for Central of Georgia Ry.; Union Station, 419 W. Broad St., for Atlantic Coast Line R.R., Seaboard Air Line Ry., and Southern Ry.; Cohen and W. Boundary Sts. for Savannah & Atlanta Ry.

Steamship Lines: Ocean Steamship Co., ticket office, 301 W. Broad St.; main office and piers, Central of Georgia Docks, for coastwise passenger service to New York and Boston. Merchants & Miners Transportation Co., main office, foot of Fahm St., for coastwise passenger service to Boston, Baltimore, Miami, and intermediate points. Augusta & Savannah Line, foot of Whitaker St., for passenger service to Augusta. Beaufort & Savannah Line, foot of Abercorn St., for passenger service to Beaufort, S. C. Freight lines: Ships leave Savannah for foreign ports with accommodations for a few passengers.

Airport: Hunter Field Municipal Airport, 5 m. SW. of city on Emmet Wilson Blvd., for Atlantic & Gulf Coast Air Line, Inc., Eastern Air Lines, and Strachan Skyways, Inc.; taxi fare, $1.

Bus Stations: 417 Berrien St. for Glennville & Savannah Bus Line; 111 Bull St. for Greyhound Lines and Savannah Beach Bus Line; 336 Drayton St. for Pan-American Bus Lines; 109 W. Broad St. for Southeastern Stages.

Taxis: 10¢ upward, according to number of passengers and distance.

Streetcars and Local Busses: Fare, 8¢.

Traffic Regulations: Right turns permitted on red light after full stop; left turns on green light only. Parking spaces marked by yellow lines.

Accommodations: Eight hotels; tourist homes throughout city, most numerous in vicinity of Whitaker and 37th Sts. Rates slightly higher during winter and early spring.

Street Order and Numbering: Streets are numbered east and west from Bull St., a north-to-south thoroughfare dividing the city. Even numbers are on the north or river side of the street, odd numbers on the south.

Information Service: Chamber of Commerce, 34 E. Bay St.; AAA, Hotel DeSoto; Travelers' Aid, Union Station, 419 W. Broad St. .

Theaters and Motion Picture Houses: Municipal Auditorium, Hull and Barnard Sts., for local productions and occasional road shows; nine motion picture theaters, including two for Negroes.

Radio Station: WTOC (1260 kc.).

Golf: Municipal Golf Club, Isle of Hope Rd., two 18-hole courses, greens fee 50¢, caddy fee 50¢; Savannah Golf Club, Moore Ave., 3 m. SE. of city, 18 holes (cards for non-members may be obtained at leading hotels for $1.50; only caddy fees charged for additional rounds); Donald Ross Golf Course, Wilmington Island, adjacent to General Oglethorpe Hotel, 18 holes, greens fee 50¢, caddy fee 50¢.

Swimming: Large artificial lake, Daffin Park, 1 m. SE. of city on Victory Dr.; Savannah Beach, 17 m. SE. of city on US 80; outdoor pool, Hotel DeSoto, SE. corner Bull and Liberty Sts.; indoor pools, Y.M.C.A., 308 Bull St., Y.W.C.A., 105 W. Oglethorpe Ave.

Polo: Savannah Polo Field, Waters Ave. Ext.

Tennis: Municipal courts in Daffin Park, 1 m. SE. of city on Victory Dr., and Forsyth Park, Bull and Gaston Sts.

Riding: Jack Reinstein's Riding Academy, E. Victory Dr.; Ranch Riding School, Bee Rd.

Annual Events: Emancipation Day parade and celebration (Negro), Jan. 1; St. Patrick's Day celebration, March 17; huckster contest, Forsyth Park, April (no fixed date); Chatham Artillery anniversary, May 1; beauty contest, Savannah Beach, May 15 or 30; Maritime Day, May 22; Interstate Sailboat Regatta, Wilmington Island, second Thursday, Friday, and Saturday in July.

For further information regarding the city see *Savannah,* another book of the American Guide Series, published in 1937 by the Review Printing Co., Savannah, and sponsored by the Savannah Chamber of Commerce.

SAVANNAH (45 alt., 85,024 pop.), built on a walled bluff overlooking the Savannah River sixteen miles from the Atlantic Ocean, is the birthplace of the Georgia colony and the oldest and second largest municipality in the state. It is a precisely planned city, showing the traditions of Georgian England in its compact brick houses, grilled gateways, and glimpses of half-concealed gardens.

Savannah is encircled by pine woods and set amid dark, moss-curtained live oaks. Because of the near-by Atlantic Ocean, the city is a stranger to snow and ice, and summer heat is tempered by cool breezes. The faint tang of salt winds, the hint of sulphur in the clear artesian water, and the odor from fish and oyster packing plants alternate with the heavy sweetness of gardenias and magnolias to make a changing but recurrent atmosphere. Luxuriant tropical plants—palmettos, oleanders, and vivid azaleas—are planted in the broad parks at the street intersections.

The city is a large seaport and one of the world's largest markets for naval stores distribution, and most of its commercial activity centers about the harbor that extends for eight miles along the Savannah River. Here wharves are crowded with thousands of bales of cotton, hogsheads of tobacco, and barrels of rosin. The shipping of these commodities often presents a scene of crowded and tumultuous life—chugging tugboats bobbing in oily red water, their shrill whistles alternating with the throaty sound of foghorns, and Negro stevedores singing as they load a waiting barge or steamship.

The plan of Savannah was based on a sketch in *Villas of the Ancients* by Robert Castell, who died in one of the English debtor prisons that Georgia was founded to relieve. From this sketch James Edward Oglethorpe,

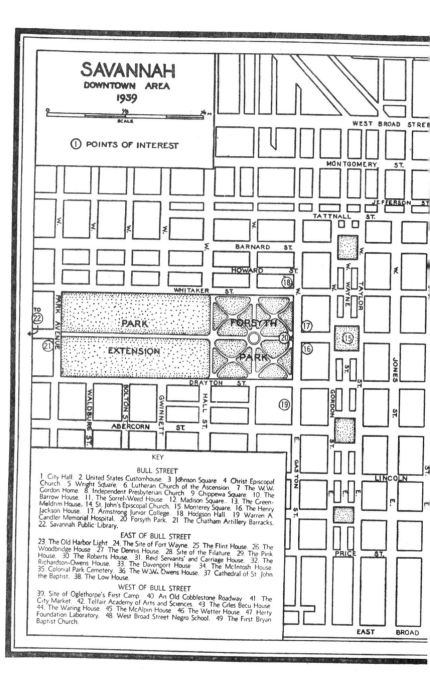

SAVANNAH
DOWNTOWN AREA
1939

SCALE

① POINTS OF INTEREST

WEST BROAD STREET

MONTGOMERY ST.

JEFFERSON ST.

TATTNALL ST.

BARNARD ST.

HOWARD ST.

⑱

WHITAKER ST.

TO
⑳

PARK

FORSYTH

⑰

⑮

EXTENSION

PARK

⑯

DRAYTON ST.

⑲

ABERCORN ST.

WAYNE

TAYLOR

JONES ST.

GORDON ST.

WALDBURG ST.
BOLTON ST.
GWINNETT ST.
HALL ST.

GASTON ST.

LINCOLN

PRICE ST.

EAST BROAD

KEY

BULL STREET
1. City Hall. 2. United States Customhouse. 3 Johnson Square 4 Christ Episcopal Church. 5 Wright Square. 6. Lutheran Church of the Ascension. 7 The W.W. Gordon Home. 8. Independent Presbyterian Church 9 Chippewa Square. 10. The Barrow House. 11. The Sorrel-Weed House 12. Madison Square. 13. The Green-Meldrim House. 14. St. John's Episcopal Church. 15 Monterey Square. 16. The Henry Jackson House. 17. Armstrong Junior College. 18 Hodgson Hall. 19 Warren A. Candler Memorial Hospital. 20 Forsyth Park. 21 The Chatham Artillery Barracks. 22. Savannah Public Library.

EAST OF BULL STREET
23. The Old Harbor Light. 24. The Site of Fort Wayne. 25 The Flint House. 26. The Woodbridge House. 27 The Dennis House. 28. Site of the Filature. 29. The Pink House. 30 The Roberts House. 31. Reid Servants' and Carriage House. 32. The Richardson-Owens House. 33. The Davenport House. 34. The McIntosh House. 35. Colonial Park Cemetery. 36. The W.W. Owens House. 37 Cathedral of St John the Baptist. 38. The Low House.

WEST OF BULL STREET
39. Site of Oglethorpe's First Camp. 40 An Old Cobblestone Roadway. 41 The City Market. 42. Telfair Academy of Arts and Sciences. 43 The Giles Becu House. 44. The Waring House. 45 The McAlpin House 46 The Wetter House. 47 Herty Foundation Laboratory. 48. West Broad Street Negro School. 49 The First Bryan Baptist Church.

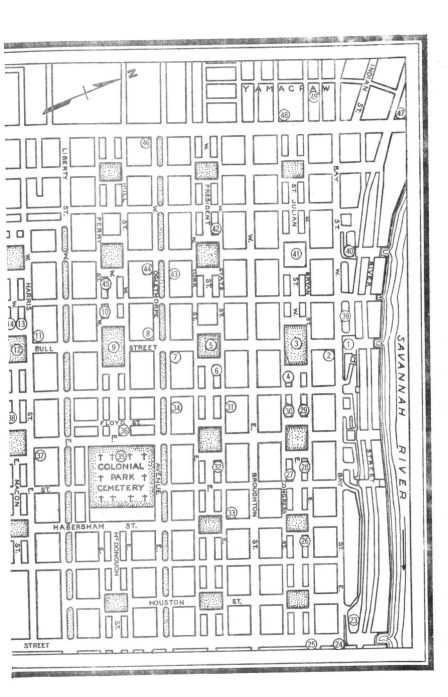

founder of the city, and Colonel William Bull, the leading engineer of Carolina, designed the Colonial city on a plan to which later builders have adhered. For all their contrasting details there is a certain uniformity in the older Georgian Colonial, Classical Revival, Greek Revival, and Victorian houses, which are built on a level with the sidewalk and often are joined in rows. Usually they have three or four stories, including a raised basement, and stairs ascending to a high stoop. Some were constructed of crude brick brought from Europe as ballast in early sailing vessels; others show in their soft colors that they were built of the celebrated Savannah Grey brick from the old kiln of the Hermitage (*see* TOUR *1*).

The most common characteristics are small entrance stoops, recessed fan-lighted doorways, delicate iron railings, and tall windows with ornate iron guards covering the lower third of their frames. Frequently an elaborately grilled balcony shows the hand of the French Royalists who fled to Savannah from the Santo Domingo rebellions of the mid-nineteenth century, and occasionally jigsaw woodwork shows the architectural influence of the latter part of the nineteenth century. High ceilings, intricately carved moldings, handsome marble mantels, and arched hallways characterize the interiors. In ante bellum times, offices, dining rooms, and service rooms were in the raised basement, while the second floor was used for drawing rooms and libraries and the upper floor for bedrooms. In the downtown areas these old houses are built close to one another, as in London, England. To the rear or side of a house there is sometimes a garden enclosed by a fence constructed of brick laid in an openwork pattern. The newer houses of the residential suburbs, though often designed in the same architectural tradition, have a different aspect because of their broad lawns and luxuriant shrubbery.

Savannah's social life is as dignified as its buildings, and in no other Georgia city is there a more widespread interest in the arts. Appreciation of painting is fostered by the art school and the frequent exhibitions at the Telfair Academy of Arts and Sciences. Leading musicians perform in a winter concert series. The literature, which began with John Wesley's *Collection of Psalms and Hymns,* now blends its traditional romanticism with twentieth-century realism. The Poetry Society of Georgia was founded here in 1923. Even more characteristic of Savannah are the earlier prose writings, which have brought forth such chroniclers as Hugh McCall and Charles Colcock Jones (*see* LITERATURE) and have aroused a lively popular interest in historical research.

Education, initiated by Benjamin Ingham's mission school and by George Whitefield's Bethesda Orphanage, has expanded to include a junior college, several private and parochial schools, and an extensive public school system. At first the colonists, who welcomed all Protestant denominations, excluded Roman Catholics because of the enmity existing between the Georgia colony and the Spanish in Florida. The city has since become the strongest center of Catholicism in Georgia, although Protestant church membership is larger.

Almost half of Savannah's population is composed of Negroes, who for the most part live along narrow streets in crowded sections. Nurses with white children, little shoeshine boys, peddlers with pushcarts, farmers with oxcarts—all are part of the Negro scene. Others drive little musical ice-cream carts, bakers' wagons with shrill bells, and trains of yellow garbage trailers that wind through this motley traffic like Chinese dragons. Throughout the city sound the loud cries of hucksters, unintelligible to the visitor not accustomed to the dialect of the 'Geechee Negro. All day these hucksters shamble through the streets with great flat baskets of fish, vegetables, and flowers balanced on their heads.

Though not a center for higher Negro education, Savannah has a number of Negro teachers, lawyers, and doctors. A branch library, seven supervised playgrounds, and a recreation center benefit children and adults. There are two modern, well-equipped hospitals: Charity Hospital, first opened as the McKane Hospital in 1893, and the Georgia Infirmary, which was opened in 1832 as the first hospital for Negroes in the United States. In the growing Negro business section are modern shops, a bank, and two newspapers. Many Negroes belong to the established denominations, while others attend churches bearing such names as First Born of the Living God, and Triumph the Church of God in Christ. Bishop Grace's House of Prayer and Father Divine's Peace Mission also are popular.

Beneath the clatter of modern industry there is always a soft but insistent undertone of the past. The city's early history is identical with that of the colony (see HISTORY), for after landing the first settlers on February 12, 1733, Oglethorpe began to lay out the town on a square tract of 15,360 acres to accommodate 240 families. He named the town Savannah, which is believed to be derived from the Sawana or Shawnee Indians who once inhabited the river valley; but, because the Spanish word *sabana* means flat country, some historians declare that this term was applied to the entire coastal plain by Spanish explorers who preceded the English settlers by almost two centuries. Protestant groups from other European countries and wealthy men paying their own way helped to give the colony a cosmopolitan population. After the cultivation of silk, wine, and medicinal herbs had failed, the colonists produced more practicable commodities and developed a lively trade with England. In 1744 the first commercial house was established, and soon afterward regular export shipments of rice, hides, and lumber were sent to England. In 1749, the year slavery was introduced, eight small bags of cotton were shipped from this town.

Savannah became the seat of government when Georgia was made a

Royal Province in 1754, and two decades of commercial growth and improved trading conditions followed. At the beginning of the Revolution the town had many unyielding Loyalists, but the hot-headed younger men set up a liberty pole before Tondee's Tavern, shouted approval of the Lexington victory, and organized a battalion headed by Colonel Lachlan McIntosh. When two British war vessels and a transport anchored off Tybee Island in January, 1776, the Royal Governor, Sir James Wright (1714-86), escaped on one of them to Halifax.

The signing of the Declaration of Independence was celebrated riotously, and in the following year Savannah became the capital of the new state. On December 27, 1778, Colonel Sir Archibald Campbell landed 2,000 British troops a few miles down the river to besiege the town, which was defended by General Robert Howe with 600 men. Failing to guard a passage through the surrounding marshes, Howe, on December 29, lost the town and more than half of his men; for this he was later court-martialed and forever divested of military prestige. Following the British occupation Governor Wright returned.

In September, 1779, a long siege was begun by Count d'Estaing's French fleet assisted by American forces under General Benjamin Lincoln, but their grand assault of October 9 was a disastrous failure, with more than 1,000 casualties. It was not until 1782, when General "Mad Anthony" Wayne's American forces struck, that the British at last evacuated the city.

After the Revolution there was another period of expansion. On October 9, 1783, the first recorded theatrical performance was given as a charity benefit at the Filature (silk manufacturing center) by a "Set of Gentlemen" under the direction of Godwin and Kidd, of Charleston, South Carolina. The program consisted of the tragedy *The Fair Penitent* and the farce *Miss in Her Teens.* The city's first playhouse was built two years later. Savannah was incorporated as a city in 1789, and after Eli Whitney's invention of the gin four years later it sprang into eminence as a cotton center. Tobacco, shipped down the river from Augusta, made Savannah a market for this commodity. The growth of surrounding plantations and the disposal of Indian lands were other factors in its expansion. In these years came provisions for water supply and fire protection, the establishment of a cotton exchange, and the incorporation of the Georgia Medical Society.

For defense during the War of 1812, Fort Wayne was strengthened, and Fort Jackson was built two miles down the river; the Chatham Artillery, the Savannah Volunteer Guards, the Republican Blues, and the Georgia Hussars were organized for duty. In May, 1814, the U. S. sloop *Peacock* captured the British warship *Epervier,* brought it into the harbor, and confiscated $10,000 in specie aboard the British ship.

The half century following the War of 1812 was an era of rapid development in transportation. In 1816 the steamboat *Enterprise* carried a Savannah party upstream to Augusta; three years later maritime history was made when on May 22, 1819, the *City of Savannah,* first steamship to cross the Atlantic, sailed for Liverpool. To lower transportation costs between the Savannah and Ogeechee rivers the Ogeechee Canal was opened in 1828. In 1843 the Central of Georgia Railway was completed from Savannah to Macon. During this period Savannah, because of its harbor, was the greatest port on the southern seaboard for cotton and naval stores.

The Mexican War of 1846 brought prominence to two Savannah men. Colonel Henry R. Jackson (1820-98), later minister to Austria and to Mexico, served as commander of Georgia's regiment, and Josiah Tattnall (1796-1871) distinguished himself at Vera Cruz in command of the Mosquito Division of the nation's fleet.

The Savannah Theater, which had opened in 1818 with *The Soldier's Daughter,* housed many famous actors and road companies during the mid-nineteenth century. Joseph Jefferson, known for his portrayal of Rip Van Winkle, served as stage manager.

During this period Savannah developed a sectionalism that made it respond instantly to the war cry in December, 1860. Now there were no Whigs and Tories to divide the city. Upon adoption of the Ordinance of Secession Savannah men seized Fort Jackson, and in March, 1861, the Confederate flag floated over the customhouse. On April 10, 1862, the 400 defenders of Fort Pulaski, occupied before secession by order of the fiery Governor Joseph E. Brown, were forced to surrender to Union soldiers. Although Fort Pulaski then became a Federal military prison, Savannah itself did not fall until 1864, when General Sherman marched through Georgia to the coast. On December 13 Sherman took Fort McAllister and on the 17th demanded the surrender of Savannah; but General W. J. Hardee and his 10,000 troops continued to skirmish three days longer before they evacuated the city by means of a new pontoon bridge to Hutchinson Island. On December 21, 1864, Union troops occupied Savannah.

With the abolition of slavery and the collapse of great plantations, the port ceased to function. But for all the poverty of Reconstruction and an appalling yellow fever epidemic in 1876 there was progress, as was shown by the increased crops, improved bank credits, and greater railroad facilities of 1879. Wealthy newcomers invested their money; cotton and tobacco prices reached their ante bellum height, and the surrounding pine forests created flourishing lumber and naval stores enterprises. With the establishment of the Naval Stores Exchange in 1882, Savannah became the leading turpentine and rosin port.

Not until the twentieth century had brought a slight decline in the production of cotton and naval stores did the city turn to manufacturing. Savannah now has more than two hundred varied industries, including a large cottonseed oil plant, a sugar refinery, a paper factory, twelve fertilizer works, nineteen lumber mills, a cigar factory, and a seafood cannery.

Savannah's prosperity, however, has always been measured by the activity of its port. During the World War, boom prices caused shipyards to be hastily built along the waterfront, but a cataclysmic fall in business followed the boll weevil's destruction of cotton in 1921. By 1926 control of the cotton pest had caused the port to regain much of its former activity. In 1938 exports, including naval stores, cotton, tobacco, corn, sugar, lumber, and other products, were valued at $19,959,909. The chief imports were fertilizer materials and petroleum products.

With all its commercial and cultural successes, Savannah gains its individual charm from its atmosphere of the past. A large and leisurely dinner at 2 P.M., sailing parties and turtle egg hunts for visitors, business conferences over iced drinks—these customs give an unhurried and genial character to this old-fashioned southern city.

POINTS OF INTEREST
(BULL STREET)

Along BULL STREET, which forms the central axis of the city, are five squares that in the original city plan were designed as centers of defense against Spanish and Indian invasion. Now two centuries old, these small parks embody Savannah's characteristic, bountiful semitropical growth subdued to a precise and formal beauty. Italian cypresses, tall cabbage palmettos, blossoming bays, and English yews are among the decorative trees that supplement a natural growth of oaks. Flower beds are bright with flame azaleas, fragrant white gardenias, and variegated pink and white camellias. Paths through the grassy plots are lined with benches, and monuments to illustrious men stand in many of the parks.

1. CITY HALL, N. end of Bull St., a massive gray-stone edifice with a green stained-glass dome, is designed in the neo-Classic style typical of civic architecture since the early part of the twentieth century; it was built in 1905 to replace a building erected in 1799. The present structure, built on two levels, is three stories high on Bull Street, but in the rear it falls away two stories lower to reach the Savannah River wharf. From Bull Street wide steps lead down to a ferry.

A tablet on the façade commemorates the sailing of the *City of Savannah,* the first steamship to cross the Atlantic. The successful use of steam in coastwise vessels inspired William Scarborough and several Savannah merchants to organize the Savannah Steamship Company which was formed on December 19, 1818. The *Savannah,* equipped with adjustable paddle wheels, was constructed at Corlear's Hook, New York, and reached Savannah on March 28, 1819. President James Monroe made a trip to Tybee aboard this vessel.

On May 22, 1819, the *Savannah* sailed for Liverpool, made a voyage to St. Petersburg, Russia, and returned home. So expensive was this expedition that its sponsors declared the vessel impracticable for commercial purposes, and it was converted into a sailing packet that plied the coast of the United States until it was lost off Long Island in 1822. In the National Museum at Washington are the log book and a cylinder of this ship, in honor of which President Franklin D. Roosevelt in 1935 proclaimed May 22 as National Maritime Day. A model of the *City of Savannah* is displayed in the Council Chamber (*open upon application to council clerk*) on the second floor of the City Hall.

Another tablet is dedicated to the *John Randolph,* the first ironclad vessel in American waters. The vessel, a commercial ship constructed of plates ordered from England, was launched in 1834, to the consternation of citizens who did not believe iron would float.

2. UNITED STATES CUSTOMHOUSE, SE. corner Bull and E. Bay Sts., a large structure of granite blocks, was designed by John S. Norris and erected in 1850 on the site of the colony's first public building. The six monolithic granite columns of the stately portico are capped with carved tobacco leaves instead of the usual acanthus. On this site in 1736 John Wesley preached his first sermon in Savannah; the event is commemorated by a tablet on the corner of the Bull Street side. The tablet on the corner of the Bay Street facade marks the site of a small frame house that Oglethorpe used for headquarters.

3. JOHNSON SQUARE, Bull St. between Bryan and Congress Sts., one of the original parks, was a center of early community life, with public buildings, stores, and a bake oven. It was named for Robert Johnson, governor of Carolina and friend of Oglethorpe. The NATHANAEL GREENE MONUMENT, in the center of the park, is erected over the grave of the famous Revolutionary general (*see* TOUR *14*). The monument, designed by William Strickland, is a tall white marble shaft on a granite base, shaft and base forming a Roman sword. The cornerstone was laid by La Fayette in 1825. A SUNDIAL commemorates the bicentennial of Georgia and honors Colonel William C. Bull, who assisted Oglethorpe in designing Savannah. Presented to the city by the Sons of Colonial Wars on February 12, 1933, it replaces the first public sundial, from which the early settlers read the time of day.

4. CHRIST EPISCOPAL CHURCH, Bull St. between E. St. Julian and E. Congress Sts., home of the first congregation organized in the colony (1733), is a

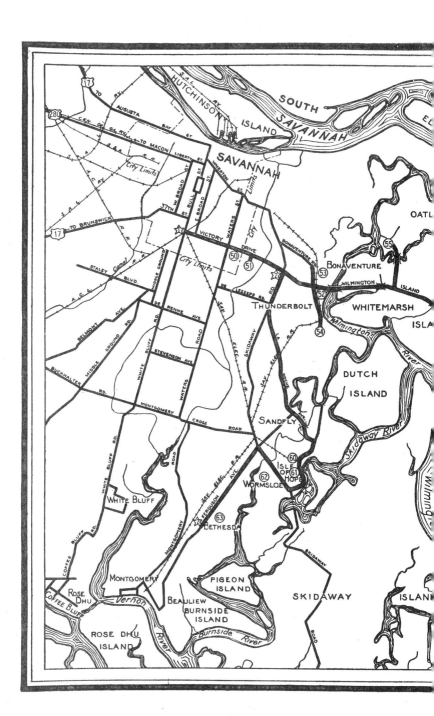

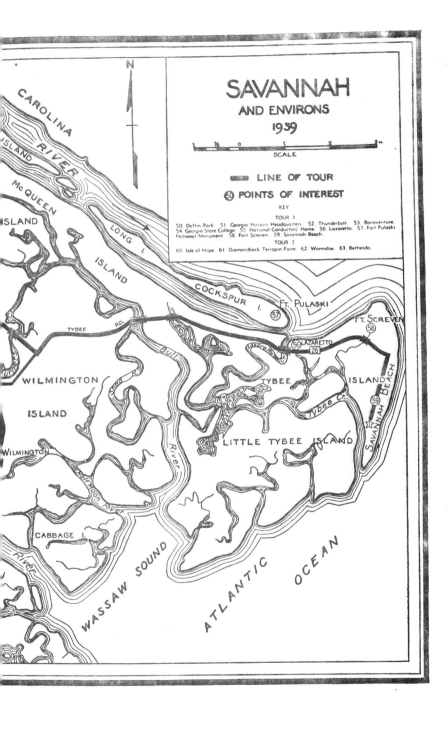

SAVANNAH
AND ENVIRONS
1939

SCALE

LINE OF TOUR

POINTS OF INTEREST

KEY

TOUR 1

50. Daffin Park. 51. Georgia Hussars Headquarters. 52. Thunderbolt. 53. Bonaventure. 54. Georgia State College. 55. National Conductors' Home. 56. Lazaretto. 57. Fort Pulaski National Monument. 58. Fort Screven. 59. Savannah Beach.

TOUR 2

60. Isle of Hope. 61. Diamondback Terrapin Farm. 62. Wormsloe. 63. Bethesda.

Greek Revival building with stucco-covered brick walls half hidden by vines. A double flight of steps leads to a large Ionic portico and above the three classic portals are panels embellished with festoons. Around three sides of the interior is a graceful balcony supported by small columns. Built in 1838 according to a plan furnished by James Hamilton Couper, it was the third edifice erected on this site. After a partial destruction by fire in 1897 it was restored the same year.

Among the early ministers was John Wesley, who came in 1736 as a Church of England missionary and established what is believed to be the first organized Protestant Sunday school in the world. His arbitrary attitude made him unpopular with both colonists and Indians, and he was indicted on ten counts for his interference in the secular affairs of the colony. He returned to England in 1737, an embittered man. The minister who followed Wesley was George Whitefield, whose benevolent disposition and many charities made him popular.

BROUGHTON STREET, which intersects Bull Street one block south of Congress Street, is Savannah's principal shopping district.

5. WRIGHT SQUARE, Bull St. between State and York Sts., another of the original squares, was laid out in 1733 as Upper Square. Later its name was changed to honor Sir James Wright, last Governor of the Royal Province of Georgia, who fled when the Revolutionary War stirred Savannah and returned later when the British captured the city. In the center of the square is the GORDON MEMORIAL, a large granite and marble monument designed by W. F. Pietch, of New York. Four pink marble columns, rising from a massive granite base, are grouped about a tall bronze urn. Above the columns are four cherubs that support a granite globe. The memorial was erected to honor William W. Gordon, an influential citizen who was the first president of the Central Railroad & Banking Company of Georgia. He lost his life while engaged in the construction of the Central of Georgia Railway.

The TOMOCHICHI MARKER, in the southeast corner of the square, honors the venerable, kindly Yamacraw chief who befriended the first settlers. On May 21, 1733, with the half-breed Mary Musgrove serving as interpreter, Tomochichi signed the formal treaty permitting Oglethorpe to settle his colonists. In April, 1734, with his wife, his nephew, and several tribesmen, he accompanied Oglethorpe to England, where he was received by King George II at Kensington and by the Archbishop of Canterbury at Lambeth palace. Excited throngs gathered to see the Indians during their four months' visit, and they enlisted valuable English Patronage for the colony. Portraits of Tomochichi show him as a man of grave, commanding presence.

6. LUTHERAN CHURCH OF THE ASCENSION, Bull St. between E. State and E. President Sts., is of mixed ecclesiastical architecture in which Gothic

predominates. Erected in 1843, the church occupies the site of a frame structure built in 1756.

The Lutheran Church in Savannah was established by refugees who fled from Salzburg, Bavaria, to Georgia because of the new colony's tolerance for persecuted protestants. Most of these Salzburgers soon went to Ebenezer, but a small number remained in Savannah and formed the Lutheran congregation in 1744.

7. The w. w. GORDON HOME (*private*), 10 Bull St., a stuccoed brick dwelling with a small Ionic portico, is an admirable example of Classical Revival architecture. Although a third story and side porch have been added, they have not marred the fine proportions of the facade and entrance portico. The interior shows numerous excellent details in the African black-marble mantels, mahogany doors, and handsome cornices. The building, originally owned by Judge J. M. Wayne, was sold before its completion in 1829 to his nephew-in-law, William W. Gordon. The house has opened its doors to such celebrities as Alexander H. Stephens, Admirals Dewey and Schley, and Presidents McKinley and Taft.

8. INDEPENDENT PRESBYTERIAN CHURCH, SW. corner Bull St. and W. Oglethorpe Ave., is a finely proportioned white granite building of late Georgian Colonial design, distinguished by its arched windows, well-designed portico, and a steeple in the Christopher Wren style. The granite Doric columns of the portico support an elaborate wooden entablature and a pediment with a shell-like design reminiscent of the Adam style. Above the portico a graceful clock tower rises from a square base through three classically adorned octagonal tiers to a tall spire. The interior is notable for the classic ornamentation of the segmental, vaulted ceiling and for the unusually high pulpit which stands before a beautiful Georgian window. In the rear the Ralph Adams Cram addition replaces the manse where in 1885 Ellen Axson, granddaughter of the pastor, became the first wife of Woodrow Wilson. The present building, constructed in 1889-90, is a copy of a former one erected 1815-19, and destroyed by fire in 1889.

The congregation was formed in 1755, about two decades after Presbyterianism was introduced into the colony by the Scottish Highlanders who were imported to defend Savannah against Spanish Florida. A branch of the Scottish Presbyterian church, it has always remained independent of the American organization.

9. CHIPPEWA SQUARE, Bull St. between Hull and Perry Sts., was laid out in 1813 and named for the Battle of Chippewa, an American victory over the British in the War of 1812. The OGLETHORPE MONUMENT, in the center of the park, is a massive bronze statue of the man whose philanthropy and

shrewdness caused Georgia to be founded. The monument, designed by Daniel Chester French with a base designed by Henry Bacon, was erected in 1910 by the state.

10. The BARROW HOUSE (*private*), SW. corner Bull and W. McDonough Sts., erected between 1835 and 1840, is an excellent example of neo-Classic architecture. Although a third story has been added and the balcony heightened, the structure retains its distinctive proportions. Handsome marble mantels and crystal chandeliers accentuate the formal beauty of the interior.

11. The SORREL-WEED HOUSE, NW. corner Bull and W. Harris Sts., now an antique shop, is a stuccoed brick structure built in 1840 for G. M. Sorrel, later a Confederate general. The building is of Classical Revival design with decorative detail resembling that of a Mediterranean villa. Strikingly designed iron grillwork ornaments the Doric portico, the balcony, and the garden fence. The living rooms are magnificent with their mahogany sliding doors, dark marble mantels, and ornate plaster medallions on the ceilings. According to the plan of old town houses the flagstone kitchen is in the basement.

12. MADISON SQUARE, Bull St. between Harris and Charlton Sts., was laid out in 1839 and named for President James Madison. The JASPER MONU-MENT, in the center of the square, honors the Revolutionary hero, Sergeant William Jasper, who won distinction by his gallantry at Fort Moultrie and was mortally wounded in the Siege of Savannah in 1779. Two OLD CANNON, at the south end, mark the junction of two early roads, one from Augusta and the other from Darien (now the Ogeechee Road).

13. The GREEN-MELDRIM HOUSE (*private*), NW. corner Bull and W. Macon Sts., is a massive stuccoed brick dwelling with Gothic Revival oriel windows, intricate ironwork, and crenelated roof. On three sides are piazzas with flagstone floors. The house, which with its garden and servants' quarters occupies an entire block, was built in 1856 by Charles Green, a British subject, grandfather of the popular novelists Anne and Julian Green. During the Federal occupation of 1864, General Sherman made his head-quarters here.

14. ST. JOHN'S EPISCOPAL CHURCH, SW. corner Bull and W. Macon Sts., a stuccoed brick edifice of Gothic Revival design, was built in 1852. In the tall wooden steeple are chimes which were saved from destruction during Federal occupation of the city by a special plea to President Lincoln.

15. MONTEREY SQUARE, Bull St. between Taylor and Gordon Sts., was laid out in 1848. Its name honors the American capture of Monterey in 1846, during the Mexican War. The PULASKI MONUMENT, centering the square, was erected in 1855 in honor of Count Casimir Pulaski, the Polish noble-man who so fervently aided the American cause during the Revolution and who met his death during the Siege of Savannah in 1779. One account states that he died near the city, another that he died aboard an American vessel. The monument was designed by Robert E. Launitz.

The houses surrounding the square, though without historic importance, are interesting for their characteristic nineteenth century architecture.

16. The HENRY JACKSON HOUSE (*private*), NE. corner Bull and E. Gaston Sts., is the home of the Oglethorpe Club. Built about 1840, with massive brownstone steps ascending to the high main floor, the house is an example of Classical Revival architecture. The large dining rooms in the basement were originally kitchens. This house once belonged to General Henry R. Jackson, charge d'affaires to Austria from 1853 to 1858, minister to Mexico during 1885-86, and author of the locally celebrated poem "The Red Old Hills of Georgia."

17. ARMSTRONG JUNIOR COLLEGE, 447 Bull St., organized in 1935, is a munici-pally supported institution with an enrollment of almost four hundred students. The MAIN BUILDING, of Italian Renaissance design, was formerly the home of George F. Armstrong and was presented to the college by his widow. A notable feature of this building is the ironwork of the en-circling fence and the decoration above the columned entrance. The AUDITORIUM, facing the Whitaker St. entrance, of white brick adorned with ironwork, was built by the city. The LANE BUILDING, adjacent to the auditorium, houses the school of finance and commerce. The structure, showing the Venetian influence in the tracery of its arched windows and its interior decoration, was formerly the George F. Cann residence and was presented to the college by Mills B. Lane.

18. HODGSON HALL (*open 2-9 weekdays*), SW. corner W. Gaston and Whitaker Sts., a stately, ivy-covered brick structure built in 1873, houses the Georgia Historical Society, to which it was given in 1876 by Margaret Telfair Hodgson in memory of her husband, William B. Hodgson. En-closed in a glass case in the main corridor is a drum used in the battles at Saratoga and Cowpens. On the walls are portraits of men and women famed in Georgia history. The hall contains a valuable collection of Georgiana, including manuscripts, maps, newspaper files, and clippings. The Georgia Historical Society, organized in 1839, has a vigorous member-ship and has published many early records and letters. From 1902 until

the completion of the public library in 1916, Hodgson Hall provided Savannah with its only free library. In 1923 a branch of the public library was established in Hodgson Hall.

Adjoining the building is an old garden planted in evergreen shrubs and fragrant with lilac-colored wisteria trailing over trellises.

19. WARREN A. CANDLER MEMORIAL HOSPITAL, W. Gaston St. between Drayton and Abercorn Sts. and extending to Huntingdon St., is the outgrowth of a hospital for seamen founded in 1819, a time when, because of growing commerce in the flourishing harbor, sailors of many nations thronged Savannah's streets. In 1835 the institution was incorporated as the Savannah Poor House and Hospital, but it is now owned by the Methodist Church and operated as a general hospital. A tall iron fence surrounds the wooded grounds, through which a center drive leads to the main building, erected in 1877 on the foundations of an earlier structure. On these grounds stands a magnificent oak, one of the finest trees in the city.

20. FORSYTH PARK, Gaston St. between Whitaker and Drayton Sts. extending to Park Ave., is a twenty-acre tract named for Governor John Forsyth. The park was laid out in 1851 according to the design of a Bavarian landscape gardener, William Bischoff. French influence shows in the garden plan and in the large white fountain in the center. In spring the park is gay with wisteria, dogwood, and azaleas, and the shrubs rustle with the scampering of squirrels and the fluttering of pigeons. Summer brings the powerful fragrance of many white magnolia blooms.

The park extends beyond its original limits through the Savannah Militia parade ground equipped with practice fields, tennis courts, and playground facilities for children. On the central walkway of this section, known as the Park Extension, are two monuments, one honoring the dead of the War between the States, the other the veterans of the Spanish-American War. The CONFEDERATE MONUMENT is a lofty sandstone pyramid surmounted by the bronze figure of a Confederate soldier. The original design for the memorial was the work of Robert Reid, of Montreal, but later much ornamentation was removed and a marble figure representing judgment was replaced by that of the soldier, designed by David Richardson. Within the iron-railed enclosure are memorial busts of the Confederate General Lafayette McLaws and Brigadier General Francis S. Barton. The SPANISH-AMERICAN MEMORIAL is a large bronze figure of a soldier overlooking the long avenue south of the park.

21. The CHATHAM ARTILLERY BARRACKS, SE. corner Bull St. and E. Park Ave., houses one of the oldest artillery organizations in continuous active

service. It is a long, low, cream brick building with double doors through which the parade ground is visible. Old records show that the company was organized May 1, 1786, by veterans of the American Revolution and that it was engaged actively in the Indian campaign the following October. It also served in the War of 1812. On the paved walk in front of the building are two brass six-pound cannon, presented to the artillery by George Washington soon after his visit to Savannah in 1791.

22. SAVANNAH PUBLIC LIBRARY (*open 9 A.M.-9:30 P.M. weekdays*), 2002 Bull St., is a massive, two-story granite structure with heavy columns flanking the entrance. Housing 56,500 volumes, it contains comfortable reading rooms, a reference room, and a children's room brightened with a mural portraying Robin Hood before his king and queen.

The institution is the outgrowth of the Savannah Library Society, organized in 1809 to replace a circulating library eleven years older. After the Georgia Historical Society was founded in 1839, the two associations occupied the same quarters, and in 1847 they were united in organization. In 1902 the joint society offered its facilities to Savannah as a public library if the city would provide for maintenance; consequently, Hodgson Hall served as the public library until 1916, when the Savannah Public Library was constructed with funds from the Carnegie Foundation. This library is one of the few Carnegie-aided institutions that does not bear the donor's name.

(EAST OF BULL STREET)

FACTORS ROW, E. Bay St. between Bull and Abercorn Sts., was named for the cotton factors who made the nineteenth century a period of flourishing trade for Savannah. To be "on the Bay" was assurance of business prestige. The old red brick buildings, straggling along the bluff, are only two stories high on the Bay Street front but are four stories in the rear where their foundations reach the wharf level. Here iron balconies overhang the river front, and iron bridges cross the cobblestones of the ramps leading to River Street. The retaining walls along the bluff are made from stones brought from England as ballast in early sailing vessels. With its steep heights, its weathered bricks, and broken ironwork dark against the water, this section suggests the atmosphere of Old World seaports.

23. The OLD HARBOR LIGHT, NW. corner E. Bay and E. Broad Sts., is a small cast-iron beacon erected in 1852 to guide ships into the harbor. It has not been used for many years.

24. The SITE OF FORT WAYNE, NE. corner E. Bay and E. Broad Sts., is now occupied by the municipal gas plant. Though built in 1762, the fort was

not of great military importance until the Revolutionary period, when it was named for the fiery patriot General "Mad Anthony" Wayne. The British strengthened it in 1779 after the city had fallen into their hands, and the Americans rebuilt it for defense during the War of 1812. Encircling a high bluff and overlooking what was once a marshy plain are the massive buttressed brick walls, built during the second alteration; they still appear redoubtable with their old black cannon, relics of the fort, pointing seaward.

The fort was built on the original site of the Trustees' Gardens, which covered ten acres. In these gardens mulberry trees were planted and experiments conducted with various exotic plants in the days when it was hoped that the Georgia colony could produce silk, wine, and drugs. In 1735 eight pounds of silk was sent to England and woven into a dress for Queen Caroline. But the silk industry did not prosper for long, and soon more practicable products replaced the mulberry trees.

25. The FLINT HOUSE (*private*), 26 E. Broad St., holds many legends of pirates and buried treasure. Here, according to tradition, died John Flint, the infamous blue-faced pirate of *Treasure Island,* hoarsely shouting, "Darby, bring aft the rum."

Like other old houses of Savannah, this one stands crowded on its lot and close to the street. A stoop extends from the sidewalk into the ramshackle structure that is now occupied by Negroes.

26. The WOODBRIDGE HOUSE (*private*), NE. corner E. St. Julian and Habersham Sts., a small, two-story frame house, is a good example of late Georgian Colonial cottage architecture. It was built about 1800, but the brick addition to the rear is of later origin. The servants' house, with its attractive roof line, dormer windows, and high brick chimney, is often sketched by artists.

27. The DENNIS HOUSE (*private*), SW. corner E. St. Julian and Lincoln Sts., formerly was owned by I. K. Tefft, a founder of the Savannah Historical Society, who was also known for his autograph collection. The Georgian Colonial house, erected in 1800, is notable for its stoops and dormer windows.

28. SITE OF THE FILATURE (Headquarters of the Silk Industry), E. St. Julian St. between Lincoln and Abercorn Sts., is now Cassell's Row, a cluster of small brick houses with high stoops and handsome iron banisters. The barnlike filature, where apprentices were instructed in silk weaving, was erected in 1751, but two decades later the industry failed and the building was converted into an assembly and dance hall.

In this hall, October 9, 1783, a group of amateurs, headed by two professional actors from Charleston, presented Savannah's first dramatic performances, *The Fair Penitent* and *Miss in Her Teens,* which were so well received that the producers remained for the season. Two years later they built the city's first playhouse, probably on Franklin Square.

29. The PINK HOUSE, 23 Abercorn St., is so named because of the pinkish stucco that covers its old brick walls. Of Georgian Colonial design, with a low-stooped, columned portico and a fine Palladian window over the entrance, it was built in 1771 for James Habersham, Jr. In 1812 additions were made, and the building became the Planters' Bank, the first state bank in Georgia. In 1865 it was used as headquarters by General York, a leader of the invading Federal forces. It is now a tearoom.

30. The ROBERTS HOUSE (*private*), 27 Abercorn St., a slate-roof brick structure built in 1840, is notable for its wrought-iron stair rail and fanlighted entrance. During General Sherman's occupation of Savannah, Federal soldiers commandeered the two lower stories while the family retired to the third floor. An octagonal room in the rear, with a marble mantel and finely carved molding, was formerly the drawing room.

31. REID SERVANTS' AND CARRIAGE HOUSE, between 112 and 114 E. State St., is visible through an open gateway. The building, partly one-story and partly two, is faced with red sandstone and has a slate roof. This typical outhouse of the early part of the nineteenth century was built about 1830 by John H. Reid, who intended to erect in front a mansion of Adam style. Because of the loss of a year's rice crop, he contented himself with a simple frame house. The carriage house is often used as a subject by local and visiting artists.

32. The RICHARDSON-OWENS HOUSE (*private*), SE. corner E. State and Abercorn Sts., was begun by an unknown architect in 1816 and finished three years later by William Jay, the celebrated young English architect. A stuccoed brick dwelling with corner quoins, arched second-story windows, and paneled parapet above the main cornice, it is praised by architects as Savannah's finest example of Classical Revival design. Notable exterior details are a beautiful wrought-iron balcony and a graceful columned entrance portico of Ionic order reached by a winding double stairway. The yard is enclosed by a balustrade with classic urns on the corner posts. Grecian details are used throughout the interior.

William Jay, at the age of twenty-three, came to Savannah in 1817 to visit his sister, Mrs. Robert Bolton, and as his first commission he built this house for Bolton's sister, Mrs. Richard Richardson. In 1825, the same year that Jay left Savannah, La Fayette was entertained in this house. Although Jay's Savannah sojourn lasted only eight years, the graceful beauty of his work strongly influenced Savannah architecture until the War between the States.

33. The DAVENPORT HOUSE (*private*), 324 E. State St., one of Savannah's best examples of late Georgian Colonial architecture, was built soon after Isaiah Davenport, son of the noted English potter, acquired the lot in 1812. Its curving, double-entrance stairs with wrought-iron banisters and its dormer windows suggest the houses of eighteenth century London. The beautiful fanlighted doorway has been pictured in national publications.

34. The MCINTOSH HOUSE (*private*), 110 E. Oglethorpe Ave., built about 1764, is generally conceded to be the oldest brick house in the state. As Eppinger's Inn it was a popular rendezvous for Colonial statesmen, but Revolutionary patriots soon closed it because of the proprietor's Tory sympathies. On August 1, 1782, after the British had evacuated the city, the Georgia Legislature held its first meeting in the Long Room on the second floor. This room, in which many important public meetings were held, was divided into a number of small rooms when the interior was remodeled. A third story and some decorative ironwork, added in the nineteenth century, have somewhat altered the Georgian Colonial simplicity of the dwelling, which stands inconspicuously amid modern commercial structures.

Later the house was occupied by Lachlan McIntosh, the Revolutionary colonel who won popularity leading Savannah's forces and lost it when he fatally wounded Button Gwinnett, one of Georgia's signers of the Declaration of Independence, in a duel that resulted from political rivalry. In 1791, during the debt-ridden McIntosh's precarious occupancy, George Washington visited in this house.

35. COLONIAL PARK CEMETERY, E. Oglethorpe Ave. at Abercorn St., laid out in 1753, was for many years the colony's only public burial ground. In its early days it was encircled by a high brick wall. No interment has been made since 1861, and the cemetery became defaced when General Sherman's soldiers used it for stabling horses. In 1896 the ground was landscaped as a municipal park. Among the distinguished men buried here are Hugh McCall (1767-1824), Georgia's first historian, and Edward Greene Malbone (1777-1807), who in his short career painted more than three hundred miniatures.

36. The W. W. OWENS HOUSE (*private*), NW. corner Abercorn and E. McDonough Sts., is one of the older houses showing the French influence

brought to Savannah in the mid-nineteenth century by French Royalists fleeing the Santo Domingo massacres. Decorative features of the old brick house are the iron balconies and the ironwork set in the lower portion of the window frames.

37. CATHEDRAL OF ST. JOHN THE BAPTIST, NE. corner Abercorn and E. Harris Sts., is one of the largest Roman Catholic cathedrals in the Southeast. The building, which shows Gothic influence, is a handsome white stucco structure with two tall spires. A feature is the iron bell of single swing and knocker. The present structure, completed in 1876, was partly destroyed by fire in 1898 and rebuilt two years later around the original walls.

38. The LOW HOUSE (*private*), 329 Abercorn St., a Classical Revival brownstone structure with an iron grillwork balustrade guarding the lower windows, was built about 1847 for Andrew Low, a cotton merchant. It is now headquarters for the Georgia Society of Colonial Dames. The front garden, retaining its original hourglass pattern, is enclosed by an iron picket fence. William Makepeace Thackeray visited this home in 1853 and again in 1856, when he came to Savannah to give his readings. A letter that he wrote at the drawing room desk speaks of the tranquillity of the city at that time and its broad, shady streets. General Robert E. Lee visited here in 1870 while he was touring the South for his health. In the drawing room on March 12, 1912, Mrs. Juliette Gordon Low (1860-1927), daughter-in-law of Andrew Low, organized a small group of Girl Guides, later called Girl Scouts. Other troops were formed, and Mrs. Low opened national headquarters in Washington the following year. On her birthday, October 31, she is honored throughout the nation as the founder of the Girl Scouts of America.

(WEST OF BULL STREET)

39. SITE OF OGLETHORPE'S FIRST CAMP, on Yamacraw Bluff, in the small park on the north side of W. Bay St., is marked by a marble bench placed by the Colonial Dames. The spot has been designated by the D. A. R. as the most outstanding historic site in Georgia.

40. An old COBBLESTONE ROADWAY, W. Bay and Barnard Sts., descends to the level of the broad river where century-old buildings with stone masonry and iron railings stand clear and commanding against the bluff.

41. The CITY MARKET (*open 9-1 Mon.-Fri.; 9-10:30 Sat.*), Barnard St. at W. Bryan St., is housed in a white-painted brick structure built in 1870, which occupies the one-and-a-half-acre site of the original market erected in 1763. In the early days Savannah housewives patronized a horsecar that

was driven into the market where purchases could be made from the car windows.

Much of the old competitive spirit is still shown by the shiny-faced Negro hucksters and white-clad clerks who jostle one another in an effort to present their wares. In addition to the cuts of meat, colorful piles of vegetables, and masses of gay flowers, there is the silver gleam of fresh fish among the mounds of food. A constant stream of trucks from other towns brings produce, which is stored in the great storage compartments on the lower floor. The market is under the supervision of the city, from which the merchants rent their stalls.

42. TELFAIR ACADEMY OF ARTS AND SCIENCES (*open 12 M.-5 Mon.; 10-5 Tues.-Sat.; 3-5 Sun. and Thanksgiving Day*), 121 Barnard St., is one of the finest art galleries in the South. The stuccoed brick building, believed to have been designed by William Jay about 1820, is a good example of the Classical Revival period; its belt cornice, high attic parapet, heavy Corinthian portico, and pedestaled figures suggest an eighteenth-century Italian villa. The small formal garden surrounding the academy is enclosed by an iron picket fence. The building, which stands on the site of the Royal Government House, was bequeathed in 1875 by Mary Telfair, sister of the original owner, to the Georgia Historical Society, which opened the academy in 1885. Since 1920 this gallery has been conducted by the Telfair Academy of Arts and Sciences Corporation.

Art classes and loan exhibitions make this academy important in the cultural life of Savannah. Much of the furniture was used by the Telfairs during their occupancy, and the dim interior with drawn curtains gives the atmosphere usually maintained in houses of the old aristocracy. Paintings, sculpture, furniture, and old costumes are only a few of the many objects exhibited. The colonial kitchens in the basement are as interesting to antiquarians as the broad, bronze-railed main stairway is to architects. No painting or museum piece is accepted without the approval of experts.

43. The GILES BECU HOUSE (*private*), 120 W. Oglethorpe Ave., is an unpretentious two-story frame structure built before 1800 by Giles Becu, the French ancestor of the present owners. Here in 1802 Mrs. Montmollin, a tenant, entertained her uncle Aaron Burr, then Vice President of the United States.

44. The WARING HOUSE (*private*), 127 W. Oglethorpe Ave., constructed of brick in 1816, is notable for its Georgian Colonial doorway, iron balcony, and fine Palladian window.

45. The MCALPIN HOUSE (*private*), 230 Barnard St., was designed and built by Henry McAlpin about 1835. Of elaborate Greek Revival design,

it is impressive because of its massive Corinthian columns and the curved sandstone steps at each end. It was constructed of Savannah Grey brick from the Hermitage kilns but has since been covered with stucco. The former owner, Aaron Champion, a wealthy banker, hid his gold hoard here in a cistern when General Sherman's forces took the city in 1864. Later he drained the cistern and recovered all his money but one ten-dollar gold piece.

46. The WETTER HOUSE (*open*), 423 W. Oglethorpe Ave., built by Daniel Remshart in 1821, was acquired by Anthony Barclay three years later. In 1839 the house was bought by Mrs. Margaret Telfair and was a part of her estate until 1890. Captain Augustus Wetter, who married into the Telfair family, lived in the house and undoubtedly was responsible for many of the later decorative details. It has housed the Savannah Female Orphanage since 1875.

One of the most elaborate residences of its day, this three-story house of stuccoed brick is notable for its decorative cast-ironwork on the encircling high stone wall, the entrance gateway, the windows, and the balustrades enclosing the first- and second-story porches on three sides. These balustrades are divided into panels, each ornamented with a medallion representing the head of a statesman, author, or poet. Equally striking details on the interior are the carved mantels of white carrara or black marble and the high windows that meet the intricately fashioned plaster molding of the ceiling.

47. HERTY FOUNDATION LABORATORY, 510 W. River St., in a low, galvanized-iron warehouse on the banks of the Savannah River, was established in 1932 as a pilot plant to demonstrate the feasibility of making paper pulp from Georgia pine. The plant was directed by Charles H. Herty (1867-1938), native Georgian and nationally known chemist, who in the face of general skepticism secured the cooperation of the Industrial Commission of Savannah, Inc., the Chemical Foundation of New York, and the State of Georgia, and carried on his experiments. Since Herty's death, this laboratory has been conducted by the Herty Foundation under the auspices of the state.

Experts have pronounced the pulp and newsprint produced from southern pine the equal of any, and successful experiments have been executed in making finer papers from gum and tupelo trees. In 1933 Herty sent pulp to the rayon mill at Rome, Georgia, where it was made into fine rayon cloth rated as high in quality as that derived from Canadian spruce. As a result of Herty's experiments, two paper mills have been established in Georgia, and others have been founded in Florida, North Carolina, South Carolina, Virginia, Louisiana, and Texas.

(YAMACRAW)

YAMACRAW, along the west side of W. Broad St., occupied almost entirely by Negroes, stands on the site of an Indian village of the same name, where Oglethorpe parleyed with the Indians. In this concentrated area live approximately three thousand Negroes, among whom are old men and women who once were slaves. Root doctors and "cunjur" folk ply their trade for a small fee, and at small shops can be purchased such remedies as Vang-Vang Oil, Lucky Mojoe Drops of Love, or Mojoe Incense to bring love and luck to the buyer and confusion to his enemies. Most of the houses are dilapidated, unpainted, and crowded.

48. WEST BROAD STREET NEGRO SCHOOL, 111 W. Broad St., the first Negro public school in Savannah, was established in 1878 by the board of education and replaced Beach Institute, founded eleven years earlier by the American Missionary Association. The building, a three-story stuccoed brick house of Classical Revival style, is another of the dwellings attributed to William Jay. Distinctive details are the Doric portico, the ironwork, the rear facade cresting, the graceful hall columns, and a white Adam mantel. The house was built about 1818 for William Scarborough, a wealthy merchant and one of the owners of the S. S. *Savannah*.

49. The FIRST BRYAN BAPTIST CHURCH (Negro), 565 W. Bryan St., dates from 1785, when Andrew Bryan, a slave who had been baptized by the noted Negro pastor George Leile, began preaching to a group of Negroes in the barn of his master's plantation, Brampton (*see* TOUR 1). He soon had a following in Savannah where Reverend Abraham Marshall, a white missionary, baptized forty-five additional members in 1788. Organizing them into the First African Baptist Church, he ordained Andrew Bryan as their first pastor. Despite many hardships, during which the Negroes resumed worship at Brampton for two years, the congregation was able to purchase the lot on which this church stands for a permanent house of worship in 1797. Outgrowing this building, the congregation moved to Franklin Square in 1832, but dissension arose during that year. Most of the members returned to the old site under the leadership of their pastor, Andrew Marshall, calling themselves the Third African Baptist Church and later the First Bryan Baptist Church. The original frame structure has been replaced by a brick building.

POINTS OF INTEREST IN ENVIRONS

(Numbers in parentheses correspond with the numbers on the Savannah and vicinity map.)

TOUR 1

*Savannah — Thunderbolt — Lazaretto — Fort Screven — Savannah Beach;
State 26, 18.5 m.*

Roadbed paved.

In the environs of Savannah attractive residential suburbs are grouped about the curve of a river or on a tree-crowned bluff. The newer houses of these suburbs are trim and smart on their well-kept lawns planted in shrubbery, and many have their own docks and boathouses in the rear. The intricate waterways and salt-water rivers afford good fishing and swimming.

Many Negroes who have found that their daily necessities may be procured with less effort along the rivers have formed permanent, self-sustaining communities near the white settlements. In these hamlets the people retain many of their early customs; the graveyards of the small churches are decorated with kitchen utensils and fragments of brightly colored glass.

State 26 leaves Bull St. at Victory Dr. **0 m.** and runs E. on this broad beautiful twin thoroughfare with a central parkway planted in scarlet azaleas and with tall palmettos dark against the sky.

(50) DAFFIN PARK, **1 m.** (R), is Savannah's largest municipal park. Among its facilities are a swimming pool, tennis courts, a stadium, and an emergency landing field.

At **1.5 m.** is a junction with Bee Rd.

Right on this road to (51) GEORGIA HUSSARS HEADQUARTERS (*private*), **0.1 m.**, a large, yellow brick building housing a unit of the 108th Georgia Cavalry. This unit is the second oldest military organization in the United States. On February 13, 1936, the Georgia Hussars celebrated their 200th anniversary, claiming that their organization is an outgrowth of the Oglethorpe Rangers, founded by General Oglethorpe on February 13, 1736, to protect Savannah against raids by Spaniards and Indians. Although it is not known when this cavalry troop became the Georgia Hussars, records indicate that the name was used as early as 1796.

At **2 m.** on State 26 is the junction with Skidaway Rd. (*see* ENVIRONS TOUR 2).

(52) THUNDERBOLT, **3.2 m.**, incorporated as Wassaw, was originally a small Indian settlement whose name was derived from the tradition that a bolt of lightning struck the ground here and started a spring. Thunderbolt

is a swimming resort and fishing village with several plants for canning shrimp, oysters, and crabs. Small yachts and launches bob up and down beside the larger shrimp boats anchored in the harbor with drying nets hung from their masts.

During the shrimping season trawlers, loaded with a day's catch, circle the wide river bend, motors chugging and nets glistening, the fishermen shouting and singing as they form a line at the pier to unload at the SHRIMP CANNING PLANT. The plant, a large shedlike structure with a pier extending into the Wilmington River, was established by L. P. Maggioni of Savannah in 1928. The shrimp are placed in a large refrigeration room until the following morning when, after a two-minute blanching process, they are picked up by the workers, boiled, labeled, and stored for marketing. Approximately three hundred workers are employed at the factory, where daily canning often exceeds 300,000 pounds of shrimp.

1. Left from Thunderbolt on Bonaventure Rd. to (53) BONAVENTURE, **0.8 m.** (R), Savannah's beautiful historic cemetery. Cloaked somberly in gray moss, the branches of old oaks meet like cathedral arches above the drives and weathered tombstones. Even in spring, when crimson azaleas and white and pink camellias lend the cemetery the beauty of a garden, it is the gray monotone of trailing moss and old stone that most truly characterizes Bonaventure. Brown fallen leaves and here and there a bright petal drift past on the slow Wilmington River.

About 1760 Colonel John Mulryne, an English gentleman, moved from Charleston, South Carolina, to this site, built a house of English brick facing the river, and cultivated a beautiful garden. It is told that when his only child, Mary, married Josiah Tattnall of Charleston, avenues of trees were planted to honor her in the form of the initials M and T. Another story recounts that in later years a fire was discovered one evening as the Tattnalls were entertaining guests for dinner. Seeing that the flames were beyond control, the imperturbable host had the table removed to the garden where, in the light of the destroying flames, he regaled his nervous guests with witty conversation as his home was consumed.

At the time of the Revolution the new state government confiscated the estate of the Royalist Tattnalls, who left the country. But the eighteen-year-old son, Josiah II, embraced the patriot cause, returned to Georgia, and joined General Nathanael Greene's army. Later the state restored to him his father's estate as a reward.

A second house was destroyed by fire in 1804. Seven years later the land was purchased by Captain Peter Wiltberger, whose wish was fulfilled when his son converted it into a cemetery in 1869. The oldest graves are those of the Tattnall family and of the French soldiers who fell in an attempt to take Savannah from the British during the Revolution.

STRANGER'S TOMB, at the entrance, was erected in memory of William Gaston, who was widely known for his hospitality. Because of his kindness to strangers, the people of Savannah honored him by building in his memory a receiving vault, where the body of any stranger who died in Savannah could be placed temporarily.

2. Right from Thunderbolt on a paved road to (54) GEORGIA STATE COLLEGE (Negro), **1.2 m.** (L), a unit of the University System of Georgia. On its twenty-five-acre campus, shaded by moss-covered oaks and bordered on the south by a tidewater stream, are twenty-eight buildings valued at $700,000. These structures are built of wood, concrete, or red brick, and most of them show the influence of either modified Georgian or Greek Revival

architecture. A few of the frame buildings were houses of the old Postell Plantation. PARSON HALL, a girl's dormitory, is an odd, one-story structure with a raised brick basement. Victorian influence is seen in the strips of wooden trellis that have the appearance of columns. Adjacent to the campus is a ninety-acre farm where students learn dairying, poultry raising, animal husbandry, and gardening. In addition to supplying foodstuffs for the college, the farm is used as an experiment station.

The institution, which has an enrollment of more than five hundred, is a four-year college, conferring the B.A. and B.S. degrees. Courses in home economics, education, and mechanic arts prepare young Negroes for useful lives in their communities. The president, Benjamin F. Hubert, is an outstanding Negro educator. The school, chartered in 1890 as a land-grant college, was opened for a preliminary session at Athens in 1891 and was transferred to this campus the following year.

Between Thunderbolt and Savannah Beach, State 26 is a causeway. Lined with palmettos and oleanders, it traverses wide marshes, wooded islands, and dark tidal rivers.

The route crosses the Wilmington River, 3.7 m., up which small craft move slowly, and passes to Whitemarsh Island. Here sea gulls glide over marshes covered with bright yellow and green grass that grows as high as three feet.

At 5 m. is a junction with a dirt road.

Left on this road across Richardson Creek to the (55) NATIONAL CONDUCTORS' HOME, 1.8 m., on Oatland Island. This institution is maintained by the National Order of Railway Conductors for the use of its members upon their retirement from active service.

State 26 crosses Turner's Creek, 6.5 m., to WILMINGTON ISLAND, which is higher than the other islands and is forested with pine and moss-covered oaks.

At SOUTH-END POINT on Wilmington Island, Confederate breastworks are still visible on the site where General A. R. Lawton massed defenses to cover approaches to Savannah from the Wilmington River. From the mouth of the river there is an excellent view overlooking Wassaw Sound, where many regattas have been held.

McQueen Island is reached by crossing Bull River, 9.4 m., the largest of the tidal streams connecting the Savannah River with Wassaw Sound and the Atlantic Ocean.

At 14 m. the rose-brick walls (L) of Fort Pulaski are visible.

(56) LAZARETTO (Sp., hospital), 14.6 m., a small community on Lazaretto Creek, was formerly the site of a quarantine station, now on Cockspur Island, and of a hospital to which slave boats brought Negroes to be examined and treated. The slaves who died were buried in unmarked graves near by. An oak grove covers the remains of the low-lying Federal breastworks used to protect the batteries that shelled Fort Pulaski in 1862.

Cars can be parked at Lazaretto and a small government launch boarded for a trip to Fort Pulaski National Monument on Cockspur Island. (*No charge on launch, 4 trips daily, hourly schedule on Sunday.*)

As the boat passes into the South Channel of the Savannah River the oak grove of a GOVERNMENT BIRD SANCTUARY is visible (R) and beyond, the TYBEE LIGHTHOUSE and FORT SCREVEN. Ahead, outlined against the sky on the detached tip point of Cockspur Island, is an ABANDONED LIGHTHOUSE, which for many years marked the river channel.

(57) FORT PULASKI NATIONAL MONUMENT embraces 537 acres of Cockspur Island and encloses one of the best preserved fortresses constructed for coast defense during the first half of the nineteenth century. The fort, facing seaward and guarding the entrance to the Savannah River, is encircled by two moats spanned by drawbridges. On the ground between the moats are breastworks, large earthen mounds overgrown with cactus, thorn ash, sweet myrtles, and cassena berries. Because of their crescent shape these mounds are called *demilunes* (Fr., half moons).

Entrance to the inner fort is through the portcullis, a dark, vaulted brick passage leading from the drawbridge. The massive brick walls of the fortification, from 7 to 11 feet thick and 32 feet high, enclose a green parade ground with officers' quarters, arched casemates, and bombproof chambers, each arranged to mount a cannon which was fired through an embrasure in the outer wall. The floors of these chambers are of Georgia pine, with all nailheads covered by wooden pegs to prevent them from giving off sparks. A four-foot layer of sand and shell covering the lead roof of the fort forms the terreplein, which serves to protect the casemates and to make an upper platform on which other guns can be mounted. In early days rain, filtering through the sand and shell, was stored in large cisterns as a water supply.

Fort Pulaski was the third fortification erected on Cockspur Island, the first being Fort George, a small block structure built in 1761 and dismantled in 1776 by American patriots. On the ruins of this garrison Fort Greene, a second small fort, was erected in 1794 but was swept away by the hurricane of 1804. The sites of these earlier structures cannot be definitely identified because time and weather have altered the shape of the island. When the Federal government made a survey of the southeastern coast in 1812, Cockspur Island was selected as the site of a new fort because of its position at the mouth of the Savannah River. The first drafts were made by Napoleon's chief engineer, Simon Bernard, who came to America to assist in planning coast defenses, and actual construction was begun in 1829. Building was principally under the direction of Lieutenant J. F. K. Mansfield, assisted in preliminary surveys by Robert E. Lee, then a young engineer recently graduated from West Point. Upon its completion in 1847 the fort was named for Casimir Pulaski, the Polish count who gave his services to America in the Revolution and was mortally wounded in the Siege of Savannah.

The shell-torn masonry at the eastern end of the fortification recalls the short, dramatic part Fort Pulaski played in the War between the States. Joseph E. Brown, Governor of Georgia, learning that Federal soldiers planned to reinforce Fort Sumter, sent A. R. Lawton, then colonel of the 1st Volunteer Regiment, to occupy the ungarrisoned Fort Pulaski on January 3, 1861. Since Georgia had not seceded from the Union, this command constituted an act of treason. The following year Federal forces fired upon the fort from eight of their batteries on Tybee Island and on April 11, after thirty hours of terrific bombardment, forced Colonel Charles H. Olmstead, the Confederate commander, to surrender. Captured with the fort were 385 officers and men, as well as ammunition and supplies. Two of the walls were destroyed, many guns dismantled, officers' quarters damaged, and powder magazines within range of the guns seriously endangered. The siege demonstrated that the older brick and masonry fortifications could not withstand the fire of the newer guns. After its surrender the fort was used for more than a year as a military prison.

Under the supervision of the National Park Service part of Fort Pulaski has been restored and the rest carefully preserved as it was at the time of its surrender in 1862. A MUSEUM in the fort contains many battle relics.

Footpaths lead west from the fort through the tropical shrubbery of the park to the SITE OF ROBERT E. LEE'S HOUSE; to BATTERY HAMBRIGHT, where guns were set up during the Spanish-American War; and finally to the section of the island called PEEPER because its shape resembles that of the small tree frog or "peeper" common to this region. Here, in a natural temple of cedars and sweet myrtles, John Wesley and his fellow colonists knelt to give thanks for a safe arrival.

(58) FORT SCREVEN, 17 m., is an army post (L) at which is stationed a battalion of the 8th Infantry, U. S. Army. From the entrance arch a private road bordered with palmettos leads to a small brick guardhouse where a sentry is always on duty. Along a circular driveway, which encloses a large green with the post flag and reveille guns in its center, are the company barracks and officers' quarters and a building and parade ground for each company. Between the officers' quarters and the sea is the post parade ground, where battalion and regimental parades are held. The post exchange, commissary, and stables stand on the western side of the post and are not encircled by the road. At a right angle turn near the completion of the circle, a road branches southeastward toward the ocean and Tybee. Near the junction of these roads (R) are the post hospital and the new theater.

The Fort Screven Reservation was acquired by the Federal government from John Screven and J. C. Rowland by Congressional acts of 1808 and 1820. Fort Screven, known at first as Camp Graham, became an active army post on March 3, 1898.

From the non-commissioned officers' quarters the circular drive leads to the TYBEE LIGHTHOUSE, which marks the mouth of the Savannah River. (*Arrangements can be made to climb the spiral stairway to see the beacon at close range.*) This lighthouse dates from Colonial times, for here in 1753 General Oglethorpe built a tower "constructed of the best pine, strongly timbered, raised upon cedar piles, a brickwork around the bottom." Before 1755 a brick tower was erected but was not lighted, and it was not until 1791 that alterations were made and a light installed. Partly destroyed and its light extinguished by Confederate forces in 1862, the lighthouse was rebuilt five years later.

The route continues over Tybee Island to the Atlantic Ocean.

At **18.5 m.** is (59) SAVANNAH BEACH.

Transportation: Savannah Beach Bus Line.
Parking: Overlooking ocean, 25¢.
Swimming: Bathhouses, bathing suits, 25¢ each.
Accommodations: Four hotels, many boarding houses, restaurants, and lunch stands.

Amusements: A dance pavilion built over the water. Concessions with amusement booths and games. Charges vary.

Savannah Beach, locally known as Tybee, has been a seacoast resort for Georgians for several generations. Along the crowded beach bright pajamas, blistered backs, and volleys of shots at revolving ducks recreate Coney Island on a smaller scale. The beach is at the southern end of Tybee Island, which is a V-shaped sand bar running 3.8 miles along the Atlantic and 2.5 miles up the Savannah River. Its flat surface is broken by a few small sand dunes, behind which are the cottages of the summer colony. Most of these cottages are built for safety on high stilts with the verandas and living quarters 10 to 15 feet above the ground.

TOUR 2

Savannah — Wormsloe — Fort Wimberley — Bethesda; Skidaway Rd., La Roche Ave., and Ferguson Ave., 11.2 m.

Roadbed hard-surfaced throughout.

Two miles E. of Bull St. Skidaway Rd. runs S. from Victory Dr. **0 m.** At **1 m.** is the junction with La Roche Ave.; L. on La Roche Ave.

(60) ISLE OF HOPE, **6 m.,** an attractive year-round settlement situated on a crescent-shaped bluff above the river, began as the summer colony of Parkersburg in 1840 and was given its present name in 1898. Steam transportation service was made available and amusement concessions were constructed and operated by the railroad. In the summer months children play in the shallow waters while their mothers sew and gossip beneath the large oak trees. Motorboats putter about the small wooden docks, where drying bathing suits and crabbing nets blow in the breeze.

At **6.5 m.,** at the narrow neck of Isle of Hope (R), is the (61) DIAMOND-BACK TERRAPIN FARM (*open 8 A.M.-12 P.M.; 8-6:30 winter; 25¢*). The farm was begun as an experiment by A. M. Barbee in 1893 and has developed until thousands of terrapins are shipped annually to northern markets. A CANNING FACTORY operated in conjunction with the farm ships shrimp and clam chowder as well as terrapin meat and soup. Many well-known sea foods are served in the restaurant adjacent to the cannery.

The beautifully marked terrapins, which are not salable until they are between five and nine years old, are kept in separate pens and fed on shrimp and fiddler crabs. Thousands are kept for breeding purposes. A novelty for visitors is the terrapin Toby, with his tricks of bowing to the ladies and playing the piano.

Immediately past the terrapin farm the road makes a sharp turn (R).

(62) WORMSLOE (*private*), 7.7 m. (L), is nationally known not only for its gardens but also as one of Georgia's few colonial plantations that have remained in the possession of the same family for two centuries. Soon after the founding of the colony in 1733, Noble Jones received from the Georgia trustees a grant of 500 acres, but it was not officially confirmed by the royal government until 1756. Jones set out mulberry trees for the culture of silkworms—hence the name "Wormsloe." Because the tract was strategically situated on the inland waterway leading south to Spanish territory, General Oglethorpe selected it as the site for a garrison. Noble Jones was placed in command of a small wooden fort built under his direction to guard the narrows of the Skidaway River. In 1763 Jones received a second grant of 500 acres adjacent to the first, but only 300 acres of this second tract are included in the 800 acres of Wormsloe.

Noble Jones, appointed captain by Oglethorpe in 1742, was a versatile man who served the colony as surveyor, treasurer, and chief justice as well as soldier. His children also achieved distinction in the early life of the colony. During the many absences of the male members of her family, Mary Jones competently supervised the plantation and on one occasion successfully defended the small fort from a sudden attack by Spaniards and Indians. His son, Noble Wimberly Jones, was a prominent physician and the first president of the Georgia Medical Society. Later owners of Wormsloe, who took privileges with the spelling of family names, distinguished themselves as doctors, jurists, and statesmen. One of the most prominent names in the history of the estate is that of George Wymberly Jones DeRenne, who began a library of Georgia history. DeRenne, born Jones, added to his name a French modification of Van Deren, the name of his maternal grandmother, and thenceforth was known as G. W. J. DeRenne.

The library begun by DeRenne was destroyed by the bummers who followed in the wake of Sherman's army, but the owner immediately began to reconstruct it. This second collection was bequeathed to his son Everard, who willed it to the state, and it now forms the basis of the literature and history collection of the library in the state capitol. Following the tradition of his father, Wymberley Jones DeRenne began in 1891 to assemble a third library, which contains rare volumes, maps, old documents, manuscripts, and engravings, and is reputedly the finest historical collection on Georgia. The Wymberley Jones DeRenne Georgia Library was housed in a white stone building at Wormsloe until its sale by Wymberley Wormsloe DeRenne in 1938 to The University of Georgia. It now forms a special collection in The University of Georgia Library at Athens.

WORMSLOE HOUSE, enlarged about the middle of the nineteenth century on earlier tabby foundations, has been recently remodeled as a residence for Dr. and Mrs. Craig Barrow. Mrs. Barrow is the daughter of Wymberley Jones DeRenne and present owner of the estate. The house, overlooking the Isle of Hope River, still contains marble mantels and many other fine interior details. The grounds, carpeted with large-leaf Algerian ivy, are shaded by lofty oaks that form a dark setting for the azalea and camellia bushes, many of which grow as tall as young trees. During the residence of Wymberley Wormsloe DeRenne, son of Wymberley Jones DeRenne, a series of formal gardens was laid out, and the estate was opened to the public until the spring of 1938.

An oak-bordered drive leads more than a mile from the arched entrance gate to FORT WIMBERLEY, a ruined tabby fortification built in 1741 to replace the earlier wooden structure guarding the narrows of the Skidaway River. It was this later fort, equipped with four brass cannon, that Mary Jones defended from a Spanish and Indian attack. The fort was approximately thirty feet square, and in places the ruined walls stand as high as eight feet. It is believed that the bastions, which extended from each corner, and the powder chamber were roofed over but that the main body of the enclosure was open. Although the tabby walls have been weathered for nearly two centuries, the embrasures through which the colonists fired are still distinct. For many months a Confederate battalion stationed here successfully prevented Federal ships from passing on the inland water route.

At 8.7 m. is the intersection with Ferguson Ave.; L. on Ferguson Ave.

(63) BETHESDA (open), 11.2 m., the oldest existing orphanage in America, occupies a group of substantial Georgian Colonial buildings set on a bluff overlooking a tidal river. The landscaping follows the plan initiated by the Trustees' Garden Club when the orphanage was opened in 1740 by George Whitefield. A small, well-proportioned GEORGIAN CHAPEL, presented in 1924 by the Georgia Society of Colonial Dames of America, is a reproduction of Whitefield's church in England.

Bethesda, meaning House of Mercy, was established as an asylum for needy boys and girls by Whitefield and James Habersham, Colonial statesman. Although the land was granted by the Georgia trustees for an orphanage, the institution functioned primarily as a school and was among the most successful enterprises of the colonists. (see EDUCATION) At the death of Whitefield in 1770 the grant was bequeathed to Selina, Countess of Huntingdon, who had rendered financial aid to the school. When she died in 1791 the orphanage was discontinued, claimed by the state government, and committed to a board of trustees. In 1801 the school was reopened by the trustees, who were members of the philanthropic Union Society. Four years later, however, the buildings burned and the property was sold, and it was not until 1855 that the Union Society purchased the property and revived the historic institution. During the War between the States the buildings were used as a military hospital, and at the close of the war were occupied by freed Negro slaves. Since its restoration to the Union Society in 1867, Bethesda has continued its work without interruption.

Jasper Spring, **1.6 m.**; Site of the Hermitage, **1.9 m.**; Union Paper and Bag Co., **2.5 m.**; Irene Mound, **5.7 m.**; Silk Hope Plantation, **5.9 m.**; Savannah Sugar Refinery, **8.3 m.** (*see* STATE TOUR *1*).

*

PART THREE

TOURS

*

TOUR I

(Charleston, S. C.) — Savannah — Darien — Brunswick — (Jacksonville, Fla.); US 17.

South Carolina Line to Florida Line, 134.7 m. — Roadbed hard-surfaced throughout, about a third concrete — Seaboard Air Line Ry. roughly parallels route — All types of accommodations in Savannah and Brunswick; limited elsewhere.

US 17, the Coastal Highway, crosses the lowest part of the Georgia Coastal Plain with its many tidal creeks and its swamps dense with cypress, tupelo, and bay trees. Giant live oaks hung with gray Spanish moss add a note of ghostly beauty. Along the route are many saltwater marshes that vary in color from the light green of tender shoots in early spring to the yellow of dying grass in fall. The higher land is wooded with pine and palmetto.

Although Spain had already laid claim to this area, Jean Ribault sailed up the coast in 1562 and gave French names to all the rivers. Spain, incensed, sent Pedro Menendez de Aviles to strengthen her claims; he reached St. Catherines Island in 1566 and established there the first garrison in Georgia. From the island, outposts spread to the mainland, which was called Guale in honor of a friendly Indian chief. The troops established presidios, near which Jesuit and Franciscan priests built missions to aid in converting the Indians.

Although King Charles II of England granted the Georgia coast to the Carolina Lords Proprietors about a century later, it was not until 1717 that a definite attempt at colonization was made. In that year Sir Robert Montgomery, a Scotsman, obtained the strip of land between the Savannah and Altamaha rivers, which he tried unsuccessfully to colonize as the Margravate of Azilia. His failure left the land a frontier of dispute between England and Spain. With the coming of Oglethorpe in 1733 a definite English civilization was established here. Later great plantations developed along the coast and flourished through slave labor until the War between the States. Some of the plantations have remained intact and their buildings have been restored by wealthy people from other sections; but many more have been divided into small farms, frequently cultivated by tenants.

In three of the coastal counties, Negroes constitute more than half the total population. Living in one- or two-room cabins, the rural Negroes sustain themselves by farming, hunting, fishing, and working in the pine forests. Many of the town Negroes are domestic servants, stevedores, naval-stores hands, and laborers in the fisheries.

US 17 crosses the red waters of the SAVANNAH RIVER, **0 m.**, the natural boundary between South Carolina and Georgia, on five concrete bridges and one steel drawbridge that link one delta island with another. Built across the islands is a high causeway lined with swamp willows and myrtles. These fertile islands, once covered with flourishing rice fields, are now part of the 12,900-acre SAVANNAH RIVER WILDLIFE REFUGE, four-fifths of which lies in South Carolina. This area was selected by the Biological Survey because it is on the Atlantic fly-way. Seventeen thousand green-winged teal and an equal number of wood duck wintered here in 1936.

On one of the largest islands is the U. S. BIOLOGICAL STATION (R) where migratory birds are studied. Opposite the station is an OLD RICE MILL, an austere three-story, gabled structure of Georgian Colonial design. Its plain brick walls, which have tiers of small windows, are relieved only by corner quoins and a delicate cornice. It is believed to have been erected about 1830 by Daniel Heyward, a rice planter. During the present century it was converted into a tavern, but it now stands vacant.

Through an entrance gate (L), 2 m., a half-mile, oak-lined drive leads past a semitropical garden to the SAVANNAH SUGAR REFINERY, one of the largest in the South. Manufacturing Dixie Crystals from raw Cuban sugar, this factory has a melting capacity of 2,500,000 pounds daily and a storage capacity of 85,000,000 pounds of raw sugar and 30,000,000 pounds of refined sugar. Five hundred men are employed in the daily production of fifty carloads of refined sugar. Around the plant is a fifteen-acre mill village of seventy-five houses, with a hospital and a hotel that has accommodations for fifty guests.

At **4 m.** is the junction with a graded road.

Left on this road to WHITEHALL PLANTATION (*private*), **0.5 m.**, on land granted to Joseph Gibbons in 1759. A green-shuttered, white frame house (L) is set in a beautiful grove of large oaks along the Savannah River.

At **5.3 m.** is the junction with a sandy road.

Left on this road to IRENE MOUND, **0.7 m.**, on the bank of Pipemakers' Creek. Archeological exploration has revealed, six feet below the surface, what is believed to have been the cellar of the schoolhouse of the Indian mission established in 1735 by John Wesley, Benjamin Ingham, and the Moravians. Near-by was the Indian village of New Yamacraw, founded by Chief Tomochichi after the white man's occupation of Savannah.

At **7.3 m.** is the junction with a narrow paved road.

Left on this road to the UNION BAG AND PAPER COMPANY PLANT, **0.3 m.**, a branch of a northern organization which is extending its field to the South because of Charles Herty's recent experiments in the manufacture of paper from Georgia slash pine pulp (*see* SAVANNAH AND NATURAL SETTING). This plant manufactures twelve million paper bags daily and employs more than a thousand people.

At **7.4 m.** is the junction with a sandy road.

Left on this road to the SITE OF THE HERMITAGE (L.), **1 m.** In the early Colonial period negotiations between Oglethorpe and Tomochichi reserved this land as the Indians' hunting ground. In 1750, however, a 100-acre tract was granted to Joseph Ottolenghe, who was employed by the trustees of the colony to further the silk industry in Savannah. The plantation, which has changed hands many times, has been used for rice culture, brick manufacturing, lumbering, and as the site for a Colonial tavern.

In the early part of the nineteenth century it was purchased by a Scotsman, Henry McAlpin, who utilized the clay soil to manufacture the Savannah Grey brick used in many structures of the city. In 1820 he facilitated shipping of his brick by constructing from the factory to the river a clumsy horsecar railroad, one of the earliest in America. For many years his beautiful, stuccoed brick manor house, with its curving, double-entrance stairway, was an inspiration to architects. Gradually, however, the place deteriorated from neglect and vandalism, and in 1936 all the buildings of this plantation were bought by Henry Ford, who razed them and used the brick in constructing his home on the Ogeechee River near Ways (*see below*). Two of the slave huts have been restored and are on display at Dearborn, Michigan. All that remains on the site of the plantation is an impressive avenue of oaks.

A small wooden shelter (R) covers JASPER SPRING, **8.7 m.,** where Sergeant William Jasper, aided by Sergeant John Newton, captured ten British soldiers who were taking American prisoners to Savannah to be hanged. Jasper was killed in the Battle of Savannah, and a large monument to him stands in the center of Madison Square in that city.

SAVANNAH, **10.3 m.** (21 alt., 85,024 pop.) (*see* SAVANNAH).

Points of Interest: Telfair Academy of Arts and Sciences, Herty Pulp and Paper Laboratory, Armstrong Junior College, Atlantic Coast Line Docks, Bethesda Orphanage, Wormsloe, and others.

Savannah is at the junction with US 80 (*see* TOUR *9*) and with State 21 (*see* TOUR *14*).

SILK HOPE PLANTATION (R), **16.2 m.,** is a part of the 500-acre tract granted in 1756 to James Habersham, who in 1750 had been appointed silk commissioner by the Colonial trustees in London. With its vast fields in mulberry trees and its gardens designed by an English horticulturist, this was a noted silk plantation until the Revolution, after which rice was cultivated until 1891. During the early part of the twentieth century lumber companies cut much of the timber.

US 17 crosses the LITTLE OGEECHEE RIVER, **17.6 m.,** one of the numerous salt-water estuaries indenting the Georgia coast. Its still, black water reflects the moss-covered branches of the black gum, oak, and tupelo trees that line its banks. This small river provides opportunities for good fishing.

At **18.5 m.** is the entrance (L) to LEBANON (*private*), formerly the Colonial holding of James Deveaux but now the property of Mills B. Lane, of Savannah, who has developed a model farm here. The two-story white clapboard plantation house with wide verandas is surrounded by semitropical gardens. It was built between 1820 and 1840 and was remodeled by the present owner.

HOPETON (L), **21.2 m.**, is a truck farm on the site of a Colonial plantation. Of the original plantation buildings, there remain only the ante bellum slave cabins; Negro laborers live in these small, whitewashed, frame huts with clay chimneys.

At **22.3 m.** is the junction with a private dirt road.

Left on this road to WILD HERN PLANTATION (*private*), **3 m.** (R), a 650-acre tract which was granted in 1756 by King George II to Francis Harris, a Savannah merchant, and remained in the same family until 1935. The original grant hangs in the house, which was built shortly after 1756 and is unchanged in appearance except for the front steps and the screening on the porch. All the old timbers, the English bricks, and some of the flooring and side paneling are still in the building. At the southeast corner of the house is a tall palm tree that was planted by Elizabeth Harris in 1780 when she came to Wild Hern as a bride. Most of the Negroes in the vicinity are descendants of the original slaves who once cultivated the extensive rice fields of Wild Hern. They have preserved the words and tunes of many spirituals peculiar to the group, and still use the old slave burial ground of the plantation.

The plantation was named Wild Hern for the Hampshire, England, estate of Mary Goodall, who married Colonel Harris. Hern is the old English contraction for heron; through an error of transcription by descendants of Harris, the estate was known for many years as Wild Horn.

The PLANT INTRODUCTION GARDEN (R), **23 m.**, is a 46-acre experiment station developed about a dense, feathery bamboo grove that resembles a low hill completely covered with ferns. The station was organized in 1920 by Barbour Lathrop who wanted to preserve the grove that had been planted here on the Chapman Plantation. This oriental variety of bamboo has a diameter of six inches by the time it is a year old. After the grove had been presented to the U. S. Department of Agriculture, other varieties were introduced, and there are now more than 150 kinds of bamboo indigenous to the temperate and subtropical zones. Some are dwarf varieties that promise to be helpful in the prevention of soil erosion. Experiments are also conducted with bamboo to determine its value as a source of pulp for paper. Bamboo canes are used in the manufacture of toothbrush and broom handles, yacht masts, flagpoles, radio aerials, and furniture. When sliced, peeled, boiled, and served in butter sauce, the tender young sprouts are delicious.

In addition to bamboo several new and little-known vegetables and fruits are grown here. Ramie, a fibrous Asiatic plant, is being studied for its cellulose content, and goldenrod, for experimentation with its latex as a possible source of rubber. Efforts are being made to develop varieties of blight-resistant chestnuts.

A marker (R) at **24.7 m.** indicates the SITE OF THE KING'S FERRY REVOLUTIONARY ENGAGEMENT. Colonel John White, with Captain George Melvin and Captain A. G. Elholm and three soldiers, on the night of October 1, 1779, determined to capture the five vessels and 130 men of Captain French, a British commander. French, intending to reinforce General Augustine Prevost and attack Savannah, had landed his forces at this point on the Ogeechee River twenty miles from the city, arranging the ships to protect him against a sea attack.

A short distance away, the six patriots built many watch fires at such intervals as to convince the British that they were surrounded by a large force. Throughout the night the stratagem was furthered by much shifting, marching between fires, and loud calls to imaginary sentinels. White then rode alone to the British camp and told French that the American troops demanded unconditional surrender as the price of his life. The frightened British commander agreed, thanking him for his humanity. The five vessels were burned and the British were conducted to Sunbury under the "protection" of two of the Americans, while White, who was ostensibly in the rear restraining his impatient forces, was collecting the surrounding militia.

US 17 crosses the Kings Ferry Bridge, **24.8 m.,** over the OGEECHEE RIVER.

At **27.3 m.** is the junction with the unpaved Ways Station Road.

1. Left on this road is WAYS, **0.5 m.** (18 alt., 100 pop.), a model community being developed by Henry Ford according to the plan of the one at Dearborn, Michigan. Beginning his operations here in 1925 with the purchase of several old plantations Ford has added to his holdings until he now has a total of 70,000 acres in Bryan and Chatham counties. Under his direction land has been cleared for gardens and a chemical laboratory has been established for research in Georgia farm products. Proposed projects are a roadside market where children may sell their garden produce or handiwork, a museum to display the industrial arts of the South, a community house in which girls may practice domestic arts, and a factory for the construction of automobile parts.

The COMMUNITY CLUBHOUSE (R), a two-story, white frame building with green trim and a wide porch extending around two sides, is of early Georgian Colonial design. A covered passage leads from the rear to an addition of the same architectural design. The house was opened in February, 1937, with a dance in the ballroom, which is finished in Georgia knotty pine with large exposed rafters. On this occasion the boys and girls danced a quadrille taught them by an instructor employed by Ford. The structure also contains a large dining room, a lounge, a reception room, and twenty guest rooms for the use of school children and their parents.

The COMMUNITY SCHOOL (R) was built by Ford to train the local people in crafts and sciences. Measuring 25 by 150 feet, the one-story building of early Georgian Colonial design contains a sawmill, an electrical plant, a machine shop, a foundry, a chemical laboratory, and home economics and woodworking equipment. The only requirement for attendance is a high standard of work and behavior. Ford assists many of the graduates of his school to attend college; these proteges are required to write to him periodically. In a large kitchen and lunchroom, soup and nourishing lunches are provided for the needy children of the vicinity. This project was formerly operated under W.P.A. supervision. A trained nurse is in attendance at all times and a doctor conducts a clinic at the school once a week.

The Ways Station road continues to the HENRY FORD ESTATE (*guarded*), **1.5 m.,** composed of the old Richmond, Cherry Hill, Whitehall, and Strathy Hall plantations, all on the Ogeechee River in a setting of large, moss-covered oaks. At Richmond, Ford has built a house of the Savannah Grey bricks he obtained from the Hermitage.

On a bluff overlooking the Ogeechee River is the SITE OF HARDWICK, **7 m.** After John Reynolds, first Royal Governor of the colony (1754-57), had selected the site in 1755, he obtained appropriations for public works and the entertainment of Indians and had William DeBrahm, noted French engineer, plan the town. The Governor initiated a movement to change the Colonial seat of government from Savannah to Hardwick, and many lots were granted and sold before the plan was abandoned. The town became a trading village and later the seat of Bryan County. After the county seat was removed in 1814, Hardwick began to decline and, despite an effort at revival in 1866, became one of Georgia's dead towns.

The SITE OF FORT MCALLISTER, **8 m.,** is on the Ogeechee River opposite Genesis Point. This earthwork, erected by the Confederates, was one of the principal defenses of Savannah and withstood attacks during 1862 and 1863. On December 13, 1864, however, the fort was taken by General William B. Hazen after Major George W. Anderson had made a gallant but unsuccessful effort to defend it with 200 men. After this defeat General Hardee withdrew his Confederate forces from Savannah.

2. Right from the junction on a dirt road to the HENRY FORD FISH HATCHERY, **0.3 m.,** one of the five hatcheries controlled by the state division of wild life. The 75-acre tract was donated to the state by Ford.

FREEDMEN'S GROVE (L), **37.4 m.,** is a Negro settlement on land deeded by the owner to his former slaves immediately after the War between the States. Although this was not a common practice, there are several instances of such gifts in Georgia.

MIDWAY, **40.9 m.** (30 alt., 98 pop.), a small, oak-shaded village, was once the religious center of a large plantation area known as the Midway District. The site is about midway between Savannah and Darien, but the name probably was derived from the English river Medway. In 1695 a group of Puritans from Dorchester, Massachusetts, moved to South Carolina to conduct missionary work among the Indians. There they founded another settlement called Dorchester, but, because of an unhealthful climate, sent scouting parties to look for a site in Georgia. In 1752 two families came to settle in the district, and by 1771 there were thirty-eight families and five single men on grants totaling more than 32,000 acres. These Puritan settlers were among the first in the colony to oppose the British. The first church, a log structure, was established in 1754. Congregational in polity but served by Presbyterian ministers, it was the religious center not only of the Puritans, but of the prosperous rice planters of the district. The roads that led to Midway became thoroughfares of fashion as the landowners drove leisurely in their carriages to the little church.

MIDWAY CHURCH (L), a white clapboarded structure, 40 feet wide and 60 feet long, is surrounded by a grove of moss-covered oaks. The exterior, reminiscent of a Colonial New England meeting house, has a double row of shuttered, small-paned windows. In the pedimented front gable end are two small circular openings. Surmounting the roof is a slender square tower with crowning belfry and octagonal spire. This building, the fourth on the same site, was erected in 1792, and the old slave gallery and high pulpit remain unchanged. For a period of six weeks in 1864 General Judson Kilpatrick's cavalry encamped about the church and made raids over the countryside. Later a part of Sherman's army used the little building as a slaughterhouse. The melodeon, used as a meat block by the soldiers, now serves as a communion table. Regular services are no longer held, but each year on April 26, Confederate Memorial Day, descendants of the early members gather for a meeting. Speeches are made, communion is received from the original service, and flowers are placed upon the graves in the cemetery across the road.

Among the early pastors of the congregation were Abiel Holmes, father of Oliver Wendell Holmes, and Jedidiah Morse, father of S. F. B. Morse. The membership of the church, which never exceeded 150 at any one time, numbered among its communicants Lyman Hall and Button Gwinnett, signers of the Declaration of Independence. With the decline of the plantation system after the War between the States, the importance of Midway ended.

In the section of the village called Black Midway is a Negro church with a wooden hand pointing heavenward from the steeple.

Left from Midway on the Dorchester road is DORCHESTER, 2 m. (30 alt., 220 pop.), settled by a group of the Puritans who came from Dorchester, South Carolina. They were the organizers of Midway Church and worshiped there until they formed their own congregation in 1781.

At 6 m. is a fork.

1. Left from the fork to the SITE OF SUNBURY, 4 m., which was established in 1758 soon after Mark Carr, friend of James Oglethorpe, had conveyed 300 acres of his original 500-acre grant to a group of trustees. They laid out a rectangular town with three public squares and 496 lots, and by 1769 Sunbury was a busy river port rivaling Savannah. Sunbury Academy, established in 1788, became the finest in this part of the state. The town began to decline with the shift of population inland and the growing importance of Savannah. It is believed that one of the earliest Masonic lodge meetings in America was held on this site in 1734 with Oglethorpe as master. Here are the REMAINS

OF FORT MORRIS, built for defense in 1776, now overgrown with wild myrtle and cedar trees. The Continental troops who garrisoned the fort offered spirited resistance to British attacks, but Sunbury was virtually destroyed.

2. Right from the fork to COLONEL'S ISLAND, 5 m., between the mainland and St. Catherines Island. In 1773 William Bartram, the botanist, explored Colonel's Island and mentioned its shell mounds in his journal:

"These sea shells, through length of time, and the subtle penetrating effects of the air, which dissolve them to earth, render these ridges very fertile; and, when clear of their trees, and cultivated, they become profusely productive of almost every kind of vegetable. Here are also large plantations of indigo, corn, and potatoes, with many other sorts of esculent plants. I observed, among the shells of the conical mounds, fragments of earthen vessels, and of other utensils, the manufacture of the ancients; about the centre of one of them, the rim of an earthen pot appeared among the shells and earth, which I carefully removed, and drew it out, almost whole; this pot was curiously wrought all over the outside, representing basket work, and was undoubtedly esteemed a very ingenious performance, by the people, at the age of its construction." These mounds have not yet been excavated on a scientific basis.

Across St. Catherines Sound, OSSABAW and ST. CATHERINES ISLANDS can be seen. These are two of the islands known to the Spanish settlers as the Golden Isles of Guale, which included only six of the chain: Ossabaw, St. Catherines, Sapelo, St. Simon, Jekyll, and Cumberland. The two northermost, Tybee and Wassaw, were never claimed by Spain.

After the voyage of Pedro Menendez de Aviles in 1566, Jesuit priests established missions and built chapels, which they abandoned within four years because of Indian uprisings and the strenuous frontier life. In 1573 their work was undertaken by hardier, brown-robed Franciscan fathers, who on errands of mercy traveled from island to island in piraguas, small canoes fashioned from cypress logs. Despite a French-incited Indian uprising in 1597, when the missions were plundered and many priests were killed, the priests' work flourished, and in 1605 King Philip III of Spain sent the Bishop of Cuba to confirm more than a thousand converts.

During the latter part of the seventeenth century, Spanish supremacy was threatened by the English and by pirates who descended upon the islands. In 1683 and 1685 Agramonte, the notorious Abraham, plundered the missions and even carried away their bells. By 1686 the Golden Isles had been virtually abandoned by the Spanish, and about 1715 Edward Teach, the infamous Blackbeard, used them as a hiding place for his loot.

With the English colonization during the eighteenth century, the islands entered upon a period of intensive agricultural and social development. Families on the islands were in communication with each other by means of dug-out cypress log canoes similar to the Spanish piraguas and rowed by four, six, or eight Negroes. The chief sporting event for the settlers was an annual regatta in which cypress dug-outs, from twenty-five to fifty feet in length, were entered for prizes as high as $10,000. Cotton succeeded rice and indigo as a leading crop until the War between the States, when the plantation owners and their slaves sought refuge on the mainland. Although many emancipated Negroes followed their former masters home after the conflict, the islands never regained their earlier splendor.

Ossabaw Island, a private game preserve and winter estate, is frequented by large sea turtles that bury their eggs in the soft sand beyond the tides to be hatched by the warm rays of the sun. Turtle egg hunts are popular along the shore on summer nights when the moon is full.

As a Spanish possession the island was the site of two missions cared for by Pedro de Lastere. By 1733 few traces of Spanish occupation remained, and in that year Oglethorpe made a treaty with the Indians, reserving Ossabaw (Ind. Obispa), as well as St. Catherines and Sapelo islands, for their use as hunting and fishing preserves. In 1747 it was deeded by the Indians to Mary Musgrove (*see below*), but after years of controversy it was ordered sold to the highest bidder by the London council. Throughout the nineteenth century this island was a private hunting preserve.

St. Catherines Island, called Santa Catalina or Guale by early explorers from Florida, was the first of the Golden Isles to be settled by the Spanish. When Menendez de Aviles came to this island he was graciously received by the Indian chief, Guale. Among the Jesuit missionaries who followed the soldiers was Brother Domingo Augustine, who in 1568 translated the catechism and wrote a grammar in the native Yamassee language. In 1680, however, the Spanish outpost was moved farther south, and pirates and hostile Indians sacked or burned all the buildings. In 1733 the island became a hunting preserve for the Indians.

In 1749 Thomas Bosomworth, who had come as a clergyman to the colony and who had married Mary Musgrove, Oglethorpe's half-breed interpreter, met with a council of seventeen *micos* (chiefs) at Frederica (*see* TOUR 1A) and induced them to acknowledge his wife Empress of the Creek and her kinsman Melatche, Emperor, since both were relatives of their former ruler, Chief Brim. Mary claimed as her right the three hunting islands, because, she declared, the Creek gave them to her and because the Colonial trustees had not paid her in full for her services nor for money she had advanced. Her claim was at first not recognized by the colony, but after ten years of delay Governor Ellis was directed to pay her more than two thousand pounds and to acknowledge her right to St. Catherines Island, upon which she was living.

The Bosomworths later sold their island to Button Gwinnett, who, it is believed, built the tabby house which has been remodeled by the present owner. The simple lines of the structure have been preserved, and the original mantels, stairways, and other details have been used wherever possible. After Gwinnett's death the island was returned to the possession of the Bosomworths, who are buried here.

The SITE OF CEDAR HILL (R), **44.9 m.**, the Colonial estate of General Daniel Stewart, Revolutionary patriot, is now owned by a paper manufacturing company that has agreed to reforest the land as fast as timber is cut. General Stewart was the grandfather of Martha Bulloch, who married Theodore Roosevelt, of New York, and became the mother of President Theodore Roosevelt and the grandmother of Mrs. Franklin D. Roosevelt.

EULONIA, **61.2 m.** (25 alt., 200 pop.), is a center of the naval stores industry. The longleaf and slash pine trees of the surrounding sandy plain are tapped for gum resin, which is distilled into turpentine, leaving a residue of hard rosin (*see* TOUR 4). Here giant live oaks arch over the highway.

At **62.2 m.** is the junction with unpaved State 131, the Darien-Crescent road.

Left on this road to CRESCENT, **2 m.** (40 alt., 16 pop.). From the crescent-shaped bluff, on which there are several summer cottages and ante bellum homes, is a clear view of CREIGHTON ISLAND and of SAPELO (Sp. *Zapala*) ISLAND, the latter the property of Richard J. Reynolds of Winston-Salem, North Carolina. During Spanish occupation it was the seat of the San Jose Mission, which became the Spanish frontier after the abandonment of St. Catherines in 1680. From 1733 to 1759 the island was reserved for the Indians. In 1786 it was purchased by five French Royalist refugees who attempted to establish a communal society. The partnership was dissolved because of dissension in 1802, and four of the Frenchmen withdrew to Jekyll Island; one retained his holdings on Sapelo. The northern end of the island was sold to the Marquis de Montalet, a refugee from the slave uprisings of Santo Domingo, who established a new home, Le Chatelet, a name corrupted by the Negroes into Chocolate.

Thomas Spalding purchased 4,000 acres on the southern end of the island and built a house, SOUTH END. Among the first to plant cotton, grow cane, and manufacture sugar, he had by 1843 become very wealthy and owned most of the island. When Spalding died in 1851, South End Plantation was left to his grandson and namesake, Thomas Spalding. During the War between the States the island was abandoned, but afterward the Spaldings moved back to the old house. Eventually it passed out of their hands and in 1914 was carefully rebuilt in all its former beauty by Howard Coffin. On Barn Creek are octagonal TABBY RUINS, believed by some to be those of a Spanish mission and by others to be the remains of old plantation sugar houses. One building has been carefully restored.

Tabby (Sp. *tapia,* mud or cement) is a building material made by grinding burned oyster shells for the necessary supply of lime and mixing the substance with sand, shells, and water. The tabby formula of Thomas Spalding called for equal parts of ground shells, lime, and sand; whole oyster shells, frequently taken from the numerous Indian mounds, were always added as a binder. Since it is known that this substance was used by both the Spanish and the English, the origin of these ruins has been the subject of much controversy.

Across the creek from the northern end of Sapelo Island is the small, heavily wooded BLACKBEARD'S ISLAND, now used as a state and Federal game preserve. It was named for Blackbeard, an English pirate, who tied his bushy black beard into small tails with ribbon. In order to inspire terror he often looped the beard tails behind his ears or stuck under his hat lighted strands of hemp dipped in a solution of saltpeter and limewater. This smoldering fiber gave the appearance of smoke coming from his ears. He began his career in the West Indies during the War of the Spanish Succession and about 1716 is thought to have made his headquarters on this island. He terrorized the coasts of Georgia, Carolina, and Virginia until he was killed in a hand-to-hand combat by a British lieutenant in 1718. From 1840 until 1910 the island was used as a Government quarantine station. In 1934 explorers obtained permission to look for the pirate's treasure, of which Blackbeard had said "nobody but himself and the devil knew where it was, and the longest liver should take all."

The route continues south through small settlements.

The RIDGE, **11.5 m.,** is a residential section where most of the houses face a tidal river.

Left from the Ridge on a shell road to the THICKET (*open*), 1.5 m., an old plantation on which are the TABBY RUINS of eight buildings. The ruins on this site are believed by many to have been the Tolomato Mission, founded in 1595 by Pedro Ruiz, and one of the largest in Georgia. At Tolomato began the Indian uprising of 1597 which spread throughout Guale. The mission, however, remained until 1686, when the Spanish retreated south of St. Marys River. Though it is known that Tolomato was located in this vicinity, the preponderance of evidence today suggests that the ruins are old sugar mills built about 1816 by William Carnochan of the Savannah firm of Carnochan and Mitchell, possibly with the aid of the wealthy planter Thomas Spalding.

The name Thicket was applied to a tract covered with myrtle and other bushes and bearing many signs of previous habitation. In 1760 Hugh Clark, an early settler, petitioned the Colonial trustees for 400 acres "at a place called the great Thicket." He evidently referred to this land, which became a Colonial plantation. In 1836 the land became the property of Charles Spalding, Thomas Spalding's son.

Those who identify the tabby structures with the sugar works call the octagonal foundations on the south the old mill house and those directly north the boiling and curing house. About sixty-five feet farther north are the ruins of an unusual structure with an arched doorway and tabby brickwork ornamentation. Some claim that the presence of cisterns indicates that it was a distillery, but those who support the Spanish mission theory believe that the structure was a church. Forty-five feet farther north are the tabby ruins of a building whose use has not been determined, and 250 feet beyond this are four tabby buildings erected to house two families.

At the Darien golf course, 16.3 m., is a junction with a dirt road; L. on this road to the junction with another road, 0.3 m.; L. on this second road, at Lower Bluff, to the SITE OF FORT KING GEORGE (R), 0.5 m., easily identified by the pits and refuse mounds of an old sawmill and by several large live oaks. Nothing remains of the twenty-foot-square, gabled blockhouse, erected in 1721 to protect the colonies from the encroachments of the French and Spanish. Garrisoned by His Majesty's Independent Company, this was the first English settlement on Georgia land. Fire almost destroyed the fort in 1727; although it was rebuilt, the pleading of South Carolina caused the removal of the troops to that colony. Upon Lower Bluff the Scottish founders of Darien landed in 1736 and built their first houses and church. In 1938 the legislature purchased the site for a state park.

The side route proceeds to Darien, 16.8 m.

DARIEN, 72.7 m. (15 alt., 937 pop.), seat of McIntosh County, is a drowsy old town on a bluff high above the northern bank of the Altamaha River. At the foot of the bluff are tabby warehouses, docks, shipyards, and canneries, about which the weather-faded little shrimp boats anchor and spread their nets to dry. Lumber rafts and old paddle-wheel dredge boats from the upper Altamaha move slowly in contrast with an occasional handsome yacht, smart in new paint. In the small mercantile section a few brick buildings stand out sharply against the older tabby structures. Old frame houses with fragrant gardens are enclosed by picket fences. Along the streets, shadowed by live oaks, pass Portuguese fishermen, Negro shrimpers who speak an almost unintelligible dialect, and lumbermen who work in the pine forests.

In 1735 the trustees for the colony procured a parliamentary grant to found a group of military colonies in Georgia for the protection of the southern frontier against the Spanish and their Indian partisans. Oglethorpe's recruiter enlisted 130 men in the Scottish Highlands, where many families had been deprived of their wealth because of the unsuccessful Jacobite rebellion of 1715. After a stormy voyage on the *Prince of Wales* these men, accompanied by fifty women and children, landed in Savannah in January, 1736. In April they proceeded down the coast where, after temporary huts had been erected, John Mohr McIntosh directed the construction of a fort in which four cannon were mounted. The settlers called the town New Inverness for their former home and the surrounding area Darien, a name that later was applied to the town. For many years the Highlanders wore their plaids and kilts and played a crude form of golf. The leaders were granted large estates, near which their relatives settled according to the Scottish custom.

Because of the large plantations and the commerce afforded by the harbor, Darien became a prosperous community. Its greatest period of development followed the War of 1812, when several large sawmills cut timber from the forests of the Altamaha for the building of navy vessels. Scores of sailboats from foreign ports took on cargoes of timber. Some of the stone ballast which they unloaded is still visible along the river bank. In 1818 the Bank of Darien was chartered and, later, branches were established in St. Marys, Milledgeville, and Macon. At one time this institution was one of the largest banks in the South.

On June 11, 1863, two Federal steamships and two gunboats landed a force of freed Negroes, burned the town, and captured a pilot boat carrying sixty bales of cotton. Rebuilt, Darien developed slowly until near the close of the nineteenth century when large quantities of cypress and yellow pine timber were shipped from this point. Although its important trade has been taken by other ports with better railroad facilities, the town still depends largely upon its waterfront industries.

Near the courthouse is OGLETHORPE'S OAK, a giant tree whose symmetrical branches are said to have sheltered an entire company of General Oglethorpe's soldiers who encamped here.

The HIGHLANDER MONUMENT (L), W. of the courthouse, is a pink marble memorial designed by R. Tait MacKenzie and erected by the Colonial Dames of the State of Georgia, the St. Andrew's Society of Savannah, and the Society of Colonial Wars. Ornamented with the

Scottish thistle and the Georgia Cherokee rose, it bears a bronze panel depicting a group of Scottish Highlanders.

The PRESBYTERIAN CHURCH was established in 1736 under the supervision of John McLeod, a minister who came with the colonists from Scotland. Although the present edifice, a brick building with a tall steeple, was not built until 1870, it contains the records of the original congregation.

The name of the wide ALTAMAHA RIVER, 75 m., is a corruption of Altama (Ind., Way to the Tama Country); Tama was a village at the point where the Oconee and Ocmulgee rivers flow together to form the Altamaha. About 1778 William Bartram searched along the lower course of the Altamaha until he found a rare species of the gordonia, a flowering tree that he and his father had discovered several years previously. From the tree that he transplanted to his Philadelphia garden, all existing specimens are believed to have been propagated (*see* TOUR 2). Despite diligent search, botanists have failed since then to find it in its native habitat—thus its popular name, the lost gordonia.

The river channels are divided by delta lowlands, known as Butler, General, and Champney islands. They were owned by Colonel T. L. Huston, part owner of the New York Yankees, until his death in 1938. The rich alluvial soils and semitropical climate of the islands make them particularly adaptable to the extensive agricultural experiments begun by Colonel Huston and continued by his son, A. T. Huston.

On the northern end of Butler Island (R) is the HUSTON HOUSE (*private*), a two-story, white frame dwelling, with dormer windows and a gabled roof designed in the manner of a New England Colonial house. The house is on the old Pierce Butler rice plantation, where the actress Fanny Kemble spent part of her time in Georgia (*see* TOUR *1A*). South of the house is an ivy-covered brick chimney (R), the REMAINS OF AN OLD RICE MILL built by Butler.

The old drainage system of the Pierce Butler plantation has been replaced by modern dikes and drainage ditches to regulate the spring and fall freshets of the river and reclaim many acres of fertile land.

Among the experiments on Butler Island is the cultivation of lemons, limes, and other semitropical products. Iceberg lettuce is grown in commercial quantities and many acres of cannas and gladioli blaze with reds and yellows when in bloom. The estate also affords excellent pasturage for a large herd of fine dairy cattle. Adjacent to the highway (R) is the milking and bottling room of a model dairy; through a glass wall the manipulation of the electrically operated machinery can be watched.

The highway, passing through heavily wooded swamp country, was built over the old roadbed of the Georgia Coast & Piedmont Railway.

At **78 m.** is the junction with a shell road.

Right on this road through a wood dense with laurel, cedar, and dogwood to SANTO DOMINGO STATE PARK (*picnic area, drives, and footpaths*), **0.5 m.** At the entrance is a wrought-iron gate, swung between concrete pylons capped with red Spanish tiles. Within this 350-acre park are giant live oaks, tall yellow pines, and many native shrubs. In winter, trails are brightened by the red berries of holly and cassena bushes, and in spring, by the blossoms of redbud, dogwood, and magnolia trees. This park, established as a memorial to the Spanish occupation of the Georgia coast, is the site of Talaxe, an Indian village, near which Spanish priests erected a mission. During Colonial days the land was part of the Elizafield Plantation of Hugh Frazer Grant and for many years was planted with rice or indigo. In 1925 it was bought by Cator Woolford, of Atlanta, who donated the land to the state.

The shell road winds through the park to the SLAVE BURIAL GROUNDS of Elizafield Plantation. The graves are decorated with bits of china, various utensils, and pieces of bright-colored glass, used by the slaves during their last illnesses or placed there to ward off evil spirits. Near by are tabby foundations, the RUINS OF THE ELIZAFIELD HOUSE.

The ADMINISTRATION BUILDING, a one-story structure of seventeenth-century Spanish design, has a patio and arched cloisters in the rear. Within the building is a museum containing arrowheads, chains, bronze and iron axes, and other relics unearthed during the improvement of the park. Some are of definite Spanish design and others were used during plantation days. Opposite the administration building is a grove of palmettos, oaks, and cedars covered with climbing wild muscadine vines. An old millstone here is used as a table.

One road leads to the picnic grounds; from this, another road leads to the remains of a rice mill, a brick chimney covered with tangled vines. The old GRANT FAMILY CEMETERY is enclosed by a moss-covered tabby wall crossed by a stile.

Another trail leads to the lagoon crossed by rustic cypress bridges. This is part of the old canal begun in 1826 by the Brunswick Canal Company to facilitate the shipping of rice, lumber, and naval stores from the Altamaha River to Brunswick. The canal was never finished, but a creek marks its course. Facing the lagoon and shadowed by cypress trees are octagonal TABBY RUINS, which some authorities believe to be the foundations of Santo Domingo de Talaxe, a Spanish mission erected in 1604; others believe that they are the remains of sugar houses used in plantation days. From the tabby ruins a trail winds through cypress forests, carpeted with many varieties of wild fern, back to the administration building.

At **4 m.** on the shell road is the ESTATE OF CATOR WOOLFORD (*private*), on the site of Hopeton, the 2,000-acre plantation of John Couper and James Hamilton. The two-story tabby house, ALTAMA, erected in 1857, is of simple design with a low front portico. Restoration, begun by William du Pont and completed by Woolford, has preserved the fine proportions of the building. John Couper's son, James Hamilton Couper, who was made manager of Hopeton in 1816, developed it into one of the most flourishing plantations along the coast. Couper was one of the first southern planters to make use of scientific methods. He set up a sugar mill with machinery imported from England in 1829. In 1834 he established a cotton seed oil mill at Mobile, Alabama, and the following year one at Natchez, Mississippi; thus he was probably the first to extract oil from cotton seed. This oil business, however, was not a financial success, and the mills were discontinued in 1836. Giving his attention to the cultivation of rice after 1838, he established a diking and drainage system that was a model for other rice growers. Since he inherited his father's plantation at Cannon's Point on St. Simon Island, he at one time had the supervision of 1,500 slaves.

A settlement, 87.4 m., has developed around two industrial plants: one manufactures veneer, crates, and other package containers; the other, one of the largest of its type in the country, extracts naval stores from pine stumps by shredding the wood and subjecting it to a steaming process.

Under LANIER'S OAK (L), 87.7 m., a gnarled live oak at the edge of the salt-water swamp, Lanier received the inspiration for his poem "The Marshes of Glynn."

The VISITORS' CLUB (*tourist information*), 88.6 m., occupies a low, Spanish-type building with arched porches, red-tiled roof, and high tower. On display are modern industrial exhibits and Colonial, Spanish, and pre-Columbian Indian relics.

At this point is the junction (L) with the paved St. Simon Causeway (*see* TOUR 1*A*).

BRUNSWICK, 90.1 m. (11 alt., 14,022 pop.), seat of Glynn County (*boating, fishing, waterfowl shooting*), is a busy seaport with the gayety of a resort city. Despite an excellent harbor afforded by Oglethorpe Bay (S) and Turtle River (W), there is no passenger steamship accommodation, but a freight line gives triweekly service to Jacksonville and tramp steamers arrive frequently to take on lumber, shrimp, naval stores, and cotton. A fleet of small motorboats, decorated by their Portuguese owners with colored pennants and figureheads, daily brings shrimp to canning and packing factories that occupy several blocks along the East River. A shipyard and a large creosoting plant are a part of the busy industrial scene.

A few houses in Brunswick are of Georgian Colonial architecture, but most are either Victorian structures or Spanish-type bungalows. Brunswick has a semitropical climate and its straight, broad streets are shaded by live oaks and divided by parkways planted with palms, dogwoods, and native shrubs. The parks and squares, part of the original plan, are named for English places and Colonial benefactors.

In 1742, six years after Frederica had been founded on St. Simon Island (*see* TOUR 1*A*), Mark Carr established a plantation on the present site of the city. It was not until 1771, however, that the council of the Royal Province of Georgia decided to build a town on the mainland. A rectangular tract of 385 acres was set aside, a survey ordered, and the town named for King George III, of the House of Brunswick (Hanover). The first lot was granted in 1772, and.Glynn Academy, one of the three oldest public schools in the state, was chartered in 1778. During the following century the town approached Savannah in importance as a port, shipping cargoes of lumber, cotton, fruit, indigo, and rice. Brunswick was prosperous in 1862, when the Confederate government ordered its evacuation because of the difficulty of fortifying it. On June 8, 1863, two Federal gunboats and a transport towing two ships sailed into the harbor but were repulsed by Confederates who had reoccupied the city.

Later the natural resources of this section attracted new settlers, who developed the lumber and naval stores industries that reached a peak in 1902; at that time Brunswick ranked first among Georgia cities in the export of lumber, second in naval stores, and third in cotton. The decline that followed because of the partial depletion of the forests and the financial depression of 1907 has been gradually dispelled. Recently a factory has been constructed to manufacture pulp paper from the fast-growing local pine.

The OGLETHORPE HOTEL, NW. corner Newcastle and F Sts., is a brick building with a wide porch and round towers. This building, designed by Stanford White and erected in 1885, has since been remodeled.

In the center of QUEENS SQUARE, intersection Newcastle and Mansfield Sts., one of the well-landscaped parks, is a large Celtic cross, a monument to James Edward Oglethorpe. A beautiful magnolia tree, planted by the Daughters of the American Revolution, is called the Liberty Tree.

The CITY HALL, 1227 Newcastle St., erected in 1889, is built of brick in the German Romanesque style. The entrance arch is constructed of large granite blocks, and a dormered clock tower rises high above the roof.

The PRESBYTERIAN CHURCH, 603 George St., erected about 1871, is a simple structure of modified Gothic design. It is the city's oldest church building for a white congregation.

WRIGHT SQUARE, intersection Norwich and George Sts., was used as a cemetery until 1850. Among the old graves is that of Benjamin Hart, husband of the Revolutionary patriot Nancy Hart (*see* TOUR *3A*). The Harts moved here after the war and aided in the development of the town.

At Brunswick is the junction with US 341 (*see* TOUR *12*).

From the bridge over TURTLE RIVER, **95.2 m.,** a tidewater arm of the Atlantic Ocean, is a broad view including the Brunswick water front and in the distance the faint outlines of ST. SIMON ISLAND (*see* TOUR *1A*) and of JEKYLL ISLAND, the smallest of the Golden Isles, now the home of the Jekyll Island Club. During Spanish occupation the Franciscan mission, San Buenaventura Gualequini, was established here. Known to the Indians as Ospo, the island was renamed by Oglethorpe for his friend Sir Joseph Jekyll, a generous contributor to the Georgia colony. In 1734 Captain William Horton, who was sent to establish a military outpost, built a tabby house here and cultivated the old Spanish fields and thousands of orange trees. The island was a military reservation until about 1768, when it was given as a Crown grant to Clement Martin. About 1802 the Frenchmen from Sapelo Island moved here and before long Poulain du Bignon, who remodeled the old Horton house, owned the whole island. On Du Bignon Creek are the overgrown earthworks of a Confederate battery.

No effort was made to repair the havoc wrought by the War between the States until 1886, when the island was bought from the Du Bignon family by a group of wealthy men from New York, Boston, and Philadelphia, who formed the Jekyll Island Club. Extending for almost a mile along the Jekyll Creek front are the magnificent homes of these winter colonists. From the palatial JEKYLL ISLAND CLUBHOUSE are bridle paths and shell roads that lead through dense forests to the individual homes and to the club beach. The ruins of the old Horton house and of the supposed Spanish mission are preserved by the club.

On the lawn of Faith Chapel, at the rear of the clubhouse, is a large iron cooking pot that was used on the *Wanderer,* the last slave ship recorded in American waters. After the importation of slaves was prohibited, ships landed Negroes on the coastal islands where they could be hidden until sold. On November 28, 1858, when the *Wanderer* anchored at Jekyll Island with more than three hundred Africans, it was seized by Government officials. A lengthy litigation followed in Savannah, when a suit was brought against the notorious Captain W. C. Corrie, of New York, and his partner, Charles A. L. Lamar, of Savannah.

BLYTHE ISLAND, 95.9 m., has been developed as a residential subdivision of Brunswick. About two-thirds of the island is privately owned. Part of the remaining 1,000 acres, which belong to the U. S. War Department, is used as a military target range.

At 100.4 m. is a junction with US 84 (*see* TOUR 5).

The DREXEL HOUSE (*private*) (L), 114.1 m., is a large frame dwelling of New England Colonial architecture on a well-landscaped tract, amid the yellow pine and hardwood forest of the hunting preserve. It was built about 1885 by a group of Pennsylvania Shakers who established a colony here and is now owned by George W. C. Drexel, a retired Philadelphia publisher.

At **117.1 m.** is the junction with a dirt road.

Right on this road to REFUGE PLANTATION (*private*), **2 m.**, a 5,000-acre tract granted by George III to John Houstoun McIntosh, who settled here in 1765. The house, built of hand-hewn timber in 1798, has a gabled roof with two dormer windows. The chamfered wood columns that support the porch roof rest upon the ground, and behind them is a balcony with wooden balustrades. Double entrance steps lead to the balcony. The old kitchen is connected with the house by a covered passage, and the brick fireplace, with its hanging rod and cooking iron, is still intact. The place is now a private hunting preserve owned by Alfred W. Jones, of Sea Island.

WOODBINE, **118.9 m.** (14 alt., 335 pop.), on the banks of the Satilla River, was incorporated in 1893 and became the seat of Camden County in 1923.

South of the Satilla River bridge is the SITE OF NEW HANOVER, a trading post established in 1755 by Edmund Gray and a group of political malcontents. The Spanish objected to this intrusion because the land between the Altamaha and St. Marys rivers had been declared neutral in 1743 by an agreement following the Battle of Bloody Marsh. The Georgia officials objected also because the settlers professed no allegiance to the colony and because the post became an asylum for refugees from justice. When threatened by military force, Gray removed his post to Cumberland Island. With this exception, this land, claimed by two nations, remained uninhabited until 1763 when it was ceded to England in the Treaty of Paris.

The small ST. MARKS EPISCOPAL CHURCH (L), erected about 1900, was built of cobblestones from the piles of ballast which the old sailing vessels discharged.

Left from Woodbine on a dirt road to BELLEVUE (*private*), **16 m.**, the once flourishing plantation of General Charles Floyd, a noted Indian fighter early in the nineteenth century and the grandfather of William Gibbs McAdoo. The tabby ruins of the old plantation house and outbuildings remain. Indications of an Indian village here are found in various shell mounds, and many believe that the old tombs, without inscriptions or dates, are those of Spanish settlers.

KINGSLAND, **130.7 m.** (34 alt., 444 pop.), was established as a flag station on the Seaboard Air Line Railway in 1894.

Left from Kingsland on State 40, a paved road, to the CAMDEN PARK RACE TRACK (*horse races spring and fall*), **2 m.**
At **4 m.** is the junction with a dirt road.
Left on this road to the junction, **2.5 m.**, with another dirt road; R. on this road to the most impressive TABBY RUINS, **4 m.**, on the coast. These ruins, two stories high and 75 feet wide by 150 feet long, stand in a grove of cedar and oak trees entwined by garlands of muscadine vines. They seem to be divided into three large rooms and were evidently of two stories. There are thirty small, vertical windows to light the second floor of the room on the north and free-standing square columns on each side of the middle room. Some authorities

believe them to be the remains of Santa Maria Mission, built about 1570 by Menendez de Aviles and his followers; others believe they were sugar houses built about 1825 by John Houstoun McIntosh, who established here during the War of 1812 a plantation called New Canaan. After the death of McIntosh the plantation was sold to Colonel Hallowes, who changed its name to Bolling-brook.

At 10.7 m. on State 40 is ST. MARYS (15 alt., 732 pop.), an old sea town occupying an eminence on the St. Marys River. A wide street lined with oaks and wind-scarred cedars leads to the docks and the beautiful wide stretch of the river. Small fishing smacks with their nets drying in the sun give the town the appearance of an Old World fishing village. The dilapidated motor bus with train wheels, which formerly operated between Kingsland and St. Marys, has been featured by Roy Crane in his comic strip *Wash Tubbs,* and the imaginary adventures of Wash and Captain Easy are followed with proprietary pride by the townspeople.

It is believed that St. Marys is the site of an Indian village, Tlathlothlaguphta, to which Captain Jean Ribault in 1562 came with some Huguenots from France to found a new town. French names were given to all points in the region, and St. Marys River was called the Seine. In 1763, after English occupation, this section was organized as St. Marys Parish. When in October, 1776, after the Declaration of Independence, the parishes were abolished and counties were created with American names, St. Marys Parish became Camden County.

Following the American Revolution, a group of settlers on Cumberland Island bought 1,672 acres for $38 and in 1788 laid out the town of St. Patrick. Each subscriber received four squares of four acres, on each of which he agreed to erect, within six months, a house of frame, log, or brick. In 1792 the town was given the name of the river beside which it was built. After its incorporation in 1802, St. Marys grew rapidly as timber was sent to shipbuilding centers for the construction of U. S. Navy vessels. Its nearness to the Spanish territory of Florida necessitated the presence of customs collectors and other Federal officials, who, with the planters, established a standard of culture unusual in pioneer Georgia. With the advent of steamships and the development of railroads, St. Marys lost its commercial prestige and today contents itself with supplying fish and shrimp to sea-food canneries.

The PRESBYTERIAN CHURCH, NW. corner Osborne and Congress Sts., is a frame structure with a high basement and a square tower. Erected in 1808, it is one of the oldest buildings in the state. At first the organization was a community church but was incorporated as a Presbyterian church in 1828. For many years it served also as a school, the Old Academy, and it still houses the library and old church records. When St. Marys was a busy seaport, smugglers from Florida often anchored in the harbor to dispose of their rum, cigars, and gin. It is said that on one occasion the crew proceeded to the Presbyterian manse, took the minister's horse, and hoisted it to the church belfry. While the townspeople, attracted by the neighing of the horse, were wondering how to get it down, the smugglers were able to land their contraband goods.

ORANGE HALL (*private*), SW. corner Osborne and Congress Sts., is a two-story house of Greek Revival design set on well-landscaped grounds enclosed by a picket fence. The porch balustrade has balusters similar in design to the columns. The immense basement kitchen has the original fireplace fitted with crane and built-in ovens. The house was built between 1832 and 1837 by Horace S. Pratt when he was serving his last term as pastor of the Presbyterian church.

The ARCHIBALD CLARK HOUSE (*private*), SE. corner Osborne and Congress Sts.,
a square, clapboard structure with a small front porch, was constructed in 1802
by Major Archibald Clark, customs collector from 1807 probably until his death
in 1848. Clark entertained Aaron Burr here, and also General Winfield Scott
on his return from the Seminole War in Florida. During the War of 1812
British soldiers arrested Clark and established their headquarters in his house.

CHURCH OF ST. MARY, STAR OF THE SEA, NW. corner Osborne and Bryan Sts.,
a Roman Catholic church, is a stuccoed building with a white clapboard steeple.
It was built in the early part of the nineteenth century for a branch of the
Bank of Darien but has since been remodeled.

A beautiful avenue of oaks leads (R) to the OAK GROVE CEMETERY, established
in 1780. It is surrounded by a low stone wall with arched gateways and
shaded by large oak trees, their trunks covered with a lichen that is rosy pink
when its brood buds appear. Many of the individual lots are surrounded by
brick walls and iron fences. Vine-covered marble slabs with French inscriptions
mark the graves of French planters who fled from Santo Domingo to escape
massacre during a slave uprising, and of Acadians banished with Evangeline.
In 1755, when the French Acadians were forced by the English to leave Grand
Pré, ten vessels set out for Georgia and South Carolina. The 400 members who
came to Savannah were not welcomed by the Protestant colony because of their
religion. In 1757, to avoid being distributed throughout the colony as inden-
tured servants, many fled to Haiti and Santo Domingo. One of the many slave
uprisings in Santo Domingo forced those who escaped death to flee, and some
came to St. Marys.

Visible from the harbor of St. Marys is the southern end of CUMBERLAND
ISLAND (*private*), the largest of the Georgia islands. It is owned almost entirely
by members of the Carnegie family, who have done much to preserve and
improve its natural beauty. Known by the Indians as Missoe and by the
Spaniards as San Pedro, Cumberland was given its present name by General
Oglethorpe at the request of Toonahowie, the adopted son of Tomochichi.
The Duke of Cumberland had given a gold watch to Toonahowie, who had
accompanied Oglethorpe to England in 1734. In 1736 Oglethorpe built Fort
St. Andrew on the northern tip of the island and a battery on the western
side to protect inland navigation, and at the southern end he erected the
larger Fort William to command the entrance of St. Marys River. In its early
days Fort William successfully resisted an attack of twenty-eight Spanish vessels
and considerable land forces. Cumberland afterward became a refuge for outlaws.

In 1932 an old canoe was excavated from the mud flats and exhibited at the
Smithsonian Institution as a relic of the Timucua Indians who formerly inhabited the island. It was a scooped-out pine log, shaped by the application
of fire and finished supposedly by shell implements.

The northern end of the island, marked by an abandoned lighthouse, is
owned by a number of people. This section was a favored summer resort from
1880 until about 1905, when pleasure seekers began frequenting the more easily
accessible beaches on Tybee and St. Simon islands. On the southern end Oglethorpe built a hunting lodge called DUNGENESS, the name of his country seat
in Kent, England. About 1784 it was purchased by General Nathanael Greene,
who erected a four-story tabby house with thirty rooms. General Henry (Lighthorse Harry) Lee, Revolutionary officer, died here in 1818 while visiting Mrs.
James Shaw, the daughter of General Greene, his former commander. In
1870 his son, Robert E. Lee, accompanied by several comrades, made a pilgrimage

TELFAIR ACADEMY OF ARTS AND SCIENCES, SAVANNAH

RAILROAD YARDS, ATLANTA

FIVE POINTS AT NIGHT, ATLANTA

WAR TANK, FORT BENNING

COLUMBUS

OLD STATE CAPITOL, MILLEDGEVILLE

THIRD STREET PARK, MACON

BROAD STREET AT NIGHT, AUGUSTA

TECHWOOD HOUSING PROJECT, ATLANTA

NEGRO SECTION, ATLANTA

JOHNSON SQUARE, SAVANNAH

OGLETHORPE STATUE, SAVANNAH

MUNICIPAL AIRPORT, ATLANTA

to the grave. The body remained at Dungeness until 1913, when it was transferred to the Lee Chapel of Washington and Lee University, Lexington, Virginia.
In 1893 the estate was bought by Thomas Carnegie, who built a large gabled
mansion on the foundation of the old Greene house.

The highway crosses the St. Marys River, **134.7 m.,** under an arch into
the State of Florida, 32 miles north of Jacksonville.

TOUR I A

*Junction US 17 — Bloody Marsh Battlefield — Sea Island — Fred-
erica; 11.5 m., St. Simon Causeway, Sea Island Rd., and Frederica
Rd.*

Bell Bus Line from Brunswick to Sea Island during summer; fare 50¢, round trip
75¢ — Shell and paved highways — Good hotel, boarding houses, cottages, and lunchrooms on St. Simon Island; fashionable hotel on Sea Island.

St. Simon Island and the small adjacent Sea Island are, with the exception of Tybee, Georgia's only coastal islands open to the public.
For many years St. Simon has been a popular summer resort for
Georgia people; the more recently developed Sea Island, offering a
luxurious hotel life, is a winter playground for northern visitors. On
these beautiful islands wooded stretches of moss-draped live oaks and
glossy-leafed cassenas mingle with colorful plantings of cerise crape
myrtles and pink and white oleanders. Evergreens and vivid flowers
grow the year round in the mild climate.

Historically, these Golden Isles are important landmarks in the New
World. Since its occupation by white men four centuries ago, St.
Simon Island has been successively under the dominion of Spain, England, the United States, the Confederate States of America, and again
the United States. As early as 1575, New World commodities, including wild turkeys, sassafras, and furs, were shipped to Europe from
the mouth of the Frederica River, and during the following century
Spanish presidios and missions flourished on the island. When English
colonists settled here in 1736, they found orange and olive groves that
had been set out by the Franciscan friars.

Although the Spanish had been moving their outposts southward for
the past half century, they resented the intrusion of England into territory claimed by their own explorers and were aroused to war; England
countered by building forts. In 1742 the Battle of Bloody Marsh as-

sured British supremacy in the New World. With the defeat of Spain, the military importance of the island ended, and the soldiers were given small grants of land. This was the beginning of the plantation system that made St. Simon Island, from the middle part of the eighteenth century until the War between the States, perhaps the most highly developed contiguous agricultural area in the country. The War between the States ended the gay plantation life here. After many of the houses had been burned and the fields laid waste, few of the old families returned. In the early 1900's wealthy northerners became interested in St. Simon, and its second era of prosperity began.

East from its junction with US 17 (*see* TOUR *1*) at the Visitors Club, **0 m.,** just north of Brunswick, the route crosses the ST. SIMON CAUSEWAY (*toll 30¢ round trip for car and driver, 10¢ for each additional person.*) Bordered with palmettos, the causeway stretches across land reclaimed from the Marshes of Glynn and tidal rivers.

GASCOIGNE BLUFF (L), **4.5 m.,** is a low, wooded, shell-covered bank overlooking the Frederica River. It is named for Captain James Gascoigne, a commander of the man-of-war *Hawk,* which convoyed the two ships bringing settlers to Georgia in 1736. Known as the Great Embarkation, this company included Oglethorpe, making his second trip to America, John and Charles Wesley, and many Salzburgers and Moravians. After leading his charges to Savannah, Gascoigne brought his sloop to St. Simon. He was placed in charge of the ships that Oglethorpe had stationed in the protected water below the bluff to defend the Georgia coast. This bluff was the scene of numerous encounters between the colonists and Spanish-Indian forces, and it was the site of two large sawmills during the era of lumber activity along the coast. Timber cut on St. Simon was used in building the first vessels for the U. S. Navy, including the frigate *Constitution,* launched in 1797 and later the subject of Oliver Wendell Holmes' poem "Old Ironsides." When the historic ship was repaired, timbers from St. Simon again were used.

Left from Gascoigne Bluff on a shell road to HAMILTON PLANTATION (*private*), **0.5 m.,** the winter home of Eugene W. Lewis, of Detroit. The two-story residence, showing New England Colonial features since it was remodeled in 1927, was built about 1880. The landscaped grounds include rose and azalea gardens, a formal garden, lily pools, and extensive lawns. The estate was first established about 1793 by James Hamilton, one of the wealthiest planters of the island, on land granted by King George II to Captain Gascoigne. According to Fanny Kemble (*see below*), the estate became "by far the finest on St. Simon Island" and in 1857 was purchased by James Hamilton Couper, who left it under the management of his brother, William Couper. After the War between the States, the estate was bought by a lumber company and a sawmill was operated here until 1906.

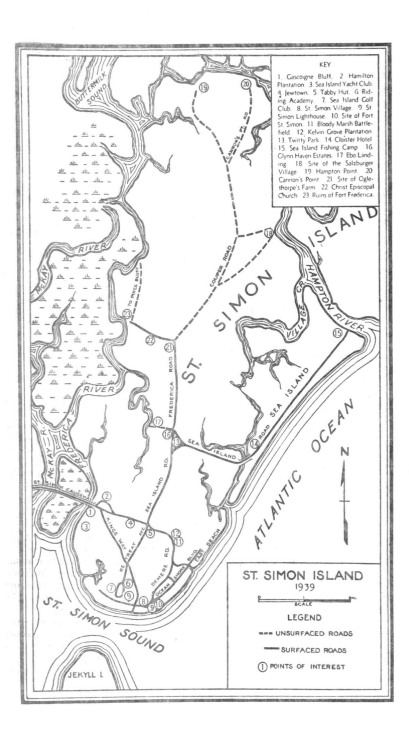

KEY

1. Gascoigne Bluff. 2. Hamilton Plantation. 3. Sea Island Yacht Club. 4. Jewtown. 5. Tabby Hut. 6. Riding Academy. 7. Sea Island Golf Club. 8. St. Simon Village. 9. St. Simon Lighthouse. 10. Site of Fort St. Simon. 11. Bloody Marsh Battlefield. 12. Kelvin Grove Plantation 13. Twitty Park. 14. Cloister Hotel 15. Sea Island Fishing Camp. 16. Glynn Haven Estates. 17. Ebo Landing. 18. Site of the Salzburger Village. 19. Hampton Point. 20. Cannon's Point. 21. Site of Oglethorpe's Farm. 22. Christ Episcopal Church. 23. Ruins of Fort Frederica.

ST. SIMON ISLAND
1939

SCALE

LEGEND

- - - UNSURFACED ROADS

——— SURFACED ROADS

① POINTS OF INTEREST

At **4.7 m.,** at the intersection with paved Kings Way, is a private road.

Right on this road to the SEA ISLAND YACHT CLUB (*reservations accepted*), **0.5 m.,** a white frame structure on landscaped lawns with curving shell drives. About two hundred yards west of the club is the Frederica River, part of the inland water route from Norfolk, Virginia, to Key West, Florida. In the protected water near the club wharf the U. S. Coast Guard has established a yacht basin and maintains both motor- and hand-power lifeboats.

JEWTOWN, **5.5 m.,** is a Negro village of small, shabby frame houses, with overgrown flower gardens and small patches of vegetables. The inhabitants, who are descendants of slaves, speak an almost unintelligible dialect. They derive most of their meager incomes from fishing and crabbing. The village developed about a store operated by Jewish merchants during the latter part of the nineteenth century and was named by Negroes who worked at the sawmill on Hamilton Plantation.

A low-ceiled TABBY HUT (R), **5.8 m.,** junction Retreat Ave. and Demere Rd., is the only remaining building of the Retreat Plantation slave quarters. Its thick, grayish walls blend into a background of moss-covered oaks.

Sea Island Road turns L. at this point.

Right **1 m.** on Retreat Avenue to the junction with Kings Way; R. (*straight ahead*) **0.5 m.** on Retreat Avenue to the RIDING ACADEMY (*horses for hire*).

SEA ISLAND GOLF CLUB (*greens fee, winter $3, summer $1.50*), **0.8 m.,** comprises two nine-hole golf courses (R); one is a typical inland links, with fairways bordered with massive oaks and pines, while the other, built along the river edge, resembles an English seaside course with sand traps and difficult water hazards. The two-story clubhouse, set in a cluster of large palms, is built around the tabby walls of an old barn which was a part of Retreat Plantation.

Retreat Plantation, once covering the southern part of the island, was the original Colonial grant to James Spalding, a Scot who came to Georgia in 1760. About 1775 the plantation, with its Colonial mansion, was bought by Major William Page, of South Carolina, who left it to his daughter Anne, wife of Thomas Butler King, planter, Congressman, and one of the organizers of the Southern Pacific Railroad. Under the supervision of the Kings, Retreat became well known for the quality of its sea-island cotton, the first grown in the United States. An olive tree, a few exotic plants, and an avenue of majestic live oaks are reminders of the beautiful plantation which John James Audubon greatly admired, when he was compelled to land on St. Simon from his schooner *Agnes*. He met King on the beach and was invited to dinner at Retreat. The old RETREAT SLAVE CEMETERY lies near the ninth green of the golf course.

Left on Kings Way from its junction with Retreat Avenue, at **2.8 m.** from Sea Island Road, is ST. SIMON VILLAGE, a permanent resort colony (*hotel, boarding houses, and cottages; fishing and crabbing equipment at St. Simon pier; deep-sea fishing, $2 a day a passenger; boat trips past Jekyll Island*). In the village are stores, novelty shops, lunchrooms, amusement concessions, and a motion picture theater. Extending into St. Simon Sound (Brunswick Harbor) from the foot of Mallory Street is the pier, from which Jekyll Island (*see* TOUR *1*) is visible across the sound. ST. SIMON LIGHTHOUSE (R), high above Neptune Park, flashes its beacon over St. Simon Sound. A light was first established at this point in 1804, marking the approach to the port of Brunswick. During the War between the States all the buildings at the light station were destroyed by Confederate forces, and it was not until 1871 that a new tower was completed. Adjacent to the lighthouse is the marked SITE OF FORT ST. SIMON, which was connected with Fort Frederica farther north by a military thoroughfare. On a bluff to the north Oglethorpe kept a guard, and on the east he erected Fort Delegal.

Left from St. Simon Village on Demere Road, which returns to Sea Island Road. On the BLOODY MARSH BATTLEFIELD, **5 m.**, the Spanish hold on Georgia territory was broken and the English dominance of southern America made secure. On June 28, 1742, a Spanish fleet of fifty-one vessels with five thousand men under Don Manuel de Montiano anchored off St. Simon Bar; after testing the bar thirty-six ships sailed into the harbor on July 5 under a four-hour bombardment from Fort St. Simon. Realizing that his troops were needed for defense, Oglethorpe spiked the St. Simon guns and retreated to Frederica; the Spanish landed and took possession of Fort St. Simon. Learning on July 7 from his rangers that the enemy was advancing upon him, the English general attacked with a force of Indians, rangers, and Highlanders and routed the Spanish. Retreating to the northern side of the marsh that he called the Grenadier Savannah, he waited in ambush for the attack that occurred about three o'clock in the afternoon. So many of the Spanish were killed or wounded that the battle was called Bloody Marsh because of the appearance of the field after the struggle. Although the Spanish still had superior forces, they were tricked by a stratagem into leaving the island. A Frenchman in the service of Oglethorpe had deserted and joined the Spanish ranks. Oglethorpe led the Spanish to believe that the deserter was a spy by sending him a letter indicating that his forces were strong and that he was expecting aid. While the Spanish, who intercepted the letter, deliberated, British reinforcements arrived from Charleston; on July 15 the enemy fleet sailed southward, never to return.

The Battle of Bloody Marsh was fought on what became KELVIN GROVE PLANTATION, owned by Thomas Cator, and later the property of James P. Postell, well-known collector of shells. The plantation is now owned by Mrs. Maxfield Parrish, wife of the celebrated painter. Mrs. Parrish, who spends the winters here, has made valuable contributions toward a knowledge of folk music by preserving the spirituals, work songs, and play songs of the island Negroes. Because these people have been out of touch with the mainland, their music is unusually free from outside influence. By encouraging the Negroes to gather in the evenings in a cabin on her plantation and sing their own melodies, Mrs. Parrish has rediscovered many forgotten tunes.

At **6 m.** on Demere Road is the junction with Sea Island Road.

TWITTY PARK, **8 m.,** on Sea Island Road, is a triangular wooded plot at the junction with Sea Island Causeway (R) and with Frederica Road (L), now the main route.

Right 1.8 m. on Sea Island Causeway is SEA ISLAND (*tennis, badminton, archery, golf, trapshooting, horseback riding, hunting, fishing, and fresh- and salt-water swimming*), a well-known resort developed by Howard E. Coffin. At the center of a group of stucco buildings on well-landscaped grounds is the

CLOISTER HOTEL (L), designed by Addison Mizner in a modified Spanish style. The three-story building with Spanish tile roof is built around tropically planted courtyards. The terrace of the Cloister Apartment Annex faces the river, where private boats can be anchored; these quiet apartments are popular with guests not interested in the gayer hotel activities. On the beach side of the hotel is the casino, overlooking the ocean, and adjoining it is an outdoor swimming pool used summer and winter. Left from the Cloister on Sea Island Drive is a residential colony along the beach.

SEA ISLAND FISHING CAMP (*fishing equipment and guides*), 6.3 m., is (L) a rustic camp overlooking the Hampton River.

GLYNN HAVEN ESTATES, 8.5 m. on Frederica Road, is a small summer colony built around a lake that is well stocked with fresh-water fish. At Glynn Haven is the junction with a dirt road.

Left on this road to EBO LANDING, 0.5 m., on Dunbar Creek, the point where cargoes of slaves were landed. On one occasion a group from the Ebo tribe refused to submit to slavery; trusting that the waters which had brought them to this country would carry them back to their native land, they were led by their chief into the water and, singing tribal songs, disappeared under the waves. Even yet Negroes will not fish in these waters, for they imagine they hear in the murmur of the river the songs of the Eboes.

At the junction with unpaved Couper Road, 10 m., Frederica Road turns L.

Right on Couper Road at 0.5 m. is the junction with another dirt road; R. here 1 m. on this second road to the SITE OF THE SALZBURGER VILLAGE. This community was settled by a group of persecuted Lutherans who accompanied Oglethorpe to St. Simon Island. These industrious people lived almost entirely from the yield of their lands, growing foodstuffs and raising mulberry trees for silkworm culture.

At 5 m. on Couper Road is a fork.

1. Left from the fork 2 m. to HAMPTON POINT, at the northern tip of the island. Here are the ruins of the house and garden of the old Hampton Plantation, one of the Georgia estates of Major Pierce Butler, a member of the Continental Congress (1787-88), of the Constitutional Convention (1787), and a United States Senator from South Carolina (1789-96 and 1803-04). Major Butler lived on this plantation during the winters from 1795 to 1815, and in 1804 was visited by Aaron Burr, who was seeking a refuge after his duel with Alexander Hamilton. His plantation was almost self-sustaining, for his slaves were engaged in tanning, shoemaking, and the manufacture of clothes in addition to their domestic and farm duties. After amassing a fortune, Butler moved to Philadelphia, and the "big house" was almost in ruins by 1838, when Pierce Butler, grandson of the founder, brought Frances Anne (Fanny) Kemble, his English actress wife, to live at Hampton. Mrs. Butler was so repelled by the institution of slavery that she voiced her hostility in bitter letters to her friends. It was the winter of 1838-39, spent here and on Butler Island (*see* TOUR 1), which she described in her *Journal of a Residence on a Georgian Plantation*. Following the War between the States, Frances Butler Leigh, Fanny Kemble's daughter, came to live on the Georgia plantations. Her *Ten Years on a Georgian Plantation Since the War* gives a softer picture of plantation life than her mother's book.

2. Right from the fork 1.5 m. to CANNON'S POINT, the site of the plantation which the Scottish John Couper, Georgia statesman, bought in 1793. He developed his plantation into what has been called Georgia's first agricultural experiment station because he planted every tree, flower, and shrub that he believed would grow in this semitropical climate. He was especially interested in his imported French olive trees which throve so well that a good grade of olive oil was produced from their fruit. All that remains of this princely estate are a few shrubs and a Persian date palm which still bears a yearly crop. The kitchen fireplace in the ruins of the old mansion has been rebuilt by the Cloister Hotel as an outdoor grill, used by guests for barbecues and oyster roasts.

Little St. Simon Island, across the Hampton River, is visible from this point.

The SITE OF OGLETHORPE'S FARM (L), 10.2 m. on Frederica Road, is indicated by a stone marker. The orange trees near-by are said to be seedlings from those planted by Oglethorpe, who cultivated oranges, figs, and grapes on his fifty-acre farm. Orange Hall, the two-story dwelling that he erected here, was the only home Oglethorpe ever owned in America, for he preferred the military atmosphere of Frederica to the agricultural and religious interests of Savannah.

Here the highway is bordered with royal poincianas, aflame with scarlet blossoms in summer.

CHRIST EPISCOPAL CHURCH (L), 10.5 m., a low, gabled, frame structure, is surrounded by the graves of early settlers and soldiers, amid a grove of moss-hung, giant live oaks. The present structure, in which regular services are still held, was erected in 1875 to replace the first church, in which both John and Charles Wesley preached. While he was fulfilling his duties as secretary to Oglethorpe on St. Simon Island, Charles had his historic quarrel with Oglethorpe which resulted in the former's departure for Savannah and, later, for England. WESLEY OAK, a large tree shading the churchyard, marks the place where the Wesleys preached to the colonists and the friendly Indians.

The RUINS OF FORT FREDERICA (R), 11.5 m., two small tabby chambers surmounted by a low parapet, are overgrown with vines and mellowed by the passage of years and the wash of the near-by river. In 1736, for purposes of expansion and defense, Oglethorpe established here as a military outpost the town and fort named in honor of Frederick, the only son of George II of England. Selecting a site on the southern branch of the Altamaha River (known locally as the Frederica River), he erected a fort on a small bluff ten feet above high-water mark, at a strategic point commanding a curve of the river. In a short time this temporary fort was replaced by a four-bastioned fortification with tabby walls.

Upon the cleared ground of a thirty- or forty-acre Indian field behind the fort, Oglethorpe built the town of Frederica in the shape of a crescent. Streets were laid off at right angles and lined with orange trees. Each soldier was given a sixty- by ninety-foot lot, on which he built a temporary bower house of palmetto leaves; these were later replaced by log houses, but the barracks and storehouse were constructed of tabby. Thickly wooded forests to the north and east, the boggy marshes of the river to the west, and the cedar log wall and moat protected the town from attack. Nothing remains of this seaport town that at one time had a thousand inhabitants.

TOUR 2

(Chattanooga, Tenn.) — Dalton — Atlanta — Griffin — Perry — Valdosta — (Lake City, Fla.); US 41.

Tennessee Line to Florida Line, 368.4 m. — Roadbed hard-surfaced throughout, one-third concrete — Nashville, Chattanooga & St. Louis R.R. parallels route between Tennessee Line and Atlanta; the Central of Georgia Ry. between Atlanta and Griffin; and the Southern Ry. between Griffin and Fort Valley, also between Cordele and the Florida Line — All types of accommodations in cities; limited elsewhere. Note: Route between Barnesville and Perry carries (1939) only State 7 markers.

Section a. TENNESSEE LINE *to* ATLANTA, *112.6 m., US 41.*

Between Chattanooga and Atlanta US 41, known as the Dixie Highway, winds through the green Appalachian Valley where the mountains, though not spectacular, have a calm beauty. This valley was the heart of the Cherokee Nation until 1838, when thousands of Indians were exiled from their Georgia homes. The highway closely follows the route taken by General Sherman in 1864, when Federal forces drove the Confederates back to Atlanta and ravaged a strip of land sixty miles wide through the state.

But few traces of war remain. In this section a considerable annual income is derived from textile mills, mining, and such farm products as cotton, corn, small grains, and fruits. The towns are attractive not for fine architecture but for their luxuriant trees and grass and for their background of distant mountains. Hills and valleys bear a thick growth of oak, shortleaf pine, gum, hickory, and fruit trees. Planting is adapted to the rolling red clay hills and the furrows are plowed in curves. Settlement is rather scattered, and Negro labor is scarce. Most of the farmhouses are unpainted, but bright flowers bloom in the grassless yards.

US 41 crosses the Tennessee Line, **0 m.,** at a point 11.2 miles south-east of Chattanooga, Tennessee.

At **1.3 m.** is the junction with an unpaved road.

Right on this road to LAKE WINNEPEESAUKEE (*free picnic grounds; fishing $1 a day; swimming 25¢ adults, 10¢ children; boats 50¢ an hour*), **1.5 m.,** a fifteen-acre lake fed by thirty-five submerged springs from which limestone water flows at the rate of 30,000 gallons an hour. The clear lake is surrounded by a circle of small oaks that provide a dark setting for its tranquil beauty.

RINGGOLD, **7.8 m.** (785 alt., 684 pop.), seat of Catoosa County, was incorporated in 1847. Seventeen years later the town was almost entirely destroyed during the fighting in this section after the Chattanooga campaign. Rebuilding has been slow, and Ringgold is now a quiet farm community.

The BAPTIST CHURCH (L), erected in the early 1840's, was one of the few buildings left standing. The two-story structure has been remodeled and enlarged, and the hand-made red bricks have been covered with pale yellow stucco.

The CATOOSA COUNTY COURTHOUSE (R), was spared during the Federal occupation because the upper floor served as a Masonic hall. According to local accounts, departing soldiers set fire to the straw on which the wounded had lain, but the flames were quickly extinguished by two Ringgold women. The three-story, red brick building, erected in the 1850's, stands in a grove of elms with whitewashed trunks. A narrow double staircase leads to the courtroom on the second floor and to the Masonic hall above it.

At **15 m.** is the junction with a graveled road.

Left on this road is the village of TUNNEL HILL, **0.3 m.** (853 alt., 211 pop.), which grew up as the result of developments by the Western & Atlantic Railroad. The town was incorporated in 1851 under a commission form of government which still exists. Once a busy railroad town, Tunnel Hill is now a quiet rural community.

Here, on November 27, 1863, the last battle of Sherman's Chattanooga campaign was fought. Patrick R. Cleburne, covering Bragg's retreat to Dalton, took up his position above a deep gorge, and Hooker, whose heavy guns had not arrived, allowed his impatient troops to attack with small arms only. Under the Confederate fire they were repulsed and forced to take cover along the railroad embankment. In 1864 Union and Confederate forces fought for possession of the railroad until the Confederates were forced back.

A strong English influence is evident in the compact old brick buildings that line the shady street. The old hotel, no longer used, is constructed of hand-made bricks covered with stucco marked off in blocks and has a second-story wooden porch jutting over the sidewalk. The depot, erected in 1848 when the railroad tunnel was begun, is built of stones dug from the embankment.

Right from Tunnel Hill about **0.5 m.** to the OLD TUNNEL (*reached by walking*

along the railroad tracks), one of the first railway tunnels in the South, built
as part of the Western & Atlantic Railroad. The old stone structure, no longer
used since the construction of an adjacent new tunnel, is so thickly covered with
bushes that it is visible only at close range. It was hewed with pick and axe
through the Chattoogata (local pronunciation Chat toóga) Ridge. Work was
begun in 1848 and the first train passed through in 1850.

DALTON, **22.7 m.** (775 alt., 8,160 pop.), seat of Whitfield County, is
second only to Rome as a manufacturing center for northwestern
Georgia. Smoke-blackened factories line the railroad tracks that run
through the heart of town, but the residential districts are clean and
attractive. Encircled by the blue ranges of the Cohutta Mountains
and planted with large trees whose branches arch across the street,
Dalton is beautiful in spring and summer, when oaks, elms, and weeping willows form a mass of blowing green. The sidewalks are bordered with broad grass plots sloping down to the street. The houses
seldom follow the classic tradition of the Deep South, but more frequently conform to the late nineteenth-century style with gables, turrets, and cupolas.

Dalton was incorporated in 1847 and became the county seat when
Whitfield County was formed in 1851. During these years the town
developed as a shipping point for the copper mined at Ducktown, Tennessee; and during the 1850's the ore was hauled to Dalton in wagon
trains.

After the Confederate defeat at Missionary Ridge late in 1863, General Bragg retreated to Dalton, where he resigned his command and
was replaced by General Joseph E. Johnston. Here Johnston wintered
and reorganized the Army of Tennessee in preparation for the coming
struggle with Sherman over Atlanta. At a religious service in Dalton
during the winter of 1863-64, General Hood was baptized by General
Polk, the Episcopal bishop from Louisiana who was later killed at the
Battle of Kennesaw Mountain.

Dalton is the center of the candlewick-bedspread industry, which
brings to northwestern Georgia an annual income of several million
dollars. The unbleached domestic is stamped with a design before it
is distributed to housewives, who draw and cut the threads and wash
the finished bedspread. Along the highway between Dalton and
Marietta tufted spreads, pillow cases, bath mats, and rugs are hung
on display from clotheslines and fences in front of the farmhouses.
The first impetus was given to the tufting industry in 1919 by Mrs.
M. G. Cannon, Jr., of Dalton, who succeeded in arousing the interest
of New York department stores in this handicraft. Many farmers have
left the fields to help their wives with tufting, and entire families sit
at work in yards and doorways. Spreads are also made in the Dalton

factories, both by hand and machinery, for sale to outside markets.

KENNER & RAUSCHENBERG FACTORY (*open to visitors*), 78 Morris St., manufactures tufted bedspreads. About 28,000 spreads are shipped every month from this factory, which employs about 350 people.

CRAFT BEDSPREAD PLANT (*open to visitors*), facing the railroad tracks, employs 375 workers in the manufacture of chenille and needlepunch bedspreads at the rate of about 45,000 monthly.

The HUFF HOUSE (*private*), 71 Selvidge St., served during the winter of 1864 as headquarters of General Joseph E. Johnston between the Chattanooga and Atlanta campaigns. Johnston's occupancy is commemorated by a small bronze plaque on the front lawn. The gray, white-trimmed cottage, with four gables, has been altered but little since that time.

RESACA, 38.8 m. (654 alt., 121 pop.), was first named Dublin by the Irish laborers who constructed the state railroad and built a large camp at the site of the present town. After the Mexican War the town was renamed by returned veterans in memory of their victory at the Battle of Resaca de la Palma. In May, 1864, this town was the scene of three days' hard fighting between Union and Confederate forces. This action was the first major engagement resulting from Sherman's turning movement through Snake Creek Gap, which forced Johnston to abandon his advanced position along Rocky Face Ridge. The Federal attacks on the Confederate entrenchments were driven back, but a further flanking move by the Federal troops caused the retreat of the smaller Confederate force. The CONFEDERATE CEMETERY here contains the graves of 500 soldiers.

The OOSTANAULA RIVER, 39 m., is spanned by a $90,000 concrete bridge (*excellent fishing for bream, black bass, goggle-eyed perch, and, in smaller quantities, rainbow trout*).

At the Calhoun city limits a rock MEMORIAL ARCH, 40.5 m., has on one side a bronze statue of a Confederate soldier, on the other that of a "doughboy." Facing the arch is a bronze STATUE OF SEQUOYAH (1770-1843), inventor of the Cherokee alphabet. The son of an Indian trader of Dutch ancestry and his Cherokee wife, Sequoyah bore the American name of George Gist, sometimes corrupted to Guess. He spent his boyhood in Tennessee and later moved to this section of Georgia. A skilled silversmith, he had his name written by a friend so that he could fashion a die to stamp his articles. This signature led him to ponder over the white men's "talking leaves," and to work out an alphabet for his people.

It is known that he spent twelve years (1809-21) devising a system of eighty-five characters, each representing a monosyllable of the Cherokee language. To preserve his work he carefully marked each symbol on a sheet of bark. One day his superstitious wife threw the sheets into the fire, but within less than a year he had reconstructed his alphabet. The Indians scorned his invention until he proved that he could communicate with his six-year-old daughter by means of the marks. The Council of Chiefs then approved his work, and soon thousands had learned to read and write. The *Book of Genesis* was printed, and a newspaper, the *Cherokee Phoenix,* was published.

In 1822 Sequoyah visited the western Cherokee in Arkansas and later moved with them to Oklahoma, where he was active in the political life of the tribe. Setting out to find the lost tribe of Cherokee who had moved West before the Revolutionary War, he visited California. On his return he became ill and died before reaching home. His name is perpetuated by the giant sequoias or redwoods of California, and Oklahoma has placed a statue of him in the Statuary Hall of the National Capitol.

Left from the Sequoyah statue on a good dirt road to a massive granite shaft with bronze plaques indicating the SITE OF NEW ECHOTA (L), **1.8 m.**, the capital of the Cherokee Nation. In 1819 the Cherokee selected this place for their assemblies, and on October 20, 1820, they met here and adopted a republican form of government. The national assembly which they formed consisted of a council and a national committee of which John Ross was elected president. On November 12, 1825, the council resolved to build a permanent capital on the assembly site, which was surveyed and marked off in lots. Business enterprises included a shoe store, a tavern, and a furniture shop. A school and a courthouse were built, and in 1828 the citizens established the *Cherokee Phoenix,* their official newspaper printed in Sequoyah's syllabary as well as in English.

Near New Echota in 1821 the Moravian church set up the Oothcaloga Mission, which continued its work among the Indians until 1833, when the missions were closed by order of the state. This was one of the maneuvers in Georgia's plan to acquire the Cherokee lands (*see* HISTORY). On December 28, 1828, the state had passed a law extending its jurisdiction over their territory. Ten years later, despite much intercession for the Cherokee and their recognition as a nation by the Federal government, Georgia succeeded in securing permission to remove the Indians. General Winfield Scott set up his headquarters at New Echota and effected, with the aid of 4,000 Federal and state troops and 4,000 volunteers, a ruthless removal of 13,000 Cherokee to the West.

CALHOUN, **42.9 m.** (657 alt., 2,371 pop.), seat of Gordon County, is a trim town, in which oaks and elms form a cool green arch above the highway. Its original name, Oothcaloga (Ind., at the place of the beaver dams), was changed in 1850 to honor John Caldwell Calhoun, Secretary of State under President Tyler. The town was incorporated in 1852. Lying in the direct path of Sherman's march, it was almost completely destroyed in 1864, but was rebuilt after the war. The town has cotton mills manufacturing sheeting and two firms distributing tufted bedspreads.

ADAIRSVILLE, 50.7 m. (708 alt., 765 pop.), has an old-fashioned town square not visible from the highway. The red brick shops have small wooden arcades that cover the sidewalk all around the square, and one shop has an upper porch finished in intricate scrollwork.

The village, approximately halfway between Atlanta and Chattanooga, Tennessee, was established in 1837 as the northern terminus of the Western & Atlantic Railroad. A large part of its population and income were lost when the repair shops, which had been built here, were removed after the line was continued to Chattanooga. The destruction of the town by Federal troops and the dismantling of a large gun and powder factory caused a further decline. A textile mill and one of the largest flour mills in the state are the principal industrial plants.

Right from the railroad station at Adairsville to the first road across the railroad tracks, 0.1 m.; R. on this road, which roughly parallels the tracks, to the junction with another road at a brick store, 5.3 m.; R. on this road to BARNSLEY GARDENS, 8.3 m. (L). Among the group of plantation buildings, in gardens now neglected, are the ruins of the handsome brick main house, begun in 1859 but never completed. Surrounded by a rank growth of trees, shrubs, and weeds, it stands roofless, its central tower crumbling, its handsomely finished Palladian windows broken and their shutters hanging loose. In the sunken garden beside it grow dwarf boxwood and a tangle of fragrant flowers.

In the early 1830's Godfrey Barnsley, English consul and wealthy merchant of Savannah, bought 10,000 acres here and built the small frame house which still stands to the right of the main structure. The construction of a permanent group of three detached brick houses was begun in 1859; only the frame house and the brick left wing are now occupied. Hand-pressed brick, woodwork from England, silver key plates, and finely wrought girandoles were used throughout the principal structure. In the tower was a reservoir for running water and in the chimney a smaller tank for hot water.

In 1859 P. J. Berckmans, a Belgian landscape artist then living in Augusta, set out flowers and rare trees, including English and Japanese yews, Nordmann's fir, and a California redwood. There are also beautiful hemlocks, Scotch rowans, and giant lindens. Many roses, growing profusely, include double varieties of the Cherokee rose.

The estate is now in the possession of Mrs. Addie B. Saylor, who owns 5,000 acres and uses the two rear houses. In one of the old kitchens, now used as a dining room, is a fireplace built to cook sufficient food for a hundred people. To the rear of the main house is an ivy-covered spring house. A path along one of the terraces is scrupulously avoided by Negroes, who insist that ghosts walk there by night.

It is generally believed that Augusta Evans Wilson used Barnsley Gardens as the setting for her novel *St. Elmo* (*see* COLUMBUS).

CASSVILLE, 62.5 m. (821 alt., 165 pop.), now an unpretentious farm community, became the most thriving town in northwestern Georgia soon after its incorporation in 1843. It had a population of 2,000 and supported the Cassville Female College and the Cherokee Baptist College for men. Its decline began when citizens, proud of their cultural institutions and fine homes, refused to allow the Western & Atlantic Railroad to enter the town. In 1864 the two colleges were burned and the town entirely destroyed by Federal cavalrymen; most of the population scattered and never returned.

A small monument left of the highway commemorates the stand made here on May 21, 1864, by Johnston against Sherman's army. More than three hundred soldiers are buried in the Confederate cemetery.

The GEORGIA ART POTTERY SHOP, 53.8 m., is a neat log cabin in which the potter makes several kinds of jars and vases, bringing out the beautiful colors of the local clay by baking. Since the heat is not absolutely uniform in an oven. fired with coal, the resulting shades are not always predictable, but blue ware is a specialty.

In ATCO, 67.2 m., a GOODYEAR TIRE AND RUBBER PLANT (*open to visitors*) employs 950 workers and uses 20,000 bales of cotton annually in the manufacture of cord and fabric. The brick plant and the mill village stand right of the highway. The white frame dwellings, similar but not identical, are neatly kept, and their gardens contain many flowers.

Right from Atco on an improved dirt road to the junction with another dirt road, 5.7 m.; R. on this road to the junction with a rough dirt lane (*impassable in wet weather*), 6.1 m.; R. on this lane to the intersection with another lane, 7.2 m.; L. about a hundred yards to SALTPETER CAVE (*adm. 25¢*), one of the few caves in the state that was ever developed commercially. It received its name during the War between the States when saltpeter was mined here by the Confederacy for use in making gunpowder; the mining was later abandoned.

The rooms that form the caverns have never been fully explored, but the recently installed electric lights show the striking stalactite and stalagmite formations characteristic of limestone caves. The main entrance leads down a long stairway into a chamber, approximately forty by sixty feet, where a small platform has been constructed for dancing. From this chamber a series of intricate passages and open caverns leads to other rooms and many stalactite formations.

The rich and varied deposits in the Bartow County mineral belt, which US 41 crosses south of Atco, include barite, bauxite, manganese, ocher, iron, brick clays, shale, talc, and limestone.

CARTERSVILLE, 69.1 m. (787 alt., 5,250 pop.), seat of Bartow County, is attractive for the well-kept appearance of its houses rather than for their architecture. The town was founded in 1832 on the site of the railroad underpass south of this point and was called Birmingham for the English coal and iron metropolis. Later it was moved northward to this site, incorporated in 1850, and named Cartersville for Farish Carter, a prominent landowner of the vicinity. Only two houses survived the Federal occupation in 1864.

ROSELAWN, Market St. (R), now the property of Madison Bell, was formerly the home of Sam Jones (1847-1906), the dynamic Methodist evangelist. The large yellow house has ornate gables; during Jones' lifetime the parlor ceiling was resplendent with clouds and floating angels.

The SAM JONES TABERNACLE, W. Main St. R. of Roselawn, where the evangelist once swayed large crowds, was erected in 1886 on property donated by the city. Like the tabernacles of the various camp-meeting grounds throughout the state, it has a dirt floor and open sides. In order to attend services many people pitched tents on the ten-acre plot surrounding the building. The structure was used for services until 1925, and many prominent ministers preached here, but it is now open only on the Fourth of July for an "all day singing with dinner on the grounds."

FRIENDSHIP MONUMENT, in a public square by the railroad tracks, is a small monument on a rock foundation, erected by Mark A. Cooper at old Etowah in 1860 as a tribute to thirty-eight "friends and creditors." During the panic of 1857, when Cooper was forced to buy his partner's interest in the Etowah Manufacturing and Mining Company for $200,000, his friends endorsed his notes. Three years later he returned the paid notes and erected the monument, which was moved to Cartersville in 1927.

1. Right from Cartersville on Main St., which follows State 61, to the junction with a dirt road, 0.2 m.; L. 0.9 m. on this road to the junction with another dirt road; L. 1.2 m. on this to the Tumlin residence (L), a two-story, yellow frame house. From this house a dirt lane leads L. a few hundred yards through cotton fields to the ETOWAH INDIAN MOUNDS, on the property of Louis Tumlin and his widowed sister-in-law, Mrs. George Tumlin (*ask directions at Tumlin house*).

Grouped about the site of an Indian village are three large ceremonial mounds and three almost indistinguishable burial mounds, all surrounded by a moat that could be flooded in times of danger. The mound upon which it is supposed a temple was built was explored by the Bureau of American Ethnology in 1882 and again in 1925-27 by Warren K. Moorehead, Director of Archeology at Phillips Academy, Andover, Massachusetts. The largest mound, which archeologists believe was constructed for the public house or chief's dwelling, has never been explored, and a cotton patch now grows on its flat top, which was once reached by an earthen ramp. Sixty-five feet high and covering almost three acres, this is one of the largest aboriginal mounds in the United States.

From the site, principally from the smallest mound, have been excavated many bodies, stone effigies of human beings and eagles, clay idol heads, bone awls, and hundreds of shells, ornaments, and weapons. Moorehead has identified the inhabitants of the village as prehistoric Indians of the Muskhogean family. Since he unearthed artifacts made of copper from Lake Superior, pottery from Tennessee, and shells from the Gulf Coast, he concluded that these Indians were traders and travelers. According to Moorehead, the mounds were built of dirt taken from the great moat.

On State 61 at Pettit's Creek, **2.6 m.**, is a junction with a dirt road; L. **1 m.** on this road to WALNUT GROVE (*private*), built in the 1840's by R. M. Young. Large boxwoods almost conceal the house of slave-made bricks with its square white columns and hanging balcony. The beautiful walnut woodwork of the interior was made from trees cut on the plantation. Walnut Grove was the childhood home of General P. M. B. Young, consul general to Russia in 1885 and minister to Guatemala and Honduras in 1893.

On State 61 at Shaw's Store, a frame structure, is the junction with the dirt Euharlee Rd., **2.7 m.**

Right (*straight ahead*) **5 m.** from Shaw's Store on the Euharlee Rd. is VALLEY VIEW (L) (*private*), its entrance marked by two stone pillars and a gate. A driveway leads from the entrance through deep woods to the house, which overlooks a wide valley. An iron gate opens on the garden, bounded on one side by Carolina cherry trees and on the other by boxwood. Dwarf box, tree box, English laurel, spruce and fir trees, crape myrtle, Cape jasmine, and forsythia grow luxuriantly.

The house, built by Colonel Robert Sproull in 1840, has six white Ionic columns on brick foundations set out from the porch. The bricks were made of red valley clay, baked by slaves on the plantation; one brick still bears the maker's handprint. The vegetable gardens, slave quarters, and brick water tower in the rear complete the picture of a plantation home.

During the War between the States the iron balustrade of the upper porch was removed by Union soldiers and carried to the Cooper Iron Foundry, where it was made into cannon balls. For three months General George W. Schofield occupied the second floor and kept his horses in the parlor below; the grand piano was used as a feed trough.

This house contains many handsome pieces of furniture made by a German cabinetmaker, as well as rare objects brought by Sproull Fouche, the builder's grandson, from Rumania, where he was an attaché of the American legation.

On the Euharlee Rd. at **6.9 m.** is the entrance to ETOWAH CLIFFS (*private*) and MALBONE (*adm. 25¢*). From three mail boxes a field road leads L. **0.5 m.** to a fork.

a. Right from the fork to Etowah Cliffs, the house built by William Henry Stiles of Savannah for a summer home. This rambling, red brick house, on a bluff overlooking a bend of the Etowah River, has spacious verandas on both floors and is surrounded by old-fashioned gardens containing boxwood, large magnolias, water oaks, and mimosa trees.

In 1838 Stiles was appointed by the Federal government to make certain payments of gold to the Cherokee and, while here on this mission, was so impressed with the beauty of the landscape that he accepted a section of the valley in payment for his services and built a frame house. In 1850 he added a wing that had walls two feet thick, made of brick molded by slaves on the plantation; another brick wing was added later.

Stiles, who served as minister to Austria (1845-49), brought many of the furnishings from Vienna; the mantels and window sills of the house are of Viennese marble. The large bedrooms, each with a lady's dressing room, contain four-poster beds, and the dining room has a fine collection of silver, old willow ware, and Bohemian glass. Almost all the furnishings were hauled to Savannah upon General Sherman's approach.

b. Left from the fork to Malbone, the summer home of Robert Stiles, brother of W. H. Stiles. The red brick house, on a tract adjoining the plantation of Etowah Cliffs, contains many beautiful paintings and much rare old furniture.

2. Left from Cartersville on US 411 to the junction with an unpaved road, 14.3 m.; L. on this road to the entrance (L) to IN THE VALLEY (*adm. 25¢*), 17.1 m., once the estate of Corra Harris (1869-1935), the Georgia novelist, who was honored by the degree of Doctor of Letters by both the University of Georgia and Oglethorpe University. She is best known for *A Circuit Rider's Wife,* a novel describing her early experiences as wife of a young minister. From the entrance the road winds 1 m. through fields and woods to the rambling log house set on a knoll surrounded by pines. A short distance from the house is the log study where Mrs. Harris wrote, and just across the lawn in front of the house is the CORRA HARRIS MEMORIAL CHAPEL, built of local stone and designed by Ralph Adams Cram, architect for the Cathedral of St. John the Divine in New York. The chapel was erected in 1936 by three nephews as a memorial to Mrs. Harris. Just inside the entrance are cabinets containing mementoes of the author's literary career; inside at the foot of the altar is her tomb.

The house stands on the site of an old camping ground of the Indians, and the living room was originally a one-room cabin built in 1830 by Pine Log, a Chero-kee chieftain for whom a near-by village is named. After her husband's death in 1912, Mrs. Harris purchased 300 acres of land and retired to write. Although the house is on a hill, she said she named it In the Valley because that year she was "in the valley of the shadow of death." The author's will requested that open house be maintained here and issued an invitation to her friends "to visit this place, not to honor me, but that they may rest here and be my guests."

At **70.5 m.** on US 41 is the junction with a private dirt road.

Right on this road a few yards to BARITE MINES (*no visitors*). The mineral is mined in open pits by means of steam shovels, loaded on tram cars, and carried to a washer where it is prepared for shipment. This heavy, non-metallic mineral, bluish-white in color, is used extensively in the manufacture of paints, rubber goods, and barium chemicals. These mines, among the largest producers of barite in the country, have been in operation since 1917, when the World War cut off importations from Germany.

At **71 m.** is the junction with a dirt road.

Left on this road, which roughly follows the banks of the Etowah River, to the COOPER IRON WORKS, 3.1 m., formerly the Etowah Manufacturing and Mining Company, about which the town of Etowah developed after the company had been established here by Mark A. Cooper in 1845. A blast furnace and foundry were constructed, as well as a rolling mill, a nail factory, a flour mill, two saw-mills, and two corn mills. The population of the town grew to 2,000, and shops, warehouses, and a hotel were built. The iron was shipped to England to be converted into steel.

The bloomery furnace (L) has walls several feet thick, and its tall chimney rises among the treetops. During the War between the States Sherman used this furnace as a powder magazine and destroyed it before passing on to Atlanta. The flour mill (R), now a ruin, was five stories high and had a daily output of from 200 to 300 barrels of flour.

After the Federal occupation the town dwindled to nothing, and the site is now known principally as an attractive picnic ground. The muddy river flows silently past the old buildings, whose stone walls have crumbled and are covered with a thick growth of running vines. In the warm seasons trumpet flowers show scarlet against the gray stones.

The ETOWAH RIVER, 71.3 m., a sluggish, muddy stream, rises in the mountains of north Georgia and converges with the Oostanaula at Rome to form the Coosa.

ALLATOONA, 77.1 m. (866 alt., 100 pop.), has been a village since the early 1830's, when gold was discovered in the vicinity. The period of greatest mining activity was during the 1840's and 1850's.

On October 5, 1864, Confederate troops attacked the ridge overlooking the Western & Atlantic Railroad tracks, which the Union forces were holding. The Federals were driven from outside parapets into their redoubts, but, after desperate fighting, the Confederate forces gave up their attack. On the night before the battle General John Murray Corse in Rome received a signal message from General Sherman's forces on the summit of Kennesaw Mountain, with instructions to hasten to Allatoona and take command of the fort on the Allatoona hills. This incident inspired the evangelist P. P. Bliss to write his religious song "Hold the Fort, for I Am Coming."

A Confederate soldier is buried in the GRAVE OF THE UNKNOWN SOLDIER (L) beside the railroad tracks. This memorial is cared for by track hands of the Western & Atlantic Railroad.

ACWORTH, 80.1 m. (915 alt., 1,163 pop.), is a small town with a line of red brick stores along the highway. The design of the frame houses, with scrollwork and gables, is that of the 1890's. Although there was a village here long before the War between the States, the town was not incorporated until 1860. Small hosiery mills are the principal industrial plants. During the Battle of Kennesaw Mountain (*see below*) Sherman made his headquarters at Acworth.

KENNESAW, 87.1 m. (1,093 alt., 426 pop.), was for many years known as Big Shanty because it was the site of the Big Shanty Distillery Company. The village was not incorporated until 1887, when it was given its present name. On June 11, 1861, Camp McDonald, a training camp for Confederate soldiers, was established here. Although numerous Union troops passed through the town, there was little action until October 4, 1864, when a Confederate force attacked a small Federal garrison and took a number of prisoners after a short encounter. Adjacent to the railroad tracks (L), marked and enclosed by a fence, is the site where the engine *General* was seized by Andrews' raiders (*see* ATLANTA).

KENNESAW MOUNTAIN (1,809 alt.), 90.8 m., is (R) divided into two peaks, Big Kennesaw and Little Kennesaw, both covered with trees. An airplane beacon on the summit is reached by means of a steep, winding road (*climb should be made on foot*). In 1939 the Federal government purchased more than two thousand acres extending westward from Kennesaw Mountain and has made plans to acquire the part of the mountain owned by the Kennesaw Mountain Memorial Association in order to incorporate the entire area into the Kennesaw Mountain National Battlefield Park.

Some historians call the Battle of Kennesaw Mountain the outstanding battle of Sherman's Atlanta campaign. After Johnston evacuated Allatoona, he entrenched his forces on Kennesaw, Lost, and Pine Mountains, which formed a triangle protecting Marietta and the railroad; the Confederate line was about two miles long, and held a very strong position. The terrain was hilly and densely wooded, with tangled vines overrunning the slopes of the mountains, and a steady rain for almost three weeks had made a concentrated advance by Union troops an impossibility. Sherman, however, divided his forces to cover all the Confederate positions and moved slowly up, attacking the line between Kennesaw and Pine Mountains on June 14, 1864. After a day's heavy fighting, the Confederates abandoned their position on Pine Mountain and by the following day were entrenched between Kennesaw and Lost Mountains. The Union troops continued to push forward, and on June 17 forced the Confederates to abandon Lost Mountain. Johnston then centered his forces on Kennesaw Mountain, with Hood covering the town of Marietta and Hardee protecting the railroad.

The Confederates were able to look down upon the Federals and observe their movements, but their high position made it impossible to do much damage by shell. For several days an incessant picket firing was kept up on both sides, and Sherman's troops continued to move slowly forward through the mud and tangled forests. On June 27 James B. McPherson attacked the Confederates near Little Kennesaw, and Thomas, about a mile south. The fighting was desperate, and the Federals were driven back with a loss of about three thousand men. The Confederate generals, Hardee and Loring, who received the brunt of the attack, were well protected by their barricades and lost only 808. Sherman then returned to his flanking movements so as to threaten Johnston's rear. This accomplished his purpose, forcing Johnston to abandon Kennesaw on July 2 and retreat to protect Atlanta. At the time of his retreat, Johnston's left was farther from Atlanta than the Union right.

MARIETTA, 92 m. (1,118 alt., 7,638 pop.), seat of Cobb County, is built about a park square in which there is a bandstand and a children's playground. In spring and fall flocks of migrating martins perch in the trees of this park. The houses face tree-shaded streets, their well-kept lawns ornamented by shrubbery and flowers. During the week Marietta has an urban aspect, but on Saturdays it has a rural air as farmers come to town to market their garden produce and buy supplies.

Although Marietta came into existence in 1832, when Cobb County was created from Cherokee land, it was not incorporated until 1834. During the 1840's the town grew rapidly, and during the 1850's hotels were built for summer visitors who came from the lower parts of the state to enjoy the cooler climate.

An old resident once wrote, "From 1850 to 1861 Marietta was the gayest, most fashionable, most flourishing, most entertaining, and fastest town in Georgia." Although Marietta is now primarily a conservative residential town, it still has a lively social life. Atlanta, twenty miles away, is so easily accessible by good highways and interurban car service that many Marietta residents work in the larger city.

In the CROSBY HOME (*private*), 509 Cherokee St., a two-story, white frame house built about 1890, are many relics and heirlooms from the families of George Washington and John Marshall. A leather-bound grammar, bearing the name of Elizabeth Frances Washington on the flyleaf, is believed to have been studied by George Washington, and two pieces of paper money are believed to have been found in Washington's purse after his death. A pair of silver candlesticks was used on the table of Chief Justice Marshall when he entertained General Washington and General La Fayette at dinner in Richmond, Virginia. Other heirlooms include steel engravings, pieces of silver, jewelry, and two lace shawls that belonged to Mrs. R. C. M. Lovell, grandmother of Mrs. Crosby. During the War between the States Mrs. Lovell accompanied her husband from Cincinnati to the White House to claim compensation for the loss of several barges of coal destroyed by Union soldiers on the Mississippi River. The charming and exquisitely gowned woman won the admiration of Mrs. Lincoln, and, after a friendly conversation with the President, Lovell was paid $85,000 for his coal.

ST. JAMES EPISCOPAL CHURCH, Church St., a stuccoed brick and stone building with an ivy-covered tower, was erected in 1842. Following the Battle of Kennesaw Mountain, the church was used as a hospital by Federal forces.

The MARIETTA NATIONAL MILITARY CEMETERY, Washington St. five blocks L. of the public square, is a well-kept plot of twenty-four acres surrounded by a high stone wall. Beneath large oak and magnolia trees, roses, petunias, and snow-on-the-mountain grow profusely amid evergreen shrubbery. There are 10,158 Union soldiers buried here, each grave marked with a headstone; at intervals are imposing monuments erected by various states to honor their dead. On top of the hill is a stone and iron bandstand where exercises are held each Decoration Day.

The CONFEDERATE CEMETERY, Powder Springs St. one-half mile south of the public square, is a section of the larger city cemetery. On the slope of a hill are more than three thousand graves indicated by rows of marble slabs, most of them unmarked. Old cedars and magnolias give an appearance of great age to this cemetery. On Confederate Memorial Day, April 26, exercises are held and school children place flowers on each grave.

At Marietta is a junction with State 5 (*see* TOUR *13*).

1. Right from Marietta at the public square on State 120 to a junction with a dirt road, 3.2 m.; L. on this winding road to CHEATHAM'S HILL (*guide service*), 3.7 m., the scene of some of the bloodiest fighting during the Battle of Kennesaw Mountain. Here the Confederate forces under General Cheatham made a desperate stand against the Federal troops—the old fortifications and breastworks are still visible. On the slope of the hill a marble arch and an impressive monument are above the tunnel that the Union forces attempted to dig beneath the Confederate breastworks on the summit. The purpose was to blow up the fortifications with a mine, but the plan was discovered and the tunnel bombarded. Both the arch and the monument were erected by the State of Illinois to honor its fallen soldiers.
Cheatham's Hill is a part of the Kennesaw Mountain National Battlefield Park, which includes the battlefields of the Kennesaw Mountain campaign. Elaborate earthworks have been restored, trails cleared, grass and shrubbery planted, and a tall flagpole has been raised. Near the entrance, in a small green frame building, is a museum that contains relics of the battle.

2. Right from the public square in Marietta on State 5, the Powder Springs Road, to the MCADOO HOUSE (R), 3.7 m., a rambling frame structure in dilapidated condition. When Knoxville, Tennessee, was captured by Union forces, the McAdoo family fled to Marietta, where the father and mother had first met. They bought this house, then called Melora, and here on October 31, 1863, was born William Gibbs McAdoo, Secretary of the Treasury under President Wilson and later United States Senator from California.
KOLB FARM (Brooks residence), 4 m., was the scene of a fierce engagement between a portion of General Hood's Confederate troops and a Union force on June 22, 1864. Driven from their entrenchments, the southern soldiers retreated to Cheatham's Hill. The central portion of the two-story, frame building is the original log house which was scarred during the battle. Trenches, still visible around the house, were built by Confederate soldiers. This area will probably be included within the Kennesaw Mountain National Battlefield Park.

ATLANTA, 112.6 m. (1,050 alt., 270,366 pop.) (*see* ATLANTA).

Points of Interest: State Capitol, Cyclorama of the Battle of Atlanta, Georgia School of Technology, Emory University, Oglethorpe University, Atlanta University (*Negro*), and others.

Atlanta is at the junction with US 78 (*see* TOUR *8*), with US 29 (*see* TOUR *3*), with US 341 (*see* TOUR *12*), with US 23 (*see* TOUR *7*), and with US 19 (*see* TOUR *6*), which unites with US 41 between this point and Griffin.

Section b. ATLANTA *to* FLORIDA LINE, *255.8 m., US 41.*

South of ATLANTA, **0 m.,** US 41 crosses an agricultural section of the rolling Piedmont region, beautiful in spring with the pink blooms of peach orchards. Most of the houses between Atlanta and Griffin were destroyed by Sherman's forces before they turned eastward a few miles above Griffin and swept on to Savannah and the sea. South of Griffin the people were more fortunate in saving their homes, although they too soon saw the wreck of the system that had raised them to power and prosperity.

Around HAPEVILLE, **7 m.** (975 alt., 4,224 pop.), the farm areas and woods were devastated during the Atlanta campaign. Hapeville, incorporated in 1891, is a suburban community, principally residential, whose citizens work either in Atlanta or in the factories of the busy neighboring town of East Point (*see* TOUR 3).

Left from N. Central Ave. on Virginia Ave. to CANDLER FIELD, **0.6 m.** (L), Atlanta's municipal airport and one of the largest in the United States. The field was developed by private capital in 1925, bought by the city in 1929, and later completed through city, county, and Federal funds. The airport provides both mail and passenger service for the Eastern and Delta air lines. A paved driveway leads from the rock entrance gates between hangars, shops, and training schools to the stucco administration building, which houses the ticket offices, executive offices, flight surgeon's headquarters, air-mail field post office, weather bureau office, and the inspection division and radio of the U. S. Department of Commerce.

The FAIR of 1850 (*adm.* 25¢), **16.2 m.,** is (R) a small but unusual historical museum owned by Colonel John West. The three buildings in which it is housed were brought from various sections of Georgia and their hand-hewn timbers were reassembled with the original wooden pegs. Included in this private collection are firearms, vehicles, household effects, clothing, and documents. Most of the relics are of the 1850's, but some represent the Revolutionary War period and some the twentieth century.

The main building was originally a dwelling, constructed with rooms on both sides of a broad, open hallway according to the breezeway or dog-trot plan. In this old house a crude cotton gin antedating Eli Whitney's invention is given a prominent place. To the right of the main building is a large cotton press, and to the rear is a campmeeting arbor transported from the mountains of northern Georgia. It is constructed of heavy beams and contains the pulpit and benches that were used under its roof for almost a century. Under this arbor is a collection of old vehicles, among which are the tasseled, glass-sided hearse which transported the body of Alexander H. Stephens,

Vice-President of the Confederacy (*see* TOUR *17*), to the cemetery, and the carriage used by the family of the fiery Georgia senator Thomas E. Watson (*see* TOUR *8*). A large tallyho, painted red and black, stands out vividly among the battered conveyances and old farm machinery. Another cabin, now occupied by the caretaker, contains firearms of both American and foreign workmanship, and in a third house to the rear are old kitchen utensils placed about a reconstructed brick fireplace.

The museum stands on the SITE OF THE BATTLE OF JONESBORO, a combat lasting two days, August 31 and September 1, 1864. It was occasioned by Sherman's attempt to cut the railroad to Macon and by the Confederate necessity for holding it. The main Confederate attack, which was repulsed, was made by Hardee's corps. On the next day a series of Union attacks were thrown back, but the Federals gained their objective and the southern army was forced to evacuate the Atlanta area.

JONESBORO, 17.3 m. (905 alt., 1,065 pop.), seat of Clayton County, has recently come into prominence because many scenes of Margaret Mitchell's Pulitzer Prize novel, *Gone With the Wind,* were laid here. According to Miss Mitchell, however, "Tara," the plantation of the story, is entirely imaginary.

Jonesboro has sawmills, a bagging and tire plant, a coffin works, and a cotton gin. There has been a town here since 1823. Called Leaksville until the Central of Georgia Railway was extended through this region in the middle of the nineteenth century, it was renamed Jonesboro in honor of one of the engineers who surveyed the line.

HASTINGS NURSERY, 24 m., comprising 1,513 acres, conducts a large seed business, specializing in roses, field vegetables, and flower seed. Along the highway is a display of evergreens and shrubs and acres of canna lilies which bloom all summer.

The HOME OF DONALD HASTINGS (*private*), a two-story brick house of Georgian Colonial design, is set back half a mile from the highway on the nursery grounds. In the rear garden are several gordonia (*Franklinia alatamaha*) plants (*see* TOUR *1*), a species discovered by William Bartram about 1768 on the banks of the Altamaha River near Brunswick. The gordonia has bright green leaves somewhat like those of a bay tree and blooms in summer with a gorgeous display of white blossoms two or three inches in diameter.

The KELL HOUSE (*private*), 29 m., was the home of Captain John McIntosh Kell, a naval officer under Commodore M. C. Perry on his expedition to Japan and later a captain in the Confederate navy, executive officer of the *Alabama,* and an adjutant general of the State of

Georgia. Standing 200 yards (L) from the highway, the simple, white frame house is unusual chiefly for its iron-railed porch, with steps at both ends. It was while visiting in this house that the Georgia poet Sidney Lanier (*see* MACON) wrote his lyric "Corn."

The GEORGIA EXPERIMENT STATION, 37.5 m., consists of 700 acres of farm and woodland and fifteen buildings in which laboratory experiments are conducted. Many farmers of this region have been taught the advantages of well-planned crop rotation; lands worn out by the exclusive growing of cotton are being restored to productivity by the planting of selected legumes.

Stoneville Number 2 Cotton, introduced by the station, has the largest yield of all cottons now being tested in Georgia's Piedmont Plateau. It has not only an increased yield but a longer staple, and matures so early that it suffers less from the boll weevil. Gasta (coined from Georgia Station) Wheat yields a barrel of flour an acre more than any other raised in middle Georgia and is now being crossed with a rust-resistant type to produce a hardier plant.

The station's work includes experiments with sheep breeding, crop foods for swine and cattle, diet and disease tests with horses, improvement of watermelons and young fruit trees, destruction of pecan parasites, and cold storage of fruit and vegetables. The muscadine grape, suitable for wine and table use, is a leading Georgia product; several new varieties of muscadines have originated here. The region around the experiment station has flourishing fields of pimientos that are canned in Griffin.

Experiment stations began to function in 1887, when an act of Congress appropriated to each state $15,000 annually for their maintenance in connection with agricultural colleges. The Georgia station was organized in Athens in 1888 and began operations on the Bates farm a year later, when Griffin donated 130 acres of land.

GRIFFIN, 39.3 m. (965 alt., 10,321 pop.), seat of Spalding County, is the center of brisk textile activities. The mills, however, have been built apart from the business and residential sections and do not mar the clean, attractive city. Along the streets and parkways rows of white and purple iris bloom in spring. Although there are numerous old houses, Griffin does not suggest ante bellum days so much as the modern, industrial South.

The land on which Griffin is built was part of the Creek territory through which the half-breed chief William McIntosh (*see* TOUR *10*) blazed a trail in 1812, when he led the lower Creek against the British. The town itself was not laid out until twenty-eight years later, when Colonel Lewis Lawrence Griffin purchased 800 acres and reserved twenty-two of them for churches, parks, and public buildings. The oldest textile mill here was built in 1883; since then three other large mills, manufacturing hosiery and underwear, have been established. In the latter part of the nineteenth century good dirt roads spurred the development of the town. Spalding County was the first in Georgia to have a concrete thoroughfare from county line to county line. Griffin is now served by an excellent system of railroads and highways. The city has an annual industrial pay roll of approximately three and one-half million dollars and is one of the most progressive small cities of Georgia.

The POMONA PRODUCTS COMPANY PLANT (*open to visitors*), on an un-named street one block R. from 9th St., is one of the largest pimiento canneries in the country, producing an average of ten million cans annually. Although the pimiento season is not long, the plant operates nine months a year by canning other vegetables and a number of fruits. During the busy season about seven hundred workers are employed.

The FIRST BAPTIST CHURCH, R. of the highway in the center of town, was erected in 1860. It is an impressive red brick building with a tall, white wooden steeple and is surrounded by an iron picket fence.

The HUNT HOME AND PRIVATE MUSEUM (*open by request*), Poplar and 8th Sts., contains costumes, baskets, pottery, brass, and a collection of early American glass that is one of the most comprehensive in the South. On exhibition are a number of flasks made for Washington, La Fayette, Lord Baltimore, and Sir Walter Scott, and an irridescent glass wine bottle taken from the ruins of Pompeii. Mrs. Robert H. Hunt (Addavale K. Hunt), the owner, is the author of *Silver Linings,* a book of verse, and *The Romance of Childhood,* a collection of stories.

The MUNICIPAL PARK (*18-hole golf course, 50¢; playground; swimming, 15¢; picnic facilities*), on S. 9th St., contains thousands of iris plants.

At Griffin US 19 (*see* TOUR 6) branches R. from US 41.

BARNESVILLE, 54.5 m. (859 alt., 3,236 pop.), seat of Lamar County, was founded in 1826 by Gideon Barnes, a popular tavern keeper of pioneer days. The tavern stood on the old Alabama Road, originally an Indian trail which, in the early part of the nineteenth century, was widened to form a highway for stagecoaches. Barnesville has two cotton mills, a pecan-shelling plant, several planing and lumber mills, and a furni-ture factory.

GORDON MILITARY COLLEGE, five blocks R. of the city square, is a non-sectarian school offering a six-year course in high school and college preparatory work. Its extensive campus and red brick buildings were formerly those of a state agricultural and mechanical school. Established in 1852 as the Barnesville Male and Female High School, this college was renamed later in honor of the Confederate general John B. Gordon. Military training was introduced in 1880. Approximately 125 boarding students and 75 day students are enrolled.

(Note: No US 41 markers (1939) between Barnesville and Perry.)

Right from Barnesville on unpaved State 18 to the GACHET HOME, **3 m.**, where General La Fayette paused for a night on his tour of the South in 1825. This two-story, rectangular, white house, built in 1823, has hand-hewn shutters, hand-carved banisters, and wooden pegs instead of nails. The interior, with its three rooms opening on each side of a broad central stairhall, is notable for its timber ceilings.

In the front yard stands a large cedar that once served as a hitching post for travelers passing over the road from Augusta to Columbus, and the staples to which the horses were tied are still visible in the trunk.

Charles Gachet, builder of the house, belonged to a wealthy French Catholic family. He studied for the priesthood, but upon reaching maturity changed his mind and went to Santo Domingo, where he was warned by a faithful slave barely in time to escape the slave uprising. After landing in Savannah about 1781, he purchased lands in Georgia.

ROBERTA, **83.2 m.** (487 alt., 449 pop.) *(see* TOUR 9), is at the junction with US 80 *(see* TOUR 9).

The FORT VALLEY NORMAL AND INDUSTRIAL SCHOOL (Negro), **99.3 m.,** was chartered in 1896 and known as the Light of the Valley. This coeducational institution, supervised by the American Church Institute for Negroes, an agency of the Protestant Episcopal church, is housed in twelve buildings, eight of which are modern brick structures. Its development has been aided by philanthropic donations from such organizations as the Julius Rosenwald and the Anna Jeanes foundations. George Foster Peabody has been a large contributor, and the Royal C. Peabody Trades Building is a memorial to his brother.

Such co-operation has made possible its transition from a small, ill-equipped elementary school to the only junior college for Negroes in Georgia accredited Class A by the Southern Association of Colleges and Secondary Schools and the Rockefeller Education Board. The school offers elementary, high school, and two years of college work, with courses in liberal arts, education, agriculture, home economics, and industrial arts. The enrollment of the high school is 219 and that of the junior college 113. A six-week summer school is conducted each year for Negro teachers in an effort to raise the state's standard of secondary education for Negroes.

Through extension courses, farmers' conferences, and public health work, this school affects beneficially the lives of more than thirty thousand Negroes each year. A graduate nurse, a Sabbath school missionary, and a farm demonstration agent visit in the community. Each Thanksgiving Day a festival is held, and many who have been aided by the school contribute to its support by gifts of money and farm produce. These donations, although decreased during the depression, in 1935 totaled $2,500.

In 1930 the principal, Henry A. Hunt, won the Spingarn Medal, given annually to an Afro-American citizen "for the most distinguished achievement in some honorable field of human endeavor." At that time Professor Hunt, a graduate of Atlanta University, had served the school for a quarter of a century.

In the Carnegie Library of the school is the American flag which was draped about the body of Abraham Lincoln·after his assassination.

FORT VALLEY, 100.3 m. (525 alt., 4,560 pop.), seat of Peach County, developed slowly around an academy and church established about 1836. When a railroad reached the town in 1851, it began to grow more rapidly and was incorporated in 1856. The town was originally called Fox Valley for the large number of foxes in the vicinity, but when the name was sent to the post office department in Washington it was misread and recorded as Fort Valley.

The beauty of the blossoming peach orchards in this section attracted so many visitors each April that an annual peach blossom festival was held here for several years. Although the festival was attended by crowds of people from other states as well as Georgia, it proved so expensive that it was abandoned during the depression of the 1930's and has not been revived.

At Fort Valley is the junction with State 49 (*see* TOUR 2B).

PERRY, 111.8 m. (355 alt., 1,398 pop.), seat of Houston County, was incorporated in 1824. Two well-preserved landmarks are the FIRST METHODIST CHURCH, a white frame structure erected in 1827, and the PRESBYTERIAN CHURCH, built in 1849. In the tower of the Presbyterian Church is a bell that has been in use for almost a century; during the War between the States it was buried in a swamp to prevent its seizure and conversion into cannon.

At Perry is the junction with US 341 (*see* TOUR *12*).

VIENNA (pronounced Vy-enna), 140.5 m. (350 alt., 1,832 pop.), seat of Dooly County, was first called Berrien and later Centreville and was incorporated under its present name in 1841. The county had been created from Creek territory twenty years earlier and named for the Revolutionary soldier Colonel John Dooly, who was killed in 1780 by Tories at his home near Augusta.

Vienna has had three courthouses since it became the county seat in 1839. The first burned in 1847 and with it all the county records. When construction was begun on a new courthouse, a large safe, designed to protect the records from future fires, was ordered; this safe was shipped by rail to Montezuma, then the terminus of the railroad, and the last twenty miles of its journey were to be made by mulecar. The safe was so heavy that the mule team bogged down several times, and the safe had to be left for a while on the road. When it finally reached Vienna, part of the courthouse wall had to be removed before it could be installed. When the third courthouse was built in 1891 the difficulties were not forgotten; the safe was put into position before the walls were completed.

Vienna is a center for pecan shelling, vegetable canning, and the shipping of truck produce. In some of the pecan-shelling plants the work is done by hand. Negro women sit on the floor, their hands moving rapidly at their work as the piles of unshelled nuts diminish. Although the town is not in the area usually called Georgia's peach section, this fruit, as well as the pimiento, is an important product.

CORDELE, 149.5 m. (336 alt., 6,880 pop.), is the seat of Crisp County and one of Georgia's newest towns. Founded in 1888 as a railroad junction, it is now served by three large lines. Industrial plants include cotton mills, sawmills, barrel factories, and a foundry and steel mill. Crisp County has 20,000 acres planted in peanuts, and Cordele, a center for the distribution of this product, maintains three large shelling plants.

Right from Cordele on paved US 280 to the HYDROELECTRIC POWER DAM AND PLANT, 6 m., built, owned, and operated by Crisp County. In 1927 a group of citizens initiated a five-year development program that included a proposed hydroelectric power dam across the Flint River, which drains an area of 3,500 square miles. An amendment to the state constitution, permitting a bond-issue election, was passed after months of bitter campaigning, in which the Georgia Power Company, a public utility, took an active part.

A bond issue of $1,250,000 for the plant was approved; construction was begun in October, 1928, and dedicatory exercises were held August 1, 1930. The Crisp County Power Commission, elected by the voters of the county, handles all the affairs of the plant, which has a 19,200-horsepower maximum capacity.

ASHBURN, 169.8 m. (450 alt., 2,073 pop.), seat of Turner County, is typical of the newer southern Georgia towns; its small frame houses are set back from wide streets and shaded by large trees. This town, surrounded by a productive agricultural region, is a poultry and livestock center.

At SYCAMORE, 172.5 m. (415 alt., 559 pop.), is the junction with State 32 (*see* TOUR 2C).

The ABRAHAM BALDWIN AGRICULTURAL COLLEGE (R), **188.1 m.,** is a co-educational junior college maintained by the University System of Georgia. Here 375 students are given a practical two-year course in scientific farming and home making. The institution, originally one of the agricultural and mechanical high schools, became the Georgia State College for Men in 1924 and the present agricultural college in 1933. Students study the demonstration and experimental work at the Georgia Coastal Plain Experiment Station.

The GEORGIA COASTAL PLAIN EXPERIMENT STATION, **188.8 m.,** also a unit of the university system, co-operates with various state and Federal agricultural agencies in promoting efficient methods of agriculture and animal husbandry. The station has 200 head of polled Hereford beef cattle. A slash-pine plot shows the rapid growth of trees under the climatic conditions of this section. Extensive experiments in crops, fertilizer, and pasture grasses are made to determine their adaptability to the Georgia Coastal Plain. As many as a thousand farmers of the surrounding region have come to this station for a tobacco demonstration.

TIFTON, **190.3 m.** (370 alt., 3,390 pop.), seat of Tift County, is a clean and prosperous town shaded by many large trees. It was incorporated in 1891, and both town and county were named for Nelson Tift, Georgia member of the United States Congress (1868-69).

Tifton is the largest tobacco market in the state; four and one-half million pounds are sold annually at an average price of 20¢ a pound. Five warehouses, comprising seven acres of floor space, are filled to capacity during the busy season of late summer. These warehouses are managed by outside capital, for the most part from North Carolina. Some of these brick or corrugated-iron structures measure as much as 150 by 500 feet. The sun, streaming through skylights in the high ceilings, brings into sharp relief the cigarette posters tacked on the walls. Although Tifton is known primarily as a tobacco market, cotton is equally important, and tomatoes, which are grown under contract with soup companies, constitute a large part of its trade.

PLANT OF THE IMPERIAL TOBACCO COMPANY (*no visitors*) of England and Ireland, First St. (R), is a handsome white building. Here the stems are removed and the tobacco dried by furnace heat to reduce the weight before exporting, as the duty in England is about $2.50 a pound.

Left from Tifton on paved State 50 to a branch of the ARMOUR MEAT-PACKING PLANT (*open to visitors*), 1.2 m., which utilizes the fine hogs raised in this section. The well-kept plant is surrounded by landscaped grounds, and visitors who can endure the odor are taken on a conducted tour.

ADEL, 213.3 m. (246 alt., 1,796 pop.), seat of Cook County, was incorporated in 1900. It is a tobacco market and also the headquarters of the Sowega (coined from Southwestern Georgia) Melon Growers Co-operative Association, owned by a group of farmers. This organization began by marketing watermelons, but now deals in fertilizers and seeds for all crops and operates a successful canning plant.

In Adel is LIME LICK, one of the numerous limesinks in southern Georgia. The small lake surrounded by trees is a popular place; the bottom has never been reached, and the lake never goes dry.

VALDOSTA, 237.2 m. (215 alt., 13,482 pop.), seat of Lowndes County, is one of the most prosperous small cities of Georgia. A railroad center with seven branch lines of three systems, it has extensive railroad shops. Other industrial establishments. include cotton mills, machine shops, feed mills, peanut-shelling plants, fertilizer works, sawmills, planing mills, and a barrel factory.

Many of Valdosta's houses have white columns and broad verandas in the old southern style, with later additions of porte-cocheres, bay windows, and octagonal turrets. In the newer sections are brightly colored Spanish-mission type bungalows in groves of oak, pine, and palmetto. In this hospitable, informal city sports are popular, and the country club, with its tennis courts and golf course, is the center of social life. The well-wooded countryside affords excellent hunting; and eighty-five clear-water lakes within easy motoring distance provide abundant water sports. Although the town is not a winter resort, it is becoming increasingly popular as a stopping place for travelers on the way to Florida.

Before 1860 the county seat, about four miles west of the present site, was called Troupville in honor of Governor George M. Troup (*see* TOUR 9). When the right-of-way of the first railroad through this section was surveyed, the engineers left Troupville off the route. The citizens lost no time in moving to the railroad, and, since they wished to honor the Governor still further, they named the new town for his estate, Val d'Osta.

GEORGIA STATE WOMANS COLLEGE, Patterson St., conducts classes in five white stucco buildings of the Spanish-mission type of architecture; the sixty-acre campus is wooded with groves of pines. Opened in 1913, this institution at first offered only two years of study, but soon arrangements were made for a four-year college course and the conferring of the A. B. degree. The school has an enrollment of about 340 and a faculty of 22.

EMORY JUNIOR COLLEGE, Patterson St., housed in three buildings of modified Georgian design on a 43-acre campus, is a branch of Emory

University (*see* ATLANTA). Like the Oxford branch (*see* TOUR *17*), it offers two years of general work in the arts and sciences as preparation for specialization at the senior college in Atlanta. The first classes were held in 1928, when the college was opened through the co-operation of the people of Valdosta, the South Georgia Conference of the Methodist Episcopal Church, South, and the trustees of Emory University.

At Valdosta is the junction with US 84 (*see* TOUR *5*).

Left from Valdosta on State 31, a graded dirt road, is LAKELAND, **18.7 m.** (approx. 200 alt., 1,006 pop.), seat of Lanier County. The town owns and operates the railroad connecting it with the Atlantic Coast Line Railroad at Naylor, ten miles away. This was originally a tramway built by a sawmill company. When the Interstate Commerce Commission ordered it dismantled in 1927, the road was purchased by the city of Lakeland in order to maintain freight service. It has been of great value in transporting the agricultural products on which the commercial activity of Lakeland depends.
Lakeland is the home of E. D. Rivers, Governor of Georgia (1936-40).

At **245.2 m.** (L) is the entrance to TWIN LAKES (*swimming, fishing, and dancing*), a resort with a hotel of Spanish design, a casino, and a tourist camp beside two large lakes surrounded by great moss-draped trees.

At **255.8 m.** US 41 crosses the Florida Line, at a point 38 miles north of Lake City, Florida.

TOUR 2A

Dalton — Chatsworth — Fort Mountain State Park — Ellijay;
34.2 m., State 2 and US 76.

Roadbed hard-surfaced between Dalton and Chatsworth; graded clay elsewhere — Limited accommodations.

Between Dalton and Chatsworth this route leads through the broad farmlands and low, timbered hills of the beautiful Appalachian Valley. The vague blue mass of the Cohutta Mountains, visible for miles across the highway ahead, takes definite shape at the entrance to the Chattahoochee National Forest just east of Chatsworth. Here peaks, almost four thousand feet above sea level, are green with a heavy growth of pines and hardwood trees. In the deep, fertile valleys are the homes of a hardy people, descendants of English settlers. Elizabethan terms are still in use not only in the ballads, but also in everyday speech.

State 2 branches east from US 41 (*see* TOUR 2) at DALTON, 0 m. (*see* TOUR 2).

SPRING PLACE, **9.6 m.** (730 alt., 186 pop.), named for the spring here, was the seat of Murray County until 1913, when the county government was moved to Chatsworth.

The SITE OF A MORAVIAN MISSION (R), established by Moravians from Salem, North Carolina, is marked by a small granite slab. In 1799 missionaries were authorized by the Society of United Brethren (Moravians) to spread their doctrines among the Cherokee; permission was granted by the U. S. Government in 1800, and the mission at Spring Place was opened March 26, 1802. The land was donated by Joseph Vann, a half-breed whom the Cherokee had made a tribal chief. The mission school, well attended by Cherokee from the near-by Cohutta Mountains and Appalachian Valley, remained open until 1833, when the Cherokee lands were distributed by lottery (*see* TOUR 2). After the Government had paid the Moravians $2,878 for the property, the building was converted into a courthouse.

CHIEF VANN HOUSE (*adm. 10¢*), across the street from the mission site (L), was built about 1790, and is now occupied by farm tenants.

According to tradition Joseph Vann fled to Georgia from the Carolinas late in the eighteenth century to escape arrest for murder. In Georgia he took a Cherokee wife and later, after he had become a prosperous trader, was made chief. Active throughout his life in furthering Christianity among the Indians, Vann befriended the Moravian missionaries and sent his children to their school. In 1838 he joined the westward march of the dispossessed Cherokee and left his home to be sold in the subsequent land lottery.

At the foot of the driveway is a D. A. R. marker recording the trial and acquittal in this house of John Howard Payne, author of the lyric, "Home, Sweet Home." After a visit to Chief John Ross in 1835, Payne, who was a champion of the Cherokee cause, had begun to study tribal customs and legends for inclusion in a Cherokee history. He was accused of sedition, seized by the Georgia guard, and imprisoned for twelve days in a log cabin near the Vann house.

The red brick dwelling, standing on high ground, is dilapidated but shows many details of fine workmanship. From a short distance the structure presents a commanding appearance with its end chimneys, its fanlighted doorway, and its fine modillioned cornice. It is said that the hand-made bricks used in construction were brought from Savannah. Their color has softened with age except where they are marred by the clinging plaster of pilasters that have been removed. It is evident that alterations have been made from time to time; the two-story wooden porch and the two rear rooms downstairs are additions of a much later date. Inside, neglect has left many marks. The Georgian mantels are cracked, and only a few fragments of the old paper cling to the walls, but there are still many interesting details of construction that remain unspoiled. Above the doorways of the lower hall are fanlights of fine workmanship, and the interior paneling is carved in elaborate designs. Beneath the recessed windows are removable panels behind which, according to local belief, treasure was hidden. Most striking of all the interior features is the hanging stairway that winds upward two stories from the center hall. In the low-ceiled attic the original plaster is defaced by the scrawled names of many visitors. The basement, with barred windows, is believed to have been used by Vann as a dungeon for disobedient Indians.

SPRING PLACE CEMETERY, 10 m., about 500 yards (L) from the highway, is planted in dark cedars and surrounded by a privet hedge. The PHOTOGRAPH MONUMENT, above the grave of Smith Treadwell, is a marble shaft with black veins that form the likeness of a human face, said to resemble a daguerreotype portrait of Treadwell. Since this likeness did not become visible until the stone had weathered for many years, the resemblance is an uncanny coincidence.

In CHATSWORTH, 11.8 m. (approx. 800 alt., 607 pop.), a trim and well-planned village, the most prominent buildings are the red brick Murray County Courthouse and the jail, which stand on a green lawn (L). The chief industry is talc mining, carried on by two local companies. The talc layers, ranging from five to fifty feet in thickness, can be traced for hundreds of feet along their strike, and are mined by digging a tunnel into the mountain until a vein is struck and then following the vein. The mineral is blasted out by dynamite and hauled in small tramcars to the grinding mills, where it is reduced to a powder of very fine mash and bagged for shipping.

Georgia talc is used in the manufacture of soapstone pencils for industrial marking, in filler materials, in foundry dusting, and in the preparation of toilet talcum powder. Although there are other talc deposits in Georgia, their mining has been unsuccessful.

From Chatsworth the mountains no longer appear a vague blue but are revealed as a solid mass of green. As the road winds upward over wooded Fort Mountain, it affords one superb view after another of the broad valley.

At **19.2 m.** is a junction with a dirt road.

Left on this road **1.8 m.** to FORT MOUNTAIN STATE PARK (*open all year; fire building prohibited except in picnic areas*). This area, comprising 2,070 acres around a rugged mountain peak, is being developed by the division of state parks under the department of natural resources in co-operation with the U. S. Forest Service. Although Georgia has much higher peaks, Fort Mountain is impressive because it rises so abruptly. The road gains more than two thousand feet in altitude in a span of three miles. A magnificent forest growth of hickory, chestnut, pine, oak, red maple, persimmon, and sourwood trees covers the mountain sides. The rhododendron, mountain laurel, dogwood, and honeysuckle that bloom along the roadside in spring are followed in fall by goldenrod and purple asters.

The graded road leads upward and becomes so steep that at **2.4 m.** it is advisable to park cars and walk about six hundred yards to the summit (2,832 alt.). From a forty-foot stone lookout tower, built by the U. S. Forest Service for detecting forest fires, is a fine panorama of the highland region. Encircling the crest of the mountain is a low stone wall, the ruins of an old fortification for which Fort Mountain was named. This wall is fifteen hundred feet long and twelve feet thick at the base, but it is very low, never rising above two feet. Pits, believed to be part of the defense works, occur at regular intervals, and there are traces of a gateway from which, presumably, a path once led to a spring thirteen hundred feet away.

A Cherokee myth about the "moon-eyed folk," a strange white people who could see only at night, is supported in part by the theory of one ethnologist that albinos lived here and built fortifications along the Tennessee River until they were conquered by the Indians. Another theory is that De Soto, on his march in 1540, erected the fortress for protection against the Indians; while still another is that British agents constructed the rampart during the American Revolution. Ivan Allen, of Atlanta, who donated 119 acres of the park land to the state, believes that Spaniards, who followed in the wake of De Soto's expedition seeking gold, built this fort to defend themselves from attacks by the Cherokee. There are records showing that gold nuggets, dug from near-by cliffs and springs, were molded by the Indians into ornaments.

ELLIJAY, **34.2 m.** (1,298 alt., 657 pop.) (*see* TOUR *13*), is at a junction with State 5 (*see* TOUR *13*).

TOUR 2B

Fort Valley — Montezuma — Andersonville — Americus; 48 m., State 49.

Roadbed asphalt-surfaced throughout — Central of Georgia Ry. parallels route — Limited accommodations.

State 49 connects towns noted for their ante bellum houses, passes the site of a large Confederate prison camp, and runs through a clay-loam section, bordered for many miles with peach orchards. In spring the countryside is pink with masses of blossoms; in harvest season it is a scene of bustling activity. Many college boys and girls find fruit packing a means of earning summer money. Work begins at six in the morning and lasts until night, since rapid handling is necessary because the fruit is perishable and the season short. At packing barns and sheds along the route, large trucks are loaded with crates of rosy, fragrant peaches for northern markets.

State 49 branches southwest from US 41 (*see* TOUR 2) in FORT VALLEY, 0 m. (*see* TOUR 2).

Memorial Highway, a five-mile stretch of State 49 on both sides of Marshallville, is bordered by camellia and crape myrtle and dedicated to the early settlers of the community.

MARSHALLVILLE, 11 m. (500 alt., 931 pop.), was settled by German colonists who had come to Orangeburg, South Carolina, in the 1730's. Almost a hundred years later their descendants decided to move farther west, and part of the group came here, where they bought thousands of acres and set out peach trees, grapevines, and flowering bulbs—especially hyacinths. The peach trees flourished and a new Georgia industry was introduced. The descendants of these early settlers have intermarried and remained aloof from other citizens of the state. They boast that their town has no lawyer, Yankee, motion picture theater, or jail.

The FREDERICK-WADE HOUSE (*private*), Main St., is a white frame structure (R) with a tall, square-columned portico and a small balcony. It was built about 1845 by Daniel Frederick, who came here in 1832 as one of the original settlers and laid out the town of Marshallville on his own land. It is the home of John D. Wade, author of biographies of Augustus Baldwin Longstreet and John Wesley.

The SLAPPEY HOUSE (*private*), Main St. (L), has a Doric portico, a fine Palladian doorway, a second-story porch, and a hipped shingle roof. It was built in the 1860's by George H. Slappey, one of the original settlers.

The MCCASKILL-RUMPH HOUSE (*private*), on McCaskill St. is a red brick structure (R) with Doric columns and a wide, second-story balcony across the front. Built about 1855, it later came, through marriage, into the possession of Lewis A. Rumph, who about 1875 developed a delicious, reddish-skinned peach with white meat. This peach, propagated from the Chinese clingstone, was named the Georgia Belle for Mrs. Belle Hall, half sister of Mrs. Rumph.

1. Left from Marshallville on Main St., which becomes a dirt road, to a junction with another dirt road, 1.5 m.; L. 3.5 m. on this second road to

WILLOW LAKE FARM, formerly the plantation of Samuel H. Rumph. The spreading, one-story white house, fronted by a beautiful garden with large boxwood plants, is reached by a walk outlined with small box. Here Samuel Rumph (1851-1922) established the first commercial peach orchard in Georgia. In 1875 he produced the large, copper-colored peach that he named Elberta for his wife. Five years later he was able to grow his new variety in commercial quantities. Propagated from a Chinese clingstone pollinated by the Early Crawford, the Elberta possesses a firm quality that is invaluable in shipping. To facilitate marketing, he invented the six-basket crate made with thin slats and devised the first refrigerated carriers. He also founded the Elberta Crate Company.

On the first dirt road, 3.5 m. from the junction, is the LEWIS RUMPH HOUSE (*private*), erected in the 1830's by Lewis A. Rumph's father, one of the first of the Orangeburg colonists. Immense boxwood plants border the front yard of the square, clapboard house, which originally had only two rooms upstairs; but two more were added after Rumph, a widower with five children, married Mrs. Benjamin D. Plant, a widow with three children. In order to separate the boys from the girls, no connection was made between the older and the newer rooms, which were reached by an additional stairway in the rear of the hall. Friends of the family insist that the barrier was no foe to romance, however, as young Samuel Rumph later married one of the Plant girls.

From Marshallville to Montezuma, State 49 follows a ridge overlooking the beautiful Flint River valley. The unusually good air circulation here tends to prevent damaging frosts and is largely responsible for the vigorous appearance of the orchards.

The narrow, two-story CROCKER HOUSE (*private*), 17.5 m. (L), was built in the 1830's. Its white boards are set flush around the porch but overlap on the rest of the house, a characteristic of many nineteenth-century houses.

MONTEZUMA, 23.9 m. (184 alt., 2,284 pop.), is a pleasant town with frame and brick houses set back from the tree-shaded streets. There are several elaborate neo-classic dwellings built during the twentieth century. One of the state's largest peach growers ships Elbertas, Hiley Belles, Georgia Belles, and Early Roses from here. In addition to peaches and the usual cotton and corn, growers also ship much asparagus and other truck produce. Among the industrial establishments are a fertilizer plant, a knitting mill, a cottonseed-oil mill, and a planing mill.

Montezuma began to develop in 1851, when the Central of Georgia Railway was built through the region, and was incorporated in 1854. In 1883, when the muddy Flint River was found to be navigable, two steamship companies were established, and the *Montezuma* and the *Ida* began making biweekly trips from here to the Gulf of Mexico. The sandy, shifting bed of the river made navigation so uncertain, however, that when the two boats sank they were not replaced.

The town site was part of the Indian reserve officially granted to

Buckee Barnard by the Treaty of Indian Springs in 1821. Buckee was a son of Timpoochee Barnard, chief of the Uchee and a major in the U. S. Army during the War of 1812; he was a grandson of Timothy Barnard, an English trader who became interpreter to the Creek and deputy Indian agent for Benjamin Hawkins. From 1780 until about 1820 Timothy owned the land of Macon County and helped lay out a stagecoach route from Columbus to St. Marys by way of this point. Because of the prominence of the Barnard family, four of Timpoochee's children were allowed to retain their land, three of the reservations being within Macon County.

OGLETHORPE, 25.9 m. (299 alt., 953 pop.), seat of Macon County, was incorporated in 1849. When the southwestern division of the Central of Georgia Railway was completed to Oglethorpe in 1851, the town expanded rapidly and was considered the "metropolis" of southwest Georgia. Its period of prosperity, however, was short-lived, the zenith of its progress being reached about 1855, a year after it became the seat of county government. The extension of the railroad to Americus and a severe smallpox epidemic resulted in the town's decline.

There are many artesian wells in this section. Prior to the installation of waterworks in Oglethorpe, one public well supplied water for most of the town's inhabitants, and housewives paid "toting" fees to have the water brought to their homes.

The COLONEL GEORGE FISH HOUSE (*private*), Randolph St., built about 1850, is a one-story structure with a high, stucco basement. Unusual features are octagonal stone chimneys and two high and narrow flights of stairs leading to a small stoop.

The HANSELL-KEEN HOUSE (*private*), Randolph St., is a square, two-story house erected in the 1840's, with a simple, pedimented classic portico, and a Palladian doorway opening on the left. An informal planting of bright flowers gives color to the front yard in summer.

The ANDERSONVILLE NATIONAL CEMETERY (*picnic grounds outside cemetery walls*), 34.9 m. (L), comprises twenty-eight acres surrounded by an ivy-covered brick wall. Limerock driveways lead through the grounds, beautiful with rolling lawns, magnolias, oaks, and willows. Indicated by small markers are the graves of 13,741 soldiers, many of whom died while incarcerated in the Andersonville Confederate Prison camp (*see below*). Throughout the cemetery are monuments erected by northern states in memory of their dead.

Right from the cemetery and across the railroad is ANDERSONVILLE, 0.2 m. (394 alt., 231 pop.). In the center of town is a MONUMENT TO CAPTAIN HENRY WIRZ, the Confederate commandant in charge of the Andersonville Prison. In 1865, soon after the close of the war, Wirz was seized in his Andersonville home and taken to Washington, D. C., where he was tried on thirteen charges by a military commission that sat for three months. Although witnesses testified that he was not responsible for the suffering and misery within the camp, he was found guilty of maliciously conspiring to kill and torture the prisoners and was hanged on November 10. Carved on the monument, erected by the United Daughters of the Confederacy as a protest against his execution, is a quotation from a speech made by Jefferson Davis in 1888: "When time shall have softened passion and prejudice, when reason shall have stripped the mask of misrepresentation, then justice holding evenly her scales will require much of past censure and praise to change places." Captain Wirz is buried in Mount Olivet Cemetery, Washington, D. C.

The ANDERSONVILLE PRISON PARK (L), 35.4 m., is the site of Camp Sumter, one of the largest Confederate prison camps. From the iron gate limestone driveways, shaded by pines, oaks, willows, and cedars, wind through the eighty-acre park, which is well maintained by the Federal government. Throughout the area northern states have erected monuments to honor their soldiers who were imprisoned here. Surrounding the prison site are the protective breastworks, now overgrown with grass. Stone posts mark the four corners of the prison stockade and white cement posts indicate its outline. In the caretaker's house, a two-story white building overlooking the park, is a picture drawn by the prisoner O'Dea depicting the hardships of the prison life. The land was presented to the United States in 1910 by the Women's Relief Corps, an auxiliary of the Grand Army of the Republic.

The stockade and hospital of the camp, built to accommodate 10,000 men, began to receive prisoners on March 1, 1864, but were soon crowded far beyond capacity. During the thirteen months the prison was used, 49,485 men were incarcerated there, as many as 33,006 at one time. Because of the crowded conditions, shortage of food in the South, and the lack of medicines, which were contraband of war, many prisoners contracted scurvy and gangrene. Others, unaccustomed to the southern diet of corn bread, contracted what is known today as pellagra. The death rate steadily increased until August 23, when it reached the appalling figure of ninety-seven for the one day. By this time, however, provision had been made to remove the prisoners to other camps or to return them to the North without the usual exchange for Confederate prisoners. By October all but 4,000 had gone. Despite attempts to counteract diseases with the few fresh vegetables obtainable and an acid beer made of molasses and corn meal, 12,462 prisoners died.

Under these conditions the morale of the men became very low, and the camp was infested with a group of marauders called Raiders. In order to protect their fellow prisoners, some of the men organized themselves into a band of Regulators who challenged the criminals to a battle. On July 3, before thousands of excited prisoners, they won in a hand-to-hand combat, but the plundering continued. After obtaining permission, the Regulators brought the Raiders before a court-martial of thirteen fellow prisoners. During the trial, which lasted several days, 125 men were convicted. Most of the Raiders were subjected to such minor punishments as running the gantlet, but the six ringleaders received a death sentence and were executed on a scaffold before a crowd of spectators.

In the center of the park is PROVIDENCE SPRING, which the Union soldiers believed to be a direct answer to prayer. In August, 1864, the prisoners were tortured by thirst when a drought dried the springs and wells that supplied their water. In their agony they prayed throughout a night and a day, and on the evening of the second day a heavy rain fell, continuing all night. The next morning a small puddle of water remained, and soon the soldiers noticed that instead of sinking into the ground this puddle grew larger. Close inspection revealed it to be another spring, clogged for years and opened by the downpour. A stone pavilion was erected in 1901 to cover the spring which has been made into a fountain.

AMERICUS, 48 m. (360 alt., 8,760 pop.) (*see* TOUR 6), is at the junction with US 19 (*see* TOUR 6).

TOUR 2C

Sycamore — Irwinville — Fitzgerald; 26.6 m., State 32 and State 107.

Roadbed unpaved — All types of accommodations in Fitzgerald; limited elsewhere.

Traversing the wiregrass section, this route passes through a distinctly rural region where small farms of diversified crops stand amid tracts of longleaf pines. The countryside is flat and somewhat swampy, with growths of scrub palmettos dotting the landscape. In spring the roadsides are yellow with tall pitcher plants and fragrant with trailing, pinkish-white honeysuckle. Near Irwinville is the site of Jefferson Davis' capture by Federal troops.

SYCAMORE, 0 m. (415 alt., 559 pop.), is at the junction with US 41 (*see* TOUR 2).

IRWINVILLE, **17 m.** (448 alt., 150 pop.), was made the seat of Irwin County in 1831 and named for Jared Irwin, the Governor of Georgia (1806-9) who rescinded the Yazoo Act (*see* TOUR *4*). In 1906 the county seat was changed by legislative act to Ocilla.

The town is the center of the IRWINVILLE FARMS, a rehabilitation project of the Farm Security Administration, which maintains offices in the building formerly used as the Irwinville Bank. The project, on ten thousand acres of the finest south Georgia lands, extends along the highway east and west from Irwinville and for several miles south on the Tifton Road. In 1934, when the project was organized, only a small part of the land was under cultivation, the major part being forest, swampland, and outlying tracts that had formerly been cultivated. After the original tenant houses had been repaired and painted, thirty-four rehabilitation families began farming on land which they hoped eventually to own. Fences were built, land cleared, and preparations made to plant the first crops. Many new houses and several barns have since been constructed. The four- and five-room cottages are of frame construction, painted white with green roofs, and are surrounded by shrubbery and flowers. Diversified farming is stressed, and the tenants are required to plant cotton, corn, tobacco, peanuts, and potatoes. The raising of poultry, cattle, and hogs also is encouraged. Each of the eighty-three families has a garden for its own needs.

According to the plan of operation, every tenant is assigned a tract of 60 to 125 acres that he is required to cultivate; the acreage varies according to the size of the family and the type of land. In their spare time the farmers do extra work, such as cutting wood, repairing implements, and clearing new ground, payment for which is applied on their rentals. All supplies, seed, and fertilizers are charged and paid later from crop proceeds. According to the supervisor's statement of November 1, 1938, none of the clients is behind in his payments, whereas thirty-three of them are entirely out of debt. After the farmers become independent by paying off all their obligations, they are released from supervision and Government aid is entirely advisory.

Left from Irwinville on the Irwinville-Abbeville Road to the JEFFERSON DAVIS MEMORIAL PARK, **1 m.,** a state park of about twelve acres commemorating the site where the President of the Confederacy was taken prisoner by Federal troops at the end of the War between the States. After seeing Davis arrested, the father of James D. Clements, one of the donors of the park site, vowed to place this ground forever in the hands of southern people. There are plans to enlarge the park and to plant a memory grove of yellow pines and magnolia trees.

The DAVIS MONUMENT, a granite shaft surmounted with a bronze bust of Davis, bears on its side a bas-relief panel depicting his capture. Davis had left Washing-

ton, Georgia, where his last cabinet meeting was held, and with his family was on
his way to a southern port. In the early morning of May 10, 1865, he was overtaken by Union soldiers and sent to Fortress Monroe.. According to his own
statement, Davis, when the Federal troops came upon him, donned his wife's
raincoat, mistaking it in the dark for his own; his wife threw a shawl over his head
and shoulders. These two garments are now kept by the War Department in a
safe in the State War and Navy Building, Washington, D. C.

To the right of the monument a small stream can be crossed by a footlog to the
skirmish ground, a hillside covered with a growth of wiregrass and tall yellow
pines. A brief engagement occurred here in the early morning of May 10 between
a detachment of the Michigan cavalry attempting to cut off the Davis party and
a body of Wisconsin cavalry on the same errand. Each, mistaking the other for
Confederate forces, opened fire, and several Federal soldiers were killed before
daylight permitted identification.

At Irwinville is the junction with State 107 (*difficult in wet
weather*), on which the route turns L.

FITZGERALD, 26.6 m. (275 alt., 6,412 pop.), is in the midst of the wiregrass section. Although the activity of the town is based on agriculture, several industries are carried on. Fitzgerald is interesting
primarily for its founding by veterans of the Union army. In 1894,
when there was a drought in the Middle West, Governor William
J. Northen of Georgia organized a relief committee that shipped flour,
corn, and meat for free distribution in the suffering states. This
friendly gesture, coming from a one-time enemy state, appealed to a
group of Union veterans who were eager to settle in the South. In
1895 the veterans formed a stock company, the American Soldiers'
Colony Association, which purchased fifty thousand acres of forest
land. Whole families, bringing their household pets and furnishings,
came to Georgia on horseback, in carriages, and in prairie schooners.
Until a city could be planned, they lived in shacks. When they
gathered in the evening to sing old camp songs, they occasionally re-
called their soldiering days and included "Marching Through Georgia."

Fitzgerald became a trading center and was incorporated in 1896.
It was laid off precisely in a square with two central bisecting avenues:
the streets bounding the square were named for Union and Confederate battleships, the streets running north and south for Federal
and Confederate generals, and those running east and west for southern trees and rivers. The hotel was named the Lee-Grant. Southerners began to move in, wartime prejudice gradually died, and the two
groups became amalgamated.

TOUR 3

(*Anderson, S. C.*) — *Hartwell* — *Athens* — *Atlanta* — *La Grange* — *West Point* — (*Montgomery, Ala.*); *US 29*.

South Carolina Line to Alabama Line, 204.2 m. — Roadbed hard-surfaced throughout, two-thirds concrete — Seaboard Air Line Ry. parallels route between Athens and Atlanta; Atlanta & West Point R.R. between Atlanta and West Point—All types of accommodations in Atlanta; limited elsewhere.

Section a. SOUTH CAROLINA LINE *to* ATLANTA, *119.7 m.*

This route crosses the upper Piedmont Plateau, where rolling hills of red clay are covered with fields of cotton and corn. Forests that once covered the entire region have been largely cleared, and the remaining trees are mostly second-growth pines. The heavy rainfall frequently makes muddy torrents of the creeks and rivers. The farms average about seventy-five acres in size, and the farmhouses are usually small, unpainted frame structures. A Government project for the prevention of soil erosion is doing much to restore the fertility of the land around Athens, a city of many ante bellum houses and the seat of the University of Georgia. Several manufacturing communities have grown up along the railroad and warehouses line the tracks. In this region occurred skirmishes during the Revolutionary War and the War between the States, and through it trekked the Indians during the Cherokee Removal.

US 29 crosses the SAVANNAH RIVER, **0 m.**, about fourteen miles southwest of Anderson, South Carolina. At this point on the river, which was established in the charter of the colony as the boundary line between Georgia and South Carolina, a ferry was operated as early as 1790, when Thomas Shockley bought a quarter acre of land to be used as the landing. On one occasion a great freshet on the Savannah washed some apples just below the ferry landing. In the spring many seedlings came up, and one of the plants saved by Shockley produced delicious fruit. The apple, named for Shockley, became a widely cultivated variety. The ferry was later known as Brown's Ferry, from a family that acquired it in the 1820's, and was operated until a toll bridge was built across the river in 1917. The bridge was purchased by Georgia and South Carolina nine years later and the toll removed.

The F. G. STOWERS HOUSE (*private*), **1.5 m.** (L), built about 1840, is one of the oldest residences in this section. On a slight rise that affords a view of the outlying territory, this single-story, white frame structure has a deep veranda adorned with small, square columns extending around three sides. The double front door is set in a Palladian frame ornamented with pilasters. The house, once surrounded by a fine grove of oak trees, is on the site of the old Oak Bower Post Office that was served by the Star Stagecoach between Athens and Anderson, South Carolina.

The NANCY HART MARKER (L), **5.4 m.**, at the intersection with a dirt road, bears a bronze tablet commemorating the bravery of the Georgia Revolutionary heroine (*see* TOUR *3A*). Both the town of Hartwell and Hart County are named for her.

HARTWELL, **6.6 m.** (838 alt., 2,048 pop.), incorporated in 1856, is the seat of Hart County, the only county in the state named for a woman. It is an attractive town with wide, well-paved streets, some of them planted with flowering shrubs and ornamental trees. Hartwell has two textile plants financed by Georgia capital and also serves as a local market and a shipping point for agricultural products, principally cotton and corn. Increasing acreage in the surrounding area is being planted in crimson clover; for the past three years a Clover Blossom Festival (*early May*) has been held to impress farmers with the commercial value of this crop. Many visitors attend to hear the guest speakers and enjoy a Georgia barbecue.

The marked SITE OF AH-YEH-LI A-LO-HEE (Ind., center of the world) (L) **9.5 m.**, was once a Cherokee assembly ground. Indian trails radiated in many directions from this point, which became an important trading post, with a large traffic in hides, furs, and blankets.

FRANKLIN SPRINGS, **21.8 m.** (approx. 750 alt., 75 pop.), was a well-known watering place before the War between the States. Now largely the property of the Pentecostal Holiness Church, it is the printing headquarters of the official church paper and Sunday school literature.

DANIELSVILLE, **33.3 m.** (760 alt., 296 pop.), seat of Madison County, was incorporated in 1818 and named for Allen Daniel, a captain in the Revolutionary Army and later brigadier general in the state militia. He donated the land for all the public buildings within the town. It is in an agricultural region where small farms are cultivated by the owners or by white tenants. There are few Negroes in this section.

In the public square is the CRAWFORD W. LONG MONUMENT, a white marble effigy of the celebrated doctor who was the first to use ether as an anesthetic during an operation. The statue, erected in 1936, the ninety-fourth anniversary of the event, shows him standing before a small cabinet. A seated figure of Dr. Long occupies the Georgia niche of Statuary Hall in the National Capitol.

At Danielsville is the junction with State 36 (*see* TOUR *3A*).

Right from the Danielsville courthouse on a dirt road to the BIRTHPLACE OF DR. CRAWFORD W. LONG (*private*), 0.2 m. (L), a small two-story clapboarded house with raised basement, tall brick end chimneys, and a low front porch supported on hand-hewn posts. In the yard are several boxwood and gardenia bushes.

Southwest of Danielsville is the 104,000-acre SANDY CREEK DEMONSTRATION PROJECT. It is a triangular area, with the towns of Commerce, Comer, and Athens as its vertices, and includes approximately a thousand farms in Clarke, Madison, and Jackson counties. This Soil Conservation Service project, begun in 1934, was the first of its kind to be set up in the Piedmont section of Georgia.

Here the various kinds of soil erosion are being checked by the planting of Bermuda grass, blackberry bushes, kudzu and honeysuckle vines, and pine and black locust trees. A large part of the work is done by C. C. C. workers, who plant trees and seedlings in the gullies, dig ditches with correctly sloped banks that turn the water into channels, build dams, and terrace the land.

To have his land protected from erosion, a farmer in this section must apply to the Soil Conservation Service office in Athens. The regional director then sends a specialist to make a survey of the farm and to help the farmer plan what crops are best suited to the soil. He also points out the fields that need terracing, the best location for drainage ditches, the lands to be converted into pasturage, and those that must be planted with seedling trees. The Federal government bears a portion of the expense, provides the equipment, and, if certain tracts of land are considered unsuitable for cultivation, helps convert them into pasture or woodland.

ATHENS, 47.7 m. (662 alt., 18,192 pop.), (*see* ATHENS).

Points of Interest: University of Georgia, Tree that Owns Itself, ante bellum houses, and others.

Athens is at the junction with US 129 (*see* TOUR *16*) and with US 78 (*see* TOUR *8*), which coincides with US 29 for about ten miles west of Athens.

WINDER, 72 m. (969 alt., 3,283 pop.), is the seat of Barrow County, created in 1914 from parts of Walton, Jackson, and Gwinnett counties. A portion of the town was formerly within each of these counties. A story is told of an altercation between two Negroes in which, within three minutes, one was shot in Jackson, staggered wounded into Walton, and fell dead in Gwinnett.

The town developed around a tavern advertised by an enormous liquor jug and was known as Jug Tavern until 1893, when it was incorporated and given its present name. It is said that the tavern furnished board and lodging for the night and all the liquor a guest could drink for only ten cents. A skirmish occurred here on August 3, 1864, between Confederate cavalry and the 14th Illinois cavalry.

Because the six textile plants of the city at one time manufactured overalls almost exclusively, Winder is sometimes called the Overall Center. For the past few years, however, the mills have manufactured men's suits, underwear, riding breeches, and blanket-lined leather jackets. Winder has also a lively trade in farm products, principally cotton, with corn ranking second.

1. Left from Winder on unpaved State 11 to the home of Mrs. Ida Wages (R), 3 m.; back of this house, 300 yards downhill, is the pre-Revolutionary CARTER HILL HOUSE (*private*), a log structure revealing the original loopholes used in defense against the Indians.

2. Right from Winder on paved State 11 to the ETHERIDGE-STANTON HOUSE (*private*), 13 m., a two-story, frame structure (L) built about 1835. It is said to have been the first dwelling in Jefferson.

JEFFERSON, 13.1 m. (800 alt., 1,869 pop.), the seat of Jackson County, was created in 1796. The town was incorporated in 1806 and had several hundred inhabitants when, on March 30, 1842, Dr. Crawford W. Long (1815-78) performed here the first operation in which sulphuric ether was used as an anesthetic. Two markers, on the front of a red brick store on the west side of the public square, indicate the SITE OF DR. LONG'S OFFICE where the operation was performed. Many persons claim, however, that it occurred out of doors under a mulberry tree that stood in front of the office. When this tree was removed several years ago, souvenirs were made from it.

After receiving his medical education at the University of Pennsylvania and serving his internship in New York, Dr. Long came to practice in Jefferson. On numerous occasions he inhaled ether for its exhilarating sensation, and, when others learned of its effect, "ether parties" became fashionable. According to Dr. Long's own account, after James M. Venable had consulted him on several occasions about removing two small tumors from his neck: ". . . I mentioned to him . . . the probability that the operation might be performed without pain, and proposed operating on him while under the influence of ether. He consented. . . . The ether was given to Mr. Venable on a towel, and when fully under its influence, I extirpated the tumor. . . . He gave no evidence of suffering during the operation, and assured me after it was over that he did not experience the slightest degree of pain from its performance."

Long remained in Jefferson for eleven years before he moved to Athens, where he lived from 1851 until his death in 1878.

The HARRISON HOTEL, SE. corner of the square, was built about 1835, probably by Joshua A. Randolph. This two-story, gray frame Greek Revival structure has verandas running the full length of the facade on both floors, forming a square-columned portico.

LAWRENCEVILLE, 89.5 m. (1,082 alt., 2,156 pop.), made the seat of Gwinnett County in 1821, is a rambling town of frame houses facing unpaved streets. It was named for Captain James Lawrence, remembered for his last words, "Don't give up the ship." These were spoken after he had been mortally wounded in an engagement between the *Chesapeake* under his command and the British *Shannon* in the War of 1812.

On September 15, 1831, Samuel A. Worcester, Elizur Butler, and other New England missionaries to the Cherokee were tried in Lawrenceville for residing in the Cherokee land and for encouraging the Indians to hold their land. Found guilty, they were sentenced to the state penitentiary, where they remained until 1833 in spite of a reversal of the verdict in 1832 by the U. S. Supreme Court.

In the corners of the courthouse square are small red brick buildings, and around the square is an iron fence. In 1849 an act of the legislature authorized the justices of the inferior court of the county to deed the four corner lots to responsible citizens, provided they build and maintain a fence around the square. The buildings are used as offices by lawyers.

HIGHTOWER TRAIL MARKER, 102 m., on the line between DeKalb and Gwinnett counties, indicates the route of an Indian trail between the sites of the present Athens, Georgia, and Gadsden, Alabama.

DECATUR, 112.9 m. (1,049 alt., 13,276 pop.), the seat of DeKalb County and a residential suburb of Atlanta, appears unlike other towns of the Old South except for the majestic oaks that shade its streets. On landscaped lawns modern brick and frame houses are interspersed with apartment buildings and somewhat older dwellings with scrollwork, turrets, and curved bay windows.

The land of this section was settled by English, Scottish, and Irish people from Virginia and the Carolinas, industrious farmers who owned few slaves. Decatur was incorporated on December 10, 1823, and soon became a prosperous town. In 1837 the citizens, disliking the smoke and clatter of trains, refused to allow the Western & Atlantic Railroad to come within the city limits. The tracks were built to the site of Atlanta, which became the railroad center of the Southeast.

On July 21, 1864, the day following the Battle of Peachtree Creek (*see* ATLANTA), General James B. McPherson brought Sherman's rear guard into Decatur and placed his supply wagons in the cemetery, about which he constructed earthworks on three sides. On July 22 General Joseph Wheeler made a fierce assault, drove McPherson through the northern limits of the town, and captured more than two hundred prisoners. Only an urgent call to support General W. J. Hardee farther west prevented the destruction of a large section of the Federal wagon trains.

The gray granite DEKALB COUNTY COURTHOUSE, the last of a series of five, was erected in 1917-18 at a cost of $110,000. Surrounded by the principal banking and commercial houses, it serves as a seat of activity for local politics and, on Saturday, as a gathering place for farmers who come to purchase their supplies for the week. Occasionally on Saturday morning the Negroes throng here to purchase old clothes at a rummage sale held on the wide concrete walks. On the lawn of the courthouse square is a mounted cannon, a relic of the Creek War of 1836. This muzzle-loading gun later belonged to the DeKalb County Artillery, organized in 1837. For more than fifty years it was used for the celebration of political and holiday occasions. On the northwest corner of the courthouse square is a small granite monument honoring Stephen Decatur, the naval hero for whom the town is named.

AGNES SCOTT COLLEGE, E. College Ave., is a college for women, with a high scholastic standing. Facing the street and overlooking an expanse of lawn shaded by oaks and magnolias are the older red brick buildings, some with wide, columned verandas. To the rear of these are the newer red brick and limestone buildings, constructed in the Collegiate Gothic style. On the campus of approximately forty-five acres are thirty buildings, including cottages for members of the faculty.

Agnes Scott's CARNEGIE LIBRARY is housed in a recently constructed red brick building trimmed with Indiana limestone; this $230,000 structure is also Gothic in style. The book stacks have a capacity of 120,000 volumes. Cubicles among the stacks permit space for individual research work, and seminar rooms provide for group study. Other features of the library are an exhibition room for paintings and a projection room for motion pictures. An outdoor reading terrace, equipped with waterproof chairs and tables and brightly colored umbrellas, is reached from the upper reading room by a stone stairway.

The college is an outgrowth of Decatur Female Seminary, organized in 1889 by members of the Decatur Presbyterian Church, under the leadership of the Reverend F. H. Gaines. It was renamed Agnes Scott for the mother of Colonel George W. Scott, of Decatur, who in 1890 donated $40,000 for a permanent endowment and six years later became its president. In 1906 the school was chartered as a college; in 1907, admitted to the Southern Association of Colleges; and in 1920, recognized by the Association of American Universities. Through appropriations of the General Education Board and of the Presbyterian church, and through private donations, Agnes Scott has acquired a substantial endowment and assets valued at $3,600,000.

In addition to their academic training, the 500 students are instructed in archery, swimming, and golf. Each year the Blackfriars, a dramatic club, produces several plays, and May Day is celebrated with an elaborate dance festival written and produced by the students.

On College Ave., directly opposite the railroad station, is VILLA

ALLEGRA (*private*), a two-story, yellow frame house with brown trim-
mings. Dr. Thomas Holley Chivers lived here for the two years
preceding his death in 1858, and at his own request was buried under
a tree in the back yard. When the property was sold, his body was
removed to the Decatur Cemetery.

Although Chivers chose medicine as a career, he is remembered
as a poet, especially for the technical innovations which are said to
have influenced Poe, Swinburne, and the French symbolists (*see*
LITERATURE).

Left from College Ave. in Decatur on Columbia Dr. to COLUMBIA THEOLOGICAL
SEMINARY (R), 1 m. Two theological buildings and four faculty houses are on
a 57-acre campus of rolling woodland. The school buildings are of red brick
trimmed with gray limestone. In addition to the bachelor of divinity degree, the
seminary offers the degrees of master of theology and doctor of theology. With
a small student body of 100 young men, excellent work is done in the fields of
biblical, historical, systematic, and practical theology.

The school was organized in 1828 at Lexington (*see* TOUR 8) by the Presbyterian Synods of Georgia and South Carolina. In 1850 it was moved to Columbia,
South Carolina, and remained there until 1927, when it was removed to Decatur. It is owned by the Presbyterian Synods of Georgia, South Carolina,
Florida, Alabama, and Mississippi and is controlled by a board of directors.

At Decatur is a junction with US 78 (*see* TOUR 8).

ATLANTA, **119.7 m.** (1,050 alt., 270,366 pop.) (*see* ATLANTA).

Points of Interest: State Capitol, Georgia School of Technology, Emory University, Oglethorpe University, Atlanta University (Negro), Cyclorama of the
Battle of Atlanta, and others.

Atlanta is at the junction with US 41 (*see* TOUR 2), with US 341
(*see* TOUR *12*), with US 19 (*see* TOUR 6), with US 23 (*see* TOUR 7), and
with US 78 (*see* TOUR 8).

Section b. ATLANTA *to* ALABAMA LINE, *84.5 m.,* US 29.

Southwest of ATLANTA, **0 m.,** the route passes through a part of the
middle Georgia section where cotton plantations formerly flourished.
In Newnan and La Grange are many ante bellum houses. Since the
War between the States several textile mills have been built in this
section and recently crop diversification has been introduced. Cotton
is still the principal product; but the red clay hills, formerly eroded
and worn out by excessive one-crop planting, are frequently green with
legumes and garden produce.

The 2nd Battalion, 22nd Infantry, is stationed at FORT MCPHERSON (R),
4.2 m., a U. S. Army post, whose red brick barracks and military
buildings are visible behind a high fence. After the fall of Atlanta,
this post was established by the Federal government on the site of the

old muster ground used by the Georgia militia—now the site of Spelman College in Atlanta. The post was named for James Birdseye McPherson, the union general who was killed during the Battle of Atlanta. In 1885 the fort was moved from Atlanta to its present quarters. The 236-acre reservation includes Camp Jessup, occupied during the World War by the 305th Motor Repair Unit and now by a detachment of the Quartermaster's Corps. The polo games, held on many Sunday afternoons in fall, attract many visitors from Atlanta to the reservation.

EAST POINT, 6 m. (1,060 alt., 9,512 pop.), once the eastern terminus of the Atlanta & West Point Railroad, was incorporated in 1887. On this site, one of the key points of the Confederate line of defense, cannon, forts, and a powder magazine were established.

COLLEGE PARK, 7.8 m. (1,060 alt., 6,604 pop.), was incorporated as Manchester in 1891, but was renamed in 1895 after the opening here of Cox College. The houses, many of which are of the late Victorian type, are dignified and neatly kept, and the railroad right of way has been beautified with grass and shrubbery.

GEORGIA MILITARY ACADEMY (L), N. Main St., visible through the Gothic entrance arch, has a 24-acre campus with well-equipped buildings, a parade ground, and athletic fields. This school was founded in 1900 by Colonel James C. Woodward. The enrollment of about 325, including a few day students, represents half the states of the Union and three foreign countries. Grammar school, high school, and college preparatory work are offered, as well as military training. The R.O.T.C. unit was established in 1916, and for twelve years the academy has been selected by the War Department as one of the fifteen honor military schools in the United States. Every Sunday afternoon at half-past three a dress parade is held. In 1920 the academy established Camp Highland in North Carolina to provide summer recreation and instruction.

PALMETTO, 23.7 m. (1,045 alt., 964 pop.), incorporated in 1854, was called Palmetto Station when, on September 21, 1864, General John B. Hood brought his 40,000 men here and began preparations for an aggressive campaign to cut the Federal lines of communication. Jefferson Davis, President of the Confederacy, visited him here, promised all possible assistance, and reviewed his troops, assuring them that they would make Sherman's retreat "more disastrous than was that of Napoleon from Moscow."

At 35.9 m. is the junction with a paved road.

Right on this road to the HETTIE JANE DUNAWAY GARDENS (*adm. 50¢; blooming season April-June; lunch, tea, or dinner by reservation at Blue Bonnet Lodge*),

7 m. This twenty-acre garden, with its masses of shrubbery and bright-hued native flowers planted on and about rugged boulders, is one of the largest rock gardens in the South. It is part of a 600-acre plantation belonging to Mr. and Mrs. Wayne P. Sewell. A single boulder covers half an acre, and it took two years to blast the solid rock foundation.

At the main entrance to the gardens is Windy Hall (L), a guest house of logs and cedar poles. Near by is the Garden Totem Pole, designed by the owner and carved from a native poplar forty-five feet high and five feet in diameter. The figures include birds, old-fashioned flowers, magnolia trees, pine cones, the head of a Negro girl eating watermelon, a Negro plowboy, a turkey, a Bible, the American eagle, the head of an Indian chief representing William McIntosh (*see* TOUR *10*), who once camped on this site, and, at the top of the pole, a dove of peace. The pole, painted by Frances Goodman, of California, was carved by a craftsman who called himself "the woodcarver of Sautee." Although he spent a year working here, he never revealed his identity and remained a mysterious character.

From Windy Hall a winding driveway lined with American Pillar roses leads to a natural amphitheater that is terraced to seat more than a thousand people. At the foot of the arena is the century-old BLUE-BONNET LODGE, a one-story building with end chimneys and a spacious living room in which are the original fireboard and beamed ceiling. The steps of the front veranda lead down into an outdoor living room, paved with flagstones laid around the trunk of a massive oak tree and enclosed with a rustic trellis on which roses grow in profusion. Surrounding the house are sunken gardens with rock-bordered lily pools and a wishing well.

The water from a natural spring flows through a series of cascades to the rock swimming pool, a natural bowl formed by the hillside slope. Seven springs have been used as a part of the landscaping plan to form a series of reflecting pools. Cedar Creek, a tributary of the Chattahoochee River, flows through the bottom lands.

At a turn of the road between Blue Bonnet Lodge and the entrance gate is the red-roofed, dark green PATCHWORK BARN, a little theater used for both amateur and professional performances. The theater has a well-equipped stage and an auditorium decorated in a rustic manner with gayly colored patchwork ceiling and comfortably upholstered pine-slab seats. The overhead lighting fixtures are made from the wheels of an old buggy. The balcony is reserved for Negroes of the plantation, who often entertain with their spirituals.

NEWNAN, **36.3 m.** (957 alt., 6,386 pop.), seat of Coweta County, is a little city of handsome ante bellum and modern houses and well-kept churches. After the formation of the county from Creek lands gained by the Treaty of Indian Springs in 1825 (*see* HISTORY), a small settlement named Bullsboro developed in 1827. Although this village was two and one-half miles to the northeast of this site, it was really the beginning of the town. In 1828 the Baptists of Bullsboro acquired several acres within the present boundaries of Newnan and built a church. Other sects followed; soon the whole village had moved to the new site, and the settlement was given its present name. Newnan became so prosperous that by the 1850's planters built large white dwellings and set up industrial plants.

Of the eight thriving mills operated in this town, seven and a part of the eighth are owned by local capital, which makes Newnan rank very high in per capita wealth. Among the industrial plants are textile mills, lumber mills, and factories making boxes and crates. Newnan is also a horse and mule market.

On the southwest corner of the courthouse square is a marker indicating that the MCINTOSH TRAIL passed through Newnan. This Indian trail ran northward from an Indian agency on the Flint River to the McIntosh Reserve in Carroll County (*see* TOUR *10*). There it connected with other trails, one running eastward by way of Indian Springs to Augusta, the other westward to Talladega, Alabama.

The CALHOUN HOUSE (*private*), 72 Greenville St., constructed in the early 1850's, is an imposing red brick house with white columns across the back as well as the front. In the rear is the old jail used to imprison unruly and runaway slaves.

ROSEMARY (*private*), 9 Jefferson St., has a front garden designed in 1859 by P. J. Berckmans, a Belgian landscape gardener. It is the only old boxwood garden in Newnan today and is dominated by two giant magnolias, one of which is entirely covered with wistaria. The flower beds are outlined by hedges of clipped boxwood, and there are also plantings of clipped tree boxwood and many flowering shrubs, including Japanese lime, sweetbay, January jasmine, forsythia, Japanese magnolia, and crape myrtle. The original cottage, built in 1823, was moved in 1914 to another part of the property so that a modern house could be erected on its site; the plan of the garden, however, was undisturbed.

A RED BRICK RESIDENCE (*private*), 73 College St., was once the Laboratory Building of College Temple, a college for women, chartered in 1854. The founder, M. P. Kellogg, came to Coweta County from Vermont in 1843 and made so great a success teaching school at Rock Springs that in 1850 he was asked to teach in the old Newnan Seminary. In 1852 he erected three large buildings, in which he opened a school having musical, primary, and preparatory departments. Kellogg offered the young ladies courses in philosophy, chemistry, and astronomy and presented the graduates with an M. A. degree. During 1864 the buildings were used as a hospital for both Union and Confederate soldiers. Because of his old age and the growing number of public schools, Kellogg discontinued his school in 1888.

At MORELAND, **42.9 m.** (937 alt., 343 pop.), is the junction with State 41 (*see* TOUR *3B*).

HOGANSVILLE, **53 m.** (715 alt., 2,355 pop.), on the old McIntosh Trail, was an industrial town even before its incorporation in 1870. A settle-

ment grew up around the village of the textile mill established here in
1828 by David Norwood. When the Atlanta & West Point Railroad
was completed in 1854, community activities began to center around
the railroad station; new settlers arrived, and it was not long before
the town was one of the best cotton markets in Western Georgia. With
the twentieth century came industrial plants, including textile mills.

South of Hogansville, at the city limits, is the 225-acre HOGANSVILLE
NURSERY, one of the largest in the South. It has a display of ornamental
trees and shrubbery extending for half a mile along the highway.

In the DUNSON MILLS (*no visitors*), 65.5 m. (L), founded in 1910,
ducks, twills, sheetings, drills, osnaburgs, and other white goods are
manufactured, as well as tire cord fabric and automobile covers. Left
of the highway dirt roads wind through the village of white frame
houses to red brick factory buildings, where about six hundred men
and women are employed.

LA GRANGE, **66.7 m.** (786 alt., 20,131 pop.), seat of Troup County, is
known for both its textile manufacturing and for the excellence of its
architecture. Here the modern, industrial South has been superimposed upon the Old South of the plantation era without destroying the
charm of the classically designed houses, luxuriant gardens, and wealth
of magnolias, water oaks, and elms.

In the early part of the nineteenth century La Grange was a settlement of log cabins. These were gradually replaced by larger houses
until, by the second quarter of the century, there were many commodious dwellings with broad, columned porches. On his visit to
America in 1825 the Marquis de La Fayette, spending two weeks in
Georgia as the guest of Governor George M. Troup, was impressed
with the similarity of the Creek lands of western Georgia to his own
estate, La Grange, in France. In his honor the town, incorporated in
1828 as the county seat, was called La Grange.

The section flourished with the growth of its cotton plantations until the War between the States. So loyal to the Confederacy were the
citizens that almost every man marched to battle. The La Grange
women, according to legend, organized themselves into a military
company named Nancy Hart for the celebrated Revolutionary heroine
(*see* TOUR *3A*). It is said that in 1865, when the defenseless city was
invaded by Wilson's Raiders, the Nancy Harts in their heterogeneous
costumes marched out to meet them, and so impressed their colonel,
who by coincidence was named La Grange, that he marched on without burning the city. La Grange remained a small, old-fashioned town
until late in the nineteenth century, when the establishment of large
textile mills caused the city to grow rapidly.

Through the city the highway follows Broad Street, which is the principal residential street and is bordered with many fine old houses.

The GEORGE HEARD HOUSE (*private*), 206 Broad St., is a two-story, white frame house of classic simplicity with double porches, tall shuttered windows, and Doric columns on three sides. It is surrounded by oaks, elms, and boxwood, and a boxwood-lined walk leads to the porch.

The SEGREST HOUSE (*private*), 311 Vernon St., visible (L) from Broad St. at the end of Trinity Ave., has been described in *House and Garden* as representative of the ante bellum South. It departs from tradition, however, in the absence of the small balcony above the entrance. Built in the 1820's, the house is of closely fitted white boards and has heavy Doric columns across its porch. The large bushes of white, pink, and variegated camellias, which bloom soon after Christmas, are typical of old southern plantings.

The OAKS (*private*), 1103 Vernon St., built in 1845, is a Greek Revival house with a facade adorned with six massive Doric columns. All timbers are mortised and secured by wooden pegs. The interior is notable for the carved mahogany stairway at the rear of the lower hall and for the mantels of black Italian marble.

BELLEVUE (*private*), 204 McLendon Ave., visible (R) from Broad St. at head of McLendon Ave., was for several years the home of Benjamin H. Hill, who purchased the site in 1853. Here Jefferson Davis was entertained, and here Hill was arrested by Federal soldiers. The white frame house, with tall Ionic columns and massive, carved cornices, stands on land once part of a 12,000-acre plantation. Boxwood hedges outline the gardens on both sides of the white-sand walk, which is flanked by superb magnolias. The interior is admired for its spacious rooms, its walnut stairway, its drawing-room mantel of black marble, and its high ceilings decorated with various floral patterns.

Benjamin Harvey Hill (1823-82), though opposed to secession, supported the Confederate cause during the war. Although he strove to protect Georgia's interests during the Federal military regime of Reconstruction, he counseled submission to the inevitable and thus lost the support of his embittered people. Nevertheless, in 1875 he was elected to the U. S. House of Representatives. A fearless and brilliant orator, he was a strong influence in persuading President Hayes to withdraw the Federal troops from the South. Elected to the U. S. Senate in 1877, he held office until his death five years later.

LA GRANGE COLLEGE (L), Broad St. extending back to Vernon St., is one of the earliest chartered institutions for female education. When it was established as La Grange Female Academy by Thomas Stanley in 1831, the cause of instruction for women was not popular. In the early days the girls came attended by their Negro mammies and wrote essays with such titles as "What is Life but Fleeting" and "Mother, Home, and Heaven." The standard steadily rose, however, and the academy was made a degree-conferring college in 1843. In 1857 it was purchased by the Methodist church. Now the college has three substantial red brick buildings and a student body of 125. Oreon Smith Hall has four ivy-covered columns known to the students as Matthew, Mark, Luke, and John.

HILLS AND DALES (*private*), Vernon St. (R), the estate of Fuller Callaway, is notable for the FERRELL GARDENS, laid out in 1827 by Mrs. Blount Ferrell. A beautiful blending of formal and informal planting, this garden is one of the show places of Georgia. With magnificent native oaks, elms, cedars, and magnolias, as well as many rare trees from foreign lands, the lower terraces are dark, mysterious, and tangled with their wistaria vines twisting through the upper branches. In spring when the wistaria blooms, the dark boughs overhead are transformed into a lavender canopy.

Through a shady grove the driveway winds from the entrance to the Italian Renaissance house of cream marble, which overlooks the older gardens with their boxwood hedges and tall trees. On the upper terrace near the house is the word *God,* laid out in large letters of dwarf box. Mottoes of the Ferrell family and of the Callaway family are also executed in this shrub.

In another section, known as the Church Garden, boxwood is planted in a harp-shaped bed with gold-leaf alternanthera for strings; an organ, a bishop's chair, a pulpit, and mourners' benches are shaped from tree box. A large Cunninghamia (Chinese fir) shades the garden, and tea olive (*Osmanthus fragrans*) bushes exude their delicate perfume. Among the foreign plants now growing here are European larches, lindens from Germany, a ginkgo tree, weeping cherry bushes from Japan, and tea bushes from China.

The marble of Italian statuary and the stone of old wells, from which water was drawn by Negro slaves in the early days, contrast with the dark green of the foliage throughout the gardens. From the older terraces pebbled paths lead to the Callaway greenhouses and cutting gardens, which in spring and summer are gay with many flowers.

The CALLAWAY MILL COMMUNITY, covering several blocks in southwestern La Grange, includes in its area some of the red brick buildings of the Callaway Mills, white frame cottages for mill employees, a community house, a Y.M.C.A., and both indoor and outdoor swimming pools. In the center of the community village is an 8-acre park surrounding the 97-foot CALLAWAY MEMORIAL TOWER, a structure of red brick and limestone with a clock on each of its four faces. It was designed in the manner of the Campanile of St. Mark's in Venice, and erected by employees in 1929 as a memorial to Fuller E. Callaway, Sr., founder of the Callaway Mills, who died in 1928. His birthday, July 15, is celebrated as a city holiday.

The Callaway Mills, established in 1900 with the building of the Unity Cotton Mills, comprise seven industrial plants in La Grange, three in other Georgia towns, and one in Alabama. In Georgia there are in the mill villages 2,071 houses, 18 churches, 4 schools, 29 stores, 7 playgrounds, 5 swimming pools, and 5 motion picture theaters. Between four and five thousand employees manufacture a hundred major products, including yarns, fabrics, tufted rugs, and men's and boys' pants.

At La Grange is a junction with US 27 (*see* TOUR *10*).

Between La Grange and West Point the land is thickly wooded in pine and oak, and small truck farms take the place of large holdings. Lettuce, tomatoes, and cabbages have to a great extent replaced cotton.

The CANNONVILLE SOIL CONSERVATION PROJECT, **70.2 m.,** is one of more than 165 similar demonstration areas in the United States, and one of five in Georgia. This project, with headquarters in La Grange, embraces an approximate area of thirty thousand acres of privately owned land between La Grange and West Point and is conducted by the Government in co-operation with the owners and operators. The purpose of the project is to demonstrate to the 175 farmers living within its area proper land-use practices to save good agricultural land that has been subject to wastage through uncontrolled erosion. All these farmers are given an opportunity to enter into co-operative agreements with the Government to test recommended land-use and erosion-control practices (77 farms were under agreement in June, 1938). The control measures being applied include terracing, contour cultivation, strip cropping, crop rotation, pasture improvement, gully control, reforestation, forest-fire control, and the retirement from cultivation of highly erosive land by planting it with trees and other vegetation.

WEST POINT, **83.9 m.** (576 alt., 2,146 pop.), on the banks of the Chattahoochee River, is an industrial town. The sidewalks are several feet above the street level, so that they can be used in time of flood. When the site of West Point was first acquired by the state in 1825 there was a trading post here known as Franklin, where both Creek and Cherokee exchanged furs for firearms and liquor. After the first store was built in 1829, the post grew into a town that was incorporated as Franklin in 1831; but, since it was the westernmost point on the Chattahoochee River in Georgia, its name was changed to West Point the following year. With the completion of the Montgomery & West Point Railroad in 1851 and of the Atlanta & West Point Railroad in 1854, West Point developed as an important cotton market. During the War between the States the town was sacked, and the toll bridge and railroad trestle were destroyed. It was the first Georgia city to be released from military control after the war, and it immediately entered a period of industrial activity.

Among the plants of West Point are an ironworks, a lumber company, and several textile mills. Here is the home office of the West Point Manufacturing Company, which comprises a bleachery and dye plant and five textile mills within a radius of a few miles, some across the state line in Alabama. This business was organized in 1866 by LaFayette Lanier, who recognized the wasted power in the Chattahoochee River. At that time the only mode of transportation to his various manufacturing plants was by river boat; in 1895, to facilitate their operation, he was instrumental in building the Chattahoochee Valley Railroad. Lanier's company furnished the duck fabrics for Admiral Richard E. Byrd's first Antarctic expedition, and more recently donated the sail material for the restoration of the U. S. Frigate *Constitution,* familiarly known as "Old Ironsides."

For many years West Point experienced heavy damage to property from the high waters of the Chattahoochee River. After the flood of 1919, Smith Lanier employed hydraulic engineers, who made surveys and recommended the construction of a lake and a series of dams to reduce the flood hazard and facilitate further industrial development in this area. A flood-control project, begun in 1933 by the C.W.A., was continued under the F.E.R.A. and finally taken over by the U. S. War Department, which spent approximately $591,000 from W.P.A. funds on stream clearance, drainage, levee construction, and bridge work.

The GRIGGS HOUSE (*private*), W. Tenth St., built about 1857, is a square-pillared, white frame house set amid cedars, boxwood, and wistaria. It is on the SITE OF THE BATTLE OF WEST POINT, which lies partly in Georgia and partly in Alabama. On a hill rising behind the house are the REMAINS OF FORT TYLER, breastworks erected to protect the city from the fire of Federal guns. General Wilson quotes Colonel La Grange's description of the fort as "a remarkably strong bastioned earthwork 35 yards square, surrounded by a ditch 12 feet wide and 10 feet deep, situated on a commanding eminence protected by an imperfect abatis and mounting two 32-pounders and two field guns." On Easter, April 16, 1865, Confederate forces under General Robert C. Tyler, who was killed, held the fort for several hours against a brigade of Federal troops under Colonel O. H. La Grange. This force was a flanking detachment of General James H. Wilson's cavalry corps which had been ordered to raid the Confederate depots and manufactories in Georgia and Alabama.

At **84.5 m.** US 29 crosses the Alabama Line at a point 23 miles east of Opelika, Alabama.

TOUR 3A

Danielsville — Elberton — (Abbeville, S. C.); State 36.

Danielsville to South Carolina Line, 39.2 m. — **Roadbed asphalt-paved except between Danielsville and Comer** — Seaboard Air Line Ry. parallels route from Comer to South Carolina Line — Limited accommodations.

State 36 crosses a land of rolling red clay hills devoted principally to agriculture. In Elbert County are several old houses associated with pioneer and Revolutionary days. The vicinity of Elberton is noted for its large deposits of granite, Georgia's second most important mineral resource.

At DANIELSVILLE, **0 m.** (760 alt., 296 pop.) (*see* TOUR 3), State 36 branches east from US 29 (*see* TOUR 3).

ELBERTON, **24.1 m.** (706 alt., 4,650 pop.), was settled during the 1780's by pioneers who came from Virginia and the Carolinas with gun and axe to open up the Cherokee lands. The town was named for General Samuel Elbert, the Revolutionary soldier who took Fort Oglethorpe and later became Governor of Georgia. When Elbert County was created in 1790 Elberton became the county seat but did not begin to prosper until a railroad was run through this section after the War between the States. Its most rapid growth began after the first granite quarry was opened in 1882. It is now the largest granite finishing and shipping point in the state. More than fifteen hundred workers are employed in the operation of the quarries and finishing sheds in the vicinity, almost all of which are locally owned. Additional stimulus to the industrial life of the town was given by the establishment of a large silk mill in 1926.

The OLIVER HOUSE (*private*), McIntosh St. (L) between Church and Edward Sts., was built in 1840. The white frame house, with its two-story gallery porch, three dormer windows, and square columns, is of an architectural type characteristic of the Louisiana low country but rarely found in Georgia. The main veranda, which is on the second floor, is adorned with banisters and reached by a curving double stairway at one side.

The HEARD HOUSE (*private*), Heard St. (R) between Thomas and Tusten Sts., is a white frame house with eight slender square columns across the facade. Extending from the hipped roof and surmounting the four central columns is a classic pediment; a small balcony overhangs the main doorway. The house was built about 1853.

The JAMES HOUSE (*private*), 340 Heard St., is the oldest of Elberton's ante bellum houses. Built about 1820, it has a gabled roof and classic portico with pediment and heavy square columns characteristic of the early Republican architecture in this section. Pleasing details are the balcony above the doorway and the banisters surrounding the floor of the portico.

Left from Elberton on State 77, a dirt road, to a junction with an unimproved country road, **1.6 m.**; R. on this second road is RUCKERSVILLE, **7.9 m.** (approx. 750 alt., 74 pop.), incorporated in 1822 and one of the oldest settlements in Elbert County. Here the Bank of Ruckersville, the first in the state to issue notes that passed at par, was established by Joseph Rucker, who is believed to have been Georgia's first millionaire.

1. Right from Ruckersville to (R) the old JOSEPH RUCKER HOUSE (*private*), **0.2 m.**, begun in 1806 on a grant received from the state in 1795. The original house was built of logs with rock and mud chimneys. In 1812 the lean-to room and shed in the rear were added and, in 1820, the right wing and permanent brick end chimneys. The fine avenue of cedars and Virginia boxwood was set out in 1825. Several years later a circular boxwood garden with crape myrtle and wistaria was planted but is now so overgrown with weeds that it is hardly distinguishable. In this house were born Tinsley White Rucker, Jr., a prominent lawyer and member for two months of the U. S. House of Representatives; and Joseph Rucker Lamar, Associate Justice of the U. S. Supreme Court.

2. Left from Ruckersville to VAN'S CREEK CHURCH (L), **0.3 m.**, organized in 1785, the second oldest Baptist church in Georgia. Dozier Thornton came into the wilderness here in 1784 to preach to the Indians and the few early settlers. At first a few hewn logs served as pews and a stump as a pulpit, but in 1800 a small cabin was built. The present church building, with clapboard exterior, two entrances, and steep gable roof, is the third on the site. Old records indicate that the church was "puritanical in creed and fanatical in government."

At **25.6 m.** is a junction with unpaved State 17.

Right on State 17 to the junction with an unimproved dirt road, **8.9 m.**; L. on this road to a gateway (R) with two tall stone columns marking the entrance to NANCY HART FOREST PARK, **10.4 m.**, maintained by local chapters of the D. A. R. as a memorial to Nancy Hart, whose courageous deeds during the Revolution have given rise to many stories. When six Tories arrived at her cabin and demanded that she cook them a meal, Nancy began preparing an old turkey and sent her daughter Sukey for water. Near the spring was a conch shell, which

Sukey used to summon her father. Meanwhile Nancy, busy with her cooking, contrived to pass frequently between the Tories and their stacked guns. She had slipped two guns through a crack between the logs when she was detected in putting out the third. The Tories sprang to their feet, but instantly Nancy pointed the gun and threatened to shoot the first man who moved. As one advanced, she killed him; seizing another gun, she fired again, and another Tory fell wounded. Hart and his neighbors, who had rushed to the cabin, wanted to shoot the captured men, but Nancy said shooting was too good for Tories; so they were taken to the woods and hanged.

Another story tells how, in order to procure information for Georgia troops concerning the enemy camp in Carolina, she crossed and recrossed the Savannah River on a raft made of four logs tied together with grapevines. On yet another occasion she is said to have donned the clothes of a man, boldly entered the British camp at Augusta, and obtained information of much value to Colonel Elijah Clarke.

Nancy Hart has been described as a gigantic, red-haired woman, cross-eyed, uncouth, and almost grotesque. Historical sources, however, indicate that, although she was six feet tall and of almost masculine build, she was a rather attractive brunette.

The park consists of five acres of the original four hundred acres granted to Benjamin Hart, Nancy's husband, and has been kept in its natural state—a woodland of dark oaks and pines, especially beautiful in spring when the white dogwood blooms. A circular driveway leads to a reproduction of the NANCY HART CABIN, a one-room, mud-chinked log cabin, eighteen by twenty-seven feet, with stone chimney, board-shuttered windows, and board doors. Through the park runs War Woman Creek, named by the Indians for Nancy Hart, whom they feared and respected. Right from the entrance just inside the park is a granite marker indicating a path that leads to the Nancy Hart Spring, where the Tories captured by Nancy Hart are said to have been hanged; its cold, clear water runs into a rock enclosure.

At **30.8 m.** is the junction with a dirt road.

Left on this road is MIDDLETON, **1.1 m.** (approx. 600 alt., 151 pop.); R. from Middleton to the junction with another dirt road, **2.2 m.**; R. on this road to (R) the WILLIAM ALLEN HOME (*private*), **5.1 m.** The two-story frame Georgian Colonial house, set well back and not visible from the road, has a long veranda with a central porch on the second story surmounted by a gable pediment. In the pediment is a fan-shaped sentinel window. Built in 1785, this is conceded to be the oldest house now standing in Elbert County.

At **7 m.** is HEARDMONT (600 alt., 350 pop.), named for Stephen Heard, acting Governor of Georgia during the Revolution. For his services he was awarded 2,343 acres of land in Wilkes County.

An old Cherokee trail once led from here to the Savannah River ford that was crossed by settlers from Virginia and the Carolinas after the opening of great tracts in this section. Here was constructed a blockhouse that aided the early settlers in repulsing the British.

ROSE HILL (L), **31 m.**, is a white frame structure with a narrow two-story central porch. The central portion of this house was originally part of the home of Stephen Heard. The spacious grounds, with their avenues of oaks and cedars, are noted throughout this section of the state. In 1895 Mrs. Eugene B. Heard established at Rose Hill the

Seaboard Railway Traveling Library, from which any resident of Elbert County can obtain books and periodicals free.

At **34.3 m.** is the junction with a dirt road.

Right on this road to the SITE OF THE STATE'S FIRST METHODIST CONFERENCE (L), **4.1 m.**, held in 1788 by Bishop Francis Asbury. Because there was a malaria epidemic in the neighboring towns, Judge Charles Tait, later United States Senator, invited Bishop Asbury to hold the conference at his plantation home. A recently constructed bungalow on the spot where the Tait home stood contains some of the original wainscoting, flooring, an old door, and an old mantel.

The congregation of BETHLEHEM CHURCH (R), **36 m.**, was organized by early Methodists of the community. The original structure, built before 1800 and known as Thompson's Meeting House, has been replaced by a new, white clapboard church set back from the highway.

At **39.2 m.** the highway crosses the Savannah River, the South Carolina Line, 19 miles west of Abbeville, South Carolina.

TOUR 3B

Moreland — Greenville — Warm Springs — Pine Mountain State Park — Tip Top; 44.3 m., State 41, State 85 and Pine Mountain Parkway.

Roadbed concrete-paved between Moreland and Warm Springs, graveled elsewhere (being paved 1939) — Central of Georgia Ry. parallels route from Greenville to Warm Springs — Bus line from Moreland to Harris — All types of accommodations at Warm Springs; limited elsewhere.

State 41 is a part of the Franklin D. Roosevelt Highway from Washington, D. C., to Warm Springs, named in recognition of the work done by the President in sponsoring the Warm Springs Foundation for the treatment of victims of poliomyelitis (infantile paralysis). It passes through a pleasant farming section, where there are large peach and pecan orchards as well as fields of cotton, corn, peanuts, and watermelons. West of Warm Springs the route crosses the Pine Mountain State Park.

MORELAND, **0 m.** (937 alt., 343 pop.) (*see* TOUR 3), is at the junction with US 29 (*see* TOUR 3).

GREENVILLE, **18.5 m.** (447 alt., 672 pop.), seat of Meriwether County, was incorporated in 1828. Honoring Nathanael Greene, Revolutionary

War general, the name of the town was originally spelled with a middle *e,* which was later dropped. Its income is derived chiefly from agricultural and dairy products and from orchards.

From HARRIS, 22.4 m. (884 alt., 106 pop.), a local bus runs to Warm Springs.

WARM SPRINGS FOUNDATION (R), 28.3 m.

Visiting Hours: 12:30-3 Sun., 1:30-3:30 weekdays.
Accommodations: one hotel at Warm Springs village, $1.50 up; tourist houses and private homes, $15 a week. Warm Springs Foundation provides rooms not in use to relatives of patients and interested visitors at a rate higher than that charged patients, who pay only costs. Guests admitted to dining room in Georgia Hall.
Transportation: Southern Ry. and Atlanta, Birmingham & Coast R.R. from Atlanta. Local bus service to Harris, a junction with commercial bus lines.
Recreation: golf course, tennis courts, and riding horses at reasonable rates.

Warm Springs, lying at the foot of Pine Mountain, is celebrated as a center for the after-treatment of poliomyelitis and as the Georgia home of President Franklin D. Roosevelt. Owned by the Warm Springs Foundation are 2,200 acres of pine and oak forests through which dirt roads, well maintained and well marked, lead to the Foundation buildings.

A large outdoor public swimming pool (*children 15¢, adults 35¢; open 9 A.M.-10 P.M., early spring to late fall*), is near the entrance (R). Beyond it is the patients' pool, presented to the Foundation by Mr. and Mrs. Edsel Ford; it is enclosed with glass so that it can be used during all seasons. Both pools are fed by a stream of perpetually warm water which, gushing from its source almost a mile below the surface of Pine Mountain, emerges at a constant temperature of 89° F. and flows at a rate of 800 gallons a minute.

From the rustic entrance gate Pine Road leads to GEORGIA HALL, so named because it was built by voluntary contributions from 50,000 Georgians. This long, one-story structure of whitewashed brick, with a portico of white Doric columns flanked by two wings, is the administration building and contains the registration desk, executive offices, dining hall, reception rooms, and recreation rooms. All entrances are level, and doors are wide enough to permit the passage of wheelchairs into the broad corridors. The decorations throughout achieve a bright, gracious informality. A well-equipped music and game room is provided for the patients, and a small craft shop is maintained for recreation and muscular development rather than for vocational training. The rear door of the building opens automatically, by means of a photoelectric cell, upon a terrace and broad lawn.

From Georgia Hall gently graded walks and pleasant roads lead to dormitories, the infirmary, the pools, and the theater where current motion pictures are shown twice a week. Seats are elevated in the rear of the playhouse, but the greater space in front of the stage is level and open for wheel chairs.

All patients pursue a rigid routine. In many cases this consists of daily exercises in the pools, swimming, rest periods, massage, and walking; in some, plaster casts or even surgery are used. The Foundation operates a school for children, and attempts to provide all facilities for normal living. Patients requiring protracted treatment can rent private cottages. Despite the presence of crutches, wheel chairs, braces, and canes everywhere, the Warm Springs Foundation has the gay atmosphere of a resort rather than that of a hospital.

A well-marked road leads to the LITTLE WHITE HOUSE (*visitors may go only to the white board fence*), the Georgia home of President Roosevelt. The round-columned white frame cottage of six rooms, built in 1932, is visible between the intervening frame garage and guest house. As the cottage faces a ravine at the foot of a heavily wooded mountain, the only approach is from the rear.

Even among the Indians, Warm Springs was known as a health resort where, according to tradition, warriors came to immerse their wounded bodies in the warm waters and soft mud. Believing that a beneficent Great Spirit stoked the fires under the earth to warm the waters, they respected the place as neutral ground where sick men could be free from attack by enemy tribes.

Late in the eighteenth century a group of Savannah residents, fleeing a yellow fever epidemic, discovered Warm Springs. By 1832 the place had become a popular summer resort and a small village had grown up near by. When Union scouts were sent by General Sherman in 1864 to burn the hotel and cottages, they were met by a quick-witted Englishman named Tidmarsh, who declared that he owned the whole of Warm Springs. Because of the strained relations between Great Britain and the Federal government, Sherman resumed his march, leaving the resort intact. In 1865, however, the buildings were reduced to ashes as a result of a bonfire of leaves lighted by Tidmarsh's wife. The resort was afterwards rebuilt and became a fashionable watering place for the aristocracy of the South during the 1880's and 1890's. In later years the property changed hands several times and finally came into the possession of George Foster Peabody, of Saratoga Springs, New York, who aided in the establishment of the Foundation.

The national prominence of Warm Springs resulted from the visits of Franklin D. Roosevelt, who came to the resort in 1921 after an attack of infantile paralysis. In 1925 he made his first extended visit and, after daily exercise in the pools, was so gratified by his improvement that he returned the following year with twenty-three patients and two medical specialists. The progress made by the patients, treated in periods ranging from five to seventeen weeks, convinced him of the value of this place as a recuperative resort.

In 1927 Roosevelt organized the Warm Springs Foundation, a non-profit corporation. Immediately he established a fund to care for patients unable to pay the regular charges, and the Foundation has reserved 50 per cent of its capacity for those who pay none or only part of the cost of their treatment. All patients are accorded identical privileges and impartial attention by the medical and nursing staff. The buildings have all been donated by philanthropic individuals or organizations.

No curative powers are claimed for the springs. The essential purpose of the Foundation has been to build up an orthopedic and physiotherapy staff and to make the best possible use of such natural advantages as high elevation, a mild and invigorating climate, and the inexhaustible flow of warm water. Dr. Michael Hoke, Georgia orthopedic specialist, lived for five years in the Little White House and assembled a staff of assistants, one of whom, Dr. C. E. Irwin, was named surgeon in chief when Dr. Hoke resigned in 1936. Affiliation with the Piedmont Hospital in Atlanta provides the patients with the equipment and services of a general hospital.

In 1933 the patients and the citizens of Warm Springs were invited to Washington for the inauguration of Franklin D. Roosevelt as President of the United States. Each year since, the larger cities of the country have held balls on his birthday, January 30, for the benefit of the Warm Springs Foundation and for research on the treatment of poliomyelitis. In the fall Mr. Roosevelt returns with his family to Warm Springs and carves the Thanksgiving turkey for his friends in the dining room at Georgia Hall.

WARM SPRINGS VILLAGE, 28.8 m. (930 alt., 400 pop.) developed as a railroad junction for the resort of Warm Springs. It was incorporated as Bullochville in 1893 and as Warm Springs in 1924.

In Warm Springs Village the route turns R. on State 85, a graveled road.

Left from Warm Springs on State 41 to COLD SPRINGS, 0.2 m., with a flow of almost mineral-free water that is well adapted to fish culture. Here the Federal government maintains a large fish hatchery, with nineteen breeding pools covering an area of approximately twelve acres. Black bass, bream, and speckled catfish are reared to restock Georgia lakes and streams. The spawning stock is free of diseases that attack fish in mineral-impregnated or polluted waters.

South of Cold Springs the highway runs through an agricultural section where peaches and pimientos are grown.

MANCHESTER, 5.2 m. (884 alt., 3,745 pop.), is an industrial town that developed around railroad machine shops established here in 1908, and was given impetus by the opening of a textile mill the following year.

At 6.5 m. is an intersection with an unpaved road; R. 0.4 m. on this road to MAGIC HILL, a hundred-yard stretch of red clay road over a spur of Pine Mountain. An automobile with motor turned off seems to coast uphill and, after passing the brow, to stop on the downgrade. Water apparently defies the law of gravitation by running uphill and draining off into a ditch on the downgrade. For a long time this place was known to the Negroes of the vicinity as Ghost Hill because some supernatural power was held responsible for their wagons stalling coming "down" and running away going "up." The hill came into state-wide prominence recently when newspapers carried stories of the phenomenon, and hundreds of people flocked to the place. Surveyors explain that the stretch of ground contains a slight knoll and that, if a car is stopped at the brow of the hill and put into neutral, it will coast for about twenty-five yards downhill. The fact that the slight slope runs in a direction different from the drainage ditch creates an optical illusion.

At 32.4 m. is a junction with the Pine Mountain Parkway (*being paved 1939*) upon which the route turns R., following the crest of Pine Mountain.

The road passes the 2,500-acre FRANKLIN D. ROOSEVELT FARM (*private*), 34.4 m. Here experiments in stock breeding and agriculture are conducted for the benefit of the farmers of this region. Two white and five Negro tenant families cultivate about 150 acres under the supervision of a manager. No cotton is planted.

PINE MOUNTAIN STATE PARK (*hiking, horseback riding, boating, fishing, badminton*) 36.9 m., is a 1,550-acre tract of heavily forested land maintained by the division of state parks as a recreational area. In spring the woods are resplendent with white dogwood, flame azalea, and delicate pink mountain laurel. One section is well known for its wild violets.

An Indian trail once led over KING'S GAP (approx. 1,175 alt.) 40.9 m., a mountain pass.

1. Right from King's Gap on a graveled park road is the SITE OF KING'S GAP VILLAGE (*picnic ground*) 0.7 m., a settlement where a post office was established in 1837 on an old stagecoach route from Columbus to Newnan. Envelopes bearing the cancellation marks of King's Gap are now sought by collectors. Since the ruins of an old water mill and tanning vats were removed during park development, a few gnarled fruit trees are the only remains of the settlement, which was abandoned when the Central of Georgia Railroad was built around the lower side of Pine Mountain.

2. Left from King's Gap on a graveled road is a junction with another graveled road 0.4 m.; L. on this road to the campground entrance of the PINE MOUNTAIN RECREATIONAL DEMONSTRATION AREA, 2 m., adjoining Pine Mountain State Park. On this 3,500-acre tract, maintained by the National Park Service, is a 23-acre lake. Here one camp for organized groups has been completed and another is under construction (1939).

ENTRANCE ARCH, UNIVERSITY OF GEORGIA, ATHENS

AGNES SCOTT COLLEGE

GEORGIA MARBLE BUILDINGS, EMORY UNIVERSIT

GLENN MEMORIAL CHURCH, EMORY UNIVERSITY

HENRY FORD BUILDINGS, BERRY SCHOOLS

RURAL CONSOLIDATED SCHOOL

BRITTAIN DINING HALL, GEORGIA SCHOOL OF TECHNOLOGY, ATLANTA

TESTING AIRPLANE MODEL IN WIND TUNNEL, GEORGIA SCHOOL OF TECHNOLOGY

STUDENTS WEAVING, BERRY SCHOOLS

N. Y. A. VOCATIONAL TRAINING

W. P. A. NEGRO LITERACY CLASS

GRADUATION, ATLANTA UNIVERSITY

PRESIDENT ROOSEVELT CARVES THE TURKEY, WARM SPRINGS FOUNDATION

FOUNDATION CLINIC, WARM SPRINGS

PINE MOUNTAIN TAVERN (L) **41.4 m.** (*rooms $2 single, $3.50 double; $21 a week; furnished stone cabins $20 a week for four*) is the recreational center of the park. This rustic stone lodge on one of the higher peaks of Pine Mountain commands a wide view of the surrounding valley.

Right from the tavern on a graveled road to PINE MOUNTAIN LAKE (*furnished log cabins $20 a week for four; picnic facilities*), 1 m., an artificial body of water covering fifteen acres within Pine Mountain State Park. On the ridge above it is a series of rearing pools for bream, rainbow trout, and bass.

TIP TOP (1,037 alt.) **44.3 m.** (*see* TOUR *10*) is at the junction with US 27 (*see* TOUR *10*).

TOUR 4

(*Columbia, S. C.*) — *Augusta* — *Louisville* — *Baxley* — *Waycross* — *Folkston* — (*Jacksonville, Fla.*); *US 1.*

South Carolina Line to Florida Line, 222.5 m. — Roadbed hard-surfaced throughout; one half concrete — Watch for cattle and pigs on the road — Atlantic Coast Line R.R. parallels route from Waycross to the Florida Line — All types of accommodations in Augusta and Waycross; limited elsewhere.

US 1 traverses a rural section that is the locale of Erskine Caldwell's *Tobacco Road* and Caroline Miller's Pulitzer Prize novel of 1933, *Lamb in His Bosom*. In the extreme southern part of the state the highway skirts the Okefenokee Swamp, a favorite laboratory for naturalists. Waycross is the only town on the route with a population exceeding 2,500.

Between Augusta and Louisville US 1 follows a Uchee trail, which later became a stagecoach route. Before the War between the States, this region was a part of the plantation belt, where slave labor was abundant for cultivating the large farms. There is a lingering charm and mellowed grace about the houses, some of which date back almost to the Revolution, but more in evidence is the sharecropper's unpainted shack with sagging porch.

Winding through the low, red clay hills, the highway bisects fields where cotton grows to a height of about three feet. In late August and early September barefoot Negroes, with red bandannas or wide straw hats on their heads and long burlap sacks slung from their shoulders, bend low over the stalks and pick the soft, white staple from the bolls.

Interspersed with fields of cotton, tobacco, sugar cane, and peanuts are farmhouses, some of them shakily balanced on rock supports. Here and there are rusty plantation dinner bells on tall poles, wells with windlasses and oaken buckets, and gourds swinging from crosspieces on high posts to provide nesting places for the martins that keep the hawks away from the chickens. Frequently the porches are boarded in to hold loose cotton piled there until enough for a bale has been picked. Instead of planting grass in their yards, the housewives sweep them clean with bundles of twigs, but even the shabbiest house is brightened with petunias, zinnias, and geraniums growing in the yards and in tin cans on the porches. Prosperity is shown on a few farms by fresh paint, new farm implements, or new lightning rods gleaming against the sky.

US 1 crosses the Savannah River, 0 m., the boundary between South Carolina and Georgia, over a free bridge.

AUGUSTA, 0.5 m. (143 alt., 60,342 pop.) (*see* AUGUSTA).

Points of Interest: The Hill, University of Georgia School of Medicine, Junior College of Augusta, Paine College (Negro), Haines Institute (Negro), Cotton Exchange, and others.

Augusta is at the junction with US 78 (*see* TOUR 8) and US 25 (*see* TOUR 15).

At 15 m. is a junction with the Bath Road.

Right on this road is BATH, 0.5 m. (410 alt., 30 pop.). This village, formerly known as Richmond Bath, developed in the early part of the nineteenth century as a summer resort because the cold, clear water of the spring supposedly possessed medicinal qualities. During ante bellum days this retreat of wealthy planters was celebrated for its old mansions and its hospitality. When malaria in low-lying Burke County caused "third day chills and fever," many families fled here. Most of the old buildings have been burned, and only the decaying manse and the well-preserved PRESBYTERIAN CHURCH remain. The church is a square white clapboard structure designed by James Trowbridge, of Boston, and built about 1820. The hand-made pulpit and pews, the slave gallery at the side, and the bell hanging in the square steeple, all remain unchanged. For eight years, beginning in 1843, the Reverend Francis R. Goulding served as minister of this church. In the manse next door he wrote *Young Marooners* and, before Elias Howe's invention, was working to perfect a sewing machine. He failed, however, because he did not place the eye of the needle near its point.

In the churchyard is the BATH CEMETERY, its oldest stone bearing the date September 20, 1816.

THE ABRAHAM (ABRAM) BEASLEY PLACE (*private*), 31.3 m. (L), probably built soon after the Revolutionary War, is an excellent example of the pioneer Georgia home. There is no proof of the exact date because all Jefferson County records were destroyed by Union troops during the War between the States.

The house, now in disrepair, is of the dog-trot or breezeway type, having two rooms connected by an open hallway. It is built of heavy hand-hewn timbers crudely squared and evened and fastened together with wooden pegs. The beam along the roof of the front porch is a solid piece of timber sixty feet long.

WRENS, 33.3 m. (423 alt., 1,085 pop.), was established in 1884, when the Augusta Southern Railroad was laid. The founder, W. J. Wren, inherited the land from his grandfather who, according to local tradition, had obtained it in exchange for two blind horses. Though chiefly a trading point for the surrounding agricultural region, the town has several planing mills, a flour mill, and a cotton gin.

Wrens was the boyhood home of Erskine Caldwell, who is known not only for his novels, including *Tobacco Road* and *God's Little Acre,* but for numerous short stories dealing with the tenant farmer. With his father, a Presbyterian minister and teacher, Caldwell visited the country people throughout the section and noted the manner in which the sharecroppers lived. When challenged for the obscenity of his work, Caldwell replied, "It is no more obscene than life." Most Georgians, however, contend that the conditions described are less general than the book implies.

Tobacco Road is the name of a dirt country road that formerly ran along a ridge from north Georgia to a point on the Savannah River below Augusta; it was used for hauling tobacco in mule-drawn hogsheads to the port, where it was loaded on boats.

POPE HILL (*private*), a white clapboard house on the eastern edge of the town, was erected about 1850. Here Jefferson Davis, after his capture by Union forces, was allowed to stop for breakfast. Although the front has been considerably altered by the addition of a porch and porte-cochere, the outlines of the original small stoop can still be seen in the paneling on both sides of the front door. During the nineteenth century the residence served as an inn and a relay station where stagecoaches changed horses.

The OLIPHANT HOME (*private*), 35.1 m. (R), is a plantation house built between 1820 and 1830. A story-and-a-half structure of wide clapboards, it has a center hall flanked by two high-ceiled rooms; later rooms have been added on each side of the front porch. The kitchen, originally standing at a distance from the house, has been moved nearer the back porch. From the rear of the "big house" a lane leads between the double row of slave cabins, which are sagging and weather-worn but held intact by their massive stone chimneys. The old gin-house still remains on the plantation. Although General Sherman's men burned near-by houses on their march to the sea, they left this place unharmed because, as the story is told, the mistress of the Oliphant house was courteous to the Federal soldiers and had food prepared for them.

The OLD WHIGHAM PLACE (*private*), 42.4 m., (R) is a gaunt, high-standing frame structure with a one-story porch jutting from the front and a kitchen ell from the side. Broad end chimneys dwindle to narrow, tall flues above the roof. An original grant in the possession of the Whigham family shows that the land was owned by that family in 1790, and it is believed that this house was built shortly after that date. The house remained in the hands of the Whigham family until 1910; the present owner maintains a pecan market catering to tourist trade.

The GOBERT HOUSE (*private*), 46.4 m., (L) was built between 1796 and 1800 by Benjamin Gobert, a political refugee from France. The one-story frame house has a steep, shingled roof and double doors opening on a dilapidated front porch. The interior has wide board ceilings and chair rails around the wall.

LOUISVILLE, 48.3 m. (337 alt., 1,650 pop.), seat of Jefferson County, succeeded Savannah and Augusta as Georgia's capital. The town was laid out in 1786 on a 1,000-acre tract purchased by the state for the establishment of a capital. The first statehouse was completed in 1796 in time for a session of the legislature, and the last session was held there in 1805 before Milledgeville became the capital.

The OLD SLAVE MARKET, Broad St., was probably built before 1800 though the exact date is not known. Hand-hewn posts support a roof approximately twenty feet square. The bell, sent in 1772 by the King of France as a gift to a convent in New Orleans, was taken by pirates and sold at Savannah, where it was bought for this slave market. Besides ringing notice of slave sales, this bell also warned settlers of Indian attacks and, after the creation of Jefferson County, called them together for sheriff's sales. This is one of the few slave markets still standing in the South.

The JEFFERSON COUNTY COURTHOUSE, E. Broad St., built from materials of the old state capitol, occupies the site of that building. In front of the courthouse is the marked SITE WHERE THE YAZOO PAPERS WERE BURNED on February 15, 1796, after an impressive ceremony in the presence of the Governor and members of both legislative bodies (*see* HISTORY). Speculative land companies had bought from Georgia 35,000,000 acres of land in the present states of Mississippi and Alabama near the Yazoo River for less than one and a half cents an acre. A state-wide wave of indignation caused the passage of a legislative act to rescind the sale and to destroy all records of the transaction. Later the U. S. Supreme Court declared this act by the Georgia Legislature unconstitutional, and in 1814 a settlement was made with the claimants.

Tradition has handed down a dramatic story of the burning of the Yazoo papers. While the crowd stood with uncovered heads, a white-haired stranger galloped up, dismounted, and proclaimed that he had come to see justice done. Saying that only fire from heaven should destroy such works of iniquity, he drew a sunglass from his pocket and held it over the pile of paper until smoke began to rise. Then he rode away, never to be seen again.

In the LOUISVILLE CITY CEMETERY, W. 7th St., is a tall granite monument marking the grave of Herschel V. Johnson, Governor of Georgia (1853-57), judge of the superior court, and a candidate in 1860 for Vice President of the United States. Near the cemetery is a small granite marker on the SITE OF LOUISVILLE ACADEMY, chartered in 1796, one of the earliest educational institutions in the state.

The ROGER LAWSON ESTATE (L), 5th St. R. of State 24, just within the city limits, has a two-story clapboard house standing on a hill at the end of a long avenue of oaks. This building, now in a dilapidated condition, has a two-story pedimented portico with upper gallery, and windows flanked by crude batten shutters. A double row of slave cabins lines the red clay road which leads to the entrance. Roger Lawson, who received this land as a grant and called it Mount Pleasant, built the house—originally a one-story structure—in 1764 and converted it into a fort during the Revolution. One of his sons was killed in a fight against Tories and Indians. In the early part of the nineteenth century, a subsequent owner enlarged the house but retained the simple design of the original structure in its paneling and wood trim.

At Louisville is the junction with State 24 (see TOUR 14).

SWAINSBORO, 78.7 m. (318 alt., 2,442 pop.), seat of Emanuel County, was incorporated in 1853. Among the industrial plants are saw mills, planing mills, cotton gins, turpentine stills, machine shops, and warehouses. Hogs, turkeys, chickens, and goats are exported in large numbers.

Swainsboro is at the junction with US 80 (see TOUR 9).

Emanuel County, created in 1812 and named for David Emanuel, Revolutionary soldier and Governor of Georgia, covers 1,000 square miles; because of its size citizens often speak of it as the State of Emanuel. The county produces large quantities of naval stores, sweet potatoes, corn, nuts, sugar cane, hay, and velvet beans. This diversity makes possible a four-year program of crop rotation, which agricultural agencies are trying to put into effect.

Below Swainsboro the road stretches through the lonely piney woods or wiregrass section, the last part of Georgia to be developed. ⸱ In the mid-nineteenth century small farmers from the Carolinas were attracted to this region by the lumber of the pine forests. Relatively few Negroes live here, and the land is worked by independent owners, who grow cotton as the principal money crop. Since the price of cotton, fluctuating from five to fifteen cents a pound, has frequently failed to meet production costs, the farmers have suffered acutely for many years. Recently, however, cigarette tobacco has been grown on a large scale, and has provided an important cash crop in the pine barrens. The planter received approximately twenty-one cents a pound for his tobacco in 1936.

LYONS, 107.6 m. (254 alt., 1,445 pop.), seat of Toombs County, was chartered in 1897. Tobacco, cotton, and corn are cultivated on the surrounding farms, and there are extensive timberlands in the area. The big-stemmed Jersey sweet potato is raised in large quantities.

Left from Lyons on US 280 is REIDSVILLE, 16.8 m. (200 alt., 631 pop.), which has been the seat of Tattnall County since 1832, although it was not incorporated until 1838. Tattnall County was named for General Josiah Tattnall, Revolutionary patriot and Governor of Georgia.

Left from Reidsville on State 147 to the new STATE PENITENTIARY, 22.8 m., a model prison constructed by P.W.A. funds under the supervision of the Prison Commission of Georgia and completed in 1936. Tucker and Howell, of Atlanta, were the architects. Outwardly this massive, dignified white concrete structure has the appearance of a modern office building. Above the two fluted columns of the entrance is a bas-relief panel by Julian Harris, a Georgia sculptor, portraying various activities of prison life. The central figure, representing Justice, is that of a powerfully built man instead of the conventional blindfolded goddess.

The building, with a frontage of 1,020 feet and a depth of 842 feet, contains 8 units with accommodations for 2,000 prisoners. The units on the right are for white prisoners and those on the left for Negroes. Young boys are separated from the more hardened type of criminal. Two large recreation fields are provided for exercise under close supervision.

Since the prison is almost completely isolated from large industrial cities, the plant was designed to be a self-sufficient unit. Ample storage space is provided for emergency as well as daily needs, and spare parts for all mechanical equipment are kept in stock. Prisoners cultivate their own food crops on a 980-acre tract of land surrounding the prison and adjoining the old state prison farm. In the machine shops they are taught trades as part of the program for rehabilitation. The state automobile tag plant was recently moved here from the old state penitentiary at Milledgeville (*see* TOUR *14*).

The plans and specifications of the building meet the standards set by the U. S. Bureau of Prisons. An agreement has been worked out with the Federal administration whereby, over a period of years, the state will pay 70 per cent of the cost, the Federal government contributing 30 per cent. The building cost $1,281,980, and equipment brings the total to $1,500,000. This prison will enable the state to abolish many of the old convict camps, which have been the target of much criticism from other parts of the country.

BAXLEY, 138.4 m. (206 alt., 2,122 pop.), seat of Appling County, was incorporated in 1875. In recent years the increased transportation facilities have made it a marketing and shipping center for the products of the surrounding area—tobacco, naval stores, lumber, pecans, and syrup. Two tobacco warehouses provide ample marketing facilities for the growers of the surrounding district. During the market season, which lasts for three or four weeks in late summer, the farmers bring their golden, aromatic leaves to the warehouse where they pile them neatly on the floor. As the auctioneer goes rapidly from pile to pile, he calls prices in a staccato manner unintelligible to the layman while the buyers signal their competitive bids. When the season is over, buyers move on to the North Carolina markets.

Resin from the slashed pines is brought to the turpentine stills to be made into hard rosin and crude turpentine. The unpainted frame sheds are crowded with barrels of amber-colored rosin, and the loading platform is gummed with resin drippings. A large copper kettle of crude resin is heated gradually; the hot vapors escape through a condensing worm that is cooled by a stream of water. The dross, chips of pine wood covered with inflammable resin, is gathered and sold for kindling. With a few handfuls of dross and a few fat pine splinters the greenest wood and hardest coal can be made to blaze quickly.

Caroline Miller was living here when she wrote *Lamb in His Bosom,* for which she secured material by talking with the farmers of this vicinity.

At Baxley is the junction with US 341 (*see* TOUR *12*).

ALMA, 156.7 m. (195 alt., 1,235 pop.), incorporated in 1926, is the seat of Bacon County, which was created in 1914.

Near Waycross the farmhouses appear better kept, and many are provided with electricity. Each has its flower plot in front, vegetable garden to the side or rear, some pecan trees, and a few cattle to provide milk and beef for home consumption.

Throughout the wiregrass section the poorer tenant farmers formerly raised "piney woods" cattle and "razorback" hogs—inferior breeds allowed to roam and graze as they could. Now, under the guidance of agricultural agencies, their livestock has been improved by proper breeding, care, and sanitation.

In HEBARDVILLE, 180.4 m. (approx. 140 alt., 309 pop.), is the mill of the Hebard Cypress Company, which has a daily sawing capacity of 150,000 feet. Until recently this company held options on the greater part of the Okefenokee Swamp, from which cypress timber was shipped by rail to be sawed and planed here.

WAYCROSS, **183.4 m.** (138 alt., 15,510 pop.), with large oaks shading the streets, is a clean, well-paved, and progressive city that owes its development as well as its name to being the converging point of nine railroads and five highways.

In 1818 settlers began to claim the land near Kettle Creek, now a part of Waycross, and to build blockhouses and fortifications for protection against the Indians. By 1825 the land had been acquired from the Indians and granted to individuals under the lottery system, initiated in Georgia in the early part of the nineteenth century after the disposal of the lands lying west of the Chattahoochee River. The officials of the state were determined that land should be parceled out in small tracts free of charge, and Governor Troup expressed their policy when he said: "Men and the soil constitute the strength and wealth of the nations, and the faster you plant men, the faster you can draw on both." After the land had been surveyed and charted into parcels, usually of 212.5 acres, it was distributed by lot. Each citizen was given one chance and heads of families two chances, but since there were more citizens than parcels of land in every lottery, many people drew blanks. As late as 1870 Waycross was only a railroad junction with fifty inhabitants and a few scattered houses, but within one generation it has become an important commercial center of southern Georgia.

Throughout a belt seventy-five miles wide, beginning at Savannah and running through Waycross to Bainbridge, bee culture has become so extensive that Georgia leads the South in the production of honey. The blossoms of the tupelo tree provide a heavy, amber-colored honey, and the small white blooms of the gallberry bushes give a clear, almost white variety. One honey establishment in Waycross has 8,500 colonies of bees in 300 apiaries.

Among the industries of the city are the production of naval stores and the marketing of furs. There are two planing mills, a pecan-shelling plant, two tobacco warehouses, and a coffin factory. Local tobacco growers take their leaves to the warehouses to be dried on long racks and stored. In 1935-36, 3,000,000 pounds sold in Waycross brought $826,000. The marketing of furs and alligator hides, formerly of commercial importance to Waycross, has greatly decreased in volume since the near-by Okefenokee Swamp was closed to hunters and trappers in 1937, for most of the pelts were obtained from that rich wild life area. Of the pelts marketed, raccoon is by far the most numerous; others are opossum, mink, muskrat, skunk, gray fox, otter, red fox, weasel, wildcat, and deer.

ATLANTIC COAST LINE RAILROAD SHOPS, on US 1 at the southern limits of the city, cover many acres of land and represent an investment of

$3,000,000. They employ hundreds of skilled mechanics and laborers and are the line's largest shops. In connection with the shops is a diversion yard, to which numerous fruit and vegetable cars are directed for icing and rerouting.

Right from Waycross on State 50 to WINONA PARK, 3 m., a popular recreation center with beautiful winding drives and a large lake surrounded by tall pines.

At Waycross is the junction with US 84 (*see* TOUR 5).

In FOLKSTON, 218.2 m. (81 alt., 506 pop.), seat of Charlton County, is the home of Dan Hebard, who controls the lumber company that formerly held an option on the Okefenokee Swamp.

At Folkston is a junction with State 23 (*see* TOUR *4A*).

US 1 crosses the ST. MARYS RIVER, 222.5 m., which is the Florida Line, at a point 39.5 miles north of Jacksonville, Florida.

TOUR 4A

Folkston — Camp Cornelia; 12 m., State 23 and an unnumbered road.

Roadbed unpaved — One hotel at Folkston, only accommodations.

This route leads to the headquarters of the U. S. Biological Survey's Okefenokee Swamp wild life refuge, a point of entrance to this swamp. Since the publication of the autobiographical *Travels of William Bartram* in 1791, the Okefenokee has been known as a region of strange jungle-like beauty abounding with plant and animal life, including varieties rarely found elsewhere.

In FOLKSTON, 0 m. (81 alt., 506 pop.) (*see* TOUR *4*), State 23 branches southwest from US 1 (*see* TOUR *4*).

At 8 m. is a junction with a dirt road; the route turns R. on this.

In CAMP CORNELIA, 12 m. (158 alt.), once the site of a lumber camp, are several log-cabin-type structures housing the headquarters of the OKEFENOKEE WILDLIFE REFUGE (*permit signed by the management, patrolman, or licensed guide required; guides essential; guide and motorboat, 1 or 2 passengers, $8 a day; 3 passengers, $10; each additional passenger, $1; bateaux or duck punts, 1 passenger, $3.50 for long trip,*

$2.50 for short trip, additional passengers, 50¢; no hunting; fishing in Suwannee Canal and certain designated lakes and prairies; old clothing advisable; best seasons: summer for fishing or bird and alligator study, winter for waterfowl, May for blossoming plants). Camp Cornelia is on Trail Ridge, which forms the eastern boundary of the Okefenokee Swamp. From this point the Suwannee, (Okefenokee) Canal, an old drainage canal leading into the interior of the swamp, is navigable by boat. Because of the dense cypress growths, passage from one side of the swamp to the other is difficult. The western side can be entered from Fargo (*see* TOUR 5) by following the Suwannee River to Billy's Island (*see below*).

The Okefenokee Swamp (120 alt.), 660 square miles of fresh water and timber, extends from a point a few miles south of Waycross to an indefinite termination several miles south of the Florida Line. It is approximately forty miles long and averages twenty miles wide. It was once the hunting ground of the lower Creek and Seminole; its name is a corruption of Owaquaphenoga (Ind., trembling earth). Geologists believe that the Okefenokee was once a salt-water sound that was shut off from the ocean by a barrier reef now called Trail Ridge, and that in its earlier stages it probably resembled the much younger Dismal Swamp in North Carolina and Virginia and the Everglades in Florida.

Despite repeated efforts to utilize its resources, the area remains an unconquered wilderness. In 1889 the Suwannee Canal Company bought the area from the state for about $62,000, intending to drain the swamp into the St. Marys River, cut the rich timber, and turn the great "prairies" (submerged trembling earth covered by a heavy growth of yellow-eyed grass) into farm lands. After more than a million dollars had been spent digging miles of canals with steam shovels and dredges, the corporation failed and abandoned the project. The next effort was made in 1908 by the Hebard Lumber Company, which forced into the swamp a railroad built on piling, with branch lines leading to the principal islands and "bays." For several years the work continued but was eventually stopped because the expense of cutting and shipping the timber became too great. The railroad is now a skeleton of rotting crossties and piling.

Of the total 479,450 acres in Charlton, Clinch, and Ware counties designated by President Franklin D. Roosevelt in 1937 as the ultimate boundary of this refuge, a tract of 293,826 acres has been acquired by the U. S. Biological Survey at a cost of $400,000, to preserve the primeval beauty of the swamp and safeguard its wild life resources. The boundaries have been posted and boat trails are being constructed (1939) to open inaccessible areas for scientific observation, but no highways will be built within the refuge, as they would impair its isolation and increase the possibility of fire. Exploitation of timber, fur, and other resources will not be permitted.

In this vast swamp, large bodies of water stretch through labyrinths of moss-covered cypress trees. White and golden water lilies, locally called "bonnets," and other flowering plants form bright splashes against the silvery, gently swaying screen of Spanish moss. The great expanse of swamp, with cypress and tupelo trees growing out of the water, is broken by several lakes and islands, by many acres of "prairies," and by "houses" (clumps of bushes and trees and an impenetrable undergrowth of berries, smilax, and muscadines growing on more solid areas).

The prairies are threaded by a maze of water runways which lead from lily-covered cypress bogs to alligator holes. Some of the prairies are named Grand, New Territory, Durdkin, Carter's, and Chase. Grand Prairie, which is perhaps the largest, covers fifty square miles and contains Gannett Lake, Buzzards' Roost Lake, Coward Lake, Sego Lake, and many smaller bays and water holes.

The houses are formed and bogs extended by a phenomenon known locally as a "blow-up." This occurs when gases, formed beneath the water by decaying vegetable matter, force masses of vegetation, some a hundred feet square, from the bottom of the water. Assisted by the rise and fall of the water level, the surface of the mass, resembling muck, rises several inches above the water and becomes covered with grass, briars, small bushes, and water weeds. When it has accumulated this covering, the entire mass floats until caught in a clump of trees; sometimes it is forced beneath the surface by the pressure of growing cypress roots. During its floating period this earth-raft collects seeds from cypress and other trees and in time develops into a house; many never become stable but sway and tremble under the slightest weight.

The old drainage canal, with its slow-moving water, is bordered by tall tupelo, cypress, and dahoon holly trees. The holly has an abundance of bright red berries in winter, and its leaves are spineless and rounded like those of the live oak. The water is colored dark brown by the tannic acid of decaying vegetable matter. At the northern end of the canal is Chase Prairie, navigable only by duck punts, small shells poled by guides who stand near the stern. The pole usually is about fifteen feet long and is terminated by two prongs used to grip the submerged masses of vegetation. The punt is shallow, drawing only four inches of water, for there are many grassy stretches to be skimmed; it is narrow so that it may thread its way between tupelo roots and the cypress "knees," as the enlargements on the roots projecting above the water are called.

Northwest of Chase Prairie is FLOYD'S ISLAND, named for General Charles Floyd, who in 1838 was commissioned to drive the Indians from the larger islands within the swamp. The camp house on the island belonged to Dan Hebard, who hunted in the swamp every year. Here, as Hebard's guests, many naturalists have spent much time studying the wild life of the Okefenokee.

Floyd's Island is one of more than twenty-five flat, white-sand islands in the swamp. They differ little from the surrounding mainland. All are covered with a thick growth of saw palmettos, huckleberries, blueberries, gallberries, sedges, and various small herbs. Longleaf and slash pines predominate in the central parts of the islands, but in the richer soil along the margins are live oak, magnolia, bay, and sweet gum trees. So dense are the bogs of muck and moss around some of the islands that it is possible to walk upon them. Here, growing to the unusual height of three feet, are great numbers of the spotted, greenish pitcher plants that ensnare small flies in their tubelike leaves by means of a sweetish liquid, imprison them with a projecting flap, and slowly digest them. Other flowers that give variety to the waterways are the blue-flowered pickerelweeds, purple water shields, and dainty white floating hearts.

On some of these islands the Seminole, driven to this fastness by invading colonists, have left mounds. A few hardy settlers later ventured here and made a meager living by marketing lumber and pine resin and by raising cattle. COWHOUSE ISLAND received its name during the War between the States, when it was used by farmers to hide their cattle from Federal troops searching for supplies. BILLY'S ISLAND, named for Billy Bowlegs, a Seminole chief, is one of the largest islands —four miles long and one mile wide. For two generations it was the home of the Daniel Lees, who for many years were the only white people living in the interior of the swamp; in their isolated home, never visited by a doctor, fifteen children were born. When timber crews first came into the swamp in the latter part of the nineteenth century, the Lees moved outside but were so homesick that they returned within a year. A lumber camp with a store, school, and motion picture house thrived for a short time on this island, but it is now deserted.

The Okefenokee is drained by two small rivers. The St. Marys drains the southeastern part of the swamp during periods of high water and winds to the Atlantic Ocean, and the Suwannee drifts southwestward to empty into the Gulf of Mexico. As the Suwannee River courses through the swamp, first through high banks and then in open channels, patches of dense shade and brilliant sunshine dapple the dark, cypress-stained water. Through the entire area the eerie stillness is broken only by splashing of waterfowl, singing of birds, bellowing of alligators, hooting and screeching of owls, and the faint rumbling of mingled sounds known as the "booming of the swamp."

Studies of the Biological Survey show that the swamp is becoming increasingly important as a winter refuge for migratory waterfowl and birds; it is visited by at least eleven species of waterfowl at various times of the year. The wood (summer) duck is a year-round inhabitant that breeds in the quiet wilderness, and in recent years the ring-necked, pintail, and black ducks have come in increasing numbers for a winter home. Mallards, canvasbacks, buffleheads, hooded mergansers, and green-winged teals are among the various winter visitors. As many as eighty-five species of birds have been recorded here in the summer and ninety in the winter. Robins, cardinals, woodpeckers, ruby-crowned kinglets, red-winged blackbirds, and brown-headed nuthatches enliven the swamp with their color and song. Other varieties are the Canada goose, barred owl, catbird, red-tailed hawk, bald eagle, osprey, Ward's heron, kingfisher, and pied-billed grebe. Fast-dwindling species such as the swallow-tailed kite, pileated woodpecker, and the Florida crane are occasionally seen. Food plants for waterfowl and birds are abundant.

Alligators, some of them eight to ten feet long, are found in the canal, the lakes, the river, and in the deeper pools of the prairies. Their deep-throated bellowing is a familiar sound throughout the swampland. Generally harmless unless prodded into attack, they are unmolested because they are useful in keeping the mud from accumulating on the lake bottoms and in building wallows that are inhabited by fish.

For many years people living near the swamp hunted deer, bears, and wildcats here and trapped otters and raccoons, marketing the pelts in Waycross (see TOUR 4). They served as guides for hunters who came to the islands seeking the Florida bear, largest mammal of the swamp. Hunts were often held at night as communal affairs, the men of the surrounding farms bringing their hounds and joining in the pursuit. The Biological Survey has limited firearms to those carried by bureau officials and state game wardens. Panthers have been found in the area, and there are such amusing novelties of animal life as little Le Conte frogs.

In the water are more than fifty species of fish, including warmouth, pickerel, short-nosed gars, suckers, perch, catfish, jackfish, and large-mouthed bass. The rare rain-water fish (*Lucania parva*) is among the many varieties of tiny tropical fish.

There is a legend that some Indian hunters, lost in the swamp, found an enchanted island. Suddenly, a group of beautiful women appeared and placed before them delicious fruits, marsh eggs, and corn pones and, warning them that their husbands would kill all intruders, pointed out a path by which the lost Indians could return safely home. No sooner did the hunters set foot on the path than the women vanished, and in spite of many efforts the Indians were never able to rediscover the island or find these "Daughters of the Sun."

TOUR 5

Junction with US 17 — Waycross — Valdosta — Thomasville — Bainbridge — (Dothan, Ala.); US 84.

Junction with US 17 to Alabama Line, 229.6 m. — Atlantic Coast Line R.R. parallels route throughout — Roadbed hard-surfaced throughout, chiefly asphalt. Watch for cattle and hogs on the highway — All types of accommodations in cities; limited elsewhere.

US 84 crosses the extreme southern part of Georgia, from the coastal country through the wiregrass section, where pine forests form the basis of extensive naval-stores operations, to the fertile western farming area, where pecans are one of the leading crops. Near Thomasville northern capitalists have restored many of the old plantations.

In the treaty signed with Oglethorpe in 1733, the Indians had agreed to permit white settlements along the coast, but retained their hunting lands in what is now western Georgia. This territory, then covered with virgin forests of hardwood and longleaf pine, was held by the Indians only by waging bitter warfare against the whites. Finally, in 1816, the territory was opened for settlement. The first homesteaders were, for the most part, farmers from Virginia and the Carolinas. Now the rich farm lands produce cotton, corn, peanuts, and sugar cane, but in the wooded sections small game, including quail, squirrels, raccoons, and wild turkeys, is still abundant, and there are a few deer.

US 84 branches west from its junction with US 17, **0. m.** (*see* TOUR *1*), at a point 10 miles west of Brunswick (*see* TOUR *1*).

The OLD POST ROAD, **16.1 m.,** designated by a granite marker at the point where it intersects the highway, was originally an Indian trail extending from St. Augustine, Florida, northward through south Georgia into the rolling country known as the Sand Hill section. Mitchell's map of 1756, now in the Library of Congress in Washington, shows this trail. During the Revolutionary War the American forces marched along it on their way to attack a British contingent at Fort Tonyn, which was somewhere south of this junction. Historians have not been able to determine its exact site. The road continued to be used as a stagecoach route and post road between Savannah and Florida until the War between the States.

NAHUNTA, 26.1 m. (66 alt., 352 pop.), developed during the latter part of the nineteenth century as a freight station, called Victoria, at the junction of the Savannah, Florida & Western Railroad with the Brunswick & Western Railroad. So much freight was consigned here to N. A. Hunter, a timber operator, that the town became known to railroad men as N. A. Hunter's siding, and shortly before 1900 was officially named Nahunta. In 1920 it was made the seat of Brantley County, which was created that year.

This area, included in the wiregrass or piney woods section, has a smaller Negro population than any other comparable area in south Georgia. The plantation system was never developed here, and the land is sparsely settled by small, independent farmers.

Logs are hauled on trucks or mule-drawn wagons to sawmills, which usually are housed in frame sheds with corrugated iron roofing and brick chimneys. A steam engine with an iron boiler generates power for the circular, coarse-toothed ripsaw, which quickly cuts off the outer part of the log as it is fed by a moving carriage. These outer slabs with the dark rough bark are used to fire the boiler, and the inner wood is sawed into planks which are stacked in triangular piles to dry. Sawdust is placed in near-by piles where it is allowed to decay. Many sawmills are temporary structures that can be moved when the local supply of logs has been exhausted.

SCHLATTERVILLE (pronounced Slaughterville), 36.8 m. (133 alt., 25 pop.), is the center for extensive naval-stores operations, somewhat decreased in recent years. From the many swamps in this locality the Hercules Powder Company of Brunswick collects large pine stumps and wreckage called stumpage, from which resin and paper pulp are extracted by a steaming process.

WAYCROSS, 49.8 m. (138 alt., 15,510 pop.) (see TOUR 4), is at the junction with US 1 (see TOUR 4).

RUSKIN, 55.8 m. (140 alt., 27 pop.), named for John Ruskin, English author and social reformer, was founded in the early 1890's by a group from Tennessee who bought 720 acres of land and established a colony here. It was so organized that all property belonged to the society; individuals brought everything they made to a general store where they also procured all supplies, paying with scrip issued by the colony. Among the enterprises were a community dining room, factories for the production of shoes, brooms, and suspenders, and a newspaper called *The Coming Nation*. A school provided educational facilities up to the twelfth grade, and a light-opera company provided entertainment. In 1901 dissension caused the experiment to be abandoned, and Ruskin now consists of only a few families who work in Waycross.

HOMERVILLE, 76.5 m. (176 alt., 1,150 pop.), is the seat of Clinch County. In 1853 John Homer Mattox established a farm on this site. It was on a stagecoach route, and the mail carrier kept a relay of horses at the Mattox place. When the Atlantic & Gulf Railroad was built through the land in 1859, Mattox granted a right of way and donated six acres of land for public buildings. The following year he succeeded in having Homerville, as he called his place, designated the county seat. The town was known as Homerville, Station Number 11, until 1869 when it was incorporated simply as Homerville.

The town is in the heart of the turpentine section. From spring until early fall the surrounding pine trees are slashed so that the resin will drip into tin cans fastened beneath the cuts, and the air is laden with the pungent smell of the dripping resin. For the conservation of the pines, firebreaks, telephone lines, and watch towers have been established in all parts of the area. The state and an association of lumbermen share the expense of retaining inspectors, who work under the supervision of the state forestry department and report by telephone to Homerville from the tops of the towers.

In the stills (*open to visitors*) the resin is distilled into naval stores—turpentine and hard rosin. Although the production of naval stores is the principal industry, this section also has much rich farm land planted in sea-island cotton or bright-leaf tobacco.

At Homerville is the junction with State 89, a graded dirt road.

Left on State 89 is FARGO, 38.4 m. (116 alt., 275 pop.). On the highway near the Suwannee River is a stone memorial to Stephen Collins Foster (1826-64), composer of "Old Folks at Home," the song commemorating that river.

At 38.9 m. is a junction with a sandy road.

Left on this road along the banks of the Suwannee River to the western boundary of the OKEFENOKEE SWAMP (*see* TOUR 4A) 48.4 m. (*accommodations at private camps; boats and guides available for trip into swamp*). The road continues across a peninsula called The Pocket, where General Charles Floyd built Fort Tattnall during an expedition against the Indians of the swamp in 1838, to JONES ISLAND, 55.4 m. At the northern end of the island is a boat landing on Billy's Lake.

VALDOSTA, 112.8 m. (215 alt., 13,482 pop.) (*see* TOUR 2), is at the junction with US 41 (*see* TOUR 2).

The source of BLUE SPRINGS, 123.9 m. (R), has never been determined exactly. Picnic pavilions and a concrete swimming pool, filled with the cold, greenish-blue waters of the springs, make this a popular summer recreational ground.

QUITMAN, 131.5 m. (173 alt., 4,149 pop.), seat of Brooks County, is a pleasant town with shaded streets and well-kept houses. Bisecting the main business street is a park, green with palms and cabbage palmettos and bright with roses that bloom the greater part of the year. Similar landscaped strips divide some of the residential streets. The town, incorporated on December 19, 1859, was named for General John A. Quitman, who had led a troop of Mississippi soldiers to aid Texas in its fight for independence from Mexico.

Quitman ships large quantities of hams, sausages, vegetables, watermelons, and cantaloupes, and is headquarters for a 225-store chain operated throughout south Georgia, Florida, and Alabama. Originating as a wholesale grocery store, this chain has been developed through the marketing of Brooks County ham and sausage. The county, still producing large quantities of corn and peanuts for fattening hogs, was known during the War between the States as the smokehouse of the Confederacy. In the many old-fashioned log and frame smokehouses here the farmers cure and preserve their meat by salting and smoking it in the traditional manner. This area was one of the first in the state to develop cold storage for the preservation of meat, with ice brought in carload lots from Savannah. Some storage houses now have electric refrigeration.

1. Right from Quitman on the Ozell Road to DRY LAKE, 12 m., so named because at intervals of two or three years it becomes dry except for one small deep hole, through which the lake drains into the underground stream that ordinarily feeds it. During the dry periods the local people gather quantities of fish left by the receding waters; when the lake refills, the fish multiply rapidly.

2 Right from Quitman on the unpaved Barwick Road to DEVIL'S HOPPER, 10 m., a privately owned cave. Leading into the cave is a ravine about seventy-five feet long, thirty feet deep, and twenty feet wide, through which trickles a tiny stream, milky with eroded limestone. From the sides of the ravine grow pines, magnolias, and oaks, with slim trunks and branches reaching upward toward the sunlight. The tops of some of the trees are level with the land surrounding the ravine. Explorers must be lowered eight feet to reach the cave; its entrance, surrounded by large limestone rocks, is big enough for an adult to enter without stooping, but the tunnel-like passage gradually becomes smaller. Hollowed out of the flinty rocks are rather large rooms, the floors and walls of which reflect the flashlights and torches used by visitors. Stories are told of futile attempts to ascertain the depth of the cave, but these investigations have never been conducted on a scientific basis. A large stream flows along the bottom of the cave.

Between Quitman and Thomasville the more prosperous farmers have tobacco barns—narrow, two-story buildings in which the large green leaves are suspended from sticks in tiers reaching to the rafters. In the late summer and early fall the air is filled with the aroma of the drying tobacco. After the leaves have dried and turned a golden brown, they are taken to market.

THOMASVILLE, 159.4 m. (250 alt., 11,733 pop.) (*see* TOUR 6), is at the junction with US 19 (*see* TOUR 6).

Much of the land in the southwestern part of the state is included in the hunting preserves of several large estates, and it is almost impossible to purchase land in this section. Some small farms here are cultivated by tenants.

GREENWOOD (*open during Rose Show in spring*), 170.8 m., is the 20,000-acre estate (L) of Mrs. Payne Whitney, of New York. It was once the plantation home of Thomas Jones, who acquired the land in 1827 and in 1835 engaged John Wind, an English architect, to build the house. It took nine years to complete the beautiful Greek Revival house, which is set in a grove of oaks, palmettos, and magnolias. It has a finely proportioned pedimented and galleried portico with fluted Ionic columns resting on the ground, a fine metal railing at the second story, and a large rosette in the pediment. Wind himself carved much of the interior woodwork, and the gardens were landscaped by Stanford White.

The palm garden (R) contains every variety of palm that grows in this locality. In rectangular beds are planted small, bright flowers, and at one end is a fountain surmounted with a classic figure. Beyond this is another garden, bordered on one side by century plants and on the other by beautiful woods. In the center is a fountain with a draped figure encircled by four other figures, and at each end is a balustrade with a background of tall shrubbery.

CAIRO (pronounced káy-ro), 173.4 m. (237 alt., 3,169 pop.), incorporated in 1870, is a progressive town with a modern business section contrasting sharply with the many old-fashioned houses in the residential district. In 1905 the town was made the seat of the newly created Grady County, which was named for Henry W. Grady, the noted Georgia orator.

Flower gardens here contain prized plants of pink and white camellias, locally known as japonicas; on cold winter days the plants are covered with canvas to protect them against frost. Many of the semitropical flowers of Florida also grow in Cairo, especially poinsettias and coral vines.

Cairo, with the largest syrup-canning plant in the state, annually ships more pure sugar cane syrup than any other city in the nation. It is said to supply approximately 98 per cent of the world's collard seed. Other industries include pecan shelling, peanut grinding, okra canning, and cucumber brining and pickling.

A center of the new tung-oil industry, the town has a mill for extracting oil from tung nuts. Approximately 200,000 tung trees grow in Grady County, which resembles in soil and climate the section of China that heretofore has produced 90 per cent of the world's tung oil. In 1908 the first Georgia tung trees were planted here and at the Georgia Experiment Station near Griffin (see TOUR 2). Tung trees, planted in groves, are beautiful in early spring with their pearl-white or pinkish-lavender blossoms. Some of the older trees are thirty-five feet high and have a limb spread of forty-five feet, but in the young groves other crops are planted between the rows. The trees bear when three years old and, because of the poisonous character of their nuts, are entirely free from pests and diseases. Tung oil has more than a hundred uses: its chief value is as an ingredient in paints and varnishes; it is also utilized in the manufacture of ink, soap, oilcloth, linoleum, auto brake linings, and insulation for cables and dynamos.

The surrounding country is one of the most fertile agricultural sections in the state and supports a variety of crops, including cotton, tobacco, pecans, and some Satsuma oranges. Dogwood, wild azalea, bay, and magnolia are plentiful, and the air is heavy in spring with the fragrance of running yellow jasmine and in summer with the white and yellow honeysuckle. Farmhouses and barns, though generally unpainted, are well maintained.

Along the highway west of Cairo are many acres planted in sugar cane that grows to a height of ten or twelve feet, with long, graceful, sharp-edged foliage topping the red or green stalks. The red variety is sweeter and more valuable for making syrup, but every farmer grows a patch of green for home consumption, because its stalk is softer and because it is easily chewed after the thick, green outer covering has been peeled off. During the sugar-cane season south Georgia boys and girls carry pocket knives with which to top and peel the stalks so that they can enjoy the sweet juice.

The sugar-cane mills along the highway are operated only during the fall months. Power is usually supplied by horses or mules walking in a circle, but some farmers use gasoline engines. After the cane stalks have been ground, the juice is boiled into syrup and the scum skimmed off with large wooden ladles. Cane grinding is often made the occasion for a picnic; the children play on the ever-growing pile of cane refuse, locally known as "pummy," and all drink the juice and sample the hot syrup.

The farmers always save some of the best cane for the coming spring planting and protect it from frost by burying it under the ground until warm weather, when the stalks are cut into various lengths and planted in rows. Every joint produces a new stalk. Since blight has injured the old-fashioned cane within the past few years, many of the farmers are experimenting with new varieties resembling sorghum.

BAINBRIDGE, **198.1 m.** (110 alt., 6,141 pop.), seat of Decatur County, is distinctive because of the large number of giant water and live oak trees along its streets and parks. The town is near the site of old Fort Hughes, an earthwork used by the troops of General Andrew Jackson during the Indian wars (1817-21) in the territory of the Flint and Chattahoochee rivers. It is believed that a white settlement was established in the bend of the Flint River as early as 1810, but the town of Bainbridge was not chartered until December 22, 1829. It was named in honor of William Bainbridge, commander of the frigate *Constitution*.

During the nineteenth century the Alligator Line of Stages, operating from Augusta into Florida, passed through Bainbridge, and hotels here served as the breakfast and supper houses of the line. The coaches, drawn by four horses, carried sixteen passengers and were always crowded, although accounts state that this transportation was slow and expensive (10 miles an hour at 10¢ a mile).

At the time of the lumber boom in the early part of the twentieth century, a thriving lumber industry made Bainbridge one of the wealthiest towns in the state. So many forests in the county were depleted, however, that agriculture superseded lumbering. The chief industries in Bainbridge now include basket and crate making, machine manufacturing, and metal casting.

At Bainbridge is a junction with US 27 (*see* TOUR *10*).

1. Right from Bainbridge on the unpaved Douglas Road to DOUGLAS LAKE (*fishing, picnicking*), 1.5 m., surrounded by a grove of longleaf pines and moss-covered oaks. The lake was formed by a series of limestone sinks.

2. Left from Bainbridge on the unpaved Tallahassee Road to the PLANT OF THE ATTAPULGUS CLAY COMPANY (*open to visitors*), 13 m. This plant, electrically operated, is one of the largest of the companies mining fuller's earth, a product used in the purification of oils.

On the bridge across the dark waters of the Flint River, **199.1 m.,** is a marker (R) designating the place where Andrew Jackson crossed in 1818, when he was conducting his campaign against the Seminole in the South.

The highway crosses the THREE NOTCH ROAD, **215.4 m.,** which was named for the three notches made on trees by advance scouts who blazed the trail as early as 1800. This road led to Fort Scott, built in 1816 on the banks of the Flint River near the Georgia-Florida Line. From this fort in 1818 Jackson launched his unauthorized campaign into Florida against the Seminole. This act, which was tacitly allowed by the Government, very nearly involved the United States in war with Spain and Great Britain because of the claims of these nations to West Florida. No trace of Fort Scott remains.

DONALSONVILLE, 218.5 m. (139 alt., 1,183 pop.), incorporated in 1897, seat of Seminole County, is the center of an area producing agricultural products, lumber, and naval stores; two of the largest peanut shellers in the state are operated here. Checker games, a popular pastime, are played in any and every shady spot during the summer months.

Left from Donalsonville on State 91, a graded dirt road, to an old SUSPENSION BRIDGE, 12 m., one of the very few remaining in the South.

In Seminole County game is plentiful, especially deer, foxes, and quail.

The CHATTAHOOCHEE RIVER, 229.6 m., the boundary between Georgia and Alabama, is spanned by a free bridge about 22 miles east of Dothan, Alabama.

TOUR 6

(Asheville, N.C.) — Blairsville — Dahlonega — Atlanta — Griffin — Albany — Thomasville — (Monticello, Fla.); US 19.

North Carolina Line to Florida Line, 363.2 m. — Roadbed hard-surfaced throughout, one-third concrete — Central of Georgia Ry. parallels route between Atlanta and Thomaston, and between Americus and Albany; the Atlantic Coast Line R.R. between Albany and Thomasville — All types of accommodations in cities; limited elsewhere.

Section a. NORTH CAROLINA LINE *to* ATLANTA; *121.5 m., US 19.*

In the northeastern section of Georgia, US 19, the Appalachian Scenic Highway, crosses a solitary and spectacularly beautiful region encompassed by darkly wooded and majestic mountains. Since no railroad has ever traversed this section, isolation has caused the settlers of the green valleys to be individualistic and boldly independent. Although Georgia as a whole is Democratic, some of the counties in this section are Republican and, during the War between the

States, gave many soldiers to the Union ranks. Confederate deserters often found sanctuary here. In some localities there is a sharp racial prejudice, and Negroes are not permitted to remain after sunset. .

Near the North Carolina Line this route passes through a segment of the Chattahoochee National Forest; in this former Cherokee Indian territory are Vogel State Park and Neel Gap, the best known vantage point in the state for views. South of the national forest lie three towns of sharply contrasting characteristics: Dahlonega, center of the only important gold mining in Georgia; Cumming, the region's most self-sufficient and independent mountain community; and Roswell, whose fine old houses were built and maintained by a once powerful aristocracy.

South of the State Line, **0 m.,** designated by a marker of Georgia marble at a point 72 miles south of Asheville, North Carolina, US 19 traverses the purchase area of the Chattahoochee (Ind., pictured rock) National Forest for twenty miles before entering the lands actually owned by the government.

MAUNEY MUSEUM (*adm. upon application to Edward S. Mauney, Post Office Bldg., Blairsville*), **6.1 m.,** is housed in a log cabin (R) set well back from the road. The display includes hand-made pioneer furniture, flintlock rifles, candle molds, bear traps, and early American tools and implements.

The NOTTELY RIVER (*cabins available*), **9.1 m.,** a small clear stream, affords excellent black-bass fishing.

BLAIRSVILLE, **11.1 m.** (1,892 alt., 298 pop.), is the seat of Union County and its only village. It was laid out in 1838 immediately after the Cherokee Removal and until 1910 was a focal point for gold-mining activities. The known deposits are still rich, but litigation over mineral rights has resulted in the suspension of most of the work. The southern section of town, at the foot of Mount Wellborn, is honeycombed with shafts and tunnels of the mines, now dangerous to enter because the shoring timbers have decayed.

Left from Blairsville on paved US 76 to the junction with a narrow country road, 5.8 m.; R. on this road 2.3 m. to TRACK ROCK GAP (approx. 2,250 alt.). On the summit of the ridge (R) are several soapstone boulders bearing many carved figures of unknown origin. According to Cherokee legends, these petroglyphs had been placed here by an earlier people before the first Cherokee entered the region.

At 8.1 m. on US 76 in Towns County — the only county in Georgia without a Negro inhabitant — is YOUNG HARRIS (1,928 alt., 316 pop.), the site of the YOUNG L. G. HARRIS JUNIOR COLLEGE AND ACADEMY (*from the girls' dormitory an 8-mile hiking trail leads to the summit of Mount Enotah*). This coeducational institution, maintained by the North Georgia Conference of the Methodist Episcopal Church, South, has brick buildings set on a wooded, fifteen-acre campus which is being landscaped by the students. The library building, constructed by the male students with bricks molded of native clay, contains the library of Sam Jones, the evangelist (*see* TOUR 2). The school owns 1,200 acres of the fertile valley, of which 200 acres are cultivated. About 100 of the 500 students pay their expenses by working on the farm and in the school. The institution, organized through the philanthropic efforts of Young L. G. Harris, of Athens, was opened in 1886 in an old storehouse.

HIAWASSEE, **16.6 m.** (1,984 alt., 169 pop.), is a small mountain town.

At **18.9 m.** is a junction with unpaved State 75 (*unsafe after rains*); R. on State 75 to a junction with a graveled road, **26 m.**; R. on this road to the SUMMIT OF MOUNT ENOTAH, **33 m.** (4,784 alt.), the highest peak in Georgia. This mountain is heavily wooded except for the bare summit, which is surmounted with the U. S. Forest Service's forty-foot lookout tower. The mountain, locally known as Brasstown Bald, was named for a near-by settlement called Brasstown, a misinterpretation of the Indian name which actually meant town of the green valley.

The MOUNTAIN EXPERIMENT STATION, **14.2 m.**, is one of the three agricultural experiment stations (*see* TOUR 2) operated by the state under the direction of the University System of Georgia. On the two hundred acres of fertile soil are the mechanics building, office and storage structures, livestock barns, and a pottery where vessels are made for the use of the station. Although experiments are conducted in the cultivation and development of apples, peaches, lettuce, grain, and truck, the specialty at the present time is the study of grape culture. The station makes tests to determine the varieties best suited to the different climates and soils, and fertilizer requirements. At the annual farmers' meeting premiums are given for the finest displays of fruits, vegetables, crops, handiwork, and cooking.

From a point at **17.1 m.** is an excellent view of Mount Enotah (*see above*), easily identified by the stone lookout tower on its summit.

The boundary of the CHATTAHOOCHEE NATIONAL FOREST (*picnic areas and camp sites with sanitary facilities, protected water, firewood; for permission to hunt and fish see supervisor at Gainesville or forest ranger at Woody Gap*) is crossed at **20.7 m.** This forest, named for the Chattahoochee River, was created on July 1, 1936, from the portions of the Cherokee and the Nantahala national forests within the State of Georgia. The gross purchase area includes 1,165,000 acres; but, since several towns and much privately owned land lie within its boundaries, the government owns only 514,772 acres. Within the forest is some of the most superb scenery in the Appalachian Highlands; in spring the beauty of the wooded mountains is intensified by blossoming laurel, azalea, and rhododendron, and in fall by gold and red foliage mingled with the evergreens. There are 136 varieties of trees, of which the most prevalent are poplar, maple, pine, hemlock, basswood, cucumber, ash, white oak, and red oak. A hardy Asiatic variety of chestnut has recently been introduced into the forest to replace the native chestnuts killed by a blight. Shrubs and plants, equally diverse, make this reserve a rich laboratory for botanists. Deer and bear are now rather scarce, but there is an abundance of quail and wild turkeys and the streams are well stocked with fish.

Here, until their removal across the Mississippi, the Cherokee lived, hunted the abundant game, and found safety in the high mountains from hostile tribes. Such names as Blood and Slaughter Mountains attest the fierceness of the battles fought in this vicinity between the Creek and the Cherokee. Exploitation of the forests by the white man, the burning of mountain growth, and the consequent erosion had greatly damaged the fertility of the region. Conservationists, however, have secured the passage of reclamation laws, and the U. S. Forest Service has improved the methods of fire and flood control, introduced scientific forestry, propagated and protected game and fish, and established recreation areas. In addition to Congressional appropriations, 25 per cent of the returns from grazing concessions, timber sales, water power, and land rentals is paid to the schools of the counties within which the forest lies, and 10 per cent is used in the construction and maintenance of roads and trails.

VOGEL STATE PARK (*hunting and fishing prohibited; 10 m. of foot trails*), 22.6 m., is a heavily wooded tract of mountain land covering 248 acres owned by the state and additional land leased from the U. S. Forest Service. The park is named for Fred and August Vogel, of Milwaukee, Wisconsin, who gave the original acreage.

LAKE TRAHLYTA (R), 22.8 m., covering an area of about forty acres at the northern entrance of the park (*cabins $20-$25 a week; free picnic grounds; swimming 10¢ for those not occupying cabins*), is formed by a fifty-foot dam across Wolfpen Creek. The surrounding mountain peaks and a profusion of natural growth reflected in the clear, green water make this a place of tranquil beauty.

Right from Vogel State Park on a winding graveled road to 22-acre LAKE WINFIELD SCOTT, 6.7 m., in a beautiful setting of hardwood trees that are reflected in the limpid waters. The lake, named for Winfield Scott, the officer in charge of the Cherokee Removal in 1838 and general in chief of the U. S. Army (1841-61), is the center of one of the Chattahoochee National Forest recreation areas.

The TOCCOA BASIN RANGER STATION (R), 10.8 m., is in a two-story white frame building (*hunting, fishing, and camping permits obtainable here*).

At WOODY GAP (approx. 3,300 alt.), 12.8 m., is a junction with the Appalachian Trail (*see* TOUR *13A*).

At 18 m. the side route rejoins US 19.

NOTTELY FALLS (L), 25.5 m., are formed by a small creek that descends 105 feet over large gray rocks into the dense shadows of the hemlocks that cover the mountain side.

The NOTTELY PICNIC GROUNDS (*comfort station, picnic shelter, outdoor fireplaces*), 25.8 m., is a twelve-acre tract within Vogel State Park. From the grounds well-marked trails lead to near-by points of scenic vantage.

US 19 crosses the Blue Ridge at NEEL GAP (*stone inn: rooms $2.50–$4 a day; 2 cabins for rent*), 26.1 m. (3,108 alt.), the southern entrance to Vogel State Park. This gap through the Appalachian Highlands affords broad views of green valleys and mountain ranges extending far into the distance. In spring and early summer the hillsides are splashed with white dogwood, flame azalea, and white rhododendron. A park service ranger stationed here gives information on the many points of interest in the region. Until recently this was called Frogtown Gap because an Indian hunter reported seeing in the pass a frog as large as a house.

The APPALACHIAN TRAIL (*see* TOUR *13A*), famous hiking thoroughfare which crosses the highway at this point, leads through the wildest and most remote parts of the mountains from the Tate Mountain Estates near Jasper (*see* TOUR *13*) to the summit of Mount Katahdin in Maine.

At 26.4 m. is a junction with a graded and well-marked foot trail.

Right on this trail through the Chattahoochee National Forest to the head of DE SOTO FALLS, 3 m., which plunge more than 400 feet down the green slope of the mountain side.

CHESTATEE KNOLL CAMP SITE (*open-air fireplaces, shelter huts, pure water*), 30.7 m., is maintained by the forest service for free use by the public.

US 19 crosses the southern boundary of the Chattahoochee National Forest, 31 m., near the SITE OF FORT FROGTOWN, an army outpost and stockade for prisoners, used by U. S. troops during the Cherokee Removal.

At 32.7 m. is a junction with paved US 129.

Left on this road at 6.2 m. is a point affording an excellent view of MOUNT YONAH (3,173 alt.), its towering cliffs crowned with a steel lookout tower for forest rangers. This land was a hunting ground of the Cherokee, who named the mountain Yonah (Ind., bear).

In CLEVELAND, 11.2 m. (1,571 alt., 498 pop.), seat of White County, is a pottery shop were many articles of old-fashioned blisterware are made. Nine gold mines are operated within this county.

Left from Cleveland on unpaved State 75 are the DUKES CREEK GOLD MINES, 18.2 m., where hydraulic equipment is used almost exclusively. One of the earliest discoveries of gold within the state was made at Dukes Creek in 1828 or 1829.

At **19.2 m.** the road enters the western side of the beautiful NACOOCHEE VALLEY (1,349 alt.), a fertile tract lying along the headwaters of the Chattahoochee and Sautee rivers. According to legend, the valley was named for Nacoochee (evening star), an Indian maiden, who came here to meet Laceola, her lover from an enemy tribe. Learning of the tryst, Nacoochee's father sent a band of warriors to overtake her. When they discovered the two lovers together, one of them drew his bow, aiming at Laceola, but Nacoochee quickly stepped before him and received the fatal arrow in her own heart. Laceola, too, was slain, and the lovers were buried together in the beautiful valley.

At **19.4 m.**, beside a bridge over the Chattahoochee River, is the junction with a country road.

Right 0.3 m. on this road across the bridge to the NACOOCHEE INDIAN MOUND, 100 yards R. of the road, on the property (*private*) of Mrs. L. G. Hardman, widow of a former state governor. This mound is 190 feet long, 150 feet wide, and 20 feet high. Exploration by the Heye Foundation in 1915 revealed a dog pot and many pottery vessels that indicate an advanced cultural development of the builders. According to tradition, this mound was the center of the ancient Cherokee town of Guaxule (pronounced Wah-zu'-lee), said to have been visited by De Soto in 1540. In 1838 American gold miners uncovered a near-by subterranean village of more than thirty log houses. The logs were well preserved and showed evidence of having been notched by sharp metal tools. It is possible that the village was made by Spanish gold seekers who penetrated this region after De Soto's ill-fated expedition.

At **21.3 m.** on State 75 is HELEN (1,400 alt., 252 pop.), a cool valley town (*two good hotels; golf course, swimming pool*) where pleasant cottages contrast with shabby old frame dwellings. The latter once housed the employees of a large mill which annually sawed more than 20,000,000 feet of lumber from the surrounding mountains. This mill was moved to Mexico, but a smaller one has been operated by local capital since the summer of 1936. After the removal of the large mill, Helen became increasingly popular as a summer resort. TRAY MOUNTAIN (4,389 alt.) is accessible by motor, and a forest service road parallels the Chattahoochee River, which abounds with rainbow trout and black bass. In this vicinity the headwaters of the Chattahoochee are clear, although farther down the water is red with mud.

PORTER SPRINGS (*hotel and cottages available*), **37.6 m.**, is (R) a quiet summer resort patronized by those seeking recreation remote from the gayer and noisier places. The springs here were discovered in 1868, and the development of the site as a resort began with the building of the rambling Porter Springs Hotel in 1876.

STONE PILE GAP, **38 m.**, at the junction with a graveled road, is a solitary stone cairn said to have been erected over the grave of Trahlyta, an Indian maiden, whose daily bathing in the waters of the spring kept her young and beautiful for many years. Unwilling to disclose the secret, she refused to marry, though she was much desired by Indian warriors who believed she would always remain young. When she was forcibly carried away by Wahsega, she faded and withered; after her death, she was buried, in compliance with her wish, at the foot of Cedar Mountain near her beloved spring. Passing Indians paid tribute by placing rocks upon her grave, and there developed a legend that a curse would fall on anyone who disturbed the cairn. When the forest service road was being graded, the cairn lay directly on the proposed route. It was said that so many tractors were wrecked and workmen injured in attempting to clear away the stones that, although they were outwardly skeptical about the curse, the engineers agreed at last to grade the road around the cairn.

At 44.9 m. is a junction with a dirt road.

Right on this road to CANE CREEK FALLS (*bathing facilities; cabins for rent; lunchrooms*) 0.7 m. The waters of Cane Creek plunge forty-five feet over the dark rocks to turn a steel, overshot water wheel that is forty feet in diameter. Rainbow trout and black bass are plentiful in the near-by pools.

A LOG HOUSE (*open on permission of owner*), 45.1 m. (L), on the summit of a low, wooded hill, is a copy of the dog-trot or breezeway type of building and was constructed of logs salvaged from several old houses. The flagstone terraces and patios are bordered with native wild flowers, and the interior contains early hand-made furniture and handicrafts.

DAHLONEGA (pronounced Dah-lahn'-e-ga), 46.9 m. (1,484 alt., 905 pop.), seat of Lumpkin County, is a trading center for mountaineers, who come to town on Saturdays to purchase their weekly supplies. The name of the town, suggested by the gold deposits of the surrounding area, is derived from Taulonica (Cher. yellow metal). Occasionally, after heavy rains, small particles of gold are found in the streets of the town.

Although it is said that a gold nugget was found in this vicinity about 1818, the gold fields were not discovered until 1828 or 1829. Almost immediately this Cherokee territory was cluttered with the shanties of rough, adventurous miners, who were followed by gamblers and swindlers. Heavy drinking, gambling, and frequent brawls became an integral part of the settlement's life. Placer mining, known here as deposit mining, utilized crude apparatus and was an inefficient process; as two men worked together, one would shovel gravel into the "long tom" or trough. After the coarse gravel had been taken out, the residue was run over the corrugated "rippler," which had indentations filled with mercury to retain the gold.

During these intrusions on Indian land, Georgia sent out the militia to protect the Indians. In 1830 the state acquired the Cherokee territory and during 1831-32 divided it into forty-acre "gold lots" which were disposed of by lottery. There was little regard for private property, however, and the miners panned gold wherever they found it.

Lumpkin County was created in 1832 and, a year later, Dahlonega was settled at a place called Licklog for a hollowed log filled with salt for livestock. New settlers were arriving daily, and soon all roads leading to the town were lined with huts. At one time there were from ten to fifteen thousand miners within a radius of a few miles. When hotels were established, Tennessee hog drovers on their way to Augusta stopped in this town and slaughtered the hogs, selling the cheaper cuts of meat to the miners and taking the hams to Augusta.

The first important discovery of gold in the United States occurred in the Dahlonega fields. The Federal government established a mint here which operated from 1838 until 1861, when it was closed because of Georgia's secession from the Union. During this period 1,378,710 pieces of gold valued at $6,106,569 were struck; every coin was marked with a D.

During the California gold rush of 1849, many of the restless adventurers who had come to Georgia moved westward. Matthew F. Stephenson, assayer of the mint, protesting against the emigration, said in praise of the local gold fields, "There's millions in it." This phrase was taken to California, where Mark Twain heard it and later made it famous in *The Gilded Age*. The section had also been depopulated by the war with Mexico, but by 1855 men had begun to return, and in 1858 the Yahoola and Cane Creek Hydraulic Company was formed by Boston capitalists. A million dollars was spent on machinery and the construction of canals and flumes. Although mining activity was halted during the War between the States, it was gradually resumed afterward and scientific processes introduced. A pronounced revival in mining took place in 1900 but was short-lived owing to the high cost of obtaining the metal. Since the increase in the value of gold within the last few years, the mines have again been opened. Of the $17,749,937 in gold taken from Georgia dirt from 1830-1933, almost $16,000,000 has come from the Dahlonega fields. In 1935 a few mines produced gold valued at $34,790.

LUMPKIN COUNTY COURTHOUSE, on the town square, is a two-story structure built in 1833-36 of brick made of native clay and painted red. The lower part of the two-story portico with its white columns is enclosed by brick walls that give an odd appearance to the old building. The S's on each facade are metal clamps placed at the ends of wrought-iron rods, inserted about forty years ago to prevent spreading of the walls.

THE WIGWAM (L), on the town square, a girls' dormitory of North Georgia College, is a large frame building of two stories and an attic upon a brick foundation. The facade has a front porch at each story, two elliptically arched doorways, and six dormer windows. For many years after its construction during the 1830's, it was the Harrison W. Riley (Eagle) Hotel.

The DAHLONEGA NUGGET OFFICE, on an unnamed street about two blocks east of the square, is a small green building with the name carved on a marble slab above the door. It contains the old-fashioned hand press on which W. B. Townsend printed the *Dahlonega Nugget*, a small-town weekly newspaper that was quoted frequently and became known to many newspaper readers throughout the United States (*see* PRESS AND RADIO).

NORTH GEORGIA COLLEGE (L), on the site of the mint, is a unit of the University System of Georgia. This liberal-arts junior college has an enrollment of 535 young men and women. After the War between the States, Federal authorities offered the old mint building to the state for educational purposes, in accordance with the Morrill Act of 1862 "donating public lands to the several states and territories which may provide colleges for the benefit of agriculture and mechanical arts." The school was opened on January 6, 1873, as a land-grant college. Known as North Georgia Agricultural College, it admitted only men until 1933, when it was reorganized by the state board of regents. Price Memorial Hall is built on the foundations of the Government mint, destroyed by fire in 1878.

At **48.9 m.**, just south of the Etowah River, is a junction with a dirt road.

Left on this road in AURARIA, **4 m.** (1,402 alt., 250 pop.), are the Bunker Hill, the Nelson, and the Auraria Gold Mines (*open to visitors*). This mining village was first called Nuckollsville for Nathaniel Nuckolls, who built a hotel here in 1832, but in 1833 it was given the Latin name for gold mine. Although the mines were closed for a time, they are now (1939) being operated.

DAWSONVILLE, **61.6 m.** (1,425 alt., 203 pop.), county seat and only town of Dawson County, is a trading center for the farmers of this vicinity. Incorporated in 1859, it was named for William C. Dawson, who served in the U. S. Senate from 1849 to 1855. The chief natural resources of the county are gold and hardwood, and the principal agricultural products are cotton, corn, small grains, apples, peaches, hay, sorghum cane, and poultry.

Right from Dawsonville on paved State 53 to a junction with an unimproved road, **2.9 m.**; R. on this road to a junction with unpaved State 43, **14.5 m.**; R. on State 43 (*several creeks must be forded, but only one is likely to drown a low-swung motor*) to Hunt Crane's farm, **15.1 m.** (L); from this point is an excellent view (NW) of beautiful AMICALOLA FALLS on the Appalachian Trail (*see* TOUR *13A*). From Hunt Crane's farm it is possible to drive **0.5 m.** farther before the rough road becomes a foot trail leading about **1 m.** to the top of the falls.

SILVER CITY, **68.8 m.** (900 alt., 127 pop.), is a rural community.

Right from Silver City on a good dirt road to the MARKED ROCK (R), **4.4 m.**, a boulder eight and a half feet long and two and a half feet high. On its rounded surface is a series of deeply carved petroglyphs made, according to Cherokee legend, by a race that preceded them here. The symbols appear to represent the deity, darkness, life, and the serpent.

CUMMING, **79.1 m.** (approx. 1,225 alt., 648 pop.), seat of Forsyth County, was founded in 1832 and named for William Cumming, an officer in the War of 1812. All Negroes were expelled from Cumming during a serious race riot in 1908, and since that time none has lived in the town. There are only seventeen Negroes and two foreign-born white people in the county.

ROSWELL, **100.7 m.** (1,000 alt., 1,432 pop.), extending for about two miles along the highway, is admired for its old houses as well as for the many mimosa trees that in early summer are covered with fluffy yellowish pink blossoms. The town was incorporated in 1854 and named for Roswell King, who came here from Darien about 1837. He bought a large tract of land and, as an inducement to settlers, offered as much as ten acres each to any of his friends who would come from Darien, Augusta, Savannah, or Charleston, South Carolina. Soon Roswell was a prosperous colony. King and his son established the Roswell Mills, one of the most successful cotton-manufacturing plants in this section until it was destroyed by General Sherman's army during the Atlanta campaign because it supplied the Confederacy with cloth. Although the mills were rebuilt after the war, Roswell has never recovered its full industrial activity and is now a small residential town with two business sections and several old residences that were used as Union headquarters and therefore saved from destruction.

COLONIAL PLACE (*private*), on a knoll at the end of Goulding St., a short unpaved street leading right from the first business district, was the home of the Reverend Francis R. Goulding, author of *Young Marooners* and *Marooners' Island*. Built by Goulding about 1857, the house is a red-painted brick structure with a Palladian doorway and white shutters. Roswell citizens claim that Goulding invented the first sewing machine and that his daughter used it for several years. However, Goulding failed to get a patent or receive official credit for the invention.

The OLD PRESBYTERIAN CHURCH (L), about midway between the two business sections, was built about 1840 under the direction of Nathaniel A. Pratt, its first minister. It is a small, white frame structure with Doric columns supporting a Greek pediment, above which is a small, boxlike bell tower. At the rear is a slave gallery, and at the opposite end is the high pulpit reached by a small double stairway. Throughout the building the original clear windows have been replaced by stained glass and the blinds removed. This church was spared destruction in the War between the States because it served as a hospital for Union soldiers. An evidence of military occupation is a cabinet door that was made into a checkerboard for the entertainment of the patients.

GREAT OAKS (*private*), across the street from the church, is a well-proportioned brick house of modified Georgian Colonial design built by Nathaniel Pratt. The walls of the house are eighteen inches thick.

In the southern business section is ROSWELL PARK, landscaped by the Works Progress Administration as a memorial to the early settlers.

BARRINGTON HALL (*private*), across the street from the southern end of the park, is set behind a grove of tall oaks. A long walkway leads to the entrance and thence left to the old English gardens, especially notable for the beautiful circular plantings of boxwood in the upper garden. The house, designed by a Connecticut architect, was built about 1842 by Barrington King, son of Roswell King. A "widow's walk" on the roof is similar to the New England "captains' walks," used as lookouts by the wives of men who had sailed on whaling vessels. Wide verandas, Doric columns, and shuttered windows extending from the floor almost to the ceiling, all recall the splendor of the old plantations.

MIMOSA HALL (*private*), on an unpaved street extending right from the park, is built of stucco-covered brick. Fashioned after a Greek temple, it has a two-story portico with four monumental Doric columns supporting a high pediment. On both sides of the walk leading to the front steps are circular plantings of boxwood and a growth of magnolia, mimosa, and oak trees. To the left is the lily-of-the-valley garden with its original plantings of boxwood, and to the rear is a wide expanse of lawn sloping gently to the flower garden. The house was built in the early 1840's by John Dunwody, one of the original settlers.

BULLOCH HALL (*private*), beyond Mimosa Hall at the foot of the street, is a Greek Revival clapboard house built about 1842 by James Bulloch. Set on a knoll in a grove of fine oaks, it has a portico with four tall Doric columns and pilasters. At Bulloch Hall, on December 22, 1853, Martha Bulloch was married to Theodore Roosevelt. Their son was Theodore Roosevelt, who became President of the United States. After the wedding the guests were served ice cream made with ice hauled from Savannah.

US 19 between Roswell and Atlanta is being beautified with flowering dogwood, tulip trees, and crape myrtles. It was dedicated as Constitution Highway on January 2, 1938, the sesquicentennial of Georgia's ratification of the Constitution.

The CHATTAHOOCHEE RIVER, **102.7 m.,** muddy with red Georgia clay, is spanned by the ROSWELL BRIDGE, a long concrete structure built in 1924.

Between Roswell and Buckhead US 19 leads through woods of pines and oaks.

The marked SITE OF THE HIGHTOWER TRAIL (L), **105 m.,** at an intersection with an unpaved road, is one of the oldest and most important Indian trails in north Georgia. It was formerly recognized as the boundary between the lands of the Cherokee Nation and the Creek Confederacy.

SANDY SPRINGS, **108.6 m.,** is a small settlement.

Right from Sandy Springs on Johnson Ferry Road across the Chattahoochee River bridge to a junction with a dirt road, 2.3 m., at a greenhouse on a hill (R); L. on this road to SOAP CREEK, 4.3 m., a small, rocky tributary of the Chattahoochee. Its name is a corruption of Old Sope, the name of a Cherokee chief who remained in this section after the removal of the Cherokee in 1838 and was buried in Sewell's Cemetery near by. The stream is crossed by SOAP CREEK BRIDGE, one of the few covered bridges still standing in the South. Reputedly built before the War between the States, it rests on foundation piers of rubble stone and spans a distance of 128 feet. Heavy hand-hewn timbers, fastened together with wooden pegs, form lattice trusses which are enclosed with vertical boards topped with a metal gable roof.

RUINS OF THE SOAP CREEK PAPER-MANUFACTURING PLANT, consisting chiefly of crumbling granite walls and fairly well defined floor plans, lie on both sides of the creek. Established soon after 1810 when this section was still Cherokee territory, the plant is believed to have been the first enterprise of its kind in the Southeast. Two mills were operated continuously in the manufacture of tissue paper, newsprint, wrapping paper, and stationery from rice, straw, shucks, cane, cotton stalks, cottonseed, and longleaf pine. Rebuilt soon after its destruction by fire during the War between the States, the plant changed ownership several times before it was closed early in the 1900's.

ATLANTA, **121.5 m.** (1,050 alt., 270,366 pop.) (*see* ATLANTA).

Points of Interest: State Capitol, Cyclorama of the Battle of Atlanta, Georgia School of Technology, Emory University, Oglethorpe University, Atlanta University (Negro), and others.

Atlanta is at the junction with US 78 (*see* TOUR *8*), with US 29 (*see* TOUR *3*), with US 341 (*see* TOUR *12*), with US 23 (*see* TOUR *7*), and with US 41 (*see* TOUR *2*), with which US 19 unites between Atlanta and Griffin (*see* TOUR *2b*).

Section b. GRIFFIN *to* FLORIDA LINE; *202.4 m., US 19.*

South of GRIFFIN **0 m.** (965 alt., 10,321 pop.), the highway crosses an area where the most important crops are cotton, peaches, and pecans.

The peach area around Thomaston is beautiful in spring when the blossoming orchards line the highway with delicate pink. In the vicinity of Albany the pecan orchards have large trees set apart at regular intervals, and annual crops of cotton, corn, hay, and peas grow between the rows.

On the lower part of this route are a popular year-round resort and a winter playground patronized by wealthy visitors. The highway has been beautified by the removal of some advertising signboards and the planting of crape myrtle and abelia bushes. Below Thomasville the Spanish moss, palmettos, and dark water of the tropics begin to appear.

ZEBULON, 11.4 m. (approx. 900 alt., 576 pop.), was incorporated in 1825 as the seat of Pike County. Both were named for General Zebulon Montgomery Pike, who was distinguished for his discovery of Pikes Peak and who was killed in action in the War of 1812. Zebulon has one of the best peach-packing sheds in the state, and the county ships between five hundred and six hundred carloads of fruit annually. There are about 300,000 peach trees in Pike County and, since the older trees do not bear well, new orchards are continually being planted.

JUGTOWN (R) 19.8 m., is a shop where jugs and pottery have been made of native clays for more than a century. The potter still uses early methods and fashions articles on his primitive wheel.

SILVERTOWN, 20.8 m. (approx. 900 alt., 2,171 pop.), is the site of the Martha Mills (*open to visitors*), a branch of the B. F. Goodrich Company, tire manufacturers. Housed in two red brick and limestone buildings, the mills represent one of the world's largest plants for the exclusive manufacture of tire cord. With 135,000 spindles in operation, 325 bales of cotton are used daily.

Eight hundred families are accommodated in houses that are individual in design and color, each being furnished with modern bathroom and kitchen equipment. The lawns and parks are trimly landscaped in a setting of pine groves and cultivated peach orchards. Recreational facilities include tennis and softball courts and a standard baseball field with a steel and concrete grandstand seating 1,500. Among the many mill villages in Georgia, this one is considered exceptionally good. The 2,000 employees of these mills refused to participate in the textile strike of 1934.

The SILVERTOWN SCHOOLS are supported largely by the Martha Mills, assisted by a small state fund. Three modern brick buildings accommodate six hundred pupils and twenty-three teachers.

A triangular CHURCH PARK, formed by the intersection of Goodrich Ave., 4th Ave. and L St., was dedicated to religious purposes when the village was laid out. The two churches, Methodist and Baptist, are built on Greek Revival lines.

The COMMUNITY CENTER, a handsome red brick building in the center of the village, houses several business enterprises and a motion picture house that seats 750.

CRYSTAL HILL (*open by request*), 4th Ave., the estate of Albert Matthews, comprises seventy-five acres of native woodland beautified by the planting of wild flowers and shrubs and by the addition of gardens, lakes, and pools. One section of the five-mile winding drive through the estate is bordered by gardenia bushes; in summer their white blooms fill the air with a heavy sweetness that mingles with the more spicy fragrance of fluffy, pink mimosa blossoms. The crystal rock formation found on the property has been used in the construction of rock gardens, pools, and a mill house. The formal gardens are outlined with hundreds of dwarf boxwoods.

THOMASTON, 26.8 m. (700 alt., 4,922 pop.), seat of Upson County, is an industrial town in the center of the peach-growing section. Since a blight lessened production in the area around Fort Valley (*see* TOUR 2), Thomaston has ranked first in the state in exports of peaches. The Mount Rose, Uneeda, Early Rose, Red Bird, and Elberta are among the favorite varieties.

Thomaston was founded in 1825 and named for General Jett Thomas (1776-1817), who built the statehouse at Milledgeville (*see* TOUR *14*) and served with distinction in the War of 1812 as captain of an artillery company under General John Floyd. In recognition of his services he was made a major general in the state militia after the war and the legislature presented him with a jeweled sword.

A textile mill and a bleachery, among the principal industrial plants of the town, continue the tradition established by Franklin Factory, founded here in 1833 for the manufacture of cotton and woolen goods.

At **41 m.** is the junction with US 80 (*see* TOUR *9*), which coincides with US 19 between this point and **45.5 m.** where US 80 branches R. (*see* TOUR *9*).

BUTLER, **55.5 m.** (650 alt., 857 pop.), seat of Taylor County, was incorporated in 1854 and named for General William Orlando Butler (1791-1880), who succeeded Scott as commander of the U. S. Army in Mexico and was nominated for Vice President in 1848. The county, created in 1852 and named for Zachary Taylor, twelfth President of the United States, included the land of Fort Laurens, which guarded an old Indian agency. This reservation, five miles square, was established in the latter part of the eighteenth century for the Creek.

ELLAVILLE, 79.8 m. (555 alt., 764 pop.), incorporated in 1859, is the seat of Schley County, which yields lumber and a variety of farm products.

Between 89.3 m. and 90.3 m. is MEMORIAL MILE, dedicated by the Garden Club of Americus to the Sumter County World War veterans. More than two hundred marble slabs have been placed at regular intervals on each side of the highway, and between them dark evergreen shrubs and scarlet poppies have been planted. When a veteran dies, a bronze plate bearing his name and rank is added to a slab.

AMERICUS, 93.3 m. (360 alt., 8,760 pop.), seat of Sumter County and one of the most prosperous towns in this area, has a neat residential section built on gently sloping wooded hills. Among its industrial plants are shirt factories, wood veneer plants, burial vault factories, canneries, creameries, gins, and lumber mills. The county, named for the Revolutionary general Thomas Sumter, was created in 1831, and Americus was founded the following year on the site of the Creek agency granary. The land of this section was well known among the Indians for its production of maize. In the cultivation of this grain, the Indians customarily bored a hole about fifteen inches deep, inserted a fish for fertilizer, and then dropped a grain of corn on the fish.

In the vicinity of Americus are bauxite and kaolin mines and thousands of acres of young pine trees. Twenty-two distinct types of soil encourage a diversity of crops.

GEORGIA SOUTHWESTERN COLLEGE is a coeducational junior college with about 350 students. Opened in 1908, it functioned as an industrial high school until 1926, when agricultural and normal courses were added. In 1929 all high school work was abandoned, and in 1932 the institution became a unit of the University System of Georgia. The four main buildings on its campus are of brick.

At Americus is a junction with State 49 (see TOUR 2B).

Left from Americus on Souther Field Road to Souther Field, 5 m., SITE OF LINDBERGH'S FIRST SOLO FLIGHT. This aviation field was used during the World War as a large training center for army pilots. After the armistice, airplanes were sold for what they would bring, some for as little as $50. In his book *We*, Charles Lindbergh says he bought his first plane at Souther Field in 1923 for $500 and made his first solo flight over this field and his first cross-country trip by a roundabout route from Souther Field to Milwaukee, Wisconsin.

In SMITHVILLE, 106.3 m. (332 alt., 777 pop.), a junction of the Central of Georgia Railway, trains stop for the customary "twenty minutes for dinner." On the porch of the frame hotel across the street from the station a Negro porter swings a large brass dinner bell. Passengers and crew hurry from the train to the dining room, where the plates are already placed on long tables. By a provision in the will of R. L. McAfee, the first owner, chicken was served every day for more than fifty years, until the original hotel burned. The proprietors of the present inn no longer limit the meals to chicken.

Between Smithville and Leesburg is a flat, sandy region.

LEESBURG, 119 m. (282 alt., 691 pop.), in 1872 became the seat of Lee County; both were named for Colonel Henry (Lighthorse Harry) Lee, who captured Augusta from the British in 1781. The surrounding agricultural area ranks high in the production of peanuts and pears.

At 127.7 m. is the junction with an unpaved road.

Left on this road to CHEHAW STATE PARK (*picnic facilities*), 1.1 m., a 600-acre tract (L) now in process of development by the state. It is enclosed on two sides by a large clear-water bayou formed by the confluence of the Kinchefoonee and Cuckalee creeks. The setting appears almost tropical, with moss-festooned trees growing along the banks of the lake. Development plans (1939) include facilities for water sports and overnight cabins to be built on the bluffs over-looking the water. Part of the land has been cultivated for many years, but will be reforested and preserved as an unbroken stand of timber.

The park, given to the state by Dougherty County, was named for the Chiha, or Chehaw, a tribe of Creek who lived here and befriended the white settlers. Arrowheads, spearheads, tomahawks, hoes, drills, scrapers, clay pipes, and stone celts have been found along the banks of one creek and in the neighboring fields. Because of the variety of workmanship in the artifacts, it is believed that this section was occupied at several distinct periods.

In the SWIFT & COMPANY FERTILIZER PLANT, 128.6 m., housed in a frame building equipped with modern, electrically operated machinery, non-acid-forming fertilizer is manufactured by about sixty employees from phosphates mined in the surrounding territory. A 900-foot well on the property has a flow of 85 gallons of mineral water a minute. Albany physicians recommend the water to patients, who often come for it from a distance of 25 miles, and the management allows all who apply in person to obtain it free.

ALBANY, 130.1 m. (184 alt., 14,507 pop.), seat of Dougherty County, is a rapidly developing city of wide streets, commanding oaks, and trim modern residences as well as older houses. Despite its languorous, semitropical setting, intensified by profuse plantings of palmettos and pink-blossoming coral vines, Albany is a lively sports town. Though not a permanent tourist colony, it is a popular stop-over point for visitors, who enjoy the golf, swimming, and dancing at near-by Radium Springs. On week ends the sidewalks are gay with beach pajamas, slacks, and flannels, while the streets are crowded with shiny, stream-lined cars full of recreation seekers.

In the surrounding region are so many acres of paper-shell pecans that several packing and shelling plants have been established in Albany. The nuts mature in October and are harvested by hand. Entire Negro families work in a grove; the children climb among the branches and shake down the nuts to their parents, who gather them from the ground. Spanish peanuts, used in candy manufacture, and the pest-proof tung nuts (*see* TOUR 5) are also produced in Dougherty County.

The site for Albany was purchased in 1836 by Alexander Shotwell, a New Jersey Quaker, who commissioned surveyors to lay out a town. In the same year Colonel Nelson Tift, accompanied by other men, brought goods from Appalachicola, Florida, up the Flint River, landed at the Albany site, and began the construction of the first log buildings. After the Indians had been removed to western territory, many white people settled here. In 1841 the legislature granted a charter, and in 1845 the *Albany Patriot,* now the *Albany News,* was first published. One of its first concerns was to dispel the current belief that south Georgia was unhealthful. Since Albany, through drainage and sanitation, has gained control of the malaria that formerly attacked its population, it has a very low death rate.

It was in Dougherty County that John Porter Fort, in 1881, drilled the first artesian well in the state. At 450 feet he obtained a flow of seven gallons a minute. This proved an important contribution to the healthfulness of south Georgia, as almost all the cities in the Coastal Plain, where the surface streams are contaminated, have since drilled wells that satisfactorily supply them with water.

The BRIDGE HOUSE, on Front St., now housing an auto-parts company, is a two-story brick building erected in 1857 by Colonel Tift at the time he built the first bridge over the Flint River. The approach to the bridge was through an archway in the center of this structure, on one side of which was Tift's office and on the other, quarters for the toll taker. Shortly before the War between the States the bridge was burned, and during the war this building was turned into a meat-packing house for Confederate troops. Later it was remodeled and richly decorated for Albany's first theater, where Laura Keene and E. A. Sothern (father of E. H. Sothern) appeared in *She Stoops to Conquer* and *Our American Cousin.* Shakespeare was presented by the Crisp family, including Charles F. Crisp (1845-96), who later served as Speaker of the U. S. House of Representatives during the fifty-second and fifty-third Congresses.

Left from Albany on paved State 50 to the CUDAHY PACKING PLANT (*open to visitors*), 1 m., opened in September, 1926. The building (L) has two stories of glass masonry set on a high concrete basement. Since the air is conditioned and the walls transmit light, no windows are needed. This plant has an annual capacity of 50,000 cattle, 350,000 hogs, 17,500 sheep, and 17,500 lambs; it produces meat, lard, hides, wool, and sheepskins, and serves as a market for butter, eggs, cheese, and poultry. The animals are slaughtered on the top floor. As the carcasses pass along moving trolleys, they are skinned, split, and prepared for the coolers without any cessation of movement. When sufficiently chilled they are passed below to the cutting floor and prepared for shipment. Almost all the beef and lamb is sold fresh, but a large portion of the pork is cured and smoked. Separate buildings are maintained for the power plant, dressing rooms for the four hundred employees, and government inspectors' offices. Livestock raisers are encouraged by the management to use improved methods of animal breeding.

RADIUM SPRINGS (*trains met at Albany on request*), 134.4 m., is a popular Georgia resort. This bowl of clear blue water, once called Skywater by the Creek, flows from an unknown depth at the rate of 70,000 gallons a minute and remains at a constant temperature of 68° F. The Indians, believing its waters had curative qualities, traveled for miles through the woods and camped in near-by villages to bathe here. White people later called the place Blue Springs. In 1925, when Barron Collier bought the property for a pleasure resort, the spring was permitted to overflow and form a lake that drains into the yellow Flint River. Both lake and river are shaded by live oaks draped with Spanish moss; when the springs are lighted at night they form a scene of weird beauty.

Flights of steps lead from the pool (*swimming 25¢*) to SKYWATER LODGE, a yellow stucco hotel with pillared porches and large outside rooms. In the ballroom on the third floor dances are held each Saturday evening. Yellow cottages scattered throughout the grounds accommodate parties of guests. The 18-hole golf course (*adm. upon recommendation of club member*) is kept in excellent condition and has been the scene of state and sectional tournaments. Wild turkeys, for which tame decoys are used, and quail are plentiful (*open season Nov. 20-March 1*). Especially popular are dove hunts (*open season Nov. 20-Jan. 31*), a new experience to most sportsmen. The resort has its own clay pigeon traps, and trapshooting tournaments are held every year. Other sports include fishing in the Flint River, tennis on the clay courts, and horseback riding along the bridle paths which lead through pine woods and open country.

RIVER BEND PARK (*swimming, dancing*), 140.3 m., on a horseshoe curve of the Flint River, affords an impressive view of the slow, tawny river. Shortly after Albany was founded, supplies were shipped to this point from Savannah by boat.

CAMILLA, 157.3 m. (167 alt., 2,025 pop.), former seat of Mitchell County, was laid out in 1857. The county was named for David B. Mitchell, Governor of Georgia (1809-13 and 1815-17), and the town, for his daughter. The marker in the center of the main street designates the SITE OF THE HAWTHORNE TRAIL, blazed in 1818 by William Hawthorne when he was seeking a short route from North Carolina to Florida. Two years later he made a trip over the trail, broadened it, and settled with his family near Cairo.

Left from Camilla on paved State 37 to MOULTRIE, 27 m. (340 alt., 8,027 pop.), seat of Colquitt County. The town was incorporated in 1859, three years after the creation of the county, and was named for General William Moultrie, who successfully defended Sullivan's Island against the British fleet when Sir Peter Parker attacked Charles Town, South Carolina, during the Revolutionary War. It is a meat-packing and watermelon-shipping center. An annual festival is held to celebrate the ripening of the watermelons, which frequently attain a length of three feet and a diameter of two feet. Georgia watermelons are grown over a wide area, but principally in the southern part of the state, where they yield an average annual income of $1,000,000.

SWIFT & COMPANY MEAT-PACKING PLANT (*open to visitors*), 1 m. N. of the courthouse, is a modern structure of brick and reinforced concrete and has the largest capacity of all such plants in the Southeast. Approximately 750 workers are employed in the preparation of meats and meat products.

PELHAM, 166.3 m. (355 alt., 2,762 pop.), began in 1870 when J. L. Hand established a sawmill and turpentine business here. The settlement that developed on the site was incorporated in 1881 and named for Major John Pelham, who commanded "Jeb" Stuart's Horse Artillery while in his teens during the War between the States. The town has peanut shelling plants, an oil mill, a canning plant, a fertilizer plant, lumber mills, and cotton gins. Approximately 6,000 bales of cotton, 300,000 pounds of tobacco, and 15,000 tons of cottonseed and peanuts are sold here annually.

CHINQUAPIN (*private*), 183.6 m., has a private road (R) lined with camphor trees that winds for miles along the wooded banks of the small Ochlockonee River to the brick residence, which is set on a beautiful cliff overlooking the river. Near by is a modern camp given to local boys for summer outings by John F. Archbold, former owner of the estate.

THOMASVILLE, 189.6 m. (250 alt., 11,733 pop.), seat of Thomas County, was incorporated in 1826, a year after the creation of the county, and, like Thomaston (*see above*), was named for General Jett Thomas. Because of its position at the intersection of three paved highways, several large companies have made it a distributing center, and its department stores resemble those of much larger cities. Sawmills, tobacco markets, cotton gins, an iron foundry, a concrete-pipe plant, and a crate and basket factory are prominent among the industrial establishments. Thomasville is also a naval-stores center where pine gum is distilled for turpentine and rosin. The recent establishment of a packing plant has given impetus to beef and dairy-cattle raising.

The winters here are short and mild, with only occasional days in which the temperature falls as low as freezing, and breezes from the Gulf of Mexico modify the heat of the summers. Flowers bloom most of the year; the telephone poles are covered with climbing Paul's Scarlet roses, and the streets are lined with Red Radiances. The annual Thomasville Rose Show (*last Friday in April*), begun in 1922, now attracts as many as 30,000 visitors. The schools, nurserymen, winter estates, and local organizations have exhibits.

Northerners began coming to Thomasville about seventy-five years ago, and from 1875 until the noted Piney Woods Hotel burned in 1900, there were many transient visitors. A number of northern capitalists bought large estates and built palatial winter homes, which are maintained in the manner of old southern plantations and provide employment for an average of three hundred people each. They include a total of 150,000 acres, of which one-fourth is under cultivation and the rest kept as hunting preserves. Many of the estates have a fine growth of unusually tall longleaf pine. Pine Tree Boulevard, completely encircling the city within a radius of two miles, passes several of these estates.

Hunting and fishing are popular sports. The preserves and the surrounding forests abound with quail, wild turkeys, deer, ducks, and doves, and numerous near-by lakes afford excellent fishing. The Georgia-Florida Amateur Field Trials for bird dogs are held in Thomasville each fall. In spring the Thomasville Horse Show and an accompanying polo series are held at Birdwood (*see below*).

On the courthouse lawn is the MCKINLEY MEMORIAL TREE, planted by William McKinley during the winter of 1895-96, prior to his election to the Presidency.

The GREAT OAK, Crawford and Monroe Sts., is one of the largest trees in the state. Estimated to be 250 years old, it has a limb spread of 146½ feet, a height of 49 feet, and a trunk diameter of 21½ feet. Recently it has been enrolled as 24th ranking member of the National Live-Oak Society, consisting of 47 tree members.

The MARK HANNA HOME (*private*), N. Dawson St., is a Victorian structure built in 1877 and later enlarged by Hanna. During the winter of 1895-96, Republican leaders came here to confer with the noted statesman and formulated the plan that carried William McKinley to the White House. McKinley was a guest in this house when he was first nominated for the Presidency.

ARCHBOLD MEMORIAL HOSPITAL, on Gordon St. near the outskirts of the city, was given to Thomasville by John F. Archbold in memory of his father, John D. Archbold. The three-story stucco building, showing

Spanish influence in its architecture, is set back on a lawn above which rise stately pines. Connected with the main building is a nurses' home given by Archbold as a memorial to his mother. The property represents a total investment of more than a million dollars, and the hospital is said to be one of the finest south of Johns Hopkins.

At Thomasville is the junction with US 84 (*see* TOUR 5).

1. Left from Thomasville on Clay Street Road to the VASHTI INDUSTRIAL SCHOOL, 2 m., housed in six brick and stucco buildings. The school has an average enrollment of 114 girls, who are given a thorough high school education in addition to training in weaving, rug making, basketry, clay modeling, and home economics. Organized in 1903 by the women of Thomasville for underprivileged girls, it was named for Mrs. Vashti Blassingame, mother of the first contributor to the school. Later it was turned over to the Woman's Missionary Council of the Methodist Episcopal Church, South.

2. Right from Thomasville on the lower Cairo Road to BOXHALL (*open during Rose Show*), 3.5 m., a 500-acre estate (R). The red brick house, set on a wide expanse of lawn, is the original structure built in 1830 by the McIntyre family. African daisies and pansies are conspicuous in the planting.

3. Left from Thomasville on State 35 to (L) HOLLYWOOD PLANTATION (*open during Rose Show*), 1 m., which is unusually beautiful because of its profuse growth. The design of the house is based upon that of Monticello, the home of Thomas Jefferson.

At 2 m. is a junction (R) with Pine Tree Boulevard, which runs for thirteen miles, completely encircling Thomasville.

BIRDWOOD (*private*), 3 m. (R), is the estate of Cameron W. Forbes, a grandson of Ralph Waldo Emerson and Ambassador to Japan, 1931-32. The spacious house is built of red brick. On the beautiful polo field, set amid a pine forest, a horse show and polo series are held each spring.

MILLPOND PLANTATION (*open during Rose Show*), 4 m., (L) was named for Linton's Mill, which was on the land when the 10,000 acres were purchased for an estate. Sixty miles of drives lead to the residence, the farm, and various gardens. The house of Spanish Colonial architecture, covered with wistaria vines and shaded by handsome oaks, is built around a large patio planted with palms and tall ferns. Leading to the right side of the house is the rose walk, a long avenue bordered by hundreds of varieties of roses against a background of climbing roses trained on posts and swinging in garlands between them. South of the house is the palm garden, a rectangular lawn bordered by many varieties of palms mirrored at one end in a reflecting pool. On the west side is a camellia garden and, near by, a grotto approached by seven lanes, each bordered by a different variety of fruit trees. On the east side a great expanse of grass, shaded by tall pines and moss-draped oaks, slopes to the millpond and boathouses.

A five-mile drive leads around the Gorge, a T-shaped limestone sink that varies from 20 to 500 feet in width and averages 40 feet in depth. In winter it is filled with water but runs dry each summer; the owner spent thousands of dollars trying vainly to dam the water.

4. Right from Thomasville on US 319 to ELSOMA (*open during Rose Show*), 3 m., a winter estate (R) of 4,000 acres. From the entrance gates, marked by a

planting of Spanish bayonets, wild azaleas, and wistaria vines, a winding drive-way leads through a growth of pines interspersed with magnolias and oaks to the house; its porch is outlined by a delicate iron railing, and several dormer windows are spaced across the high pitched roof. Beyond the open terrace on the south side is an old-fashioned garden with beds of narcissi, snowdrops, camellias, azaleas, and tea olives. The property once belonged to Colonel A. T. McIntyre, one of the first settlers.

INWOOD PLANTATION (*open during Rose Show*), across the road (L) from Elsoma, is a 1,000-acre estate with entrance gates banked in native shrubs, flowers, and trees. A circular drive, bordered by a clipped hedge and magnolia trees, leads to the low, rambling stucco house and the near-by azalea and rose gardens. The south terrace is outlined with a low hedge of tea olives, which bloom all spring and summer with small, fragrant, white flowers. Between the terrace and the beautiful lawns stretching to the pine woods is a formal garden accented by boxwood and camellia plants. In spring the heavily scented banana shrubs lend their fragrance to the air.

MELROSE (*open during Rose Show*), 4.9 m., the estate (R) of H. M. Hanna, financier of Cleveland, Ohio, is bordered by fences on which Cherokee roses and yellow jasmine vines are trained. Wide expanses of lawn, spreading from the winding approach to the house, are shaded by large oaks, magnolias, redbuds, crape myrtles, and flowering peach trees. The residence is a rambling, buff-colored frame house trimmed in white and covered with wistaria. The central portion, constructed of logs and covered with clapboards, was on the site when H. M. Hanna, Sr., bought the estate in the 1890's.

Among the plantings is the White Garden, a sunken grassplot bordered with a hedge of white pittosporum and planted with white azaleas, camellias, snow-drops, and pansies. From this area white marble steps lead to the Pink Garden of azaleas, camellias, and roses. The Rose Garden, west of the house, has a hedge of Louis Philippe roses.

Also on the estate are a red brick, white-columned house built by Hanna for his daughter; a "show boat" (motion picture theater), entered by a gangplank across a pool; and white cottages for the employees. The barn and outhouses are in groups like the quarters of an old plantation.

PEBBLE HILL (*open during Rose Show*), 5.4 m., is an estate (R) enclosed by fences covered with Cherokee roses. The planting is in harmony with the natural setting of pine forests. The rambling, whitewashed brick house, three stories in height, has deep eaves and shows the influence of several types of architecture. From the residence paths lead to camellia gardens, a wild flower garden, a swimming pool, and a camphor-tree maze. The land was granted to James Johnson in 1810, and the central portion of the present house was an earlier residence, built in 1855.

The red brick MILLION DOLLAR BARN has white classical columns and doorways covered with ivy. This barn, built for a fine herd of Jersey cows, is equipped with every device for the scientific handling of the animals and has radios to provide music for the cows while they are being milked. The courtyard where the cattle are shown is surrounded by a serpentine wall on which wistaria is trained.

On WINSTEAD (*open during Rose Show*), 5.4 m., the approach (L) to the house is by way of a quarter-mile avenue bordered with magnolia and dogwood trees. The house, a remodeled Greek Revival structure, is set behind a white picket fence and a low privet hedge. Along the brick walkway inside the fence are dwarf boxwoods, and behind the row of boxwoods are flower beds with a background of cedars, kumquats, and banana shrubs. The lawns are shaded by magnolias, oaks, hollies, Irish yews, and tea olives.

(Greenwood, another well-known estate in the Thomasville section, is described on Tour 5.)

At **202.4 m.** US 19 crosses the Florida Line at a point 8 miles north of Monticello, Florida.

TOUR 7

(Franklin, N.C.) — Clayton — Clarkesville — Cornelia — Gainesville — Atlanta; US 23.

North Carolina Line to Atlanta, 118.4 m. — Roadbed hard-surfaced throughout, chiefly concrete — Tallulah Falls R.R. parallels route between N. C. Line and Cornelia; the Southern Ry. between Cornelia and Atlanta — All types of accommodations — Many summer hotels and boarding houses.

US 23 crosses a corner of the Chattahoochee National Forest in the lower slopes of the Blue Ridge Mountains, which vary in altitude from 800 to almost 5,000 feet. The broad views of wooded valleys, with blue mountain ranges, waterfalls, and clear, calm lakes combine to make this one of the most beautiful regions in the state. At times the road winds along the sides of wooded slopes, brightened in spring by the delicate pink and white blossoms of mountain laurel and rhododendron and in fall by brilliant red and yellow leaves.

This northeastern corner of Georgia is a popular summer resort area, where many private cottages, summer hotels, and fishing camps have been built along the shores of lakes. In the valleys some of the land has been cleared for pastures, truck gardens, and apple or peach orchards. Few Negroes live in this section, and most of the small farms are cultivated by white owners.

Near Gainesville are rolling foothills, where agriculture is extensive and industry well advanced. There are several small but prosperous factory towns along the southern part of the route.

US 23 crosses the North Carolina Line, **0 m.,** at a point in the CHATTAHOOCHEE NATIONAL FOREST (*see* TOUR 6) more than thirteen miles south of Franklin, North Carolina.

At **0.7 m.** is a junction with a graveled road.

Left on this road, which curves around the hillsides and sometimes dips sharply into a valley, to ESTATOAH FALLS (R), **3.1 m.,** formed by the waters of Middle Creek cascading between the feathery foliage of hemlocks.

Many points along the road afford sweeping views of valleys and surrounding hills. Occasionally sheep and cows can be seen grazing in pastures enclosed by split-rail fences. The mountain woodlands are redolent with the clean, sharp scent of pine and the earthy odors of damp mold.

At **9.6 m.** is a junction with a dirt road.

Left on this road to RABUN BALD, **12.6 m.** (4,717 alt.), the second highest peak in the state. The summit affords views of three states, North Carolina, South Carolina, and Georgia.

RABUN GAP, **2 m.** (approx. 2,100 alt., 205 pop.), a small settlement in a narrow pass through the highland, was formerly known only for its surrounding scenery, but in recent years has become important for its vocational school.

The RABUN GAP-NACOOCHEE SCHOOL (R), **2.3 m.**, is a junior college that offers two years of agricultural training. The red brick buildings are set on a hill with the mountains as a background, and the 1,600-acre school farm for practical demonstration lies on the opposite side of the highway in a circular valley at the head of the Little Tennessee River.

The nucleus is the boarding school and farm of 200 acres where young men and women students pay for their education by farm and domestic work. In the outer circle of 1,400 acres is the farm settlement school, where whole families receive both agricultural instruction and a living in return for their labor. Fourteen families, admitted in rotating groups for five-year periods, are each provided with forty acres of land, a model six-room cottage, a barn, and outhouses. Under approved methods of agriculture the farms are operated on a sharecrop basis and the farmers assisted in marketing their products, purchasing supplies, and keeping accounts. Adjacent to the boarding school farm is the day school, through which vocational education is extended to the children of the surrounding district. This was the original school, begun in 1920 by the consolidation of two country schools. The institution is supported by appropriations of state and Federal funds and by private donations.

US 23 crosses the TENNESSEE RIVER, **4 m.**, which rises in the mountains of Georgia but is little more than a creek in its short course in the state.

From the northern boundary of Clayton, **8 m.**, is an excellent view of BLACK ROCK MOUNTAIN (R), its bald summit rising sharply above the wooded lower slopes.

CLAYTON, **9.3 m.** (1,959 alt., 798 pop.), is a well-kept town whose main street is lined with frame hotels that provide good accommodations for the summer visitors. They hike up Black Rock and Pinnacle Mountains and participate in the old-fashioned square dances of the mountaineers. At these dances urban people in fashionable city clothes mingle with the mountaineers in overalls and ginghams. As the sheriff calls the figures, all stamp and whirl through the dances, clapping time to the music.

Clayton was incorporated in 1823 as the seat of Rabun County, which had been created in 1819 from Cherokee lands. This town has the highest precipitation in the state (70.07 in.); its high elevation and low temperature cause immediate condensation of the moisture in the warm breezes from the Atlantic and the Gulf of Mexico.

The town has been a summer resort for more than twenty-five years. Within a radius of a few miles there are twelve lakes (*boating, swimming, fishing*), six of them formed in the process of power development. Camping facilities of the Chattahoochee National Forest (*see* TOUR 6) also are easily accessible, and bream, black bass, and rainbow trout are plentiful in the mountain streams.

Rabun County, with little agriculture and few industries, is a typical mountain region, settled principally by New Englanders who previously had lived in the mountains of Virginia, and by a few Tories who escaped to the mountains during the American Revolution. When the Cherokee were removed to Oklahoma in 1838, a few escaped, and some who intermarried with white settlers have descendants still living in the county.

During the 1880's and 1890's efforts were made to develop the mining of mica, gold, and corundum, but the inaccessibility of the region made operations unprofitable. From 1908 to 1920 the Georgia Power Company purchased 20 per cent of the best farming land for power development. Recently more than half the total area of the county has been withdrawn from cultivation for inclusion in the Chattahoochee National Forest. Since paved highways have made the mountain lakes of this region accessible, it seems probable that recreation will become its chief source of income.

1. Left from Clayton on War Woman Rd. to SCREAMER MOUNTAIN, 2 m. (2,925 alt.), named for an Indian who broke away from his tribe during the Cherokee Removal and fled screaming to the mountain.

At 3 m. is WAR WOMAN DELL (*picnic facilities*). A small brook, crossed by several bridges, runs through the grounds, and a compactly built shelter of logs provides protection from rain. The road, the dell, and the creek are named War Woman, not for Nancy Hart but for another Georgia heroine, an Indian woman who was friendly to the whites and is said to have walked twenty miles in four hours to warn the early settlers of a proposed raid.

On a farm (L) is DICK'S CREEK TUNNEL, 7 m., dug through a granite mountain by pick and shovel prior to 1860. The tunnel was planned as a passage for the Black Diamond Railroad to haul coal from the mines of Tennessee to the Savannah port. Though 80 per cent complete, it was abandoned during the War between the States and work has never been resumed.

2. Right from Clayton on US 76 to LAKE BURTON, 7 m. (*cabins and water sports*), created when the Georgia Power Company impounded the waters of

the Tallulah River for power development. With a shore line of sixty-five miles, this is the largest and highest of six lakes so formed. A new graveled road (L) leads down the lake shore to LAKE RABUN, another of the Georgia Power Company's lakes.

TIGER, 11.9 m. (approx. 1,800 alt., 137 pop.), is named for a Cherokee chief, Tiger Tail. The names of Tiger Mountain, Tiger Creek, and Tiger Church all originally had "tails."

LAKEMONT, 17.3 m. (approx. 1,700 alt., 75 pop.), a small settlement, serves as the post office for a summer colony on the shores of Lake Rabun.

At 17.6 m. is a junction with a graveled road.

Right on this road to the LAKEMONT SUMMER COLONY, 1 m., composed principally of Atlanta people. Houses of wood or local stone, each with its own boathouse and bathing pier, are built on spacious grounds along the wooded slopes that encircle Lake Rabun. In summer this beautiful lake, with its clear waters reflecting the surrounding mountains, is a busy thoroughfare of canoes, motorboats, and aquaplanes.

Winding US 23 crosses the Tallulah River, 17.7 m., and runs parallel to it for almost five miles before recrossing it. Tallulah is an Indian word of unknown origin. It has been interpreted as meaning *terrible*. The bed of the river is rugged and almost dry because the flow from Lake Rabun has been diverted by means of Terrora Tunnel, cut 5,300 feet through a large mountain.

SAW TOOTH, 22 m., a flag station on the Tallulah Falls Railroad, is the outlet for Terrora Tunnel that supplies water for the powerhouse (R).

South of Saw Tooth the road parallels Tallulah Lake (R) for one-half mile, but an abundant growth of short-needle pines occasionally screens the dark green waters.

The highway crosses the power dam, 22.6 m., that impounds the waters of the Tallulah River. To the left, over the sheer rock precipice of 1,000 feet, the river once formed a beautiful falls. Now only a small stream trickles over the sharp rocks and flows through the deep gorge that was earlier cut by the torrent of rushing water. Tallulah Tunnel, also cut through the heart of a mountain, diverts the course of the Tallulah River for more than a mile. Below the tunnel the Tallulah and Chattooga Rivers join to form the Tugalo River, dammed in two places to create Lakes Tugalo and Yonah.

TALLULAH FALLS, 22.7 m. (1,629 alt., 105 pop.), is a small settlement on the Tallulah River near the southern end of the dam.

TALLULAH FALLS INDUSTRIAL SCHOOL, INC. (*open 9-5*), 23 m., owned and operated by the Georgia Federation of Women's Clubs, occupies (R) fourteen rock and timber buildings grouped upon stone terraces on the side of Cherokee Mountain. From this point are sweeping views, not only of the near-by Georgia mountains, but of the distant blue ranges of Tennessee, North Carolina, and South Carolina.

The school, which opened in 1909 with twenty-one pupils and one teacher housed in a small building, now has a student body numbering three hundred, a faculty of fourteen, and five hundred acres of land, with a plant valued at $250,000 and an endowment of $100,000. The institution is operated under the state school system and receives public funds, but it is also aided by generous private donations and, in crafts and home economics, by the Smith-Hughes Fund.

The curriculum includes courses from the first through the eleventh grade. Special emphasis is placed on religion, recreation, and social training. The students earn their maintenance by doing domestic, agricultural, and industrial work; occasionally the institution houses whole families, the parents supporting themselves in the same manner. Approximately one-third of the students come from remote districts and live at the school, while the remaining two-thirds are day students.

GREY EAGLE'S CHAIR, on the grounds of the school, is roughly carved from solid rock and weighs 500 pounds. It is said to have been the council chair of the Cherokee and was left on the property of a mountain man who sat in council with them. A descendant of this man lent the chair to the school on condition that it be neither sold nor given away, but remain forever the property of Grey Eagle, a chief of the Cherokee.

TALLULAH POINT, 23.1 m. (2,000 alt.), is a vantage point for the best view of TALLULAH GORGE, which extends in a huge semicircle from Tallulah Dam. The steep, rugged walls of the canyon are covered with a natural growth of trees and shrubs. In the distance (NE) Rabun Bald in Georgia and Round Mountain in South Carolina are visible on clear days.

At 23.4 m. is a junction with a dirt road.

Left on this road to the TALLULAH POWER PLANT, 0.4 m. (*open 7-5; for adm. phone from booth at top of cliff; guides*). An inclined railroad along the 608-foot wall of the canyon affords passengers a magnificent view of the gorge. Power generated here is distributed in Alabama, Tennessee, North Carolina, and South Carolina, as well as in Georgia.

A granite marker (R), 39.8 m., at the entrance to Clarkesville indicates that this is the supposed ROUTE OF DE SOTO when, with 500 Spanish and Portuguese soldiers and 200 Cherokee burden bearers, he passed through this region in 1540. So confusing are the varied accounts of his travels that historians have been unable to establish conclusively the exact places that he visited. It is believed that De Soto

entered the region now Georgia at its southwest corner, marched in
a northeasterly direction in search of gold, and stopped at an·Indian
village somewhere between the present Augusta and Columbia, South
Carolina. "Thence he marched northwestward," writes E. M. Coulter
in *A Short History of Georgia,* "and either entered North Carolina
before he turned to the southwest, or he took a shorter cut through the
Nacoochee Valley of northern Georgia. It seems rather certain that
he departed down the Coosa River, passing by the future location of
Rome."

CLARKESVILLE, 35.9 m. (1,372 alt., 617 pop.), seat of Habersham County,
was named for John C. Clarke (1766-1832), Revolutionary soldier and
Governor of Georgia (1819-23). This small town, in an almost level
valley among the mountains, was a fashionable summer resort in the
nineteenth century. Apple and peach orchards are cultivated extensively in the county. At intervals along the highway are fruit-packing
houses, frame buildings resembling barns, where pinkish-yellow peaches
or bright red apples are graded and packed in the fall. Clarkesville
ships about 100,000 bushels of apples and 135,000 bushels of peaches
annually. Although there are mineral deposits in this section, only
kyanite is mined.

DEMOREST, 41 m. (1,469 alt., 730 pop.), developed about PIEDMONT
COLLEGE (L), one of the earliest schools for mountain boys and girls.
This accredited four-year college confers the bachelor's degree in liberal
arts, science, and law, and has an average enrollment of about 400
students from 14 states and Cuba. Founded in 1899 by a Methodist
circuit rider, it is now under the auspices of the Congregational church.
Since the denomination has few adherents in the South, the financial
support, other than tuition, comes chiefly from New England. The
college, enlarged and reorganized in 1903, has buildings and equipment
valued at $30,000.

DEMOREST SPRINGS, in a public park 150 feet L. of the highway, is a
group of six mineral springs. They are within a few feet of one another, marked with metal plates describing their mineral properties, and
surrounded by a wall of concrete.

CORNELIA, 44.5 m. (1,537 alt., 1,542 pop.), incorporated in 1887, is in
the center of the apple-growing section of northeastern Georgia and
advertises this fact with a large RED METAL APPLE, set on a concrete
shaft about ten feet high beside the railroad station. Cornelia is known
over the entire state as the home of the Big Red Apple.

The road from Cornelia to Baldwin is lined with apple orchards.
Throughout the summer and fall, cider is sold at roadside stands.

At Cornelia is a junction with State 13 (*see* TOUR 7*A*).

GEORGIA TUBERCULOSIS SANATORIUM (R) 51.3 m. (approx. 1,500 alt.), comprises a large main building, a smaller one for Negro patients, a dormitory for children, quarters for the nursing staff, and a 375-acre farm cultivated to supply the sanatorium with vegetables, beef, poultry, and dairy products. Profits from the sale of surplus agricultural products are added to the annual state appropriation of $240,000 and the fees of paying patients for maintenance of the hospital.

The actual bed capacity of the sanatorium is 300, but thousands of patients are treated yearly through the facilities of the hospital and clinic. Approximately 75 per cent of the patients are treated free of charge. Since there is always a long waiting list, no case considered hopeless is accepted and, if X-ray examinations reveal no improvement at the end of six months, the patient is dismissed. An important adjunct to the sanatorium is the traveling clinic extension service, originated in 1930. Specialists from the institution travel throughout the state in automobiles equipped with X-ray machines and make examinations at community centers and schools in an effort to detect and give early treatment to incipient cases.

In NEW HOLLAND, 68.9 m. (approx. 1,200 alt.), a textile mill established in 1898 operates 60,000 spindles in the manufacture of duck and heavy sheetings and uses annually from 22,000 to 24,000 bales of cotton. The New Holland Spring here was once the site of a well-known summer resort.

GAINESVILLE, 70.5 m. (1,254 alt., 8,624 pop.), in the foothills of the Blue Ridge, is the seat of Hall County, created in 1818 and named for Lyman Hall, one of the three Georgia signers of the Declaration of Independence. On Saturday afternoons farmers from the surrounding countryside park their cars or wagons around the public square and market their produce; mill workers stand in groups on the street corners; and fashionably dressed young women and military students in cadet-gray uniforms from the near-by schools fill the shops and drug stores. With its varied industries, Gainesville is one of the most economically sound and progressive towns of northern Georgia.

Incorporated in 1821, it was named for General Edmund P. Gaines, who as commandant of Fort Stoddart in Alabama arrested Aaron Burr, defended Fort Erie in the War of 1812, and served in the Black Hawk and Seminole wars. At first the town grew slowly, but in 1848 it attracted settlers because of its proximity to the gold fields of Dahlonega (*see* TOUR 6). The greatest stimulus to development, however, came after the War between the States with the construction of the Charlotte & Atlanta Air Line Railroad, now the Southern Railway. About 1874 the Piedmont Hotel was built to accommodate summer visitors. The installation of a municipal power plant in 1889 made Gainesville the first town south of Baltimore to have electrically lighted streets. During the 1890's farm produce was brought into the town from the mountains in such quantities that Gainesville became an important chicken and egg market. The establishment of a cotton mill in 1901 and a hosiery mill in 1933 continued its development.

On April 6, 1936, a terrific tornado struck three miles west, and ravaged a path eight miles long and about a mile wide through the heart of the town. Nine hundred and ninety-two structures were destroyed or damaged, 950 people were injured, 786 made homeless, and 170 killed. Property loss was estimated at $16,000,000. This was the second major disaster in the history of Gainesville; a tornado in 1903 had resulted in the loss of many lives and much property.

Through the aid of city and county organizations co-operating with the W.P.A., about $3,000,000 has been spent on rehabilitation. The public square has been landscaped and replanted and the surrounding business houses renovated. Through a Government project, 125 houses have been built, 50 for white people and 75 for Negroes. Marks of the tornado are still evident, however, on numerous structures, especially where new bricks have been used to replace parts of damaged walls.

BRENAU COLLEGE, E. Washington St., one block R. of highway, is a woman's school, housed in 39 buildings on a campus of 350 acres. A natural park with three lakes, a Japanese garden and pagoda, and ten miles of bridle paths provide recreation for the 350 students. Brenau was chartered in 1878 as the Georgia Baptist Seminary and opened in 1879. In 1886, because of heavy indebtedness, it was sold to A. W. Van Hoose to be operated as a private nonsectarian school. H. J. Pearce bought a half interest in 1893 and acquired sole possession in 1913. In 1917 the school was deeded to a board of trustees, who secured an endowment of $700,000 through the contributions of Mrs. Aurora Strong Hunt and others. The college offers degrees in music and oratory as well as in the liberal arts.

Right from the post office on Green St. to a fork, 0.9 m.; R. to a second fork, 1.2 m.; L. from the second fork on Riverside Dr. to RIVERSIDE MILITARY ACADEMY, 2.5 m., a military preparatory school rated as an honor school by the U. S. War Department since 1923. Its twelve buildings, most of them constructed of red brick in Gothic design, are on a 250-acre campus near a bend of the Chattahoochee River. The fraternity houses on Riverside Drive are attractive white frame buildings. The school was established in 1907, and in 1913 became the property of Colonel Sandy Beaver. It has an average enrollment of 500. During January, February, and March, classes are held in winter quarters at Hollywood-by-the-Sea, Florida. Academic work meets the requirements of the Southern Association of colleges and secondary schools.

The FACTORY OF THE CHICOPEE MANUFACTURING CORPORATION (R), 74 m., established in 1927, produces Johnson & Johnson surgical supplies. The spacious brick, stone-trimmed mill building is surrounded by broad green lawns. The mill village (L), designed by engineers and landscape architects, is outstanding among communities of this type and is widely known as a model. All the houses are constructed of tapestry brick and equipped with modern conveniences. The community is provided with a large store, a clubhouse for entertainments, an athletic field, a swimming pool, and playgrounds. A farm operated by the company supplies fresh eggs, milk, and poultry through the community store.

FLOWERY BRANCH, 80.5 m. (1,122 alt., 418 pop.), built along the highway, is the site of a furniture-manufacturing plant. A green frame building (L) houses the HIGH ACRES GUILD (*open to visitors*), manufacturers of inlaid woodwork, pottery, and hand-woven rugs and bags. From the waste products of knitting mills, this guild daily produces 200 rugs and 600 bags that are shipped to several foreign countries as well as to many parts of the United States. The story is told of a Georgia woman who received a bag from a friend in Holland. Upon examining it, she was astonished to find that it bore the trade-mark of the High Acres Guild.

At 84.8 m. is a junction with a paved road.

Right on this road in BUFORD, 4 m. (1,205 alt., 3,357 pop.), is a large tannery and factory making harness, riding equipment, men's shoes, and glue. This company, established in 1873, employs mostly native Georgians, including many deaf-mute workers. In the environs of Buford more than 2,000 acres are devoted to the cultivation of rye, grown to supply the straw filling for horse collars. Straw, hides, and tanning material amounting to $4,500,000 are used each year.

ATLANTA, 118.4 m. (1,050 alt., 270,366 pop.) (*see* ATLANTA).

Points of Interest: State Capitol, Georgia School of Technology, Emory University, Oglethorpe University, Atlanta University (Negro), Cyclorama of the Battle of Atlanta, and others.

Atlanta is at the junction with US 41 (*see* TOUR 2), with US 341 (*see* TOUR 12), with US 19 (*see* TOUR 6), with US 29 (*see* TOUR 3), and with US 78 (*see* TOUR 8).

TOUR 7A

Cornelia — Toccoa — (Greenville, S. C.); State 13.

Cornelia to South Carolina Line, 25.9 m. — Roadbed hard-surfaced throughout — Southern Ry. parallels route — Limited accommodations.

State 13 leads through the foothills of the Blue Ridge. Beautiful timberlands of pine and oak are broken by small farms, with patches of cotton, corn, and vegetables growing on the steep hillsides. In recent years important educational institutions have been established in this neighborhood and tourists have made the section a popular summer resort.

State 13 branches east from US 23 (*see* TOUR 7) in CORNELIA, **0 m.** (1,537 alt., 1,542 pop.) (*see* TOUR 7).

From a point at approximately **14.7 m.** CURRAHEE (Ind., standing alone) MOUNTAIN (1,740 alt.), an outlying peak of the Blue Ridge chain, can be seen in the distance (L).

TOCCOA, **17.7 m.** (1,094 alt., 4,602 pop.), seat of Stephens County, is a prosperous mountain town, incorporated in 1875. According to some authorities, Toccoa is an Indian word meaning beautiful; but according to James Mooney, author of *Myths of the Cherokee,* it means Catawba Place and was named for a tribe of Indians who lived peaceably just east of the Cherokee territory and used this locality as a trading center. Older residents tell of plowing up many Indian artifacts, including pottery, beads, pipes, and weapons.

Toccoa serves as a trading center for the surrounding productive farm and orchard area. Four furniture factories utilize the oak, pine, and poplar timber from the mountain forests and the abundance of hydroelectric power generated at the near-by Yonah Dam. Textile mills manufacture a coarse grade of cotton cloth, work pants, and riding breeches.

TOCCOA ORPHANAGE, Franklin St., an undenominational institution, was founded in 1911 when the Reverend A. C. Craft opened his house to homeless children. Since then the orphanage, supported entirely by private donations, has grown until it now houses seventy-five children in seven frame buildings. Ninety acres of land are cultivated in food crops.

1. Left from Toccoa on State 17, a paved road, to the junction, **1 m.,** with an unpaved road, which winds among low hills; L. on this road to TOCCOA FALLS INSTITUTE, **1.4 m.,** an accredited four-year high school for boys and girls. It

408

was founded in 1911 as a nonsectarian institution by the Reverend R. A. Forrest, a Presbyterian minister. In 1936 the student body numbered 103 and the faculty 12. During the two-hour work period required daily of each pupil, the boys have constructed the fourteen frame buildings now used by the school. A farm and a dairy on the 382-acre tract of land surrounding the school supply much of the food for the students.

Toccoa Falls Park, developed on the land owned by the school, is a beautiful wooded tract where 486 varieties of plants have been found.

At 1.8 m. a footpath (R) leads 100 yards to TOCCOA FALLS (*adm. 10¢*), formed by Toccoa Creek as it cascades in a thin veil of mist over a precipice 186 feet high. When the white foam glistens in the sunlight against the moss-covered rocks, or when the wind blows the mist in a series of waves, the scene is one of great beauty. One path leads to the rock wall behind the falls, and another follows a rustic stairway to the top, which affords a view of Toccoa and the surrounding country. Below the falls the ravine through which the creek flows is banked with masses of fern, brightened in spring by rhododendron and mountain laurel. Like so many other high precipices, this one has its legend of the Indian maiden disappointed in love. On the face of the rock is a dark spot said to have appeared at the moment she leapt from the cliff.

2. Left from Toccoa on the unpaved Prather Road to the PRATHER HOUSE (*private*), 6 m., one of the three houses that Devereaux Jarrett, who came to north Georgia from Virginia and accumulated a large amount of property, built about 1850 for his children. The two-story, hip-roofed white clapboard house, crowning a high hill that overlooks the Tugalo River, has a wide piazza with square white columns on the front and two sides. A small, balustraded balcony overhangs a Palladian doorway. In this house General Robert Toombs (*see* TOUR 8), Secretary of State for the Confederacy, took refuge on his flight from Union soldiers after the downfall of the Confederacy. Hidden by his friend, Major Joseph Prather, he was not discovered; later he sailed for Europe. He returned and died without having taken the oath of allegiance to the United States.

At 24.1 m. is the junction with the unpaved River Road.

Left on this road to JARRETT MANOR (*adm. 25¢*), 0.3 m., a large, two-story frame house (R) built in 1775 by Jesse Walton. Soon afterward the Walton family, with the exception of one member, was massacred by Indians. The house was then bought by James R. Wylie, who sold it to Devereaux Jarrett about 1800; it has since remained in the possession of the Jarrett family. For a number of years before the War between the States, the manor was used as an inn on a stagecoach route and was called Travelers' Rest.

The house measures 100 feet across the front and is flanked by massive end chimneys, one of brick and the other of stone. Twin flights of stone steps lead to the low, columned porch. Despite the fact that its hand-hewn clapboards have never been painted, the house is well preserved.

The interior is so constructed that the rooms open one into another without a central hallway, and each of the three front rooms opens directly on the porch. The old kitchen in the basement has a flagstone floor and a large fireplace. In the attic are slits used by early inhabitants to fire on Indian intruders. Handmade tables, beds, and cupboards show fine carving, and English locks bear the royal crown and crest; relics include a powder horn, candle molds, snuffers, and saddlebags that belonged to George Jarrett, and records of the family real estate and business transactions bearing the names of George Walton, Robert Toombs, Alexander Stephens, and Jefferson Davis.

State 13 crosses the Tugalo River, **25.9 m.**, about 61 miles west of Greenville, South Carolina.

TOUR 8

(Aiken, S. C.) — Augusta — Washington — Athens — Monroe — Atlanta — Villa Rica — Tallapoosa — (Heflin, Ala.); US 78.

South Carolina Line to Alabama Line, 242 m. — Roadbed hard-surfaced throughout, chiefly concrete — Georgia R.R. parallels route between Augusta and Thomson; Seaboard Air Line Ry. between Athens and junction with US 29; Southern Ry. between Atlanta and Alabama Line — All types of accommodations in cities; limited elsewhere.

Section a. SOUTH CAROLINA LINE *to* ATLANTA, *174.7 m., US 78.*

US 78 crosses the low, red-clay hills of the Piedmont Plateau, where fields of corn and cotton are separated by forested tracts. This upper portion of Georgia's broad cotton belt was once divided into large plantations, and in Washington and Athens there are still many ante bellum columned houses. Even when shabby, they have an enduring beauty in their settings of magnolia trees, boxwood, and flowers.

Stone Mountain, with its colossal but unfinished Confederate Memorial, is on this route.

US 78 crosses the SAVANNAH RIVER, **0 m.**, the boundary between South Carolina and Georgia, 17 miles southwest of Aiken, South Carolina.

AUGUSTA, **0.5 m.** (143 alt., 60,342 pop.) *(see* AUGUSTA*)*.

Points of Interest: The Hill, University of Georgia School of Medicine, Junior College of Augusta, Paine College (Negro), Haines Institute (Negro), Cotton Exchange, and others.

Augusta is at the junction with US 25 *(see* TOUR *15)* and with US 1 *(see* TOUR *4)*.

HARLEM, **23.1 m.** (542 alt., 784 pop.), is the junction with State 47, a sand, clay road.

Right on State 47 to Appling, **10.2 m.** (263 alt., 300 pop.), the seat of agricultural Columbia County, laid out in 1790. In front of the courthouse is the GRAVE OF DANIEL MARSHALL, a Baptist missionary who baptized many converts and established several churches.

Right from Appling on a dirt road *(difficult in bad weather)* to the junction with a country road, **10.9 m.**; R. on this road to another junction, **12.6 m.**; L. on this road to a third junction, 12.8 m.; R. on this to old KIOKEE CHURCH, 13.3 m., a square building of hand-made brick with rough stone steps. It was erected in 1772 to house the congregation of the Anabaptist Church of the Kiokee, organized that year by Daniel Marshall and incorporated in 1789. The interior, with its hand-hewn pews and slave gallery, has the austerity of the pioneer house of worship.

Once Marshall, a commanding figure with white locks and earnest mien, while kneeling to lead public worship, was arrested on the charge of preaching in St. Paul's Parish, in violation of an act of 1758 establishing the Church of England as the official religion. His spirited defense so impressed his hearers that the constable was converted to his faith and the magistrate became his friend. He was allowed to continue his work unmolested until his death in 1784.

THOMSON, 36.2 m. (540 alt., 1,914 pop.), seat of McDuffie County since 1879, was incorporated in 1820 and named for J. Edgar Thomson, a Philadelphia engineer who surveyed the route of the Georgia Railroad. In the town are box and basket factories and a textile plant that manufactures men's work pants and shirts. Less than half of the county's 180,000 acres are under cultivation, and these are worked chiefly by sharecroppers.

HICKORY HILL (*private*), about two blocks L. from the Methodist Church (R), is the 100-acre estate of Thomas E. Watson. The grounds are surrounded by a wooden fence topped with a single strand of barb-wire. From the main gateway a path leads past a circular lily pool to the house, set in a deep grove of trees. Four white columns support the roof of the gabled pediment; above the ornate recessed doorway is a small balcony, and on each side is a large screened porch. The house was erected soon after the War between the States and in 1900 was bought by Watson, who added the Greek portico.

Thomas Edward Watson (1856-1922) was a controlling factor in Georgia politics for a quarter of a century. Known as the Sage of McDuffie, he inspired in his adherents an intense, almost fanatical, devotion, and in his opponents, who regarded him as a demagogue, an equally violent hatred. Although he died in 1922, candidates for office are still careful not to offend his following. In 1890 he was elected to the U. S. Congress, where he advocated the use of automatic couplers on railroad cars and introduced the first resolution for rural free delivery service. For his support of the latter an association of rural mail carriers is planning (1939) to buy his estate and preserve it as a memorial.

Embittered by a defeat that he attributed to a false count, Watson withdrew from the Democratic party and became identified with the Agrarian movement, fostering the county unit system of voting in Georgia to assure power to the rural element. The farmers whose cause he championed were inveterate readers of his *Weekly Jeffer-*

sonian. In 1896 Watson was a candidate for Vice President of the United States on the Populist party ticket with William Jennings Bryan; in 1904 he entered the campaign for President on the same ticket. He died while serving in the U. S. Senate, to which he had been elected on the Democratic ticket in 1920.

Thomson is at the junction with State 12 (*see* TOUR *17*).

At **47.2 m.** is a junction with a dirt road.

Right on this road to the office and shaft of the COLUMBIA GOLD MINES, **0.2 m.** The metal was discovered here in 1823 by two English miners. About 1830 the property was bought by Jeremiah Griffin, who used hand mortars and pestles for stamping the ore obtained by sluicing and washing. To expedite his work, Griffin set up Georgia's first stamp mill in 1833. The following year he produced $80,000 in gold bullion. Although there have been many changes of ownership, the Columbia Mines have been worked since 1843.

At **58.7 m.** is the junction with State 47, a topsoil road.

Right on this road to SMYRNA CHURCH (Methodist, but originally Presbyterian), **4 m.,** one of the oldest congregations in the state. The original building was probably a rough log structure like most of the early meeting houses. In February, 1793, John Talbot deeded two acres of land to the congregation, and a frame building was erected shortly afterward. This second building was replaced by the present white clapboard structure about 1910.

Right from Smyrna Church on the Old Augusta Road to a point at **1 m.;** R. from the road about **0.3 m.** in the woods to the GRAVE OF ABRAHAM SIMONS, a Jewish Revolutionary soldier, who in compliance with his own request was buried in a standing position with his musket at his side so that he could shoot the devil. In 1827 his widow, Nancy Mills Simons, married the Reverend Jesse Mercer and used the Simons fortune to establish Mercer University, a Baptist institution in Macon.

At **5 m.** on State 47 is MOUNT PLEASANT (*private*), once part of the John Talbot plantation. The two-story frame house, built about 1790, has its four original end chimneys; the stoop has been replaced by a low-roofed porch. The farm now belongs to J. L. Burdette, who discovered in the attic an early model of Eli Whitney's cotton gin (*see* TOUR *14*). Parts of other models have been found in the surrounding fields.

Not more than fifty feet left of the house is a two-room, barnlike structure, ELI WHITNEY'S WORKSHOP, in which he perfected his cotton gin. The marks on the windows were made by iron bars that protected his models from those trying to steal his secret. Through the narrow grated windows visitors were able to watch the cotton flying from the gin but could not see the machine. Since the inventor believed that women were not capable of understanding the process, he allowed them to enter the shop. It is said that Edward Lyon, disguised as a woman, gained admittance and later betrayed the secret to his brother John, who made further improvements and began to manufacture the machines in Columbia County. After long, expensive litigation, Whitney's prior claim was established.

An old plantation road leads from Mount Pleasant to the adjoining MILLER-WHITNEY PLANTATION, where the Eli Whitney workshop stood till 1810 when it was moved to its present site. After his invention of the cotton gin in 1793, Whitney formed a partnership to manufacture the "cotton engines" with Phineas Miller, who tutored General Nathanael Greene's children and later married his widow (*see* TOUR *14*). In 1796 Miller bought 822 acres of land so that Whitney might perfect his model in seclusion. Here the inventor built his workshop, perfected his machine, and established the first public gin. He made machines for cotton growers on a royalty basis, but Georgia planters, angered by the high 33⅓ per cent toll, preferred to get their gins from those who had stolen Whitney's ideas.

In 1811 the Wilkes Manufacturing Company erected on this land a two-story building for the manufacture of cotton cloth. Bolton's Factory, as it was then known, was one of the first textile plants established in the South.

WASHINGTON, 60.7 m. (618 alt., 3,158 pop.), seat of Wilkes County, was laid out in 1780 and for a time was the principal town in the up-country north of Augusta. Many fine old houses and the narrow, tree-shaded streets give this town unusual charm. Such commercial enterprises as cotton factories and textile mills were long discouraged by its citizens, but recently a shirt factory has been established and is operated by northern capital.

The streets of the town are so well marked that a stranger can find his way without difficulty. The highway follows Robert Toombs Avenue, on which are many of the oldest houses.

The FRANKLIN HOUSE (*private*), 359 E. Robert Toombs Ave., erected about 1840, is a handsome, white board structure with massive Doric columns. The house is placed with a side toward the street and is sheltered by several fine old trees. At one time the lot comprised extensive acreage, but parts of the land have been sold and now only an average-sized city lot remains.

The SAMUEL BARNETT HOUSE (*private*), set back (L) from the street on Robert Toombs Ave. opposite the Franklin House, is a two-story frame house with a broad, one-story porch. Built in 1820, it was later occupied by Samuel Barnett, who served as railroad commissioner of Georgia in 1879. When the father of Woodrow Wilson came to Washington as visiting pastor to the Presbyterian church, he frequently brought small Woodrow with him to stay a few days with the Barnetts.

The ROBERT TOOMBS HOUSE (*private*), Robert Toombs Ave. (L), erected between 1794 and 1801, was bought and remodeled by Robert Toombs on January 1, 1837, and has remained in the possession of the Toombs family since that time. Two-story Doric columns adorn the veranda, and French windows lead into cool, high-ceiled rooms where the furnishings remain much as they were in the 1860's.

The house is easily identified by Toombs Oak, a large, gnarled tree around which the paved sidewalk curves in a semicircle. This is the tree from which Union troops vainly hoped to hang the fiery rebel general.

Robert Augustus Toombs (1810-85), statesman, orator, and military officer, was born in Wilkes County and later made his home in Washington. After graduating from Union College, Schenectady, New York, he established a law practice that was interrupted by a half dozen terms in the Georgia Legislature. In 1844 he was elected to the U. S. House of Representatives, where he was influential in passing the compromise acts of 1850 that did much to quiet the southern unrest arising from the Wilmot Proviso. In 1853 he became a United States Senator, and upon the eve of the War between the States he advocated secession. Appointed Secretary of State of the Confederacy, he resigned in 1861 after a short term of service to become commander of a Georgia brigade in Virginia; in this capacity he distinguished himself for bravery at Antietam. After the war had ended, General Toombs, refusing to swear allegiance to the Union, escaped to New Orleans (*see* TOUR 7*A*) and became a refugee in London. Upon his return to Washington in 1867 he rebuilt his law practice and fought for the maintenance of popular rights. He dominated the legislative conference of 1877 that repudiated the carpetbag rule and revised the state constitution.

Toombs was a brilliant orator with a gift for terse phrasing. His convivial and robust laughter gained for him many friends throughout the nation as well as in his home town, where stories are still told of his extraordinary personality. His home was seldom without guests. After the war, when the townspeople sought to build a hotel in Washington, he indignantly opposed it, saying, "If a respectable man comes to town, he can stay at my house. If he isn't respectable, we don't want him here at all."

The PRESBYTERIAN CHURCH (L), Robert Toombs Ave., is a white clapboard structure built about 1826. The Greek Revival style is evident in its small Doric columns. In this church the father of·Woodrow Wilson preached on several occasions.

The HOME OF MRS. SARAH HILLHOUSE (*private*), Robert Toombs Ave. just opposite the Presbyterian Church, is a rambling, white frame house of two stories, with a long veranda flanked by wings, each containing one room. Set far back from the street, the house is almost hidden among large magnolia trees. Sarah Hillhouse, who once lived here, succeeded her husband as editor of the *Monitor* on his death in 1804. She was the first woman newspaper editor in the South.

The ALEXANDER HOME (*private*), N. Alexander Ave., a two-story brick house (R) set far back from the street, was built in 1804 by Felix and William Gilbert.

The PRESBYTERIAN POPLAR, on the Alexander estate, is the tree under whose branches occurred, on July 22, 1790, the ordination of the Reverend John Springer, the first Presbyterian minister ordained on Georgia soil.

ST. PATRICK'S ROMAN CATHOLIC CHURCH (R), N. Alexander Ave., was built in 1830 to serve the parish organized in 1790 at Locust Grove (now Sharon). The small brick building is now a ruin overgrown with ivy. Interments are still made occasionally in the churchyard.

The THOMAS WINGFIELD HOUSE (*private*), on State 17 just within the corporate limits of the town, was built in the 1790's. The house (R), set on broad grounds, is an excellent example of Greek Revival architecture, with wide verandas and tall Doric columns. Enclosing the front yard is a picket fence, with a gate fastened by chain and weight. In the rear the slave quarters of the early 1800's stand much as they were in that period.

THOMAS HOLLEY CHIVERS TREE, Chapman St. at end of the pavement on S. Alexander Ave., stands in the dooryard of the house where Thomas Holley Chivers (*see* TOUR 3) lived in 1852. This holly tree, now of unusual height, was planted by Chivers, a poet and friend of Edgar Allan Poe.

MARY WILLIS LIBRARY (*open*), Liberty St. at Jefferson St., the first free public library established in Georgia, occupies a red brick building (L) erected in 1887. It was presented to Washington and Wilkes County by Dr. Frank Willis as a memorial to his only daughter.

The WILKES COUNTY COURTHOUSE, on the N. side of the public square, a gray brick building of Flemish design, was erected in 1904 on the approximate site of the old Heard House, where Jefferson Davis held the last cabinet meeting of the Confederacy on May 5, 1865. On the second floor of the courthouse the local chapter of the United Daughters of the Confederacy maintains a museum of war relics, including the camp chest used by Jefferson Davis and a uniform and trunk that belonged to General Toombs.

On the courthouse grounds is set the capstone from Bolton's Factory (*see above*), established in 1811 on Upton's Creek.

PEMBROKE POPE HOUSE (*private*), W. Robert Toombs Ave., is a handsome Greek Revival building (R) with large Doric columns. The grounds are beautiful with magnolia and dogwood trees. The estate embraces the SITE OF HAYWOOD (R. of the house), the birthplace of Eliza Frances Andrews (1840-1931), botanist, author, and educator.

ST. JOSEPH'S HOME FOR BOYS (L), on an elevated site at the convergence of W. Robert Toombs Ave. and Lexington Ave., is a Roman Catholic orphanage built on the site of the estate of Jesse Mercer, the Baptist minister for whom Mercer University was named. The frame house facing the highway is the old Mercer home, now used as the rectory. Additions have been made to the rear of the house to provide dormitory space. The small park in front is called Mercer Park.

LEXINGTON, 85.2 m. (756 alt., 455 pop.), seat of Oglethorpe County, was incorporated in 1806 and named for the town in Massachusetts. Three governors of Georgia—George Mathews (1793-96), Wilson Lumpkin (1831-35), and George R. Gilmer (1829-31 and 1837-39)— were from this county.

The LUMPKIN HOUSE (*private*), on the eastern edge of town, is the old home of Joseph Henry and Wilson Lumpkin, brothers who became prominent in state politics during the nineteenth century and were co-founders of the Lumpkin Law School, now a part of the University of Georgia.

The PRESBYTERIAN CHURCH, one block R. from the highway, serves what is believed to be the oldest Presbyterian congregation in the Synod of Georgia. The original church, known as Bethsalem, was organized in 1785 two miles from town. When the church was moved to Lexington in 1822, the members erected on this site a white frame building that was replaced by the present structure in 1896.

Across the street from the church is the old PRESBYTERIAN MANSE where the Reverend Thomas Goulding, the father of Francis Goulding, conducted the first classes of Columbia Theological Seminary during his ministry of the church. Later the school was moved to Columbia, South Carolina, and in 1927 it was established on its present site in Decatur (*see* TOUR *3*).

In the outskirts of Lexington, two blocks L. from the courthouse, is the old GEORGE R. GILMER HOME (*private*). Gilmer was twice Governor of Georgia; during his second administration the Cherokee were finally moved to lands west of the Mississippi River. The house, set far back from the road in a grove of cedars, oaks, and cherry laurels, is a two-story white clapboard structure with a Doric-columned portico. The main body of the house was built about 1800, and the two-story wing was added in 1840 when Gilmer bought the place. The two iron foot scrapers were made by one of his slaves.

On each side of the walkway is a mound of uncut stones found by Gilmer in a now unknown grotto near town. In his book *Georgians,* he expresses the belief that these stones are relics of a pre-Columbian race. On the stoops of the main entrance are quantities of mica, quartz, and inferior amethyst, which he gathered in the surrounding woods and fields.

CRAWFORD. 88.2 m. (approx. 757 alt., 538 pop.), named for the Georgia statesman William H. Crawford (*see below*), developed around the railroad station intended to serve Lexington, whose citizens had objected to the noise and smoke of the locomotives. The CRAWFORD MEMORIAL (R), next to the railroad station, is a granite shaft presented to the town by Colonel Charles J. Haden, of Athens, and unveiled in 1933.

The SITE OF WOODLAWN (R), 88.8 m., was Crawford's old plantation home during the latter half of his life. The house, built by him in 1804, burned down in 1936 at the time the Crawford Memorial Association was planning to make it the center of a memorial park. In a plot here enclosed by a stone wall is the GRAVE OF WILLIAM H. CRAWFORD (1772-1834).

He was a United States Senator, Minister to France, Secretary of War under Madison, Secretary of the Treasury under Monroe, and a leading Democratic-Republican candidate for the Presidency in 1824. A kindly but sternly righteous man, he fought two duels in the 1800's in support of his principles. President Monroe visited him at Woodlawn in 1819, when, according to tradition, they discussed the policies which led to the formulation of the Monroe Doctrine. After a stroke of paralysis, Crawford retired from public life and practiced law in Lexington.

CHEROKEE CORNER (R), 93 m., was so named because here the boundary line between the Cherokee and the Creek lands formed an angle from which distances were reckoned. This was in accordance with the survey of 1773, when much of their land was ceded to the white people by the Indians. Behind the old Methodist Church is the Cherokee Corner Marker.

ATHENS, 101.8 m. (705 alt., 18,192 pop.) (*see* ATHENS).

Points of Interest: University of Georgia, Tree that Owns Itself, ante bellum homes, and others.

Athens is at the junction with US 129 (*see* TOUR *16*) and with US 29 (*see* TOUR *3*), which unites with US 78 for about ten miles.

MONROE, 129.2 m. (910 alt., 3,706 pop.), seat of Walton County, was incorporated on November 30, 1821. Approximately half of the population gains its livelihood from the town's two cotton mills.

The HOME OF HENRY D. MCDANIEL (*private*), McDaniel St., is a large, red brick structure with classic portico. McDaniel was a captain in the Confederate army and a Governor of the state (1883-86).

Adjoining the spacious grounds of the McDaniel house is the SELMAN HOUSE, a notable example of Greek Revival architecture, built in the early 1800's by Walter Briscoe, a pioneer settler. The original front stoop has been replaced by a wide veranda extending across the front and along two sides. There is a small balcony above the main entrance, and the doorways on both stories are surmounted with beautiful fanlights. Overhanging mimosa and black locust trees border the winding walk that leads to the house.

STONE MOUNTAIN (1,686 alt.), **158.4 m.**, is the largest exposed granite dome (L) in North America. The mountain rises 650 feet above the surrounding Piedmont Plateau, is about two miles long, has a circumference of more than seven miles at the base, and is estimated to weigh about 1,250,000,000 tons, although geologists believe that the mass appearing above ground is only a fraction of the entire granite formation. Its gray, almost bare, elliptical surface is given a greenish cast by the profuse growth of moss and lichen.

According to geologists, Stone Mountain was formed about two hundred million years ago as a subterranean molten mass, and its gradual appearance above the earth's surface has been due to erosion of the overlying soil. Running throughout the dome in two principal directions and giving the surface a streaked appearance are crevices formed probably by the contraction of the rock in cooling. The sides of the mass have been streaked by iron oxide and organic matter carried down by rain water from the top.

Before Georgia was settled, Stone Mountain had been used as a signal tower by the Indians of this section. In 1790 Alexander McGillivray, the half-breed Creek chief, met here the tribesmen who were to accompany him to New York to treat with Government officials. By 1825 white settlers had a stagecoach terminus at the mountain and a hotel at the western base. The place became a popular resort, and before 1842 Cloud's Tower, 165 feet high, was erected on the summit to afford visitors broader views of the surrounding country. The mountain was in the possession of various white owners until 1880, when it was acquired by Samuel Hoyt Venable, who quarried the granite for use in the construction of bridges, buildings, and roadways. In the 1920's the Ku Klux Klan held state-wide conclaves on the top of the mountain.

Until recent years there remained upon the crest some large boulders piled in regular formation and believed by some to have been the ruins of an old fortress or perhaps a sacrificial altar used by some prehistoric race. To prevent injury to the workmen carving the CONFEDERATE MEMORIAL on the sheer northeastern wall, most of the loose stones were rolled down the mountain side.

The unfinished figure of Robert E. Lee on his horse Traveler measures from the crown of the general's hat to the hoof of his mount 130 feet, approximately the height of a ten-story building. Appearing in rough outline are the head of Jefferson Davis (L) and that of Stonewall Jackson (R). Tons of granite, removed during the carving, form a pile reaching from the base of the mountain almost to the foot of the memorial.

Across the road from the memorial is a small museum, where information is given and souvenirs are sold. The museum contains a model of the project work and plaster molds of some of the figures, including those of Lee, Jackson, and Davis. A study of these working models reveals some of the difficulties of the sculptors; against so vast a background the figures need to be of gigantic size and require an appreciable change of scale from head to foot, since the feet are so much nearer the eyes of the spectator.

In 1915 the United Daughters of the Confederacy invited Gutzon Borglum to consider the practicability of carving on the mountain a colossal figure of General Robert E. Lee. The plan he submitted portrayed Confederate forces, led by their generals, seemingly emerging from a depth within the surface. The plan was accepted and the Stone Mountain Monumental Association organized. Samuel H. Venable, with his sister, Mrs. Frank T. Mason, and his nieces, Mrs. Priestly Orme and Mrs. Walter G. Roper, donated the northeastern side of the mountain, a gift valued at more than $1,000,000, and on May 20, 1916, it was dedicated as a memorial.

Before carving began in 1923, the workmen had traced the outlines of the giant figures from a photograph projected upon the mountain side. This projection, one acre in size, was made from a two-inch stereopticon slide by means of a specially prepared triple-lens projection lamp. Daily thereafter Borglum was suspended by steel cables over the mountain side, where he not only closely supervised the work of his artists and stone cutters but also did much of the carving himself. On January 19, 1924, the head of Lee was unveiled.

Soon afterward a violent quarrel disrupted the Stone Mountain Monumental Association. Borglum, unwilling to have his unfinished work completed by anyone else, destroyed all his working models except a completed figure of Jefferson Davis and left the monument on which he had worked for seven years. The association engaged another sculptor, Augustus Lukeman, who began work on his placid, classical design of soldiers going across the face of the mountain. When another head of General Lee had been completed, the earlier work was blasted away. By this time the funds had been exhausted and public enthusiasm had cooled.

The site for a new memorial has been offered to the city of Atlanta by Venable and his associates. Gutzon Borglum has created a new design and the state has endorsed the project, but no work has yet (1939) been undertaken.

At **159.4 m.** is a junction with a paved road.

Left on this road at **0.5 m.** to a junction with a footpath; L. on this among granite boulders and scrub pines up the gradually sloping southwestern side of Stone Mountain to the summit, **1 m.**

AVONDALE ESTATES, **168 m.** (approx. 1,025 alt., 535 pop.) (*see* TOUR *17*), is at a junction with State 12 (*see* TOUR *17*).

DECATUR, **168.9 m.** (1,049 alt., 13,276 pop.) (*see* TOUR *3*), is at a junction with US 29 (*see* TOUR *3*).

ATLANTA, **174.7 m.** (1,050 alt., 270,366 pop.) (*see* ATLANTA).

Points of Interest: State Capitol, Cyclorama of the Battle of Atlanta, Georgia School of Technology, Emory University, Oglethorpe University, Atlanta University (Negro) and others.

Atlanta is at the junction with US 41 (*see* TOUR *2*), with US 19 (*see* TOUR *6*), with US 29 (*see* TOUR *3*), with US 23 (*see* TOUR *7*), and with US 341 (*see* TOUR *12*).

Section b. ATLANTA *to* ALABAMA LINE, *67.3 m., US 78.*

West of ATLANTA, **0 m.,** the highway winds through sweeping hills and broad, forest-bordered fields. Dark cedars, somber pine groves, dun fields, and unpainted, slate-colored farmhouses are brightened in spring by the pink and white of blossoming fruit trees, in fall by the white of cotton. In some places the yellowish clay banks along the roadside sparkle in the sunlight with mica particles.

In the towns along the route are the gleaming oil tanks and smoking chimneys of new factories. Most of these villages have no central squares, but sprawl along the railroad; their main streets are lined with stores that have tin awnings projecting over the sidewalk and with frame cottages having jigsaw banisters around their porches. The newer brick bungalows often have copper-screened porches and composition roofs of gaudy colors.

The highway crosses the sluggish red waters of the CHATTAHOOCHEE RIVER, **10.5 m.,** which inspired Sidney Lanier's poem "The Song of the Chattahoochee."

AUSTELL, **17.9 m.** (927 alt., 963 pop.), an industrial town incorporated in 1885, was named for General Alfred Austell, who founded in Atlanta in 1865 the first national bank in the southern states.

1. Right from Austell on paved State 6, in CLARKSDALE, **1.6 m.** (approx. 920 alt., 600 pop.), is the CLARK (O.N.T.) THREAD COMPANY FACTORY, of Newark, New Jersey. In the large, red brick mill building (L), about 600 people are employed. To the left of the mill, electrically lighted drives wind through the industrial village.

2. Left from Austell on a good dirt road to FACTORY SHOALS (*picnicking, swimming, boating, and fishing*), **3.5 m.,** a recreational development named for

The Constitution
of The
Confederate States of
America

We, the people of the Confederate States, each State acting for itself, and in its sovereign and independent character, in order to form a permanent Federal Government, establish justice, ensure domestic tranquility, and secure the blessings of liberty to ourselves and our posterity — to which ends we invoke the favor and guidance of Almighty God — do ordain and establish this Constitution for the Confederate States of America —

ARCADE OF FORT PULASKI, COCKSPUR ISLAND

TABBY RUIN OF FORT FREDERICA, ST. SIMON ISLAND

BURNING THE YAZOO ACT

SEQUOYAH MONUMENT, NEAR
CALHOUN

SIGNERS' MONUMENT, AUGUSTA

INDIAN EFFIGY PIPE FROM BULL CREEK VILLAGE EXPLORATION, COLUMBUS

INDIAN DOG POT FROM BULL CREEK VILLAGE EXPLORATION, COLUMBUS

INDIAN MOUND, OCMULGEE NATIONAL MONUMENT, MACON

CONTRABANDS IN THE WAKE OF SHERMAN'S ARMY

OLD SLAVE MARKET, LOUISVILLE

BATTLE OF ATLANTA, CYCLORAMA, ATLANTA

END OF RUN—THE STOLEN ENGINE, THE "GENERAL," ABANDONED

MIDWAY CHURCH, MIDWAY   OLD EXECUTIVE MANSION, MILLEDGEVILLE

"LITTLE ALECK'S" BEDROOM IN LIBERTY HALL, ALEXANDER H. STEPHENS STATE PARK

the Manchester Cotton. Mills, destroyed by Federal forces during the War between the States. Tall trees grow within the enclosure formed by the brick walls that are overgrown with flowering vines.

LITHIA SPRINGS (*tourist cabins; 9-hole golf course, 25¢*), 18.9 m., is a picnicking resort (L). Water from the spring, which is enclosed within a circular concrete wall and sheltered by an open pavilion, flows at the rate of three gallons a minute. It is bottled in Atlanta and sold in various cities. On the surrounding land are numerous gray boulders, some fantastically shaped. During the latter part of the nineteenth century this resort was known as Salt Spring and was popular with southerners in summer and northerners in winter. A short railroad brought visitors from Austell to the Sweetwater Park Hotel here.

LITHIA SPRINGS VILLAGE, 20 m. (1,054 alt., 222 pop.), developed because of the near-by spring. During the 1880's Henry Grady (1850-89), orator and journalist (*see* ATLANTA), became actively interested in the resort and was instrumental in establishing here the Piedmont Chautauqua and building a large auditorium to accommodate the crowds it drew.

DOUGLASVILLE, 26.8 m. (1,250 alt., 2,316 pop.), seat of Douglas County, was incorporated in 1875 and, like the county, was named for Stephen A. Douglas, Lincoln's opponent. On this site was an Indian village called Skinned Chestnut, for a large, peeled chestnut tree that stood here at the intersection of several Indian trails.

The NEW HOPE PRIMITIVE BAPTIST CHURCH (R), 37.1 m., was organized in 1826, the year the Creek were moved from this region. This plain, white frame building, recently erected, is said to contain the original pulpit and pews. The service here has remained virtually unchanged for the last 110 years, and the ceremony of foot washing is still performed upon occasions.

VILLA RICA (Sp. rich town), 38.1 m. (1,156 alt., 1,304 pop.), is the oldest town in northwest Georgia. Gold discovered here in 1826 attracted settlers. Within ten years after the discovery of the ore, placer mining produced 20,000 pennyweights of gold. Incorporated in 1830, Villa Rica was at first called Hix Town for the local innkeeper. It was at that time one and a half miles north of the present site, but when the Georgia Pacific Railroad (now the Southern Railway) was run through the region the settlers moved to the railroad. A cottonseed-oil mill and gin are among its industrial plants.

West of Villa Rica US 78 is divided into US 78 S. and US 78 N., now the route.

BREMEN, **52.9 m.** (1,416 alt., 1,030 pop.), is an industrial town incorporated in 1883 and named for the German city. The recent establishment of several mills has contributed much to its growth. The town developed at the intersection of the Georgia Pacific Railroad with the Chattanooga, Rome & Columbus Railroad, later bought by the Central of Georgia Railway.

At Bremen is the junction with US 27 (*see* TOUR *10*).

TALLAPOOSA, **61.9 m.** (1,159 alt., 2,417 pop.), was incorporated in 1860 but grew slowly until 1884, when northerners became interested in developing the gold, silver, copper, and other mineral deposits found here, and in building a resort around a spring of lithia water. In 1887 the Tallapoosa Land, Mining & Manufacturing Company was formed; lakes, parks, drives, and 8,000 city lots were laid out; industries were established; and excursions were run from Kansas City, Chicago, New York, and other cities. This boom reached its peak in 1891, when the partial depletion of the mines and the confusion of involved litigation caused a decline.

The old LITHIA SPRINGS HOTEL, on Head Ave. half a mile L. of the highway, is a rambling frame building of 130 rooms and is almost bare of paint. The wide porch with ornamental banisters and the many gables and turrets are characteristic of the late Victorian period, as is the golden-oak paneling of the interior. Three families live in this old structure that remains from the boom days when promoters tried to develop a resort here. At the foot of the hill (R) is one of the springs for which the inn was named.

US 78 crosses the Alabama Line, **67.3 m.**, about 35 miles east of Anniston, Alabama. This line was designated as the western boundary of Georgia in 1802 by a treaty between the state and Federal governments. According to its terms, Georgia ceded all lands west of the line (the present states of Alabama and Mississippi) to the United States. In return, the Federal authorities agreed to extinguish all Indian claims to lands within the state "whenever it could be peaceably done on reasonable terms" and to transport the Indians westward. This provision almost resulted in war between Georgia and the United States (*see* HISTORY). The Cherokee Removal was not completed until 1838, although the Upper Creek had been forced out in 1825-26.

TOUR 9

Savannah — Dublin — Macon — Talbotton — Columbus —
(Montgomery, Ala.); *US 80.*

Savannah to Alabama Line, 286.3 m. — Roadbed hard-surfaced throughout, chiefly
concrete — Watch for cattle on highway in eastern part of route — Dublin, Macon &
Savannah R.R. parallels route between Dublin and Macon; Central of Georgia Ry.
between Geneva and Columbus — All types of accommodations in Savannah, Swainsboro, Macon, and Columbus; limited elsewhere.

Section a. SAVANNAH *to* MACON, *185.3 m., US 80.*

On the outskirts of Savannah US 80 is lined with burlap and cotton
bag factories, tanneries, fertilizer plants, and paper mills, as well as
acres of marshy land covered by pines, scrub palmettos, and moss-hung
oaks. The sandy soil is not well adapted to agriculture, and the
highway has been constructed over reclaimed land. Large cotton,
turpentine, oil, and tobacco trucks, going to and from Savannah, speed
past old mule-drawn wagons that creak along the shoulders of the
highway with only two wheels on the pavement.

Alternating with the unpainted dwellings of Negroes and of tenant
farmers are the larger and better planned houses of landowners.
Yards in the smaller rural communities are bright with petunias,
zinnias, and roses; in the marshes, weeping willow trees droop gracefully. Small game is plentiful in the surrounding fields, and the sluggish Ogeechee River, spreading through heavily wooded swamps,
provides good fishing.

Midway across the state the route runs through almost level country,
dips at times into hollows at creek levels, and traverses a sandy terrain
of scrub oaks and scrawny pines, known as the "pine barrens." The
soil is poor for cultivation, and farmhouses are widely separated.

SAVANNAH, 0 m. (21-65 alt., 85,024 pop.) (*see* SAVANNAH).

Points of Interest: Telfair Academy of Arts and Sciences, Armstrong Junior
College, Atlantic Coast Line Docks, Herty Pulp and Paper Laboratory, Bethesda
Orphanage, Wormsloe, and others.

Savannah is at a junction with US 17 (*see* TOUR *1*) and with State 21
(*see* TOUR *14*).

POPPY GARDEN, **5 m.**, is aflame each summer with poppies, grown
from seed brought by a Gold Star Mother from France and planted in
memory of her son.

Jencks' Bridge, 21.4 m., spans the dark and sandy-bottomed Ogeechee River which runs through swampy pine lands. Near the bridge is a FISHING CAMP (*tourist accommodations; fishing, picnicking*); shad caught here are marketed in Savannah or shipped to the North.

STATESBORO, 52.6 m. (218-250 alt., 3,996 pop.), was laid out in 1803 as the seat of Bulloch County, but records of the superior court show that its first session was held here in 1797. During the American Revolution the Whig settlers, outraged by the raids and encroachments of Daniel McGirth, a Tory spy, cornered McGirth and his followers in a swamp near by and killed many of them. This act rid the settlement of Tory sympathizers. Statesboro was on the line of General Sherman's march to the sea during the War between the States, and Federal soldiers encamped here for a short time.

The town has a meat-curing plant, gins, lumber mills, cotton warehouses, and wholesale produce and grocery houses. Because of the abundance of deer, ducks, quail, and doves in the Ogeechee River Valley, Statesboro attracts many Georgia sportsmen during the hunting season.

Left from Statesboro on State 73 to GEORGIA TEACHERS COLLEGE, 1.5 m., a unit of the University System of Georgia. The five red brick buildings are set on a large campus, planted with trees and shrubbery and containing two lakes and an amphitheater. Formerly operated as one of ten district agricultural and mechanical schools in the state, the institution was converted into the Georgia Normal School in 1924. In 1929 the name was changed to South Georgia Teachers College and in 1939 to its present name of Georgia Teachers College. Degrees are given in the sciences and liberal arts; the enrollment is almost six hundred.

At 59.2 m. is a junction with US 25 (*see* TOUR *15*).

The CANOOCHEE BAPTIST CHURCH (R), 82.8 m., a severe, gabled, white clapboard building erected in 1818, has undergone no alterations. In the cemetery near the church a number of pioneer settlers are buried.

SWAINSBORO, 90.2 m. (318 alt., 2,422 pop.) (*see* TOUR *4*), is at the junction with US 1 (*see* TOUR *4*).

DUBLIN, 130.3 m. (106 alt., 6,681 pop.), seat of Laurens County, is a widely spread town with a vigorous, prosperous atmosphere. During the latter part of the eighteenth century, before this section of the state was opened to settlers, a lumbering community developed here, as lumber, cut from the piney woods, was floated down the Oconee River. The town was incorporated in 1812, the year it succeeded Sumterville as the county seat, and was named by an Irishman, Peter (Jonathan) Sawyer, who gave the land for the public buildings. As the distributing point for freight brought up the Oconee River, Dublin was at one time more important than Macon, but it declined when the Central of Georgia Railway was built and the people of the county forbade its passage through the town.

Lumber from the oak, gum, and tupelo trees of the surrounding forests is shipped from Dublin to be used in high-grade cabinet work, including tables, radios, and wall paneling. The oak lumber, as well as that from hickory and ash trees, is used by a local factory for making handles and vehicle rims. Laurens County originally grew little besides cotton, but since the ravages of the boll weevil in the early 1920's, the farmers of the county have devoted an increasing amount of their land to the production of corn, peanuts, and sweet potatoes.

Right from Dublin on State 29 (N. Jefferson St.) to HUNGER AND HARDSHIP CREEK, 0.4 m., believed to be the site of an Indian village. During a great drought, many of the tribe died of famine, and the survivors moved away.

At 0.4 m., just north of the creek, is a junction with the unpaved Blackshear Ferry Road; R. on this road to SESSION'S LAKE (*open during summer; outdoor fireplaces, cabins; small fee for swimming*), 3 m., supplied with water by a large creek and several artesian wells.

From BLACKSHEAR'S FERRY, 6 m., a wooden flatboat has served for generations in crossing the muddy Oconee River. It was built, tradition says, by members of the Lost Colony of Roanoke in North Carolina. The ferry was taken over by David Blackshear soon after he came to Georgia from North Carolina in 1790 and settled across the river at Springfield. During the Indian troubles in 1793, Blackshear joined with the other colonists along the Oconee, then the Georgia frontier, to suppress the Creek. In 1796 he was appointed justice of the peace and in 1812 was made a brigadier general. He served throughout the War of 1812 and was state senator from Laurens County from 1816 to 1825.

VALLAMBROSA, 137.3 m., was one of the estates of George M. Troup. All that remains of the house are a few crumbled ruins, but a spring house, built by slaves for Oralie, Governor Troup's daughter, has been preserved by the D. A. R. Troup, who served as Governor of the state between 1820 and 1826, vigorously urged the Federal government to remove the Indians from Georgia. Although by an agreement of 1802 (*see* TOUR 8) the United States had promised to remove the Indians, when Troup took office in 1823 little or nothing had been done toward carrying out the agreement. Letter after letter from the Governor to the Federal government brought only excuses and additional delays. Finally, Governor Troup wrote, on April 24, 1824: "If nullified by the act of one party, the other party is dissolved—both are free to declare the resumption of his former rights—give us back our lands and we will give you back your money." When this, too, was ignored by the Government, he issued the ultimatum: "We have exhausted the argument. We will stand by our arms," and ordered the state militia to be in readiness to meet Federal troops at the border. The matter was finally settled, without recourse to arms and in a manner satisfactory to Georgia, by the Cherokee Removal of 1838.

JEFFERSONVILLE, **161.3 m.** (526 alt., 692 pop.), seat of Twiggs County, is a marketing center for pecans and the site of valuable kaolin beds.

Left from Jeffersonville on an unpaved road to the RICHLAND BAPTIST CHURCH, **5 m.** The earliest extant minutes of the church cover the period from 1811 to 1821. The large, white frame building with square columns was constructed in 1845 when membership numbered only a hundred. Separate doors lead to the slave gallery, which extends around three sides. The most valued possession of the church is the original communion service, more than a hundred years old. There are also a pulpit, a table, and a bench used by the congregation before the present building was erected.

DRY BRANCH, **175.3 m.** (approx. 370 alt., 100 pop.), is the center of a kaolin-mining district. Several mines, their bleak board walks white with dust, lie along the highway. Some have been idle for several years, but those at Dry Branch produce annually 100,000 tons of kaolin and ship from 100 to 400 tons daily to many parts of the United States. This clay is used principally as a paper filler and in the manufacture of ceramics and firebrick.

At **181.5 m.** is a junction with State 87 (*see* TOUR *9A*).

At **183.4 m.** is the entrance to the Ocmulgee National Monument (*see* TOUR *9B*).

MACON, **185.3 m.** (334 alt., 53,829 pop.) (*see* MACON).

Points of Interest: Home of Sidney Lanier, Mercer University, Wesleyan Conservatory, and others.

At Macon is a junction with US 341 (*see* TOUR *12*) and with US 129 (*see* TOUR *16*).

Section b. MACON *to* ALABAMA LINE, *101 m., US 80.*

Just west of MACON, **0 m.,** US 80 crosses a prosperous farming section producing cotton, corn, watermelons, and pecans. Midway between Macon and Columbus is a sandy, thinly populated region of unproductive farms and stunted trees; in this area, however, are a number of widely separated old houses that, though unpainted, are well built and quite distinct from the usual tenant house. Near Columbus and the valley of the Chattahoochee River is another region of prosperous farms.

KNOXVILLE, **25.6 m.** (640 alt., 183 pop.), seat of Crawford County, lies to the right of the highway, which passes through the outskirts of town.

On the courthouse square (L) is the JOANNA TROUTMAN MONUMENT, a granite boulder with a bronze marker, erected to the memory of the Georgia girl who designed the Lone Star Flag of Texas. In 1835 Joanna, then a girl of sixteen, learned that a group of Macon men were going to Columbus to join the Georgia battalion, composed of 120 men, who had volunteered to aid Texas in its fight for independence. She made a white silk flag displaying one blue star and presented it to them as they passed through Knoxville. On January 8, 1836, the flag was unfurled at Velasco, Texas, and on March 8 was hoisted over Fort Goliad, when news arrived from Washington that Texas had been recognized as an independent republic. Because the flag played so prominent a part in the fight for freedom, it was adopted by the first congress of the new Republic of Texas as its official flag.

The flag was easily soiled so its colors were reversed to a white star on a blue background, which is still the state flag of Texas. After Santa Anna, the Mexican general, had been defeated, army officers sent Miss Troutman several pieces of his silver as tokens of regard and appreciation. In 1913 Texas officials removed her body from Crawford County to the state cemetery at Austin, Texas, and erected a bronze statue to her memory.

ROBERTA, 26.6 m. (487 alt., 449 pop.), is a trading village for farmers. In the center of town, one block L. of the highway, is the BEN HAWKINS MONUMENT, erected in 1930 by the U. S. Government to commemorate the life and services of this Indian agent.

Roberta is at the junction with US 41 (*see* TOUR 2).

At **41 m.** is a junction with US 19 (*see* TOUR 6), which unites with US 80 to a junction at **45.5 m.**

LEONARD HOUSE (*private*), **63.3 m.**, set back from the road (L) and approached by a curved drive, was built about 1845 from lumber that was carefully selected for uniformity of grain. The two-story stucco house, with a hipped roof and a small balcony over the front door, is surrounded by a two-story colonnade.

TALBOTTON, **64.3 m.** (726 alt., 1,064 pop.), seat of Talbot County, was laid out in 1828. During the middle of the eighteenth century the town was an educational center with two schools, LeVert and Collingsworth institutes, that offered advanced courses.

An EPISCOPAL CHURCH, on the highway one block S. of the courthouse square, erected in 1848, is considered one of the finest examples of Tudor Gothic architecture in the state. All the nails used in its construction were hand-forged and all the lumber was hand-hewn. The old-fashioned pipe organ with a hand pump is in perfect condition and is still in use.

About one-half block NW. of the courthouse square is a little frame cabin, the first American HOME OF LAZARUS STRAUS. Driven from Bavaria in the Revolution of 1848, Straus landed in Philadelphia where he bought a small stock of china and then journeyed southward, peddling his wares. When he arrived in Talbotton in 1852, he opened a small store. After the War between the States, Straus and his three sons established a crockery business in New York City and in 1874 took over the crockery department of R. H. Macy & Company, becoming sole owners of the establishment in 1896. One of the sons, Oscar, became Minister to Turkey under President Cleveland and Secretary of Commerce in the Cabinet of President Theodore Roosevelt.

Serving as a community center is STRAUS-LEVERT HALL, College St., one block E. of the highway, a large frame building with tall Doric columns around three sides. It was formerly LeVert College, established in 1859 and named for Octavia Walton LeVert, granddaughter of George Walton, one of the three Georgia signers of the Declaration of Independence. The building was restored in 1930 by the sons of Isadore Straus.

The PERSONS COTTAGE (*private*), near the southern limits of the town, is an ante bellum house (R) with a pyramidal roof. Characteristic of this type of house are the wide central hallway, large rooms with high ceilings, and spacious veranda. All the doors, mantels, and transoms are hand-carved. The pyramidal roof appears on several other houses of the town.

Between Talbotton and Geneva, US 80 runs through a sandy country where the vegetation is dwarfed.

GENEVA, 72.4 m. (581 alt., 179 pop.), was a stagecoach stop during pioneer days.

Left of the railroad is the MORRIS HOUSE, built before 1840 and operated as Kookogy's Tavern for about seventy-five years.

Between Geneva and Columbus, Negroes can often be seen washing their clothes near a flowing spring or small creek and beating them with "battlin' sticks." Their equipment consists of a large iron pot for boiling the clothes and a wooden block over which the boiled garments are battered vigorously with wooden paddles. This method of washing clothes is common throughout the rural sections of the state.

COLUMBUS, 100.5 m. (250 alt., 43,131 pop.) (*see* COLUMBUS).

Points of Interest: St. Elmo, Wynnton School, Bibb Manufacturing Company Plant, and others.

Columbus is at a junction with US 27 (*see* TOUR *10*).

US 80 crosses the Chattahoochee River, 101 m., the Alabama Line, 80 miles east of Montgomery, Alabama.

TOUR 9A

Junction US 80 — Cochran — Eastman, 58.4 m.; State 87.

Roadbed asphalt-surfaced except for about 12 miles between Cochran and Eastman — Southern Ry. approximately parallels route — Limited accommodations.

Between a surburban section of Macon and the town of Eastman, State 87, the Cochran Short Route, traverses a region once thickly populated by pre-Columbian Indians. It leads through a wide expanse of slightly rolling farm land and forests of pine and oak that supply lumber companies with fine timber.

State 87 branches south from its junction with US 80 (*see* TOUR 9), **0 m.,** at a point about 4 miles east of Macon.

At **0.2 m.** is a junction with Riggins Mill Road.

Left on this road to a junction with another road, 0.7 m.; L. on this second road to the TRAINING SCHOOL FOR NEGRO GIRLS (L), 1.2 m., a state institution for delinquents under eighteen years. The school was sponsored by the Georgia Federation of Colored Women's Clubs and the building erected in 1936 at a cost of $45,000; in March, 1937, the legislature provided for its maintenance. Both elementary schooling and industrial training are provided.

At **1.5 m.** on State 87 is the junction with a dirt road.

Right on this road to the entrance to the LAMAR MOUNDS AND VILLAGE SITE, 1.5 m., a part of the Ocmulgee National Monument (*see* TOUR 9B). Before the coming of the Creek the Lamar village was probably occupied by the powerful Hitchiti tribes that had lived on the Ocmulgee hundreds of years before De Soto's journey in 1540. Ethnological studies indicate that these people, although they had divergent customs, were of the same linguistic stock as the Creek and were of Muskhogean origin.

A study of their arts, industries, and materials indicates that they attained a high level of cultural development, that their life was well adapted to swamp dwelling, and that they were agriculturists as well as hunters and fishermen. Vast quantities of animal remains and the small stores of maize and beans are evidence that they were primarily hunters. A study of 100,000 potsherds collected from the Lamar village reveals a sharp contrast in design and general features with the pottery from the Macon Plateau (*see* TOUR 9B). The Lamar Indians made large cooking and utility pots decorated with ornate designs by pressing the pots with wooden paddles or stamps before firing them.

The Lamar site, which has two mounds about 20 feet high and 100 feet wide lying 200 yards apart, exactly fits the description of an "ancient Creek village" as sketched by William Bartram in his *Travels* (1793). The conical SPIRAL MOUND (Mound B), although it has not been explored, is considered unusual because of its truncated top and the spiral path that runs counter-clockwise from the level of the plain to its summit. This mound was possibly used for ceremonial purposes. Encircling the base is the collar, formed by a slight ridge of earth, and on the summit are surface indications of a building that probably will be reproduced by the park service. The pyramidal MOUND A also has a truncated summit, which implies that it, too, was the foundation of a temple. It has been altered in shape by erosion, modern cultivation, and partial exploration. An earth ramp leads to the summit of the primary structure. Cross-sectional studies of about one-sixteenth of the mound reveal that it was built in at least two stages.

Small elevations in the surrounding meadows proved to be house sites. One excavated site exhibited many details of structure and revealed much of the daily life of the villagers. The house was constructed of small sapling timbers inserted upright in puddled blue-clay floors packed hard by the treading of many feet. Material found on the floors indicates that the irregularly spaced wall posts had been thatched with cane and that the thatched roof had been covered by a thin layer of reddish clay loam. Enough data were found to show that these houses, from twenty to twenty-five feet square, were of rather flimsy construction and that they were built on artificial earth mounds with ramped sides. They were of a type not found in the uplands and are thought to have been inhabited at a different time from those of the Macon Plateau. On the floors were found whole pottery vessels, flint implements including highly polished greenstone celts, a pot of charred beans, and several piles of burned corn-cobs. It is evident that these houses had been hastily abandoned because of fire, which no doubt spread rapidly in the dry thatch.

At 4.8 m. on State 87 is a junction with a sandy road.

Right on this road to BROWN'S MOUNT, 0.2 m., the most striking topographical feature in the sweep of hills overlooking the Ocmulgee River. The high shelf of 1,000 acres rises 180 feet above the plain. In 1870 Charles C. Jones, Jr., historian, described walls and ditches which signified that an Indian fortification once occupied the summit. Excavations of a red-clay knoll have revealed a round Indian council chamber, thirty feet in diameter and similar to that of the Ocmulgee National Monument. It has the same arrangement of clay seats, only eleven of which remain. No trace of a platform has been found, but the central fire altar is in good condition. Extensive collections of pottery and other artifacts have been taken from around the council chamber. Fossil remains discovered here indicate that this region was at one time a part of the sea bed.

At 5.1 m. on State 87 is a junction with a dirt road.

Left on this road to a junction with another dirt road at Bond's Store, 0.2 m.; R. on this to a junction, 1.1 m., with a very poor country road that runs through the yard of a Negro's house; R. on this road to SHELL ROCK CAVE (R), 1.3 m., a large rock shelter with a high shelving roof of limestone. More than twenty varieties of shell-life fossils indicate that it also was once covered by the sea. Several species of extinct starfish have been found, as well as millions of bryozoa, minute stick-like forms found in the composition of limestone. Thick beds of ashes and charcoal under the debris of the floor indicate habitation by Indians at some time. Many shards, artifacts, and charcoal beds excavated at the cave entrance indicate that the cave dwellers did most of their cooking outdoors. Pottery showed a close relationship to that of both the Napier and the Swift Creek villages, and a combination of pottery and flint suggested the Lamar culture mixed with some other. Many implements were made of beautiful red flint or jasper. At a depth of nine or ten feet a thick cluster of rocks weighing three or four tons mark a section of the cave which had collapsed.

COCHRAN, 40.2 m. (342 alt., 2,267 pop.), seat of Bleckley County, was in early days known as Dykesboro, but in 1870 when incorporated it was renamed for Arthur Cochran, who ran the first train through its boundaries. Cotton gins, a textile mill, a lumber mill, and a cold-storage plant are its chief industrial units.

MIDDLE GEORGIA COLLEGE, 41.2 m., a coeducational, accredited junior college of Georgia's university system, is on the brow of a hill against a background of tall pines; its red brick, Georgian Colonial buildings are grouped about a court landscaped with shrubs and grass. This site has been occupied by an educational institution since 1885, when New Ebenezer College was opened. In 1917 the state established an agricultural and mechanical school, which burned in 1928. That same year the present buildings were erected and the institution was re-opened as Middle Georgia College. It has an enrollment of 403.

EASTMAN, 58.4 m. (357 alt., 3,022 pop.) (*see* TOUR *12*), is at a junction with US 341 (*see* TOUR *12*).

TOUR 9B

Junction with US 80 to Macon Mounds Section of Ocmulgee National Monument; 1.1 m.

Dirt roads and paths.

The Macon Plateau is a part of the OCMULGEE NATIONAL MONUMENT, a memorial to the Indians of Georgia, supervised by the National Park Service; the other part, the Lamar Mounds and Village Site (*see* TOUR *9A*), is two and a half miles south. Analysis of the great mass of material taken from the land indicates the existence of several cultural periods. These range from the simple civilization of the hunting people, who lived on the Ocmulgee terraces at a period far antedating the era of agriculture, pottery making, or mound building, to the advanced culture of the Creek, principally the Kasihta and Coweta tribes who returned after 1670 to the Ocmulgee, their former home, from the Chattahoochee, where the Spaniards recorded finding them in 1665.

The monument road branches south from its junction with US 80, 0 m., (*see* TOUR *9*) at a point about two miles east of Macon.

Near the parking area, 0.4 m., it is planned (1939) to erect a combined administration and museum building. From this point paths lead west to MOUND D, an almost oval plateau 150 feet long, 125 feet wide, but only 8 feet high. Originally square, it was made of white or tan-colored sand, covered with a 14-inch surface of red clay that served to prevent erosion. On the flat top had been erected a series of three public buildings, probably the residences of chieftains. More than six hundred post molds, some definitely adzed and showing the course of the wall timbers, indicate that the floors of the houses had been super-imposed. There is evidence that the rough walls of these houses were partly covered with red clay sod and that the floors were made of hard-packed yellow clay. In the floor of one of them were small clay-lined cache pits, probably used as a granary. A profiled cross-section of the mound is contemplated by the National Park Service as a permanent exhibit.

The PREHISTORIC CORNFIELD, uncovered in the same mound, has the appearance of a modern plowed field, owing to the custom of having hillocks for corn culture in straight or slightly curving continuous patches with undulating troughs and crests. Two small beaten paths, running diagonally through the cultivated plot, indicate a division of the tract into smaller segments. This prehistoric field is significant because it is one of the two examples recorded for North America in archeological literature and is the only one sufficiently well preserved to be of interest to the layman.

An important discovery in the exploration of the Mound D area is the COUNCIL CHAMBER, a room forty-two feet in diameter and enclosed within a low, red clay wall. Against this wall, opposite the entrance, is a large clay platform in the shape of an eagle with folded wings; from this platform fifty yellow clay seats extend around the inner wall. No seats similar in form have been found in any other ceremonial structure of the American Indians. Carved upon the front of each seat is a small dish-shaped receptacle, possibly used to hold paraphernalia for religious ceremonies, and in the exact center of the chamber floor is a large clay-lined fire pit containing ashes and charcoal. A worn depression near the rim of the bowl is believed to be the place from which ceremonial fires were replenished. Charred timbers found on the floor were part of the roof structure, which was supported by four large posts set in deep pits equidistant from the central fire bowl. From the debris on the floor archeologists learned that the roof was covered with reed matting or thatch over which at least three feet of red clay had been mounded, leaving space only for a smoke hole directly above the fire bowl. The thatched roof has now been reconstructed. This lodge, with no nearer examples of similar structures than the Pawnee and Arikara lodges of the western plains, throws new light on the ceremonial structures of the Southeast.

From Mound D the road continues past MOUND E (R) to another parking area, 1.1 m., from which a path leads to MOUND B (L), three-fifths of which was cut away by railroad excavations. About nine feet high and seventy feet wide, the exposed profile made by the railroad cut shows that it is a composite structure of several mounds built one upon the other. About three feet from the top a heavy band of red clay runs through the mound. The middle section has slumped markedly, filling in a large excavation that possibly had been a pit house or underground lodge before the mound was built.

From Mound B the path leads fifty feet to the almost square MOUND A, whose flattened summit rises forty feet above the level of the Macon Plateau and a hundred feet above the level of the river plain. Although it has suffered from erosion, it is one of the highest mound pyramids in the United States and is an awe-inspiring monument to the industry of the prehistoric builders. To avoid cutting away the mound, a shaft ten by fifteen feet was sunk from the top. At a depth of eighteen feet there was a clay platform with lines of post molds indicating a large house site. At a depth of twenty-eight feet excavation was discontinued because heavy rains had undermined portions of the sand body in the interior of the mound. Evidence indicated that Mound A, like Mound C, had been built in successive stages and that buildings had been constructed on the clay platform of each mound.

Later exploratory trenches, dug into the side of the mound from the east rim of the plateau, uncovered evidence of a large projecting apron of earth from the plateau level to the top of the mound. The profiled cross-section of the trenches revealed house sites and refuse pits which indicated the occupation of the plateau before the mound was built.

Beginning at the southeastern toe of Mound A and following along the slope to the extreme east of the middle plateau are four terraces forming an extensive amphitheater overlooking the swamps below. The purpose of the terraces is not definitely known, but it is conceivable that they formed a fortified ramp which served to protect the Macon Plateau. By cutting exploratory trenches through their slopes, archeologists found that these terraces were artificial and that they were built over pits found in a large trench which extended around Mound D, starting at one side of Mound A and returning to another side of the same mound (*see below*).

From the second parking area a path (R) leads to MOUND C, the first to be explored; it has been left only partly excavated to show in profile its complex structure. Archeological data reveal that it antedates the journey of De Soto in 1540. Originally 30 feet high and more than 250 feet long, it was partly destroyed in 1841 when the Central of Georgia Railway was laid and again in 1877 when the cut was widened. When exploration was begun, workers first removed the slump dirt from the cut-away portion to enable archeologists to study the structure, which was found to be a composition of five mounds, built one upon another, with a colorful mosaic of clay bands covering the summit and slopes. The colors of the lower bands ranged from yellow to blue and bluish-yellow to slate-gray, but the topmost was a three-foot band of brilliant red clay. The significance of this possibly deliberate use of colored mosaic is not understood. The main portion of each mound was composed of basket-laid sand, and evidences of each basket load were seen in the freshly cut profiles. Post molds and other materials found in the top of each mound indicated that some sort of structure had been built on each summit. A CLAY-MOLDED STAIRWAY of fourteen steps leads from the ground level to the summit of the first or core mound. These steps, about six feet wide, show worn surfaces where human feet trod for generations.

From the original red clay soil beneath the first mound six tomb burials were troweled out. In some cases the sides of the tombs were lined with bark or small saplings, and in others, with upright logs which are indicated by the dark soil that filled the cavities left by the decaying logs. The bodies in the tombs had been previously exposed until advanced decomposition had set in; then skin and muscles were stripped from the bones, which were wrapped in skin or bark and laid away in the log tombs. The distribution of many shell beads and disc-shaped bone beads over the burials suggested a woven blanket. Little pottery and few flint artifacts were found, but the bone tools included needles, awls, and skewers, and the ornaments, gorgets, pendants, and ear plugs. In the slopes of the successive mounds were found evidences of secondary burial in bark and skin wrappings. Burials that intruded into the slopes of the last mound contained glass beads, knives, and brass trinkets, evidently obtained in trade with early Europeans. There were also many large conch shells and shell cores perforated and strung as necklaces.

Slight exploration of the several extensive villages around Mound C has revealed quantities of pottery and flint artifacts indicating that some of these Muskhogean villages were inhabited as late as the Colonial period. The inhabitants who buried their dead in the exposed slopes of the last mound were either of the Hitchiti Indians (*see* TOUR 9A), whom the Creek said they found in the territory, or of the Creek themselves after they returned from the Chattahoochee.

Extending for more than a mile around the rim of the Macon Plateau are two continuous excavations following the general contour of the land except on the west slope, where erosion has destroyed a short span. The inner line or trench has half partitions at regular intervals, while the outer line is a series of large oval pits. Dug into the red clay, they became filled with soils from which quantities of pottery, flint artifacts, and a few fragments of human bones have been taken. The pits excavated in the floor of the second line vary in depth from three to twelve feet and have an average width of twenty-five or thirty feet. Occurring at regular intervals, they seem to have been part of a plan, but some have been disturbed by tree roots. At intervals large round pits, from one to five feet in depth, are excavated in the floors. Definite post molds in the red clay floors are found beneath the accumulated soil, and occasionally irregular areas of burned clay suggest some sort of hearth in the floors. The earliest explanation of them was that the dugouts were quarries from which clay was obtained for mound building and house construction. Another is that they were fortification trenches enclosing the top of the plateau as a place of refuge in time of siege. The third is that they were underground houses. This last theory assumes that the red clay excavated was put on the roof as a sod.

At the foot of the south slope of the plateau there is a break in the two lines of dugouts, cut by the large OCMULGEE SPRING, from which workers spent months removing a mucky black mud. In the process of cleaning they found evidence that this was the source of water supply for the Indian inhabitants. Continuous around this south slope are pits different in construction from the others. Here they are built in lean-to fashion with their rear walls fastened into the plateau itself and their floors overlooking the low marsh lands below. There are indications of beaten trails leading from them down to the spring.

There is some evidence that the plateau was inhabited in historic times. Excavations on top of the middle section revealed, just below the surface, small trenches two feet deep and one and a half feet wide. When excavated by troweling, this small trench was found to have held posts which formed a regular, five-sided stockade, with logs laid horizontally rather than inserted vertically in the ground, as in the frontier forts built about 1800. Inside was a discolored area with log molds that outlined the storeroom. There was evidence that the posts of the stockade wall had been pulled up and that the cabin had been demolished instead of burned. Both inside and outside the stockade wall were found numerous Indian burials, most of which were primary burials, in which the flexed or extended bodies were interred with many objects. The presence of rusty parts of flintlock rifles, bullet molds, iron knives, swords, and axes suggested military occupation; and glass beads, clay pipes, brass and copper ornaments, and irridescent pieces of glass revealed trade relationship between the Indians and early European settlers. A flattened piece of silver bearing the coat of arms of Phillip IV of Spain was found inside the stockade, and one of the swords from an Indian burial resembled the weapons used by the Spaniards late in the seventeenth century.

From a study of these objects archeologists have identified this stockade as a trading post built between 1690 and 1715 by English traders from Charleston, South Carolina. Pottery, artifacts, and burials identify the people with those on the Chattahoochee River where Spanish historians found them in 1665. The National Park Service plans (1939) a reconstruction of the stockade and storeroom, for this trading post promises to throw light on several Indian migrations which occurred between De Soto's expedition in 1540 and the Yamassee Wars of 1715.

Further exploration of the middle plateau east of the trading post site uncovered successive lines of post molds indicating a series of six large houses, forty feet square and with rounded corners. No clay was used either on the floors or on the roofs. Examination of the catalogued material implies that these houses were made by plateau dwellers who occupied the site before the period of the trading-post Indians.

The pottery of the Macon Plateau is plain and lacks the glossy finish and highly ornate, paddle-marked designs found at the Lamar Village site. Some vessels have impressions of baskets or nets that were used either to mold or mark them before they were baked. They lack the strength of the Lamar pottery, are rough and crudely finished, and are therefore considered as belonging to a less advanced era. Prepottery flint implements, excavated from a considerable depth in the plateau soils, comprise scraping and cutting tools intended for skin dressing. The technique of their manufacture resembles that of the Old Stone Age in Europe and that of the flint implements found in the western plains of the United States in association with Pleistocene mammals.

TOUR 10

(Chattanooga, Tenn.) — Rossville — Rome — La Grange — Columbus — Cuthbert — Bainbridge — (Tallahassee, Fla.); US 27.

Tennessee Line to Florida Line, 363.3 m. — Approximately 40 per cent of route concrete-paved; remainder graded dirt or treated gravel — Central of Georgia Ry. roughly parallels route between Fort Oglethorpe and Carrollton, and between Chipley and Columbus; Seaboard Air Line Ry. between Columbus and the Florida Line — Limited accommodations except in larger towns.

Section a. TENNESSEE LINE *to* COLUMBUS, *212.2 m.,* US 27

Near the Tennessee Line US 27 crosses a region of superb forests and commanding mountains. On the upper part of the route, the sheer sandstone cliffs of the Lookout Range contrast with the dark, wooded ridges of the Appalachian Mountains; in the vicinity of Rome, less rugged mountains rise behind the cornfields and orchards of the Appalachian Valley, with its muddy, meandering rivers. Between this valley and Columbus, Georgia's second largest industrial city, is the rolling, red clay land of the Piedmont Plateau.

Along this route are a soil conservation area, a farm resettlement project, a prosperous textile area, and a well-known mountain school.

There are reminders of both pioneer and wealthy planter; huts almost as crude as those of the early settlers are only a few miles from some of the state's finest Greek Revival mansions.

ROSSVILLE, 0 m. (approx. 750 alt., 3,230 pop.), an industrial suburb of Chattanooga, Tennessee, is on the boundary line between Tennessee and Georgia. The town was named for John Ross, a man of mixed Scottish and Indian ancestry who for almost forty years was head of the Cherokee Nation.

ROSS HOME (*open*), Government St. one block L. of post office, is an unpainted, weather-beaten clapboard house that has been altered but little since its erection about 1770 by the Scottish grandfather of John Ross. Its severe simplicity is somewhat relieved by a front porch and a stone end chimney.

In this house John Ross (1790-1866) kept a post office after he had come to the village as a young man, and there is an unsubstantiated story that an underground passage connects the dwelling with a cave where Cherokee leaders held secret councils. Ross, whose Indian name was Kooweskowe, was only one-eighth Cherokee and served under Andrew Jackson, but he steadfastly defended the rights of the Indians

437

to their lands and accompanied them in the Removal of 1838. His wife, a full-blooded Cherokee, was among the many who died on the march. He devoted his entire life to the education and mechanical training of the exiled people.

FORT OGLETHORPE, 2.8 m. (approx. 800 alt.), bisected by the highway, is a U. S. military reservation of 810 acres. Established in 1903, it was named in honor of James E. Oglethorpe, founder of Georgia. Eight hundred and sixty men of the 6th Cavalry are at the garrison, and a group of buildings, parade grounds, barracks, and officers' quarters represent an outlay of approximately $2,000,000. During the World War the fort was a mobilization and training center.

CHICKAMAUGA PARK (*free guide service*), 3.6 m., established in 1890 by an act of Congress, is the Georgia portion of the greater Chickamauga and Chattanooga National Military Park of 8,456 acres lying within the states of Georgia and Tennessee. For more than three miles the highway runs through the Chickamauga area of 5,562 acres planted with trees and flowering shrubs. The Battle of Chickamauga, fought in 1863, has been commemorated by markers, monuments, tablets, and cannon. The physical features of the park, both open fields and heavily wooded acres, have been restored virtually as they were at the time of the battle.

In the Administration Building are a battlefield museum and a historical library of the War between the States. Some of the chief points of interest in the Chickamauga area are SNODGRASS HILL, where General George H. Thomas made his stand; BATTLE LINE ROAD, scene of the terrific fighting of September 20, 1863; BLOODY POND, whose water is said to have turned red with the blood of the soldiers; BROTHERTON HOUSE, where a break occurred in the Union line; KELLY FIELD, scene of heavy fighting during the battle; state monuments of Alabama, Georgia, Florida, South Carolina, and Kentucky; and WILDER TOWER, erected in memory of Wilder's Union brigade, from the top of which there is an excellent view of the park.

The Confederate general, Braxton Bragg, evacuated Chattanooga on September 8, 1863. The Union general, W. S. Rosecrans, believing that Bragg was falling back to Rome, divided his own army in an attempt to trap Bragg between two fires. Finding to his surprise that the Confederates had concentrated for an attack on these divided ranks, he quickly reunited them before Bragg's subordinates had made the attack, as ordered. The opposing lines were then drawn up facing each other across Chickamauga Creek. General James Longstreet was on his way from Atlanta with reinforcements that would make the Confederate total 70,000; reinforcements also were being sent by Johnston from Mississippi. Rosecrans had an army of 55,000.

On September 18 skirmishing occurred at Reed's and Alexander's bridges, and during the night almost two-thirds of Bragg's men crossed to the west side of the creek. General Thomas, who held the extreme left of the Union line on the slopes of Missionary Ridge, attempted to capture a Confederate brigade on the morning of the nineteenth and encountered fierce resistance. Sharp artillery fire continued all day along the line.

During the night Longstreet and Hindman arrived with reinforcements. The attack was planned for daybreak of September 20, but a dense fog delayed it until later in the morning, when General John C. Breckenridge opened the engagement with a charge that was intended to interpose a large force between Rosecrans and Chattanooga. Fighting was severe and losses were heavy on both sides. The furious Confederate charges against the log and earthen breastworks of the Union lines met with varying degrees of success. The Federals were able to repulse the repeated assaults on their left, but at the Brotherton house Confederates poured through a gap created by the withdrawal of a division to reinforce Thomas. Rosecrans retreated to Rossville, where he halted the Federal rout, reformed his lines, and drove the Confederates back. The Union army then withdrew in order to a position nearer Chattanooga, and Bragg took possession of Lookout Mountain and Missionary Ridge.

Following the Battle of Chickamauga and after the arrival of Grant and Sherman, occurred the battles of Orchard Knob, Lookout Mountain, and Missionary Ridge. All these are commemorated by reservations within the confines of the greater park, and can be reached from Chattanooga.

At **7.1 m.** is the junction with a paved road.

Right on this road is CHICKAMAUGA VILLAGE, 2 m. (750 alt., 1,715 pop.), on a site known to the Indians as Crawfish Spring. In 1891, when the town was incorporated, it was given its present Indian name, a corruption of Tsikamagi, the meaning of which is unknown. The principal industrial plants of the town are a textile mill and a bleachery.

The GORDON LEE HOUSE (*private*), on Cove Rd., is a handsome, twelve-room, grayish-red brick structure built in the 1850's by James Gordon, grandfather of Gordon Lee, United States Congressman (1905-27). A wide walkway, bordered on each side by two rows of maples planted about 1880, leads to the handsome Greek portico with its four well-proportioned, Roman Doric columns. Constructed of brick made by slaves, the house has walls eighteen inches thick. The interior has been remodeled and the second-story veranda replaced by a balcony. In 1863 General Rosecrans made his headquarters here, and later the house was used as a Union hospital. To the rear (R) is an ivy-covered brick smokehouse and to the side (L) are two of the twelve slave cabins which constituted the "quarters."

The GORDON LEE MEMORIAL HIGH SCHOOL, adjoining the Lee house on property donated by Gordon Lee, is a boarding and day school for boys and girls. On the twenty-acre campus, sodded in bluegrass, is a crescent-shaped drive which leads past the six red brick buildings. Students are given training in both high and grammar school subjects. Upon his death in 1927 Gordon Lee bequeathed $250,000 to the town for the school.

CRAWFISH SPRING, in a wooded ravine across the street from the Gordon Lee High School, is a clear spring that flows from the natural rock. It was given its name by the Indians in honor of Chief Crawfish. After the invention of the syllabary by Sequoyah (*see* TOUR 2), the Cherokee Nation was divided into districts, each with a council house similar to the white man's courthouse; about 1820 on the bluff above the spring the Indians built a log structure that was used by the county officials when Walker County was created in 1833. Here Fort Cumming, a blockhouse stockade, was built by the U. S. Government in 1836 to aid in the removal of the Cherokee to the West (*see* TOUR 2). The land surrounding the spring was later bought by James Gordon, who settled here in 1836.

LA FAYETTE (pronounced La-Fay'-et), 22 m. (871 alt., 2,811 pop.), was established as the seat of Walker County in 1835 under the name of Chattooga, later changed to Benton, and then to La Fayette in honor of the French general. Its development was accelerated when the Chattanooga, Rome & Columbus Railroad was built through the town in 1888. A purchasing center for farmers, it is now the site of two textile plants and one large hosiery mill operated by local interests. During the War between the States many skirmishes occurred here. On June 24, 1864, there was a bloody battle between 1,500 Union troops under Colonel Louis D. Watkins, who occupied the town, and about 1,600 Confederates under Brigadier General Gideon J. Pillow and Colonel Charles G. Armistead. The Confederate forces, who were on their way to interrupt the Federal lines of communication between Atlanta and their base of supplies in Chattanooga over the Western & Atlantic Railroad, attacked and had taken the town when they were hastily routed by Federal reinforcements under Colonel John T. Croxton.

TRION, 33.5 m. (800 alt., 3,289 pop.), was named for a trio of La Fayette businessmen who first settled here in 1847. The town, incorporated in 1863, escaped Federal destruction, but its development was retarded by the accidental burning of its mills in 1875. It now has a large textile mill and glove factory.

In SUMMERVILLE, 39.5 m. (668 alt., 933 pop.), incorporated in 1839 and the seat of Chattooga County, are a large textile mill and a knitting mill that manufactures children's hosiery. This was a scene of fighting during the Chickamauga campaign, and on October 18, 1864, a skirmish occurred here when General Hood marched northward into Tennessee.

In the ROCK MUSEUM (*open*), owned by Dr. F. W. Hall, is a collection of stones from every state in the Union and from many foreign countries. The specimens range in weight from pebbles of less than an ounce to a seven-ton block of granite from Stone Mountain (*see* TOUR *8*). In the collection are rocks from a battleground of Flanders Field, from the Potter's Field of Jerusalem, from the grave of Buffalo Bill, from the Mayan temples of Honduras, and from the Josef Glacier. One rock was taken from the foundation of the Alexandria Academy, established in Alexandria, Virginia, by George Washington and later attended by Robert E. Lee; another, from a historic site of India, was presented by Mahatma Gandhi. Embedded in a rock from Pompeii is an ancient Roman coin.

Right from Summerville on Lyerly St. to State 48, an unpaved road; R. on State 48 to the STATE FISH HATCHERY (*open 6-6 daily; picnicking, boating, fishing*), 4.1 m., about 300 yards L. of the highway. The hatchery propagates more than 2,000,000 rainbow trout each year and black bass and bream in limited numbers. Water is supplied by a single limestone spring with a flow of 1,800 gallons a minute. A feature of the grounds is an old mill with a large overshot wheel.

The road passes through the village of MENLO, 9 m. (850 alt., 355 pop.), and continues up the slopes of Lookout Mountain to CLOUDLAND PARK (*resort hotel, swimming, golfing, dancing for guests*), 13.2 m., on the almost level summit of the mountain (2,000 alt.). From this point is a magnificent view of the rugged countryside; the steep escarpment on the eastern margin of the Lookout Plateau descends in sheer cliffs for several hundred feet. A few cottages have been built by summer tourists.

From Cloudland an unpaved road leads to HIGH POINT, 17.2 m., a large boulder that overhangs the valley and is an exceptionally fine vantage point for views.

South of Summerville the highway enters a rolling agricultural section. From TAYLOR'S RIDGE, 42.8 m. (approx. 1,425 alt.), is a view of the Appalachian Valley and Lookout Mountain to the northwest.

The Gate of Opportunity (R), 61.5 m., is the entrance to the RRY SCHOOLS (*open 8-6 weekdays; guide service through buildings and grounds, $1*). The fenced grounds extend for about eight miles along the highway. Replacing the log cabin in which Miss Martha Berry began her work are sixty impressive buildings housing four distinct units: separate schools for boys and girls, a college, and a project for child and adult education.

From the gate the Road of Opportunity, a broad avenue of elms planted by Miss Berry and her first pupils, leads to the white Administration Building. The campus, covering 150 acres of a 32,000-acre tract of forest and farm land, is landscaped with flower gardens and lawns. Shady walks and pleasant drives connect the buildings, some of which are Georgian Colonial in design, some Greek Revival, some Gothic, and others adaptations of the early log cabin. The MOUNT BERRY CHAPEL (nonsectarian) is a brick structure of Georgian Colonial design seating 1,600 persons. The entrance is through a lofty front tower topped with a pedimented and arched belfry of three stages. Above the entrance is a fine Palladian window.

From the Administration Building a drive leads R. to Berry College, a group of white-columned, red brick buildings that are visible from the highway. This unit was opened in September, 1926, for young men and women from rural districts who were not financially able to attend other colleges. A member of the American Association of Colleges, it provides academic instruction and requires a year of training in agriculture or industry.

From the Berry College campus the driveway leads to the rustic log cabins of MARTHA BERRY SCHOOL FOR GIRLS, also visible from the highway, and turns R. to the Gothic stone buildings donated by Mr. and Mrs. Henry Ford for high school and college girls. A medieval effect is created by the gargoyles ornamenting the towers and cornices. In the library is a stained-glass window depicting scenes from Shakespeare's *Twelfth Night*. Wood carving is used effectively throughout the buildings, which are constructed of stone quarried near Rome. Among the exhibits of this school are woolen and cotton articles woven by the girls.

From this school the Road of Remembrance leads to a lake fed by mountain springs, to barns where pedigreed cattle are bred, to fields where food crops are cultivated, and through forests to MOUNT BERRY SCHOOL FOR BOYS, where 300 students, including mature men, receive high school training.

From the School for Boys, drives lead to the Community House of the POSSUM TROT RURAL COMMUNITY, founded in 1935. In three classroom buildings a model rural graded school, conducted for local children, serves as a practice school for student teachers. At Possum Trot entire families are given a measure of formal education, as well as instruction in farming. It was here that Miss Berry, performing much of her early religious work, became known as the Sunday Lady.

Right from Possum Trot, on the hilltop of Mount Berry (1,900 alt.) within the bounds of the school property, is the HOUSE OF DREAMS, a cottage in which Miss Berry entertains faculty members, visitors, and students.

These schools for rural people charge an annual fee of $150 for high school work and $200 for college training but provision is made for many students to work their way. Those paying the cash fee complete the nine-month term in scheduled time, but the others work out their tuition during the summer. In order to cover expenses, the school must contribute $400 for each student, and the annual sum required for maintenance exceeds $150,000.

More than 1,300 students from eleven states are matriculated in the four schools, half of them doing college work. In the work period—two 8-hour days a week—these boys and girls care for the grounds, cultivate the farms, or work in the carpenter shops, laundries, dairies, and kitchens. The 140 faculty members, many of whom are Berry graduates, all live on the campus and carefully supervise the students. Girls are not permitted to leave the grounds unchaperoned. Bible study and regular attendance at Sunday school are required of all students.

Miss Martha Berry began her work by telling Bible stories to the children of her father's tenants. Next she opened a day school in her study, and rode on horseback through the mountain regions to organize sewing classes, Sunday schools, prayer meetings, and other day schools. With the aid of Miss Elizabeth Brewster, she established a school in a large log cabin on her 300-acre farm. With five boys she opened her first boarding school on January 13, 1902. The boys hewed pine trees, hauled logs, and built a school for girls, which was opened on Thanksgiving Day, 1909. By this time she had exhausted her personal funds and began enlisting the aid of her friends, the merchants of Rome, and various philanthropists.

Epidemics, crop failures, and a disastrous fire have not deflected Miss Berry from her purpose. She has been granted honorary degrees by eight prominent colleges and has received many other tributes. In 1925 the President of the United States presented her with the Roosevelt Medal; in 1929 she was given the $5,000 Pictorial Review award; and in 1931, as a result of a nation-wide poll, she was selected as one of the twelve outstanding women in America.

More than 10,000 people visit the Berry Schools each year. During the pilgrimage, held usually once a year but at no fixed time, invited guests are welcomed with an unusual candlelight ceremony. From their special train on the spur track at Mount Berry Station, the guests are conducted along the winding road to the campus through a long double line of students holding lighted candles, whose flickering light outlines the serious faces of the girls and boys against a background of dark pines.

ROME, 63.5 m. (614 alt., 21,843 pop.), seat of Floyd County and the leading industrial city of northwest Georgia, is surrounded by the fertile, rolling plains of the Rome Valley. Its seventy-five industrial plants—including textile and lumber mills, a stone foundry, a cottonseed oil mill, and a factory that makes a disc plow invented by a Rome citizen—are built away from the principal business section, which is on a peninsula where the confluence of the Etowah and Oostanaula rivers forms the Coosa. From this point the residential sections spread in all directions. Built among several rounded hills, the city has wide streets lined with commodious, old frame houses and new brick bungalows and shaded by oak and elm trees.

Because Hernando De Soto, in 1540, is believed to have spent almost a month on the site of Rome, a section of the city was once called De Soto. When the first settlers came to north Georgia in the early nineteenth century, they found here the Indian village of Chiaha, which was a center for negotiations between the Federal government and John Ross, chief of the Cherokee Nation, during the period preceding the Cherokee Removal. Although huts and wigwams were replaced with substantial frame houses, the town was overrun by vigilance committees, outlaws, land speculators, and unruly Indians until the Indians were removed in 1838.

The town was founded in 1834 and succeeded Livingston as the county seat in the following year. Its name, drawn by lot, was suggested because it was built upon seven hills as was ancient Rome. The Cherokee Female Institute, later called the Rome Female College, was founded here in 1853. When Chattanooga, Tennessee, was chosen as the terminus of the Western & Atlantic Railroad, the Rome Railroad, chartered as the Memphis Branch Railroad in 1839, was built to connect with the Western & Atlantic at Kingston. Stagecoach lines and post roads were established over Indian trails in north Georgia to join other routes at Athens, Milledgeville, Macon, and Augusta. Although the steamboat *Coosa* came up the river from Greensport, Alabama, and the locally built *William Smith* was operated for a time, river traffic never flourished.

Rome has always been supported almost equally by agriculture and industry. Even in its early days it was a cotton market and had thriving tanneries. In 1855 the Noble family from Pennsylvania established an iron works here, which later made cannon for the Confederacy. The machine lathe that ground these cannon is still in use at the Davis Foundry and Machine Shop.

In May, 1863, Colonel Abel D. Streight, coming up from northeastern Alabama with 1,466 men, prepared to attack Rome. This force was pursued for five days and nights and captured near Rome by 410 men under General Nathan Bedford Forrest, who by a stratagem convinced Streight that he was outnumbered. In May of the following year, at the beginning of his Atlanta campaign, General Sherman dispatched cavalrymen under General Kenner Garrard and General Jefferson C. Davis to take Rome. A small Federal force occupied the town during the summer, and in September Sherman sent troops under General John Murray Corse to hold Rome against expected Confederate attacks. On his way to Resaca, Sherman stopped in Rome on October 12; on October 28 he returned to the city and from headquarters here directed his forces until November 2, when he withdrew to Kingston. On November 10 evacuation was begun, and that night all mills, factories, and any establishments that might be of use to the Confederates were destroyed.

Rome has been flooded numbers of times by the high waters of the three rivers. In 1886 the city was so deeply inundated that a steamboat traveled up Broad Street, but the streets in the main business section have been raised since that time and levees have been constructed.

On Neely Hill, 5th Ave. (US 27) and E. 2nd St., and visible from every part of town, is the brick City Clock Tower, erected as a reservoir in 1871 and abandoned when it became inadequate for the city's water supply. An electric fire alarm system has been connected with the clock, and the transmitting antennas for the police radio system have been placed on the tower.

In front of the Municipal Auditorium, Broad St. at 6th Ave., one block L. of the highway, is the CAPITOLINE WOLF, a bronze reproduction of the famous Roman statue showing the wolf suckling Romulus and Remus. It was presented by Premier Benito Mussolini when the Georgia city was selected as the site for a mill of the Tubize-Chatillon Corporation, an Italian company.

On the lawn of the auditorium is the BATTEY MONUMENT, a memorial to Dr. Robert Battey (1828-95), a surgeon and pioneer in using ovariotomy as a means of correcting a pathological condition. He is honored by the medical world as the developer of Battey's Operation. In Rome, on August 27, 1872, he performed an oophorectomy by abdominal section that is described in medical journals as "without precedent."

ST. MARY's CATHOLIC CHURCH, N. Broad St. between 9th Ave. and Smith St., suggests a medieval Gothic country chapel. The simple granite building, set back on an elevated lot, is without ornamentation except for a large crucifix and the carved words *Venite Adoremus* above the doorway. Behind the altar is a sixteenth-century oil painting, *Il Giorno,* of the school of Correggio, showing the Madonna and child, Mary Magdalene, and St. Jerome. The canvas was presented to the church by Princess J. Eugenia Ruspoli, of Rome, Italy, a sister of Miss Martha Berry.

THE CHIEFTAINS (*private*), 80 Chatillon Rd., is a two-story house of white clapboards laid over the log cabin built in 1794 by Major Ridge, a Cherokee leader whose English name probably was derived from his military rank in the Creek War of 1814. At first a supporter of John Ross against the eviction of the Indians, he later changed sides and on December 29, 1835, signed a treaty at New Echota by which the Cherokee ceded all their lands east of the Mississippi. When his people were moved westward in 1838, he accompanied them, but in the following year he was shot in accordance with the tribal law that inflicted the death penalty for the sale of lands without the full consent of the tribe.

Major Ridge's trading post and ferry made these grounds a tribal gathering place. Hundreds of Cherokee often gathered on the lawn before the house, and negotiations leading to the Treaty of 1835 were made here. A stone marker has been erected by the W.P.A.

On Chatillon Rd. just beyond The Chieftains is the TUBIZE-CHATILLON CORPORATION MILL, a branch of the Italian company. One of the most important rayon plants in the South, it has a capital of $10,000,000 and employs 1,500 people. The 478 red brick houses of the village accommodate 2,400 people.

The FORREST STATUE, at the junction of Broad St. and 2nd Ave., is a memorial to General Nathan Bedford Forrest, brilliant Confederate cavalry leader.

THORNWOOD, Alabama Rd., is an ante bellum house with a Greek portico, whose white columns bear notches and initials carved by Union soldiers. It was originally Colonel Alfred Shorter's home.

SHORTER COLLEGE, Shorter Hill off Alabama Rd., was founded in 1873 as the Cherokee Baptist Female College and named for its benefactor Colonel Shorter in 1877. This woman's college, with an enrollment of 250, has a high scholastic standing, is accredited by both the Southern and American Associations of Schools and Colleges, and confers the A. B. degree. In 1911 the college was moved from the buildings now occupied by the high school into the simple red brick buildings high on a hill overlooking Rome and the winding rivers. With Mount Alto and Lavender Mountain in the distance, the campus is a point of scenic vantage.

MYRTLE HILL CEMETERY, S. Broad St. across bridge, is on a conical hill that rises abruptly from the junction of the rivers. In this old cemetery are the graves of three founders of the city; and marked by a simple stone of Carrara marble is the GRAVE OF MRS. WOODROW WILSON, who was Ellen Axson, of Rome. Wilson met Miss Axson, the daughter of the Presbyterian minister, while visiting relatives in this city. In a lower corner near the street is the GRAVE OF THE KNOWN SOLDIER of the World War. Because the body of Charles W. Graves was the last returned from France, the Federal government planned to bury it in Arlington Cemetery, but his mother requested burial in Rome.

The SEVIER MONUMENT, intersection Pennington Ave. and Branham Ave., was erected in honor of General John Sevier (1745-1815), who defeated a band of Indians at the foot of Myrtle Hill in October, 1793.

Sevier was a founder of the Watauga Association, Governor of the State of Franklin (1785-87), Governor of Tennessee (1796-1801 and 1803-09), and a member of the U. S. Congress (1789-91 and 1811-15). He died in what is now Alabama near Fort Decatur while on a mission to the Creek. A legend has been handed down regarding his rescue from the trial in which he was charged by North Carolina with treason (c. 1787). A friend disguised as a rustic placed Sevier's own mare, noted for her speed, in front of the open courthouse door, strode into the court, and interrupted the trial. In the ensuing confusion Sevier was able to leap on his horse and escape.

1. Right from Rome on State 20 to the junction with a wooded road; L. on this road to RADIO MINERAL SPRINGS, 3 m., a small summer resort at the foot of Mount Alto. Left from Radio Mineral Springs on a well-marked road to the MOUNT ALTO SCENIC LOOP, a 25-mile route winding among high, wooded ridges northwest of Rome and reaching the SUMMIT OF MOUNT ALTO (1,529 alt.), which affords an excellent view of the surrounding valley. The route returns to Rome on US 411.

2. Right from Rome on US 411 S. to the DARLINGTON SCHOOL, 2.5 m., a boys' preparatory school, founded in 1905 and named for Joseph P. Darlington, a teacher in an earlier school in Rome. Its red brick buildings with limestone trim are grouped about a beautiful lake on a wooded campus of approximately eighty acres. The student body numbers two hundred and the faculty seventeen.

On WATER CRESS FARM, 7.9 m., cress for local consumption and northern markets has been raised for more than fifty years.

CAVE SPRING, 13 m. (662 alt., 723 pop.), on Little Cedar Creek in Vann's Valley, has broad streets shaded by oaks, bays, and weeping willows. Settlement was begun in 1826 and the town was incorporated in 1852. Two blocks L. of the main street is the CAVE (open 8 A.M.-11 P.M., adm. 10¢; free picnic grounds). The chambers in this series of limestone caves are equipped with stairs and bridges that lead to a deep pool and various rock formations. The water from a spring that flows from the cave is piped to supply the town. A smaller spring, about fifty yards from the cave, flows naturally from the hillside and forms a shallow stream that supplies water for a large rock swimming pool.

A short distance from the cave is the GEORGIA SCHOOL FOR THE DEAF, housed in simple red brick buildings. Established by legislative act in 1847, the school was opened on July 1, 1848. Georgia began education of the deaf and dumb in 1835, when several children were sent to the American Asylum at Hartford, Connecticut. In 1846 the principal of Hearn Manual Labor School at Cave Spring accepted four pupils from the state and this led to the establishment of the state institution here.

AGATE SOIL CONSERVATION PROJECT, with headquarters in Rome, comprises 30,000 acres in Floyd and Polk counties and is one of five projects designated as demonstration areas in the Federal soil and water conservation program. Within the project boundaries are 287 farms ranging in size from 15 to 1,500 acres. Their owners cooperate with the soil conservation service by utilizing their land according to the plan worked out by the experts. Throughout the area many acres of abandoned land have been planted in permanent cover crops and designated as permanent pasture or forest land. Approved farming methods, selected crops, especially kudzu, a leguminous forage and hay crop, and new uses of crops have been introduced.

The acreage given to lespedeza, alfalfa, and crimson clover has been greatly increased. Strip cropping has resulted in one-third of the cultivated land being covered throughout the year by some thick-growing crop that retards the running off of the water and holds the silt washed from the clean-tilled soil. Many thousands of check dams have been constructed in gullies to stop erosion. As a demonstration area, the project affords the farmers of northwest Georgia an opportunity to see recommended practices in operation under conditions similar to those found on their own farms.

LINDALE, 65 m. (652 alt., 3,380 pop.), is an industrial settlement dependent upon the modern, well-equipped textile mills of the Pepperell Manufacturing Company. In the village of identical frame houses is a large brick community auditorium, containing game rooms, a motion picture theater, a tearoom, and a large tiled swimming pool.

CEDARTOWN, 81.2 m. (809 alt., 8,124 pop.), seat of Polk County, was the site of a Cherokee Indian settlement named for the numerous red cedars growing in the vicinity. When the town was incorporated in 1854, several wealthy planters had already built homes here. It was not until the 1920's, however, that its chief industrial expansion occurred; in this period a well-known textile company and a national tire and rubber company established branches here. Other industrial plants are cottonseed-oil mills, marble shops, and phosphate mines.

BIG SPRINGS, in a large, well-landscaped park on Wissahickon Ave. two blocks from the courthouse, has a daily flow of 8,000,000 gallons. The springs supply the water for Cedartown and its industrial plants.

BUCHANAN, 97.9 m. (1,295 alt., 429 pop.), seat of Haralson County, was chartered in 1857 and named for President James Buchanan.

BREMEN, 105.4 m. (1,416 alt., 1,030 pop.) (see TOUR 8), is at the junction with US 78 (see TOUR 8).

CARROLLTON, 117.3 m. (1,095 alt., 5,052 pop.), made the seat of Carroll County in 1829, was incorporated in 1856 and became an enterprising commercial center. The citizens are so independent that in the past generation the town was known as the "Free State of Carroll." Busy textile mills and comfortable homes indicate the town's prosperity.

The county lies in a fertile agricultural section, worked by thrifty farmers, most of whom own their farms and maintain a high record for productivity. On Saturdays, when the farmers throng the public square, the mules are unharnessed and allowed to eat their hay from the backs of the wagons.

Right from Carrollton on College St., which becomes State 8, to the entrance of WEST GEORGIA JUNIOR COLLEGE, 1.2 m., a unit of the University System of Georgia. "This co-educational institution was organized in 1907 as the Fourth Congressional District Agricultural and Mechanical School and was made a junior college by the board of regents in 1933." The enrollment is 428. On the campus are four red brick buildings with white columns, and ten feet from the entrance is the MCINTOSH MONUMENT (R), erected to General William McIntosh, leader of the Creek Nation. This monument was originally a mounting block at his home (*see below*).

ROOPVILLE, 127.2 m. (1,253 alt., 260 pop.), is a settlement built around a granite quarry.

1. Right from Roopville on an unpaved road to GOAT ROCK, 1 m. The deep holes carved in its surface were used as mortars for grinding corn by Creek Indians who inhabited this region until 1825. The vicinity is rich in Indian relics, chiefly arrowheads and spear heads, tomahawks, and pottery shards.

2. Left from a tourist camp in Roopville on an unimproved dirt road to the SITE OF THE MCINTOSH RESERVATION, 10 m., on which is a monument marking the SITE OF CHIEF WILLIAM MCINTOSH'S HOUSE. This tract of one square mile was given to McIntosh after he had effected cession of Creek lands to the state by the Treaty of Indian Springs, February 12, 1825 (*see* TOUR *12*).

McIntosh, a man of Scottish and Indian ancestry, joined the American forces in the War of 1812, served in the Florida campaign, and became a brigadier general. He was a cousin of Governor George Troup (*see* TOUR 9), whose violent efforts to evict the Creek almost caused war between Georgia and the National government. The Treaty of Indian Springs kindled a faction of the Creek Nation to hatred of McIntosh; Menawa, a rival leader, was appointed his executioner. On April 30, 1825, Menawa led more than a hundred braves to the McIntosh house and commanded all white people to leave. Chilly McIntosh, son of the chief, escaped with the white visitors. When only McIntosh and his second-in-command remained, they were driven out by fire into a fusillade of rifle bullets that killed them instantly.

FRANKLIN, 141.1 m. (695 alt., 312 pop.), seat of Heard County, on the Chattahoochee River, was a village as early as 1770 but was not incorporated till 1831. It has changed little since western Georgia was a frontier country; streets are unpaved, and the small frame stores encircling the courthouse have wooden or tin roofs extending over the sidewalk. The town is dependent on the farm products and timber of the county, which is somewhat isolated because of the complete absence of railroads.

Left from Franklin on State 34 to FLAT ROCK CAMPGROUND, 3 m., where Methodists of the section gather during August for ten days of religious meetings, with four services each day. The large tabernacle was built of logs in 1855 and its roof covered with 9,000 shingles made by hand. In the eighteen small cabins with straw-covered dirt floors campers live during the session. Approximately a hundred acres surrounding the campgrounds have granite deposits from which tombstones have been cut for more than a hundred years.

In old PROSPECT CEMETERY (L), 146.9 m., small sheds, covered with pink rambler roses, have been built over the century-old graves to protect them from the weather.

At LA GRANGE, 162.5 m. (729-786 alt., 20,131 pop.) (*see* TOUR *3*), is a junction with US 29 (*see* TOUR *3*).

TROUP COUNTY PRISON (R), 169.5 m., stands on bleak grounds encircled by a steel-wire fence topped with barbwire. Within this enclosure are a central two-story stucco building, portable frame barracks, and a kennel for bloodhounds. The Negroes are segregated from the white prisoners. When weather permits, the convicts in horizontally striped uniforms work on the roads each day.

Robert W. Burns, author of *I Am A Fugitive from A Georgia Chain Gang,* was quartered here before his escape. This book, published while he was at large, describes the sweatbox, stocks, and brutal floggings that he claims were administered to the convicts. His statements have been vigorously denied, and are still a matter of controversy. This book, especially after its adaptation to the screen, aroused interest in prison reform and in the extradition laws of the various states.

TIP TOP, 185.6 m. (1,037 alt.), a pass over nine-mile-long Pine Mountain, is a vantage point for a broad, pleasant view of the bordering valleys. Although the mountain rises only 200 to 400 feet above the surrounding uplands, its highest point is 1,395 feet above sea level.

At Tip Top is the junction with the Pine Mountain Scenic Highway (*see* TOUR *3B*).

Left from Tip Top on a macadamized road is the PINE MOUNTAIN VALLEY RURAL COMMUNITY, 2 m., a rehabilitation project established by the F.E.R.A. The project area comprises approximately 13,000 acres in a fertile, well-wooded valley, bounded on the north by Pine Mountain and on the south by Oak Mountain, and accommodates approximately 200 families. The project was planned to be self-liquidating, and the individual homesteads are being bought by monthly payments that will extend over a period of twenty years. Its affairs are guided by a board of directors; one member is selected from the community, the others are connected with national, state, and local welfare work. The directors have three objectives for the people of this community: to give them opportunities for work, to enable them to produce most of their subsistence, and to provide them with means to supplement their incomes through agricultural and industrial activities.

Individual homesteads vary in size from three acres near the community center to thirty-six acres in outlying areas. The smaller homesteads are occupied by the tradespeople and the larger by farmers, of whom there are 135. All settlers are encouraged to produce food and feed crops, poultry and live stock for sale and home use. Similar in design, though not identical, are the simple, four-to six-room frame cottages, equipped with electric lights and modern plumbing. One hundred and one families living within a radius of one and a quarter miles receive their water from a central deep well, but those beyond this limit have individual wells and electric pumps. In the front yards are roses, dogwood trees, and ornamental shrubbery. A few sagging, unpainted dwellings, in which the families formerly lived, emphasize the difference between the new houses and those found on many impoverished Georgia farms.

Since crop diversification and the self-sustaining farm are ideals of this community, about 5,600 acres are under cultivation in general farm products. Of this acreage, the corporation owns a community farm of 1,500 acres, on which it conducts various enterprises for the benefit of the settlers, whose salaries are paid from the profits. The dairy farm has a barn housing two hundred Jersey cows, the enclosures of the beef cattle farm contain two hundred animals, and the poultry plant has twenty laying houses and twenty brooder houses. Peach and plum orchards and vineyards of scuppernong and muscadine grapes have begun bearing. Since the region produces a great variety of fruits and vegetables, there is also a plant for the processing and preservation of these food products.

The timberlands of Pine Mountain Valley, covered with a good growth of trees, both natural and planted, are valuable for timber and firewood and as parks and wild life preserves. With the increased interest in paper pulp following the experiments of Herty (*see* SAVANNAH), the rapid growth of pines may prove a valuable source of income in the future. There is an abundance of hardwood, including hickory, ash, and several varieties of oak. The softer woods, such as poplar and chestnut, are less plentiful. Several hundred thousand slash and longleaf pine seedlings are grown in the valley nursery and transplanted annually.

At the community center, from which roads radiate to the homesteads, are the elementary school and recreation buildings. The high school children are taken by bus to Hamilton and Shiloh. The recreation building contains a spacious auditorium-gymnasium, stage, club rooms, kitchen and well-equipped library. In a near-by shop is made much of the furniture used by the settlers. A large steel building is used as a warehouse and trading post.

Religious activities are inter-denominational. There are two farmers' 'bs, an active woman's club, boy and girl scout groups, and other community organizations. Special emphasis is given to health education and disease prevention. The corporation employs a nurse, and physicians from near-by towns hold clinics at the community center.

HAMILTON, 188.9 m. (778 alt., 438 pop.), incorporated as the seat of Harris County in 1828, has several old frame houses built before the War between the States.

Right from Hamilton on an unpaved road to BLUE SPRINGS (*open by special request*), 3.5 m., the 8,000-acre estate of Cason Callaway, industrialist of La Grange. The bird sanctuary contains pheasants and other birds unusual in this section.

LAKE HARDING (*cabins and boats available*), 10.5 m., has a 150-mile wooded shore line with many houses. This lake, which covers an area of ten square miles, was created in 1926 by BARTLETT'S FERRY DAM, owned and operated by the Georgia Power Company.

South of Hamilton US 27 follows an Indian trail through one of the last sections in Georgia taken by the white man.

COLUMBUS, 212.2 m. (250 alt., 43,141 pop.) (*see* COLUMBUS).

Points of Interest: St. Elmo, Wynnton School, Bibb Manufacturing Company Plant, and others.

At Columbus is a junction with US 80 (*see* TOUR 9).

Section b. COLUMBUS *to* FLORIDA LINE, *151.1 m.*

South of COLUMBUS, 0 m., the land has been seriously eroded, which has caused great suffering not only on the farms but in the towns. The ravages sometimes show in spectacular canyon formations. In the undamaged areas the land produces an abundance of cotton, pecans, peanuts, and garden truck, and the woods and muddy streams are popular for hunting and fishing. This region, once occupied by Creek Indians, was settled later than most of Georgia, not by wealthy planters but by farmers, lumberjacks, and trappers.

At 3.5 m. is a junction with State 85 (*see* TOUR 10A).

CUSSETA (pronounced Ku-see'-ta), 18.7 m. (540 alt., 343 pop.), was a small village called Sand Town when it was made the seat of the newly created Chattahoochee County in 1854. Incorporated the following year, the town was named for Kasihta, the largest of the Muskhogean Indian trading towns, which had formerly been near by.

LUMPKIN, 39.5 m. (approx. 500 alt., 1,103 pop.), named for Wilson Lumpkin, Governor of Georgia (1831-35), became the seat of Stewart County in 1828 and was incorporated in 1831.

More than 40,000 acres of land in Stewart County have been rendered unproductive by erosion. A study of the soil revealed that below the rich humus topsoil is a 100-foot stratum of very loose clay-sand overlying a layer of blue marl, a harder clay limestone. If the humus covering is worn away, water seeping through the sand to the marl carries the sand with it into the Chattahoochee River and causes a cracking that occurs first about ten feet below the surface. In many places the marl limestone has been worn away almost completely and immense gullies several miles long and from 100 to 200 feet deep have been formed. It is estimated (1939) that almost half of the agricultural land of the county has been so eroded. On a few scientifically farmed tracts the erosion has been checked by terracing and planting kudzu vines in the ditches.

In the thinly settled farm region surrounding Lumpkin are many good examples of the breezeway (also known as dogtrot or saddle-bag) type of house, in which two units are connected by a roof built across an open central passageway. Lean hounds sleep in the shade of the open passageways, and chickens scratch in the bare, sandy yards. Red clay gullies, bordered by pine trees and broom sedge, stretch from the road far back into the fields.

Left from Lumpkin on unpaved State 27 to PROVIDENCE CAVERNS, 7.5 m., known as the Grand Canyons of Georgia. The term applies more specifically to the second and largest canyon. The central basin of this octopus-shaped cavern covers more than 3,000 acres, and the chasm is about 300 feet wide and 200 feet deep. Although the gullies are a spectacle of destruction, their great size and the delicate colors of their vertical walls give them a strange beauty. Red, yellow, brown, mauve, lavender, jade, ochre, orange, and chalk-white appear in the different strata of the soil; white and yellow predominate.

It is believed the erosion began less than fifty years ago, and the gullies have formed with almost unbelievable rapidity until they have become a serious menace. Red clay, blue marl, shell, and a yellow clay have yielded readily to the devastation, and now the erosive process is eating through a layer of chalk. Trees, leaning outward and awry, cling perilously by their roots to the perpendicular walls. Small islands, which have not yet given way, rise like pinnacles from the bottom of the vast gully, and on these a few small pine trees struggle upward. It is predicted that within a few years the two caverns will meet across the road.

South of Lumpkin the highway is an improved sand-clay road (*slippery in wet weather*).

At 51.4 m. is the junction with a narrow, rough dirt road.

Left on this road to GRIER'S CAVE, 1 m., in a limestone hill surrounded by a forest of pines and oaks. The opening is a small hole in the ground less than one yard in diameter.

A descent of about ten feet leads to an elevated limestone floor that slopes sharply downward on all sides. The roof of the cave is so low in places that visitors must crawl. Near the entrance the originally glistening white lime deposits have been darkened by the smoke of torches used by explorers, but far inside the crystals gleam and sparkle in the torchlight or show ghostly white in the gloom. A stream flows through the lower portions. The temperature of the cave remains almost constant, and the condensation of warm air rising from the cave in winter looks like smoke. The extent of this cavern is unknown; some boys, exploring here recently, found an exit several hundred yards from the entrance.

CUTHBERT, 59.3 m. (446 alt., 3,235 pop.), seat of Randolph County, is on the fertile plateau between the Flint and Chattahoochee rivers. Soon after the county had been created in 1828, log houses formed a village that was incorporated in 1834.

A winery, a cannery, and cotton and lumber mills are the principal industrial establishments; hunting, fishing, and gardening are the chief recreations. The town is given an old-fashioned dignity by its older houses, which are sturdily built with thick walls, limerock chimneys, spacious verandas, and tall, shuttered windows. Some have columns and Greek porticoes.

The TOOMBS HOUSE (*private*), on Lumpkin St., built about 1836, was one of the first two frame houses erected in the town. The entrance portico of this white clapboard house has two square columns, a small hanging balcony, and a Greek pediment.

The W. E. KING HOUSE, also called the Thornton Place (*private*), on College St., is a modernized ante bellum house with six Doric columns supporting its hipped roof. Palladian doorways open on the front porch and small overhanging balcony.

ANDREW COLLEGE, on College St. about three blocks W. of the square, is a women's junior college with an enrollment of 110 controlled by the South Georgia Conference of the Methodist Episcopal Church, South. Founded in 1854, it is one of the oldest denominational schools for women in the United States. The red brick buildings are set on a thirteen-acre campus shaded by oak and pecan trees. When these buildings were used as a hospital during the War between the States, the college continued to function and classes were conducted in private homes.

On Lumpkin St. in the yard of the George McDonald House is the MCDONALD PECAN, believed to be Georgia's oldest pecan tree. Although more than a century old, it is said to yield from 200 to 1,200 pounds of nuts annually.

At **72.1 m.** is the junction with State 37.

Right on State 37 is FORT GAINES, **13.2 m.** (166 alt., 1,272 pop.), seat of Clay County, established in the early 1800's and named for the stockaded fort here. The tranquil little village on a bluff overlooking a bend in the Chattahoochee River suggests a medieval fortress. The white frame building of the Woman's Club is on the highest point between two dugouts which were once used as lookout posts by Indians.

On the bluff, about 100 yards R. of the Woman's Club House, is a large iron cannon used during the War between the States. The deep hole behind the cannon was a powder deposit.

At the foot of the bluff a graceful cantilever bridge spans the Chattahoochee River. Right of the bridge on a large knoll is the SITE OF FORT GAINES, a log fort occupied and successfully defended by General Edmund Gaines during the Indian wars.

In the town is the old DILL HOUSE, built, according to tradition, by a young girl who was captured by Indians but who was so beautiful that the chief would permit no one to harm her. When the Indians returned from raiding expeditions with sacks of money, they kept the gold coins but threw away the paper currency; this the young girl gathered up. Each day, on the horse the Indians had given her, she ventured farther away from the camp until one morning she rode to the banks of the Chattahoochee River and swam across. She was rescued by men from Fort Gaines and later adopted by a family living there. Some years afterward she married General John Dill and used the paper currency to build a beautiful house. This old structure, remodeled and greatly altered, is now a hotel known as the Puckett House.

BLAKELY, 87.8 m. (275 alt., 2,106 pop.), seat of Early County, was founded in 1821 and named for Captain Johnston Blakely, naval officer in the War of 1812. He was the commander of the *Wasp* which mysteriously disappeared at sea after having made the most severe depredations on English commerce of any one naval vessel during the war. Among Blakely's industrial plants are a hardwood mill, several small sawmills, turpentine stills, and a large peanut-shelling plant.

Blakely has become an important peanut center since the coming of the boll weevil in 1921 caused a decrease in cotton production. Until that time peanuts were grown chiefly for stock feed, the vines being baled and the nuts left in the ground for hogs to root. With the development of new uses and the establishment of a steady market, peanuts have become one of the state's most profitable crops. In July small, light-yellow blossoms appear on the vines, and nuts begin to form in clusters on the roots. Before the nuts are fully matured, quantities are gathered and, while still soft, are boiled in salty water to be sold along the streets of the town. In August the plants are pulled and stacked around poles to dry. About four weeks later the nuts are picked, and the vines are compressed into bales of hay. Mechanical planters, pickers, and balers, often owned by a co-operative group, are moved from farm to farm to serve the growers. The nuts are sold either to a mill, where the oil is extracted by a cooking process, or to a peanut-shelling plant. Here, after being separated by a shaker from vine particles and foreign matter the nuts are taken to shellers, which rapidly separate the kernels from the hulls. The kernels are then carried on conveyers through a line of workers who sit on each side and pick out the imperfect nuts. From the conveyers the nuts fall into chutes that carry them to a lower floor, where they are placed in bags and weighed, ready for shipment to processing plants and candy factories. The capacity of a plant with five shelling machines is approximately twenty-five tons a day.

On the courthouse square near the Confederate monument is a CONFEDERATE FLAGPOLE, erected in 1865. Twice it has been broken by storms, but it is now reinforced with copper wire and set in a concrete base.

A map published in 1820 shows an old Federal road passing through the county. It is also called the Jackson Trail, because General Jackson's troops in 1818, under the command of Colonel Haynes, crossed the Chattahoochee River from Fort Mitchell in Alabama to Columbus and then followed this road down to Fort Scott.

Right from Blakely on a dirt road to three INDIAN MOUNDS, 6 m., near Little Colomokee Creek on the Mercier Plantation. Two of these are twenty-five to thirty-five feet high and conical in shape. A few years ago a hole was dug in the center of the largest mound to a depth of six feet, where a stratum of human bones was found. Here souvenir hunters occasionally find arrowheads and other relics of an ancient civilization.

In COLQUITT, 108.5 m. (175 alt., 832 pop.), created as the seat of Miller County in 1856 and named for Judge Walter T. Colquitt, Georgia statesman and United States Senator, is a trading center for farmers. Checker games are played around the square, and horseshoes are thrown at the numerous pegs placed in the courthouse yard.

BAINBRIDGE, 130.3 m. (119 alt., 6,141 pop.) (*see* TOUR *5*), is at the junction with US 84 (*see* TOUR *5*).

At 151.1 m. US 27 crosses the Florida Line, 21 miles north of Tallahassee, Florida.

TOUR 1OA

Junction US 27 — Fort Benning; 6 m., State 85.

Roadbed asphalt-surfaced.

State 85 branches south from US 27 (*see* TOUR *10*), 0 m., at a point 3.5 miles southeast of Columbus (*see* COLUMBUS).

From the entrance to Fort Benning Reservation, 4.5 m., a tree-shaded drive, crossing Upatoi Bridge, leads to Outpost No. 1.

FORT BENNING, 6 m. (*open 7 A.M. to 9 P.M. daily; visitors register at Outpost No. 1; permits from provost marshal required to visit points on reservation outside the post; information at Post Public Relations Office; speed limit, 15 to 30 m.p.h., rigidly enforced; dress parade Fri. afternoons; polo matches Sun. afternoons during winter; weekly fox hunts and boar hunts during season*), is the largest infantry post in the United States. Established as an army training camp during the World War, it became the infantry school in 1919, and since that time $22,000,000 have been spent to transform it from a temporary, ramshackle wartime camp into a modern post with more than three hundred buildings and fifty miles of broad, paved streets. Young trees and shrubbery are planted with military precision about the buildings and in some of the open spaces. Fort Benning has a population of 8,500; the 6,500 officers and soldiers on active duty represent all branches of military service except cavalry and heavy artillery. The post was named for the Confederate General Henry L. Benning, of Columbus. The buildings of the garrison are concentrated within a relatively small area, but the reservation itself covers 97,000 acres of rolling, wooded land crossed by many streams. Fort Benning has well-distributed fire departments, a telephone exchange, a bakery, a refrigeration plant, a central heating system, two libraries, a children's school, two theaters, a baseball field, a golf course, tennis courts, a bowling alley, a skating rink, and three swimming pools.

Troops stationed at the camp make up the units necessary for maneuvers, which are directed by student officers. Theory is tested by maneuvering companies under all possible combat conditions, and examinations are worked out, not with pencil and paper, but with men. The 29th Infantry, assigned to demonstration work, is the only peacetime regiment maintained at full war strength. Other branches of the military service, such as the tank battalions, signal corps, artillery, air corps, chemical warfare service, and medical corps, are used in maneuvers to demonstrate co-ordination with the infantry. Each year 200 to 400 officers, ranging in rank from second lieutenant to colonel, take the nine-month training course that makes them eligible for instruction at the Command and General Staff School, the Army War College, the Army Industrial College, or for foreign military college assignments on an exchange basis. Short courses are offered also to enlisted men and officers of the National Guard and reserve officers, who come each year from all parts of the United States.

On the reservation is a forest nursery with a 12,000,000-tree capacity and a 5,000-acre erosion-control project. Since the reservation forms one of the largest game preserves in the South, hunting is a popular sport. Fox hunting, particularly, is a traditional feature of the social life.

The POST CHAPEL, Sigerfoos Rd., is a white, stucco-covered building with a tall spire in the Georgian Colonial style. Although the chapel is undenominational, it provides facilities for Roman Catholic, Protestant, and Jewish religious services. In the nave is a confessional booth, a canopied pulpit, a tablet showing the Ten Commandments, and a small model of the Ark of the Covenant.

DOUGHBOY STADIUM, on an unnamed street R. of the chapel, was erected by soldier labor through subscriptions of the various infantry units and has a seating capacity of 8,000. General Pershing turned the first shovelful of dirt and poured the first batch of concrete for the structure.

The 29TH INFANTRY BARRACKS, Vibbert Ave., two blocks from the NW. corner of the stadium, immense brick buildings with wide front porches, house 2,133 men; these are the first barracks ever erected by the U. S. Army to quarter an entire war-strength regiment. The two units, each occupying a full block, are built around large courts. One of them, 2,528 feet long, was described by Robert Ripley in his *Believe-It-Or-Not* as having the longest porch in the world.

The CAMPBELL KING HORSE SHOW BOWL AND STABLES, NW. corner Anderson St. and Upton Ave., provide officers and members of their families with horses for riding, jumping, polo playing, and hunting.

The 24TH INFANTRY BARRACKS, Anderson St. and Wold Ave., house a Negro regiment quartered at Fort Benning since 1922. It was organized at McKavitt, Texas, in 1869 and "has soldiered around the world." At one time this regiment's band was the largest in the U. S. Army and won favorable comment from John Philip Sousa.

The buildings of the TANK SCHOOL within the Tank Area, Wold Ave., are of reinforced concrete and steel with four sheds for tank storage. This is the only tank school of the U. S. Army.

The OFFICERS' CLUB, Morrison Ave. five blocks SE. of the Tank Area, is a low, spacious, yellow stucco building with a series of arches and a red tiled roof. In the rear is a tiled swimming pool.

The ACADEMIC BUILDING, opposite the Officers' Club, is used as headquarters of the post and accommodates the academic department of the Infantry School. Its cost exceeded $500,000.

CALCULATOR'S MONUMENT, rear of the Academic Building, was erected to a crippled dog, the mascot of the Infantry School. A bronze tablet bears this inscription:

> Calculator
> Born?
> Died—August 29, 1923
> He made better dogs of, us all.

The U. S. POST HOSPITAL, Wold Ave., has a staff of some of the foremost medical authorities of the U. S. Army and is one of the finest hospitals in the South. Its normal capacity is 250 patients. Here enlisted men are trained in the technicalities of X-ray, violet ray, and kindred work. A number of those showing special aptitude are sent to Carlyle Barracks, Pennsylvania, and other medical centers for further study.

RAINBOW ROW, extending R. from Wold Ave., named in honor of the American Rainbow Division of the World War, is a residential avenue for captains and higher ranking officers. In keeping with the name of the street, each of the stucco houses is painted a different color.

The COMMANDANT'S HOUSE, Vibbert Ave., is a spacious, white-columned structure set apart in a large grove of spreading oaks and tangled shrubbery. The site was once occupied by the Kasihta Indians.

The INFANTRY SCHOOL MUSEUM, Vibbert Ave., in the Department of Experiment Building, contains a collection of American and foreign war relics, including American uniforms and small arms of all periods from Revolutionary days through the World War, a display of early and modern types of pistols, a *lantaka* or Moro swivel cannon from the Philippines, and various souvenirs of European battlefields.

TOUR 11

(Chattanooga, Tenn.) — Trenton — Rising Fawn — (Fort Payne, Ala.); US 11.

Tennessee Line to Alabama Line, 23.6 m. — Roadbed graded dirt; condition poor in some places — Southern Ry. parallels route throughout — Limited accommodations.

Crossing the extreme northwestern corner of the state, US 11 passes through the narrow limestone valley that lies between Lookout and Sand mountains, the southern end of the great Appalachian Plateau. This rugged region is separated from the rest of Georgia by mountain barriers and formerly could be reached only from Tennessee or Alabama; in 1939 State 2 was extended from La Fayette (*see* TOUR 10) to the top of Lookout Mountain.

The inhabitants, almost all of whom are native white, are dependent on the fruit and vegetables they raise on their 100- or 150-acre farms. These people were never part of the slaveholding plantation life, and their continued isolation has only increased their aloofness till they now have little in common with the rest of the state. Many of them belong to the Sanctified (colloq., Holy Roller) church and express their religious emotions with shouts and gesticulations, though in daily life they are somewhat taciturn.

From about 1860 until 1908 coal was mined in this section, and after 1874 the smelting of iron ore was an important industry. Since mining was abandoned in the 1900's, two small lumber mills have been the only industrial plants. The towns are little more than hamlets of small frame houses and garden patches, with corn stalks and fruit trees growing along the main streets. Herds of sheep graze in hilly pastures separated by old stone fences.

US 11 crosses the Tennessee Line, **0 m.,** at a point 6 miles southwest of Chattanooga, Tennessee.

LOOKOUT MOUNTAIN (L), ranging in height from 1,750 to 2,392 feet, probably received its name from the high cliffs that afforded a vantage point for observing approaching Indians. Its steep slopes are capped with almost vertical sandstone cliffs, rising from two hundred to three hundred feet and presenting unscalable walls cut into deep gullies by streams flowing from the top of the mountain into the valley. Although the broad plateau at the summit of the ridge is, for the most part, sparsely settled, there is a residential colony at the northern end.

SAND MOUNTAIN (1,630 alt.), is (R) much larger than Lookout Mountain and extends far to the southwest. This mountain plateau is more thickly populated than the other because its farms are more productive.

TRENTON, **10.8 m.** (735 alt., 370 pop.), was made the seat of Dade County in 1840. At that time it was called Salem, but the following year its name was changed to Trenton. The county was created in 1837 and named for Major Francis Langhorne Dade, who, with his entire force, was killed in the Seminole War in Florida.

Right from Trenton on a country road are several ABANDONED COAL MINES, about **5 m.** It has been estimated by the state geological survey that the coal fields of Dade County contain deposits sufficient to supply the needs of Georgia for at least two hundred years. This coal is valuable for furnace and industrial needs, but is too fine for satisfactory use in grates. The deposits still supply some of the Trenton citizens, although mining was discontinued about 1908 because of inaccessibility to markets. During the latter part of the nineteenth century, when convicts were leased to private individuals, numbers of prisoners served sentences in the Dade County coal mines under wretched conditions.

Southwest of Trenton the dark cedars and bare gray cliffs are a somber scene in winter, but in spring the roadsides are resplendent with white dogwood blossoms, golden-centered white Cherokee roses, and pale pink laurel and rhododendron. The fragrant white and yellow flowers of the honeysuckle vine cover the clay banks; ferns, anemones, trilliums, and wild violets grow in the deeper woods. In autumn the forest is beautiful with the warm, rich colors of hickory, beech, sweet gum, oak, and chinquapin contrasting with the darker pine foliage. The chestnut trees that once grew luxuriantly here have all been killed by blight.

RISING FAWN, **20 m.** (793 alt., 246 pop.), was known as Hanna in 1870 when the Wills Valley Railroad, now the Alabama Great Southern, was run through the village. Its name was then changed to Staunton and later to Rising Fawn.

Left from Rising Fawn on the Newsom Highway, a narrow, graveled road, to the RUINS OF THE RISING FAWN FURNACE (L), **1 m.,** erected in 1874. It had a daily capacity of fifty tons and was operated until about 1910.

At this point the Newsom Highway turns left and, ascending Lookout Mountain, partly encircles JOHNSON'S CROOK, **5 m.**, a great wooded amphitheater formed by a horseshoe bend of the mountain and bounded on all sides except the south by rugged cliffs.

At the top of Lookout Mountain is a junction, **6 m.**, with unpaved State 157, a new scenic highway, running from Chattanooga, Tennessee, over the mountain to Gadsden, Alabama; L. on this road to SITTON'S GULCH (L), **11.6 m.**, about eight hundred feet deep, a half mile wide, and four miles long. In 1938 about fourteen hundred acres around the gulch were set aside as a wild life refuge and recreational area. This land was a gift from the citizens of Dade County aided by Chattanooga friends who were interested in the region.

The gulch, little known even in Georgia, is a majestic sight because of its imposing dimensions and its gray sandstone walls that have been worn perpendicular by Bear Creek. In June these walls are crowned by pink blossoms of rhododendron. Deep within the gorge a magnificent waterfall plunges with a muffled roar in one sheer drop to the bottom of the gorge. Against the massive, grimly commanding gray cliffs, this cataract, with its clouds of shimmering spray, has a delicate and almost unearthly beauty.

US 11 crosses the Alabama Line, **23.6 m.**, at a point 23 miles northeast of Fort Payne, Alabama.

TOUR 12

Atlanta — McDonough — Forsyth — Macon — Perry — Hawkinsville — Brunswick; 293.4 m., US 341.

Roadbed hard-surfaced, one-third concrete; watch for cattle and hogs in the r...—Southern Ry. parallels route between Atlanta and Jackson, and between Eastman **and** Brunswick; Central of Georgia Ry. between Forsyth and Macon — All types of accommodations in Atlanta, Macon, and Brunswick; limited elsewhere — Note: US **341** markers not yet erected (1939); State 42 markers between Atlanta and **Forsyth,** US 41-State 19 between Forsyth and Macon, US 41-State 11 between **Macon and** **Perry.**

Section a. ATLANTA *to* MACON, *92.9 m., US 341.*

Through a section that is typical of the Piedmont Plateau of middle Georgia, this route passes red-clay hills, pine woods, pecan groves, and fields of corn and cotton. There are few evidences of luxury but many of good living; barns are unpainted but well stored with fodder; gardens, though not trimly kept, are green with abundant vegetables. The few ante bellum houses remaining are stoutly built and spacious but not elegant.

This land was a stronghold of the Creek before they were evicted by a series of treaties (*see* HISTORY). After they had been removed in 1821, the section became a thriving cotton-plantation area. General Sherman covered part of this route in his march to the sea after the burning of Atlanta. After the war the plantations were divided into small farms, but the section remained agricultural. Industrial development is, for the most part, small and local.

ATLANTA, **0 m.** (1,050 alt., 270,366 pop.) (*see* ATLANTA).

Points of Interest: State Capitol, Cyclorama of the Battle of Atlanta, Georgia School of Technology, Emory University, Oglethorpe University, Atlanta University (Negro), and others.

Atlanta is at the junction with US 78 (*see* TOUR 8), with US 29 (*see* TOUR 3), with US 41 (*see* TOUR 2), with US 23 (*see* TOUR 7), and with US 19 (*see* TOUR 6).

MCDONOUGH, **28.1 m.** (861 alt., 1,068 pop.), like the usual county seat, radiates from the courthouse square. The town developed around a trading post built on land obtained from the Creek by the Treaty of Indian Springs in 1821. Early settlers here came from the Carolinas by way of Madison over a stagecoach route that followed an old Indian trail, now Key's Ferry Road. The village was incorporated in 1823 as the seat of Henry County and was named for Thomas Mac-Donough, the naval officer who had defeated the British on Lake Champlain, September 11, 1814. Citizens claim that the *Jacksonian,* the town's first newspaper, which was established in 1828, was the first journal to advocate Andrew Jackson for the Presidency. By the time of the War between the States, McDonough was large enough to send two companies to the front.

After the Battle of Atlanta, July 22, 1864, General Sherman divided his army for his march to the sea. One division came through McDonough, destroyed property, and burned the court records. The town was again overrun with soldiers on August 30, when 20,000 Confederates encamped here in preparation for an attack on the Federal troops at Jonesboro.

Although the commerce of McDonough is based primarily on agriculture, industry has made some headway. The chief manufacturing establishments are two hosiery mills and two plants that make filing machines. Several of the houses built soon after the incorporation of the town are still standing.

A CORK TREE in the front yard of Judge T. J. Brown's house, Jonesboro St., is almost a century old, measures two feet in diameter and approximately sixty feet in height, and is covered with cork nearly two inches thick. During the administration of President James K. Polk the U. S. Department of Agriculture attempted to introduce cork trees into this country for their commercial value. Acorns were imported from Spain and distributed throughout the southern states. One of the trees that grew in this yard was killed in 1899.

JACKSON, **45.7 m.** (697 alt., 1,776 pop.), seat of Butts County, was incorporated in 1826 and named in honor of James Jackson, Governor of Georgia from 1798 to 1801. It is an unusually clean and well-kept town. Its large frame houses, with cupolas and jigsaw carving, are freshly painted, and their yards are neat and trim.

The First National Bank of Jackson, facing the square, stands on the SITE OF THE ROBERT GRIER HOME. Although it is not known exactly when Grier's *Almanac* was begun, residents of Butts County have copies published as early as 1810. Grier died in 1848 and is buried in the family burial ground at his old home near Stark, about five miles northeast of Jackson.

Left from Jackson on unpaved State 16 to the junction with a country road, **8 m.**; L. on this road to a fork, **8.3 m.**; R. from the fork to the junction with another dirt road, **9 m.**; R. on this to LLOYD SHOALS DAM, **9.2 m.**, erected on the Ocmulgee River in 1910 by the Central of Georgia Power Company (merged with the Georgia Power Company in 1928). This dam, 100 feet high and more than 500 feet long, develops 22,000 horsepower.

The river is curbed for approximately fifteen miles, and the backwater covers more than 3,000 acres of land, leaving many small islands in the large reservoir. The lake has been stocked by the government with bream, trout, perch, and migratory ducks and geese.

HOLINESS CAMPGROUND (R), **50.3 m.**, has been in use since 1890. A hotel, a tabernacle, and approximately 300 cottages are provided for the thousands of people who gather here every August for revivals of "the old time religion."

The entrance (R) to INDIAN SPRINGS STATE PARK (*hotel open May 1-Oct. 15; casino, museum, 9-hole golf course, outdoor swimming pool, bowling alley, foot trails*) is at **51.5 m.** When Douglas Watson, a government scout, paused here in 1792 to investigate an odor which he attributed to burnt gunpowder, he found a sulphur spring fed by a small but steady flow from the walls of rock. It had long been known to the Indians, who gathered here to drink the water for its curative properties. In 1800 Creek under General William McIntosh, a halfbreed chief, encamped here.

On January 8, 1821, the Creek signed a treaty here ceding to the U. S. Government most of their land between the Flint and Ocmulgee rivers as far north as the Chattahoochee. They reserved only a few small tracts, including 1,000 acres surrounding this spring. In another treaty signed here by McIntosh on February 12, 1825, the Creek relinquished all their remaining holdings within the boundaries of Georgia in exchange for $400,000 and acre for acre west of the Mississippi. Although McIntosh negotiated this treaty as leader of the Creek Confederation, the Upper Creek repudiated his action and later executed him (*see* TOUR *10*).

The state disposed of all the Indian lands except ten acres called the Indian Springs Reserve, which was leased to individuals for development as a summer resort. After the Wigwam Hotel burned in 1921, the popularity of the resort waned. In 1933 the citizens of Butts County purchased 122 acres adjoining the reserve and gave it to the state for a park. The 152 acres now constituting Indian Springs State Park have been extensively improved with rock buildings and walks, and thousands of native trees and shrubs have been planted under the supervision of the state forest service.

An old WATER-POWER GRISTMILL, on the highway (R) near the spring, was built in 1873 and called the Alberta Mill. It still has its original grinding rocks and large water wheel. ROCK CASTLE, the old Collier house near by, was built in 1853. Although rock was plentiful in Georgia, comparatively few houses were constructed of this material because expert stone masons were rare. A stone MUSEUM, assembled by the park service in conjunction with the Butts County Historical and Archeological Society, contains Indian artifacts and relics.

The VARNER HOUSE (*private*), a large frame building (L) with a long one-story veranda, was erected as a hotel in 1821 under the supervision of McIntosh and Joel Bailey. It has been changed little and still contains some of the original furnishings and the register desk on which the treaty was signed. Beside the porch is McIntosh Rock, the large boulder upon which O-potto-le-yo-holo stood while making a speech of protest against the treaty.

FORSYTH, **67.5 m.** (704 alt., 2,277 pop.), seat of Monroe County, is built about a large open courthouse square bordered by red brick buildings with second-story roofs jutting over the sidewalks. It was incorporated in 1822 and named for John Forsyth, Secretary of State under President Jackson and President Van Buren. Its growth was accelerated when the Monroe Railroad was built from Forsyth to Macon in 1834, since products of the vicinity were shipped to Macon for redistribution to other points by means of the Ocmulgee River. Forsyth raised half the capital stock of $200,000 for this railroad, now merged with the Central of Georgia, and became the first inland town of the state to be made accessible by a navigable waterway. Its industrial plants include a cottonseed-oil mill, three cotton mills, and two lumber mills.

HILL ARDIN (*private*), two blocks R. of highway on S. Lee St., built in 1822, is a Greek Revival house with fluted door facings and elaborate cornices. The interior is notable for a spiral stairway built of mahogany brought from South America. In the flower garden is a cork tree a hundred years old.

BESSIE TIFT COLLEGE, on a sixty-five-acre campus two blocks L. of the public square, is a woman's college controlled by the Georgia Baptist Convention. Its rambling red brick buildings, with wide verandas ornamented with white columns, are set on a broad expanse of lawn. Founded in 1847 as a private school, it was taken over by the Georgia Baptist Convention in 1898, and in 1907 its name was changed to honor its benefactress, Mrs. Bessie Willingham Tift. This college, which confers the A. B. degree, has an enrollment of 250 students.

Right from Forsyth on unpaved State 42 to the STATE TEACHERS' AND AGRICULTURAL COLLEGE, 1.3 m., an institution offering high school and junior college work to Negroes. Its five buildings are grouped on a 226-acre campus. Under the control of the University System of Georgia, the school provides superior training at an exceptionally low cost, tuition being $3 a month and board and room $9. In addition to the usual academic work, courses in agriculture, carpentry, and home economics are offered. Special emphasis is placed on the normal course which includes practice teaching in a primary and elementary school attended by the Negro children of the vicinity. For the school year 1938-39, there were 174 high school and 112 junior college students in the institution.

The school, with seven pupils, was opened on May 9, 1902, by William Merida Hubbard in the Kynett Methodist Church. The work of this young Negro attracted the attention of the secretary of the American Mission Association, which made a donation of $25 a month to his school. In 1904 a tract was purchased and the first building erected. With the assistance of contributions from the General Education Board and the Federal government under the Smith-Hughes Act, the school continued to grow; in 1922 it became a state institution, called the Agricultural and Mechanical School. Throughout its history the institution has helped the Negro farmers of Monroe County by setting up various agricultural projects.

At 84.7 m., begins a mile stretch, known as the MEMORIAL MILE, which is part of the Dixie Highway Road of Remembrance extending from Sault Sainte Marie, Michigan, to Miami, Florida. At regular intervals along both sides of the memorial mile are cement posts about two feet high, each with a bronze marker bearing the name and record of one of Bibb County's World War soldiers. Pecan trees, crape myrtles, and spirea bushes beautify the spaces between the markers, and poppies and zinnias add color during the summer. When the 5,000-mile Dixie Highway was completed, both southern and northern women had become interested in beautifying it as a World War memorial. In February, 1922, the Dixie Highway Road of Remembrance Association planted the first trees here.

WESLEYAN COLLEGE (R), 86 m., at Rivoli, was the first college in the world chartered to grant degrees to women. Incorporated on December 23, 1836, as the Georgia Female College, the school was opened in Macon on January 7, 1839, under the supervision of the Georgia Conference of the Methodist Episcopal Church, South, and in July, 1840, eleven young women were graduated. In 1843 its name was changed to Wesleyan Female College, but later the middle word was dropped. Maintained today by the North Georgia, South Georgia, and Florida Methodist Conferences, Wesleyan has an enrollment of more than 250 young women working for the A. B. degree. In 1928 the college was moved here, where 170 acres of rolling woodland provide a beautiful setting for the twelve brick and marble buildings of Georgian Colonial design. The original buildings in Macon are occupied by the Wesleyan Conservatory of Music (*see* MACON).

Wesleyan, popular with foreign-born Methodists, was attended by the three Soong sisters, who later married prominent officials of China. Mei-ling, Madam Chiang Kai-shek, was tutored at Wesleyan for four years before she attended Wellesley, from which she was graduated. Ching-ling and Ai-ling were both graduated from Wesleyan.

Right of the entrance is the CANDLER MEMORIAL LIBRARY, similar in architecture to the Hermitage in Savannah. This library, a gift of Judge John Candler, of Atlanta, in memory of his parents, contains 21,108 volumes. Several large reading rooms provide a seating capacity of 250. On the ground floor is the Georgia Room, which holds a 1,200-volume collection of Georgiana presented to Wesleyan by Orville A. Park, trustee of the college and president of the Georgia Bar Association in 1918. Rare first editions and autographed copies of books now out of print are included. Among valued relics are a desk used by Sidney Lanier and a copy of the first diploma awarded by Wesleyan.

GEORGIA ACADEMY FOR THE BLIND (L), **90.6 m.,** is housed in a red brick building with a modified Greek portico. An average of 130 pupils from pre-school age to twenty-one receive instruction in trades, home economics, and music, as well as academic training by the Braille system.

In 1851 a movement for the establishment of an institution for the blind of the state was brought before the public by the Macon press. A beginning was made possible by private donations, and a small school with four pupils was set up the same year. In 1852 the school was accepted by the state and received legislative appropriations. During the War between the States it was moved to Fort Valley while the school building, then in downtown Macon, was being used as a hospital. The present building, modeled after that of the Philadelphia Institution for the Blind, was erected in 1906 at a cost of $100,000.

MACON, **92.9 m.** (334 alt., 53,829 pop.) (*see* MACON).

Points of Interest: Home of Sidney Lanier, Mercer University, Wesleyan Conservatory, and others.

At Macon is a junction with US 80 (*see* TOUR 9) and with US 129 (*see* TOUR *16*).

Section b. MACON *to* BRUNSWICK, *200.5 m., US 341.*

South of MACON, **0 m.,** US 341 descends from the Piedmont Plateau into the Coastal Plain, where the trees gradually begin to show gray hanging moss, the streams become dark and sluggish, and the hills fall away into level ground. The sandy loam of this section responds readily to fertilizer, and the mild climate makes it possible to produce a variety of crops during most of the year. Diversified farming, however, is a relatively new development and, although vegetables, fruits, and nuts are grown in abundance, cotton still predominates. This route also crosses the wiregrass or piney woods section, where sawmills and turpentine stills appear at intervals along the highway and in the small towns.

PORTERFIELD (*open*), **7.7 m.,** is the 25-acre estate (L) of James H. Porter, of Macon. This Normandy farmhouse is built of painted white brick, with rough-hewn beams, stucco trim, and brown Brittany roof tiles. Porter, assisted by J. D. Crump, vice-president of the American Rose Society, has planted extensive rose gardens to test the possibilities of successfully planting the different varieties in southern gardens. Beneath arches covered with ramblers, verbena- and pansy-bordered paths lead between sections divided into 100 diamond-shaped beds, each containing 25 bushes of the variety being tested. The Duchess of Wellington, Madam Butterfly, and Radiance roses are especially beautiful.

Another Memorial Mile of the Road of Remembrance (*see above*) begins at **8.1 m.**

In ECHECONNEE, **11.2 m.** (approx. 340 alt., 60 pop.), is a pottery shop that uses the old-fashioned potter's handwheel.

The road between Echeconnee and Cordele runs through part of Georgia's peach section, and in late March and April pink blossoms border the highway. The copper-colored Elberta and the lighter-colored Hiley Belle are the most popular varieties produced in this section. During the harvesting season, May to July, peaches are sorted, packed, and shipped in thousands of crates to many parts of the country. Packing houses (*open to visitors*), sometimes little more than loosely constructed sheds, appear at frequent intervals.

PERRY, **27.9 m.** (365 alt., 1,398 pop.) (*see* TOUR 2), is at a junction with US 41 (*see* TOUR 2).

CLINCHFIELD, **34.9 m.** (approx. 350 alt., 160 pop.), is an industrial community developed about a CEMENT-MANUFACTURING PLANT (*open to visitors*). The settlement, formerly called Coreen, was the site of a small limestone plant. In 1924 a Portland cement corporation, finding the material mined here suitable for their needs, bought the land, renamed the settlement, and built a plant occupying twenty acres along the Southern Railway.

The office and laboratory are housed in a stucco and tile building just within the entrance. Several other concrete and steel structures, which form two parallel lines along the railroad, are visible from the highway. These include raw storage and crusher buildings, waste-heat boilers, three kilns, a finishing mill, and fourteen concrete silos, arranged to permit a continuous flow of material in the successive stages of manufacture. Smaller buildings house the electric power plant and service shops.

From **35.4 m.** is a view of the QUARRY FACE (L), one-half mile long and about forty-five feet high. Here the raw products are loaded into cars by steam shovels and conveyed to the plant over an industrial railroad. This quarry supplies Ocala limestone, the principal raw material of the cement, and, from the upper levels, fuller's earth, a secondary material.

HAWKINSVILLE, **47.8 m.** (235 alt., 2,484 pop.), on the bank of the Ocmulgee River, is the seat of Pulaski County and was named for Benjamin Hawkins. Hawkins was a member of the Continental Congress and was appointed (1796) by Washington as superintendent of all the Indians south of the Ohio. His headquarters were in Georgia, first at Fort Hawkins near Macon, then at Old Agency on the Flint River in Crawford County, where he is buried. He was so eager to teach the Indians improved methods of agriculture that he brought his slaves to Georgia and operated a model farm as a demonstration project, quite like those now maintained by the department of agriculture's extension service.

On July 3, 1936, Hawkinsville celebrated its centennial, recounting the early days when the settlers lived in log cabins and carried on trade by means of small barges on the river. It is still a trading center, and its chief industries are cotton ginning, peanut shelling, and cheese making. Most of the houses are frame, ornamented with Victorian gables and scrollwork.

One block R. of the highway on State 11 is the marked SITE OF THE JACKSON TRAIL (R), which Andrew Jackson followed in 1818 when he invaded Florida to suppress the Seminole. One block farther south is the marked SITE OF THE BLACKSHEAR TRAIL (L), laid out in 1814 by General David Blackshear (*see* TOUR 9). This was the first road in Pulaski County, and documentary evidence indicates that Jackson followed the same course.

About one block from the highway on State 26 is an S-shaped MEMORIAL BRIDGE (L) spanning the Ocmulgee River and dedicated to the World War veterans of the county. Here General Oglethorpe crossed the Ocmulgee in 1739 on his way to confer with the Indians at Coweta Town near Columbus.

EASTMAN, 66.8 m. (357 alt., 3,022 pop.), seat of Dodge County, was named for William Pitt Eastman, who gave the land on which the town is built. The first store was operated in the old depot of the Macon & Brunswick Railroad in 1871, two years before the town was incorporated. At that time lumber milling and turpentine distilling were the chief enterprises, but cotton and pecan cultivation have superseded them in recent years. The modest bungalows bordering the highway have a trim appearance, and the park opposite the courthouse square is beautiful the year around with shrubs and evergreens.

Eastman is at the junction with State 87 (*see* TOUR 9*A*).

HELENA, 85.4 m. (247 alt., 963 pop.), was created when the Scottish citizens of McRae (*see below*) refused a right of way to the Southern and Seaboard railways. Helena became the junction for the two railroads, and rivalry between the two towns has been intense since that time. They are called, however, the twin cities of McRae-Helena, for a stranger never knows when he has left one town and entered the other.

MCRAE, 86.3 m. (230 alt., 1,314 pop.), seat of Telfair County, was settled in the middle of the nineteenth century by a band of Scottish Presbyterians who came from the Carolinas where they had settled on their arrival from the old country. These people gave staunch support to South Georgia College, a school that was discontinued when the Emory Junior College was opened at Valdosta in 1928.

The town is the focus of farming operations in the vicinity. Because the county is in a fertile area, agricultural products are diversified, and truck farming, dairying, and poultry raising bring considerable profits. Within the county ten large stills (*see* TOUR 4) annually produce large quantities of spirits of turpentine. Crossties, each bringing $1, are shipped from the hardwood swamps at the rate of 2,000 a week. Many acres in this section are planted in dewberries, a large and coarse-seeded variety of the blackberry that ripens early. Crates in truckload and carload lots are sent to the markets of the larger cities, and in the picking season 300 men, women, and children are employed.

McRae is the home of Eugene Talmadge, Governor of Georgia (1933-37). While state commissioner of agriculture he built up a strong following among the farmers and met all opposition with a bluntness and vigor that endeared him to some and made bitter enemies of others. During his terms as Governor, Talmadge adopted a "Georgia cracker" manner and a use of colloquial terms that appealed to farmers. When making a speech he usually took off his coat to show his red suspenders; an identical pair was presented to all visitors at the Governor's mansion.

Left from McRae on an unpaved road to LITTLE OCMULGEE STATE PARK, **2.4 m.**, a 1,395-acre tract of land partly donated by the citizens of Telfair and Wheeler counties. From the entrance an unpaved but improved road leads two and a half miles directly across the park. Foot and motor trails to be constructed (1939) will lead from this road into the dense oak and pine forests. Near the entrance a hand-hewn frame building, fastened together with wooden pegs, will serve as a combination clubhouse, administration building, and lunchroom. Camping cottages and a dance pavilion will be built, and facilities for boating, swimming, fishing, picnicking, and other outdoor recreations will be provided. Since the land on the east adjoining the Little Ocmulgee River is low and flat, many acres are inundated during periods of excessive rainfall. Plans for the park provide for the construction of a large earthen dam in order to form a lake by flooding the lowlands. Trees are being reset, shrubbery planted, building sites established, and buildings erected.

LUMBER CITY, **104.1 m.** (146 alt., 1,043 pop.), on the Ocmulgee River (*fishing and swimming*), was incorporated in 1889. It is sometimes called Artesian City because the city's water supply is obtained from fifty-six artesian wells. A number of sawmills make this town the largest shipping point for pine and hardwood lumber in this section of the state. Sand pits three miles from the town produce quantities of sand suitable for building and concrete work. A free camping site near the town is transformed each spring into a gay and colorful village by a band of gypsies who park their cars beneath the pines and pitch their tents here.

HAZLEHURST, **111.3 m.** (256 alt., 1,378 pop.), seat of Jeff Davis County, was incorporated in 1891. The town was first settled in the late 1850's, when the Macon & Brunswick Railroad was begun, and was named for the engineer who surveyed for the railroad. Hazlehurst is a tobacco market for the eastern part of the tobacco belt.

BAXLEY, **128.7 m.** (206 alt., 2,122 pop.) (*see* TOUR *4*), is at the junction with US 1 (*see* TOUR *4*).

Southeast of Baxley is the wiregrass section, which slopes gently toward the Atlantic Coast. In this part of the state there are no stock laws, and many hogs are branded and put out to graze until hog-killing time in the winter.

In JESUP, 160.2 m. (100 alt., 2,303 pop.), incorporated in 1878 and the seat of Wayne County, the sandy streets are shaded by giant oak trees. The principal sources of income are farming, naval-stores production, and lumber milling.

LOVER'S OAK, with a limb spread of 150 feet, is one of the oldest trees in the state.

Jesup is at a junction with State 38 (*see* TOUR *18*).

Right from Jesup on unpaved State 23 to the junction with a dirt road, **16 m.**; R. on this road is MCKINNON, **17 m.** (65 alt., 81 pop.), a community settled by twenty-five families of Finns in 1920. On their 3,000-acre tract of swampland they produce staple crops and vegetables, raise poultry, and operate a dairy. The farm is cultivated by the community as a whole, profits and losses are shared equally, and all members, regardless of the work done, receive the same wages. A commissary provides needed supplies and serves as a local market for some of the farm products. All implements and all land are jointly owned except the lots on which the private homes of the members are built.

BRUNSWICK, **200.5 m.** (11 alt., 14,022 pop.) (*see* TOUR *1*), is the junction with US 17 (*see* TOUR *1*).

TOUR 13
(*Knoxville, Tenn.*) — *Blue Ridge* — *Ellijay* — *Canton* — *Marietta; State 5.*

Tennessee Line to Marietta, 95.9 m. — Roadbed hard-surfaced throughout, about one-third concrete — Murphy Branch of the Louisville & Nashville R.R. roughly parallels route — Limited accommodations.

Between the Tennessee Line and the mining and textile areas around Marietta, this route crosses ridges of the Copperhill basin and the wooded mountains of the Chattahoochee National Forest area and of the Tate region. In spring the mountains are pink with the delicate shades of rhododendron, laurel, and blossoming fruit trees. In autumn the oak leaves, turning a russet color, contrast with the gold of hickory and the dark green of pines and hemlocks, and the meadows are colorful with goldenrod, daisies, and wild asters. The Tate region is noted for its valuable marble deposits and its summer resorts.

In the mountainous northern sections, the early settlers laboriously cultivated their own stony lands, owned few slaves, and remained politically and socially aloof from the slave-holding cotton planters. There are few Negroes. Some of the northern counties poll a strong Republican vote in this otherwise solidly Democratic state.

State 5 crosses the clear TOCCOA RIVER, 0 m., the boundary between Georgia and Tennessee, at a point about a hundred miles south of Knoxville, Tennessee.

Between the Tennessee Line and Ellijay State 5 runs through the purchase area of the Chattahoochee National Forest (*see* TOUR 6).

MCCAYSVILLE, 0.1 m. (1,500 alt., 1,969 pop.), is inhabited principally by employees of the mines and smelters of a copper company across the river in Copperhill, Tennessee.

For several miles southeast of McCaysville there is a great stretch of waste land where escaping sulphuric fumes from the smelters have destroyed plant life and heavy rains have washed away all the fertile soil. The steep slopes of more than 100,000 acres in Georgia and Tennessee are as barren as deserts and have been worn down by erosion to the basic mineral formations and igneous rocks. Although the scene is one of desolation, it has a certain stark beauty when the sunset paints the ridges in bold colors.

BLUE RIDGE, 11.6 m. (1,751 alt., 1,190 pop.), seat of Fannin County, was incorporated in 1887 but remained unimportant until 1895, when the Louisville & Nashville Railroad was brought here. It is a trim little town, a center for farming, timbering, and mining operations. The beauty of the surrounding mountains has made it popular as a summer resort. This vicinity was a stronghold of the Cherokee, whose occupancy is attested by the arrowheads, spear points, and pottery found here.

Left from Blue Ridge on paved US 76 to LAKE BLUE RIDGE (Lake Toccoa) (*hunting; fishing, June to Oct.; swimming; boating*), 3.6 m., formed by impounding the Toccoa River with an immense earthen dam, along the crest of which the highway passes. The narrow lake, twelve miles long, is the largest in the state and has a brilliant blue color, unusual in Georgia. Its 102-mile shore is privately owned and is a popular site for summer homes. Rainbow trout, bream, and smallmouthed black bass are plentiful; the muskellunge, locally known as jackfish, is relatively abundant, and specimens have been caught weighing as much as eighteen pounds and measuring forty inches in length. During the winter months wild ducks and wild geese are hunted at the lake, and wild turkeys in the near-by mountains. Although Virginia white-tailed deer are frequently seen in these ranges, the state game laws prohibit hunting them until 1940.

ELLIJAY, 27 m. (1,298 alt., 657 pop.), seat of Gilmer County, is a pleasing, well-kept village built around a grass-covered square with a rock fountain. It is named for a Cherokee village on this site that was called Elatseyi (Ind., place of green things), probably suggested by the valleys of the Ellijay and Cartecay rivers. Rainbow-trout and black-bass fishing is excellent along these rivers, which converge near Ellijay to form the Coosawattee River. The town was incorporated in 1834, two years after the creation of the county.

In addition to shipping many varieties of apples to middle western markets, Ellijay produces a good grade of Elberta peaches and cans fruits and vegetables. During late March and early April pink peach blossoms and white apple blossoms are beautiful against the darkly wooded mountains.

Ellijay is on the southern boundary of the Chattahoochee National Forest Purchase Area (*see* TOUR 6).

Here is a junction with US 76 (*see* TOUR 2A).

At 28.9 m. (R) is a GRISTMILL with a large overshot water wheel that is still in use.

Beneath JASPER, 47.5 m. (1,500 alt., 563 pop.), the seat of Pickens County, are the Georgia marble beds. This trading center for farmers was incorporated in 1857 and named for Sergeant William Jasper, a Revolutionary hero (*see* TOUR 1).

Left from Jasper on State 108, an unpaved but improved road, to the junction with another dirt road, 0.3 m.; R. 1.7 m. on this road is Long Swamp Creek. Just east of the creek a trail leads downstream for a hundred feet and then up the slope of the mountain for seventy-five feet to COVE MOUNTAIN CAVE (*dangerous without a local guide*). The unlighted caverns have been partly explored and contain many chambers with rock formations, streams, and pools.

State 108 winds through a mountainous region of dense forests and deep ravines to the entrance of the TATE MOUNTAIN ESTATES, 10.4 m., a resort development. Right 0.2 m. on a winding graveled road is (R) a public PICNIC GROUND.

At 1.5 m. is the junction with another road. Left on this road to LAKE SEQUOYAH (*golf course, tennis courts, shooting boxes, water sports, and fishing, for lodge guests and residents only*), named for the Indian who created the Cherokee syllabary (*see* TOUR 2). A small summer colony, with homes owned principally by Atlanta people, has been developed on the shores of the lake, which is heavily stocked with black bass and bream.

At 2.7 m. from State 108 on the first graveled road, which completely encircles MOUNT BURRELL (3,300 alt.), is (R) CONNAHAYNEE LODGE (*open May 20-Oct. 31*), crowning the treeless summit of the mountain. This rambling, two-story chestnut log building with a stone foundation is set in the midst of attractively landscaped grounds. From the lodge flagstone walks lead to many vantage points, from which the surrounding area is visible for many miles on all sides. To the north are the towering peaks of Tickanetly Range; to the northeast are the distant ranges of the Great Smoky Mountains of Tennessee and North Carolina; and to the northwest, rising above the lowlands of the Appalachian Valley, is the distant plateau of Lookout Mountain. To the south, past the foothills of the Piedmont region, Kennesaw and Stone mountains, fifty and eighty miles away respectively, are visible on a clear day.

Throughout the woods of the slopes and valleys are azalea, blood-red Indian paintbrush, rhododendron, laurel, and trailing arbutus. There is an abundant growth of holly, dogwood, and galax, many red and white oaks, and hickory, beech, birch, and pine trees. The wild life of the estates includes turkeys, quail, ducks, deer, and pheasants. Wildcats and other predatory animals are being exterminated.

At 8.7 m. on this graveled road is the summit of MOUNT OGLETHORPE (3,290 alt.), a bald mountain crowned by a white marble shaft erected as a MEMORIAL TO GENERAL JAMES E. OGLETHORPE, founder of Georgia. This peak affords a spectacular view.

Mount Oglethorpe is the terminus of the 2,050-mile Appalachian Trail (*see* TOUR *13A*).

South of Jasper the steps and walks of even the smaller houses along the highway are of marble, which contrasts strikingly with the informality of the buildings.

Near TATE, **52.5 m.** (approx. 1,300 alt., 1,548 pop.), the home of the Georgia Marble Company, is a marble vein that is a solid block three-eighths of a mile wide, four miles long, and from a twenty-sixth to a half of a mile deep. Although the stone has been quarried for fifty years, only the surface of a few acres has been removed. The marble, in various colors—several shades of pink with intricate veins, light and dark grays, dark blue, and white—is remarkably free of impurities, fine-grained, and durable as well as beautiful. Georgia marble has been used in forty-six states, Mexico, Canada, Cuba, and Italy. Among the buildings constructed of it are the federal reserve banks of Cleveland, Detroit, and Atlanta; the state capitols of Utah and Rhode Island; the Corcoran Art Gallery and the Lincoln Memorial in Washington, D. C.; the Field Museum of Natural History in Chicago; and the Stock Exchange addition in New York.

In 1840 the first marble was quarried here by Terry Fitzsimmons; in 1850 Tate, Atkinson, & Company was formed; and in 1884, when the Georgia Marble Company was organized by northern capitalists, extensive improvements in methods of quarrying were made. Because of poor transportation facilities this organization did not succeed, and in 1905 the company was sold to Sam Tate, who owned the property. At first the quarrying was done by means of diamond drills and saws, but now steam drills, channeling machines, derricks, and traveling cranes are used to cut and move the blocks.

The employees live near the quarry in company-owned homes, many with garden plots and garages. As the community is not incorporated, there are no city taxes. Schools, churches, and recreational fields are provided, but employees must comply with certain restrictions concerning dancing and the use of alcohol.

BALL GROUND, **59.5 m.** (approx. 1,200 alt., 706 pop.), incorporated in 1883, developed about a small settlement where the Marietta & North Georgia Railroad established a station. At Ball Ground are a marble-finishing plant, a monument works, and several sawmills and cotton gins. The village was named for a large field where the Cherokee played a native game that developed into modern lacrosse. The ball used by the Indians was made of a piece of scraped deerskin, moistened and stuffed with deer's hair, and strongly sewed with deer sinews. The rackets were approximately two feet long, the flattened lower end resembling the palm of the hand.

CANTON, 71.1 m. (894 alt., 2,892 pop.), seat of Cherokee County, was incorporated in 1833 as Etowah, but the following year it was named for the Chinese city because two prominent settlers who had arrived in 1831 engaged in silk culture, an industry that flourished for a time. Although a public school, known as Etowah Academy, was begun in 1833, Canton remained a very small village until the Marietta & North Georgia Railroad was run through the town in 1879. The *Cherokee Advance,* a weekly newspaper established in 1880, gave the town so much publicity that lowlanders began to spend their summers in this mountain town.

R. T. Jones (1850-1937), grandfather of the golfer Bobby Jones, lived in Canton. Known to the townspeople simply as Mr. R. T., he was influential in the development of the town and the surrounding counties. As early as 1880 he acted as banker for Canton; in 1891 he was instrumental in having a marble-finishing works established here; in 1892 he founded a bank, of which he was elected president in 1894; and in 1899 he established a textile mill. About one-third of Canton's population works in the two units of the local mill.

MARIETTA, 95.9 m. (1,118 alt., 7,638 pop.) (*see* TOUR 2), is at the junction with US 41 (*see* TOUR 2).

TOUR 13A

North Carolina Line — Neel Gap — Amicalola Falls — Mount Oglethorpe; 100.7 m., Appalachian Trail.

Accommodations: At intervals of about 10 miles are stone or log huts that provide shelter for from 4 to 8 people. Camp sites, springs of drinking water (widely separated), and points of interest are marked. The nearest settlements are mostly to the north and west of the trail. A few stores for food supplies — Watch for rattlesnakes and highland moccasins.

The Appalachian Trail is a 2,050-mile hiking route running along the crest of the Appalachian Highland between Mount Katahdin in

Maine and the summit of Mount Oglethorpe in north Georgia. It is well blazed and identified by metal markers bearing the symbol of thirteen affiliated Appalachian Trail clubs. On the hundred-mile Georgia section of the route, maintained by the U. S. Forest Service and the Georgia Appalachian Trail Club, are a site of an Indian battle, a national game refuge, and a spectacular waterfall.

The trail passes through a region beautiful for its dense woodlands, its cascades, and for the deep blue color of the Appalachian Highland when seen from the eastern plateau. It is because of this hazy, almost violet hue that the range is called the Blue Ridge. The crests are not level like those in Virginia, but are frequently broken by rounded peaks with the well-worn, gentle slopes characteristic of all old mountains. Although the peaks rise gradually, some are 2,500 feet above the surrounding 2,000-foot elevation. Except for an occasional bald summit or an exposed rock cliff, the entire region is covered densely with hardwoods and conifers including pine, spruce, and hemlock.

Many small, rapid streams cross the forests that are gay in spring with the pale pink of rhododendron, the white of dogwood, and the vivid colors of wild azalea. In autumn the deeper hues of oak and maple, gum and hickory enrich the somber landscape.

This part of Georgia was occupied by the Cherokee Nation until 1838, when the Indians were forcibly exiled (see TOUR 2). In intelligence and general culture the Cherokee were one of the most highly developed tribes within the present boundaries of the United States. Several mounds, a few scattered pictographs, and such musical place names as Enotah, Hiawassee, Toccoa, Unicoi, and Chestatee are among the souvenirs they have left.

The Appalachian Trail crosses the North Carolina Line, **0 m.**, over RICH KNOB MOUNTAIN (about 4,000 alt.), which has a trail shelter near its summit, and immediately enters the CHATTAHOOCHEE NATIONAL FOREST (see TOUR 6).

At DICK'S CREEK GAP, **8.6 m.** (2,668 alt.), is a junction with US 76 (see TOUR 7), the Henry Grady Scenic Highway. This gap can be reached from Clayton (see TOUR 7) or Blairsville (see TOUR 6).

SNAKE MOUNTAIN, **9.5 m.** (3,365 alt.), has a log shelter hut with enclosed fireplace and bunks to accommodate four to eight people.

South of Snake Mountain the crest of the Blue Ridge falls to a relatively low "sag," which in mountaineer dialect is known as the "Swag of the Blue Ridge." In one of the most isolated highland sections, the "swag" is a vantage point for broad, spectacular views. On the east is the placid expanse of Lake Burton (see TOUR 7), and on the west ridge upon ridge extends to the Great Smoky Mountains.

The Montray Appalachian Trail Shelter, **19.9 m.**, is on the northern side of TRAY MOUNTAIN (4,398 alt.). The summit, **20.1 m.**, is a scenic vantage point popular with hikers.

INDIAN GRAVE GAP, **22.5 m.** (about 3,400 alt.), was named for the isolated stone cairn in the level portion of the gap at the junction of the trail with a forest service road. This rounded mound, about two feet high and eight feet in circumference, supposedly marks the grave of an Indian.

UNICOI GAP, **25.3 m.** (2,963 alt.), at the junction of the trail with State 75, can be reached from Cleveland on the south and Young Harris and Hiawassee on the north (*see* TOUR 6). State 75 follows the route of a Colonial trail, which British soldiers from Charleston, South Carolina, and Augusta followed to Fort Loudon on the Tennessee River near the present site of Knoxville. In 1812 a company, formed by coastal traders interested in commerce with the Cherokee Nation, graded the trail and made a toll road called the Unicoi Turnpike. After this time a trading post was established in almost every village throughout the Cherokee land.

ROCKY KNOB, **28.7 m.** (about 3,600 alt.), has an Appalachian Trail shelter, a spring, and an excellent camp site.

CHATTAHOOCHEE GAP, **30.5 m.** (about 3,600 alt.), is within a hundred yards of the spring (L) that is the source of the Chattahoochee River. Throughout its upper course the river is clear, but it becomes muddy long before it reaches Atlanta.

Left from Chattahoochee Gap on the Enotah Trail to the junction with an unblazed path, **0.3 m.**; L. on this path about thirty yards to an old CAVE HOUSE, entered by an opening in the face of a steep cliff. This entrance is protected by an artificial stone wall of dry masonry covered with dense, slow-growing lichens. Within the cave, which is large enough for several men to stand erect, are the ashes of long-dead fires. The presence of lichens indicates that the structure has stood for many years, and several theories have been advanced to account for its occupancy. Some people believe that it was a place of refuge for Indians during the Cherokee Removal; others, that it was occupied by fugitives from military service during the War between the States; and yet others, that it was the habitation of desperadoes who are known to have raided this region in the 1830's, during the days of the Dahlonega gold rush.

On the Enotah Trail at **5.5 m.** is the bald summit of MOUNT ENOTAH (4,784 alt.), known locally as Brasstown Bald (*see* TOUR 6), the highest peak in Georgia.

TESNATEE (Ind., wild turkey) GAP, **41 m.** (3,138 alt.), in an isolated and rugged region, was until 1923 the only entrance to the Nottely River valley from the south.

NEEL (FROGTOWN) GAP, **46.8 m.** (3,108 alt.), is at the junction with US 19 (*see* TOUR 6) and the southern entrance of VOGEL STATE PARK (*see* TOUR 6).

BLOOD MOUNTAIN, **48.9 m.** (4,463 alt.), is a scenic vantage point popular with sightseers because of its easy accessibility from Neel Gap. On its summit, the highest point of the Appalachian Trail in Georgia, is a stone shelter for hikers.

The name of the mountain commemorates a legendary Indian battle fought on its slopes. Near the summit is the ROCK HOUSE, a cave extending about fifty feet into the native rock. According to Cherokee legends, the cave entrance gave access to the subterranean dwellings of Yunwee Chuns Dee (Ind., little folk), a spritelike people whose magic music was heard on the mountain slopes. Other fabulous people of this region were the Nunne-hee, an invincible race of normal size who always aided those lost or injured on the wild mountains. Cherokee children were the special wards of the kindly Nunne-hee folk. Within recent years Indians have been known to return to search for treasure said to be hidden in the Rock House.

BLOOD AND SLAUGHTER GAP, **49.6 m.** (approx. 3,850 alt.), the pass between Blood and Slaughter mountains, is the site of the traditional battle for which the mountains were named. During a fierce engagement here the Cherokee are said to have defeated the Creek who were encroaching upon their territory. Many arrowheads and spear points have been found in the gap.

WOODY GAP, **56.8 m.** (approx. 3,300 alt.), is marked by a "TOTEM POLE" carved with symbols of stream and timberland—a fish, a pick, a dogwood blossom. Erected by the forest service, the pole is topped with the sturdy figure of a forest ranger.

Right from Woody Gap on a paved forest service road to the TOCCOA BASIN RANGER STATION (*see* TOUR 6), 2 m. (*telephone and telegraph service; first aid station; store*).

From Woody Gap an alternate route leads straight ahead through open fields to the SUMMIT OF BLACK MOUNTAIN, 0.5 m. (about 3,800 alt.), which affords a magnificent view. A fire lookout tower and a guard's house are on the top.

The main trail follows the south side of Black Mountain.

HIGHTOWER GAP (about 2,900 alt.) is at **70.6 m.** About 200 yards L. of the gap is the source of the Etowah River, which in its upper course is locally called the Hightower River. Both names, as well as that of the gap, are corruptions of Itawa, a Cherokee word believed to be derived from Italwa (Creek, the town where).

Right from Hightower Gap on a graveled forest service road to the CHATTA-HOOCHEE GAME REFUGE RANGER STATION (*emergency accommodations; first aid;*

telephone and telegraph service), **0.5 m.** The state department of wild life maintains a small fish hatchery here and a rearing pool for trout.

Southwest of Hightower Gap the trail follows a forest service road along the eastern boundary of the CHATTAHOOCHEE GAME REFUGE, a 20,000-acre state and Federal game and wild-life preserve. Black bears, recently introduced into this region, are rare, but visitors often encounter white-tailed deer, wild turkeys, or ruffed grouse. Although the streams through this area are filled with rainbow and brook trout, the management permits fishing only at stated periods.

HAWK MOUNTAIN, **71.6 m.** (3,619 alt.), lies within the game refuge. On its bald summit are provisions for shelter, a steel watchtower, and the forest ranger's house.

SPRINGER MOUNTAIN, **77.8 m.** (3,820 alt.), on the edge of the game refuge, has on its northern slope a log shelter enclosed on three sides. Under the eaves of the hut on the open side is a large fireplace for the use of campers.

Until the second decade of the twentieth century, when rural churches became more widely distributed, people from several counties gathered on this mountain once each year for religious services that lasted a week or two. The mountaineers trudged daily over the rough roads of this wild land. Natives still point out PULPIT ROCK, which was used by the preacher.

Although it is in the midst of the Georgia highland region, Springer Mountain is the southernmost peak of the Blue Ridge, which runs northwest from this point into North Carolina. South of Springer Mountain the trail follows the crest of Amicalola (Ind., tumbling water) Ridge.

The trail leaves the Chattahoochee National Forest at a shelter hut (L), **84 m.**

AMICALOLA FALLS, **84.3 m.**, is little known because of its isolation. It is formed by a clear mountain creek plunging 729 feet down the eastern side of Amicalola Ridge in sparkling cascades and is generally considered one of the most beautiful sights in the state (*see* TOUR 6).

A country store (*staple provisions*), **89.3 m.**, marks the junction with unpaved State 43, which affords access to the trail from Ellijay (*see* TOUR *13*) on the west, and from US 19 (*see* TOUR 6) on the east.

At **94.7 m.** is the junction with a dirt road (L), now the route.

1. Right on this road to JASPER, **10 m.** (1,500 alt., 563 pop.) (*see* TOUR *13*), which is at the junction with State 5 (*see* TOUR *13*).

2. Straight ahead across this road is an alternate route through the TATE MOUNTAIN ESTATES, **2 m.** (*see* TOUR *13*).

Left on the dirt road to MOUNT OGLETHORPE, **100.7 m.** (*see* TOUR *13*), the southernmost peak (3,290 alt.) of the main mass of the Appalachian Highland and the terminus of the Appalachian Trail.

TOUR 14

Eatonton — Milledgeville — Louisville — Sylvania — Savannah; 199.3 m., State 24 and State 21.

Roadbed hard-surfaced, mostly asphalt, except about 10 miles between Waynesboro and Sylvania, and 3 miles between Sylvania and Springfield — Savannah & Atlanta R.R. parallels route between Waynesboro and Savannah — All types of accommodations in Savannah; limited elsewhere.

This route reveals the sharp contrast between the typical old southern towns in the western part of the route and the newer sawmill villages near the South Carolina Line. As capitals of the state, both Milledgeville and Louisville were centers of wealth and social life in ante bellum days. The stately old houses of the plantation era are seen only in the towns, as the route does not follow the roads of early days.

Near Sandersville are valuable kaolin deposits. Much of this gently rolling sandy land is forested, and in the lowlands trees are covered with hanging moss. Although there are some pecan orchards, the principal crops are cotton and corn. The farmhouses in this thinly settled section are generally small and unpainted.

In the area south of Sylvania, lumber and turpentine are the principal industrial products, and the small towns with their frame houses sprawled along the railroad tracks look almost like frontier settlements. At intervals the road passes through pine forests where the scenery is so monotonous that it appears to be moving on a revolving belt. The sight of an occasional cultivated field or a black snake or a large terrapin in the road affords the only variety. Where the land in the low country is swampy, the oak trees are draped in moss.

Near Savannah the road approaches some abandoned settlements of the Salzburgers, Bavarian immigrants who played an important part in the early history of the state.

South of EATONTON, **0 m.** (approx. 575 alt., 1,876 pop.) (*see* TOUR *16*), State 24 and US 129 (*see* TOUR *16*) are united. At **2 m.** State 24 branches L.

MILLEDGEVILLE, 21 m. (326 alt., 5,534 pop.), laid out in 1803 as the site of the state capital, retains the precision of its original plan. Three twenty-acre plots were called Capitol, Government, and Penitentiary Squares, and another plot "reserved for public uses" was later made into Cemetery Square. These squares enclose an area of sixteen city blocks in which are most of the old houses. Capitol and Cemetery Squares are little changed, but the penitentiary has been removed and its site is now occupied by the Georgia State College for Women. Government Square is used as a recreation ground by the college.

The houses of Milledgeville typify the development of early nineteenth-century southern architecture. The earliest structures had small single-story stoops; the next had two porches, one above the other, with superimposed columns. When the Greek portico with full two-story columns was introduced, the second-story porch became a balcony; still later, mansions were built with broad, many-columned verandas that sometimes extended around three sides of the house. The well-proportioned classic portico with an elaborate doorway is more characteristic of Milledgeville homes, however, than are the spacious porches seen frequently in Athens and Washington. Although most of these houses are set too near the street, they still give an impression of serenity and aristocratic self-assurance.

In 1934 the city council voted to make Milledgeville a bird sanctuary, and the fact that birds are protected here is announced on all highways leading into the town.

It is believed that this section was settled by the Hitchiti Indians before the coming of the Creek, and some historians have sought to establish a point on the eastern bank of the Oconee River, about six miles from the present city, as the site of a village which Hernando De Soto visited in 1540. A near-by Indian council place called Rock Landing was later the unloading point for all goods brought up the river.

Near the landing is the SITE OF FORT FIDIUS, the largest garrison of Federal troops south of the Ohio, which was established here in 1793. Other forts constructed within the next few years included Fort Wilkinson, a few miles north, where representatives from thirty-two Creek towns signed the Indian treaty of 1802 and thereby ceded the lands of this section to the state.

When the newly acquired Indian territory was being developed under the land-lottery system, Louisville seemed too far east to remain the capital; consequently, in 1803 the legislature created this town near the center of the state and named it for John Milledge, Revolutionary soldier, who was then Governor. In 1807 the transfer of the treasury and the state records from Louisville to Milledgeville was made by wagons, escorted by a troop of cavalry sent from Washington, D. C., and Milledgeville became the second Georgia town to be laid out as a state capital.

On his march to the sea in 1864, General Sherman spared the city except for burning the state penitentiary. In 1868 Atlanta was made the capital, but some of the state institutions have remained in Milledgeville. From 1871 to 1879 the old capitol building served as the Baldwin County courthouse; since that time it has been used for educational purposes.

The HARRIS HOME (*private*) 400 block W. Montgomery St., was built by Judge Iverson Louis Harris in 1832. The two-story frame dwelling, with heavy chimneys and a front porch ornamented with Victorian banisters, pendants, and brackets, stands close to the oak-shaded street. Judge Harris planted the double row of oaks on Clarke and Hancock Streets so that he might walk to his office down a shaded avenue.

The GEORGIA STATE COLLEGE FOR WOMEN (*open 9-5; guides obtainable at bursar's office*), bounded by Clarke, Montgomery, Hancock, and Wilkinson Sts., was created by legislative act in 1889 as the Georgia Normal and Industrial College and was opened in 1891. Many private schools had failed to open after the War between the States and there was need of a college with low tuition fees; consequently, the institution grew rapidly. In 1917 the legislature changed the charter to permit the granting of degrees, and in 1922 the school was given its present name and became the chief women's college of the state system.

On a spacious campus shaded by old oak trees are the twenty buildings of the college. Most of them are of red brick trimmed with limestone and adorned with white Corinthian columns. Ten dormitories accommodate 1,500 students.

The INA DILLARD RUSSELL LIBRARY (*open*), on the college campus at Clarke and Montgomery Sts., is a stately building with Corinthian columns supporting a Greek pediment. The library, with a capacity of 100,000 volumes, has an excellent collection of books on Georgia history and a valuable file of old newspapers. On the top floor of this building is the GEORGIA HISTORY MUSEUM (*open*), begun by Amanda Johnson, head of the department of history. It contains a letter from Jefferson Davis, original stamps of the British Stamp Act, and Indian artifacts.

The BROWN-STETSON-SANFORD HOUSE (*private*), Wilkinson St. between Greene and Washington Sts., was erected in 1812. This square, clapboard structure of post-Colonial design has a hipped roof, a stately, two-story Greek Revival portico with square Doric columns at the first story and slender Ionic columns above, supporting a pediment, and a fanlighted doorway. Massive chimneys lend dignity to the building.

Within are beautiful inlaid mantels, paneled wainscotings, old furnishings, and a circular staircase. This house was originally a part of the United States Hotel, a fashionable hostelry in the years when Milledgeville was the state capital. Since 1857 it has been a private residence.

The OLD EXECUTIVE MANSION (*open 9-5 by appointment*), center of block on Clarke between Hancock and Greene Sts., is one of the finest and best preserved of the old Greek Revival houses in Georgia. Visible beyond a garden planted with oaks, boxwood, and iris is the impressive Ionic portico topped with a classic pediment. Pilasters at the corners accentuate the simplicity and dignity of the house, and a small cupola adds to the height. Back of the square entrance hall is a rotunda, fifty feet high, with a dome decorated in gold and a mezzanine floor with a mahogany railing. The old salon has been converted into two rooms, each containing a black marble mantel and a center plaster medallion from which hangs a handsome chandelier.

The design of the house, constructed in 1838 at a cost of $50,000, was based upon that of Palladio's Villa, built in Italy during the fourteenth century. An entry in the state treasurer's report, dated March 20, 1837, reads: "John Pell, $100 for the best plan for a house for the residence of the governor, as approved by the committee." An identical check made to C. B. McCluskey on April 19, 1837, leaves doubt as to whether one of these men designed the mansion or whether they collaborated. Up to 1879 it served as the home of eight successive Georgia governors and since 1890 has been the home of the presidents of the Georgia State College for Women.

The SANFORD-POWELL-BINION HOME (*private*), W. Greene and Clarke Sts., is a handsome clapboarded Greek Revival house with fourteen Doric columns around the front and sides. Exceedingly well kept, it is set on a small lawn planted with beautiful shrubbery and shade trees. The house was built about 1825 by General John Sanford, who surrounded it with boxwood gardens and built many greenhouses. The original plan specified only four columns, but as building progressed, the number grew. The general was often heard to chuckle and say, "Got to sell another slave; my wife wants four more columns."

The WARD-BEALL-CLINE HOUSE (*private*), 305 W. Greene St., is an irregular, white clapboard house with four Ionic columns. The hip and mansard roof, the "widow's walk" or railed platform on top of the house, and the balustrades around the first and second floor gallery porches give it an ornate appearance. The columns belonged to the house as originally built, but the elaborate balustrades have been added. The date of the building is not known, but a record of the legislature in 1838 shows that the house was leased for the Governor while the executive mansion was being built. The unusual openwork brick wall enclosing the garden once surrounded the entire block. An old lamp to the left of the entrance was used in Savannah during early days.

The WILLIAMS-ORME-CRAWFORD HOUSE (*private*), S. Liberty and Washington Sts., built in 1820, is distinctive for its two slender Doric columns, delicate fanlighted doorways, simple balcony, and massive end chimneys. The house is well preserved and little changed from its original condition.

The WILLIAMS-JONES-FERGUSON HOUSE (*private*), S. Liberty and Washington Sts., a white frame post-Colonial house with excellently proportioned front doors opening upon a central portico and hanging second-story balcony, was built in 1817 by Peter J. Williams. The boxwood hedges surrounding the lot and the wistaria vines clinging to the old trees were planted in the original garden soon after the house had been built. Among the rare plants are two spikenard trees, one blue and the other pink. Within the house are many old furnishings, valuable paintings, and files of the *Georgia Journal,* a newspaper founded in Milledgeville in 1809 and merged with the *Macon Messenger* in 1847. For a while it was published by Fleming Grantland, a kinsman of Mrs. Ferguson.

The house claims a ghost that followed the Williams family from Wales to Virginia in 1715, and then migrated with them to Georgia. There is another legend that a fabulous treasure is buried on the grounds.

MILLEDGEVILLE CEMETERY, at the end of Liberty St., is a peaceful, secluded place made beautiful by shrubs, flowers, and trees, including Norway spruces, Chinese yews, and Italian cypresses. The GRAVE OF GENERAL JETT THOMAS, an officer in the War of 1812, is marked by a monument. An old-fashioned slab built two and a half feet above ground marks the GRAVE OF DAVID BRYDIE MITCHELL, Governor of Georgia (1809-13 and 1815-17). In the Lamar lot, identified by a tall monument, are the GRAVE OF ZACHARIAH LAMAR, a wealthy and influential farmer and merchant of ante bellum Georgia, and the GRAVE OF L. Q. C. LAMAR, SR. (1797-1834), a prominent lawyer and the brother of Zachariah Lamar. The oldest date recorded on a tombstone is 1804. The site of the first church (Methodist) erected in Milledgeville is indicated by a marker in the cemetery.

Within his family's brick vault a young man named Fish, who was facing dishonor for a crime of which he was innocent, is said to have locked himself to die. Each year hundreds of people visit the vault and peer into the deep keyhole of the marble door to see the key in the lock on the inside.

The OLD DARIEN BANK, Wilkinson and Greene Sts., is a severe two-story, red brick building with a gable roof and walls two and a half

SAVANNAH BEACH

ANGLING IN A NORTH GEORGIA STREAM

POSSUM HUNT

QUAIL HUNTING

HIKERS ON THE APPALACHIAN TRAIL

BOAT RACING ON A NORTH GEORGIA LAKE

NEGRO BASEBALL GAME

WAITING FOR A LOAD OF COTTON AT THE GIN

GOLF, SEA ISLAND

SWIMMING POOL AND BEACH, SEA ISLAND

QUAIL BREEDING FARM

WILD DEER, SOUTH GEORGIA

WILD DUCKS, PINE MOUNTAIN STATE PARK

TENNIS, SEA ISLAND

SANFORD STADIUM, UNIVERSITY OF GEORGIA

feet thick. Two short flights of steps on the front and a small stoop on the right side serve as entrances. The building, erected about 1820 as a branch of the Bank of Darien (*see* TOUR *1*), has served many purposes. In 1825 it was the Masonic lodge hall in which La Fayette was entertained. After 1834 it was used as the printing office of the *Federal Union,* a newspaper established in 1825 and combined with the *Southern Recorder* in 1872 to form the *Union Recorder,* which is still being published. Since the War between the States it has served as an apartment house, the barracks for Georgia Military College, and a tearoom. It is now the Darien Hotel. According to an unsubstantiated story, the committee which drew up the Ordinance of Secession met in this building.

OLD STATE CAPITOL (now Georgia Military College) (*open*), bounded by Wayne, Elberton, Franklin, and Greene Sts., near the business section, is a weathered gray stone building of Gothic Revival design with battlemented crestings. The main building, constructed by Jett Thomas and John Scott at a cost of $60,000, was completed in 1807 in time for the legislative session. One wing was added in 1828; the other, in 1837.

The secession convention met in this building on January 16, 1861. Since four states had already seceded from the Union, national attention was focused on Georgia's decision. Ex-Governor George W. Crawford, United States Senator Robert Toombs, and T. R. R. Cobb, younger brother of Howell Cobb, upheld the keynote of this convention: "We can make better terms out of the Union than in it." Alexander Stephens (*see* TOUR *17*), later Vice President of the Confederacy, Ex-Governor Herschel V. Johnson, and Ben H. Hill, later United States Senator, opposed secession. After three days of debate, the Secession Act was passed and signed by the members of the convention.

By the time Sherman reached Milledgeville most of the state documents had been removed from the capitol. The remaining books and papers were scattered, but many of the more important records were later recovered. During their occupation of Milledgeville, the Union troops held a mock session of the legislature in which they repealed the Secession Ordinance.

The entrance gates on the north and south are built in the same architectural style as the old capitol, and their three pointed arches and battlemented tops serve as fitting frames for the old building as seen from the streets.

To the right of the main driveway is the LA FAYETTE BOULDER, marking the spot where General La Fayette was entertained at a Georgia barbecue on his visit to the capital in March, 1825.

In 1879 the old statehouse was given to the newly-created Middle Georgia Military and Agricultural College, set up as a unit of the state university system. The school, renamed in 1900 the Georgia Military College, is now a preparatory school and junior college with a good military rating. The old statehouse contains the administrative offices and classrooms; the barracks to the left have accommodations for 300 pupils.

On the twenty-acre college campus is the gray stucco Georgia Military College Grade School, S. Wayne St., erected in 1926 and designed in the same architectural style as the old state capitol.

ST. STEPHENS PARISH CHURCH (*open upon application to church secretary*), S. Wayne St., also on the campus, is a small, frame, Gothic Revival structure built in 1843. In 1864 the building was partly destroyed by Union soldiers who used it for stabling horses, poured syrup down the pipes of the organ, burned some of the pews, and damaged the altar. The hand-carved chairs and altar, which replaced the old ones when the church was restored, are still in use. Beautiful memorial windows are behind the pulpit.

The SCOTT HOME (*private*), 300 block N. Jefferson St., a large, two-story frame house built about 1828, has a front door made of a hundred tiny pieces of wood representing almost every variety of tree grown in Georgia. This residence contains some old and valued records of the Revolutionary War and the War between the States. Many old costumes are carefully preserved. The bracketed cornice, louvered dormers, and latticed porch are later additions.

1. Right from Milledgeville on State 22 to the GEORGIA TRAINING SCHOOL FOR BOYS (*open*), 1.2 m., a reform school (L) for delinquents. On a 600-acre tract the state has erected seventeen buildings, of which three are substantial concrete structures. The institution cares for an average of 150 boys between the ages of ten and sixteen. About eighty-five of the inmates are white; most delinquent Negroes are confined in regular penal institutions. Regular common-school training through the seventh grade is provided, as well as courses in agriculture, reforestation, shoe repairing, and woodworkng. The institution was created as the Georgia State Reformatory in 1905 and its present name was adopted in 1919.

The GEORGIA STATE PRISON (R) 2.8 m., is housed in twenty-five buildings on a 4,000-acre farm. The main building is a rambling, red brick structure surrounded by well-kept grounds. Executive officers occupy the front of both floors. On the first floor are the dining halls, print shops, and machine shops. On the second floor are separate dormitories for white and Negro male prisoners. The women prisoners are housed in camps about a mile away. The large brick building (R) at a considerable distance from the main building is scientifically equipped to care for male tubercular patients, both white and Negro. The number of such patents, however, is small.

The greater part of the 1,000 inmates are white. Prisoners, though well cared for, receive no wages for the labor required of them. The diversified crops and livestock raised by the prisoners provide food for the entire institution. Negro women work in the fields, and white women sew for all the prisoners. All are allowed to listen to radio programs, and once a week motion pictures are shown. Church services are held each Sunday.

2. Right from Milledgeville on State 29 to a junction with a paved private road, 1 m.; L. 0.6 m. on this road to the GEORGIA STATE HOSPITAL (*open weekdays 9-11 and 2-4*); its sixty buildings accommodate more than 6,000 mental patients and 712 employees. On the 2,500 acres of land are numerous flower gardens and groves of oak and pine trees. The main building, set on a wide expanse of rolling lawn, has a large circular dome and an Ionic-columned portico. To the rear and sides of the main building are dormitories, recreation halls, infirmaries, cottages for nurses and doctors, and the hospital farms. The act establishing the institution was passed by the legislature in December, 1837. The hospital, at first known as the Lunatic Asylum of the State of Georgia, was opened in November, 1842.

On State 29 is LOCKERLY (*private*) at 1.3 m., a Greek Revival house (L) built by Judge Daniel R. Tucker about 1839. The commodious, square, stone house, with its six massive Doric columns, stands on an eminence and is surrounded by old-fashioned boxwood gardens and magnolia trees. Extending across the front of the yard is a wrought-iron fence made in England. Judge Tucker, reputed to be the wealthiest man in the community, was ordered by Sherman's soldiers to reveal the hiding place of his silver. Tucker outwitted the Federals by giving directions to one of his plantations a few miles south although the silver was actually hidden beneath the smokehouse in the back yard here. As the direction given was on the line of march, the soldiers never returned.

At 1.8 m. is a junction with the Henry Dawson Allen Memorial Drive. Right on this to (R) ROCKWELL MANSION (*private*), 1.9 m., built about 1830 by Colonel W. S. Rockwell. The wide expanse of lawn, surrounded by a wrought-iron fence with handsome gateways, is shaded by many beautiful oak and magnolia trees. A long flight of steps leads to the central portico, which has four Ionic columns and a delicate grillwork balcony flanked by two Doric pilasters. Especially notable is the elliptical arch fanlight above the door. One of the owners of this house was Herschel V. Johnson, Governor of Georgia in 1853 and candidate for Vice President of the United States in 1860.

The SITE OF OGLETHORPE UNIVERSITY, 2.5 m., is now occupied by the Allen Invalid Home, a private sanitarium for mental cases. A manual training school was opened here in 1835 and a year later was taken over by the trustees of the newly chartered Oglethorpe University, organized by the Presbyterian Church. Forced to close in 1862 when the students were conscripted for the Confederate Army, Oglethorpe never reopened here but was refounded in Atlanta in 1916 (*see* ATLANTA).

THALIAN HALL (*open*), erected (R) by the Thalian Literary Society, is the only school building which remains, and it is now used as one of the hospital buildings. On the second floor is the SIDNEY LANIER ROOM, which the poet occupied as a student.

In the Scottsboro community, 5 m., is the SCOTT-CARTER-FURMAN-SMITH HOUSE (*private*), a white clapboarded structure built by General John Scott in 1806. The porch extending around two sides of the long house is covered with wistaria, and the house itself is almost hidden from view by large trees. In 1813 Colonel Farish Carter bought the house and made many improvements, among which was the double "breezeway" which forms a cross passage through the center of the house. In some of the rooms heavy damask curtains and furniture remain as they were in ante bellum times. Carter made presents of building lots from his plantation to many of his friends who lived in the southern part of the state. They built houses for occupation during the summer; thus the Scottsboro community was formed.

At the Cooperville School (R), **8.8 m.**, is a junction with another dirt road; R. on this road to the STEVENS POTTERY (*open 9-5 weekdays*), **9.8 m.**, in a small village of the same name. This plant, housed in eight or nine long brick buildings, was organized in 1861 by Crawford and John Henry Stevens. Between eighty and a hundred people are employed in the manufacture of such products as firebrick, hollow tile, and pipe. Much of the material used is obtained from near-by clay pits. In front of the general offices is a large stone wheel, the first crusher used in the factory. Fine pottery and brick made here in the nineteenth century are still in use in many houses and buildings throughout the state.

State 24 and State 22 unite for 4.2 miles east of Milledgeville.

At **23.1 m.** is the junction with an unimproved dirt road.

Left on this road to the junction with another dirt road, **3.1 m.**; R. on this second road to another junction, **3.4 m.**; L. on this third road to the MITCHELL-MCCOMB HOUSE (*private*), **4.3 m.** A cedar-bordered driveway (L) leads from the stone and tabby entrance posts to the white weatherboarded house, of a transitional type of architecture combining Georgian Colonial and Classical Revival styles. The two-story portico, rising above the roof of the first floor, has two orders of columns, Doric below and Ionic above, and fanlighted doorways open on each porch. The date 1823 stamped on the gutters indicates the approximate time in which the house was erected. David B. Mitchell, Governor of Georgia 1809-13 and 1815-17, built the house, called it Mount Nebo, and fitted it out with lightning rods tipped with gold—some say with gold dollars. His slaves carved the mantels and interior woodwork. A graceful mahogany stairway curves to the second floor at the rear of the semicircular reception hall.

After Mitchell's death in 1837 the property was sold to Robert McComb and came to be known as McComb's Mount. For generations the Mount was well known for the hospitality of its owner, who gave fashionable parties and picnics. It is said that Uncle Ned, a slave on this plantation, had been brought from North Carolina without his wife, Aunt Silvy. Years afterward a wagonload of slaves happened to stop at the Milledgeville hotel on its way south. Uncle Ned saw Aunt Silvy and reported the fact to his master, who reunited the old couple.

At **25.2 m.** is the eastern junction with State 22 (*see* TOUR *14A*).

BOYKIN HALL (*open*), **31 m.**, a two-story white frame house (L) set well back from the road, was built by Samuel Boykin in 1830. It has a large Palladian doorway with a fanlight above and a portico ornamented with two Doric columns. At the time it was built it was the only painted house in the community and was known as the White House. Today the plantation is called the Indian Island Farm and Ranch for the INDIAN MOUNDS on the plantation, from which artifacts have been sent to the Museum of the American Indian, Heye Foundation, in New York City.

At **39 m.** is a junction with a side road.

Left on this road to a large KAOLIN MINE, **1 m.**, which has been worked over a period of eleven years but must soon be abandoned because quicksand and water have been reached in almost all parts of the area. Although digging must be done by hand in most mines, the fine, chalklike clay in this section is so pure that it is unnecessary to have the various layers separated, and steam shovels are used.

SANDERSVILLE, **50.6 m.** (445 alt., 3,011 pop.), seat of Washington County, was established in 1796 and incorporated in 1812. As an outpost of Georgia's early white settlements, the town suffered many Indian depredations. Like its neighboring towns, Sandersville is pleasantly old-fashioned in its architecture and shady streets.

1. Right from Sandersville on S. Harris St. to the junction with a little-used, unpaved street just within the city limits; R. on this street to the junction of three roads, 0.2 m. The central road leads to the LIME SINKS, 0.3 m., sunken places from twenty to twenty-five feet deep through which a bluish milky stream flows into the hillside. The extent of the caverns running back into the hillside is unknown, but it is said that they stretch beneath the entire town of Sandersville. Starfish and other marine fossils have been found near these sinks, which are caused by the dissolution of the lime contents of the soil.

2. Left from Sandersville on Harris St. to a junction with unpaved State 15; L. on State 15 is WARTHEN, 9 m. (490 alt., 150 pop.). In this town is the well-preserved WARTHEN JAIL of hewn logs, in which Aaron Burr was held overnight when being taken to Virginia in 1807 to face trial for treason. This small structure, ten by fifteen feet, was built about 1783.

LOUISVILLE, **76.6 m.** (337 alt., 1,650 pop.) (*see* TOUR *4*), is at the junction with US 1 (*see* TOUR *4*).

Between Louisville and Waynesboro, State 24 is known as the Nancy Hart Highway. A story relates that over this road the Revolutionary War heroine (*see* TOUR *3A*) came to rescue her son-in-law, Thompson, who had killed an insolent wagoner with a blow of his sword and was confined in the jail at Waynesboro. After one of her visits, the door of the jail was found ajar and the prisoner had vanished.

WAYNESBORO, **102.3 m.** (261 alt., 3,922 pop.) (*see* TOUR *15*), is at the junction with US 25 (*see* TOUR *15*).

State 24 between Waynesboro and Sylvania is called the George Washington Highway because President Washington and his escort traveled this route in 1791 from Augusta to Savannah.

The DELL HOUSE (*private*), **133.5 m.**, is about 200 yards (R) from the highway at the end of a dirt road. This simple, two-story, white frame building was constructed about 1815 with hand-hewn beams joined with wooden pegs. The house is the sole remaining structure of Jacksonboro, a village founded in 1794 as the first seat of Screven County. George White, in *Statistics of the State of Georgia* (1849), says of Jacksonboro: "The place had formerly a very bad character. It was reported that in the mornings after drunken frolics and fights you could see the children picking up eyeballs in tea saucers."

In 1830 Lorenzo Dow, an itinerant evangelist, came to Jacksonboro to conduct a meeting in the Methodist church. The citizens, considering him eccentric, not only prohibited his holding services but refused to give him shelter. Finally he was taken in at this house, then owned by the Goodall family. The next morning the townspeople escorted Dow across the rustic bridge and forbade his returning to the village. Indignant, the evangelist took off his shoes, shook the dust from them, and pronounced a curse upon everybody in Jacksonboro except the Goodalls and their home. After the removal of the county seat to Sylvania in 1847 Jacksonboro soon became a deserted village in which only the Dell house remains.

SYLVANIA, **139.2 m.** (238 alt., 1,781 pop.), was established in 1847 as the seat of Screven County. Its name, derived from *silva* (Lat., forest), was suggested by the wooded land on which it was built. Its chief industries are lumbering, from which fortunes have been made, and cotton cultivation, for which Screven County has one of the highest production records in the state. There are twenty cotton gins and eleven warehouses in the county.

At Sylvania is the junction with State 21, now the route. South of Sylvania State 21 passes through a level, pine-woods country, where there is an occasional farm or lumbering settlement.

SPRINGFIELD, **171.9 m.** (80 alt., 402 pop.), seat of Effingham County, was founded in 1799 and named for a mineral spring discovered in a near-by field.

RINCON (pronounced Rink'-on), **179 m.** (75 alt., 317 pop.), is a small town in a turpentining section.

Left from Rincon on the Ebenezer (Jerusalem Church) Road (*rough but passable*) to a fork, **1.3 m.**; L. from the fork to the junction with another road, **5 m.**; R. on this road to JERUSALEM CHURCH, **8 m.** The red brick building, completed in 1796, has a white boxlike steeple above the front of a high-pitched roof. This old church, in its setting of moss-covered trees, is the only building remaining of the once thriving Lutheran settlement of New Ebenezer.

The trustees of the colony invited the persecuted Salzburgers of Bavaria to come to Georgia, promising to pay their expenses, to allot each family fifty acres of land, and to provide for them until crops could be produced. The seventy-eight who came in 1734 were so pleased to have a home that they named their town Ebenezer (Heb., stone of help); but the soil proved so unproductive that, despite the arrival of 150 more refugees, the town did not prosper. In 1736 the colonists began to migrate to a high ridge near the Savannah River, where they formed another settlement and called it New Ebenezer. As other colonists arrived, this new town grew rapidly and its silk culture prospered. During the American Revolution, when New Ebenezer was occupied by the British, houses were burned, gardens were destroyed, and the church was used as a hospital. Efforts made after the war to regain its former prosperity were defeated by the failure of the silk industry and the rising importance of Savannah. New

Ebenezer claims to have had the first orphanage and the first organized Sunday school in the state.

The GOSHEN METHODIST CHURCH, **182 m.**, organized in 1822, is still active. Its building is the only remnant of the old settlement of Goshen which also declined with the rise of Savannah.

At **183.5 m.** is a junction with the dirt Rice Hope Plantation Road (*private*).

Left on this road to the SITE OF MULBERRY GROVE, **3 m.**, the former estate of General Nathanael Greene (1742-86), who succeeded Gates as commander of the southern army. The land, originally the estate of the loyalist lieutenant-governor, John Graham, was confiscated after the Revolution by the new State of Georgia and presented to Greene who had lost his estates by endorsing notes to secure supplies for the troops when he was quartermaster general. The general died here on June 19, 1786, but a tradition of lavish hospitality was maintained at this house until 1864, when the plantation was devastated by Sherman's army. In 1791 George Washington was a guest of his friend Mrs. Greene, and while living here in 1793 Eli Whitney invented his cotton gin.

On leaving Yale in 1792, Whitney (1765-1825) came to Georgia to serve as a tutor in a Savannah family, but on his arrival found the place filled. Having made the acquaintance of Mrs. Nathanael Greene on board the ship coming south, he was invited to make his home at Mulberry Grove. One morning he overheard a remark: "There is a fortune in store for someone who will invent a machine for separating the lint of cotton from the seed." Since he looked interested, Mrs. Greene pointed to him and said, "You are the very man, Mr. Whitney, for since you succeeded so well in repairing my watch, I am sure you will have the ingenuity to make such a machine." The young man made his own tools, shut himself in an improvised workship (*see* TOUR *8*), and devoted an entire winter to the task. The first machine he showed to Mrs. Greene had a revolving cylinder with hooks which caught the cotton and pulled it through a slit in a metal plate, leaving the seed behind; but there was no contrivance for throwing off the separated lint which wrapped around the cylinder. Mrs. Greene, seeing the difficulty, picked up a clothes brush, applied it to the teeth of the machine, and caught the lint upon it. "You have solved my problem!" delightedly exclaimed Whitney. "With this suggestion the machine is complete."

SAVANNAH, **199.3 m.** (21-65 alt., 85,024 pop.) (*see* SAVANNAH).

Points of Interest: Telfair Academy of Arts and Sciences, Armstrong Junior College, Atlantic Coast Line Docks, Herty Pulp and Paper Laboratory, Bethesda Orphanage, Wormsloe, and others.

Savannah is at the junction with US 80 (*see* TOUR 9) and with US 17 (*see* TOUR *1*).

TOUR 14A

Junction with State 24 — Sparta — Crawfordville; 44.9 m., State 22.

Roadbed asphalt-surfaced between State 24 and Sparta; dirt road between Sparta and Crawfordville — Georgia R.R. parallels route — Limited accommodations.

This route runs through a section which was developed in the latter part of the eighteenth century under the cotton plantation system. It is so remote from the main thoroughfares and railroad centers that it has retained much of its old-fashioned atmosphere. The area is primarily agricultural and produces cotton, livestock, feed crops, and pecans. Most of the farms are large and are worked by sharecroppers among whom Negroes predominate.

State 22 branches north from its junction with State 24 (*see* TOUR *14*), **0 m.**, at a point about 4 miles east of Milledgeville.

SPARTA, **20.8 m.** (557 alt., 1,613 pop.), was incorporated in 1805 as the seat of Hancock County. Overlooking the tree-shaded square of the business section is the usual red brick courthouse of late Victorian design. The narrow, unpaved streets of the residential section are bordered with elms and lined with clapboard houses built during the early decades of the nineteenth century. Although they have not been carefully maintained, many of these old houses still suggest the pleasant manner of living and the prosperity of the planters who erected them. Rabun Street, the oldest and most attractive of the residential streets, is often called Maiden Lane because young ladies from the female seminary used to walk here beneath the trees.

Dairy products and large quantities of lumber are shipped from the surrounding country, while eighteen sawmills and four planing mills operate in the town. Although much cotton is cultivated around Sparta, diversified farming according to advanced agricultural methods is being introduced through the local soil conservation and improvement association.

The JUDGE LITTLE HOUSE (*private*), 223 Broad St., originally a one and one-half story log structure and later covered with clapboards, is believed to have been built before 1812 by Timothy Rosseter, a surgeon of the Revolutionary army. The porch and projecting one-story wings were added about the time of the War between the States.

The MIDDLEBROOKS HOUSE (*private*), 510 Rabun St., has an elliptical front walk bordered with bulb flowers and shaded by dark cedars. A large Greek Revival house with a slender Doric colonnade supporting a pedimented portico, it was built as a dormitory for the Sparta Female Academy, founded in 1832. By 1837 the academy, which was one of the first schools for girls in the South, had 121 pupils and 5 teachers; the older girls were taught "philosophy, chemistry, French, astronomy, literature, and electricity." In 1838 when the institute was renamed the Sparta Female Model School, the method of teaching developed at the Rensselaer School (now the Rensselaer Polytechnic Institute) in Troy, New York, was adopted. Under this system actual experiments and lectures were conducted by the students—an early version of the modern "learning by doing" system.

The old SPARTA POST OFFICE, Broad St. at the public square, houses some of the county offices. The exact date of its erection is not known, but the hand-made bricks of its walls indicate that it is one of the oldest buildings in the town. It is said that a tree which once stood here had suspended from its branches a barrel in which inebriates, their hands and feet protruding through small holes, were swung until they became sober.

The DRUMMER'S HOME, across the street from the old post office, was constructed in 1851 of hand-made brick. The wide front veranda of this long, rectangular hotel has eight square columns rising to the height of the second-story roof, and the basement has walls thirty-six inches thick. It was originally called the Edwards House for James B. Edwards, early settler and soldier of the War of 1812, and was noted for its good food.

The SAYRE-REESE-OLIVER HOUSE (*private*), at the end of a short street branching R. at the traffic light, is a two-story Greek Revival house with Doric portico. The facade of this gray brick house has been covered with stucco and outlined to resemble concrete blocks. When the house was built in the earlier part of the nineteenth century, an addition was planned. The house was never completed, however, and the recessed, fanlighted doorway, flanked by Doric pilasters, remains on the side, thus giving an unbalanced appearance to the facade. The windows are protected on the outside by old-fashioned green shutters and are shaded on the inside by white blinds with little silver knobs and old hasp fastenings. The graceful stair rail is of mahogany.

The TERRELL HOUSE (*private*), 839 Jones St., is a two-story, clapboarded structure with a beautiful elliptical fanlight over the front door. The irregularities of the fluted Ionic columns, carved from heart pine, indicate their hand-made origin. The house was built by William Terrell, an early settler from Virginia, while he was a United States

Congressman (1817-21). The original small entrance stoop was later extended, making a porch across the front. In the rear is an old smoke-house of field stones.

The WYNN-CLINCH HOUSE (*private*), on Jones St. N. of the railroad (L), is a notable white Greek Revival house set on a hill. When it was recently repainted, the green shutters were removed and the Doric columns, supporting the broad front portico, were stripped of their ivy. Built during the first decade of the nineteenth century, the house was later acquired by Major Henry A. Clinch, a Confederate officer who achieved renown at Vicksburg, Mississippi.

Left from Sparta on State 16, the unimproved road to Eatonton, to Shoulder Bone Creek, 7.5 m.; on its banks is the marked INDIAN TREATY SITE. This agreement signed on November 3, 1786, by the Creek and the State of Georgia would probably have ended the Oconee War, if it had not been repudiated by the Indians under the leadership of the half-breed chief Alexander McGillivray.

HARRIS MILL, 7.6 m., on the bank of Shoulder Bone Creek, was erected in 1881 on the site of an earlier mill that had been destroyed. The water house and dam are of cut stone, and the mill itself is of heart pine, unpainted but without a trace of decay. One beam, hand-hewn from a single timber, is eight by twelve inches, and forty-five feet long. On one of the uprights, about ten feet from the floor, is a mark cut to show the height of a flood in 1887. For many years farmers of this section have depended on Harris Mill to grind their corn and wheat. Recently a small shingle mill has been installed here.

The HAROLD ROUNTREE HOUSE (*private*), 22.8 m., is a story-and-a-half Georgian Colonial farmhouse type of structure (L) with louvered shutters at the windows. Both the exterior and interior walls are of wide boards. The date of its erection is unknown, but it has been established that Aaron Burr spent the night here in 1807, probably after his arrest in Mississippi, when Federal authorities were taking him to Richmond, Virginia, for trial. In the back yard occurred the first legal hanging in Hancock County; the condemned was a Negro woman who had poisoned five people.

At this point is a junction with State 15.

Left on State 15 to a marked INDIAN TRAIL, 4.8 m., the route followed by the Creek and other tribes in traveling from Columbus to Augusta.

The MOUNT ZION METHODIST CHURCH (L), 6.3 m., is a white frame structure with four square columns, wide floor boards, and covered keyholes. In 1812 Joseph Bryan, an early settler from Connecticut, influenced Nathan S. S. Beman to come to Mount Zion, then a prosperous community, to organize a Presbyterian church. The present building, erected about 1850, became the property of the Methodists in 1903, when the Presbyterian congregation combined with that of Sparta.

Near the church was the noted Mount Zion Academy, a coeducational preparatory school organized about 1813, with "Classical, English, and Female departments." Nathan S. S. Beman, the Presbyterian founder, maintained severe discipline by means of the rod. In 1855 the institution became the Mount Zion

High School under the leadership of the Reverend C. P. Beman, who had been the first principal of Midway Seminary, which later became Oglethorpe University.

At **27 m.** on State 22 is a junction with a dirt road.

Left on this road at a school building of the Springfield community, **9.9 m.,** to a junction with another road; R. on this road to the CAMILLA-ZACK COUNTRY LIFE CENTER, **10 m.,** a project originated and operated by the Negroes of the community under the direction of Zack T., Benjamin F., and Moses Hubert. It was organized in 1931 and named for the founders' parents, Camilla and Zack Hubert. The community center, a log house set in a pine grove, is equipped with modern appliances, has large fireplaces with hand-wrought andirons, and contains a number of African relics. In the cabin community members hold social functions; Boy Scout troops, girls' clubs, and sewing clubs meet; and the men of the farmers' club discuss advanced methods of agriculture. Adjoining the community center is the newly constructed health center, where classes in health and sanitation are held and where doctors and nurses from Sparta conduct a clinic each month. A Negro physician and a registered nurse serve the community at all times.

Of the 75 farm families in the community, 40 own their small farms of from 50 to 150 acres each. In the aggregate, Negro land holdings here amount to from 12,000 to 15,000 acres. A threshing machine and a tractor are used by the farmers in rotation. Zack T. Hubert, who is a county farm agent, assists the farmers in planning and marketing their crops. Though a community enterprise, the project is in no sense communal, since each farm is strictly an individual undertaking. In 1936 the community store declared its first dividend of 10 per cent. Plans for a community loan association are being formulated. The county-supported school for the Negro children of Springfield comprises high school as well as the grades, which is unusual in Georgia. White residents of the county are proud of the undertaking and eager to show it to visitors.

The summer session of the Georgia State College (Negro) (*see* SAVANNAH) is held at Springfield. The six-weeks' season marks the crest of the year's activity; three hundred adult students and from thirty to forty grammar school children attend classes under twelve teachers. Classes fill the log cabin, the school building, and the church, and many of the students live in tents. Camps for boys are directed by the Boy Scouts and the Y. M. C. A.; Camp Camilla is conducted for girls.

In POWELTON, **35.8 m.** (approx. 500 alt., 75 pop.), an old village, the houses show no Greek Revival influence, but are simple farmhouse types of one or two stories. They are all of frame construction and most of them are unpainted.

The BAPTIST CHURCH (R), at the turn of the road, serves a congregation organized on July 1, 1786, with Silas Mercer as pastor. The white frame auditorium with two towers is the original church edifice, but the Sunday school rooms are of later construction. The church minutes, complete except for nine months of 1852, are carefully inscribed in great ledgers. Among the many important church conferences held here was that which organized the Georgia Baptist Convention on June 27, 1822. Near by is a slave cemetery, with graves marked by rough slabs of field stone. The Negroes buried here were members of the church and once occupied the rear pews.

CRAWFORDVILLE, **44.9 m.** (616 alt., 840 pop.) (*see* TOUR *17*), is at the junction with State 12 (*see* TOUR *17*).

TOUR 15

(Saluda, S. C.) — Augusta — Waynesboro — Millen —Junction with US 80; US 25.

South Carolina Line to junction with US 80, 75.2 m. — Roadbed hard-surfaced through-out, about one-third concrete — Central of Georgia Ry. parallels route — Limited accommodations.

This route runs through the most fertile cotton section of the state. Long green watermelons and fragrant yellow cantaloupes are grown in abundance, and garden truck of all kinds is produced. Many acres of pecans are planted near Waynesboro. In this level sandy country US 25 occasionally crosses a long red hill, from the crest of which there is a wide view of farm lands and distant hillsides wooded in pine and scrub oak. In the cool, swampy hollows, the dark but clear creeks are bordered with dense growths of bay, cypress, and water oak hung with gray moss.

Although many of the small tenant farmhouses along the highway are sagging and unpainted, they are brightened all summer by flowers growing about the doorways and by the cerise blossoms of crape myrtles. Some of the cabins, built on the sites of stately plantation houses, are surrounded by trees and shrubbery that were planted when the houses were built. In the vicinity of Waynesboro and Millen are many prosperous-looking farmhouses, some with their own windmills and water tanks. The houses in the towns are attractive with neatly trimmed hedges and lawns.

US 25 crosses the Savannah River, 0 m., the boundary line between South Carolina and Georgia.

AUGUSTA, **0.5 m.** (143 alt., 60,342 pop.) (*see* AUGUSTA).

Points of Interest: The Hill, University of Georgia School of Medicine, Junior College of Augusta, Paine College (Negro), Haines Institute (Negro), Cotton Exchange, and others.

Augusta is at a junction with US 78 (*see* TOUR *8*) and with US 1 (*see* TOUR *4*).

At **3.6 m.** is a junction with the Old Savannah Road.

Left on this road to the COTTAGE CEMETERY (L), 3 m., about a fifth of a mile from the highway; here is the GRAVE OF JOSEPH EVE (1760-1835), inventor of a roller cotton gin which was used in the Bahama Islands as early as 1787 to gin long-fibered cotton. Eve moved to Richmond County in 1810 and built his home, "The Cottage." Here he manufactured gunpowder, some of which is said to have been used by American forces in the War of 1812; experimented with steam and was granted patents on two steam engines, one in 1818 and the other in 1826; and in 1823 published a book of poetry.

At **5.2 m.** is a junction with Tobacco Road (*see below*).

Left 1.9 m. on this road to the SITE OF NEW SAVANNAH, on a bluff of the Savannah River. During the latter part of the eighteenth century, this was an important point for the shipment of tobacco, and scores of boats were loaded from warehouses near by. With the decline of river traffic, however, all trace of the settlement's activity vanished. In 1935 the section sprang into new growth when the Federal government began deepening the Savannah River channel between Augusta and New Savannah. A lock and dam were completed at this point in 1937 at a cost of about two million dollars.

At **9 m.** is a junction of US 25 with the unmarked, red clay TOBACCO ROAD, the locale of Erskine Caldwell's novel (*see* TOUR *4*). This road once followed a ridge from north Georgia to New Savannah. During the latter half of the eighteenth century, the growing of tobacco was a major factor in the development of the Southeast, and pioneers from Georgia and the colonies to the north trundled tobacco over this road in mule-drawn hogsheads to the port; here it was loaded on boats for shipment down the muddy river to Savannah. The men also brought furs and grain to be traded for necessities. These swashbuckling pioneers, traveling in caravans and cracking rawhide whips, gained the name of "Georgia crackers," a term now applied to all Georgians. Tobacco Road runs through a sparsely populated region between indifferently cultivated fields and occasional dilapidated shacks. This section has been planted in cotton since the introduction of that crop in the early part of the nineteenth century, but because of the low price of cotton and the destruction caused by the boll weevil, tobacco is again being raised extensively.

Left on Tobacco Road to Gracewood Road, **0.2 m.**; R. on this road **0.1 m.** to the GEORGIA TRAINING SCHOOL FOR MENTAL DEFECTIVES (R), housed in eight cream-colored concrete buildings and several frame structures. This well-equipped state institution, opened in 1921, now takes care of 350 boys and girls from six to eighteen years of age. The boys are taught dairying and farming, and the girls learn sewing, laundering, and telephone exchange operating. In addition to its 325-acre tract, the institution acquired a 450-acre farm about four miles away on the Old Savannah Road in 1929.

WAYNESBORO, **31.5 m.** (261 alt., 3,922 pop.), seat of Burke County, laid out as a town in 1783 and incorporated in 1812, was named for General Wayne, known as "Mad Anthony" because of his daring exploits. He served in Georgia during the Revolution and later moved to the state, where he was elected to the U. S. Congress in 1791. After serving less than one term, he was unseated because of a charge of fraudulence in the election. He did not enter the campaign in the new election. Waynesboro's houses vary in architecture from the dignified Greek Revival type to the modern bungalow. Once part of the old plantation belt, where the landowners kept many slaves, the town still has a large Negro population.

At Waynesboro is a junction with State 24 (*see* TOUR *14*).

For many years Burke County has led the state in acreage and production of cotton, but in 1938 it ranked second, with a total of 21,755 bales ginned.

Left from Waynesboro on the unpaved McBean Road to the junction with the Girard Road, **4.8 m.**; R. on the Girard Road to the junction with a third dirt road, **9 m.**; R. on this to a junction with a fourth road, **9.4 m.**; R. on this road (*narrow, sandy, and virtually impassable in bad weather*) to a junction with a fifth road, **15.7 m.**; L. on this road to a junction with a sixth road, **16.5 m.**; R. on this road to a point at **17.2 m.** (*cars must be parked*); about 200 yards L. is SHELL BLUFF, an unusual geological formation. Here, high above the Savannah River, are many giant oyster fossils (*Ostrea georgiana*) from 12 to 15 inches long. Authorities claim that the bed, stretching a thousand feet along the river, is of the Eocene age and that it was formed when the Coastal Plain of Georgia was submerged beneath the sea. The landing at Shell Bluff was important when steamboats plied the river between Augusta and Savannah. The road, now little frequented, was then the main artery of trade, used to haul tobacco and other commodities to and from the landing. A section of Confederate breastworks, though covered with trees and vines, is plainly visible.

At **43 m.** is the junction with a dirt road.

Right on this road to the junction with another road, **3.1 m.**; L. **0.1 m.** on this road to (R) BELLEVIEW PLANTATION (*private*). Set among fine old oaks and a profusion of flowers, this two-story clapboarded house with its flanking wings is one of the most notable Colonial structures in this section. Porter Carswell, who owns the place, has in his possession a warrant for the survey of the land, dated 1766, and a grant from King George III to Samuel Eastlake, dated 1767. Since Eastlake was the surveyor, it is probable that the land was granted in payment for his services. The house is believed to have been built the following year, and the estate has since remained in the possession of the same family.

Built of heart pine and cypress, the house is in a state of perfect preservation. Though altered from time to time, it retains the authentic lines of the pioneer houses, with sloping roof supported by square columns, front porch, and extensive wings at both sides. The southern wing, a modern addition, is in keeping with the rest of the house, even to the wide floor and ceiling boards. The brick in the massive end chimneys is hand-made, and every piece of timber is hand-hewn; the frame is joined with wooden pegs. The structure is painted white with green trim.

The characteristic severe plainness of the interior is relieved by the beautiful old furniture. At several places are bullet holes made during the skirmish at Buckhead Creek in the War between the States. General Sherman is known to have tied his horse to a large rosebush beside the door. All of the outbuildings and many of the neighboring houses were burned at that time, but Belleview was spared, presumably because many women and children from Waynesboro had taken refuge here.

On the first dirt road is BUCKHEAD BAPTIST CHURCH (R), **6.5 m.**, a white frame structure built about 1800. Four simple, square columns rise from the ground to the roof, and steps extend across the entire front. The church was organized in 1778. It was here in 1831 that the Georgia Baptist Convention passed a resolution to organize the school that became Mercer University (*see* TOUR *17*).

The road crosses BUCKHEAD CREEK, **6.7 m.**, where a skirmish occurred during the War between the States, when Sherman's cavalrymen under General Kilpatrick were pursued by Confederate forces under General Wheeler. To bar Wheeler's progress, Kilpatrick partly burned the bridge across the creek, but Wheeler, with quick ingenuity, had pews brought from the church to replace the burned flooring. New pews are the only modern note in the church.

MAGNOLIA SPRINGS, **46.5 m.**, is a picnic resort a short distance L. of the highway. The spring has a flow of 2,800 gallons of clear mineral water a minute and has been developed as a swimming pool (*adm. 10¢*). This is the SITE OF CAMP LAWTON, a Confederate prison established during the fall of 1864 to relieve the congestion at Andersonville Prison (*see* TOUR *2B*). Across the stream are the breastworks erected for the protection of the prison area.

Directly across the highway is the MAGNOLIA SPRINGS FISH HATCHERY (R), opened under state direction in 1935. Here millions of fish are raised annually for distribution to Georgia streams. To the rear of the hatchery are a number of LIME SINKS, geological curiosities which often appear suddenly when the lime content of one layer of the soil is dissolved by moisture, thereby causing the surface to cave in. In this way, a pond may be created overnight. Some of the sinks are more than thirty feet deep, the sloping sides overgrown with wild flowers. The bottom usually is filled with a milky or clear blue pool, in which are numerous fish.

MILLEN, **52.4 m.** (160 alt., 2,527 pop.), seat of Jenkins County, was first called Seventy-Nine because it is seventy-nine miles from Savannah. In 1836 the town was given its present name for Captain John Millen, a civil engineer of the Central of Georgia Railway, which passed here on its route from Savannah to Atlanta and formed a junction with the branch to Augusta. The town has developed around this junction.

Right from Millen on unpaved State 17 to the junction with a dirt road, **10.4 m.;** R. on this road is BIRDSVILLE, **14.4 m.**, a small village that grew up about the ancestral estate of the Francis Jones family. The tract of land was a grant from King George III of England. The avenues about Birdsville are lined with giant oaks almost two centuries old. Still standing at the crossroads are pre-Revolutionary buildings which made the Jones house the center of a small village. The small, gabled frame building was used as the inn, stage stop, and post office; here the members of the community gathered to learn news of the outside world. Here, too, is a log building which once served as the dining house. In the carriage house near by is an old silver-mounted postilion coach, with sliding glass windows.

The JONES HOUSE (*private*), of hand-hewn pine timbers with mortised joints held by wooden pegs, was built (R) in 1762; additions in the Greek Revival style were completed in 1847. On the facade of this two-story house are four tall Corinthian columns, capped and based with iron, which support a central pedimented portico. The mantels are hand-carved and secured with wooden pegs.

At the rear of the manor house is the JONES FAMILY CEMETERY, the resting place of the woman who preserved the old home from destruction. During the War between the States, General Sherman's men had overrun the plantation, stripped it of its treasures, and started to burn the house. Having no desire to outlive her home, the mistress refused to leave her bed where she lay ill. Because of her persistence the soldiers extinguished the fire, already mounting from a room in the lower story.

At **75.2 m.** is the junction with US 80 (*see* TOUR 9), at a point 6.6 miles west of Statesboro.

TOUR 16

Athens — Watkinsville — Madison — Eatonton — Macon; 91.3 m., US 129.

Roadbed hard-surfaced throughout; a few short sections of concrete — Central of Georgia Ry. parallels route — All types of accommodations in Athens and Macon; limited elsewhere.

US 129 is a speedway through an agricultural land where fields of cotton, corn, and sorghum are interspersed with peach orchards and groves of oak and pine. Once a part of the plantation belt, this section has many old houses which, even when shabby, have an enduring charm. Few remain along the country roadside, but the towns are particularly notable for their examples of ante bellum architecture.

ATHENS, **0 m.** (662 alt., 18,192 pop.) (*see* ATHENS).

Points of Interest: University of Georgia, Tree that Owns Itself, ante bellum homes, and others.

Athens is at the junction with US 78 (*see* TOUR 8) and US 29 (*see* TOUR 3).

WATKINSVILLE, 5.4 m. (approx. 750 alt., 425 pop.), seat of Oconee County, is a quiet community. The town was founded as the seat of Clarke County in 1802 and became the seat of Oconee County when it was formed from Clarke in 1875.

Opposite the courthouse is the EAGLE HOTEL, a rectangular building with a two-story loggia. It is known that in 1789 the building was used as a blockhouse for protection against the Cherokee and was called Fort Edwards. Later it was covered both inside and out with wide boards and greatly enlarged. It has been a tavern since 1801.

MADISON, 28 m. (667 alt., 1,966 pop.), seat of Morgan County, was incorporated in 1809 and named for President James Madison. Beneath the arching branches of large oak trees, the streets have a quiet, restful beauty. Tall, white columns and broad, graceful doorways of old houses recall ante bellum days. George White, writing of the town in 1845, said, "Madison, Georgia, is the wealthiest and most aristocratic village on the stagecoach route between Charleston and New Orleans."

Morgan County has always been an agricultural area, and Madison is its trading center. The only industrial interests are a few small lumber mills.

The BURNEY HOME (*private*), 339 N. Main St., is a two-story, white Greek Revival house set among cedars and magnolias. The portico has six fluted Doric columns and a delicately designed balcony that overhangs the entrance; the doorways on both floors are decorated with sidelights and heavy lintels. The house was built about 1845, but additions have since been made to the left and to the rear.

SNOWHILL (*private*), on the old Agricultural College Rd., was the home of Lancelot Johnson, inventor of one of the first machines for crushing cottonseed. This device, patented before 1832, contributed to the rapid development of the cottonseed-oil industry. Snowhill is a two-story, white frame house with a deep, columned portico. The main body of the house has a very steep roof that Johnson once had painted with a combination of cottonseed oil and white lead; the effect produced suggested the name Snowhill. The wings are said to have been built by Johnson for two of his sisters whom he supported but required to maintain separate households. Especially noteworthy are the fine hedges of boxwood.

On the public square is the BRASWELL MONUMENT honoring Benjamin Braswell, who in 1817 provided in his will that thirteen of his slaves be sold to provide "for education of indigent white children" of the town. The sale of the slaves brought $3,595, which was increased by

investment and still provides an income for the purchase of books and
supplies for needy children.

TRAVELERS' INN, 147 S. Main St., now a tourist home, is a large, two-
story, white house with green blinds.   Built about 1850, it is one of the
best examples of Greek Revival architecture in the town.   Of the six
columns supporting the roof, two are square and four are fluted Doric.
The doorway, which has a transom and sidelights, is framed with
slender Doric columns.

The PRESBYTERIAN CHURCH, 210 S. Main St., erected about 1810, is a
small structure with three entrance doorways encased in heavy frames.
The hipped roof is topped with a small, square tower.

The KOLB HOME (*private*), 218 S. 2nd St., is a handsome early Victorian house, built in 1851 of timbers cut and fitted in Augusta and
hauled to Madison by oxcart.   The roof of the square front porch is
supported by two Doric and two square columns, and the sidelights of
the front door are of Venetian glass.   The geometrical boxwood
gardens, with dwarf hedges varied by an occasional box tree, are
brightened with roses and lilies, Japanese magnolias, cherry laurel, and
January jasmine.   The barn in the service yard is flanked with a
vegetable garden and an orchard.   The original early Victorian furnishings are still in the parlor, and the old cisterns, installed by the first
owner to supply the house with running water, are still in use.

The STOKES-MCHENRY HOME (*private*), 240 S. 2nd St., is a two-story,
gray frame house with green blinds.   Delicately wrought latticework
adorns the piazza that extends across the entire front of the house.
The doorway is flanked with pilasters ornamented with unusual
circular motifs.   The house, built between 1830 and 1840, contains many
of the early furnishings, and a recent restoration of the interior has
made it one of the show places of Madison.

THURLESTON (*private*), 455 Dixie Highway Ave., is a two-story white
clapboarded house, said to have been built on the Butler plantation
near Madison, taken down in 1818, and moved to town.   The facade,
of Georgian design, is adorned with fluted pilasters and topped with
three gables.   The house, occupied by descendants of the first owners,
contains much of the old furniture.   A large oak tree on the grounds
has been named the Joyce Kilmer Oak, for the author of the poem
"Trees."

BONAR HALL (*private*), 512 Dixie Highway Ave., a two-story brick
house with Victorian ornamentation, is set 200 yards from the road
on a 100-acre tract.   A broad walk leading to the entrance and encircling the house is bordered with beds of bulbs, and the formal
gardens to the left contain boxwood and rare shrubs.   The house was
built about 1845 by Colonel John Walker, who used bricks made by

slaves at his own kiln. The roof is of copper and doorknobs are of silver. To the rear of the house are an old brick kitchen and a slave house.

Madison is at the junction with State 12 (*see* TOUR *17*).

At **43.7 m.** is a junction with a good dirt road.

Right on this road to the Indian EAGLE MOUND, **1 m.**, a mass of loosely piled stones in the shape of an eagle with outspread wings. It measures 102 feet from head to tail and 120 feet across the wings. The body, 10 or 12 feet above the surface of the ground, is 60 feet long and 35 feet wide. The proportions of the mound, distinguishable only from a height, correspond amazingly well to those of an eagle. The stones of the body are larger than those of the head, and the stones of the wings are graduated in size; thus the likeness to the bird is emphasized. The mound has been described by Matthew W. Sterling of the Bureau of American Ethnology as the "most perfect effigy mound in North America." The Farm Security Administration, which owns the property, has cleared the land of undergrowth and constructed an 85-acre lake near by. Two other eagle mounds in Georgia attest the awe in which the Indian held this bird.

EATONTON, **49.7 m.** (approx. 575 alt., 1,876 pop.), seat of Putnam County, was incorporated in 1809 and named for William Eaton, Revolutionary officer and naval agent to the Barbary States. The town was settled by owners of large plantations and became a seat of ante bellum culture. A number of old houses remain. Some of the older Negroes who gather around the town square on Saturdays are not unlike Uncle Remus, the popular character created by Joel Chandler Harris (*see* ATLANTA), who was born in Eatonton on December 9, 1848, and lived in Putnam County until young manhood. Before the War between the States the region around Eatonton was devoted chiefly to the cultivation of cotton, but now the farmers take an active interest in dairying and in the improvement of livestock.

The JOEL CHANDLER HARRIS MONUMENT, on Jefferson St., is near the eastern entrance to the courthouse. Although Harris' character Uncle Remus is a composite creation, many of his traits were those of Uncle George Terrell, an old slave who baked ginger cookies in his Dutch oven to sell in Eatonton on Saturdays. The children of the planters liked to visit the old man's cabin and sit before a snapping fire amidst the spicy smell of the cakes, listening to his stories.

The WARDWELL HOUSE (*private*), SW. corner Jefferson and Sumter Sts., was built in 1848 as a branch of the state bank but later was remodeled into a residence. The two-story house, built of red brick with very thick walls, still contains an old vault with ribbed ceiling and heavy doors. The present owners have several of the old banking house keys, which appear to be made of bronze and weigh almost a pound each.

The BRONSON HOUSE (*private*), 103 Madison St., built about 1830, has a porch with well-proportioned columns around three sides. It has no front yard but stands directly on the street. Within recent years extensive additions have been made to the rear of the house.

The SLADE HOUSE (*private*), 112 Madison St., built between 1830 and 1840, is a two-story brick dwelling with Ionic columns of molded cement, surrounded by a brick wall and an iron fence. The columns are reproduced in miniature on each side of the doorway.

The T. G. GREEN HOUSE (*private*), La Fayette St., built about 1845, is the best-preserved old house in town. It has Corinthian columns, a Palladian doorway, and a hipped roof. The garden is bordered with a beautiful boxwood hedge.

PANOLA HALL (*private*), across from the public library on N. Madison St., is a two-story, white-columned Greek Revival house built before 1850. It was the home of Benjamin W. Hunt, scientist and horticulturist, who came to Georgia from New York in 1876. An underground passage leads from a pergola in the grounds to a storm pit in the basement of the house. The gardens are planted in palms and other tropical plants, and, although the place is untenanted and unkept, it still has an air of distinction. Hunt developed a variety of fig and one of scuppernong, or fox grape, that bears his name.

Left from Eatonton on State 16 to the junction with a dirt road, 1.3 m.; L. on this road to BRIAR PATCH FARMS, 5 m., a small project started by the F.E.R.A., transferred first to the Resettlement and then to the Farm Security Administration. Twenty-one selected families and a manager occupy the farms, which average 110 acres each. Because most of the soil on this 10,000-acre tract has been depleted by years of cotton production, various soil-building crops are being planted and much of the area is now pasture land. The acreage granted to each family varies with the productivity of the land. The residences are neat, one-story, white frame cottages, with tiny entrance porches and green blinds. Near them are substantial barns, poultry houses, and fenced-in gardens. All structures—including the combined cannery and vocational-training building, the administration building, and the community center, which is also used as a school—were constructed as a relief project supervised by Government engineers.

Briar Patch Farms are operated on a co-operative basis under the supervision of a project manager, but the farmers are not restricted in choice of markets. The residents draw upon Federal funds for livestock, farm tools, fertilizer, seed, and subsistence, but their indebtedness with interest is charged each year against their crop yields. The aim of the administration is to help each farmer to become independent and eventually to own the farm on which he lives. None (1939) is behind in his payments.

At 51.7 m. is a junction with State 24 (*see* TOUR *14*).

GRAY, 75.6 m. (533 alt., 653 pop.), was made the seat of Jones County in 1905. In the county's 6,000 acres of peach orchards is an individually owned orchard with 100,000 trees. Two canneries here employ about

500 persons at the height of the season and buy pimientos under contract from the farmers.

Left from Gray on State 22 is the village of HADDOCK, **6 m.** (approx. 500 alt., 336 pop.); R. from Haddock on a dirt road to the BLOUNT HOUSE (*private*), **7 m.**, one of the best examples of ante bellum architecture in the state. This fine old house is of white clapboards with unusual corner pilasters of the Doric order and two tall columns extending from the corner of the small front porch to the overhanging cornice. Opening on both the porch and the balcony are wide paneled doors with unusually fine fanlights. An "eyebrow" window is placed at the south end of the attic. The ceilings and interior walls are ornamented with plaster medallions and cornices of acanthus leaves, and a spiral staircase with mahogany handrail winds from basement to attic. On each side of the fireplace in the living room are semicircular alcoves outlined with gilded acanthus leaves. It is believed that the house was built for John W. Gordon, a brigadier general in the state militia (1835-39), and was designed by Daniel Pratt, a New England architect who became the first great industrialist of Alabama. Construction was begun in 1828 and completed five years later.

CLINTON, **77.6 m.** (approx. 650 alt., approx. 200 pop.), was the seat of Jones County from 1807, when the county was created, until 1905, when the government offices were removed to Gray because Clinton had no railroad facilities. Before the War between the States the town was surrounded by large plantations and was a center of wealth and culture. The first iron foundry in the state was established here and manufactured 900 cotton gins a year. It was destroyed by General Sherman's forces on their march to the sea. The Clinton Female Seminary, founded in Clinton in 1828 by Thomas B. Slade, lost prestige and declined when Wesleyan College was opened in Macon several years later.

The CLINTON METHODIST CHURCH is one of the oldest churches in middle Georgia, and Macon people attended services here before there was a church in their city. The land on which the church and cemetery stand was deeded to the congregation in 1821. About 1882 the church was remodeled and the slave gallery removed.

LOWTHER HALL (*private*), set on a wide sweep of green lawn shaded by elms and cedars and enclosed within a white picket fence, is a handsome building of post-Colonial design. It was built in 1822 and, like the Blount house, is believed to have been designed by Daniel Pratt. The hip-roof, clapboarded structure has small-paned, shuttered windows, a small Roman Doric portico, and a graceful elliptical fanlight above the entrance door. A transomed door at the second story opens on the roof of the portico.

GEORGIA BAPTIST COLLEGE (L), **85.8 m.**, provides high school and junior college courses for Negro boys and girls; theological training is also given. It was founded in 1889 through the efforts of the Reverend E. K. Love, pastor of the Savannah Baptist Church, and placed under the

Missionary Baptist Convention in 1915. At the Baptist convention held in Athens in 1935, the school was placed under the supervision of a chartered board of white trustees responsible for administrative procedure. The college is maintained by donations from the General Missionary Board and the Georgia Baptist Convention and by private contributions.

The campus contained 235 acres until recently, when 30 acres were deeded to the city of Macon for development as a recreational park. On the southwestern side of the school grounds, which were a part of the great plantation called Wilburn Hill, are breastworks set up to check the advance of General Sherman. The original main building, once the plantation house, was totally destroyed in 1921, when it was set on fire by a demented woman; the present two-story building was erected the next year.

MACON, **91.3 m.** (334 alt., 53,829 pop.) (*see* MACON).

Points of Interest: Home of Sidney Lanier, Mercer University, Wesleyan Conservatory, and others.

At Macon is a junction with US 80 (*see* TOUR 9) and with US 341 (*see* TOUR 12).

TOUR 17

Thomson — Crawfordville — Madison — Covington — Avondale Estates; 128 m., State 12.

Roadbed hard-surfaced, about one-half with concrete — Georgia R.R. roughly parallels route — Limited accommodations.

State 12 traverses a section developed late in the eighteenth century with the growth of the middle Georgia cotton plantations. Although these plantations have long since been broken up into small farms cultivated by owner or tenant, survivals of the past are evident along the route in a memorial park, the site of a century-old university, and the classic ante bellum houses of Warrenton and Covington. The region between Covington and Avondale Estates contains vast stores of granite, and the quarrying of this stone is a thriving industry.

THOMSON, **0 m.** (540 alt., 1,914 pop.) (*see* TOUR 8), is at the junction with US 78 (*see* TOUR 8).

The unpaved streets of WARRENTON, 12.1 m. (500 alt., 1,289 pop.), are bordered with large old oak trees and its lawns and gardens are carefully tended. The seat of Warren County since 1797, it was named for General Joseph Warren, Revolutionary patriot of Massachusetts and author of the *Suffolk Resolves*, who was killed at the Battle of Bunker Hill. The town grew up around a seven-acre plot of land given to the county for a permanent courthouse and jail. It was incorporated as a town in 1810 and as a city in 1908. Early in the nineteenth century Warrenton was on the stagecoach route between Augusta and Milledgeville. When the Georgia Railroad was built through Camak, a few miles to the north, a car drawn by mules was operated between the two towns; in 1868, when the Macon branch of the railroad was built, mule-car service was discontinued.

An extract from Adiel Sherwood's *Gazetteer of the State of Georgia* of 1837 records: "In this town [Warrenton] lived for a number of years, Dr. Bushnell, formerly of Saybrook, Connecticut, inventor of a submarine vessel called the 'Turtle.' By this instrument great damage was done to the British ships during the Revolutionary War."

The WALKER HOUSE (*private*), Main St., built in 1820, is a white clapboard house (L) with green blinds and an intricate balustrade. It is admired by architects for its fine proportions.

The MCGREGOR HOUSE (*private*), one block R. from the public square, is a two-story, gray stuccoed brick building, originally of Georgian Colonial design. The entrance stoop of this early nineteenth-century house has been replaced by a Greek portico with four Doric columns. A cement and stone wall, with iron gateway, surrounds the spacious gardens, which contain fine boxwood and many cherry laurels trimmed into symmetrical shapes.

The WARREN COUNTY JAIL, adjacent to the *Warrenton Clipper* office, is a gaunt rectangular brownstone structure built about 1800. The iron bars of the small windows are so wide that little light can penetrate between them.

The W. W. PILCHER HOUSE (*private*), 209 Main St., is a two-story, white frame structure with Corinthian portico. Although the house has been remodeled since its erection in the early 1800's, the original framework has been retained. When General La Fayette stopped in Warrenton in 1825 a masked ball in this house was the first of the entertainments.

Right from Warrenton on an unpaved country road to Camak, 3.7 m. (578 alt., 345 pop.); R. from Camak on a dirt road to the junction with another road, 5.1 m.; L. on this road to a ROCK-CRUSHING PLANT, 8.2 m., the largest in the state. This $350,000 plant has a daily crushing capacity of 60 carloads of granite obtained from the near-by quarry.

CRAWFORDVILLE, **32.7 m.** (616 alt., 840 pop.), seat of Taliaferro County, was incorporated in 1826. One block from the courthouse is the ALEXANDER H. STEPHENS MEMORIAL STATE PARK. On a slight knoll just north of the entrance to the park stands LIBERTY HALL, a two-story white frame structure with a wide porch across the front and an ell of two rooms at the rear. The grounds surrounding the house are planted with shrubs and flowers to resemble the original garden. Directly in front of the house is the ALEXANDER STEPHENS MONUMENT, an Italian marble figure on a granite base, and to the left is ALEXANDER STEPHENS' GRAVE enclosed by a wall.

Stephens purchased Liberty Hall in 1845 from the estate of Williamson Byrd, a relative of his stepmother. In 1872 the old house was torn down, except the two rear rooms, to allow space for the present structure, which has been restored as nearly as possible to its original condition. Stephens' bedroom on the first floor contains his walnut furniture, the round table where he worked, and his wheel chair. The flowered ingrain carpet has been repaired, and the blue-and-gold-striped wallpaper has been reproduced. The massive chairs of the dining room have been duplicated from a single remaining chair of the original set. In the library at the rear, Stephens wrote *A Constitutional View of the Late War between the States* (1868-70). At the head of the steps leading from the dining room to the second floor is a chamber known as the Tramps' Room, with beds for wayfarers who had no money for lodging. If these visitors were present at mealtime they were welcomed to the family table.

To the rear of Liberty Hall are the slave quarters, wine cellar, smokehouse, woodhouse, wash house, and chicken house, all restored. One cabin, marked "Eliza's and Harry's House," and containing the old furnishings, recalls the story of Eliza, the cook, who was so much in love with Harry, the slave of a neighbor, that "Marse Aleck" bought him for her.

Alexander Hamilton Stephens (1812-83) was born in Taliaferro County. After graduation from the University of Georgia in 1832, he studied law, entered state politics, and was elected to Congress in 1843. He was Vice President of the Confederacy during the War between the States, after which he retired to Liberty Hall. Here he was arrested by Union soldiers and taken to Fort Wayne in Boston Harbor, where he was detained for several months. Elected to the U. S. Senate in 1866, Stephens was disqualified because of his affiliation with the Confederacy, and he remained out of active politics until 1882, when he became Governor of Georgia.

A small, frail man with a shrill voice and indomitable courage, he never weighed more than a hundred pounds and spent the last years of his life in a wheel chair. Although a leader of the Confederacy, Stephens was outspoken in his opposition to secession. Affectionately called Little Aleck, he was widely known for his unfailing hospitality and for the generosity with which he spent large sums to educate under-privileged young men and women.

The state park consists of two divisions: the 20 acres surrounding the house, and the 243 acres given in part by the town of Crawfordville for a recreational section.

Memorial Drive overlooks a picnic area containing a circular wading pool fed by two cold, clear springs. Mercer Drive leads to LAKE LIBERTY (*boating and swimming 25¢*). A bathhouse, built in the same style as Liberty Hall, is equipped with showers, lockers, and rest rooms. On Camp Drive is a 62-foot lookout tower, having a steel framework covered with wood. On the first three floors are lounging rooms; on the fourth, a 3,500-gallon water tank to supply the park; and on the fifth, an observation room for fire prevention. Along Sunset Drive there are other picnic areas where shelters and barbecue pits are provided.

The ALEXANDER H. STEPHENS MEMORIAL RECREATIONAL DEMONSTRATION AREA, adjoining the state park, is under the jurisdiction of the National Park Service. In the 1,000-acre tract of rolling wooded land is a lake with boating, swimming, fishing, and picknicking facilities. Camps are available for organized groups.

At Crawfordville is a junction with State 22 (*see* TOUR 14A).

Beside a railroad crossing is JEFFERSON HALL (*private*), **43.3 m.,** a well-proportioned two-story Greek Revival house (L) with Ionic columns. The doorway is decorated with ornamental woodwork and surmounted with a wide fanlight. This house, built by Lemuel Greene about 1830, became the center of a thriving village of the same name when the Georgia Railroad made its terminus here about 1838. After the railroad had been extended to Augusta, the village began to decline, and Jefferson Hall is now the only remaining house.

BUFFALO LICK, **44.1 m.,** is named for a rock with a salty taste that attracted buffaloes in the early days of the colony. William Bartram (1739-1823) described this place in his *Travels,* published in 1791. Here is the marked CREEK AND CHEROKEE COUNCIL SITE, where meetings were held culminating in the Treaty of Augusta in 1773. The survey of the lands ceded by the Indians to the state began at this place.

UNION POINT, **44.6 m.** (644 alt., 1,627 pop.), is the central point of the Georgia Railroad between Augusta and Atlanta and the junction with a branch line to Athens.

Left of the highway at a railroad crossing is a HOSIERY MILL that has beèn in operation for thirty-five years and is owned largely by local capital. About 575 workers are employed and produce each month 65,000 pairs of hose.

On Carlton Ave. is (R) HAWTHORN HEIGHTS (*private*), named for the hawthorn hedge which surrounds the eight-acre lot. Built 1867-69, the house has a Greek portico in front and a tiled terrace on one side. A tea bush on the front lawn is one of those sent to Washington, D. C., from Japan by Commodore Perry when he opened the ports of that nation in 1854.

Right from Union Point on the unmarked, dirt Washington Road to the RED-MAN THORNTON HOUSE (*private*), 2.6 m., on the crest of a hill (L). The two-story hip-roof structure has a pedimented portico supported by square rough stone columns. Although the walls between the studding are of brick, the exterior is finished with weatherboards. Until this house was built, the only dwellings in Greene County had been log cabins. Here Redman Thornton, a Baptist minister, was born in 1805.

At 2.8 m. is the junction with another dirt road; L. on this to the junction with a third dirt road, 4.6 m.; L. on this road to the BETHESDA BAPTIST CHURCH, 5.1 m., a two-story brick building, with two corner entrances, erected in 1817. At one end of the interior is the old slave gallery. Many of the Negroes, upon the consent of their owners, were received as members.

The church was organized in 1775 and until 1817 was known as Whatley's Mill Church. In early days the minister, who was responsible for law and order in the community, required the members of the congregation to bring their guns to service for protection against Indian uprisings. The minutes show that four militiamen stood guard at each service. The graveyard near by has been in use since the founding of the church.

At 50.4 m. is the junction with an unpaved road.

Right on this road is PENFIELD, 7.5 m. (approx. 650 alt., 184 pop.), where Mercer Institute, a Baptist school offering classical and theological training, was opened on January 14, 1833. The institution was operated as a manual labor school in which students earned part of their expenses by doing farm work on the 450-acre tract of land. The movement to start the school was begun in 1827 when Josiah Penfield, of Savannah, left the Georgia Baptist Convention $2,500 for the education of young ministers, on condition that a like amount be raised. Its establishment was due, to a great extent, to the efforts of the Reverend Adiel Sherwood, Baptist minister and author of the *Georgia Gazetteer,* and to the beneficence of Jesse Mercer, a prominent Baptist clergyman who aided the school with money his wife had inherited from her first husband, Abraham Simons (*see* TOUR *8*). In 1837 the institution was chartered as a university, including an academy, a college, and a theological seminary. In 1871 it was moved to Macon (*see* MACON).

The GRAVE OF JESSE MERCER and three of the original buildings constructed of hand-made brick are still on the campus. Mercer Chapel, now used as the PEN-FIELD BAPTIST CHURCH, is a Doric-columned structure with a Greek pediment. Within are the original pews and a gallery that extends around three sides and divides in half the tall windows. Science Hall, in appearance much like the chapel, is used as a public school building, and Ciceronian Hall, the old literary society building, serves as a school auditorium and community house.

In GREENSBORO, 51.9 m. (598 alt., 2,125 pop.), seat of Greene County, are large cotton mills owned by local capital. The town was laid out for the site of the University of Georgia soon after the creation of the county in 1786. One hundred acres were reserved for the school, and lots were sold for business houses and residences, but before construction began Athens was chosen as the seat of the university.

Greensboro is on the site of one of a series of forts built in Greene County to protect the state from the Creek whose reservation was west of the Oconee River. From 1786 until 1802 the county was a buffer between the civilized east and the frontier west where land speculation was rife. From 1789 to 1796 more than three times as much land as the state had acquired from the Indians was granted to speculators. Elijah Clarke, Revolutionary general and Indian fighter, who already owned many acres, saw in the unsettled conditions an opportunity to seize more land for himself and to set up another government. Through the influence of Citizen Genêt, representative of the French Republic, he assembled a group of adventurers to help the French take Florida from the Spanish. When the chimerical scheme failed, he marched his hungry men to the Indian land, built forts, laid out a town, and made plans to set up an independent government called the Trans-Oconee Republic. Since Greene County lay beside the land of the new republic, its citizens bore the brunt of anxiety over the new military regime. Despite protests and threats from the Federal and state governments, Clarke continued to hold his ground. Finally President Washington ordered the tolerant Georgia government to deploy troops, and they forced Clarke and his men to surrender by cutting off all sources of supplies.

Greensboro, an early cultural center, has produced some noted citizens. While living on a plantation near the town, the Reverend Adiel Sherwood (1791-1879) wrote the first of his four editions of *A Gazetteer of the State of Georgia,* now a source book in Georgia history. Augustus B. Longstreet (1790-1870), politician, writer, preacher, and college president, practiced law here as a young man.

The COBB-DAWSON HOUSE (*private*), East and South Sts., is a square, two-story frame structure with a hipped roof. At the entrance on each street there is a small porch with Ionic columns. The doorways, ornamented with sidelights and fanlights, lead into wide hallways which cross in the center of the house. The garden at the rear is planted with luxuriant shrubbery and beautiful trees covered with wistaria. The house was built by Thomas W. Cobb in 1810 and in 1829 was sold to William C. Dawson, who succeeded him as United States Senator.

Diagonally across from the Cobb-Dawson House is the HOME OF

THOMAS J. BOWEN (*private*), who charted the Yoruba country in Africa for the British, put the Yoruba language in writing, served as a missionary in Brazil, and fought in the Indian wars of 1836.

The GREENE COUNTY COURTHOUSE, Main St. (R), a large three-story brick structure with Greek Doric columns, was built in 1848 on a lot acquired from the trustees of the University of Georgia. To the rear of the courthouse is the OLD GREENE COUNTY JAIL, built about 1807 and used until 1895. The walls of the two-story granite structure are two feet thick, and the cells, dimly lighted from small grated windows, are veritable dungeons. On the upper floor is a trap door through which condemned prisoners were hanged.

Left from Greensboro on paved State 15 is SILOAM, **6 m.** (approx. 600 alt., 269 pop.); L. at the brick stores for one block to another dirt road; R. on this road to the junction with another road, **10.5 m.**; L. on this third road to BETHANY PRESBYTERIAN CHURCH, **12 m.**; the congregation was organized about the time of the formation of Greene County in 1786. In the little cemetery adjoining the church are the graves of many Revolutionary soldiers. Here in 1886 James Woodrow, Presbyterian clergyman and uncle of Woodrow Wilson, was accused of heresy following the publication of his address "Evolution," in which he denied any essential conflict between science and the Bible. Woodrow, courageously defending his views, was exonerated by the Augusta Presbytery, but later the decision was reversed by the state synod, and he was finally forced to resign his position.

At MADISON, **74.3 m.** (667 alt., 1,966 pop.) (*see* TOUR *16*), is a junction with US 129 (*see* TOUR *16*).

COVINGTON, **98.9 m.** (763 alt., 3,203 pop.), seat of Newton County, was incorporated in 1822 and named for Leonard Covington, a general of the Revolutionary War. Originally it served as a trading center for large planters, but with the development of cotton mills it has become a prosperous, small industrial center and a cotton market for the farmers of the country.

The founding of two schools showed an early interest in education. In March, 1835, the Georgia Conference Manual Labor School was opened in Covington with thirty students and with Stephen Olin as president. This was the result of "Uncle Allen" Turner's suggestion, made in the annual Methodist Conference held in Washington, Georgia, in 1834, that an industrial institution was needed in the state. When Emory College was opened in 1836 the school was moved to Oxford. In 1851 the Southern Masonic Female College was established as a finishing school. The old building served as a hospital during the War between the States and in 1887 was taken over by the city school system. It has since been replaced by a new structure.

On State 12, here known as Floyd Street, are several well-preserved ante bellum houses.

The MCCORMICK NEAL HOME (*private*), 501 Floyd St., is a beautiful white frame house of Mississippi planter design. It stands on a high basement of brick; a long flight of steps leads to a portico with small fluted Doric columns. The decorative doorway and long windows emphasized by green blinds are distinctive features.

The USHER HOME (*private*), 300 block Floyd St., a white frame structure with six Doric columns across the front, is a fine example of the Greek Revival style. The entrance ornamented with Doric pilasters, the small hanging balcony, and the long windows flanked by green blinds are characteristic details. Built about 1840, the house was occupied for many years by Jack Henderson, son of the Confederate general.

The HOUSE OF GENERAL ROBERT J. HENDERSON (*private*), L. of Floyd St. two blocks E. of the square, is a large, frame, Greek Revival structure with fluted Doric columns. The house was built by Carey Wood, an early settler and the father-in-law of Henderson (1822-94), who was made a brigadier general for bravery under Joseph E. Johnston in North Carolina.

DIXIE MANOR (*private*), 3 blocks from State 12 at the intersection of Monticello and Church Sts., is a red brick house. The small recessed portico has four Ionic columns and a small balcony. When it was erected in 1859 by Colonel Thomas Jones, the brick cost $10,000; it was sold for $3,800 soon after the War between the States.

TURNER MEMORIAL BUILDING, Monticello and Floyd Sts., has a portico with four Doric columns extending over the sidewalk. It was first erected in Oxford to serve as a hotel, but the residents of the town were so hospitable that there were no guests for the hotel. Later it was torn down and rebuilt here, to be used as a store and office building.

1. Left from Covington on State 81 is PORTERDALE, 3.2 m. (600 alt., 3,002 pop.), a prosperous mill town on the Yellow River. The frame houses of 2,700 employees line each side of the highway. Three large mills manufacture seine twine, rubber hose yarn, tire cord, tire fabric, and materials for work suitings. These mills were established in 1868 and manufactured cotton and woolen fabrics.

At 4.9 m. is a junction with a dirt road; R. on this road to OLD SALEM CAMPGROUND, 9.2 m., where interdenominational camp meetings are held each year. On a rolling hill is the OLD SALEM TABERNACLE, built in 1854 with hand-hewn beams mortised and secured with wooden pegs. As is customary with such structures, the sides are left open to the weather. Behind the tabernacle is a long row of camp houses, called tents, and a sidewalk sheltered by wooden awnings. At the foot of the hill across the road is a spring enclosed in a springhouse.

The first camp meeting was held at Salem by Methodists in 1828, the grounds being rented for $10 or $15. Five years later sixty acres were purchased, and in 1836 an additional five acres including the spring were donated. Since there were no railroads at the time the campground was established, people came in wagons from long distances to attend the two-weeks' services, and used their wagon sheets as tents.

Outstanding ministers of the Methodist church who have preached here include Bishop J. O. Andrew (1794-1871), Bishop George F. Pierce (1811-84), and Bishop Atticus G. Haygood (1839-96). For a number of years camp meeting has opened on the first Sunday in August, with Bishop Warren A. Candler preaching, and is the occasion of a large gathering from Georgia and other states. This series of meetings has been held annually, except for the four years of the War between the States. It is well attended by people of other denominations as well as Methodists, especially Presbyterians and Baptists.

The "hell-fire and damnation" school of preaching is fast being supplanted by study courses in religious education and social trends. One feature of the service, however, remains unchanged: the preacher is expected to give a lengthy sermon. This opportunity is relished by visiting city ministers who have been forced during the year to shape their discourses to the taste of urban congregations. Here at camp meeting, although there are four services each day, the sermons regularly exceed an hour in length. Hot weather, palmetto fans, flies, and the intermittent cries of infants accompany the service. At noon bountiful dinners are served.

Near the highway on a corner of the campground is KITTY'S COTTAGE, a small, white clapboarded house with green shutters and roof. The interior, appointed with old furniture, contains pictures of Bishop James Osgood Andrew and other Methodist leaders, painted by Lewis Gregg of Atlanta, and books on southern Methodism. The house was built in 1842 at Oxford (*see below*) and was removed to this site in December, 1938. It was the home of Bishop James Osgood Andrew's slave, Kitty, who was indirectly responsible for the schism in the Methodist Episcopal church.

Kitty was bequeathed to Bishop Andrew by a friend in Augusta and was to be sent to Liberia at the age of nineteen, but when the time came she refused to go. At the General Conference held in New York in 1844, Bishop Andrew was accused of owning slaves (Kitty and slaves belonging to his wife) and was formally requested "to desist from the exercise of his office so long as this impediment" remained. Prior to this time the fact that laws in Georgia and other states made it impossible for ministers to free their slaves had been recognized by church statute. But the 1844 conference was obdurate. As a result, the delegates from the South withdrew, a convention of representatives from the southern conferences was held in Louisville, Kentucky, and the Methodist Episcopal Church, South, was established as a separate body.

2. Right from Covington on paved State 81 is OXFORD, 1.1 m. (801 alt., 537 pop.), a college town of sandy, oak-shaded streets lined with houses, several of which are as much as a hundred years old. The town developed with Emory College, which was the focal point for all activities, and by a sort of tacit understanding the larger part of the town council has always been composed of faculty members. During the War between the States, Confederate officers occupied the town, and school buildings were used as a hospital. Older townspeople tell the story of Zora Fair, of Oxford, a Confederate heroine, who, disguised as a mulatto, penetrated the Union camp in Atlanta and obtained important information. Confederate officials, believing her to be a crank, failed to take advantage of her information, and she died brokenhearted a few years later.

EMORY JUNIOR COLLEGE (L) is on the old campus of Emory College. Through the efforts of Ignatius A. Few, the Georgia Methodist Conference was induced to broaden the field of the old Manual Labor School at Covington. As a result, a charter was obtained on January 25, 1836, for an institution to be named Emory College in honor of Bishop John Emory of the Methodist church. The following year the cornerstone for the first college building was laid on the 1,400-acre campus in Oxford. In 1914 Emory College became the College of Arts and Sciences of Emory University (*see* ATLANTA) and in 1919 was moved to the new campus. The old buildings at Oxford were used for Emory Academy until 1928, when the junior college was established here as a unit of the Emory University system. The junior college has an enrollment of almost two hundred.

From the stone entrance posts a dirt road leads around the quadrangle, surrounded by ten buildings and shaded by trees planted by graduating classes.

SENEY HALL (L) is a three-story Victorian building of red brick, erected in 1881 through contributions from George I. Seney, New York philanthropist. In the tower is a bell bearing an odd Spanish and Latin inscription and engravings of a crucifix and the Virgin Mary. It is said that the bell, originally taken from one of the ships of the Spanish Armada, was presented to Alexander Means in 1841 by Queen Victoria as a token of her interest in the advancement of learning.

EMORY CHAPEL (*open*) has been in use since its construction in 1873. The entrance portico of the small, brown cement building (L) is adorned with Doric pilasters and sheltered by a small gabled roof.

PHI GAMMA HALL (*open*) is a cream-colored stucco building (L) with a high basement, its simplified Greek Revival facade having two fluted Ionic and two square Doric columns. It was built about 1851 for the Phi Gamma Literary Society, one of the two societies organized in 1837 by Few. There was great rivalry between the members, who engaged in serious and prolonged debates.

FEW HALL (*open*), with four square Doric columns, a pilastered doorway, and a double row of windows on the sides, was erected (R) soon after Phi Gamma Hall for the Few Literary Society.

Left from Emory College entrance gates on State 81 (R) is the HOME OF ALEXANDER MEANS (*private*), a two-story frame structure set well back in an oak grove and surrounded by an iron fence. The first four rooms were built of hand-hewn logs before Oxford was a town, but the house was later weatherboarded, and additions have been made at various times without regard for architectural symmetry. The square-columned portico and the pilastered doorway are evidences of Greek Revival influence. Means (1801-85) served as superintendent of the Manual Labor School in Covington, became the fourth president of Emory, and later taught chemistry at Emory and the Atlanta Medical School. He was far in advance of his time in realizing the possibilities of electricity. In 1852, while at Emory, he made what is believed to be the first electric light bulb in America. An electrostatic machine, probably the one used by Means, is in the university museum.

On a dirt road opposite the Means house is the TREE THAT OWNS ITSELF, a beautiful white oak, one of two such trees in the state (*see* ATHENS). Although it grew on the sidewalk, the city officials considered it so beautiful that they deeded to the tree the small surrounding plot of ground so that it might never be cut down.

The DIXON HOME (R) (*private*), a two-story white house with small porches on each floor, is set far back from the street. It was built about 1836 and is one of the best preserved houses in town.

OLD EMORY CHURCH (*private*), on Wesley St., is a white frame building (L) with two projecting wings forming a cross. The structure was dedicated by Bishop William Capers in 1841, used as a Confederate hospital from 1862-64, completed in 1876, and restored by Bishop Candler in 1932. For years this was the only house of worship in town, and was used by both students and towns-people.

BRANHAM HEIGHTS (*private*), on Wesley St., is a two-story frame structure (L) with a Greek portico and two Doric columns. Built in 1840, it came into the possession of the Branham family in 1855. In this house Lucius Q. C. Lamar (1825-93) left his wife and children while he was seeking aid for the Confederacy in England and Russia. Lamar had lived in Oxford with his mother when he attended Emory College and had married Virginia, the daughter of Augustus Longstreet. He practiced law in Covington and other Georgia towns before he moved to Mississippi and became a United States Senator; he was almost alone in advocating a closer union between the North and the South after the War between the States. Appointed Secretary of the Interior in 1885, he resigned three years later to become an Associate Justice of the U. S. Supreme Court.

CONYERS, 110.3 m. (909 alt., 1,495 pop.), seat of Rockdale County, was incorporated in 1854. It was the first town in the state to test and win a case for prohibition; the first to have a law requiring people to keep their livestock confined; and the first to have a Presbyterian campground.

Rockdale County was named for an immense vein of granite or granite-gneiss underlying the soil for 450 square miles and projecting above the surface in many places. Very little granite is quarried near Conyers, an essentially agricultural section. Tenant farmers, living in small, unpainted houses, grow cotton, corn, and garden truck, and raise cows and chickens.

At 116.4 m. is a junction with a side road, marked by granite entrance posts.

R. on this road to LITHONIA, 0.1 m. (954 alt., 1,457 pop.), known for its granite-quarrying industries. Many of the houses and stores of this DeKalb County town are constructed of gray stone from quarries within a radius of five miles. The Lithonia stone is a highly metamorphosed form of gneiss, believed by some to be older than the Stone Mountain granite (*see* TOUR 8). Although it is used to some extent for building and monumental purposes, most of it is crushed for highway construction and railroad ballast, and often the gritty particles are sold to be added to chicken feed. DeKalb County ranks next to Elbert County in the production of granite.

1. Right from Lithonia on an unmarked dirt road to PINE MOUNTAIN, 1 m., where quarries (*open to visitors*) have been in operation since 1883 and are among the largest and best equipped in the state. The mountain is sometimes called Little Stone Mountain, for one side has been blasted away, leaving a sheer wall 114 feet high that resembles Stone Mountain.

2. Right from Lithonia on another unmarked dirt road to the QUARRY (*open to visitors*) of the Consolidated Quarries Corporation, 3 m. The solid granite face of this quarry, 1,000 feet long and 111 feet high, is periodically blasted. For this purpose, holes 6 inches in diameter are drilled 100 feet and filled with 16,000-pound charges of dynamite, which loosens about 75,000 tons of stone. By means of electric shovels the rock is loaded on trucks and hauled to the crusher, from which a belt conducts it through revolving and vibrating screens that separate

it into sizes ranging from two inches down. The oversized stones are crushed again by a cone crusher. From the stock piles, underground conveyers carry the stone to the loading bin where it is given a final washing and screening and dumped by means of an automatic hopper into freight cars. Some of the crushed stone is made into granite-concrete brick for building purposes.

Between Lithonia and Avondale Estates many outcroppings of granite are visible. Along the Georgia Railroad, which parallels this route (R), gondola cars stand filled with crushed stone, or large cranes load heavy granite blocks on flatcars. Many houses along the route are constructed of native granite.

AVONDALE ESTATES, 128 m. (approx. 1,025 alt., 535 pop.), a residential suburb of Atlanta, was incorporated in 1927. A park (L) is planted with shrubbery and rose crape myrtle; beyond are streets lined with modern brick and wide-board houses, each having a landscaped lawn. The stores (R) are of Tudor-Gothic design. Tennis courts and a swimming pool, with a constant flow of cold spring water, provide recreation for the suburban residents.

At Avondale Estates is a junction with US 78 (*see* TOUR *8*).

*

PART FOUR

APPENDICES

*

Chronology

1540 Hernando de Soto marches from Florida through part of Georgia and crosses the Savannah River at Silver Bluff, near Augusta.

1560 Tristan de Luna and 300 Spanish soldiers cross Coosa River and search for gold in north Georgia.

1562 Jean Ribault of France explores Georgia coast.

1566 Pedro Menendez de Aviles builds fort on Santa Catalina (St. Catherines) Island.

1573 Franciscan friars build mission on Cumberland Island.

1595 Franciscans build missions on St. Simon and Jekyll islands and mainland.

1663 Charles II grants to lords proprietors of Carolina land between 31° and 36° N. lat., including present territory of Georgia.

1689 All missions abandoned, forces being withdrawn to strengthen garrison at St. Augustine, Fla.

1717 "Margravate of Azilia" granted to Sir Robert Montgomery; fails through lack of settlers.

1721 Fort King George, first English settlement in territory, built at mouth of Altamaha River.

1732 George II grants charter authorizing settlement of Georgia by imprisoned debtors; first Great Seal made.

1733 February 12. James Edward Oglethorpe and his colonists settle at Yamacraw Bluff; greeted by Tomochichi, Indian chief.
May 14. Italian Piedmontese arrive to teach silk culture to colonists.
May 21. Chiefs of Creek Nation sign treaty ceding to Oglethorpe and colonists all land between Savannah and Altamaha rivers.
July 7. Savannah town court organized; first jury empanelled.

1734 March 17. Salzburgers from Bavaria settle at Ebenezer.
April 7. Oglethorpe sails for England with Tomochichi and several Indian chiefs.

1735 January 9. Trustees establish ban on rum and slaves in Georgia.
May. Moravian immigrants settle on Savannah River.
Augusta founded.

1736 January. Scottish Highlanders settle Darien.
February 5. John and Charles Wesley arrive at Savannah with Oglethorpe.
February 18. Fort established at Frederica.
August 11. Charles Wesley returns to England.

1737 Oglethorpe appointed commander in chief of His Majesty's forces in Georgia and South Carolina.
December. John Wesley returns to England.

1738 George Whitefield and James Habersham arrive at Savannah.

1740 March 25. George Whitefield lays first brick of Bethesda Orphan House.
May 10. Oglethorpe captures Fort San Diego, near St. Augustine, Fla.

1741 Georgia divided into two counties: Savannah County, north; Frederica County, south.

1742 July 7. Oglethorpe, with small band of colonists, defeats large Spanish force at Battle of Bloody Marsh, St. Simon Island.

1743 Oglethorpe leaves Georgia permanently.
Government of Georgia changes from military to civil status, directed by a president and five councillors; Frederica County abolished; William Stephens becomes first president of Colony.

1744 First commercial house in Georgia established by James Habersham and Francis Harris.

1749 Trustees allow introduction of slaves into colony.

1751 First Colonial Assembly meets at Savannah.

1752 June 23. Trustees surrender charter.
Midway settled by Puritans from Dorchester, S. C.
Estimated colonial population 4,000 to 5,000, including 1,500 Negroes.

1754 Georgia becomes a royal province; Capt. John Reynolds, British Navy, appointed first royal governor.
October 29. Reynolds arrives at Savannah.

1755 First house of commons, elected by Georgians, convenes at Savannah.
Four hundred Acadians banished from Nova Scotia arrive; sent to South Carolina the following spring.

1758 Assembly declares official adherence to Church of England. Georgia is divided into eight parishes.

1761 George III proclaimed King with great ceremony in Savannah.

1763 April 7. The *Georgia Gazette,* Georgia's first newspaper, issued at Savannah.
October 7. Boundaries of Georgia extended to St. Marys River on south and Mississippi River on west.
November 10. Peace treaty signed at Augusta with all Indians in Georgia.

1766 February. Stamp Act riot in Savannah.
Estimated population 10,000 whites and 7,800 Negroes.

1768 Benjamin Franklin appointed Georgia's agent in England.

1772 First Baptist church in Georgia founded at Kiokee Creek.

1773 Creek and Cherokee Indians sign treaty at Augusta ceding to Britain 2,100,000 acres in Georgia.

1775 January. First Provincial Congress meets at Savannah; Archibald Bulloch elected president.
May 11. Patriots seize store of powder at Savannah.
May 13. Lyman Hall presents credentials as delegate from Georgia, and is seated by Continental Congress as representing only his own parish, St. Johns.

May 17. Continental Congress places all of Georgia except St. Johns Parish under ban of colonial nonintercourse.

June 22. Council of Safety elected by Savannah citizens.

July 4. Second Provincial Congress meets at Savannah; Archibald Bulloch reelected president; official Council of Safety appointed.

July 20. Continental Congress rescinds ban of colonial nonintercourse.

July. Georgia schooner takes 9,000 pounds of powder from British vessel.

September 13. Continental Congress seats three Georgia delegates: Houstoun, Bulloch, and Zubly.

1776 February 11. James Wright, Royal Governor, escapes arrest and boards British ship.

April 15. Third Provincial Congress adopts temporary constitution. Lyman Hall, George Walton, and Button Gwinnett sign Declaration of Independence.

1777 February 5. First state constitution ratified by Constitutional Convention in Savannah; parishes replaced by counties; president replaced by governor; new seal adopted.

May 8. John Adams Treutlen elected first state governor.

May 16. Button Gwinnett mortally wounded in duel with Gen. Lachlan McIntosh.

1778 July 24. Edward Telfair and Edward Langworthy sign Articles of Confederation.

November. British troops invade Georgia.

December 29. Savannah captured by British.

1779 January. Whig government removed to Augusta.

January. British capture Augusta.

February 14. British defeated at Battle of Kettle Creek.

February 28. British evacuate Augusta.

July 13. Governor Wright returns to Georgia and reestablishes royal rule.

July 24. Supreme Executive Council elected by Whig assembly to exercise executive power instead of governor; John Wereat elected president.

September. Colonial troops aided by French fleet lay siege to Savannah.

October 9. Savannah defenders repulse attack; Count Pulaski and Sgt. William Jasper mortally wounded.

1780 January 4. Richard Howley appointed governor by Whig assembly in opposition to Supreme Executive Council.

February 3. Heard's Fort declared temporary capital by Governor Howley.

June. Augusta retaken by British.

1781 British expelled from Augusta by Col. Henry (Lighthorse Harry) Lee, Gen. Andrew Pickens, and Col. Elijah Clarke.

1782 British forces withdrawn from Savannah; seat of government reestablished in Savannah.

1783 February 15. Edward Telfair, John Houstoun, and Gen. Lachlan McIntosh authorized to adjust northern boundary of Georgia.

May 31. Creek and Cherokee cede lands west of Tugalo River.

July 31. Legislature establishes Richmond Academy at Augusta, oldest existing chartered school in Georgia.

Georgia extends jurisdiction to Natchez district along Mississippi River.

1784   February 25. University of Georgia endowed, granted 40,000 acres of land.

1785   January 27. University of Georgia chartered.
Augusta Chronicle founded.
Georgia organizes Bourbon County along Mississippi River.

1786   Augusta becomes temporary seat of government.
Sea Island cotton introduced on Georgia coast.

1787   Boundary line established between Georgia and South Carolina.
Four of Georgia's six elected delegates attend Constitutional Convention at Philadelphia: William Few, Abraham Baldwin, William Pierce, and William Houstoun; Few and Baldwin sign Constitution.

1788   January 2. Georgia ratifies Federal Constitution, the fourth state to do so.
February 1. Chatham Academy at Savannah chartered.

1789   May. New state constitution adopted.

1790   Population of Georgia 82,548 (U. S. Census).

1791   President Washington visits Augusta and Savannah.

1793   Eli Whitney invents cotton gin at home of the widow of General Nathanael Greene near Savannah.

1795   January. Georgia legislature passes Yazoo Act, whereby state relinquishes claims to 35,000,000 acres of land in present states of Alabama and Mississippi at price of less than 1½¢ an acre.
February 25. Joseph Habersham becomes Postmaster General of U. S. (1795-1801).
May. Seat of government removed to Louisville.

1796   Yazoo Act rescinded and all documents pertaining thereto burned before state capitol at Louisville.

1798   Georgia abolishes African slave trade and interstate slave trade, in new state constitution.
Act of Congress separates Mississippi territory from Georgia.

1799   Present seal of Georgia adopted.

1800   Population 162,686 (U. S. Census).

1801   First building of University of Georgia erected.

1802   All Georgia lands west of Chattahoochee and of a line running north from the mouth of Uchee Creek to Nickajack Creek ceded to United States.
Creek, by Treaty of Fort Wilkinson, cede tracts south of Altamaha and west of Oconee rivers.

1803   Land lottery system inaugurated by act of legislature.

1804   Milledgeville declared new seat of government.
Georgia Medical Society incorporated.

1805   Creek, by treaty, cede their remaining lands east of Ocmulgee River except a strip in Old Ocmulgee Fields.

1806   Fort Hawkins, site of Macon, built.

1808   Site for penitentiary selected in Milledgeville.

1810   Population 252,433 (U. S. Census).

1812   Georgia coast towns fortified after United States declares war on England.

1814   General Andrew Jackson forces Creek to sign treaty ceding land in southern Georgia.

1815   August 1. William H. Crawford appointed U. S. Secretary of War.
       Bank of the State of Georgia in Savannah chartered.
1816   April. Regular steamboat transportation begins on Savannah River.
       October 22. Crawford appointed U. S. Secretary of the Treasury (1816-25).
1818   Creek cede 1,500,000 acres south of Altamaha and about headwaters of Ocmulgee.
       Tennessee-Georgia boundary line established.
1819   May 22. The *Savannah*, first steamship to cross Atlantic, leaves Savannah for Liverpool.
       Senator John Forsyth becomes United States Minister to Spain (1819-23).
1820   Population 340,989 (U. S. Census).
1821   Creek cede all their lands east of Flint River.
1824   Charter obtained for Savannah and Ogeechee Canal.
1825   February. By Treaty of Indian Springs, Creek cede all their lands in Georgia to U. S.
       April 30. William McIntosh, Creek chief, slain by Indians for promoting cession of Creek lands.
       Sequoyah, Cherokee Indian, invents syllabary.
       La Fayette visits Georgia.
1826   January. Creek chiefs sign new treaty at Washington, ceding to the State of Georgia all lands but 300,000 acres of land east of the Chattahoochee River.
1827   November 15. All remaining Creek lands ceded to U. S. for $28,000.
       Cherokee adopt a constitution at their capital, New Echota.
1828   December 20. Georgia legislature extends state jurisdiction over Cherokee country.
1828-29   Gold discovered in north Georgia.
1829   Senator John M. Berrien becomes Attorney General of United States (1829-31).
1830   Population 516,823 (U. S. Census).
       Legislature decrees no white person may live in Cherokee country without license.
       First medical college in state organized in Augusta.
1831   Missionaries to Cherokee imprisoned after refusing to obtain license; case brought before U. S. Supreme Court.
       Cherokee lands surveyed by Georgia for distribution by lottery.
1832   Georgia ignores U. S. Supreme Court decision. Cherokee country divided into ten counties.
1833   January. Missionaries released by clemency of Governor Lumpkin after swearing allegiance to Georgia.
       Georgia R. R., first to be built in state, chartered.
       Central of Georgia Ry. chartered.
       Alabama-Georgia boundary line agreed upon.
1834   Senator John Forsyth becomes U. S. Secretary of State (1834-41).
1835   Oglethorpe College at Milledgeville chartered.
       Congressman James M. Wayne becomes Associate Justice of U. S. Supreme Court (1835-67).

December. By New Echota Treaty, Cherokee cede to state all their lands in Georgia.

1836 Emory College chartered.

Wesleyan College chartered as Georgia Female College.

Western & Atlantic R. R. chartered, to be built at state expense.

1837 Mercer College chartered.

Terminus of Western & Atlantic R. R. located at present site of Atlanta.

Branch mint built by United States at Dahlonega.

1838 Last of the Cherokee removed from Georgia.

1840 Population 691,392 (U. S. Census).

1842 First operation using ether as anesthetic performed by Dr. Crawford W. Long at Jefferson.

State Sanitarium for the Insane erected at Milledgeville.

1843 Settlement at terminus of Western & Atlantic R. R. chartered as Marthasville.

First train runs from Savannah to Macon over Central of Georgia Ry.

1844 Methodist church divided into Northern and Southern Conferences over slavery question.

1845 Georgia organizes its first supreme court; Joseph Henry Lumpkin, first chief justice.

Marthasville incorporated as town of Atlanta.

1846 Georgia sends 898 men to the Mexican War.

1849 Governor George W. Crawford becomes U. S. Secretary of War (1849-50).

1850 Population 906,185 (U. S. Census).

1857 Former Governor Howell Cobb becomes U. S. Secretary of the Treasury (1857-60).

1858 Legislature appropriates $100,000 annual income from Western & Atlantic R. R. to maintain free elementary schools.

1860 Population 1,057,286 (U. S. Census).

Secession meetings in Georgia begin.

1861 January 3. Fort Pulaski seized by order of Governor Brown.

January 19. Georgia secedes from the Union.

January 23. Georgia Congressmen resign seats.

January 24. Federal arsenal at Augusta surrenders to Governor Brown.

February 9. Alexander H. Stephens elected Vice President of the Confederacy.

March 16. Georgia adopts Confederate constitution.

March 23. Georgia adopts new state constitution.

November 24. Admiral Dupont, U. S. N., takes Tybee Island.

1862 April 10. Fort Pulaski taken by Federal forces.

1863 September 20. Federal forces defeated at Battle of Chickamauga.

1864 May 4. General W. T. Sherman opens campaign in Georgia.

May 15. Battle of Resaca.

June 14. Lieutenant General Leonidas Polk, the "fighting bishop," killed at Pine Mountain.

June 27. Battle of Kennesaw Mountain.

July 7. General John B. Hood succeeds General Joseph E. Johnston.

July 20. Battle of Peachtree Creek.

July 22. Battle of Atlanta. General J. B. McPherson and Major General W. H. T. Walker killed.

July 28. Battle of Ezra Church.

August 31. Battle of Jonesboro.

September 2. Sherman occupies Atlanta.

November 14. Sherman burns Atlanta and starts on march to the sea.

December 22. Sherman occupies Savannah.

1865 May 10. Jefferson Davis, President of the Confederate States, captured near Irwinville.

October 26. Secession Ordinance repealed by convention at Milledgeville.

December 9. Thirteenth Amendment, abolishing slavery, ratified by legislature.

1866 Georgia accepts Whitner-Orr line as Georgia-Florida boundary.

State superintendent of education appointed.

1867 April 1. Federal troops under Major General John Pope occupy Third Military District, including Georgia.

December 9. Constitutional convention meets at Atlanta.

Ku Klux Klan appears in Georgia.

Atlanta University, first of Georgia's Negro colleges, granted charter.

1868 March 11. Convention adopts new state constitution; declares Atlanta state capital.

April 20. People ratify new state constitution; Rufus Bullock elected governor.

July 21. Legislature ratifies Fourteenth Amendment; civil government restored.

July. Six Georgia Congressmen take seats in national House of Representatives; Senators not seated before Congress adjourns.

September. Negro members expelled from legislature.

1869 March. Georgia rejects Fifteenth Amendment.

March 5. Georgia Congressmen excluded from national House of Representatives.

December 22. Georgia again under military control.

1870 Population 1,184,109 (U. S. Census).

February 2. Fifteenth Amendment ratified by legislature with Negro members again in attendance; Fourteenth Amendment reratified.

July 15. Georgia readmitted to Union.

October 13. Legislature establishes state department of education.

December. Congressmen reseated in national House.

1875 State board of health organized.

1877 New state constitution adopted (still in force); Atlanta established as permanent capital by referendum.

1879 Flag of state of Georgia adopted by legislature.

1880 Population 1,542,180 (U. S. Census).

William Burnham Woods becomes Associate Justice of U. S. Supreme Court (1880-87).

1881 International Cotton Exposition held in Atlanta.

1885 Georgia School of Technology chartered.
1888 L. Q. C. Lamar becomes Associate Justice of U. S. Supreme Court (1888-93).
1889 Present state capitol at Atlanta opened.
      Agnes Scott College established as Decatur Female Seminary.
1890 Population 1,837,353 (U. S. Census).
      Chickamauga and Chattanooga National Military Park established by Congress.
1893 Hoke Smith appointed Secretary of Interior by President Cleveland (1893-96).
      Congressman Thomas E. Watson secures first appropriation for rural free delivery.
1895 International and Cotton States Exposition held in Atlanta.
1897 State library commission established by legislature.
1898 Georgia contributes three regiments to Spanish-American War.
1900 Population 2,216,331 (U. S. Census).
1901 Federal penitentiary established in Atlanta.
1902 Martha Berry Schools for mountain children founded.
1904 Thomas E. Watson nominated for President of U. S. on Populist ticket. Nominated again in 1908.
1907 State-wide prohibition adopted.
1908 Convict leasing system abolished.
1910 Population 2,609,121 (U. S. Census).
1911 Joseph R. Lamar becomes Associate Justice of U. S. Supreme Court (1911-16).
1912 Girl Scouts of America founded at Savannah by Juliette Low.
      High schools made part of state school system.
1914 Sixth District Federal Reserve Bank established in Atlanta.
1915 Juvenile courts established in counties with population of 60,000 or more.
1916 State highway commission created.
1917-18 Two Army and two National Guard training camps established; 93,321 men and 238 army nurses from Georgia enter World War.
1918 Georgia ratifies Eighteenth Amendment.
1919 State board of public welfare created.
1920 Population 2,895,832 (U. S. Census).
      Georgia ratifies Nineteenth Amendment.
1921 Boll weevil first seriously damages cotton crop.
1922 Fort Benning, largest infantry training school in the world, established near Columbus by Federal government.
1925 Candler Field, first airport in state, established at Atlanta.
1926 High Museum of Art established in Atlanta.
1927 Franklin D. Roosevelt organizes Warm Springs Foundation.
1928 First commercial airways system in Georgia completed.
      First concrete-paved state-line-to-state-line highway in Georgia completed.
1930 Population 2,908,506 (U. S. Census).
      Atlanta University consolidates with Spelman and Morehouse colleges.

1931 Reorganization bill passed, consolidating state departments and establishing university system.

1937 March. State department of natural resources created.
Legislature establishes minimum seven-months' term for public schools, with free textbooks.
State planning board organized.
Social Security Act adopted by Georgia.

1938 State prohibition law repealed.

1939 State board of penal corrections created.

Bibliography

GENERAL INFORMATION

American Automobile Association. *Southeastern Tour Book.* Washington, D. C. 1938. 408 p. illus., maps. See pp. 67-85. Issued annually.

Candler, Allen D., ed. *Georgia: Comprising Sketches of Counties, Towns, Events, Institutions, and Persons, Arranged in Cyclopedic Form* . . . ed. by ex-Governor Allen D. Candler and General Clement A. Evans. Atlanta, State Historical Assn., 1906. 3 v. ports.

Woodward, Emily, ed. *Empire: Georgia Today in Photographs and Paragraphs.* Atlanta, Ruralist Press, Inc., 1936. 182 p. col. front.

DESCRIPTION AND TRAVEL

Bartram, William. *Travels through North and South Carolina, Georgia, East and West Florida* . . . Philadelphia, James & Johnson, 1791. 520 p. front., plates, map. New edition pub. by Macy-Macius, New York, 1928. (American Bookshelf).

Cooney, Mrs. Loraine Meeks, comp. *Garden History of Georgia, 1733-1933.* Atlanta, Peachtree Garden Club, 1933. 458 p. illus. (incl. plans), bibl.

Coulter, E. Merton, ed. *Georgia's Disputed Ruins.* Chapel Hill, Univ. of North Carolina Press, 1937. 275 p. front., illus., maps. Contains articles on the tabby ruins of the Georgia coast, archeology of Elizafield ruins, and cultivation of sugar cane.

Kemble, Frances Anne. *Journal of a Residence on a Georgian Plantation in 1838-1839.* New York, Harper; London, Longman, Greene, 1863. 434 p.

Knight, Lucian Lamar. *Georgia's Landmarks, Memorials and Legends* . . . Atlanta, Byrd Print. Co., 1913-14. 2 v. fronts., plates, ports.

Leigh, Mrs. Frances Butler. *Ten Years on a Georgia Plantation Since the War.* London, R. Bentley & Son, 1883. 347 p.

Longstreet, Augustus Baldwin. *Georgia Scenes, Characters, Incidents, etc. in the First Half-Century of the Republic.* New York, Harper, 1897. 297 p. front., illus. 1st pub. 1835.

Lovell, Mrs. Caroline Couper. *The Golden Isles of Georgia.* Boston, Little, Brown & Co., 1933. 300 p. front., plates, ports., maps, bibl. Describes St. Simon and Sapelo islands.

McQueen, A. S., and Hamp Mizell. *History of Okefenokee Swamp.* Clinton, S. C., Jacobs & Co., 1926. 191 p. front. (map), plates, ports.

Matschat, Mrs. Cecile Hulse. *Suwannee River; Strange Green Land.* New York, Toronto, Farrar & Rinehart, Inc., 1938. 296 p. illus. (incl. maps). (Half-title: The Rivers of America; editor, Constance Lindsay Skinner.)

NATURAL SETTING

Burleigh, Thomas D., and W. R. Mattoon. *Common Forest Trees of Georgia.* Athens, 1923. 80 p. illus. (Georgia State College of Agriculture. v. 12, No. 7. Bulletin no. 291.) A pocket manual.

Davis, D. W. *Georgia Wild Flowers and Laboratory Manual.* Ann Arbor, Mich., Edmonds Bros., Inc., 1938. 174 p. illus.

Georgia. Department of Education. *Natural Resources of Georgia.* Atlanta, 1938. 222 p. illus.

Georgia. Geological Survey. *Physical Geography of Georgia,* by Laurence La Forge, Wythe Cooke, Arthur Keith, and M. R. Campbell, with int. by S. W. McCallie, State Geologist. Prepared in co-operation with U. S. Geological Survey. Atlanta, 1925. 189 p. illus., maps. (Bulletin 42.)

——*Preliminary Report on the Geology of the Coastal Plain of Georgia,* by Otto Veatch and Lloyd William Stephenson. Prepared in co-operation with U. S. Geological Survey under the direction of T. Wayland Vaughan. Atlanta, 1911. 463 p. illus., maps. (Bulletin 26.)

Georgia. State Board of Game and Fisheries. *Some Helpful Georgia Birds.* Atlanta, 1928. 55 p.

Greene, Earl R. *Birds of the Atlanta, Georgia, Area, Distribution, Migration, and Nesting.* Atlanta, 1933. 46 p. illus. (Georgia Society of Naturalists. Bulletin no. 2.)

Wright, Albert Hazen. *Life Histories of the Frogs of Okefenokee Swamp, Georgia.* New York, Macmillan, 1931. 497 p. illus.

ARCHEOLOGY AND INDIANS

Caughey, John Walton. *McGillivray of the Creeks.* Norman, Univ. of Oklahoma Press, 1938. 385 p. facsim., bibl. (Half-title: Civilization of the American Indian.)

Floyd, D. B. *New Yamacraw and the Indian Mound Irene.* Savannah, 1936. 26 p.

Foreman, Grant. *Sequoyah.* Norman, Univ. of Oklahoma Press, 1938. 90 p. plate, port., facsims. (Half-title: The Civilization of the American Indian.)

Heye, George H., F. W. Hodge, and George H. Pepper. *The Nacoochee Mound in Georgia.* New York, 1918. 103 p. illus. (Contributions from Museum of American Indian, Heye Foundation, v. 4, no. 3.)

Kelly, A. R. *A Preliminary Report on Archaeological Explorations at Macon, Ga.* Washington, Govt. Print. Off., 1938. 68 p. (U. S. Bureau of Am. Ethnology. Bulletin 119.)

Moorehead, Warren K. "Exploration of the Etowah Site in Georgia." (In *Etowah Papers.* New Haven, Pub. for Phillips Academy by Yale Univ. Press; London, H. Milford, Oxford Univ. Press, 1932.)

United States Congress. *Indian Affairs, May 12, 1789-Oct. 5, 1814* and *Indian Affairs, Dec. 6, 1815-March 1, 1827.* Washington, Gales and Seaton, 1832 and

1834. Vols. VII and VIII in *American State Papers;* documents, legislative and executive of the Congress of the United States, authorized by both houses and prepared by representatives for each.

Walker, Robert Sparks. *Torchlights to the Cherokees: The Brainerd Mission.* New York, Macmillan, 1931. 339 p.

HISTORY AND GOVERNMENT

Andrews, Eliza Frances. *The War-Time Journal of a Georgia Girl, 1864-1865.* New York, Appleton, 1906. 387 p. illus. from contemporary photographs.

Avary, Mrs. Myrta Lockett. *Dixie after the War* . . . New York, Doubleday, Page & Co., 1906. 435 p. illus. from old paintings, daguerreotypes, and rare photographs.

Avery, Isaac W. *The History of the State of Georgia from 1850 to 1881* . . . New York, Brown & Derby, 1881. 754 p. ports. (incl. front.), facsim.

Bolton, Herbert E., ed. *Arrendondo's Historical Proof of Spain's Title to Georgia.* With introduction, "The Debatable Land," by Herbert E. Bolton and Mary Ross. Berkeley, Univ. of California Press, 1925. 382 p. illus., maps.

Brooks, Robert Preston. *History of Georgia.* Boston, New York, etc., Atkinson, Mentzer & Co., 1913. 444 p. illus., map.

The Colonial Records of the State of Georgia. Comp. by Allen D. Candler. Atlanta, published by various state printers, 1904-16. 26 v. in 28 parts.

The Confederate Records of the State of Georgia. Comp. by Allen D. Candler. Atlanta, C. P. Byrd, State Printer, 1909-11. 5 v.

Cooper, Walter G. *The Story of Georgia.* New York, Am. Historical Society, Inc., 1938. 4 v. fronts., illus., plates, ports., maps, bibl. Vol. 4, biographical.

Coulter, E. Merton. *A Short History of Georgia.* Chapel Hill, Univ. of North Carolina Press, 1933. 457 p. front., illus. (incl. maps), plates, ports., facsim., diagr., bibl.

Dugat, Henry. *Life of Henry W. Grady.* Edinburg, Texas, Valley Printery, 1927. 150 p. front. (port.), plates.

Egmont, John Perceval, 1st Earl. *Manuscripts of the Earl of Egmont: Diary.* London, His Majesty's Stationery Office, 1920-23. 3 v. (Historical Manuscripts Commission). Contains day by day account of the transactions of the Georgia trustees by the 1st Earl of Egmont, their first president.

Ettinger, Amos Aschbach. *James Edward Oglethorpe, Imperial Idealist.* Oxford, Eng., Clarendon Press, 1936. 348 p. front., plates, ports., fold. map.

Evans, Lawton B. *A History of Georgia for Use in Schools.* New York, Cincinnati, etc., Am. Book Co., 1908. 360 p. front., illus., double map. (State History series) 1st pub. 1898.

The *Georgia Historical Quarterly.* Pub. by Georgia Historical Society . . . v. 1-23. Mar. 1917-Mar. 1939. Savannah, 1917-1939, 23 v.

Georgia Historical Society. *Collections of the Georgia Historical Society.* Savannah, printed for the society, 1840-1916. 9 v. in 13 parts.

Gilmer, George Rockingham. *Sketches of Some of the First Settlers of Upper Georgia, of the Cherokees, and the Author.* Americus, Georgia, Americus Book Co., 1926. 458 p. 1st pub. in 1855.

Gosnell, Cullen B. *Government and Politics of Georgia.* New York, T. Nelson & Sons, 1936. 248 p. diagr., bibl.

Johnson, Amanda. *Georgia as Colony and State.* Atlanta, Walter W. Brown Pub. Co., 1938. 1064 p. illus. (maps), diagrs., bibl.

Jones, Charles Colcock. *The History of Georgia.* Boston, New York, Houghton, Mifflin & Co., 1883. 2 v. fronts., ports., maps, plans.

Knight, Lucian Lamar. *Georgia's Bi-Centennial Memoirs and Memories* . . . Published by the author for private distribution, 1931-33. 4 v. ports.

——*A Standard History of Georgia and Georgians.* Chicago, New York, Lewis Pub. Co., 1917. 6 v. fronts., illus., plates, ports., double geneal. table. Vols. 4-6, biographical.

Lanning, John Tate. *The Diplomatic History of Georgia; a Study of the Epoch of Jenkins' Ear.* Chapel Hill, Univ. of North Carolina Press, 1936. 275 p. front., ports., fold. maps, bibl. (Publications of Univ. of Georgia.)

McElreath, Walter. *A Treatise on the Constitution of Georgia* . . . Atlanta, Harrison Co., 1912. 700 p.

McCain, James Ross. *Georgia as a Proprietary Province; the Execution of a Trust.* Boston, R. G. Badger, 1917. 357 p. bibl.

Northen, William J., ed. *Men of Mark in Georgia:* A Complete and Elaborate History of the State from its settlement to the present time, chiefly told in biographies and autobiographies of the most eminent men of each period of Georgia's progress and development. Atlanta, A. B. Caldwell (publisher), 1907-12. 7 v., ports.

Page, James Madison. *The True Story of Andersonville Prison; A Defense of Major Henry Wirz.* In collaboration with M. J. Haley. New York and Washington, Neale Pub. Co., 1908. 248 p. front., portraits.

Pendleton, Louis Beauregard. *Alexander H. Stephens.* Philadelphia, G. W. Jacobs & Co., 1908. 406 p. front. (port.), bibl. (Half-title: American crisis biographies, ed. by E. P. Oberholtzer.)

Phillips, Ulrich Bonnell. "Georgia and State Rights, a Study of the Political History of Georgia from the Revolution to the Civil War . . ." (In Am. Historical Assn. *Annual Report for 1901.* Washington, 1902. maps, bibl. v. 2, pp. 1-224.)

——*The Life of Robert Toombs.* New York, Macmillan, 1913. 281 p. front. (port.).

The Revolutionary Records of the State of Georgia. Comp. and pub. under authority of the Legislature by Allen D. Candler. Atlanta, Franklin-Turner Co., 1908. 3 v.

Spruill, Julia Cherry. *Women's Life and Work in the Southern Colonies.* Chapel Hill, Univ. of North Carolina Press, 1939. 434 p. illus. Covers the colonial period from the earliest days to the time of the Revolution.

Thompson, C. Mildred. *Reconstruction in Georgia, Economic, Social, Political, 1865-1872.* New York, 1915. 418 p. bibl. (Studies in History, Economics, and Public Law, ed. by Faculty of Political Science of Columbia University. vol. 64, no. 1.)

White, Rev. George. *Historical Collections of Georgia* . . . New York, Pudney & Russell, 1854. 683 p. illus., plates, ports.

Woodward, C. Vann. *Tom Watson, Agrarian Rebel*. New York, Macmillan, 1938. 518 p. plates, ports., bibl.

TRANSPORTATION

Hinton, E. H. *A Historical Sketch of the Evolution of Trade and Transportation in Macon, Ga.* Atlanta, 1912. 56 p.

Johnston, James Houstoun, comp. *Western and Atlantic Railroad of the State of Georgia.* Comp. in pursuance of legislative action 1925. Atlanta, Stein Print. Co., State Printers, 1931. 364 p. front., plates, ports., fold. map, facsim. diagrs.

Phillips, Ulrich Bonnell. *A History of Transportation in the Eastern Cotton Belt to 1860.* New York, Columbia Univ. Press, 1908. 405 p. illus., maps, tables, bibl.

AGRICULTURE

Brooks, Robert Preston. *The Agrarian Revolution in Georgia, 1865-1912.* Madison, Wis., 1914. 129 p. maps, bibl. (Bulletin of Univ. of Wisconsin, no. 639. History Series, V. 3, no. 3.)

Johnson, Charles S., Edwin R. Embree, and W. W. Alexander. *The Collapse of Cotton Tenancy.* Chapel Hill, Univ. of North Carolina Press, 1935. 81 p. bibl.

Moore, A. N., J. K. Niles, and R. C. Campbell. *Credit Problems of Georgia Cotton Farmers.* Experiment, Ga., Georgia Agricultural Experiment Station, 1929. 56 p. tables. (Bulletin 153.)

Raper, Arthur. *Preface to Peasantry; a Tale of Two Black Belt Counties.* Chapel Hill, Univ. of North Carolina Press, 1936. 425 p. front., illus. (maps), plates, diagrs. Describes effects of the New Deal in Greene and Macon counties, Georgia.

SOCIAL AND ECONOMIC CONDITIONS

Bryan, Malcolm H., and Thomas J. Askew, comp. *Readings to Accompany a Course on Contemporary Georgia.* Athens. Div. of Publications, Univ. of Georgia, 1935. 520 p. illus., maps, fold. table, diagrs. Photolithographed.

Chambliss, Rollin. *What Negro Newspapers of Georgia Say about Some Social Problems, 1933.* Athens, Ga., 1934. 117 p. bibl. (University of Georgia Phelps-Stokes Fellowship Studies, no. 13.)

Citizens' Fact Finding Movement. *Bulletins.* Atlanta, 1938-39. Published occasionally.

Couch, W. T., ed. *Culture in the South.* Chapel Hill, Univ. of North Carolina Press, 1935. 711 p. Contains 31 essays (by Broadus Mitchell, George Fort Milton, Donald Davidson, Bruce Crawford, B. A. Botkin, Charles W. Pipkin, etc.).

Davidson, Elizabeth H. *Child Labor Legislation in the Southern United States.* Chapel Hill, Univ. of North Carolina Press, 1939. 312 p. Covers the last half century and deals particularly with the four leading textile states of North Carolina, South Carolina, Alabama, and Georgia.

DuBois, W. E. Burghardt. *Black Reconstruction: an Essay toward a History of the Part Which Black Folk Played in the Attempt to Reconstruct Democracy in America, 1860-1880.* New York, Harcourt, Brace & Co., 1935. 746 p. bibl.

Evans, M. G. *The History of the Organized Labor Movement in Georgia.* Reprint from abstracts of theses, Humanities Series, V. 8. Chicago, Univ. of Chicago Press, 1929-30. 9 p.

Fanning, J. W. *Negro Migration, a Study of the Exodus of the Negroes* between 1920 and 1925 from Middle Georgia Counties . . . Athens, Univ. of Georgia, 1930. 39 p. diagrs. (Georgia University Phelps-Stokes Fellowship Studies, no. 9.)

Gordon, Asa H. *The Georgia Negro: a History.* Ann Arbor, Mich., Edwards Bros., Inc., 1937. 426 p. illus. (incl. ports.). Lithoprinted.

National Emergency Council. *Report on Economic Conditions of the South.* Prepared for the President [Franklin D. Roosevelt] (by the National Emergency Council, Lowell Mellett, executive director). Washington, Govt. Print. Off., 1938. 64 p.

Odum, Howard W. *Southern Regions of the United States.* Prepared for the Southern Regional Committee of the Social Science Research Council. Chapel Hill, Univ. of North Carolina Press, 1936. 664 p. maps, charts, tables.

Phillips, Ulrich Bonnell. *Life and Labor in the Old South.* Boston, Little, Brown & Co., 1929. 375 p. front., illus., maps, diagr.

EDUCATION

Boogher, Elbert W. G. *Secondary Education in Georgia, 1732-1858.* Philadelphia, 1933. 452 p. bibl.

Bowden, Haygood S. *Two Hundred Years of Education: Bicentennial, 1733-1933, Savannah, Chatham County, Georgia.* Richmond, Va., Dietz Print. Co., 1932. 381 p.

Byers, Tracy. *Martha Berry: the Sunday Lady of Possum Trot.* New ork, London, Putnam, 1932. 268 p. front. (port.), plates. An account of educational endeavor in the Mount Berry schools.

Coulter, E. Merton. *College Life in the Old South.* New York, Macmillan, 1928. 381 p. front., plates, maps, bibl. Based on the University of Georgia.

Dabney, Charles William. *Universal Education in the South.* Chapel Hill, Univ. of North Carolina Press, 1936. 2 v. fronts., illus. (maps), plates, ports, facsims., diagrs., bibl.

Johnston, Richard Malcolm. *Early Education in Middle Georgia.* Washington, Govt. Print. Off., 1896. 35 p. U. S. Bureau of Education. Report of the Commissioner of Education. Chapter 42.

Jones, Charles Edgeworth. *Education in Georgia.* Washington, Govt. Print. Off., 1889. 154 p. plates. U. S. Bureau of Education, Circular of Information. 1888, no. 4.

RELIGION

The *Christian Index. History of the Baptist Denomination in Georgia.* Comp. for the *Christian Index.* Atlanta, J. P. Harrison & Co., 1881. 887 p. illus., ports., fold maps.

Fries, Adelaide L. *The Moravians in Georgia, 1735-1740.* Raleigh, N. C. Printed for the author by Edwards & Broughton, 1905. 252 p. front., plates, ports., maps, plans.

Jones, Rev. Charles Colcock. *The Religious Instruction of Negroes.* 4th ed. Princeton, N. J., Printed by D'Hart & Connolly, 1832. 38 p. A sermon delivered before associations of planters in Georgia.

O'Connell, Rev. Jeremiah Joseph. *Catholicity in the Carolinas and Georgia, Leaves of Its History. A.D. 1820-A.D. 1878.* New York and Montreal, D. & J. Sadlier & Co., 1879. 647 p. port. of author.

Ragsdale, B. D. *Story of Georgia Baptists.* Atlanta, printed by Foote & Davies Co., 1932-38. 3 v. front., plates, ports., bibl.

Smith, Rev. George G. *The History of Georgia Methodism from 1786 to 1866.* Atlanta, A. B. Caldwell, 1913. 430 p. plates, ports.

Stacy, Rev. James. *A History of the Presbyterian Church in Georgia.* Elberton, Ga., Press of the *Star,* 1912. 404 p. plates, ports.

FOLKLORE

Darby, L. "Ring Games from Georgia." *Journal of American Folklore.* April-June, 1917, v. 30: 218-221.

Harris, Joel Chandler. *Told by Uncle Remus: New Stories of the Old Plantation.* New York, Grosset & Dunlap, 1905. 295 p. illus. by A. B. Frost, J. M. Conde, and Frank Uerbeck. Other books by Harris also contain folklore material.

Henry, Mellinger E. "Nursery Rhymes and Game-Songs from Georgia." *Journal of American Folklore.* Jan.-Mar., 1934, v. 47: 334-340.

Jones, Charles Colcock. *Negro Myths from the Georgia Coast Told in the Vernacular* . . . Boston and New York, Houghton, Mifflin & Co., 1888. 171 p.

Redfearn, S. F. "Songs from Georgia." *Journal of American Folklore.* Jan.-Mar., 1921, v. 34: 121-124.

Smiley, Portia. "Folk-Lore from Virginia, South Carolina, Georgia, Alabama, and Florida." *Journal of American Folklore,* July-Sept., 1919, v. 32: 357-383.

LITERATURE AND JOURNALISM

Brantley, Rabun Lee. *Georgia Journalism of the Civil War Period.* Nashville, Tenn., 1929. 134 p. illus. (map), fold. facsims. (Half-title: Contributions to Education of George Peabody College for Teachers, no. 58.)

Damon, S. Foster. *Thomas Holley Chivers, Friend of Poe.* New York, Harper, 1930. 305 p. illus.

Dean, Austin F. *Observations from a Peak in Lumpkin County, or, The Writings of W. B. Townsend.* Oglethorpe University, Oglethorpe Univ. Press, 1936. 342 p.

Edwards, Harry Stillwell. *Eneas Africanus.* New York, Gosden Head, 1932. 32 p. illus., map.

Harris, Mrs. Julia Florida Collier. *The Life and Letters of Joel Chandler Harris.* Boston and New York, Houghton, Mifflin & Co., 1918. 620 p. col. front., plates, ports., facsims., bibl.

Hart, Mrs. Bertha Sheppard. *Introduction to Georgia Writers.* Macon, J. W. Burke Co., 1929. 322 p.

Lorenz, Lincoln. *The Life of Sidney Lanier.* New York, Coward-McCann, Inc., 1935. 340 p. front. (port.), bibl.

Smith, Charles Henry. *Bill Arp's Scrap Book: Humor and Philosophy.* Atlanta, J. P. Harrison & Co., 1884. 405 p. portraits.

Suddeth, Ruth Elgin, ed. *An Atlanta Argosy: an Anthology of Atlanta Poetry.* Atlanta, Franklin Print. Corp., 1938. 175 p.

Wade, John Donald. *Augustus Baldwin Longstreet; a Study of the Development of Culture in the South.* New York, Macmillan, 1924. 392 p. front. (port.), bibl.

Wynn, William T., ed. *Readings in Georgia Literature.* Atlanta, T. E. Smith & Co., 1937. 352 p. illus., (ports.). With biographical sketches and notes.

ARCHITECTURE

Denmark, Ernest Ray. *Architecture of the Old South.* With foreword by Lewis E. Crook, Jr.; photographic plates illustrating the better work between 1640 and 1850. Atlanta, Southern Architect & Building News, 1926. 72 plates.

Howard, Mrs. Annie Hornady. *Georgia Homes and Landmarks.* Atlanta, Southern Features Syndicate, 1929. 186 p. illus.

Kimball, Sidney Fiske. *Domestic Architecture of the American Colonies and of the Early Republic.* New York, Chas. Scribner's Sons, 1922. 314 p. illus., plans.

Lanning, John Tate. *The Spanish Missions of Georgia.* With illus. by Willis Physioc. Chapel Hill, Univ. of North Carolina Press, 1935. 321 p. front., illus., fold. map., bibl. (Publications of Univ. of Georgia.)

Major, Howard. *The Domestic Architecture of the Early American Republic: the Greek Revival.* Philadelphia and London, Lippincott. 1926. 236 p. illus. (incl. plans), plates, col. front.

COUNTIES, CITIES, AND TOWNS

Cate, Margaret Davis. *Our Todays and Yesterdays: a Story of Brunswick and the Coastal Islands.* Rev. ed. Brunswick, Ga., Glover Bros., Inc., 1930. 302 p. front., illus. (incl. ports., maps), bibl.

——*Sketches of Coastal Georgia; Midway, Sunbury, Darien, Brunswick, St. Marys.* Brunswick, Ga., Glover Bros., Inc., 1931. 25 p. illus.

Harden, William. *A History of Savannah and South Georgia.* Chicago, Lewis Pub. Co., 1913. 2 v. illus.

Hines, Mrs. Nelle Womack, comp. *A Treasure Album of Milledgeville and Baldwin County, Georgia.* Macon, G. W. Burke Co., 1936. 52 p. illus. (incl. ports., plan, facsim.).

Hornady, John R. *Atlanta, Yesterday, Today and Tomorrow.* Atlanta, Index Print. Co. for Am. Cities Book Co., 1922. 442 p. illus., plates.

Johnson, Gerald White. *The Undefeated.* New York, Minton, Balch & Co., 1927. 120 p. front. Describes Stone Mountain Confederate Memorial.

Jones, Charles Colcock, and Salem Dutcher. *Memorial History of Augusta, Georgia* . . . Syracuse, New York, D. Mason & Co., 1890. 569 p. ports.

Reed, Wallace P., ed. *History of Atlanta, Georgia* . . . Syracuse, N. Y., D. Mason & Co., 1889. 702 p. ports.

Telfair, Nancy. *A History of Columbus, Georgia, 1828-1898.* Columbus, Historical Pub. Co., 1929. 572 p. illus. With biographical sketches.

Wilson, Adelaide. *Historic and Picturesque Savannah.* Boston, Pub. for subscribers by Boston Photogravure Co., 1889. 258 p. front. (facsim.), illus.

Note: Histories of the following counties have been published by various organizations and individuals: Baldwin, Bartow, Camden, Carroll, Charlton, Chattahoochee, Cherokee, Clarke, Clinch, Cobb, Coffee, Colquitt, Coweta, Crisp, Dodge, Dougherty, Floyd, Fulton, Gordon, Hart, Irwin, Jackson, Jefferson, Lamar, Lumpkin, Macon, Marion, Pickens, Pike, Pulaski, Talbot, Thomas, Troup, Turner, Upson, Walker, Ware, Washington, Whitfield, Wilkinson, and Worth.

Index